AMERICAN
FOUNDATIONS

AMERICAN
FOUNDATIONS

Roles and Contributions

HELMUT K. ANHEIER

DAVID C. HAMMACK

editors

BROOKINGS INSTITUTION PRESS
Washington, D.C.

Library of Congress Cataloging-in-Publication data

American foundations : roles and contributions / Helmut K. Anheier and David C. Hammack, editors.
   p.   cm.
Includes bibliographical references and index.
Summary: "Assesses comprehensively the impact and significance of philanthropic foundations in the United States and their effect on American culture and society covering areas such as education and research, health care, social welfare, arts and culture, religion, social movements, and international affairs"—Provided by publisher.
  ISBN 978-0-8157-0339-6 (hardcover : alk. paper)
  1. Endowments—United States. I. Anheier, Helmut K., 1954– II. Hammack, David C. III. Title.
HV91.A665 2010
361.7'6320973—dc22
                                           2009053991

Contents

Social Movements

List of Tables and Figures

Tables

Figures

Acknowledgments

This volume has benefited from the advice, support, and contributions of many individuals and organizations. We endeavor to acknowledge and thank all of them here. In the ultimate analysis, the coeditors alone are responsible for the final publication.

Advisory board: Alan Abramson, William Bowen, Craig Calhoun, Emmett Carson, Paul DiMaggio, Sara Englehardt, Virginia Esposito, Joel Fleishman, Barry Gaberman, Joseph Galaskiewicz, Vartan Gregorian, Paul Grogan, Peter Hero, Warren Ilchmann, Stanley N. Katz, Leslie Lenkowsky, Sylvia Matthews, Steve Minter, Ed Pauly, George Penick, Alicia Phillip, Kenneth Prewitt, Benjamin Shute, Bruce Sievers, Adele Simmons, John G. Simon, James Allen Smith, Pamela Waters, Burton Weisbrod, Bill White, Julian Wolpert.

Research and editorial support: Jocelyn Guihama efficiently managed practical details; Kathleen Mills and Elise Hagesfeld provided invaluable editorial assistance on the many drafts. Eve Garrow, David B. Howard, Marcus Lam, Erik Miller, Tia Morita, Jennifer Mosley, and Tiffany A. Willey made many helpful contributions. We would also like to thank our editorial and production team at Brookings Institution Press: Larry Converse, Katherine Kimball, Mary Kwak, Carlotta Ribar, Janet Walker, and Susan Woollen.

We gratefully acknowledge the following for their expertise and support of this endeavor: Burt Barnow, Joseph J. Cordes, Eugene Steuerle, and Burton Weisbrod for their input on methodology at the beginning of this project; Sara Englehardt, Steve Lawrence, and the entire research team at the Foundation

Center, who provided invaluable support; Phil Buchanan and the staff at the Center for Effective Philanthropy; the Aspen Institute and the Pocantico Conference Center of the Rockefeller Brothers Fund for providing facilities for meetings that allowed the authors and editors not only to envision but also to debate the project as it moved forward.

This project was initiated and generously supported by the Aspen Institute's Nonprofit Sector and Philanthropy Program. It also benefited from support from the Mandel Center for Nonprofit Organizations at Case Western Reserve University and the UCLA School of Public Affairs.

PART I

Introduction

1

American Foundations: Their Roles and Contributions to Society

DAVID C. HAMMACK AND HELMUT K. ANHEIER

What have independent grant-making foundations contributed to the United States? What roles have foundations played over time, and what distinctive roles—if any—do they fill today? Are new roles for foundations currently emerging? This volume presents the product of a three-year effort to answer these questions.

America's grant-making foundations are significant by many measures. They numbered more than 112,000 in 2008, held more than $627 billion in assets, and had grown substantially over more than two decades. They command substantial resources even in the midst of the 2008–09 financial crisis.[1] Entitled to considerable tax benefits and exemptions, and free from direct responsibility to shareholders and voters, foundations enjoy exceptional independence. They can invest the assets they hold, subject to modest restrictions and to an annual tax, generally 2 percent of investment income. So long as they give a minimum amount each year for "charitable purposes" defined in very broad terms, avoid enriching their donors or staffs, and do not directly support candidates for political office or lobby directly for specific legislation, American foundations can largely do as they please.

1. Number and total assets of foundations from the National Center for Charitable Statistics (nccsdataweb.urban.org/PubApps/profileDrillDown.php?state=US&rpt=PF [July 28, 2007]). The global financial crisis of 2008–09 is a reminder that as holders and investors of charitable funds, foundations are not exempt from external market forces.

American law and practice define *charity* in wide terms. As the Internal Revenue Service puts it, "The term charitable is used in its generally accepted legal sense," which "includes relief of the poor, the distressed, or the underprivileged; advancement of religion; advancement of education or science; erecting or maintaining public buildings, monuments, or works; lessening the burdens of government; lessening neighborhood tensions; eliminating prejudice and discrimination; defending human and civil rights secured by law; and combating community deterioration and juvenile delinquency."[2] Unlike an operating charity such as a school, hospital, research institute, social service agency, or museum, a foundation's board may, in almost all U.S. states, shift funds from one activity to another at any time.[3] And foundation grants add up to a considerable total: the Foundation Center has estimated that in 2007, American foundations gave away more than $42 billion.[4]

Among all industrial societies, the United States has long granted the most scope to philanthropy. While foundations exist in many countries—most prominently in Germany, the United Kingdom, Italy, the Netherlands, and Japan—the United States stands out: in no modern society are foundations more numerous, and nowhere have they become so prominent and visible. Compared with

2. See "Exempt Purposes: Internal Revenue Code 501(c)(3)," January 2009 (www.irs.gov/charities/charitable/article/0,,id=175418,00.html).

3. Many organizations call themselves foundations, including hospitals and other operating charities (such as the Cleveland Clinic Foundation); supporting organizations controlled by state universities, public schools, and operating charities; and annual fund-raising entities (such as the March of Dimes Birth Defects Foundation). This book focuses on the three thousand larger independent grant-making foundations that have paid staffs and take the legal form of a nonprofit corporation (or, rarely, a legal trust) established to give money for purposes deemed "charitable" under U.S. law, either indefinitely or over a specified period; compare the Foundation Center's definition at "What Is a Foundation?" (http://foundationcenter.org/getstarted/faqs/html/foundfun.html [November 12, 2009]). We include foundations created by force of law, including conversion foundations created when profit-seeking firms purchase nonprofit health insurers or hospitals or, more rarely, under other circumstances. Under U.S. law independent foundations are self-governing and institutionally separate from government. These foundations are also independent of business firms and are distinct from "company foundations" in holding their own substantial assets, in the autonomy of their governing boards, and in their complete separation from the obligation to help a sponsoring firm make a profit. Under federal law, a foundation may not be used for the "private inurement" of a donor, trustee, or staff member or of members of their families. Thus we are not considering the special foundations that are allowed to hold family assets in some European nations. Most foundations receive all of their donated assets at their creation, but all may grow by investing their "corpus," and many receive additional gifts over time. The Tax Reform Act of 1969 gives community foundations the status of "public charities," exempt from certain regulations and fees, if they receive each year in new gifts from multiple donors at least 5 percent of the three-year running average of the value of their assets.

4. Estimated grant total from the Foundation Center, "Foundation Growth and Giving Estimates," 2007 (http://foundationcenter.org/gainknowledge/research/pdf/fgge07.pdf).

their counterparts in Europe and Asia, the philanthropic foundations of the United States look back to a longer and more continuous history.

In this book, however, our concern is not to explain why so many foundations have appeared in the United States or why they are more numerous and more influential here than in other countries. Instead, we ask, What difference have they made over time, and what difference are they making today? What have they contributed to American society over time, and what are they contributing today? How did foundations achieve impact in the past, and how are they attempting to make a difference today?

The Approach Taken in This Volume

In seeking answers to these questions, we asked each of our collaborators in this book to evaluate several hypotheses advanced by previous research, presented more fully below, paying particular attention to the resources available to foundations, the fields they engage, and the contributions of other institutions, whether government agencies, nonprofits, professionals, or business firms, to those fields. Research on the roles, performance, and contributions of businesses and public agencies fills libraries and is the focus of distinct academic disciplines. A more limited but rapidly growing literature considers nonprofit organizations.[5] By contrast, the foundation, as a distinct organizational form, has received much less scholarly attention. Whereas foundations have from time to time been praised or damned in sweeping terms from one perspective or another, we contend that precisely because foundations have sought to do many different things over several distinct periods of American history, broad generalizations are neither illuminating nor useful.[6] In this book, we are taking a more nuanced approach, being mindful also of heightened policy interest in foundations—in the causes they choose to support, in their potential to advance fields ranging from culture, education, and health to religion, the arts, social services, and effective government, and in their potential abuse.

When we began to explore foundations' roles and gauge their contributions, we quickly concluded that foundation impact, whatever it might be, could best

5. See Powell and Steinberg (2007); Salamon (2002b); Anheier (2005); Heydemann (2002).

6. The diversity of fields in which foundations work, the limited resources of foundations in relation to the sizes of their fields, the complexity of defining and measuring impact, all pose severe challenges of method. Challenges also derive from the wide range of criteria proposed for evaluating foundations: social and economic welfare in general, for example, the standard of living and the life chances of the largest possible number of people; social equality; the preservation of religious traditions and cultural diversity; excellence in research, writing, and the arts; the overall amount of total philanthropic giving for charitable causes; and the level of social engagement. See also the comments on method in Margo (1992, pp. 207–34).

be assessed in the context of particular fields at particular times. Ideally, we see "impact" in causal terms, as a measure of the effectiveness of specific activities intended to bring about sustained and observable change. But given the wide range of foundation purposes, the complexity of the changes they seek, the small size of foundation funds in relation to their fields of action, the limitations of the available data, and also the limited resources available for this project, we decided to combine qualitative and quantitative approaches by focusing on large grant-making foundations, while also noting other types such as community foundations; considering several quite diverse fields over extended periods of time; and using consistent approaches that take account of the best current analyses of work in the fields that foundations address.[7]

The larger independent and community grant-making foundations are at the core of discussions about the contribution of foundations to American society. More than half of all independent grant-making foundations have less than a million dollars in assets. We focus not on these small foundations, which are numerous but whose total assets amount to just 3 percent of all foundation holdings, but on the largest 5 percent, which hold the bulk of philanthropic assets.

Foundations as Institutions

Large grant-making foundations are important not just for their wealth but also because they are notable institutions. Institutions make ideas and practices regular, routine, almost solid. They can provide a measure of predictability and a sense of consequence. Institutions define realities, concert resources, enhance or frustrate the power of those who work through them and with them, and generally help shape their environments.

Foundations are important institutions because they enable donors to reserve and invest charitable funds, to set terms for their distribution, to provide funds to one or many grantees over time, and to shift funds from one charitable activity to another. Foundations are also important because they focus grant-seekers'

---

7. A wealth of reliable data is now available, especially from the Foundation Center and the National Center for Charitable Statistics. We are all too well aware of the limitations to the available data and the costs associated with gathering more. Contrary to conventional laments, many serious studies of foundation impact have been published by historians and social scientists, as the reference list demonstrates. Much of what we would ideally want to know is not measurable, and even though some data are available, data that would allow direct evaluation of cause and effect are not. Multiple purposes make it difficult to identify the true intentions of many foundation programs. Those who seek to promote change often, quite appropriately, must take indirect approaches. So far as possible, we have sought to unpack foundation staff and trustee intentions and to learn how they themselves have tried to evaluate their success. In current language, we have sought to understand the underlying theory of change brought to bear by foundation leaders in particular cases.

attention. In their financial capacity, foundations contribute in a minor way, together with individual and corporate donors and certain government agencies, to what some describe as a grants economy that provides about a fifth of the income of America's nonprofit organizations.[8] In their civic capacity, foundations (like associations and nonprofit organizations) constitute sources of wealth, influence, and initiative independent of government and business. Foundations can help individuals discharge religious obligations and moral commitments, provide a secure basis for minority religious and cultural and scientific interests, and enable ambitious people to exchange economic wealth for social recognition and prestige.

Clearly, foundations do much more than give away money: when society permits, they can confer legitimacy and worthiness on, as well as enhance the recognition and status of, a donor. In conjunction with policymakers, tax authorities, judges, accountants, religious leaders, pundits, and many others, foundations can make real Americans' divergent and changing ideas as to what is really charitable or valuable. Foundations can shape the actions of others by granting money and defining particular activities, purposes, achievements, and people as worthy of gifts, grants, awards, and prizes.

Ancient and medieval foundations in Europe and the Ottoman Empire supported the saying of prayers; the preservation, copying, and study of sacred texts; the education of religious leaders; the symbolic feeding of the poor (especially widows and orphans); and the religious care of the sick and dying.[9] Modern foundations continue to do all that, and they also reward heroism, good citizenship, writing on many topics, artistic endeavor, and scientific and applied research. When conditions have been favorable, modern foundations have successfully introduced public awareness campaigns, encouraged new social behavior, launched self-sustaining organizations, and even reorganized entire fields of activity.

U.S. foundations once helped define limits and indirectly served to maintain social barriers within American society by confining their gifts largely to white men. Since the civil rights and women's movements, many American foundations have instead sought to eliminate such limits and reduce barriers by emphasizing their willingness to include African Americans, Hispanics, Native

8. In 2005 foundations themselves provided about 1 percent of the income of the charitable nonprofits; other private donors contributed about 12 percent; government agencies added another 9 percent in the form of grants. Government also paid for services provided by nonprofits through processes that are quite distinct from grant making. In 2005 foundations gave a total of $36.5 billion to all recipients; a substantial portion of this went to religious entities, state universities and other government agencies, and individuals rather than to charitable nonprofits. Blackwood, Wing, and Pollak (2008).

9. On ancient foundations, see Veyne, Murray, and Pearce (1990).

Americans, members of other minority communities, and women among their grantees and among their trustees, as well—as a matter of course.

The existence of the foundation as an institution gives a donor an alternative. A donor who wishes to give outside his or her family and friends can give directly to a religious institution or other operating organization (or its endowment) or to an individual. A donor can also place funds in a foundation to be given over time to a developing field, a complicated project, or a cherished purpose, or to be given in a field—such as the production of works of art or literature; the mounting of theatrical, musical, or dance performances; or the celebration of religious rites and duties—in situations where stable organizations are lacking. Any person can also, of course, decide to make no gifts at all. To focus on foundations is to focus on just one of the legal and institutional instruments that the United States makes available to its donors.

U.S. foundations act chiefly through nonprofit organizations; in an important sense, giving money to a foundation is an alternative to giving to an operating charitable nonprofit organization, religious or secular. U.S. foundations also often give to state universities, public schools, county hospitals, national museums, and other government entities. Hence it is important to consider the implications of the fact that donors can give through foundations as well as directly to nonprofit organizations or agencies of government. Foundations can reinforce the autonomy of a nonprofit by providing distinctive sources of income; they can enable a nonprofit to launch a new initiative, to expand, even to pursue some difficult-to-fund course. Foundations can enhance the ability of a government entity to do its work. But foundation demands can also limit nonprofit autonomy and exert controversial influence on public agencies. Because foundations have the power to expand or contract their funding in accordance with their own purposes, they can help their grantees expand—and they can also lead grantees to distort their missions.

One of our key findings, not sufficiently appreciated in general discussion, is that as nonprofit organizations and government agencies have grown in recent decades, foundations have grown much more slowly and have, as a result, become less important. Over the past forty years, private colleges, not-for-profit hospitals, state universities, county hospitals, nonprofit job training centers, and similar entities have dramatically increased their earned income. They have also benefited since 1966 from increased federal funding through Medicaid, Medicare, federal grants and loans to college students, and massive federal investment in job training. Huge increases in other federal programs, ranging from the National Science Foundation and the National Institutes of Health to subsidies for housing and support for the disabled, have produced a steady increase in government funding for nonprofits as well as for state and local schools, hospitals, clinics, and other agencies.

Meanwhile, private giving of all kinds, including giving to and through foundations, has not increased in relative terms but has remained quite steady at a little less than 2 percent of disposable income.[10] Thus in recent decades American foundations have been operating in a new and rapidly changing environment in which their resources have been declining relative to the resources devoted to the fields with which they engage. For nonprofit organizations, earned income now amounts to three or four times as much as all private donated income.[11] And, if we count medical insurance payments as "earned," even though they are heavily subsidized and regulated by the federal government, earned income also exceeds government funding of nonprofits by about 50 percent. "Charitable" American nonprofits gain that designation through the character of the services they provide and through the spirit of their operations, more than through reliance on private donations. This has always been true to a considerable degree; it is now more true than ever.

So we began this project knowing that impressive though they are, foundation assets are small and declining in relation to the fields and the needs they seek to address. Previous work had also made it clear in a general way that, precisely because their assets are limited, the most effective foundations have always demonstrated notable creativity and strategic thinking.[12] Foundations that achieve real impact must have a shrewd understanding of the dynamics of the fields in which they operate and a thoughtful mastery of ways to use limited funds with maximum leverage. Even as foundation assets have seen relative decline, federal and state regulation of activity in most fields relevant to foundation interest has greatly increased. With increased wealth, Americans can and do pay for more and more of the kinds of services that foundations support. Today's foundations must adapt their strategies and tools, perhaps even downsize their ambitions, and in any case carefully reconsider the fields and issues they choose to address. In so doing, autonomy in the use of assets gives foundations their great potential. Our ambition here is to begin to develop a more precise empirical assessment of how foundations use their exceptional position, and with what impact.

Roles and Contributions

As they seek to make an impact, foundations above all distribute money. Foundations have also been able to offer resources that are less tangible than money but that under the right circumstances can be even more valuable. Through

10. Burke (2001).
11. Salamon (1999).
12. See Hammack (2006); Fleishman (2007); Frumkin (2006); Anheier and Leat (2006); Andrews (1973); Cuninggim (1972); Nielsen (1972); Wheatley (1988); Lagemann (1999).

longevity, consistency, and good judgment—and, more generally, through the basic terms of their programs—foundations can confer honor, prestige, or authority, and in this way they can encourage desired behaviors and actions. Sometimes foundations have done this by offering prizes for notable achievement; sometimes by supporting research, creative work, or collegial activity; sometimes through scholarships designed to attract newcomers into a field. Some foundations have sought to make a mark even more programmatically, by devoting resources to operating institutions that seek their own distinctive reputations for excellence.[13]

It is important to consider not just what foundations provide in the way of money and other resources but also intent and method. As has been noted, in legal terms, all foundation grants must be "charitable"; in practice, foundation approaches can be seen as attempting to contribute to society in three main ways: through relief of immediate needs, through philanthropy, or through control.[14]

Relief of immediate need occurs when foundations pay for services or goods that benefit others—for example, characteristically, the poor or the disabled—within an existing framework. Counterproductive efforts of this sort encourage dependency—or are insufficient. We identify two chief forms: complementarity, whereby foundation gifts supplement tax funds and individual gifts in paying for services or goods for otherwise undersupplied groups; and substitution, whereby foundation grants replace tax funds and individual gifts in providing services or goods.

Philanthropy describes foundation efforts to create something new in one of three ways: innovation in social perceptions, values, relationships and ways of doing things, which has long been a role ascribed to foundations, although any effort to innovate can fail and can yield negative as well as positive results; original achievement in the arts, in science, and in the study of society; and social and policy change, whereby foundations foster recognition of new needs, seek to bring a wide range of perspectives to the table, and encourage discussion of structural change in the interests of such general social goals as efficiency,

13. As in the current cases of the Getty Foundation with its art museums and related programs, the Duke Endowment's support for Duke and three other universities and colleges, and the Howard Hughes Medical Endowment (whose federal charter specifies that it is not legally a foundation) with its own laboratories and related grant programs, as well as the classic case of the Russell Sage Foundation's support of various research and publication programs in the fields of social work and social policy and of the regional plan of New York and New Jersey, from World War I through World War II, the Carnegie Endowment for International Peace, and the Carnegie Foundation for the Advancement of Teaching.

14. Role classification is informed by Weaver and others (1967); Nielsen (1972); Karl and Katz (1981); Hammack (1999); Prewitt (1999a); Kramer (1987); Salamon (1995); Anheier and Daly (2005); Frumkin (2006).

equity, peace, social and moral virtues of all kinds, law and order, or economic growth. Control can also take three forms: preservation of traditions and cultures, whereby foundations hold and distribute funds intended to preserve and encourage valued beliefs and commitments; redistribution, whereby foundations voluntarily redistribute wealth from the rich to the poor; and asset protection, whereby a foundation holds, invests, and distributes funds for use by other charitable institutions or for particular charitable purposes.

Foundations do not only give money away; they also invest. Regulations have changed over the years, but some foundations have always sought to contribute to society through what are now called program-related investments as well as through grants. Some of the earliest program-related investments were intended to help young craftsmen and farmers establish themselves, to demonstrate the practicality of higher standards in housing design and construction, or to subsidize office and meeting space for charitable organizations. Foundations have also sought to promote local economic growth through their investments as well as their gifts.

A number of authors have suggested that foundations have significant comparative advantages over other institutions.[15] Independence from both market considerations and election politics might well enable foundations to contribute to society in four distinct ways. They can be social entrepreneurs, identifying and responding to needs or problems that for whatever reason are beyond the reach or interest of market firms, government agencies, and existing nonprofit organizations. They can act as institution builders, identifying coalitions of individuals and organizations capable of action across existing sectors, communities, regions, and borders; mediating conflicts, convening, and assuming the role of honest broker; and offering financial resources as well as knowledge and insights to help new entities (and sometimes entire groups of new institutions) become self-sustaining. Foundations can also serve as risk takers, investing where there is great uncertainty and a return is doubtful; foundations can be especially well placed to support new departures in research, scholarship, writing, and the arts and in vital questions that are not yet in the mainstream. Finally, foundations can be value conservers, supporting practices, virtues, and cultural patterns treasured by donors but unsupported by markets or legislative majorities.

We set ourselves to identify the general significance of each sort of contribution. Is it true that relief of immediate need is especially significant for many smaller foundations, though even large, change- or control-oriented foundations often make donations intended to relieve need created by disasters, economic

15. For example, Douglas and Wildavsky (1978); Prewitt (2001); Anheier and Leat (2006); Fleishman (2007).

depressions, and war? Are we correct to think that foundations hold such small amounts of wealth relative to government expenditures that we can find few if any cases of outright substitution? Foundations often do supplement government and private provision of goods and services for the poor: to what extent is this the case? Even in meeting immediate need, foundations can act as social entrepreneurs when they devise more effective arrangements for relief or when they challenge outdated notions that define one population as more worthy than another. How often does this occur?

Those who have written about American foundations have neglected the foundation role in controlling charitable and philanthropic resources, but this role is an important one, not only for the classic foundation purpose of preserving traditions and cultures and for protecting assets. Are we right about this? Is it correct to conclude that given the small sum of assets foundations hold relative to national wealth, their capacity for redistribution from the rich to the poor is very limited?

Many writers celebrate foundations' philanthropic roles, especially the encouragement of innovation and social change. We would also call attention to foundations' roles in supporting original achievement and in encouraging careful thought about policy in the broader sense of frameworks and approaches to help the formulation of legislative action. Are we right about this? Perhaps it should go without saying that it is exceptionally difficult for any institution to bring about real innovation, social or policy change, or truly notable achievement.

We hypothesize that foundations can achieve the greatest impact when they act as social entrepreneurs, institution builders, risk takers, and value conservers—or, in slightly different terms, that foundations are most effective when they act as neutral intermediaries (with no direct market or electoral interests) that possess independent financial and other assets, mobilizing resources for needs that will not otherwise be met or purposes that would not otherwise win support.

But the evidence also makes it clear that these are difficult tasks to accomplish, and that their impacts are difficult to measure. Donors, regulators, courts, and American society at large recognize a wide range of activities as appropriate for foundations. Some American cultural traditions emphasize the stewardship of resources for the future; others take the view that available funds should largely be devoted to immediate need. Which of these is best or most effective or most valuable or most appropriate is widely debated, not least among different religious communities. Because people place varying values on different foundation activities—as is appropriate in a free society—we do not think it is possible to identify any one best foundation practice. But we do believe that some foundation efforts have made especially effective use of the institution.

In addition to comparative advantages, we also ask about the disadvantages associated with foundations. Among those that have been suggested in the literature,[16] we see the following as most critical:

—Insufficiency, when foundations lack resources adequate to their proclaimed goals. This disadvantage becomes acute when the foundation fails to recognize its own limitations.

—Particularism, an inappropriate favoring of one group of beneficiaries based on value preferences. U.S. law forbids discrimination on the basis of race or gender but allows foundations to require that beneficiaries meet religious, geographical, or appropriate ability tests. Criticism arises when such tests are imposed in arbitrary fashion or for an ulterior discriminatory purpose.

—Paternalism, the substitution of a foundation's judgment for that of its beneficiaries—in particular, the attitude that the foundation knows what is good for those it seeks to support. This charge is often linked to the alleged aloofness and elitism of foundations.

—Amateurism, the making of decisions by (often well-meaning) dilettantes who possess only a cursory understanding of the fields and issues they address.

Once we had defined terms and developed these hypotheses, we invited colleagues to write authoritative analyses of the contributions of American foundations in eight distinct fields. For each field we commissioned a study of the changing contexts in which American foundations have worked; for seven fields, we also commissioned contemporary studies based in part on data from the Foundation Center.[17] We were able to include most of the fields in which foundations have been most active over the years, including K–12 education, university-based research, medical research and medical care, social welfare, international relations, arts and culture, religion, and social movements relating especially to class, gender, and race. Limited resources and a lack of previous studies prevented the inclusion of other important fields, including the environment, population studies, energy, the press and public information, and many specific social welfare fields, ranging from the needs of children to aging and housing. While we paid extensive attention to questions of race and gender, we treated those matters in the context of foundation work in the various applied fields.[18]

16. Nielsen (1972, 1985); Salamon (1987, 1995); Anderson (1988); Fleishman (2001); Hammack (2006); Frumkin (2006). We leave aside here the abuse of the foundation for legally proscribed self-enrichment and dynastic wealth preservation purposes.

17. For information on our data sources, see appendix A.

18. In several cases, we have been able to draw on excellent work by others; see the lists of references for this volume and for our companion book (Hammack and Anheier, forthcoming).

The contributors include sociologists, historians, political scientists, and economists. All are excellent independent researchers in their own disciplines. Several write on the basis of practical experience, having played senior leadership or advisory roles at a wide range of foundations, from the venerable Milbank Memorial Fund and the Russell Sage Foundation to the Century Foundation and Chicago's Joyce Foundation, from the J. Paul Getty Trust and the Ford Foundation to the Robert Wood Johnson Foundation and the newly formed New York State Health Foundation. But all write as independent, if unusually well-informed, researchers, not as advocates for the foundations.

The Importance of Context

Several influential recent accounts have emphasized the remarkable continuities in the history of American foundations.[19] The studies in this book persuade us, however, that America's foundations themselves have changed less over the past hundred years than the contexts in which they operate—contexts of two sorts, to be precise. Foundations operate in specific fields, so the character of each field that a foundation addresses provides one key context. Theological education, for example, offers possibilities and challenges quite different from those entailed by public health, by elementary and secondary education, or by a concern for the arts or the elimination of poverty.

Foundations also operate in real time, and each period imposes its own critical political and economic context. Foundations have a long history—we date the earliest recognizable American foundations to the 1790s—and we observe four sharply distinct periods: the sectarian, particular-purpose era of the nineteenth century; the classic institution-building era of the first half of the twentieth century; a postwar period of struggle for strategy and relevance that lasted into the 1990s; and, if we are correct, the present time, with its acceptance of foundation variety and its focus on measurable and sustainable results. For each field, for each period, external realities—not least, the general climate of public culture and opinion, expressed through state laws and court decisions even more than through federal policy—have shaped the sorts of things foundations could do and the sorts of contributions they could make. The record of foundation work, and in fact the record of serious analysis of foundations, is longer, fuller, and richer than is often suggested. We believe that today's foundations, and today's foundation watchers, can—and, if they are responsible, understand that they should—learn from the past.[20] But to do so, they must consider the

19. See, for example, Fleishman (2001, 2007); Prewitt (2001); Dowie (2001).

20. F. Emerson Andrews directed the Russell Sage Foundation's early studies of foundations before launching the Foundation Center; he titled his 1973 memoir *Foundation Watcher* (Andrews 1973).

context of time and field, and they must consider present realities as they think about what might be relevant from past experience.

The Sectarian, Particular-Purpose Foundations of the Nineteenth Century

Because a foundation is a legal device for holding, investing, and over time paying out money for the support of charitable purposes, it is wealth and sustained focus that make foundations impressive. The lists of the largest and otherwise most notable foundations of the particular-purpose era of the nineteenth century include religious, educational, local economic development, and arts endowments that are sometimes omitted from discussions of the field but that actually meet most if not all the elements of the definition of a foundation.[21]

What did nineteenth-century foundations contribute? In organized religion, literature, the arts, the sciences, and popular and collegiate education, endowed funds and early foundations played strongly innovative philanthropic roles as social entrepreneurs and institution builders. They also worked to advance cherished values and to create opportunities for individual achievement. Through their funds in support of education and the clergy, they helped create America's Protestant denominations. Funding from foundations and endowments allowed colleges to increase their usefulness by moving into new areas of teaching, public service, and research, including science. Foundations expanded opportunities for popular self-education. Some foundations sought to invest strategically in local economic development. In the notable cases of the Peabody Education Fund (for the South) and the Carnegie libraries, they worked effectively for policy change. In most of these areas foundations did not substitute for, or complement, nineteenth-century governments, because those governments did not take the provision of opportunities for religion, scientific research, the arts, or, in most cases, higher education to be among their responsibilities.

Nineteenth-century endowments and funds certainly did not escape criticism. Every religious movement, every denomination, indeed organized religion itself, had critics and detractors. Every cultural and educational initiative evoked

21. For fuller detail on nineteenth-century foundations, see Hammack and Anheier (forthcoming). The Massachusetts Hospital Life Insurance Company (active after 1825) combined the functions of a trust company, an insurance company, and a charitable endowment. It donated a full third of its often considerable profits to the Massachusetts General Hospital. Related arrangements continue: according to its website, the United Methodist Development Fund "provides first-mortgage loans to United Methodist churches, districts, city societies, district unions, mission institutions, or conference church-extension agencies for the purchase of sites and for the purchase, construction, expansion, or major improvement of churches, parsonages, or mission buildings. . . . The UMDF accepts investments from United Methodists, sends them an interest check twice a year, then lends that money to United Methodist churches for new construction and/or renovation" (http://gbgm-umc.org/who_we_are/ecg/umdf/ [September 2008]). Of course, under twentieth-century tax law, the United Methodist Development Fund is not technically a foundation.

criticism. Lowell Institute lectures and Carnegie libraries greatly increased opportunities for many Americans to help themselves. Yet few nineteenth-century charities challenged contemporary treatment of African Americans or women. Much nineteenth-century philanthropy by foundations and proto-foundations was indeed particularistic, amateur, paternalist, elitist.

Classic Institution Building in the Early Twentieth Century

Most accounts of the history and character of American foundations derive from the classic institution-building period, the first half of the twentieth century, and most of the essays on context in this volume pay a good deal of attention to this period. General-purpose grant-making foundations became legal (on a state-by-state basis) only with the rise of nonsectarianism and science and the formation of exceptionally large fortunes at the end of the nineteenth century. The best-known foundations of this era—the several created by Andrew Carnegie and by John D. Rockefeller and his associates, together with the Rosenwald Fund, the Milbank Memorial Fund, the Russell Sage Foundation, the Twentieth Century Fund, the several Guggenheim foundations, and the Alfred P. Sloan Foundation—did much to shape the basic institutions of American public and higher education, medical research and education, and scientific research. They succeeded by backing national cadres of institution builders and by funding and conferring legitimacy and prestige on new and reformed academic, professional, and research institutions. In their core fields, they found strong partners in certain regional foundations, in the rising professions, in industry, in the state legislatures, sometimes in the White House.

Over the first half of the twentieth century these foundations, as well as many others, also made substantial efforts in the fields of social welfare, the delivery of health care, the improvement of elementary and secondary education for children from disadvantaged families, housing and regional planning, the promotion of particular virtues and the suppression of particular vices, the arts, and international relations. But in those fields foundations often worked at cross-purposes with one another and also encountered powerful countervailing forces. Finding few effective partners, some foundations did help, in several cases, to create notable communities of would-be change agents who struggled to make a difference.

Most accounts of foundations strongly emphasize the Carnegie, Rockefeller, and allied national foundations, and for good reason: during this dramatic period, these foundations held a large share of all foundation assets and pursued the most striking set of agendas. But another group of large foundations played different roles. Several of these, especially around the Great Lakes and in the West—including the Cleveland Foundation, the Chicago Community Trust, the Kresge Foundation, the Charles Stewart Mott Foundation, the

Buhl Foundation, the Children's Fund of Michigan, the Field Foundation, the Amherst Wilder Foundation, the Lewis W. and Maud Hill Foundation, and the Charles Hayden Foundation, as well as quite a number of smaller regional funds, such as the Maurice and Laura Falk Foundation in Pittsburgh, the Louis D. Beaumont Foundation in Cleveland, the El Pomar Foundation in Colorado, the Katie and Thomas Haynes Memorial Educational Fund in California, and the Harold K. L. Castle Foundation in Hawaii—intervened within their own spheres to advance the national foundations' efforts to institutionalize modern medicine and scientific research.

But many other regional foundations in these years sought less to advance modernization than to build selected regional institutions. Most notable, perhaps, were efforts in Cleveland and elsewhere to develop the community foundation and the community chest (the predecessor of the United Way movement) into substantial regional fundraising organizations, and the efforts of the W. K. Kellogg, Mott, and some other foundations to expand public health, local hospitals, public libraries, and public education in rural areas and small towns. Also worth particular notice were the successful uses of foundations to build arts organizations ranging from the National Gallery, the Juilliard School, and the Metropolitan Opera to the Cranbrook School, Longwood Gardens, and the Kimbell, Nelson-Atkins, and Huntington museums. Meanwhile, most of the nineteenth-century denominational foundations continued to grow and were joined, during the 1920s, 1930s, and 1940s, by new Baptist and Methodist foundations in the South. The Duke, Danforth, Lilly, and many other regional foundations, especially but by no means only in the South and the West, also emphasized their religious commitments.

As our colleagues Pamela Barnhouse Walters and Emily A. Bowman (chapter 2), Steven C. Wheatley (chapter 4), and Daniel M. Fox (chapter 6) make clear, the most notable foundations did much to build America's modern institutions in education, scientific research, and the professions. Many regional foundations built local institutions in these fields and helped connect them to national networks. National as well as regional foundations also continued to support the main Protestant denominations and to make other contributions to organized religion—a neglected field that Robert Wuthnow and Michael Lindsay (chapter 14) begin to explore. Donors used foundations to advance other cherished cultural values, especially, as James Allen Smith (chapter 12) shows, by creating new organizations for the arts and, as Steven Heydemann and Rebecca T. Kinsey (chapter 10) demonstrate, in the field of international relations.

Efforts during these years to encourage systematic reforms in the delivery of health care, secondary education, social welfare, race relations, and family and recreational life produced decidedly more mixed results, as our colleagues Fox, Walters and Bowman, and Wolfgang Bielefeld and Jane Chu (chapter 8), as well as others, argue.[22] Opposition from general practitioners drove foundations from the health policy field. The New Deal overwhelmed strong foundation support for private social work agencies and for control over the social work profession. Having done much to create public school systems supported by local tax revenues and to integrate public schools with private and public colleges, foundations found themselves unable to persuade the school systems to adopt new policies. Foundation resources were insufficient to diagnose in a timely way the factors that brought the Great Depression, to maintain peace after World War I, to spread Christianity around the globe, to equalize access to education for African Americans or anyone who lived in a rural area, or to raise moral standards. And in the absence of any systematic regulation, not a few donors used foundations largely to enrich themselves and to preserve wealth for their families.[23]

Struggle for Strategy and Relevance in the Postwar Period

By the early 1950s, American foundations were operating in a new context. A great expansion in the role of government, sustained prosperity, and the very success of earlier foundation efforts to build new, sustainable systems of key institutions all worked together to reduce foundation influence. New issues demanded attention: the reconstruction of Western Europe, the cold war, and the collapse of the European colonial empires; the African American civil rights movement; the persistence of poverty; the new women's movement. Large new nonsectarian foundations had been a dramatic new presence on the American scene in the first two decades of the twentieth century, but fewer new foundations appeared in the 1930s and 1940s, and when their numbers rose again in the 1950s and 1960s, congressional hearings and new legislation sharply slowed the creation of new foundations. Whatever their field of action, for several decades foundations struggled to redefine their place in America's civil society.

It is easy to forget how extensively Americans transformed their governments in the 1930s and 1940s. State and even municipal governments had traditionally taken the lead in most areas of domestic policy. Before the New Deal, the federal government had almost nothing at all to do with questions relating to scientific research, higher education, health and medicine, elementary and secondary education, or social welfare and family relations. These were exactly the fields in which American foundations were then making their most notable contributions.[24]

22. Harlan (1958); Hammack and Wheeler (1994); Sealander (1997); Anderson and Moss (1999).

23. Goulden (1971); Nielsen (1972, 1985); Troyer (2000).

24. Joel Fleishman notes the foundation support in this period of work to eliminate hookworm and to develop insulin and the Pap smear test; historians of American science credit the Rockefeller and several other foundations with building research capabilities that during the early years of World War II made possible the Manhattan Project, the effort to develop radar and sonar, and the rapid advance of American aeronautics (Kohler 1991).

By the early 1950s, federal agencies were providing overwhelmingly more money than foundations in most of these fields. The federal government did not crowd out the foundations: rather, its enormous resources and the nation's new policy commitments transformed every field, so that research, higher and professional education, hospital care, and funds for the relief of the unemployed, the elderly, and the very poor could do far more than ever in the past. Meanwhile, across the nation, state and local governments, including school and other special districts, had during the Depression added sales and income taxes to their traditional property-tax revenue bases and now raised more money than ever for education, welfare assistance, and recreation.

The transformation of America's health, education, and welfare systems slowed during World War II and the early years of the cold war, but the success of the civil rights movement and the passage of Great Society legislation in the mid-1960s revived the process. In just two years, 1965 and 1966, Congress passed the historic Civil Rights and Voting Rights acts, created Medicare and Medicaid and a new national system of grants and loans for college students, greatly expanded federal support for job training and other antipoverty initiatives, expanded the National Science Foundation, and established the National Endowments for the Arts and the Humanities.

Meanwhile, although American incomes continued to be unequal, average per capita income, measured in dollars of constant purchasing power, was growing steadily, from about $9,000 in 1960 to more than $23,000 in 2000.[25] Increased family incomes, which allowed for disproportionately increased spending on health care, school tuition, the arts, and other nonprofit services, combined with steadily increasing government spending to make possible rapid growth in nonprofit employment.

The remarkable increases in private spending and government funding allowed foundation-funded fields to grow rapidly, at a time when foundation assets were growing slowly or stagnating and private giving was failing to move above its post–World War II peak of more than 2 percent of disposable income.[26] Private giving, including foundation giving and giving influenced by foundation example, had accounted for a considerable share of nonprofit employment between 1900 and 1950. It accounted for a much smaller, and rapidly decreasing, share thereafter.[27]

Market forces and federal funding requirements also imposed new constraints, limiting the possibilities for foundation influence on nonprofit organizations and

25. Statistical tables can be found at "Economic Report of the President: 2008 Report Spreadsheet Tables" (www.gpoaccess.gov/eop/tables08.html [July 9, 2008]).

26. Foundation Center data suggest that foundation assets grew little in relation to U.S. gross domestic product between the mid-1960s and the late 1980s. See also Burke (2001).

27. Hammack (2001).

government agencies. Because federal priorities could and did change from year to year, from Congress to Congress and from president to president, foundations and other private donors could not be sure how their initiatives would fit into a changing scene, as our colleague Steven R. Smith has shown.[28] In the 1940s, 1950s, and 1960s, large portions of the funds appropriated under the G.I. Bill, the Hill-Burton hospital construction act, the National Defense Education Act, and the legislation of the Great Society went directly to existing—and to some extent foundation-shaped—nonprofit organizations and government agencies. Sometimes, as with the Head Start program, housing for the elderly, and the community development field, federal funds went to nonprofit organizations newly created to provide new services to previously underserved populations.

Then in the 1970s and 1980s, Congress dramatically shifted the bulk of this funding to voucher and voucherlike and loan programs. This change enabled patients, the disabled, the elderly, students, and others to act more like consumers in a marketplace and significantly increased public support for federally funded programs. From the start, Medicaid and Medicare left it to patients (and those who advised them) to select hospitals, clinics, doctors, and treatments, then paid for the services rendered.[29] Over the next two decades, Congress shifted other federal programs to this model, including student aid (increasingly involving loans), job training, and help in overcoming substance abuse. Food stamps and rent supplements, Medicaid, and disability payments supplemented or replaced existing welfare programs.

Federal funds came with strings. New rules imposed standards on the design of buildings and facilities; provisions for employee and public health and safety; program design; staff training, licensing, and certification; and institutional accreditation. They also enforced the newly established civil rights of women and minorities in hiring and promotion and in receipt of services. The U.S. Supreme Court affirmed that Congress had the power to set such rules. In every field, funding arrangements—fee structures, insurance arrangements, local taxes, streams of state and federal funds—as well as the standards and interests of professionals and other workers, shaped the provision of services in ways that, once established, were not easy to change.

All this forced the reconstruction of the fields in which foundations had long been active. And it forced foundations to reconsider their strategies.

Criticism of foundations inevitably increased as foundation efforts to change health care, education, family services, and other arrangements challenged the rapidly growing ranks of people whose interests as consumers, providers,

28. Smith and Lipsky (1993); see also Gronbjerg (1993).

29. Medicare and Medicaid only reimburse for approved services rendered by accredited hospitals and licensed providers. Medicare and Medicaid greatly expanded the health care market but increased that market's regulation.

employees, and taxpayers were vested in these fields. Some criticism was the political product of cold war–era fears such as those exploited by Senator Joseph McCarthy. Efforts to use foundations to shield family wealth from taxes and to maintain dynastic control over business firms—efforts that, as we have noted, grew rapidly in some quarters during the 1950s[30]—also provoked criticism. These critiques, together with complaints about the political activism of a few foundations, culminated in the Tax Reform Act of 1969, which increased public reporting requirements and formalized restrictions on the political activities of foundations.[31]

Together, changes in the fields foundations addressed as well as in their own positions led to a great deal of rethinking about appropriate roles. Greatly reduced relative wealth and other postwar conditions simply did not allow foundations to play the dramatic institution-building roles that had been available to them in the century's early decades.

As the chapters in this book demonstrate, foundations made many contributions during recent decades, but their contributions went in many different directions. Their contributions cannot be summed up in a phrase like "supported the creation of American denominationalism and the public library system" or "built major institutions in public education, higher education, medicine, international relations, and research." Nor did foundations in the postwar decades play decisive roles in most of the fields examined in the previous section.

Acceptance of Foundation Variety and a Focus on Sustainable Results in the Present Period

By the 1990s American foundations were experiencing renewed growth in numbers and resources, yet they found themselves in ever more complex and challenging fields, fields now heavily populated by institutions that had grown even larger in size and capacity. And while foundations grew, other sources of funding—notably, consumer and government spending—continued to grow faster. No longer able to play the sometimes dominant institution-shaping roles for which they had long been most celebrated and criticized, foundations entered a new era marked by increased transparency, an emphasis on achievable results, creative efforts to address the failures of government as well as of the market by enhancing civil society's capacity for self-organization, and an acceptance of the extraordinary diversity of foundation size, approach, and purpose.

30. Troyer (2000).

31. Although the Carnegie and Rockefeller foundations and their leaders, the Russell Sage Foundation, and the Twentieth Century Fund provided notable counter-examples, most foundations had traditionally insisted on privacy, even secrecy. The law did not require more. For this reason, there are hardly any reliable measures of the numbers or assets of foundations before the late 1970s.

Several of the studies in this volume, together with other evidence, persuade us that foundations are indeed entering a new period. Both foundations and their publics are coming to accept that foundations are widely diverse and varied, in size, focus, purpose, approach, and operations. Both foundations and their publics increasingly understand that foundation resources—even, as Bill Gates insists, those of the very largest—are and will always be quite limited in relation to the fields they address. Moreover, both foundations and their publics are interested in realistic claims and measurable results. Given their limited resources, many foundations are putting a renewed emphasis on creative efforts to mobilize collaborators and exert leverage.

At the beginning of the new millennium, American foundations find themselves in a situation that is dramatically different from that of the classic foundation period of the early twentieth century. In relation to the fields they address, foundations now have significantly less money. Other nonprofit and government institutions, often with far greater resources, occupy those fields. Early in the twentieth century, few families had been able to afford to send their children to high school, let alone college or professional school—or to pay for the limited medical care then available, or to provide private assisted-living services for infirm elderly parents. By 2000 greatly increased prosperity changed those circumstances for as much as half of the American population. And while federal government funding had been almost entirely absent from health care, education, and social services before the New Deal and the Great Society, the federal government now directs at least 5 percent of the entire U.S. economy toward work in those fields. Before the 1960s few federal regulations affected those fields: by the 1990s federal rulebooks and court decisions imposed extensive controls on the operations of every entity engaged in the fields of health, education, and welfare.

Responding to these new realities, foundations have come to redefine their ambitions and their practices. While foundations continue to use the legal forms that allow them to define their missions broadly as embracing "social welfare" in general, increasingly they address specific, specialized needs in well-defined niches. Collectively, foundations have taken on an ever-widening array of purposes; individually, increasing numbers of foundations are undertaking more precisely defined activities toward goals that can be specified and monitored.

Most postwar foundations had their origins in earlier decades, and many postwar foundation leaders had continued to think in terms of earlier eras. They understood their work in ways derived from nineteenth-century religious and community charity or from foundations' remarkable prewar institution-building achievements. Almost half of today's thirty largest foundations, by contrast, received their funds not in the first thirty years of the twentieth century but in the last twenty. Most new donors did not make their fortunes by accepting the status quo. They have come onto the scene after most of the changes detailed in the preceding pages and long after the notable achievements of the institution builders of the twentieth century's early decades.

Foundations have increased their commitment to transparency in many ways. Some of these are collective. The Foundation Center has continued to expand and enhance the information it provides not only about grant making but about foundations in general. The National Center for Charitable Statistics has created easily available data sets and summary sources of statistics. Foundations provided large start-up funds for the GuideStar website, which makes available to anyone the forms that foundations—and indeed nonprofits of all kinds—must file annually with the U.S. Internal Revenue Service. As access to this information increased, the Internal Revenue Service, working closely with Independent Sector (an umbrella organization for American nonprofits), the National Center for Charitable Statistics, and others, has substantially revised, clarified, and expanded its data collection activities. The Indiana University Center on Philanthropy has developed a continuing survey of American's charitable beliefs and actions,[32] and other research centers around the country monitor patterns and trends of the U.S. nonprofit sector.

Many individual foundations have taken moves toward increased transparency that fit with their own missions. The Robert Wood Johnson Foundation, the Wallace Foundation, and others have taken to publishing, or posting on the web, extensive evaluations of their programs. Like an increasing number of foundations, the Jessie Ball duPont Fund undertakes and publishes extensive studies of the fields it addresses.

Foundations increasingly link their emphasis on transparency to their growing commitment to evaluating impact and achieving measurable results. For the Annie E. Casey Foundation, to take one example, this has meant developing the notable Kids Count measures of child welfare, as well as identifying and encouraging wide attention to the plight of children in foster care who age out of government-funded support on their eighteenth birthdays and must immediately become self-supporting. For the Pew Charitable Trusts, it has meant significant investment in gathering and making available information about the press. We could multiply examples in many directions. Key actors at the Ford, Annenberg, Thomas Fordham, Walton Family, and other foundations engaged in the renewal and reform of elementary and secondary education have created an extensive literature on the challenges and possibilities of foundation work in that set of fields.[33] They are far from achieving consensus on what works, but they have done much to inform discussions of policy and practice.

32. Center on Philanthropy Panel Study, "Center on Philanthropy Study Panel" (www.philanthropy.iupui.edu/Research/COPPS/ [November 13, 2009]).

33. See, for example, the contributions to F. M. Hess (2005b); Bacchetti and Ehrlich (2006); Domanico and others (2000); Glennan and others (2004).

The creative efforts of many foundations to address what they see as the failures of government attracted a great deal of favorable attention during a period in which the market often seemed to enhance civil society's capacity for self-organization. Several foundations have expressed a renewed emphasis on social entrepreneurship and have worked to define new philanthropic instruments, even to promote for-profit approaches to the solution of social problems. The desire to move beyond regulation was of course very much in tune with mainstream thinking in business and policy analysis during the 1980s, the 1990s, and the early years of the twenty-first century. The 2008 collapse of so many American and international financial institutions has raised many questions about deregulation and has made governmental solutions seem more attractive. But as we see it, foundations have been responding not just to current fashion but to serious analysis of social change and to very real changes in their own position.

Not surprisingly, California's Silicon Valley has strongly fostered new philanthropic approaches, although other urban centers, including New York, Los Angeles, Chicago, Houston, and Seattle, have seen similar developments. The creation of the microchip and software industries, the dot-com boom of the mid-1990s, and the rise of the Internet as a business tool drew attention to new business models even as they created extraordinary new private wealth. The rapid success of start-up companies ranging from Intel, Microsoft, Hewlett-Packard, eBay, and Google—like the earlier successes of Benjamin Frankin, the Lowells, George Peabody, Andrew Carnegie, John D. Rockefeller, Julius Rosenwald, and Henry Ford—derived in large part from entrepreneurship. Like their philanthropic predecessors, several of the recent donors have channeled their entrepreneurial spirit into new forms of philanthropy.

Pierre Omidyar, the founder of eBay, and the Google.org foundation seek to break down what they view as outmoded distinctions between philanthropy and business.[34] They and others insist that general solutions to social problems require "going to scale" in ways best mastered by some of the largest, most rapidly growing corporations. Several Google initiatives, not unlike a number of the initiatives of the Bill and Melinda Gates Foundation and the projects of Bill Clinton's foundation, have emphasized the strategic application of technology, science, and medicine to global problems of health, climate change, and education. Other initiatives promoted by Omidyar and eBay cofounder Jeffrey Skoll, as well as by the much older Surdna Foundation and many others, hope to identify individual young "social entrepreneurs," mentor them, and encourage them to pursue distinctive careers.

34. Douglas McGray, "Network Philanthropy," *Los Angeles Times Magazine*, January 21, 2007; see also Omidyar Network (www.omidyar.net).

Current leaders of several other recently established foundations (the Gates, Ewing Marion Kauffman, and United Nations foundations, for example) as well as leaders of several older foundations—Cleveland, Hewlett, and many others—have added their own calls for imaginative, entrepreneurial approaches to foundation philanthropy.[35] Some of these call for new initiatives directed toward the creation of new organizations, new practices, even new orientations for the economies of entire regions. Others insist that foundations can make perhaps their greatest impact by acting to increase the capabilities of existing organizations. Foundations have funded several important initiatives in this last direction, including those of Grantmakers for Effective Organizations, the Center for Effective Philanthropy, and the Stanford Social Innovation Review.[36]

It is not yet clear whether available resources will suffice to achieve the more expansive ambitions of the new foundations. These ambitions reflect a belief that civil society has a greater capacity for self-renewal and less need for government than most foundation leaders had believed during earlier eras.[37] Some advocates of new initiatives also (and controversially) call for a reconsideration of the long-settled distinction between philanthropic and profit-seeking activities. Many argue that foundations can achieve the greatest impact by acting as social entrepreneurs and risk takers as well as institution builders and value conservers.

Yet while many foundations celebrate the capacity of civil society for self-organization, others continue to emphasize that there can be no alternative to using the regulatory and funding capabilities of government if society is to make progress toward improving health, the environment, or opportunity for all. Our colleagues document a number of creative and effective foundation efforts to find ways to make government more effective. They cite important cases in

35. See, for example, Brest and Harvey (2008), and Brest's blog, "Strategic Philanthropy," November 13, 2008 (www.huffingtonpost.com/paul-brest/strategic-philanthropy_b_143675.html).

36. The search for effectiveness is a strong, continuing thrust in the foundation field, although it will take changing form from time to time. The leaders of one interesting initiative wrote in November 2008 that "unfortunately, in the past few years the funding environment for GivingNet's category of nonprofit work, philanthropy infrastructure, has been dramatically reduced. This type of funding goes in cycles, and we rode a great wave of 'operational effectiveness' funding from [a number of foundations]. . . . The board and management of GivingNet have decided that it is best to complete the organization's original program on a high note, declare a limited victory, and thus allow all involved to re-focus resources and energy on future opportunities." Community Foundations of America, "The Impact of Giving" (http://communityfoundationsonline.net [December 2008]).

37. The most recent example is the 2008 launch of the World Wide Web Foundation. Seeded with a $5 million grant from the John S. and James L. Knight Foundation, the WWW Foundation hopes to raise enough to become an important catalyst for the future development of the web in ways that will allow access by and benefit underserved, economically deprived communities throughout the world.

elementary and secondary education (involving the Annenberg, Walton, and many other foundations), in arts education (notably by the Wallace Foundation), in health (involving the R. W. Johnson and the Henry J. Kaiser Family foundations and the Milbank Memorial and other funds), in the reform of welfare, and in the effort to reduce poverty (involving the Ford, Annie E. Casey, Rockefeller, and many other foundations).

It would be wrong to conclude on a note that suggests that all foundations subscribe to any single set of approaches. Instead, we step back for a moment to emphasize the extraordinary diversity of foundation size, approach, and purpose and to suggest that acceptance of that diversity is increasing. Recent decades have seen a remarkable and still little-studied flowering of religious foundations devoted not only to the oldest-established mainline Protestant denominations but also to evangelical Protestantism in many of its varieties, to the many dimensions of Judaism, and even to Catholic causes that had long made minimal use of foundations.[38] The liberal National Committee for Responsive Philanthropy critiques the field from a progressive standpoint; the Philanthropy Roundtable and the Capital Research Center comment from the right. In its efforts to provide an umbrella for the entire field, the Council on Foundations has set up a number of specialized committees. Foundation program officers have organized a large and increasing number of grant makers in particular fields ranging from aging and the arts to the environment and health to the U.S. International Grantmaking project.

Hence it is no surprise that those who call for new foundation approaches do not speak with a single voice. Some emphasize transparency and accountability to the widest public; others emphasize results (in fields they deem of preeminent importance) above all. Whereas some of the proponents of entrepreneurialism tout their projects with impressive enthusiasm, others urge modesty.[39] Several notable foundation leaders have called, quietly as well as eloquently, for renewed emphasis on fidelity to valued religious or cultural traditions.[40] Government-sponsored hospital conversion funds often emphasize their commitment to equality. While many of the most vocal contributors to the debate are based on the West Coast or in New York, the W. K. Kellogg, Charles Stewart Mott, Kresge, Lilly, MacArthur, Cleveland, and other midwestern foundations

38. Many religious foundations are small, as our colleagues Wuthnow and Lindsay note; but even among the thirty largest, the Lilly Endowment and the Tulsa Community Foundation pay special attention to Protestantism (among other religious and secular causes), while the Harry and Jeanette Weinberg Foundation pays special attention to certain Jewish institutions. A notable recent development is the creation of foundations to support Catholic Charities in Cleveland and several other dioceses.

39. See Karoff (2004); also Cuninggim (1972).

40. The Lilly Endowment is notable in its efforts to maintain religious and cultural traditions.

continue to redefine their efforts to expand opportunity for self-improvement. The most rapid foundation growth is occurring in the South.

What does seem different from the past are the acceptance of limitation, the search for leverage, the emphasis on such intangible foundation resources as reputation and the ability to convene, enhanced transparency, openness to new approaches, and the embracing of foundation diversity. We see all this both in the new foundations and in many of those that are larger and established. Could it be, as the chapters in this volume suggest, that at the beginning of the twenty-first century, the institution of the philanthropic foundation is finding a new role?

PART II

Exploring Roles and Contributions

2

Foundations and the Making of Public Education in the United States, 1867–1950

PAMELA BARNHOUSE WALTERS AND EMILY A. BOWMAN

Public education was one of the early forms of American social provision.[1] Indeed, by the mid-nineteenth century primary education was fully institutionalized as a state responsibility in most of the country.[2] Once established, public responsibility for American schooling continued to expand; public high schools were commonplace in much of the United States by the first decade of the twentieth century. The exception to these patterns is the South. There, public responsibility for elementary education was not firmly established until the late nineteenth century, and public secondary education remained underdeveloped, especially for blacks, until well into the twentieth century.[3]

While most accounts of the history of American education acknowledge that public schooling originated when the public sector absorbed a preexisting mix of private academies and charity schools, the further development of state systems of education is generally depicted as a wholly state effort.[4] In fact, as this chapter

---

1. Skocpol (1992).

2. Cremin (1951); Kaestle (1983); Spring (1990).

3. Anderson (1988); Bullock (1967); Knight (1922); Leloudis (1996); Link (1986, 1992). Scholarly definitions of what states constitute the South often differ. In the context of discussion of underdeveloped southern responsibility for public schooling in the late nineteenth century, however, the South is generally considered to consist of Virginia, North Carolina, South Carolina, Georgia, Florida, Alabama, Mississippi, Louisiana, Texas, Arkansas, and Tennessee. See Dabney (1936, pp. 56, 78).

4. Cremin (1951); Kaestle (1983); Tyack (1974).

demonstrates, the creation and institutionalization of public elementary and secondary education in America was actually a joint public-private effort.[5] More specifically, private foundations provided funding to build public education in the South, and throughout the country they spearheaded and underwrote reform efforts that institutionalized "modern" forms of schooling that remain taken for granted to this day. Foundations, in short, decisively shaped public policy about the provision of education.

Foundations have been active in the field of public education since 1867 and played a formative role in the creation of the modern state system of public elementary and secondary education—a task that was more or less complete by the time the United States entered World War II. Despite their appearances as private, politically neutral institutions, foundations were deeply intertwined with the public sphere. Foundations' political work extended far beyond the complementary role of delivering social services outside of the public sector that public authorities (federal, state, or local) could or would not provide.[6]

Throughout the period considered here, foundations primarily played the role of promoting change in official state policy concerning access to and content of public education. Depending on the political circumstances under which they were trying to act, they deployed three main strategies to do so (see table 2-1). When they were political outsiders without good access to the public officials who controlled public education, foundations adopted a strategy of state infiltration, which involved getting inside the state and using their considerable private resources to call forth new state responsibilities for public education. When foundations enjoyed good access to education policymaking circles, they used a variety of forms of political suasion to shape the decisions of education policymakers. When they set their sights on reforming the content of instruction in the nation's schools—practices controlled by thousands of school districts rather than a single national political authority—foundations succeeded when they bypassed the public sector and instead relied on market interventions to effect widespread change. Eight major foundations, employing these strategies, devoted some or all of their attentions to public schooling before the mid-twentieth century.[7]

---

5. Foundation work related to higher education took a different course and is the subject of separate discussion in chapters 4 and 5.

6. See, for example, Powell and Clemens (1998); Jackson (1990); Douglas (1987).

7. These philanthropic foundations had very large financial resources and were active in shaping formal schooling systems between 1867 and 1950. Andrea Walton (2005) and others have advocated for broader definitions of both foundation activity and education, but we rely on more traditional definitions of philanthropy and education in our analysis of foundation involvement in public education. Our focus is on foundations with regional or national agendas and influence rather than those with local or statewide missions, the most important of which were the Chicago Community Trust, the Cleveland Foundation, and the M. S. Hershey Foundation (Pennsylvania).

Table 2-1. *Foundation Strategies for Influencing Public Education Policy, 1867–1950*

Foundation strategy	Characteristics	Context	Examples
State infiltration	Places contingencies on provision of funds to the state and inserts new officials within state bureaucracy	Provides limited possibility for cooperation between foundation actors and local or state political officials	Peabody Education Fund (with Slater Fund); Rosenwald Fund; General Education Board (with Jeanes Foundation and Phelps-Stokes Fund)
Political suasion	Uses good public standing and social research findings to influence state policymakers	Foundation actors and policymakers are on good terms and share policy objectives	General Education Board (with Jeanes Foundation and Phelps-Stokes Fund); Russell Sage Foundation
Market intervention	Bypasses political actors altogether by introducing new practices through the national marketplace	Foundation actors have national goals, but meaningful policy is decentralized	Carnegie Foundation for the Advancement of Teaching

An Overview of the Eight Major Foundations

Foundation efforts in the field of public education before the mid-twentieth century fall into two general categories: some sought to solve what they saw as a problem of insufficient access to public schooling, others to reform public schools to do a more effective job of educating America's youth. When the first of these foundations, the Peabody Education Fund, was founded in 1867, the access problem was a southern problem. Solving that problem occupied foundations working in the field of public education until the turn of the twentieth century, and all of them confronted the challenge of being outsiders to the region.

In 1867 the northern merchant-banker George Peabody established the first significant American foundation, the Peabody Fund, whose purpose was to bring public education to the South.[8] A legal framework for public schooling in the South was established in the same year: as a condition of readmission to

8. Andrews (1961); Ayres (1911); Curry (1969); Kiger (2000); West (1966).

the Union; federal authorities required southern states to draft new constitutions that repealed laws prohibiting the education of blacks and established state responsibility for public schooling.[9] The depletion of southern states' treasuries by the war, however, posed a significant obstacle to realizing those responsibilities. Thus Peabody provided substantial private funds for school construction, for salaries for state education bureaucrats, and for public relations efforts intended to promote the cause of public schooling. These funds, though, were contingent on financial contributions from state and local authorities and required public authorities to agree to assume responsibility for the ongoing operation of the school systems it helped build. Peabody's actions, especially its funding for school construction and for government bureaucrats' salaries, blurred the line between public and private and allowed it to, in effect, infiltrate the state, to work from the inside to effect a change in public policy.

In its education work in the South, the Peabody Fund was joined in 1882 by the John F. Slater Fund for the Education of Freedmen, intended to promote public education for African Americans by helping to train an adequate cadre of teachers for black schools.[10] Because Slater funds were given to church and private teacher-training schools, and because its endowment was significantly lower than the Peabody's, the Slater Fund had a far weaker impact on the trajectory of public responsibility for schooling than did the Peabody Fund.[11]

By 1902, when John D. Rockefeller used part of his Standard Oil fortune to establish the General Education Board (GEB), public authority over and fiscal responsibility for public schooling were institutionalized practices in the South, but southern school systems were still underdeveloped compared with those in the rest of the country. The GEB brought the Rockefeller family's considerable financial resources—$53 million in contributions between 1902 and 1909—and political clout to bear, first on the educational inadequacies of the South and later on what they perceived to be educational problems throughout the country.[12] The GEB took a page from the Peabody Fund's book by providing private funds for school construction contingent on contributions from the local community and for salaries of various public education bureaucrats. Their greatest contributions, however, were their public relations work in support of expanded state responsibility for public education in the South and their use of "scientific philanthropy"—demonstration projects and social research—as a tool for influencing education policy decisions nationwide. Their greatest successes came, therefore, from respecting the line between public and private by acting as

    9. Foner and Brown (2005); Knox (1947).
    10. Andrews (1961); Fisher (1986); Kiger (1956); Newbold (1928).
    11. The Slater endowment was $1 million, the Peabody's $3 million. Ayres (1911).
    12. Ayers (1992); Bond (1934); Bullock (1967); Coon (1938); General Education Board (1915, 1916); Harlan (1958); Leloudis (1996).

civic-minded outsiders to the state who sought to help education policymakers make the right choices.

The distinctive educational needs of southern blacks continued to call forth new foundation activity well into the twentieth century. The Anna T. Jeanes Foundation was established in 1908 with a gift of $1 million to aid Negro rural schools, and the Phelps-Stokes Fund was established in 1911 with a gift of $1 million to, among other goals, promote the education of Negroes in the South.[13] The work of both funds came to be coordinated and administered by the GEB, however, making it impossible to distinguish either their contribution or their means of shaping education policy or practice from the overall efforts of the GEB.[14]

The most significant new foundation of the twentieth century devoted exclusively to the cause of better public education for southern blacks was established in 1917 by the northern philanthropist Julius Rosenwald with an initial contribution of $4 million. The major thrust of the Rosenwald Fund was to stimulate the creation of public elementary schools for blacks in the rural South.[15] To this end, Rosenwald deployed the same strategy of making funding contingent on contributions from nonfoundation sources that had proved effective for the Peabody Fund. Given Rosenwald officials' status as political outsiders trying to improve educational opportunities for blacks in a region that had recently reasserted white supremacy, infiltrating the state with private money was most likely the only way they could have realized their objective.

The final significant foundation actors in the field of American public education before the mid-twentieth century were two of national scope that were not centrally concerned with K–12 education but nonetheless had significant influence on public elementary and secondary schooling. Consider first the Russell Sage Foundation, established in 1907 with a gift of $10 million from Russell Sage's widow, Margaret Olivia Sage. The Russell Sage Foundation hoped to stimulate elected officials and the public to make better policy decisions by using social research to identify the causes of pressing social problems. Although not devoted primarily to education work, the two best-known of the many surveys supported by the Russell Sage Foundation, the Pittsburgh Survey in 1907 and the Springfield Survey in 1914, both included careful investigations of public schools.[16] These surveys, and others like them, included recommendations to the public for action to remediate the problems identified. Russell Sage findings and recommendations took the scientific philanthropy approach pioneered by the GEB to new heights.

Finally, some of the most lasting curricular practices of public secondary education in America originate in a foundation devoted to higher education: the

13. Anderson (1988); Ayres (1911); Kiger (1956); Leavell (1933); Parker (1972).
14. General Education Board (1915).
15. Anderson (1988); Ascoli (2006); Hanchett (1988); Strong and others (2000).
16. Harrison (1916, 1931).

Carnegie Foundation for the Advancement of Teaching. Established by the U.S. Steel founder Andrew Carnegie in 1905, with endowments totaling $25 million dollars over its first three years, the foundation devoted its funding exclusively to higher education.[17] Nevertheless, by intervening in the marketplace of higher education the foundation realized a spectacular degree of success in its goal of helping to standardize American secondary education.[18] In two separate efforts, the Carnegie Foundation shaped college admissions requirements, which, in turn, changed and standardized high school curricula throughout the country. First, in the second and third decades of the twentieth century it used contingencies placed on its funding of institutions of higher education to put in place new high school course requirements for college admission. Second, by helping to fund the development of the Educational Testing Service in the 1940s, it promoted standardized college admissions testing.

Foundation Strategies for the Development of Public Education

In this section we describe in more detail the three strategies foundations adopted to advance their goals of expanding and reforming public education in the period before the mid-twentieth century, and we analyze the ways in which deploying them allowed foundations to exert a significant influence on the development and institutionalization of public K–12 education in the United States. We examine the limits and possibilities inherent in each strategy with selective illustrations of foundation activities during this period.

Infiltrating the State

State governments throughout the South were faced with the formidable task of constructing systems of public schooling practically from scratch in the aftermath of the Civil War. The South had boasted many private academies for affluent whites before the Civil War, along with a few "free" schools for poor whites, but little or no formal schooling existed for blacks. During the war, many former slaves established and operated schools in Union-occupied areas, and other schools for southern blacks were established by the Union Army itself or by northern missionary and benevolent societies.[19] At war's close in 1865,

17. Lagemann (1983).
18. Kliebard (1995).
19. Anderson (1988); Bond (1934); Bullock (1967); Curry (1969). These societies were not foundations as foundations are typically defined. They were nongovernmental and nonprofit, but they did not meet other conditions commonly established for counting as a foundation, that is, "having a [significant] principal fund of its own, managed by its own trustees or directors" (Andrews 1961, p. 157). Furthermore, their focus was the provision of short-term relief for acute social problems rather than remediation of the root causes of social problems.

the U.S. Congress created the Bureau of Refugees, Freedmen, and Abandoned Lands (know as the Freedmen's Bureau), which until 1870 operated, with federal funds, a system of free schools for blacks that coexisted with black-run schools and with schools established by northern societies. None of these forms of schooling new to the South were popular with most white southerners, however, and all bypassed local and state public authorities entirely.[20]

When George Peabody established the Peabody Education Fund to promote public education in the South for both black and white children, he eschewed the policy of supporting individual private schools—the strategy of the missionary and benevolent societies—in favor of building a strong public system.[21] Private monies would help get public school systems started, but over the long term public schools had to be supported through public means. Indeed, the fund intended to work in a way that required the state to assume responsibility for the schools and education programs it helped initiate. The Peabody Fund used the financial resources it could offer to stimulate state action and responsibility: it provided only a portion of the money needed for support of a school and made the contribution of even larger sums by southern state and local governments a condition of its assistance. "The chief benefit did not arise from what the Fund gave, but from what it induced others to give and to do. . . . In many instances, the towns soon assumed all the expense, the schools became self-supporting, and thus the timely and judicious aid gave permanence to schools which continued to flourish after the fostering external help was withdrawn."[22] This model, which the Peabody Fund termed "partial succor," would long outlive the fund itself as a strategy to create a public commitment while securing more money for public schools than foundations alone could provide.

Peabody used a different form of state infiltration to help build state administrative capacity. Throughout the late-nineteenth-century South, state government bureaucracy was too limited in size to be effective, in the view of Peabody Fund officials. The fund therefore initiated a program of paying the salaries of state agents for public education—agents who were placed inside the state bureaucracy and who functioned in all respects as state officials.[23] It also undertook efforts to increase state officials' authority. Most notably, Peabody Fund agents required that all requests for aid for individual schools be endorsed by the state superintendent, who was also required to specify the amount that should be allotted.[24]

20. Bullock (1967); Vaughn (1974).
21. Peabody explicitly rejected the charity model; instead of seeking "to relieve pauperism," he sought to "prevent it" (Curry 1969, p. 15).
22. Curry (1969, pp. 40–42).
23. Curry (1969).
24. Black (1961, p. 39).

As northerners, the principals paid by the Peabody Fund could not directly participate in southern politics. The fund accomplished its goals by using private funds to leverage educational commitments from public officials and by cooperating with local leaders. What did the Peabody Fund accomplish through these means? There is no doubt that in the first decade and a half of the Peabody Fund's operation, the framework for free public education for blacks and whites was laid and means were established for funding the schools, increasing the authority of state bureaucrats, and building state administrative capacity.[25] Peabody Fund trustees, reflecting in 1880 on their first thirteen years' work, concluded that they had helped bring about "one of the most marvelous revolutions of the century. . . , namely, the incorporation, into organic and statute laws, of systems of free public schools [in the South], backed by a sustaining public sentiment."[26]

As political outsiders to the South who chose to work within the political framework and culture of the South, Peabody officials accommodated the racial "color line" favored by white southern leaders. For example, the Peabody Fund opposed mixed-race schools on the grounds that whites' refusal to attend them would thwart the development of public schooling throughout the region.[27] Even more important, its monies were used to the greatly disproportionate benefit of white schools and white students, despite its intent to benefit children of both races. Early annual reports from the fund do not provide detailed listings of school-by-school expenditures, but a summary of Peabody spending for 1867–80 shows that only 6.5 percent of the $1.2 million disbursed during that time was allocated to black schools.[28] Furthermore, in 1871 the Peabody Fund adopted an explicit policy of supporting black schools at two-thirds of the rate established for white schools—at a time when salaries of black and white teachers were identical.[29] This systematic underfunding of schools for blacks is ironic, given the Peabody Fund's adamant opposition to racially mixed schools on the grounds that racial integration was not necessary for racial equality, a goal it supported.[30]

In the last two decades of the nineteenth century, Peabody officials, having in their view succeeded in establishing public systems of education in the South, turned their attention, in part, to further strengthening the state education sector. First, they turned away from funding construction of new elementary and secondary schools, focusing instead on increasing the number of qualified public

25. Bullock (1967); Foner and Brown (2005); Knight (1922).
26. Curry (1969, pp. 77–78).
27. Bullock (1967, p. 122); West (1966, p. 15).
28. West (1966, p. 4).
29. Bond (1934, p. 131).
30. Bond (1934, p. 131).

school teachers by partly funding teacher training institutes and normal schools, some in the private sector. Second, they escalated their practice of increasing the number of state education personnel by paying salaries of various forms of state agents. Both strategies are extensions of Peabody's earlier efforts to build state administrative capacity.[31] Once again, they used their private funds to place new personnel inside the state bureaucracy.

As with its funding for school construction, however, the Peabody Fund's allocations for teacher training disproportionately benefited whites.[32] Furthermore, it closely aligned the curricula of black normal schools (but not white normal schools) with principles of industrial education. Industrial education for blacks was intended to prepare students for manual labor, especially agricultural and domestic work, and black teachers were expected to "stand as exemplars [to their students] of the 'dignity of labor.'"[33] Industrial education in black normal schools was supposed to "adjust" blacks to their inevitable future roles as manual laborers.[34]

The strategies pioneered by the Peabody Fund for "infiltrating" the state were taken up by other education foundations that worked in the South. The Peabody Fund's efforts to expand state administrative capacity by paying the salaries of new state officials was accelerated after the establishment of the General Education Board in 1902, when the GEB joined with the fund in this mission (along with the Slater Fund and the Jeanes Foundation, the activities of which were closely coordinated by the GEB).[35] These new public authorities included state supervisors of rural schools; supervising teachers for black rural schools, who eventually came to function as assistant county superintendents; and state agents for Negro education.[36] In the period from 1924 to 1938, the GEB again escalated its efforts to build state administrative capacity by making grants to establish new administrative units in state departments of education throughout the country.

The foundation that made perhaps the most systematic use of the state infiltration strategy, however, was the Rosenwald Fund. When Julius Rosenwald surveyed the state of southern education in the second decade of the twentieth century, he saw that large numbers of southern blacks, especially in rural areas, still did not have access to public elementary schools.[37] To meet, at least partly, the educational needs of black southerners that were being ignored by the state

31. Ayres (1911); Curry (1969); Leavell (1933); West (1966).
32. West (1966, p. 12).
33. Anderson (1988, p. 55).
34. Anderson (1988, p. 36).
35. Parker (1972).
36. Harlan (1958, p. 254).
37. Anderson (1988); Anderson and Moss (1999).

(and, to some degree, by the GEB and the other foundations that worked collaboratively with them), in 1917 Rosenwald established the foundation that bears his name for purposes of stimulating "public authorities to take a larger share of social responsibility."[38] Rosenwald followed the partial succor model pioneered by Peabody: the fund supplied a relatively small proportion of the monies needed to construct a new school, and the bulk was provided by the local school district and by donations from the black community.[39] By the time it ended its school construction efforts in 1930, the Rosenwald Fund had significantly altered the landscape of public schooling in the South: one-fifth of all rural schoolhouses for blacks in the South were Rosenwald schools, and about one-third of all rural black students were educated in one.[40] As of 1930 more than 600,000 African American students were enrolled in 4,762 Rosenwald schools scattered across the rural South.[41]

Because Rosenwald officials were trying to moderate, in effect, the extremes of the Jim Crow system in an era in which southern blacks had been stripped of all political influence, they too had to accommodate the very color line they were trying to challenge. This accommodation was manifested in two principal ways. First, whereas Peabody's partial succor method had required contributions from state and local treasuries, Rosenwald's school construction program required contributions from local black communities as well as from public sources. Blacks were therefore subject to a double taxation: they paid taxes that were disproportionately used to fund white schools, and then they made private contributions—often substantial ones—toward construction of needed public schools for their communities.[42]

Second, the Rosenwald Fund emphasized—indeed, required—a form of education for blacks designed to prepare them for manual labor: industrial education.[43] Rosenwald schools had to follow

> simple, efficient plans carefully worked out by representatives of the Fund in co-operation with school authorities. They were to provide not only formal and theoretical "book larnin'" but also practical work and to have

38. Embree and Waxman (1949, p. 17). The neglect by state authorities of the educational needs of southern blacks was made possible by the disfranchising campaigns of the late nineteenth-century South that stripped blacks of the vote and reestablished white supremacy (Kousser 1974).

39. Strong and others (2000).

40. "Conference of Trustees and Guests, Julius Rosenwald Fund, April 29, 1928," box 135, Julius Rosenwald Fund Papers.

41. "Rosenwald Fund: Rural Schoolhouse Construction Report to July 1, 1930," box 2, folder 25, Una Roberts Lawrence papers.

42. Anderson (1988); Hanchett (1988); Strong and others (2000).

43. Anderson (1988).

at least one room for shop or home arts and two acres of land available for farm gardens. In addition to their lessons, the girls were expected to learn sewing and cooking and the boys farming and simple work with tools.[44]

In fact, after the fund's work was well established, it had a uniform architectural blueprint for all Rosenwald schools that included space specifically allocated to "industrial" training.

The Rosenwald Fund suspended its schoolhouse construction program in 1932, noting that provision of schooling for blacks in the South was not yet adequate nor were blacks yet receiving their share of state educational appropriations. Nonetheless, the trustees and officers of the fund felt that they had done a great deal toward stimulating a public commitment to black education.[45] They decided to discontinue the program to prevent state overreliance on outside aid for the finance of education for blacks. It was time for states in the South to assume "full responsibility for the schools of this section as an integral part of public provisions for the education of all the people."[46]

Although partial succor was the Rosenwald Fund's primary strategy, it also continued Peabody and General Education Board efforts to increase state authority: Rosenwald established and paid the salaries of both white and black assistants to the white "Negro agents" within state education bureaucracies, and it mandated that funding requests go through state departments of education. These actions contributed to the establishment of a competent network of administrators, including some African Americans, who would continue to advocate for increased state funding of public schools for blacks long after the Rosenwald initiative ended.[47]

Major foundation activity to improve access to public elementary and secondary schooling in the South came to a close with the end of Rosenwald's school construction program in 1932, largely because foundations considered that by around 1930 public education was on firm institutional footing throughout the country.[48] Illustrating the guiding principle of foundation activity articulated by Horace Coon—"When the State steps in, the foundation steps out"—foundations pulled back from direct social provision.[49]

44. Embree and Waxman (1949, p. 39).

45. As they had: throughout the entire course of the Rosenwald Fund's program, state and local government contributed more than three times as much as the Rosenwald Fund toward the cost of schoolhouse construction (Bullock 1967, p. 144).

46. Embree and Waxman (1949, p. 57).

47. Hanchett (1988, pp. 406–07).

48. Access for southern blacks remained a problem, however. Southern blacks did not enjoy adequate access to public secondary schools until after World War II (Anderson 1988, pp. 187–237).

49. Coon (1938, p. 55).

Political Suasion and Scientific Philanthropy

By the time Rockefeller established the General Education Board in 1902, blacks had been disfranchised in most southern states and white supremacy was firmly reestablished.[50] With an agenda that placed far greater priority on the educational needs of white southerners than of black southerners and emphasized industrial rather than classical education for southern blacks, the priorities of the GEB were generally in line with those of white political elites.

The resulting ability of the GEB to work "cooperatively" with state officials allowed them access to southern policymaking circles that had been heretofore unknown to political outsiders. In the first published account of its own activities, the board described its cooperative stance: "[The GEB] felt its way cautiously, conscious of the difficulty, complexity, and delicacy of the situation. It hoped to aid, not by foisting upon the South a program from outside, but by cooperating with Southern leaders in sympathetically working out a program framed by them on the basis of local conditions and local considerations. [The Board] has cooperated, not interfered."[51]

The most significant result of establishing the confidence and trust of white southern leaders was the GEB's ability to partner with them in a campaign of mass persuasion intended to convince what it saw as the "better class" of white southerners that public education was a good thing and that they should tax themselves at the levels necessary to support it. As one element of this campaign, the GEB funded state university positions for specialists in secondary education who traveled throughout the state as evangelists for the cause of public secondary education, "making speeches, holding conferences, playing one town against another."[52] Through these and other efforts, they helped engineer the great educational awakening of the South in the early twentieth century that provided a firm basis in public taxation for white public schools in the region.[53] After 1915, the triumph of southern educational progressivism (for whites) accomplished, the GEB largely ceased efforts to fund public elementary and secondary schools, in the South and elsewhere.

By the first decade of the twentieth century, the principle (if not the practice) of universal access to state-funded and state-controlled public elementary and secondary education had been firmly established in each state of the Union.[54] With the access problem largely solved, foundations turned their attention to remedying

50. Kousser (1974).

51. General Education Board (1916, p. 14).

52. Coon (1938, p. 135).

53. Kousser (1980); Leloudis (1996).

54. As our prior discussion emphasizes, southern blacks did not have universal access to public elementary schooling, much less public secondary schooling, until the 1930s.

deficiencies in public education throughout the nation. The major debate was over curriculum, both its content and its organization: What instructional content, organized in what way, would best serve the nation's public schools?

The major foundations attempting to solve national educational problems adopted two main strategies for accomplishing their goals that took advantage of the generally favorable access they had to political decisionmakers. First, they tested innovative model programs, whose effectiveness could be demonstrated to policymakers in state and local school districts. Second, they sponsored educational research and disseminated their findings widely in hopes of influencing policymakers' decisions. Professional education associations were important channels for disseminating research findings and the best practices presumed to follow from them.

It was the General Education Board that pioneered these new strategies for influencing education policymaking throughout the nation. For instance, they undertook the first demonstration efforts by establishing "model programs in school supervision, teaching training, curriculum design, and student health" in hopes of triggering widespread state adoption—a strategy best illustrated by their farm demonstration efforts.[55] Within a few years of the GEB's founding, its trustees became convinced that low levels of agricultural productivity in the South were the primary impediment to establishing a sound basis in public taxation for public schools. Hence they funded a far-reaching initiative in farm demonstration work, intended to champion "scientific agriculture as a technique that would earn farmers the extra money necessary to gain their support for additional taxation."[56] By undertaking a "quiet alliance" with the U.S. Department of Agriculture between 1906 and 1914, their efforts contributed to the passage of the federal Smith-Hughes Act in 1917, which provided federal funds for programs of "vocational education of less than college grade in agriculture, home economics, and trades and industry . . . to girls and boys in all rural states."[57]

This act marked the first time that "federal funds became a significant resource to be used for educational purposes"—the first significant assumption of responsibility by the federal government for public elementary and secondary education—and it resulted in the creation of countless numbers of vocational education programs in public schools throughout the country.[58] What had originated as an effort to bolster the tax base for southern education had a far broader effect: it transformed school curricula throughout the country.

The GEB was also the pioneer of a method its directors described as "scientific philanthropy": reliance on expert knowledge, statistics, and social research

55. Leloudis (1996, p. 151).
56. Sealander (1997, pp. 44–45).
57. Bullock (1967, p. 138).
58. Sealander (1997, p. 52).

to identify the causes of social problems and to plan actions to correct them.[59] The foundation that most fully relied on social research as a means of influencing policymakers, however, was the Russell Sage Foundation.

By investigating and making known the facts behind pressing social problems, the Russell Sage Foundation, established in 1907, hoped to stimulate elected officials and the public to make better policy decisions. Unlike the GEB, however, the Russell Sage Foundation did not allocate its own funds for new forms of social provision. For the remediation of social problems, the Russell Sage Foundation relied on the state. Indeed, each survey and investigation outlined steps public officials should take to solve the problems, often including education reform. These findings and recommendations appear to have led to changes in education policy. In his recounting of the accomplishments of the Springfield Survey, for example, Shelby Harrison identifies fourteen distinct ways in which public school officials made improvements suggested by survey findings.[60]

Other Russell Sage Foundation studies and recommendations brought about widespread changes in American educational practices. Through its department of education, the Russell Sage Foundation first documented and dramatized the problem of unacceptably large numbers of overage students in American public schools and set about finding a solution to the problem by conducting some of the earliest experiments in educational measurement and assessment.[61] Two important changes to the organization of schooling nationwide resulted, in part, from the Russell Sage Foundation's efforts. First, school districts throughout the country adopted a policy of age-grading (accomplished by what is often referred to as social promotion) to keep children of similar ages together as they progressed through the grades. But age-grading created new problems even as it solved an old one: it increased the heterogeneity of academic achievement on the part of students within a single grade level. The solution to this problem was widespread application of the newly developed measurement scales and ability tests, the results of which were used to group children by ability levels within grades and to track students into a newly differentiated curriculum.[62] The Russell Sage Foundation's efforts were partly responsible for the rapid adoption of ability testing for classification purposes: by 1926 most urban public school systems in the country used some sort of ability test to assign students to ability groups.[63] Age-grading, ability grouping, and tracking remain key organizational features of American schooling at present, albeit contested ones.

59. Dabney (1936); Leloudis (1996).
60. Harrison (1916, pp. 21–22).
61. Ayres (1909); Harrison (1949); Resnick (1981).
62. Ayres (1912); Chapman (1981).
63. Chapman (1981).

Market Interventions That Shaped Education Policy

In their quest to remedy national deficiencies in public education, there were limits to foundations' ability to shape the political decisions of education policymakers in one state and locality after another. The American system of public education was not a true system; there was no national political authority to administer, fund, or regulate schooling practices in the individual states, much less in the thousands of individual school districts. Under these circumstances, some foundations marshaled market forces as an indirect means of better regulating American public schooling. The efforts of the Carnegie Foundation for the Advancement of Teaching to solve what it saw as a problem of mismatch between the high school and the college in the early twentieth century illustrate this strategy.

Andrew Carnegie's vision was to make the Carnegie Foundation for the Advancement of Teaching "one of the great agencies not only in dignifying the [teacher's] calling but also in standardizing American education."[64] Although the foundation focused its efforts on improving higher education, its policies and practices trickled down to significantly affect high school education. The Carnegie Foundation's initial undertaking was setting up and funding a system of pensions for collegiate faculty (a system that would eventually become the financial services company TIAA-CREF). In so doing, one of the foundation's first undertakings was to define what a college was. In its first annual report, the foundation noted that higher education institutions would not be considered colleges for their purposes—and hence worthy of and eligible for Carnegie Foundation funds—unless admitted students had received a full "four years of academic or high school preparation."[65] In 1906 the foundation proposed a division of the high school curriculum into what came to be called "Carnegie units" in order to scientifically and efficiently measure students' college readiness. Preparing for college became synonymous with completion of a prescribed set of Carnegie units. Because colleges wanted to be defined as pension eligible, they began to use the Carnegie unit to define their admission requirements, and as secondary education expanded, high schools began to design their curriculum and graduation requirements to match the Carnegie unit system. Their efforts led to a nationwide standardization of high school instruction.

Not everyone was happy with the standardized and academically focused high school curriculum that the Carnegie Foundation had helped bring about. Between 1933 and 1940 the General Education Board undertook a "coordinated national effort" to develop "more flexible curricula for the public high

---

64. Lagemann (1983, pp. 37–38).

65. Carnegie Foundation for the Advancement of Teaching (1906, p. 38).

schools."[66] Concerned that the lack of adaptation of schooling "to any immediate practical end" was partly responsible for the economic dislocations of the Depression, the GEB worked to design and promote, throughout the country, a high school curriculum "responsive to the needs of a rapidly increasing school population."[67] The GEB combined a strategy of public suasion with a strategy of scientific philanthropy in hopes of convincing those charged with making policy decisions for secondary schooling to change the standard curriculum, but it failed to turn back the Carnegie Foundation's successes.

In their efforts to unshackle high schools from the overly narrow classical academic curriculum the Carnegie Foundation advocated, the GEB followed loosely in the survey tradition brought to prominence by the Russell Sage Foundation: it mobilized "a corps of prominent consultants to provide a private, confidential assessment of American educational needs."[68] Working with several other national educational organizations, the GEB funded and produced a series of educational surveys. With the report in hand, it launched a nationwide campaign, not unlike the campaign it had successfully undertaken to promote the great educational awakening in the (white) South in the first two decades of the twentieth century. The GEB's attempts to cultivate education bureaucrats and other public officials were unsuccessful, however; when the GEB terminated its work in general education in 1940, it had "failed to restructure American education as [it] had boldly planned."[69] Remaking the content of high school curricula throughout the country—a policy matter in the hands of thousands of local school districts—proved too daunting a task. In the context of our present consideration of using the marketplace to regulate American public education, this failure demonstrates the limits of explicitly political strategies in a context in which there is no overarching political authority responsible for education policymaking.

Although the high school curriculum organized around Carnegie units survived the GEB's attempts to dislodge it, by the late 1930s the Carnegie Foundation was no longer satisfied that the Carnegie unit system was a sufficient means of measuring students' readiness for college. In 1938 the foundation published "The Pennsylvania Study," the results of a ten-year extensive testing program of students, that encouraged the use of standardized testing rather than Carnegie units for measuring student competence. Again, with its eye on improving higher education, the foundation recommended that colleges use entrance examination scores—rather than the simple completion of fourteen Carnegie units—as the primary determination of admission.

66. Biebel (1976, p. 3).
67. General Education Board (1964, p. 49).
68. Kliebard (1995, pp. 182–83); Lagemann (1983, p. 113); Biebel (1976, p. 8).
69. Biebel (1976, p. 20).

Carnegie's influence might have been inconsequential had it not followed this policy recommendation with another market intervention. In 1947 the Carnegie Foundation joined with the American Council on Education and the College Entrance Examination Board to create the Educational Testing Service, a private centralized agency to design and implement college entrance exams. Taking its Scholastic Aptitude Test quickly became a rite of passage for college-bound high school students, and high schools began to shape their curricular offerings to best prepare their students for that rite. Once again, a foundation brought about a degree of standardization of the high school experience by intervening in the marketplace of higher education.

Conclusion

Early American foundation activity focused primarily on the creation of a social welfare program that philanthropists considered to be of critical importance: an adequate system of public schools. Significantly, four of the seven "great foundations" that existed in 1910 were devoted to promoting and expanding elementary and secondary public education, primarily in the South.[70] Even more significant, the single largest foundation, the General Education Board, which accounted for well over half of the total endowments of those seven foundations, was devoted entirely to education. The development of public education in the United States, and state policy concerning access, curriculum, and funding, especially in the South, cannot be understood apart from the role played by early American foundations.

Throughout the period considered here, the primary purpose of the K–12 education work in which foundations engaged was to change state education policy and to stimulate the state to take on greater responsibility for the funding and regulation of public elementary and secondary education. That is, foundations harnessed their considerable resources for purposes of shaping state policy concerning public education, one of the most important social goods the state provided during this era. By providing private funds for partial support of public educational endeavors and using private resources to influence state policymaking, foundations helped bring about a public education system that might more accurately be described as a public-private hybrid, especially in its early years.

How did foundations go about trying to realize their goals, given the decentralized nature of responsibility for and authority over public education in the United States? As discussed previously, they adopted one of three strategies with

70. Described in Ayres's 1911 book of the same title.

respect to state authorities to bring about changes in public education policy and practice. Where there were limited possibilities for working cooperatively with local and state political officials, foundations effectively used contingencies on the provision of their funds for school construction to call forth new commitments from public officials, and they helped remake the state bureaucracy from the inside out by placing new officials within it. This strategy of state infiltration proved useful to northern foundations working in the American South to literally build the framework for public schooling. When foundation actors were on good terms with policymakers—either because they had good political standing themselves in the policy arena in question (for example, GEB efforts to change federal policy with respect to vocational education in the early twentieth century) or because their objectives were consistent with those of the policymakers they were trying to influence (for example, the GEB and local and state officials in the South working hand in glove on a campaign of mass propaganda)—they were able to use political suasion, sometimes backed up by social research findings, to influence policymakers' decisions.

When deployed in the late-nineteenth- and early-twentieth-century South, these strategies of state infiltration and political suasion came at a price, given that they depended on political outsiders' maintaining cooperative relationships with local officials. Even as they worked to improve public educational opportunities for blacks, foundations' efforts reinforced racial inequalities. For example, the Peabody Fund's proportionately greater spending on schools for whites helped institutionalize racial inequality in public education expenditures as well. Although the General Education Board's public relations and propaganda campaign in the South was responsible for the southern educational awakening of the first decade of the twentieth century, which resulted in a reasonably well-funded and expansive system of public elementary and secondary schooling, it was an effort that benefited whites at the expense of blacks and thus contributed to the further institutionalization of white supremacy in the postdisenfranchisement South. The Rosenwald Fund's insistence that its schools be devoted to industrial education contributed to a practice throughout the South of excluding blacks from opportunities for a classical education.

As foundations' ambitions became increasingly national in scope but focused on policy matters out of the hands of national political authorities, the radically decentralized nature of American public education presented significant limitations to any political strategy for effecting change in education policy or practice. The most effective strategy for foundations under these conditions was to bypass political actors (state and local officials) altogether in favor of intervening in the education marketplace. Ironically, the single most effective change in the practice of public elementary or secondary education throughout the country resulted from interventions in the marketplace of higher education on the part of the Carnegie Foundation for the Advancement of Teaching.

When all is said and done, however, perhaps the most important question is, what did foundations accomplish in the period from their inception through the first half of the twentieth century? The Peabody Fund, the Jeanes Foundation, the Phelps-Stokes Fund, and the Rosenwald Fund helped build public schools for whites and blacks in the postbellum South and contributed in significant ways to increasing the educational administrative capacity of southern states. The Slater Fund helped provide adequate numbers of trained teachers for the newly built public schools for blacks. The General Education Board was instrumental in putting public schooling on a firm tax basis and greatly expanding access to public schools for whites. As a result of efforts by the General Education Board, the Russell Sage Foundation, and the Carnegie Foundation for the Advancement of Teaching, public schools significantly changed their organizational practices and the content of their curricula: among other things, they incorporated vocational education into the high schools; they turned to age-graded instruction; they adopted a differentiated curriculum for high schools and used newly developed ability tests to assign high school students into curricular "tracks"; and they adopted a standard classification scheme for high school courses, based on Carnegie units.

Despite its failure in the 1930s to remake the high school curriculum, the General Education Board—the largest of the foundation actors working in the field of public education during the period considered here—left the biggest mark on American education. It is thus fitting to close our assessment of the contributions of foundations to the development of American public education with an illustration of the board's influence. Writing in 1938, Coon offered the following assessment:

> Not only does [the GEB] control the direction of its own large funds, but its policy of contingent giving places it in position to control the direction of nearly all large expenditures in the field of American education. . . . Thus, the policies and ideas of the Rockefellers, their board, and their agents control and permeate American education. It is not necessary for anybody connected with the Board to suggest policies or to express ideas. Everybody related to American education knows very well what they are. Today every teacher, professor, student, is touched in some manner by one or more projects financed by the Board.[71]

71. Coon (1938, p. 150).

When we extend our gaze beyond the GEB and consider the collective impact of the eight major foundations that worked in the field of public education before the mid-twentieth century, and with the benefit of a longer time horizon than Coon's, we see that they continue to touch schools, students, and education personnel throughout the United States. These early education foundations made decisive contributions toward the institutionalization of state responsibility for public schooling, and they helped put in place the routinized organizational structures of public schooling that remain recognizable today.

3

Catalysts for Change? Foundations
and School Reform, 1950–2005

ELISABETH CLEMENS AND LINDA C. LEE

From the early nineteenth century through World War II, American foundations developed a varied repertoire of strategies, beginning with a model of
the foundation as charity and later expanded to include conditional giving, otherwise known as partial succor, to leverage additional support and the "outsider
within" strategy of subsidizing new kinds of public officials or experts, training
personnel, demonstration projects, and scientific research.[1] Pursuing strategies
of complementarity, philanthropy provided more and better schools for those
children not well served by public education, exemplified by foundation efforts
to expand supply or to make schooling more equitable for black students in
the South and Hispanic students in the Southwest.[2] Yet as public provision of
schooling expanded, foundations withdrew from the partial succor model and
began to develop new theories of giving and models of transformation to promote innovation and policy change.

By the 1950s foundations faced a very different situation from that which confronted the Peabody Education Fund after the Civil War or the General Education Board in the Jim Crow South. To a considerable extent, the public provision
of education from kindergarten through twelfth grade was set in place.[3] Since

1. Havighurst (1980); chapter 2, this volume.
2. Getz (1992); Rose and Stapleton (1992).
3. By 1940, 74.6 percent of all five- to nineteen-year-olds were enrolled in school (75.6 percent
of whites, 68.4 percent of nonwhites). Enrollment rose to 78.7 percent in 1950 and 88.6 percent in
1960. By 1990, 92.6 percent of this age group was enrolled in school. Snyder (1993, p. 14).

midcentury the aims of foundation giving have focused on better or different education rather than simply more or even more equitable schooling. This change of emphasis coincided with greater involvement in education by the federal government, driven by judicial decisions such as *Brown v. Board of Education* in 1954 and new laws such as the National Defense Education Act of 1958 and the Elementary and Secondary Education Act of 1965.

To promote better or different education, foundations now confront an elaborate set of legal constraints, a developed set of operating schools, and greatly expanded public spending which decreases the financial leverage afforded by even the most generous of foundation grants. The increase in federal intervention has also generated denser interconnections across levels of government, linking federal programs to state departments of education and to individual districts and schools. These ties are complicated by the professional associations, unions, commercial companies, and institutions of higher education that are also involved in providing different components of primary and secondary education.[4] Consequently, foundation efforts to promote change or improvement now require attention to the systemic properties of education systems.

From Partial Succor to School Reform

In response to the changed character of elementary and secondary education, postwar philanthropic projects adopted new approaches. By midcentury, grants began to shift from support for established programs (libraries, arts education) to investment in instructional innovation. While foundations remained committed to equal educational opportunity, donors such as the Ford Foundation supported efforts to develop innovative curriculums, teacher training programs, and even novel uses of space within schools.[5] Ford's Great Cities Schools program of the 1950s and the Comprehensive School Improvement programs of the 1960s represented major efforts to improve urban education, projects that complemented both the commitment to racial equality in the wake of *Brown v. Board of Education* and the focus on alleviating poverty at the core of Lyndon Johnson's Great Society programs.

Foundations no longer relied so heavily on cultivating local and state political elites, a concern that had been central to strategies of partial succor. Instead, they built alliances with national policy elites and cultivated community support by advocating for the decentralization of school district control in the spirit of the "maximum feasible participation" of the poor.[6] Many of these programs focused on improving the quality of teachers and of the infrastructure to support

4. Rowan, Barnes, and Camburn (2004).
5. Mead (1972).
6. Economic Opportunity Act of 1964, Section 202(a)(3).

them.[7] But foundations increasingly combined a technical focus on pedagogical innovation with support for transforming the governance of local districts. Multifaceted approaches, reformers argued, could "form a critical mass sufficient to overcome the inertia of traditional school systems and allow the introduction of the helpful but largely unimplemented projects of the past."[8] Through the Public Education Fund, for example, the Ford Foundation supported—or "seeded"—more than fifty local funds intended "to bring attention, energy, creativity, resources, and, ultimately, improvement to many of the nation's long-neglected and isolated low-income minority school districts."[9] These efforts represented an important addition to the foundations' tools for education change: the creation and mobilization of new actors and networks at the local level. In these projects, foundations acted neither as charities nor as instruments of public policy but as catalysts for change—organizational, institutional, and political.

This style of ambitious transformative philanthropy is now prominent in the field of primary and secondary education. The crisis of education over the past two decades has challenged the central role of government in public schooling. Particularly in the wake of the 1983 publication of the *Nation at Risk* report, which framed the state of public education as a national emergency, foundations and business groups have been called to take a central role in salvaging the public schools.[10] More recently, this intensified focus on elementary and secondary education has produced a significant shift in the cast of characters. Foundations with a long history of involvement (including Ford, Carnegie, and Rockefeller) have reduced their roles as newer foundations (most notably the Bill and Melinda Gates Foundation and the Walton Family Foundation) have surged to the top of the list of foundations giving to K–12 education.[11] These new major donors are guided by distinctive models of change, signaled by a new set of metaphors: "an important lever," "like a small rudder steering a large ship," and, most important, "catalyst."[12] To address the impact of foundation giving we need to understand how foundation grants act as catalysts, setting off cascades of transformation in deeply institutionalized systems of education.

Patterns of Philanthropic Giving

Although foundations have long been involved in elementary and secondary schooling, their contributions have grown significantly since the 1980s.

7. Fraser (1992).
8. Havighurst (1980, p. 12).
9. Bergholz (1992, pp. 516–22).
10. Leif (1992); Sabourin (1992).
11. Colvin (2005); F. M. Hess (2005a).
12. F. M. Hess (2005a).

According to the Foundation Grants Index (and acknowledging the problems created by its shifting categories), grants directed to elementary and secondary education increased from roughly 3 percent of total giving in 1980 (of a sample of large grants) to 3.5 percent in 1989 and to approximately 4.5 percent by 1998. This increase in the overall share of grants going to schools has been accompanied by a much more direct involvement of foundations in efforts at school reform. The prominence of elementary and secondary education in the field of philanthropy has been further heightened by major initiatives supported by large donors such as the Annenberg and Gates foundations.

Estimates of current annual private contributions range from $1.2 billion to $2 billion—an impressive sum, but only a tiny fraction of the $427 billion of public money devoted to public K–12 education each year.[13] Data from the Foundation Center for 2001 provide a second snapshot of the philanthropic landscape (see appendix B). Almost three-quarters of grants to K–12 education came from foundations located in only ten states, with two states—New York and Washington, the latter dominated by the Gates Foundation—accounting for more than one-fourth of the national total.

The geographical concentration of grants awarded reflects the financial prominence of a relatively small number of individual foundations active in the area of elementary and secondary education. In 2001, for example, just twenty foundations accounted for 45 percent of grants in K–12 education; Gates and Lilly alone gave more than 20 percent of the national total. The receipt of foundation largesse is also geographically concentrated, although slightly less so than the giving. Ten states received 62 percent of all 2001 grants of more than $10,000. Three states—California, New York, and Indiana (reflecting the local orientation of the Lilly Foundation)—received one-third of the dollars conveyed by foundation grants of more than $10,000 in 2000.

A relatively small number of states attract the lion's share of foundation grants for elementary and secondary education, regardless of the scale of the grant. This reflects the even greater concentration of foundations that give. In the area of elementary and secondary education, foundations in only ten states account for almost 75 percent of the total dollars given and 63.6 percent of the total grants given. By state, the lists of largest givers and largest receivers overlap to an impressive degree. For instance, Washington is second on the list of giving states—reflecting the presence of the Gates Foundation—but eleventh on the list of receiving states, while the District of Columbia enjoys the greatest discrepancy between giving (ranking in the twentieth slot) and receiving (ranking seventh in the nation). In some cases, this close geographical match between giving and receiving reflects a kind of philanthropic particularism, exemplified by the

13. 2002 figures (Greene 2005, pp. 53–54).

Lilly Foundation's focus on its home state of Indiana. But there are also impressive transfers of philanthropic grants across state lines. The geographic proximity of foundations that give and nonprofits that receive may also reflect the coevolution of these organizations in particular communities that develop a preference or a capacity for participation in the philanthropic economy.[14]

Looking at foundation grants by the cities that receive them, a similar picture of concentration appears. The top ten cities accounted for almost one-third of the total foundation dollars (of grants in excess of $10,000) but only one-quarter of the total number of grants.[15] These cities received a large proportion of foundation dollars and also larger-than-average grants. This disparity reflects both the decision by a number of major foundations to focus very large grants on systemic urban school reform and the close relationships between foundations and particular cities—for example, the Albertson Foundation with Boise, Idaho, and the Lilly Endowment with Indianapolis.

Finally, what is the intended purpose of all this giving? The Foundation Center's coding system can be used to create a rough approximation of the purposes that motivate philanthropy. Regarding the question of impact, the grants for school reform are particularly interesting. These grants are explicitly intended to bring about change at the level of schools as organizations and districts as systems, to leverage broad changes in the system of public education. For the largest foundations active in the area of elementary and secondary education, significant school reform has emerged as a top priority. School reform accounts for 22.6 percent of all grant dollars to K–12 education and is dominated by large grants (741 of them) given by large foundations (see table 3-1). The bulk of the funding—86.4 percent of grant dollars—comes from only twenty foundations.[16] Among these twenty, a good number are also among the top twenty foundations in terms of overall giving to elementary and secondary education. For these givers to school reform, the average grant size is approximately $615,000 (a pittance compared with gifts in the millions found in endowment-building grants to higher education). This compares with an average of just less than $140,000 for all foundation grants for any purpose within secondary or elementary education.

14. Among the ten cities receiving the greatest total grants, only New York and Chicago have a higher percentage of grants given than their percentage of grant dollars received. This may reflect the combination of some very large grants with a large number of smaller grants given by local foundations or received by the many nonprofit organizations in these locales.

15. $423 million went to the top ten cities: New York ($106 million), Indianapolis ($71 million), Washington, D.C. ($50 million), Chicago ($42 million), Atlanta ($35 million), Los Angeles ($26 million), Houston ($25 million), Sacramento ($25 million), Boise ($20 million), and Boston (almost $19 million). Indianapolis, Sacramento, Boise, and Boston are also state capitals.

16. Gates topped the list at 37.4 percent of giving for school reform, followed by Annenberg (15.5 percent), the Wallace Foundation (5.6 percent), and the Ford Foundation (4.8 percent).

Table 3-1. *Foundation Grants, by Primary Purpose, 2001*

NTEE code	Primary purpose of grant	Total grant dollars	Share of total grant dollars (percent)	Total number of grants	Share of total grants (percent)
B20	Elementary and secondary education	446,013,935	34.3	3,156	33.9
B2R	Elementary and secondary school reform	293,127,923	22.6	741	8.0
B25	Secondary school and education	162,738,002	12.5	1,411	15.2
B24	Elementary school and education	64,234,289	4.9	682	7.3
B56	Teacher school and education[a]	50,976,673	3.9	292	3.1
B90	Education, services[a]	47,024,302	3.6	586	6.3
B28	Education, special[a]	37,513,156	2.9	467	5.0
B82	Scholarships, financial aid[a]	33,376,068	2.6	161	1.7
B12	Education, fund-raising[a]	27,346,745	2.1	422	4.5
B92	Reading[a]	25,546,605	2.0	196	2.1
	Other codes[a, b]	111,889,966	8.6	1,186	12.8
	Total	1,299,787,664	100.00	9,300	99.9[c]

Source: Data from Foundation Center Statistical Database 2001.

a. Grants with these primary codes were included if the secondary code was B20, B2R, B25, or B24.

b. These include education followed by Management (B02), Government (B17), Single organization support (B11), Alliance (B01), Association (B03), Gifted students (B27), Volunteer services (B16), PTA groups (B94), Reform (B07), Administration/regulation (B04), Community/cooperative (B95), Public policy (B06), Research (B05), Public education (B15), Information services (B14), Alumni groups (B84), Equal rights (B13), Testing (B93), ESL programs (B63), Bilingual programs (B70), as well as Drop-out prevention (B91), Libraries (school) (B72), Early childhood education (B21), Child development, education (B22), and Libraries/library science (B70).

c. Total is less than 100.00 owing to rounding.

These snapshots of foundation giving and receiving for K–12 education suggest different ways of asking about the impact of philanthropy. The answer depends on whether the focus is on the typical grant (the modal size falls between $10,000 and $100,000) or the largest grants (over $10 million). Do we care about the typical grantee, which receives between $10,000 and $100,000 a year, or those grantees that are magnets for much larger philanthropic contributions? What about the broader context of grant-giving and grant-receiving organizations? One-third of foundation grants for elementary and secondary education go to locations outside the top ten states, and three-quarters go to cities and towns other than the ten largest recipients of such grants. There is certainly no reason to think that grants given to organizations working in these philanthropically sparser locales will have the same consequences as those that enter into the relatively dense philanthropic communities that have developed around centers of donative support for schooling.

In addition to these relatively smaller and relatively scattered grants, a number of major foundations have particularly close relationships to one city or state. As previously mentioned, Lilly directs most of its almost 10 percent of the national total to cities and towns in Indiana. On a smaller scale, the Benwood Foundation has worked with the schools of Chattanooga, Tennessee, to produce promising results by focusing on the recruitment, support, and retention of excellent teachers.[17] Philanthropy may matter in different ways when foundation efforts map so directly onto the community networks and public institutions that shape education. Finally, a number of cities—New York, Washington, D.C., and Chicago most prominent among them in 2001—receive philanthropic dollars in the form of many different grants. Efforts such as the Annenberg Challenge of the 1990s not only gave grants for city-level school reform, they also required matching grants from other donors and public agencies. In these prominent cases of urban school reform, many different foundations are simultaneously or sequentially involved in efforts to transform elementary and secondary education.

Across many of the nation's school systems, foundations have been welcomed, for the most part, in a time of tight public funding, the perceived failure of public schooling, and the need for innovation and reform. Yet foundations have learned to tread carefully, particularly in relation to the demands that they place on individual schools for either detailed reporting or rapid demonstration of improvements in test scores.[18] This challenge is particularly daunting when gifts are linked to philosophical visions of school reform or understandings of effective pedagogy. With the growing scale of public education budgets and the increasing complexity of education systems, it is difficult for even the most generous philanthropic gifts to leverage significant and systematic change.

Theories of Implementation and Change

Total dollars do not capture the possibilities for leveraging change in education. The 2001 ranking of foundations that donated to elementary and secondary education illuminates the field in a moment of transition. Traditionally significant participants, such as Ford, Carnegie, and Packard, were in the process of scaling down their education programs. At the same time, newly prominent foundations—notably, the Gates and Walton Family foundations—were

---

17. "Benwood Initiative Fosters Teacher Quality through Professional Incentives," *Educational Innovator* 40 (December 1, 2003).

18. Sabourin (1992).

engaging with educational issues with growing intensity and generosity.[19] These newer participants brought not only new funds but new theories of change.

Just as early American foundations had distinctive repertoires, contemporary foundations have elaborated models to inform their support of education reform. Chester Finn and Marci Kanstoroom identify four general theories that dominate contemporary discussions of education improvement and reform: first, change will follow from extra resources and increased flexibility; second, change requires the provision of expertise, technical assistance, and social support from outside of the school system; third, change requires greater centralization, enhanced control, and explicit standards; and fourth, change will follow from marketlike systems of choice, driven by the preferences and judgments of parents and students as consumers of educational services.[20]

The competition-driven fourth model critiques more traditional theories of change and, in particular, the assumption that public schools can reform themselves if they have the resources to do so. Advocates of competition, such as the Walton Family Foundation, the Children's Scholarship Fund, and Children First America, argue that such efforts to work with public systems for reform will inevitably be defeated by the entrenched interests and institutional inertia of existing school systems.[21]

Missing from this list of change theories is an explicitly political model of institutional transformation. This silence resonates with the technocratic character of many claims for education improvement; yet as Seymour Sarason argues, changing schools—like changing any other organization—involves changing power relationships.[22] This reticence, which is not restricted to the role of foundations in education reform, signals a point of tension between philanthropic efforts and the character of schools as public institutions, governed by democratic processes and standards of accountability.

In elaborating various theories of change, each of these models directs attention to the design of the intervention rather than the character of the object, the schools or school systems that are to be changed. Yet the effect of a treatment depends jointly on the intervention and its object. As David Tyack and Larry Cuban conclude in their study of American education reform,

> The typical rational and instrumental assumptions of education reformers fail to give due weight to the resilience of schools as institutions. This

19. Colvin (2005).

20. Finn and Kanstoroom (2000, p. 53). The Finn and Kanstoroom list also brackets questions of "going to scale" (see Rowan, Barnes, and Camburn 2004).

21. Tyce Palmaffy, "Charities Throw Money at Schools, But Is Reform Just a Matter of Cash?" *Investor's Business Daily,* May 17, 2000, p. 24.

22. Sarason (1990, p. 5).

institutional structure probably has more influence on the implementation of policy than policy has on institutional practice. The grammar of schooling is the result of previous reforms that had, and continue to have, powerful political constituencies and a strong foundation in the social expectations about schooling held both by educators and by the general public.[23]

In the wake of the attention given to the $500 million Annenberg Challenge, foundations have been much more explicit in articulating models of change in conjunction with major gifts to K–12 education.[24] But implementation is shaped by more than the overall theory of change. Both philanthropic experience and the large body of research on public policy implementation underscore the need for attention to both the design of the grant and the process of implementation. In both dimensions, the challenges faced by foundations are similar to those confronted by government agencies, particularly those implementing policies adopted and funded at one level of government but requiring cooperation with other governmental agencies or private organizations to produce results.[25]

In these relationships—where an entity offers funds to a local government or private organization to produce an outcome desired by the funder—both the federal government and the philanthropic foundation are effectively outsiders to political and social systems (a situation shared by foundations since the Peabody Fund's first efforts to promote education in the defeated South). Consequently both must leverage change without creating enmity or provoking hostility from those with stakes in the system as it currently operates. Foundation efforts to promote education reform predictably meet resistance: teachers and administrators contest the loss of autonomy, neighborhoods are committed to local schools, parents support particular pedagogies or activities. As Sarason notes in arguing for the irreducibly political nature of reform,

> Like almost all other complex traditional social organizations, the schools will accommodate in ways that require little or no change. This is not to say that the accommodation is insincere or deliberately cosmetic but rather that the strength of the status quo—its underlying axioms, its pattern of power relationships, its sense of tradition and therefore what seems right, natural, and proper—almost automatically rules out options for change in that status quo."[26]

23. Tyack and Cuban (1995, p. 134).

24. Meg Sommerfeld, "Annenberg Schools Program Yields Millions, but Gets Mixed Results," *Chronicle of Philanthropy* June 27, 2002, p. 12.

25. Selznick (1949).

26. Sarason (1990, p. 35).

Because foundation discourse is relatively silent about political processes, difficulties that could be anticipated can easily flare into local conflicts.[27] The Heinz Foundation, for example, pulled grants from Pittsburgh schools following disagreements with the district leadership, and the Gates Foundation terminated funding to the Seattle schools after turnovers in the superintendent's office.[28] Foundations may also find themselves allied with the losing side in local contests, as Annenberg did in Chicago when a coalition dedicated to a decentralized, participatory vision of school reform was effectively outmaneuvered by the mayor, who imposed a dramatically centralized model of reform tightly linked to accountability through testing.[29]

In addition to highlighting the politics of implementation, studies of public policy illuminate the organizational infrastructure for getting results, complicated by the sequences of decisions and activities of multiple public agencies and private organizations. In their influential study of a federal economic development grant to the city of Oakland, California, Jeffrey Pressman and Aaron Wildavsky made a simple arithmetic point.[30] Even if there is an 80 percent probability that every agreement needed for successful implementation will be made, the probability of final agreement falls below 50 percent as soon as four agreements are required. Imagine that foundation A desires to improve education in town Z. To do so, foundation A negotiates a grant with nonprofit B (the first agreement—to the extent that B is a coalition, the favored recipient of the Annenberg Challenge and a number of other major initiatives, the agreements required are multiplied).[31] Nonprofit B develops a plan to implement in partnership with school district C (the second agreement).

This agreement might require waivers from either the teachers union or the state department of education, candidates for the third agreement. Provided that all these agreements are made, the nonprofit and school district must work with individual schools to implement the proposed reform (the fourth agreement). Although this is a relatively short chain of cooperation—and using odds of 80 percent, despite the expected opposition from at least some with commitments

27. Hewlett is one exception, explicitly incorporating politics into its "logic model" of change. The Broad Foundation is another, with programs focused on governance and school leadership as well as a commitment to the role of labor unions.

28. Debra E. Blum, "Three Pittsburgh Foundations Halt Grants to Schools," *Chronicle of Philanthropy*, July 25, 2002, p. 18; Donna Gordon Blankinship, "Gates Foundation Waiting to See How Seattle Schools Do before Granting More Money," *Associated Press State and Local Wire*, October 21, 2002; see also Jenkins and McAdams (2005).

29. Russo (2000).

30. Pressman and Wildavsky (1984, p. 107).

31. Foundations' preferences for coalition building and collaboration—and the avoidance of controversy—may minimize the possibility of achieving significant change. F. M. Hess (2005b).

to the current system—the odds of aligning a foundation's intent with full consent from an individual school—four in ten ($0.8 \times 0.8 \times 0.8 \times 0.8 = 0.41$)—are sobering and low.

But the odds are definitely greater than zero. Given the deep concern about the quality of American education, many foundations—and teachers and parents and local politicians and district administrators—have made serious efforts to produce significant improvements in schools and educational outcomes. Presuming that foundation, nonprofit, school district, union, legislature, and individual school all agree on a plan for reform, what shapes the likelihood of success in producing the desired outcome? A short list of answers might begin with something obvious: Whatever is to be implemented must be clearly specified and provisions made for an adequate infrastructure for implementation. If the intervention is a new curriculum, the presentation of that curriculum must be specific so that all the teachers are following the same plan, and there must be provision for training teachers and monitoring their use of the new curriculum.[32] Without these provisions, any finding that the new curriculum did or—more likely—did not improve educational attainment is meaningless. The effects attributed to the curriculum are just as likely to have been produced by a flawed approach to implementation.

Even the clearest and most specific design, however, has little chance of success if it is at cross-purposes with the interests of those responsible for its implementation. Ann Chih Lin makes this point in her study of education reform in an unusual setting.[33] Remedial education programs for prisoners, she demonstrates, will be poorly implemented and ineffective if they are not understood to support the primary goals of those working in prisons: the preservation of order, the safety of officers and prisoners. But where remedial education serves these purposes—by creating an incentive system that may be used to reward good behavior, by mitigating the boredom that can fuel violence—prison guards may embrace education as an instrument that supports their primary concern with maintaining order. Consequently, unless attention is paid to the practical interests and concerns of those charged with implementing a new program, those interests will reshape the reform so that it serves other purposes: schools almost always change reforms.[34] As Lin observes, "Evaluators tend to expect that organizations can be changed to accommodate programs, while organization theorists tend to explain that programs are inevitably changed by the organizations implementing them."[35]

32. Rowan, Barnes, and Camburn (2004).
33. Lin (2000).
34. Tyack and Cuban (1995, p. 61).
35. Lin (2000, p. 8).

New Models of Philanthropy and Change

Given these many challenges, how can all this philanthropic giving have an impact on education? Over the past decade, most answers to this question invoke metaphors that capture how small interventions can have relatively large effects: rudder, lever, catalyst.[36] In one variant, these arguments echo the method of partial succor central to the Peabody Foundation's efforts to expand public schooling in the South after the Civil War; philanthropic gifts would be tied to public or community contributions. But as Jay Greene argues, "Most education philanthropy is not actually guided by a feasible strategy to redirect future public expenditures."[37]

In current philanthropic practice, the targets of matching grants are just as likely to be other foundations or private donors as public agencies. The use of foundation grants to leverage other donations rests on a different model of leverage through the mobilization of mediating organizations. In many cases, the imagery of change involves the foundation facilitating or mediating or convening a conversation among other organizations and political actors who will ally to create beneficial change. While foundation accounts typically highlight the constructive processes of mobilizing coalitions in support of change, grants may also have the potential to demobilize or disrupt ongoing practices and relationships in the system targeted for change.[38] This possibility, as many have noted, raises important questions about the intersection of philanthropic efforts and democratic accountability.

The emphasis on mobilizing coalitions and convening stakeholders reflects a widely held assumption that solutions will emerge out of the sustained interaction of those who are most familiar with a particular situation and most committed to improvements. This contrasts with a traditional foundation commitment to an expert-led model of change—in particular, one in which experts discover best practices, which are then disseminated to the organizations actually involved in providing services. Historically, this research-development-diffusion-utilization model has been used to describe the relationship between university researchers and education practitioners.[39] But a related model of innovation and

---

36. The rudder, lever, and catalyst trope is exemplified by a recent discussion of foundation leadership in the Pittsburgh schools: "In Pittsburgh, the foundations had no authority over the mayor, school board, media, or voters, yet their leadership set in motion a chain of events that had substantial impact on all other players" (Heifetz, Kania, and Kramer 2004, p. 23). The funds withheld represented only 0.5 percent of the district's budget (Heifetz, Kania, and Kramer 2004, p. 24), so the key questions concern the processes involved in setting in motion the chain of events.

37. Greene (2005, p. 58).

38. Heifetz, Kania, and Kramer (2004, p. 22).

39. Rowan, Barnes, and Camburn (2004).

diffusion has shifted the initial phases of research and development to the inter-action of foundations and their grantees. In these programs, foundation grants may be tied directly to the implementation of a particular model of reform—the "small schools" sponsored by the Bill and Melinda Gates Foundation are a prom-inent example—and the model is then refined through rigorous monitoring and evaluation of the outcomes of the supported activities. Other foundations, such as the William and Flora Hewlett Foundation, contribute simultaneously to the development of theory on the part of researchers and the implementation and evaluation of those theories in practice.[40]

Finally, some foundations have sought to transform elementary and second-ary education by intensifying the competition confronting existing institutions and practices. This approach has taken clearest form in foundation support for school choice, either through direct funding of scholarships for private schools (for example, the Walton Family Foundation) or through research and advo-cacy for systems of public school choice (for example, the Gates Foundation). In each case, there is a market model of systemic change: freed from requirements to attend one particular school, citizen-consumers will choose among multiple options, new entrants will offer distinctive choices, and in the process the most desirable options will survive while suboptimal education organizations will fail. Increasing the choice for individual students is the mechanism that sets in motion a virtuous cycle of systemic change.

In each of these cases, the potential effects of foundation grants have also been shaped by increased attention to accountability. Following the imagery of rudder, lever, and catalyst, this emphasis translates into rapid and direct feedback processes or course corrections. Foundations monitor the implementation of programs they have funded and then pull or extend funding based on results—either indicators of process or final outcomes. By intensifying the feedback from initial grant to subsequent foundation decisions, this model of monitoring increases the importance of rapid results and raises the stakes in getting the "lag" correct by having an accurate estimate of how long it will take for a program to produce observable results.

Partial Succor Revisited

In the current debate over the efficacy of education philanthropy, the premises of the partial succor model have come under serious scrutiny. As Finn and Kansto-room explain, these premises undergird one major theory of change: that change can be effected through "the provision of expertise and stimulus from outside to a system that is assumed to lack both but to be willing and able to change if

40. Hewlett (1999, p. vii).

supplied with these missing elements."[41] This assumption, they argue, informed much of the effort supported by the Annenberg Challenge, a $500 million effort leveraged by matching gifts and contributions, to improve public education in nine major cities. The extraordinary generosity of the gift, combined with the difficulty of demonstrating positive educational achievements associated with it, has fueled considerable reflection on how foundations may give effectively.

One strategy has involved multiple foundations combining their efforts in a single change initiative, thereby minimizing the cross-pressures on the schools or districts that receive grants. The sense that more money can make a difference remains, but there is attention to coordinating the efforts of multiple donors. This emphasis on coordination and consensus shaped the Annenberg Challenge, which required matches from other donors and public agencies, thereby building partnerships such as the $50 million, five-year joint sponsorship with Hewlett in the Bay Area School Reform Collaborative.[42] The Gates Foundation has been a particularly prolific cooperator, multiplying the impact of its own large gifts (totaling $15 million) by combining them with $10 million from the Meyer Memorial Trust in Oregon and with donations from a number of corporate and family foundations in Kansas City's Partnership for Regional Education Preparation.[43] Gates, Michael Dell, other donors, and the Communities Foundation of Texas collaborated to the tune of $130 million in creating "a massive new initiative called the Texas High School Project, which is designed to boost graduation rates and college readiness at low-performing schools."[44]

In an important respect, these foundation-led collaborations can go beyond simply multiplying the size of the total gift to creating a legacy of increased philanthropic and charitable support for local schools. This has been an explicit object of the Lilly Foundation's CAPE initiative, an effort to create Community Alliances to Promote Education throughout Indiana.[45] In some cases, however, large foundation grants can have the opposite effect by crowding out or, as one nonprofit executive put it, "intimidating" other donors whose largesse does not come in multimillion-dollar packages.

Another variant on this approach focuses on building the capacity of nonprofit organizations to play an ongoing role in education improvement and innovation. Yet this may come about in two quite different ways: from considering

41. Finn and Kanstoroom (2000, p. 54).

42. Hewlett Foundation (2001, p. 16).

43. Susan Nielsen, "Big Donors, Small Schools," *Sunday Oregonian,* December 4, 2005, p. E4; Joe Robertson and Dawn Bormann, "Initiative for Schools Takes Shape," *Kansas City Star,* December 1, 2005.

44. Vanessa Everett, "Donors Offer $130 Million to Texas High Schools to Boost Graduation Rates," *Beaumont (Texas) Enterprise*, November 13, 2003.

45. See www.lillyendowment.org/ed_cape.html (January 17, 2007).

nonprofits as either the ends of philanthropic support or as the means, either targets or tools. For some donors, notably the Hewlett Foundation, this strengthening of nonprofit organizations is an end in itself, designated as one of its three fundamental values: "a vibrant democratic society requires an array of strong nonprofit institutions that allow citizens to come together to express and further their various concerns and interests."[46] In light of this commitment, Hewlett has been unusually forthcoming with long-term operating funds for nonprofits, rather than focusing its grants on specific projects.

All foundation grants inevitably add money. Thus strategies of partial succor continue to influence philanthropic initiatives in elementary and secondary education. Yet in current practice, there is a great deal of theorizing about what can follow from adding money or from shaping the conditions under which additional resources are introduced into existing education systems. The most basic of these consequences follows from the relationship-building emphasis inherent in requirements of consensus and collaboration among grantees in a community. Foundations increasingly seek to build coalitions and to create new capacities for collective action around educational issues. While these changes are often described in neutral language—as collaboration and consensus—the creation of new networks that sustain collective action may have political consequences. In addition, the widespread concern for K–12 education has drawn a number of foundations more directly into the world of politics and advocacy. In 2001 the Gates Foundation opened an office in Washington, D.C., and has been increasing its donations to advocacy groups, in conjunction with both its education and global health initiatives.[47] Thus education philanthropy—particularly grants to reform public school systems—brings foundations into politics.

Mobilization and Disruption

Collaboration and consensus building create ties, they build networks. In the process, such programs provide participants not only with resources for their direct activities but also with standing in a newly recognized community of concern for elementary and secondary education. Because so many of the largest grants for school reform have required the formation of new coalitions as lead grantees, many of their most obvious legacies have been at this level. As a number of evaluations have noted, the most important impacts of foundation grants for education reform may be on the nonprofits and networks organized around this issue. As one study of Annenberg's New York challenge concluded, "The

46. Hewlett (2001, pp. ix, xi).
47. Ian Wilhelm, "A View Inside the Gates," *Chronicle of Philanthropy*, November 11, 2004, pp. 12–15.

largest impact is likely to be seen not in the schools, but in the [four] nonprofit organizations that were recipients of the funds." Three "are now larger and better established," while the fourth broke away from a sponsoring organization and is now both larger and independent.[48]

Finally, one foundation's gift may create a legacy for other foundations. In Kansas City, for example, Gates is working with a number of corporate and family foundations in a project "focused heavily on training teachers, small student work groups and strengthening relationships between schools and family." In 2006 the president of the Ewing Marion Kauffman Foundation, which had been supporting First Things First since 1997 with a $14 million foundation grant, announced that the foundation was stepping aside as a major investor, but that the Partnership for Regional Education Preparation–Kansas City was "the happy outcome of the process." He continued, "We're delighted with what's emerging. We're delighted Gates has come along."[49]

A series of philanthropic legacies can also mean the layering of one reform after another. Tyack and Cuban argue that this produces the "fragmented centralization" that now characterizes many large systems.[50] Thus the degree of coordination across philanthropic projects has important implications for governance at the level of individual schools, districts, and states:

> When programs find constituencies, claim district support, and then pile up gradually alongside (or atop) one another, the collection of 'focused' initiatives can actually make it more difficult for districts to maintain coherence. The gradual accretion of such gifts can bog down decision making and create fragmentation between conflicting fiefdoms. . . . The weight of accumulated initiatives and grant conditions poses one more constraint on burdened district officials, educators, and would-be reformers.[51]

The status of foundation grants as discretionary money in fiscally strained public school districts raises clear and obvious questions of democratic accountability evident in those cases in which foundation decisions have destabilized existing political relations. In one prominent incident, the Heinz Endowments, the Grable Foundation, and the Pittsburgh Foundation jointly announced that they were discontinuing support of Pittsburgh's school system in 2002 because "they had completely lost confidence in the ability of the local school board to run the district." Controversy ensued, but within two years a new majority on the school board was actively implementing initiatives recommended by

48. Domanico and others (2000, p. 14).

49. Joe Robertson and Dawn Bormann, "Initiative for Schools Takes Shape," *Kansas City (Mo.) Star*, December 1, 2005.

50. Tyack and Cuban (1995, p. 78).

51. F. M. Hess (2005a).

a mayor's commission that had brought together civic leaders, business elites, and representatives of the three foundations. As the city's paper concludes, the foundations' decision to withdraw funding served "to concentrate minds on the seriousness of the board's dysfunction . . . and provided helpful context for the grassroots effort that led to the victory of several new board members, breaking the old majority and bringing the hope of better times."[52]

Because public schools are embedded in local and state politics, the ability of foundation grants to nurture new coalitions or "concentrate the mind" by under-lining shortcomings can have significant potential to leverage change. A grant that is small in relation to the total budget may nevertheless have multiplicative effects by way of facilitating political realignments and reevaluations. The Gates Foundation has engaged in direct dialogue with public school leaders. Both its words and its awards clearly establish that the foundation looks for reliable part-ners who share its vision of how to achieve change in public schools. Repeatedly, the foundation has declined to extend—and has even cut—grants to districts where the leadership appears either in disarray (as in nearby Seattle) or less than committed to the small high school initiative.[53] After announcing grants to a number of districts in Washington state but declining to extend its grants to Seat-tle, "foundation leadership said it was focusing most of its attention on districts that have the potential to become models in high school education. Seattle is not ready to fit that description because of financial issues and leadership changes."[54]

This stern stance toward district leadership may energize coalitions for reform within districts. This appears to have happened in Los Angeles, where the super-intendent "has endured criticism from some school board members, education experts and local politicians for not pushing more aggressively to reform high schools. Until he did, many said, the Gates Foundation would not lend its sup-port as it has to several other urban districts."[55] Foundation officers responded to this criticism, arguing that the success of the superintendent's school construc-tion and curriculum reform efforts had been necessary foundations for projects that could be funded by Gates. This insistence on finding partners who are both effective and committed to the foundation's goals has been a central element of the Gates program for leveraging significant change through its grants.

---

52. Quoted in Heifetz, Kania, and Kramer (2004, pp. 21–22). Given the growing influence of business models of philanthropy, the question is what to make of the Schumpeterian element of "creative destruction." Is this an appropriate, or necessary, component of any project of institu-tional change?

53. Heather Knight, "Gates Money Pulled from Small Schools," *San Francisco (Calif.) Chroni-cle*, October 22, 2005, p. B1.

54. Blankinship, "Gates Foundation Waiting to See."

55. Joel Rubin and Jean Merl, "L.A. District Thinks Small in Reform," *Los Angeles Times*, November 3, 2005, p. B-3.

The demand for reliable partners aligned with foundation goals can draw donors into local district politics. The relationship of foundations to education reform is potentially troubling with respect to concerns for democratic accountability. As one editorial writer in Oregon has complained about Gates funding for small high schools in the state, "Two generations ago, the ideal high school was a factory. One generation ago, it was a shopping mall. Today, the ideal is whatever the rich people will give us."[56] Yet in light of historical evidence, foundations are probably right in paying close attention to political alignments. As Tyack and Cuban document in their survey of a century of American education reform, initiatives that have significant political support are much more likely to result in lasting changes.[57]

Innovation and Diffusion

The imagery of foundation-sponsored experimentation and innovation developed in the wake of the partial succor methods that dominated the first decades of efforts to expand education in the South. As the president of the Hewlett Foundation has noted, "The solutions to serious problems are seldom known with anything close to certainty. The Foundation must therefore be prepared to experiment and take risks in its philanthropic activities. This, too, entails clear objectives and measures of success, without which we cannot know how the risk eventuated. It also requires a willingness to acknowledge and learn from failures." He further noted, "In the case of systemic school reform, however, foundations have taken quite varied approaches to experimentation."[58]

In the most prominent philanthropic effort of the 1990s, the Annenberg Challenge adopted an open and bottom-up understanding of experimentation. The Annenberg funds were given to different local coalitions, which developed models for change that suited their particular situation.[59] Critical evaluations have since characterized this as "letting a hundred flowers bloom," but given the great uncertainty about what can actually be done to improve education, this permissive approach to experimentation may not have been unreasonable. Hewlett appears to represent an approach to experimentation that is more centrally monitored, if not fully dictated from above. The Hewlett president has explained that the foundation "typically seeks impact on a large scale. . . . In addition to strengthening the fields in which the Foundation works, strategies that the Foundation employs to achieve large-scale impact include demonstration or

56. Nielsen, "Big Donors, Small Schools."
57. Tyack and Cuban (1995, p. 107).
58. Hewlett (2001, p. ix).
59. Domanico and others (2000, p. 1).

pilot projects and their replication; research and evaluation to assess the effectiveness of particular theories or strategies of change; and the dissemination of knowledge for the benefit of professionals, citizens, and policymakers."[60] One distinctive characteristic of Hewlett's self-description is the emphasis on foundation giving in the process of developing and testing explicit causal theories with respect to complex social and environmental problems.

Some foundations have taken a much more explicit leadership role in developing interventions to promote more effective schooling. In this respect, the landscape of education philanthropy changed significantly in 2000 when the Bill and Melinda Gates Foundation, as of 2004 the world's wealthiest foundation, added a program in education to its already significant efforts in fields such as global health.[61] Two precursor foundations—the William H. Gates Foundation and the Gates Learning Foundation—had been involved in educational projects through scholarships for minority students and the promotion of technology in the schools.[62] But with the new and enlarged Gates Foundation, efforts were focused on producing significant improvements in high school education.

Unlike either Lilly or Annenberg, the Gates Foundation rejected community-based models of change. Instead, it began with a model of education reform drawn from the "small school movement."[63] A three-year review of the small-school program begins by stating that

> the Bill & Melinda Gates Foundation's theory of change addresses the need for whole K–16 system change, stressing the importance of the individual relationships high school students forge with each other and with the adults in their schools. Building on its experience and recent research, the foundation has established key partnerships with state education agencies, school districts, and other organizations to improve high school graduate rates by promoting the new 'three R's'—rigor, relevance, and relationships. The three R's are derived from a number of key attributes of effective schools.[64]

Specificity in both program design and procedures for implementation are highly valued as the foundation focuses "its school efforts on 'well-specified school models that provide really strong support,' including a well-developed curriculum and instructional approach."[65]

60. Hewlett (2001, p. xiii).
61. Wilhelm, "A View Inside the Gates."
62. Wilhelm, "A View Inside the Gates."
63. Domanico and others (2000, pp. 5–6).
64. National Evaluation of High School Transformation (2004, p. 2).
65. Erik W. Rubelen, "Gates High Schools Get Mixed Review in Study," *Education Week*, November 16, 2005.

Gates grants are accompanied by extensive evaluation efforts, which provide feedback to modify the foundation's strategy for giving. In the case of small high schools, evaluations in the first three years found small but significant improvements in reading and language, advances in terms of the "learning culture" of small schools, but little or no movement with respect to mathematics achievement. School autonomy is another issue on which Gates has shifted its position, relaxing its insistence on small school autonomy in the face of evidence.[66] While the Gates Foundation effectively chose a "national champion," its insistence on rigorous and continuous evaluation provides a method for adjusting and refining the model at the heart of its exceptionally large investments in education reform.

Competition

While many philanthropic projects involve working with schools and districts to bring about reform, others seek to use competition both to provide alternatives and to generate additional pressure on public schools to implement change. Within public education, school choice programs, particularly charter schools, receive "the largest share of charitable grants given by foundations in the area of K–12 education."[67] Charter schools represent an intermediate form of exit from public school systems: publicly funded yet often independently governed (and owned), these schools may be understood as catalysts for change within public systems or as gateways to a more privatized system of education. The creation of charter schools, therefore, has required considerable change at the level of state policy, where provisions for mandatory education have been altered to allow for novel systems of financing and governance. A number of foundations have been active in this policy effort, particularly by supporting think tanks dedicated to educational choice.

Foundations have straddled the public and privatizing versions of school choice. The Gates Foundation has been a prominent supporter of creating small schools within public systems, thereby building the infrastructure for a different form of school choice. The Walton Foundation, by comparison, has focused on supporting scholarships for children to attend private schools and thereby exit the public system altogether. In some cases, choice (and even exit) is linked to a model of leveraging improvement in the public schools through competition; for other funders, support for choice is embedded within a strategy of diminishing support for public education and moving toward a more privatized system of education.

66. Rubelen, "Gates High Schools Get Mixed Review."
67. F. M. Hess (2005b, p. 44).

Conclusion

What has been learned about the role of philanthropy in the field of K–12 education and, more specifically, in the latest round of efforts at systematic school reform and improvement? Much of the giving for primary and secondary education falls into the roles described by the editors of this volume: private school endowments, scholarships to private schools, and "extras" for public schools all conform to the model of charity by providing substitutes to, or extensions of, existing programs. The larger grants linked to school reform, however, embrace a rather different set of ambitions. While grants may provide something that is missing from existing public education—funding, personnel, or expertise—they are informed by models of change that link these relatively small supplements of assets (in comparison with the magnitude of public spending) to broader processes of transformation.

The idea that philanthropy can leverage significant change in public education has a long history. In the nineteenth century, the partial succor strategy used philanthropy as a matching grant to elicit state and community financing for public education, particularly for racial minorities. By the middle of the twentieth century, the foundation strategy for school reform came to rely on the anticipated partnership with government: foundations would fund innovation and experimentation, and government would take charge of introducing effective programs to schools. This division of labor within the research-development-diffusion-implementation model could be sustained only so long as there was a reasonable expectation of additional public funding for successful projects. In the changed political and fiscal environment since the 1980s, this assumption was no longer tenable, and philanthropists embraced new models of change in which they simultaneously engaged in the support of innovation and used their capacity to mobilize other actors to create pressures for more expansive adoption and systemic transformations.

A survey of major school reform projects amply documents the difficulties of pursuing multiple philanthropic strategies and demonstrates why such multifaceted efforts are necessary in order to intervene in complex and entrenched social systems. Embedded in local politics, family strategies, career trajectories, and national economic concerns, the challenge of mobilizing effective philanthropic support for education reform is daunting. Thus one of the most important contributions of large-scale education philanthropy involves mobilizing new actors and reorganizing alliances. Even if the specific reform supported by a foundation has few discernible effects, the process of framing school reform as a major issue for city or state policy and mobilizing new alliances (and oppositions) around reform can have lasting effects, such as establishing the quality of education as a key indicator for evaluating the performance of politicians. The catalytic effect of foundation funding may be to create a moment of visibility and volatility around public education such that many other actors—activists interested in redressing problems of poverty, real estate developers interested in urban gentrification, municipal governments concerned for property tax revenues and job quality—all have an opportunity to discover stakes within public education.

4

The Partnerships of Foundations and Research Universities

STEVEN C. WHEATLEY

In 2005 the Carnegie Foundation for the Advancement of Teaching celebrated its centennial with worry. One of the great exemplars of the impact of scientific philanthropy on education, the foundation found itself questioning whether foundations could any longer have a productive role in the advancement of teaching, especially in higher education.

The question had become urgent since the Atlantic Philanthropies and the Pew Charitable Trusts, both sizable endowments with creditable records of university grant making, announced their withdrawal from higher education—the most visible evidence of a more pervasive change. It was therefore understandable that the Carnegie Foundation, so prominent in developing foundation-university partnerships, anxiously commemorated its centennial. It organized conferences, commissioned papers, and published a volume focused on bridging the perceived chasm between the once tightly connected realms of foundation philanthropy and research universities. Despite disagreement by some of those interviewed for *Reconnecting Education and Foundations: Turning Good Intentions into Educational Capital*, the authors did find evidence of that disengagement, especially among the largest foundations. [1]

"In the early years of the twenty-first century," the authors conclude, "a number of foundations appeared to grow weary of support for education and more hesitant about the assumption that education institutions can deliver on their

---

1. Bacchetti and Ehrlich (2006, p. 18).

promise of leveraging philanthropic funding into individual and societal prog-ress."[2] For philanthropists and "philanthropoids" (career foundation officers), the golden age of university and foundation cooperation was between the 1890s and World War II, when philanthropists and philanthropic foundations were the most influential forces in higher education, linked in a common project that mutually reinforced institutional ambitions. They were the most concentrated, nimble, and strategic donors. Their interventions and policy choices had great effect on a developing field. And the influence was reciprocal. As the essayist Dwight Macdonald has observed, "[Foundation leaders] have proved more responsive to the values . . . of the academic concerns on whose borders they operate than to those of the rich men who founded them."[3] The linkage of foun-dations and universities has been, perhaps until now, one of the tighter institu-tional pairings in American public life.

This alliance was so durable that the rise of sustained federal funding for higher education after World War II did not dissolve the systemic influence of the largest foundations. Francis Sutton, a former Ford Foundation deputy vice president, refers to the period from the 1950s to 1970s as a "silver age" of phil-anthropic influence, when foundations, most notably the new and enormous Ford Foundation, focused their energies and donations on what they felt were key points of leverage in a system for which they felt responsible.[4] But in the early twenty-first century, all that once glittered seems tarnished. Foundation philanthropy and higher education have both become mature industries, with all that term implies of stasis. In this situation, according to a report in the *Chroni-cle of Higher Education*, "foundations and colleges are on the road to Splitsville."[5]

Some foundation leaders qualify this view. Alison Bernstein, a vice president of the Ford Foundation, notes that "the most frequently cited data do not sug-gest that there has been a decrease in foundation support for higher education." Indeed, she maintains, foundations and philanthropists "continue to view higher education as the catalyst for new ideas and critical knowledge building, and for challenging societal structures in every aspect of human life." That said, she does acknowledge smaller increases in foundation contributions and cautions that education leaders "need a new understanding of what foundations can and can-not offer" and must "tailor their advancement strategies to the new core values of . . . grant makers," values that include "impact analysis" and development of "critical new ways of thinking and being."[6]

2. Bacchetti and Ehrlich (2006, p. 4).
3. Macdonald (1956, p. 165).
4. Sutton (1999).
5. John L. Pulley, "Crumbling Support for Colleges," *Chronicle of Higher Education,* March 29, 2002.
6. Alison R. Bernstein, "Is Philanthropy Abandoning Higher Education?" *The Presidency,* Octo-ber 2003.

Bernstein's analysis raises the question: How do we measure the relationship between foundation philanthropy and higher education? In dollars donated? In interlocking leadership and boards of trustees? By these measures, the contributions of foundations to American higher education continue to be significant. Foundation grants to higher education form a substantial portion of foundation giving, and while those grants may be a shrinking percentage of university receipts, no development office will give up on this source. The Foundation Center reports that in 2004, U.S. foundations donated more than $7 billion to higher education institutions, which made up 22 percent of total foundation giving to U.S.-based institutions of $31.8 billion.[7]

A key element of philanthropy's decisive role has been conceptualizing American higher education as a system and maintaining or modifying the dynamics of that system. To some observers, invoking the idea of an American "system" of higher education may require a throat-clearing pause. The sociologist Edward Shils ascribes the excellence of American universities to their "sovereignty, affluence, and tradition," with sovereignty being understood as independence from systemic direction or regulation.[8] This chapter focuses on foundations' efforts to influence the American university systemically—to go far beyond support for individual projects. More than a century ago, John D. Rockefeller declared the need to "promote a comprehensive system of higher education in the U.S."[9] Foundations helped define that system as one that mixed public and private institutions and resources, on the one hand, and mixed market mechanisms with fidelity to professional academic standards, on the other. From its consolidation in the early twentieth century, this system has been remarkably stable in balancing market, professional, and political power. One hundred years later, however, many note signs of disequilibrium in the system. Whether philanthropic foundations will play an equally influential role—or what type of role they might play—in this new stage is a significant and unanswered question.

The Foundation-University Partnership in the First Half of the Twentieth Century

In the early twentieth century, philanthropic foundations played a critical role in setting the terms for the development of the emerging university system. They helped establish the idea of a competitive, national framework and set the standards by which institutions would compete and be measured. They reinforced decisions to combine research and teaching—graduate and undergraduate

7. Bacchetti and Ehrlich (2006, p. 488).
8. Shils (1973, pp. 6–27). Quoted in Graham and Diamond (1997, p. 68).
9. Quoted in Shils (1979, p. 28).

education—in one set of institutions. While one could imagine that the involve-ment of private philanthropic foundations would widen any division between tax-supported and private universities, in fact the opposite was the case: founda-tions encouraged a common framework for public and private universities.

Historians have extensively analyzed and documented the decisive role of foundations in shaping the research university in the golden age of philanthropic influence, extending from the late nineteenth century until World War II. Jug-gling the three attributes noted by Shils—sovereignty, affluence, and tradition—the largest foundations used affluence as a means to help universities discover and enshrine traditions of research and academic value and to give them some insulation from, if not sovereignty over, a purely commercial competition.

Foundations and research universities formed a natural alliance, reciprocal in personnel and in influence. There was a ready synergy between the science advanced by the new universities and the scientific philanthropy that distin-guished the new, more analytically rigorous foundations from the merely ame-liorative charity of the past.[10] Universities provided philanthropists with the per-sonnel, prestige, and objects with which to develop their own new organizations and procedures. University presidents were prominent members of the early boards of the Rockefeller and Carnegie philanthropies.[11] After the philanthro-pists withdrew from the direct management of the foundations they had created, university presidents and leaders were the most likely candidates to fill those positions.

Confronting the nineteenth-century heritage of "a loosely defined higher education universe" of colleges and academies that were universities more in aspiration than in fact, philanthropists and the university presidents with whom they partnered sought to rationalize and standardize institutional categories.[12] Andrew Carnegie wanted to establish a pension scheme for college teachers, but doing so required defining what a "college" was. Henry Smith Pritchett, the president of the Massachusetts Institute of Technology and the first president of the Carnegie Foundation for the Advancement of Teaching, worked with other activist leaders to use pensioning as a springboard for promulgating benchmarks and, eventually, rankings for all of tertiary education. But this was only the first step in a larger effort to decree the shape of the emerging American univer-sity. The education reformer Abraham Flexner, working with the Carnegie and Rockefeller foundations, redefined the relationship of professional education to the university, requiring that faculty be academic researchers and not local pro-fessional luminaries.[13]

10. See Rosenberg (1997) and Karl and Katz (1987).
11. See Hollis (1938, pp. 86–97).
12. Bowen and others (2005, p. 26).
13. See Bonner (2002); Wheatley (1988); Lagemann (1983, pp. 59–83); Fox (1980).

Standard setting, however, was not the conclusion of the philanthropic project. It was the necessary condition for introducing the second defining quality of the developing system of higher education: competition. Nineteenth-century higher education had been defined by the market for student tuition dollars. While president of MIT, Pritchett worried that "in no other institution have the commercial tendencies of our national life been more strongly reflected than in our college-universities," to the detriment of professionalized research.[14] Without any external standards regulating this market, the competition among institutions to fill their classrooms produced a downward spiral in admissions criteria, curricular requirements, and the quality of faculty appointments.

With the inauguration of the Carnegie Foundation for the Advancement of Teaching in 1905, Pritchett was in a position to write some new rules for the game. At their first meeting, the trustees of the new foundation were presented with a memo by Pritchett stating that "the most important question with which the Board has to deal . . . is that of determining what educational standard shall be set up."[15] The new foundation defined standards, faculty qualifications, student admissions criteria, and curricular organization as eligibility criteria for admission to the pension scheme it would provide.

These new standards not only sought to regulate the market for tuition but also set up new axes of competition among institutions: for highly trained faculty, prestige, and philanthropic dollars. Pritchett promised Carnegie he could make the new foundation "one of the Great Agencies for standardizing American education."[16] Education reformers hoped that the foundations would "do what in Germany the government does—develop a policy & offer inducement enough to force its acceptance."[17]

The demands of the new competition were well understood by all players. Columbia University's president Nicholas Murray Butler said in 1921, "We have arrived at the point where [capital resources] must be increased unless we are going to stand still—and we cannot stand still because to stand still in this particular endeavor means to fall back."[18] "Make the peaks higher!" admonished Wallace Buttrick, a long-serving Rockefeller officer. Raising the quality and character of the most prominent universities would have a systemic effect precisely because the bulk of colleges and universities could now be plotted on standings and rankings. It was vital, according to Flexner, that there be an apex of institutions characterized by "uniformity . . . in respect to type, organization, and ideal" that could be emulated by aspiring institutions.[19] Hierarchy was an

14. Quoted in Lagemann (1983, p. 30).
15. Quoted in Lagemann (1983, p. 39).
16. Quoted in Lagemann (1983, p. 123).
17. Abraham Flexner, quoted in Wheatley (1988, p. 59).
18. Quoted in McCaughey (2003, p. 303).
19. Buttrick and Flexner quoted in Wheatley (1988, p. 86).

essential feature of the system, but so was fluidity. While rankings were stable, they were sufficiently porous to allow for new entrants and rising stars.

The intensifying competition among universities for prestige and visibility increased enormously the marginal utility of foundation grants. University suppliants were therefore more prepared to pay whatever institutional "price" was asked by the foundations in terms of reshaping their own structures and practices. This would be especially true if, as was often the case, foundation grants were linked to gifts from local philanthropists such as Edward Harkness in New York, Julius Rosenwald in Chicago, or George Eastman in Rochester.

Part of establishing a system was creating the intermediary mechanisms that could reinforce standards, measure achievement, and signal new directions. A set of national bodies dedicated to these purposes indeed emerged. The National Academy of Sciences was energized by the creation within it of the National Research Council. Foundation grants were crucial to sustaining two fledgling organizations, the American Council of Learned Societies and the Social Science Research Council. Together, these three agencies formed a genuine national academy. Foundation officials also supported the Association of American Universities in its efforts to rank institutions "in the general interest of education."[20] There was further systematization, including the development of standardized testing, such as the Scholastic Aptitude Test (now the SAT Reasoning Test) and the Graduate Record Exam (GRE), developed under the auspices of the Carnegie Foundation for the Advancement of Teaching.[21]

Foundation officers promoted competition between public and private institutions. The Carnegie Foundation's faculty pension scheme, originally limited to private institutions, was soon opened to state-sponsored colleges and universities. Within the Rockefeller philanthropic boards, Abraham Flexner ardently campaigned to include public institutions among those the foundation supported. By doing so, he noted, "we not only escape bureaucratic uniformity but we obtain a wholesome competition."[22] He continued: "Cities and states are all rich enough to do these things without foundation aid, as far as mere wealth is concerned. They don't do it, because they haven't been educated up to it, and the most effective way to educate them is to stimulate them by a conditional gift. This strengthens the university authorities whether they deal with individuals or states."[23]

As foundation officers experimented with what Ellen Condliffe Lagemann refers to as different "technologies of influence," they debated differing

20. FPK to Adam Leroy Jones, July 23, 1923, folder 17, box 47, series III.A, Carnegie Corporation of New York Archives, Columbia University (hereafter CCNYA).

21. Lagemann (1983, pp. 94–121).

22. Quoted in Wheatley (1988, p. 104).

23. Quoted in Wheatley (1988, p. 105).

conceptions of foundation roles and the place of the philanthropic professional.[24] Should foundations restrict themselves to sizable grants focused on institutional transformation, or build programs through a series of smaller grants, each being a piece of a larger mosaic? Those favoring larger grants bemoaned the "scatteration" of energy and resources on discrete, smaller activities.[25] "We are really in many cases a University playing hide and seek in other [universities' buildings]," lamented one Rockefeller program officer.[26]

While some denounced smaller grants as turning foundations into "the single largest distributor of chicken feed in the world," others defended the practice by noting that "there is at least one instance in which chicken feed is not despised, and that is by a starving chicken."[27] This latter view of the foundation as an active innovator working through existing institutions would carry the day after the 1969 Tax Reform Act helped reshape the organizational culture of many philanthropies.

Foundations, Universities, and the Federal Government, 1945–1970

In the quarter century following World War II, the federal government became the major—though selective—source of funding for higher education, and the responses of universities to that new funding reshaped them in important ways. *Science: The Endless Frontier,* by MIT dean Vannevar Bush, succeeded in convincing President Harry Truman and Congress to enter into the support of university research through the National Science Foundation in 1950.[28] The parallel growth of research support from the National Institutes of Health, the Department of Defense, and later the National Aeronautics and Space Administration helped establish the norm of the federal grant university so celebrated by Clark Kerr. Later, with the Great Society, funding for the humanities and the arts became part of the government's university support. While federal grants for research benefited universities through one channel, federal student aid assured additional revenue through another.

From the 1940s through the 1970s the size and ambition of American higher education escalated. Foundation leaders did not abandon their systemic focus but adjusted to the growth of federal and state spending by finding new points of leverage. There remained a large space for the persistence of foundation influence, for while the federal government became a supporter of research and

---

24 . Lagemann (1983, pp. 57–58).

25. Lagemann (2006, pp. 56–58).

26. Alan Gregg, memo, 1937, quoted in Wheatley (1988, p. 184).

27. Alan Gregg, memo, 1937, quoted in Wheatley (1988, p. 183).

28. *Science: The Endless Frontier,* National Science Foundation (www.nsf.gov/od/lpa/nsf50/vbush1945.htm [November 16, 2009]).

(primarily through student aid) of education, its policy interventions were ad hoc and happenstance. As the historian John Thelin has commented, "There were nationwide trends without national policy."[29]

Foundation leaders were well aware that federal funding had displaced foundation dollars as the largest supply of venture capital for higher education. John Gardner, the president of the Carnegie Corporation, told its trustees that "when the National Science Foundation moves into a field . . . it puts up funds on a scale which dwarfs anything the Corporation can do." It was therefore essential to consolidate and target resources on those points where one could find "the most leverage in moving one or another field ahead."[30] As the largest foundations repositioned themselves in the decades following World War II, they continued to conceive of themselves as working at a systemic level. Foundations made a series of interventions into higher education that were focused on balancing and rounding out the system in relation to the new variable of federal funding. Those interventions included the strengthening of private education and support of the humanities. They also sought to provide leadership for the system through agenda-setting commissions.

While the entry of the federal government into the funding of American higher education had significant consequences, this change was, according to Clark Kerr, a "vast transformation without a revolution."[31] American higher education remained a mixed political economy, with both public and private institutions receiving public and private funds through a series of competitive markets for research grants, student tuition, and general development. Some, however, had envisioned a more thoroughly changed system; that vision can be seen in the recommendations of President Truman's Commission on Higher Education.

The Truman Commission

Many individual campuses participated in the efforts to mobilize human resources and research during World War II. With the passage of the Serviceman's Readjustment Act of 1944—what became known as the G.I. Bill—it did not require much imagination to foresee that the national government would henceforth play a larger role in higher education. Shaping that role, and, by extension, reshaping the role of private education institutions and leadership, became an urgent issue. In 1945 George Zook, of the American Council on Education, warned that if academic leaders did not give concerted thought to the role of the federal government in higher education, "we may some day wake up to find . . . as the result of patchwork and piecemeal legislation, a distorted

29. Thelin (2004, p. 270).
30. Lagemann (1989, p. 186).
31. Kerr (2001, p. 34).

and disjointed policy in education which represents neither the considered judgment of education leaders nor the needs of our country."[32] One year later, Zook was given an opportunity to develop a comprehensive vision when he was appointed chairman of the President's Commission on Higher Education.

President Truman charged the commission with the task of "reexamin[ing] our system of higher education in terms of its objectives, methods, and facilities."[33] The commission's report and recommendations were issued under the title *Higher Education for American Democracy*. With the rhetorical propulsion that investing in education preserved democracy, the report advocated a sustained and active role for the federal government in the development of a system of higher education that could serve an ever-larger portion of the population. According to the commission, the federal government must become "a strong, permanent partner in the system of financing higher education."[34] The federal government should provide student aid, support for operations, and assistance for capital projects while also developing an enhanced system of community colleges, more adult education, and increased studies of foreign cultures so as to reap "the real advantages of cultural diversity."[35] Many of these recommendations would be adopted in years to come, albeit in exactly the piecemeal and patchwork fashion that Zook had lamented.

The commission also sought to balance its argument for a broad expansion of federal action with acknowledgment that any reformed system must remain pluralistic. Great attention was given to the role of voluntary, intermediary organizations—such as learned societies, national federations, and accrediting agencies—that together developed standards for curriculum, faculty promotion, and scholarly achievement. "In this country," the commission stated, "governmental agencies have been relatively ineffective in systematizing and improving the work of colleges and universities," whereas private voluntary organizations had a strong record. The report saw, however, a "danger inherent" in the "monopoly" of private authority and called for a leading, but not dominant, role for the federal government.[36]

Still, the commission's vision clearly implied a predominantly public system of higher education. While "private colleges will, in the future as in the past, contribute immeasurably to the expansion and improvement of our facilities for

32. Zook (1945, pp. 1–2).

33. President Harry S. Truman, "Letter of Appointment of Commission Members," July 13, 1946, in President's Commission on Higher Education (1947), vol. 1, *Establishing the Goals*.

34. President's Commission on Higher Education (1947), vol. 5, *Financing Higher Education*, p. 43.

35. President's Commission on Higher Education (1947), vol. 1, *Establishing Goals*, p. 17.

36. President's Commission on Higher Education (1947), vol. 5, *Financing Higher Education*, p. 43.

higher education . . . in the nature of things, the major burden of equalizing educational opportunity must rest on publicly supported institutions."[37]

Finally, the commission was forthright in arguing for an end to racial and religious discrimination in college and university admissions—a stance that reduced the political attractiveness of the comprehensive vision. Truman, suffering politically and anticipating a vigorous challenge in the 1948 presidential election, felt in no position to push for an education program likely to provoke significant opposition.

The report imagined a fundamentally different profile of the American university developing over the following decades, one in which higher education would become a largely public enterprise, with private institutions maintaining a perhaps prestigious but limited corner of the system. Many distrusted that vision. In 1947 the Rockefeller Foundation supported an Exploratory Committee on the Financing of Higher Education with a different agenda from that of the Truman Commission, which seemed to threaten private higher education. Two years later, the Rockefeller Foundation asked the Carnegie Corporation to join in support of a new body, the Commission on the Financing of Higher Education, that would build on the work of the Exploratory Committee in providing a counter to the call for direct federal support for institutions of higher education, as opposed to support for research only.

The Carnegie Corporation's president, Charles Dollard, while calling the new commission's work "very persuasive," held out a slightly more nuanced view. He suggested to the commission that federal support for research did pay its full share of indirect costs and that the distinction between public and private could be overdrawn. "In terms of admission policies, sensitivity to the national interest and general operation, the distinction is not very meaningful," he wrote. "The independent institutions are really public in the sense that they exist solely for the purpose of training the country's best brains and advancing knowledge on all fronts to the end that our whole society would be a healthier one."[38]

While George Zook's project to promote federal support for the whole system of higher education proved too unwieldy, MIT's Vannevar Bush did not propose a new organizational technology. His proposal for what became the National Science Foundation seemed familiar because it built on the pattern of selecting and supporting discrete research projects that foundations had established. For the same reasons, foundation leaders found that adjusting to the increase in federal research support was not difficult, and relations with the National Science Foundation were cooperative. In 1952 Alan Waterman of the science foundation met with Carnegie president Dollard and reported that

37. President's Commission on Higher Education (1947), vol. 1, p. 44.

38. Charles Dollard to Laird Bell, February 27, 1952, folder 20, box 47, series III.A, CCNYA.

almost every national organization in the field of higher education had appointed a committee to consider the impact of government contracts on universities. . . . After discussion it was the sense of the meeting that [Waterman] should take the initiative in calling together the [chairmen] of these committees in the hope that some order might be brought out of the existing chaos. . . . [The] ideal solution would be that the [National Science Foundation] would take the responsibility for an overall review of this problem, hopefully with the cooperation of the other agencies concerned.[39]

Dollard agreed with the approach and considered withholding Carnegie support from efforts that were not coordinated with the new federal entity.

Support for the Humanities

Another foundation project aimed at rounding out both the postwar university and the federal establishment of university support was the campaign for the humanities that culminated in the creation of the National Endowment for the Humanities in 1965. While the natural and social sciences first achieved definitive form within the research university, the humanities had an earlier history as a self-conscious field of study. "Theirs is the story," writes the historian Lawrence Veysey, "not so much of the creation of professions from scratch, as of the transition from an older, long existing professional outlook and mentality to newer, more specialized versions of it."[40]

In the 1920s the Rockefeller Foundation created a humanities division that supported research and public programs in the classics, regional history, and Native American studies. But there seemed to be an undercurrent of dissatisfaction. In 1949 the foundation's retiring president, Raymond Fosdick, lamented to his successor, "I am conscious that in this difficult field our performance falls short of our ideals," even though the program was "excellent, so far as it goes," despite the officers' inclination to describe it in "fuzzy" terms. "Somehow we aren't addressing ourselves to the core of the question—the spiritual hunger and aimlessness of our generation. How do we meet it? I don't know the answer, but I feel the lack of it every time an item in the humanities is presented to the Trustees."[41]

In the late 1950s, the Harvard professor Howard Mumford Jones sought to be the Vannevar Bush of the humanities, and foundations supported him in

39. Note for the Record, October 3, 1952, folder 17, box 47, series III.A, CCNYA.

40. Veysey (1979, p. 58).

41. Raymond Fosdick to Chester I. Barnard, February 7, 1946, folder 177, box 23, series 900, record group 3, Rockefeller Foundation Archives, Rockefeller Archive Center, Sleepy Hollow, New York.

doing so. A midwesterner who never earned a doctoral degree, Jones was one of the founders of the field of American studies and one of the leaders of the American Council of Learned Societies. When the council approached insolvency in the 1950s, he beseeched the Rockefeller and Carnegie foundations to rescue the organization, not as an end in itself but as one building block of a national infrastructure supporting the humanities, an infrastructure that should include federal funding. Grants from the same foundations supported the Commission on the Humanities, a group of scholars and business and organizational leaders whose conversations Jones used as grist for his book-length essay titled *One Great Society: Humane Learning in the United States.*[42]

Jones's essay sought to present the practical benefits of the humanities that would justify public support. "Americans," he noted, "have developed an enormous respect for exact knowledge," and it is humanistic knowledge that produces most reference books, dictionaries, encyclopedias. "Without the activity of [humanities] scholars, about one third of our available information about man would . . . grow more untrustworthy . . . and . . . eventually disappear."[43] A new Commission on the Humanities, appointed in 1963 by the American Council of Learned Societies, the Council of Graduate Schools, and the United Chapters of Phi Beta Kappa, elaborated Jones's argument in its brief for the creation of a national humanities foundation. "Democracy demands wisdom of the average man," declared the commission's report. "Without the exercise of wisdom, free institutions and personal liberty are inevitably imperiled. To know the best that has been thought and said in former times can make us wiser than we otherwise might be, and in this respect the humanities are not merely our, but the world's best hope."[44] This was, indeed, a project with international implications. "World leadership of the kind which has come upon the United States cannot rest solely upon superior force, vast wealth or preponderant technology. Only the elevation of its goals and the excellence of its conduct entitle one nation to ask others to follow its lead."[45]

Congress ultimately accepted the commission's argument that "during our national life the activities of society as a whole and of government in particular have been greatly extended,"[46] and it created the parallel national endowments for the humanities and the arts in 1965. These new agencies were, in many ways, legatees of a line of foundation programming stretching back to the 1920s. The Rockefeller Foundation had continued for some time to nurture this

42. Jones (1959). There is an entry on Jones by Robert L. Gale in volume 12 of the *American National Biography* (New York: Oxford University Press, 1999).

43. Jones (1959, pp. 20, 22).

44. American Council of Learned Societies (1964, p. 4).

45. American Council of Learned Societies (1964, p. 5).

46. American Council of Learned Societies (1964, p. 7).

"corner of the academic marketplace."[47] The foundation's Humanities Division was instrumental in helping to develop a network of campus-based humanities centers. After the National Endowment for the Humanities suffered from the retrenchment in federal funding that took place in the early 1970s, the Rockefeller Foundation in 1978 convened a new Commission on the Humanities, chaired by Richard Lyman, the president of Stanford University, who was named to the foundation's presidency in the course of the commission's work. The commission's recommendations included calls for "public and private [funders] . . . to establish adequate collaboration in order to identify priorities for funding" and for the endowment to recognize the "federal responsibility" of "sustaining projects and institutions over the long term."[48]

Challenge Grants for University Development

In the 1950s and 1960s two Ford Foundation programs helped solidify the financial base of private higher education and demonstrated the potential for fundraising at new levels. These programs incubated practices such as prospect identification, campaign sequencing, and the creative deployment of matching funds that have become standard elements in the armory of university development.

In 1955–56, with the first sale of the Ford Foundation's stock in the Ford Motor Company (equities that had not been previously traded publicly), the scale of the foundation's endowment became apparent. With memory of recent congressional investigations of foundations still fresh, the foundation decided to accelerate its grant making lest it seem to violate its charitable purpose. It distributed $260 million among the more than six hundred accredited private institutions of higher education to raise faculty salaries eroded by inflation. While some regarded this largesse to have been purely mechanical, and the money to have, more or less, disappeared without a trace, these grants did increase the impact of the foundation in higher education. They also contributed to the foundation's self-perception by raising the comfort level of the trustees with sizable grants on a national scale. It was explained to them that "it can take as much staff work to give a $3,500 Guggenheim Fellowship as to give $3,500,000 to a well-known university." By 1960 more than half of the foundation's total giving—$646 million of $1.2 billion—had gone to higher education.[49]

In 1960 the Ford Foundation began what became known as the Special Program in Education, aimed at "strengthening American higher education by strengthening specific universities." Carefully targeted foundation grants, with calibrated matching requirements, could stimulate in matching funds three or

47. Menand (2001, p. 1).
48. Commission on the Humanities (1980, pp. 156, 176).
49. McCaughey (1984, pp. 169–71). See also Geiger (2004b, pp. 110–57).

four times the basic grant amount. "Our present income picture enables us to carry on a broad program in the basic undergirding of higher education," foundation staff observed, "while at the same time, we continue the more specific, pin-pointed programs aimed at improving parts of the educational system."[50]

The assumptions justifying the program attest to the systemic ambitions of the foundation. These are

> That the strengthening of American higher education is one of the primary means by which the foundation pursues its objective of advancing human welfare
>
> That the continuation of the established dual system of public and private support for higher education is essential to the welfare of the nation
>
> That the foundation most appropriately performs its role in society when it supports primarily privately supported higher education (in the belief that the state should and will provide the bulk of the funds necessary for publicly supported higher education)
>
> That regional peaks of excellence in privately supported higher education are essential to nationwide intellectual vigor and growth, overall academic and institutional freedom, and broad equality of educational opportunity.[51]

Over seven years, the Special Program awarded $349 million in challenge grants to sixteen research universities and sixty-one liberal arts colleges, grants that resulted in $990 million in matching donations.[52] By 1967 McGeorge Bundy had succeeded Henry Heald as Ford's president and had come to the conclusion that "the present needs of Deans and Presidents, strung end to end, would go three times around the endowment of Ford Foundation without a pause for breath."[53] Foundation staff also concluded that the program had achieved its aim of demonstrating that universities "can greatly expand the scale of their support." Indeed, the pace of university advancement was growing exponentially. "There is now at least a tendency to make intensive fund-raising a chronic, perennial matter, maintained at new levels by permanent, enlarged development offices, rather than by an intermittent series of convulsive episodes called 'drives,'" it was noted. "If this tendency should spread further, the challenge grant format may not be as useful a model in the future as it was when the Special Program began."[54]

50. Special Program in Education, HTH notes, March 1960 trustees meeting, file 010407, Ford Foundation Archives (hereafter FFA), pp. 4, 6, 7.

51. "Special Program in Education Assumptions," file 010407, FFA.

52. Rueben Frodin, "A Review of the Special Program of Capital Grants to Universities and Colleges," September 20, 1968, Report 0001347, FFA.

53. Ford Foundation (1967).

54. F. C. Ward to McGeorge Bundy, "Memorandum on the Special Program in Education, for discussion by the Education Committee of the Board on September 25th," August 3, 1968, file 010407, FFA.

Setting the Agenda

As the Ford Foundation closed down its Special Program in Education in 1967, the Carnegie philanthropies began an effort to refine the system's design. Its attempt to set the agenda extended to the development of metrics for making the system comprehensible. The Carnegie Foundation for the Advancement of Teaching developed the classification scheme that retains its influence today. This new taxonomy was intended, as Hugh Graham and Nancy Diamond put it, to "identify the different functional types of institutions and legitimize their differences."[55] It was to be a classification, not a ranking (institutions were listed alphabetically and by state within categories), and to be comprehensive for all of postsecondary education. Still, the new classifications helped reinforce the prestige order of higher education. "The nationalization of higher education tended to establish a single standard of excellence," writes historian Thomas Bender, "the model of the research university."[56]

Despite, or perhaps because of, having been a growth industry during the previous two decades, colleges and universities were, in the late 1960s, living beyond both their current income (their operating budgets) and their future income (projected earnings from endowments).[57] The Carnegie Commission on Higher Education, established in 1967 with financing from the Carnegie Corporation and sponsorship from the Carnegie Foundation for the Advancement of Teaching, was originally conceived as another study of higher education's financing. Its mandate became much broader when Clark Kerr was appointed its chairman. "The systematic analyses sponsored by the Carnegie Commission produced the most comprehensive depiction of the American system of higher education that it is ever likely to receive," notes Roger Geiger.[58] Carnegie Corporation president Alan Pifer pointed out proudly that the commission "is serving a highly important national purpose" as "the only sustained, comprehensive attempt there has ever been in this country to place the entire field of higher education under review and to formulate a coherent set of policy recommendations for its development."[59] Because he had "the gnawing feeling that there will be a tremendous vacuum in higher education when the Commission does expire," in 1973 Pifer put in place the Carnegie Council on Policy Studies in Higher Education as a "continuing enterprise that at a very high level involves itself with sustained study of policy issues."[60]

55. Graham and Diamond (1997, p. 53).

56. Bender (1997, p. 5).

57. Thelin (2004, pp. 318–19); Lagemann (1989, pp. 226–30).

58. Geiger (2004b, p. 199).

59. Quoted in Lagemann (1989, p. 229).

60. Memorandum EAD to DZR, April 7, 1971, folder 7, box 46, series III.A, CCNYA; see also Mayhew (1973).

The Efflorescence of the University System

In the quarter century between 1945 and 1970, American colleges and universities became more numerous, more complex, and richer. In the prosperous 1950s and 1960s, the growth rate of the aggregate income of all institutions of higher education was twice that of the gross national product.[61] But for all the financial, ideological, and demographic tumult, there was relatively little change in the structure, governance, or systemic aspects of U.S. higher education.[62] As universities competed for faculty, students, and support, "distinctions among different types of institutions, so far as the professoriate was concerned, began to be sanded down," observes the intellectual historian Louis Menand.[63] "The competition is unbelievable," complained Washington University chancellor Thomas Eliot to F. Champion Ward, a Ford Foundation officer. "The St. Louis branch of the University of Missouri just offered one of our professors, who now gets paid $20,000 a year, a position carrying a salary of $27,000. When [the professor being wooed] pointed out that they had no library resources, [the public university wooers] replied that Washington University's library was a very fine one, and they would use it!"[64]

The growth of federal funding for aspects of higher education increased rather than diminished the power of market forces. The 1972 amendments to the 1965 Higher Education Act allocated "vast new sums for student aid" but not, as universities had hoped, in the form of support to be distributed by institutions.[65] Instead, Congress mandated that what became known as Pell grants be portable awards issued to students who could "vote with their feet" in choosing the college or university that would ultimately receive the federal funds. Higher education lobbying groups had sought block grants to colleges and universities, but in an act the university leadership saw as "treason," the Carnegie Commission on Higher Education endorsed portability.[66] Equally important was the parallel development of new programs of federal student loans along the same lines. The federal government thus underwrote an enlarged market for student tuition, just as the National Science Foundation, the National Institutes of Health, and other federal grantors had enlarged and enriched the market for research support.[67]

---

61. McCaughey (1984, p. 176).

62. Altbach (2005, p. 25).

63. Menand (2001, p. 9); see also Graham and Diamond (1997, pp. 99–103).

64. Thomas H. Eliot to F. Champion Ward, February 21, 1969, section 4, grant file PA 6500-256, reel 1785, FFA.

65. Kerr (2001, p. 114).

66. Thelin (2004, p. 324).

67. See Zemsky, Wegner, and Massy (2005, pp. 163–77).

Foundation leaders searched harder for points of leverage but still expected to find them. "In my view," wrote Carnegie Corporation president Pifer to his education officers,

> we must, for at least some significant part of our higher education money, stop thinking of the Corporation as a *source of funds* to which individual institutions, education associations, agencies which serve higher education, etc. can lay claim and begin consciously to think of it solely as a *source of new ideas and initiatives*, particularly in regard to the subject of productivity. We should be asking ourselves not just the question of how institutions can become more productive but how groups of institutions, or even the entire system, can save significant sums of money without serious erosion of quality. We should also keep to the fore the question of what we can do that others can't or won't.[68]

The New Endless Frontier: The University Marketplace

Any concern that higher education would be conclusively shaped by federal policy evaporated in the 1970s as political, economic, and demographic forces undid the conditions that had opened up higher education after World War II. The disruptions on campus in response to the Vietnam War and the civil rights struggle soured many state and federal legislators on colleges and universities. The unsteady economy of the 1970s revealed that many universities were fiscally overextended and not prepared to deal with what Earl Cheit of the Carnegie Commission called "a new depression in higher education."[69] Demographic changes aggravated the situation. In 1975–76, with the crest of the baby boom graduating from college and the artificial stimulation of draft deferments ending, enrollment in higher education declined absolutely for the first time since 1951, when the initial surge from the G.I. Bill had played out.[70]

The political and economic unraveling also loosened the alignment of foundation and university leadership. The complementary roles they had played in the structure of higher education policymaking were now changing. But the rise of federal funding had not displaced the foundations. Rather, over thirty years an effective partnership had developed in which foundations reinforced the mixed public-private character of the system, even as federal funding became

68. Staff Committee on Higher Education, memorandum AP to DZR, RHS, EAD, March 31, 1975, Administrative Records Policy and Program, folder 9, box 7, series I.D, CCNYA; emphasis in original.

69. See Cheit (1971).

70. Thelin (2004, p. 321).

increasingly important. Foundations provided resources for the development of neglected segments of the university (area studies, the humanities) that could then make their claim on federal funding. Projects such as the Carnegie Commission on Higher Education showed how foundation philanthropy, in partnership with elements of the university elite, could have an agenda-setting role. This triangulation of academic, foundation, and federal influences flourished in an environment of growing resources, but the chillier climate of the 1970s altered the ecology that sustained that interaction. The last quarter of the twentieth century saw the steady rise of market forces as the primary variable in the university system. Even though maintaining a vigorous private sector had been the goal of previous philanthropic policies, philanthropic professionals found the university system less congenial as it became, in effect, increasingly privatized.

In the 1970s a changing economy and new public policies led universities "to the understanding that their survival depended on being more responsive to market forces."[71] A 1982 report of the Association of American Universities recognized the need for "finding policies that minimize, to the extent possible, institutional dependency on long-term governmental commitments."[72] Indeed, in the decade between 1978 and 1988, universities doubled the allocation of their own budgetary resources to the direct support of research, an increase of more than $1 billion.[73]

As university presidents confronted student disruptions in the late 1960s, the Tax Reform Act of 1969 and the hearings that led to it were a parallel ordeal for foundation leadership. Presided over by Representative Wright Patman, the hearings revealed what some regarded as a level of self-dealing bordering on corruption in smaller, less visible foundations and self-confidence bordering on arrogance in leadership of the most visible philanthropies. The resulting legislation increased regulatory scrutiny of foundations and, for the first time, levied a modest tax on them to cover the cost of that regulation. More consequential was the persistent uneasiness produced among foundation leadership, who were reminded that their institutions existed amid the interstices of the tax code. Foundation officials recalled an "atmosphere of terror" and resolved to develop new practices of openness and transparency to enhance the public legitimacy of the foundation form.[74]

Peter Frumkin's study of the institutional reaction of foundations to the 1969 crisis reveals several important changes in the organizational culture of the largest foundations. First, the foundation career became "professionalized" in the

---

71. Zemsky, Wegner, and Massy (2005, p. 4).
72. Rosenzweig and Turlington, (1982, p. xi.)
73. Measured in constant 1988 dollars. Graham and Diamond (1997, p. 120).
74. Frumkin (1999, p. 72).

sense that previous foundation work became an increasingly important quali-fication for service as a foundation officer or director. In the 1960s, as Robert McCaughey observes, "it was a rare [foundation] staff member who did not have a personal tie with one of the major universities, most often Chicago, Harvard, Yale or Columbia, or was not giving some thought to moving back into the university world after a tour with the [Ford] foundation."[75] Frumkin's study shows that in the 1970s and 1980s, the percentage of foundation staff hired from university positions declined by 50 percent, while the share of those with previous foundation positions increased nearly 200 percent. Foundation staffing increased significantly, as did the share of foundation expenditures devoted to administrative costs.[76]

The exaltation of evaluation and impact was a second dimension of profes-sionalization. Foundations received a friendlier but still critical review of their role in American life from the Commission on Foundations and Private Phi-lanthropy, known as the Peterson Commission. Organized at the initiative of John D. Rockefeller III in 1968, the commission's report, issued in 1970, became something of a rejoinder to the Patman hearings. It affirmed the positive potential of the foundation role and pointed to, among other historic achieve-ments, foundations' "unrivaled achievements in higher education." The report also spotlighted a number of problems in the management and investment prac-tices of foundations but most emphatically urged them to concentrate on "new and different approaches to problems" rather than "sustaining on-going, normal activities."[77]

The ideology of philanthropic foundations had always placed a high quotient on the values of innovation and impact, but these qualities were now elevated to be weapons of institutional self-defense. If the public were to have confidence in the efficacy of foundation philanthropy, then foundation officers needed to demonstrate the results of programs and grants. These changes naturally refo-cused the sights of foundation officers. If their careers were to depend on devel-oping portfolios of discrete and inventive programs, then there was increased incentive to focus on smaller projects. Dedication to the long-term curation of a complex, ongoing system could be seen as hazardous to professional and insti-tutional health.

The focus of foundation leadership and staff, however, shifted slowly. In the 1970s, there was still an impulse to broker public-private cooperation in steering the university system. In 1977 six major foundations sponsored *Research Univer-sities and the National Interest,* a report written by fifteen presidents of research

75 . McCaughey (1984, pp. 179–80).

76. Frumkin (1999, p. 87).

77. Commission on Foundations and Private Philanthropy (1970, pp. 118–19).

universities, that argued for "a renewed and stronger partnership between the government and the major research universities."[78]

But by 1979 Earl F. Cheit, then at the University of California, Berkeley, and Theodore E. Lobman of the William and Flora Hewlett Foundation wrote a technical report for the Ford Foundation and the Carnegie Council on Public Studies in Higher Education that opened with a chapter titled "The Diminishing Influence of Private Foundations." "Foundation influence has declined not only because less money is available," the report observed, "but also because there are far more claimants for it," even as "colleges and universities are far more developed and less susceptible to major change." Even so, the authors found that donations to higher education formed a major portion of foundation largesse, ranging (depending on the stratum of foundations examined) from 33 to 40 percent of total grants made.[79]

As the conception of the higher education system as essentially market driven became the reigning view, the close cooperation between public and private funders was less central to management of the system. Geiger contrasts the studies of two federal commissions separated by only a quarter century. In 1972 the National Commission on the Financing of Postsecondary Education expected the federal government to ensure access to higher education, especially given the contemporary financial weakness of colleges and universities. The 1997 National Commission on the Cost of Higher Education "assumed a market environment" as the defining dynamic and tailored its recommendations to market mechanisms.[80]

Social and economic conditions in the 1980s created a window of opportunity for elite private institutions to distinguish themselves. With a slowdown in inflation, an increase in the premium attached to obtaining higher education, and the growing wealth of already affluent families, private colleges and universities found they could increase tuition costs with no decline in applications. Over time, these responses to the changing market for higher education have worked their way through the system into the public sector. As state legislatures have reduced their contributions, public research universities have sought to increase tuition to remain competitive with private institutions. The powerful image of higher education as a market system is such that there is almost a positive value to increasing tuition, as many potential consumers have come to equate price with quality. At the same time, market-driven increases in the cost and price of higher education have eroded public confidence in these institutions.[81] As the economist, foundation president, and former college president

78. Ford Foundation (1967), p. vi.
79. Cheit and Lobman (1979, pp. 6, 24).
80. Geiger (2004a, p. 28).
81. Clotfelter (1996, pp. 8–11).

Michael McPherson puts it, "Individual colleges and universities are prisoners of the competitive situation in which they find themselves."[82]

This is the context for the frustration expressed in the Carnegie Foundation for the Advancement of Teaching's centennial volume mentioned at the beginning of this chapter. Raymond Bacchetti of the Hewlett Foundation has observed that "foundations and institutions of higher education can behave like carnival bumper cars in the ways they careen, collide, momentarily lock together, and then move off cheerfully in new directions." Foundations look outward, colleges inward, he notes. Bacchetti imagines conversations with representative foundation program officers who are sure to state that "universities are mightily indifferent to goals foundations might have," goals that need to be achieved in a relatively short time period because "foundation staff members are expected to show accomplishments quickly and [b]oards normally want to lead flexible foundations."[83] The clashing time horizons of foundation officers and university leaders point to the larger divergence of their professional and institutional projects. Once orbiting the same cluster of values and ambitions, universities are now in the gravitational pull of the academic marketplace, while foundation officers circle the guidestar of innovation.[84]

The primary change is in the frame of reference. In 1960 Ford Foundation president Henry Heald stated that "the strengthening of American higher education is one of the primary means by which the Foundation pursues its objective of advancing human welfare."[85] In 2000 William Richardson, president of the W. K. Kellogg Foundation, posited different institutional priorities when he wrote that "strengthening higher education institutions and the effectiveness of their individual leaders is of great importance to the work of the Foundation, but it is not our central concern. Kellogg support for institutions of higher education is premised on their role in serving communities and society at large, not merely on their preservation and enrichment as institutions."[86] In 1973 Carnegie president Alan Pifer identified seven foundations with substantial programs concerning the policies of American higher education.[87] A review of the websites of those same foundations in 2007 finds that none of these seven identify American higher education as a central element of their work.

There are of course exceptions to this trend. The Andrew W. Mellon Foundation is the most notable. Created in 1969 by the merger of two foundations

82. McPherson (2005, p. 82).
83. Bacchetti and Ehrlich (2006, pp. 251, 258, 253, 259).
84. Clotfelter (2006) analyzes this divergence.
85. Quoted in Geiger (2004b, p. 110).
86. William C. Richardson, foreword to Astin and others (2000), p. vi.
87. The Carnegie, Ford, Kellogg, Exxon Educational, and Edna McConnell Clark foundations, the Rockefeller Brothers Fund, and the Lilly Endowment.

endowed by the children of Andrew W. Mellon, the Mellon Foundation developed and maintained deep engagement with higher education. Led by, successively, former presidents of Williams College, Princeton University, and the University of Chicago, the Mellon Foundation has concentrated its work on such fields as the humanities, graduate education, and the changing dynamics of scholarly communication in the digital age. The Mellon Foundation is distinctive as a relatively new foundation choosing to engage the university system.

It will be interesting to learn whether the new program adopted by the Rockefeller Foundation in 2006 brings a return to engagement with American higher education. In 2005 the foundation, so instrumental in forming the U.S. university system, asked a "program strategy task force" to outline how it might "intervene with the highest impact" in higher education to bring about "transformational change." While the task force's report did note that "the capacity to acquire, generate and apply knowledge is perhaps the crucial factor in the improvement of the human condition," it considered only fleetingly the health of the university system, noting that "at present, the U.S. has the best research universities in the world" and that "maintaining an innovative advantage may be easier than building one." The report also suggests that both poor and wealthy nations should "invest deeply in knowledge-building infrastructure," without suggesting that role for the foundation.[88]

Foundations and Universities in the Twenty-First Century

The relative scale of institutional resources is one mark of the changing relations between foundations and universities. In 1960 the total endowment of all colleges and universities in the United States was $5 billion, and the endowment of the Ford Foundation was greater than the total endowments of the five richest universities in the country. In 2007, the Ford Foundation's endowment stood at $11 billion, while the endowment of Harvard University alone was $30 billion. Universities now begin development campaigns with goals in the billions. Any hardheaded foundation officer or trustee might conclude that the work of his or her institution in this realm is now finished. Beyond financial issues, that officer might echo the idea that today's university structure is "an indigestible hodgepodge" in which constructive and innovative intervention is impossible.[89]

But if the diminished engagement of foundations with the university system follows from professional and institutional pressures, higher education still presents challenging policy problems, including the growing privatization of public colleges and universities, a more commercialized and politicized research

---

88. "New Conceptions, New Directions," Rockefeller Foundation (www.rockfound.org/about_us/news/2006/111006conceptions_directions.pdf [November 16, 2009]), pp. 1, 2, 19, 22.

89. Rhodes (2001, p. 33).

system, challenges in access to higher education, and a teaching force increasingly composed of faculty with "contingent," that is, untenured, appointments.[90] Some analysts see such changes "transforming higher education to an extent not seen since the end of World War II."[91] Who or what will shape this transformation?

James Duderstadt, president emeritus of the University of Michigan, has identified one answer. He states that "a market-driven restructuring of higher education" is "driving changes at an unprecedented pace, perhaps even beyond the capacity of our colleges and universities to adapt. There are increasing signs that our current paradigms for higher education—the nature of our academic programs; the organizations of our colleges and universities; the way we finance, conduct, and distribute the services of higher education—may not be able to adapt to the demands and realities of our times."[92]

Although in 1947 the President's Commission on Higher Education foresaw an essentially public system, sixty years later the relative prospects of public and private research universities seem reversed. In the early twenty-first century "obtaining adequate financial resources is a particularly acute problem in public universities. Even the strongest and most prestigious of these institutions struggle to compete with their private counterparts for students, faculty, and research money."[93] In 1998 Clark Kerr, who had trumpeted the paradigm of the federal grant university thirty years earlier, commented that "the future of research universities (and all of higher education) appears to be substantially bifurcated, with one fork (the private) generally pointed level or even up and the other generally down."[94] Roger Geiger describes "the paradox of the marketplace" in which "universities find that insatiable needs and increasing competition constrain their freedom of activity."[95] It is a situation in which "the costs of universities have shifted from public to private sources, including gifts from alumni and other individuals. Privatization has not merely been fiscal; it has also meant that revenue streams are now more closely linked with university functions, limiting the discretion of university leaders. Competition has also become keener, driven by the increased reliance on private revenues and, more fundamentally, by the national integration of the university system."[96] "Massive and growing inequality," Geiger declares, "seems to rule in the private sector in the twenty-first century."[97]

90. Finkelstein and Schuster (2001); Finkelstein (2003).
91. Zusman (2005, p. 115).
92. Duderstadt (2004, p. 60).
93. Bowen and others (2005, p. 249).
94. Kerr (2001, p. 186).
95. Geiger (2004a, p. vii).
96. Geiger (2004a, p. 261).
97. Geiger (2004a, p. 42).

The relationship of the university system to the marketplace was also the focus of the 2006 report of the Commission on the Future of Higher Education appointed by secretary of education Margaret Spellings. The report warns of "unwarranted complacency" in current discussions of colleges and universities. "American higher education," it declares, "has become what, in the business world, would be called a mature enterprise: increasingly risk-averse, at times self-satisfied, and unduly expensive."[98]

Both the 2006 report and that of its predecessor commission sixty years earlier call for increased engagement of the federal government with higher education. But while the Truman Commission argued for increased funding for a broad set of initiatives aimed at both research and education, the Spellings Commission recommends increased federal regulation targeted toward the operation of the education market and presents the case for a more forceful federal role in increasing the market-driven character of higher education and, indeed, privatization. Secretary Spellings has cast the U.S. government less as a supporter of the university system than as a consumer of educational services. Noting that federal funds provide roughly one-third of the support for higher education, she regrets that "we don't ask a lot of questions about what we're getting for our investment in higher education." "It is time," she declares, "to examine how we can get the most out of our national investment."[99] In contrast, Robert Zemsky, a prominent analyst of higher education and a member of the Spellings Commission, notes the "missed opportunity" of the commission's narrow focus on the relation of student achievement to tuition charges. Reflecting on his own testimony before the commission, he writes, "I also came to understand just how important it was to begin talking, in almost singular terms, about an American higher education system—huge, complex, diverse. . . . There really is a need for a national dialogue, one that treated higher education as a whole by asking, 'How do the parts relate to one another?'"[100]

The debate over the future of higher education echoes the questions that the first generation of foundation philanthropists and their advisers grappled with: What is the relative role of public goods in the marketplace? How can a decentralized and seemingly unresponsive market-driven system of higher education be adjusted so that the equilibrium resulting from competition is a public good?

---

98. Commission on the Future of Higher Education (2006, pp. vi, ix).

99. Quoted in Doug Lederman, "The Future of Higher Ed," *Inside Higher Ed,* September 20, 2005 (www.insidehighered.com/layout/set/print/news/2005/09/20/spellings [November 16, 2009]).

100. Robert Zemsky, "The Rise and Fall of the Spellings Commission," *Chronicle of Higher Education,* January 26, 2007, p. B9.

Those questions recall the sociologist Burton Clark's triangular matrix for schematizing the governance of university systems.[101] The three points of the triangle represent government regulation, the authority of academic leadership, and market forces. Philanthropic foundations help position the American university system roughly in the center of that triangle, although certainly more toward the shared axis of academic values and market forces. In the late nineteenth century, individual philanthropists—Johns Hopkins, Leland Stanford, John D. Rockefeller—supported the ambitions of Dwight Gilman, David Starr Jordan, and William Rainey Harper to transform the market of higher education from one of destructive commercial competition to virtuous competition for prestige. To do so, they needed to systematize higher education, an arena from which the federal government was absent.

After World War II, the leading philanthropic foundations found a role in a new institutional ecology in which the federal government had become a major funder, while still maintaining their ambitions of systemic influence. Those ambitions, however, now seem more limited, even as the dynamics of higher education are changing again. Over the course of the twentieth century, the gravitational pull of the market moved the system more toward that corner of the triangle of influence, a trend that some political forces wish now to intensify, with uncertain consequences. "In higher education, the existence of an informed outside force, like foundations, has unmistakably yielded a net gain for the universities and society," wrote Ford president Henry Heald in 1963.[102] In the marketplace of today, however, past performance is no guarantee of future results.

101. Clark (1983).
102. Heald (1963, p. 7).

5

Foundations and Higher Education

PETER FRUMKIN AND GABRIEL KAPLAN

American philanthropic foundations have a long history of supporting higher education. It is a domain in which foundations have focused tremendous resources over time.[1] Although foundation dollars make up only a small part of higher education revenues, they constitute more than a quarter of all foundation giving. And nearly all foundations report some giving to higher education.[2]

Funding higher education has proved attractive to foundations for two very different reasons. The first is that higher education has long been seen as a critical gateway to greater opportunities.[3] By supporting colleges and universities, foundations can increase the life chances of young people who often start out with considerable disadvantage. To many, higher education appears to be the great equalizer in American society.[4] The second reason stems from the desire of many foundations to support the advancement of knowledge and institutional excellence.[5] Colleges and universities are often where medical and scientific breakthroughs originate and where the arts and letters are nurtured. As a consequence, and as chapter 4 suggests, over time foundations have been major donors to core research and teaching programs in higher education.[6] These two .

1. Bremner (1988); Sealander (1997).
2. Lawrence and Marino (2003).
3. Lucas (1994); Veysey (1965).
4. Lee (1963).
5. Fosdick (1989); Geiger (1990).
6. Karl and Katz (1981).

rationales are, of course, quite different, and it may be useful to think of them as constituting two poles: one focused on access and social change and the other on core capacity and institution building.

While the second pole is familiar and straightforward enough, the first is more complex. Paradoxically, higher education is both a sensible and an unlikely place for foundations to pursue a social change agenda grounded in increasing access and opportunity. On one hand, colleges and universities are indeed the access points to the middle class and to increased lifetime earning potential. It is only logical that foundations wanting to address inequality and lack of opportunity would focus their attention on higher education. If the doors of colleges and universities could be opened more widely, a large number of young people long lacking access to ladders of opportunity could be given new possibilities for self-improvement and advancement.[7] Some institutions have also reached out to the neighborhoods that surround their campuses and attempted to bridge large divides of class and race.[8] These efforts, along with progressive policies in the areas of recruitment, have made it possible for higher education to inject into its more traditional work an element of social change.

On the other hand, colleges and universities seem uniquely ill equipped to serve donors interested in promoting change. Higher education is full of large and intransigent institutions that have entrenched procedures and defined cultures.[9] Work within this environment requires patience and a willingness to accept compromises. Moreover, colleges and universities are not, by their nature, oriented toward social change. Their missions rarely include controversial social and political goals. Tenure protects academic freedom, but the more mundane reality is that academic freedom is rarely fully exercised. The largest universities are deeply committed to scientific discovery and basic research, pursued according to the academic ethos. Gifts to colleges and universities can and often do seek simply to increase the capacity of institutions to do this work at a high level.

In examining the role foundations have played in higher education over time, it may be useful to ask to what extent change-oriented foundation giving has or has not competed with core capacity and institution-building support. Although higher education and foundations have been linked for more than a century, it is unclear which of these two major objectives foundations have sought more to achieve through their funding of universities and colleges. It is also not obvious how foundations go about the work of delivering grant support to higher education, the role they play in the operation and organization of higher education, and the influence they have on university behavior. One thing is clear: the

7. U.S. Department of Education (2006).

8. Julianne Basinger, "A Promoter of Town-Gown Cooperation Finds Development May Be Her Undoing," *Chronicle of Higher Education*, June 2, 2000, p. A41.

9. Barley, Meyer, and Gash (1988).

current landscape of foundation philanthropy in higher education has changed a great deal, and the major funders in this sector represent a different set of actors with potentially different social objectives from those who helped launch the American university's dominance in the twentieth century.[10]

In seeking solutions to these puzzles, we focus on the higher education sector more broadly than does the preceding chapter, which looks at foundations' role in support of research universities during the first two-thirds of the twentieth century. Our definition of higher education includes all four-year institutions accredited to grant bachelor degrees in the liberal arts and sciences by the regional accrediting agencies.[11] It also includes community colleges. Hence we expand our view beyond research universities to consider the broad range of activities and organizational types within the higher education sector. This allows us to look at four-year degree-granting institutions as a sector operating alongside that of postsecondary vocational education and junior and community colleges.[12]

This expansive but defined scope is justified by the very different missions pursued by four-year and two-year higher education institutions in the United States. Our analysis takes into consideration four-year liberal arts colleges, a sector populated by older elite institutions with a broad social spectrum represented in the student body, as well as less well established schools with a narrower spectrum of students drawn primarily from the ranks of the middle class. We also examine the role of foundations in relation to a class of institutions known as comprehensives. These are often modern offshoots of the state land-grant colleges, teachers colleges, and regionally based institutions.

This wide range of grant patterns across the full spectrum of higher education institutions gives us an opportunity to explore the predominant focus of foundations giving, whether on increasing access and opportunity or on supporting core needs connected to institutional capacity. This chapter reviews and analyzes grant data compiled by the Foundation Center (specifically, the FC Stats data for 2001) to identify the most frequent targets and purposes of grant awards. It also addresses a related question: What have been the guiding purposes of foundation activity in higher education?

10. Karl and Katz (1981).

11. There are six regional accrediting agencies that certify college and university programs so that students are eligible for federal financial aid programs: the Middle States Association of Colleges and Schools, the New England Association of Schools and Colleges, the North Central Association of Colleges and Schools, the Northwest Association of Schools and Colleges, the Southern Association of Colleges and Schools, and the Western Association of Schools and Colleges.

12. The Foundation Center data we examined exclude grants to museums associated with colleges or universities, theologically oriented stand-alone institutes, and university-affiliated medical centers. They also include some endowment entities that are only loosely affiliated with higher education institutions and scholarship pass-through vehicles.

Current Trends in Philanthropy toward Higher Education

In executing our research strategy, we used existing data to examine foundation activity along five dimensions: type of recipient organization, largest givers and largest recipients, type of grant support, beneficiary population, and grant purpose or field of activity. We use the descriptive data to paint a portrait of the field by looking at the way these five dimensions intersect.

Recipient Type

To begin, we employed the National Taxonomy of Exempt Entities classification codes. Using a variable that codes the purposes of the grant recipient organization, we then selected all institutions that were identified as serving some kind of higher education purpose—in particular, those identified as undergraduate colleges or universities. But we also selected institutions identified as two-year colleges and organizations formed for their support, such as public university foundations, and entities that function as financial aid or scholarship organizations. Our first objective was to identify where foundations directed their resources by mapping funding with the organizational purpose of the recipients.

The data show that more than 72 percent of foundation dollars were granted to universities (57 percent) and colleges (15 percent), while only 9 percent went to more specialized organizations that focused on technical or professional education. Only 2 percent of gifts and grants supported community colleges, which are typically seen as the entry point to higher education for poor and traditionally underserved communities. In institutional choice, at least, foundations appear to favor core capacity and institution building over access and opportunity.

Givers and Recipients of Largest Gifts

To sketch the landscape of major foundation grants to higher education, we compiled a table of the largest foundation grants in the field over almost forty years. These grants ranged in size from $50 million to $1 billion (see table 5-1). The list of foundations making these grants includes many of the largest foundations in the United States. Represented are both old-line foundations that have been active in the field of higher education for decades and newer entrants that have only recently turned their philanthropic attention to higher education.

By and large, most of the recipient organizations are tier-one research universities. There are two likely explanations for this preponderant favor shown to the largest and most prestigious institutions in American higher education. The first is that these are the only institutions with the size and operational capacity

Table 5-1. *Largest Grants to Higher Education, 1967–2004*

Foundation	Recipient	Grant amount (dollars)	Year
Bill and Melinda Gates Foundation	Gates Millennium Scholars program[a]	1 billion[b]	1999
Gordon and Betty Moore and the Gordon and Betty Moore Foundation	California Institute of Technology	600 million	2001
F. W. Olin Foundation	Franklin W. Olin College of Engineering	460 million	1997
Mr. and Mrs. William Hewlett and the William and Flora Hewlett Foundation	Stanford University	400 million	2001
Walton Family Charitable Support Foundation	University of Arkansas at Fayetteville	300 million	2002
Tom Monaghan and the Ave Maria Foundation	Ave Maria University	200 million	2002
Ingram Charitable Fund	Vanderbilt University	178 million	1998
Alfred E. Mann and the Alfred E. Mann Foundation	University of Southern California	112.5 million	1998
W. M. Keck Foundation	University of Southern California[a]	110 million	1999
Lilly Endowment	Indiana University at Bloomington	105 million	2000
Eli and Edythe L. Broad Foundation	Broad Institute[a]	100 million	2003
L. Samuel and Aline W. Skaggs	Scripps Research Institute	100 million	1996
David and Lucile Packard Foundation	Stanford University, Lucile Salter Packard Children's Hospital	100 million	2001
Abramson Family Foundation	University of Pennsylvaniaa	100 million	1997
Annenberg Foundation	University of Pennsylvania, Annenberg School for Communication	100 million	2002
Annenberg Foundation	University of Southern California, Annenberg School for Communication	100 million	2002
Danforth Foundation	Washington University in St. Louis	100 million	1986
Danforth Foundation	Washington University in St. Louis	100 million	1997
Duke Endowment	Duke University[a]	74 million	2005
Frederick and Sharon Klingenstein Fund	Mount Sinai School of Medicine[a]	75 million	1999

Foundation	Recipient	Grant amount (dollars)	Year
Joseph and Bessie Feinberg Foundation	Northwestern University Medical School[a]	75 million	2002
W. M. Keck Foundation	California Institute of Technology	70 million	1985
Bill and Melinda Gates Foundation	University of Washington at Seattle	70 million	2003
W. M. Keck Foundation	California Institute of Technology	65.3 million	1991
Roy J. Carver Charitable Trust	University of Iowa[a]	63 million	2002
Joseph C. Bancroft Charitable and Educational Fund	University of Mississippi	60 million	1997
Lilly Endowment	Indiana University at Bloomington	53 million	2004
Arnold and Mabel Beckman Foundation	California Institute of Technology	50 million	1986
William H. Gates Foundation	Columbia University School of Public Health	50 million	1999
Zanvyl and Isabelle Krieger Fund	Johns Hopkins University	50 million	1992
W. M. Keck Foundation	Keck Graduate Institute of Applied Life Sciences	50 million	1997
Jeffry M. and Barbara Picower Foundation	Massachusetts Institute of Technology[a]	50 million	2001
Cummings Foundation	Tufts University[a]	50 million	2004
Walton Family Charitable Support Foundation	University of Arkansas	50 million	1998

Source: "Major Private Gifts to Higher Education since 1967," *Chronicle of Higher Education,* August 29, 2008 (http://chronicle.texterity.com/chronicle/almanac200809/?pg=33 [November 16, 2009]).

a. Full amount of gift not yet received.

b. Value of gifts is based on information from institutions or donors at the time the gifts were promised. In cases of stock, property, art, and other non-cash donations, actual value may have increased or dropped since gift was pledged or received.

to handle large gifts. The second is that these are the institutions that have the longest-standing relationships with the foundation world. Examples of these strong ties include the lasting associations between the Danforth Foundation and Washington University in St. Louis, the Lilly Endowment and Indiana University, and the William and Flora Hewlett Foundation and Stanford University. A handful of the grants do represent novel entrants to higher education. Examples of these kinds of gifts include the large grants to Ave Maria University, the Olin College of Engineering, and the Gates Millennium Scholars program.

Table 5-2. *Top Twenty-Five Recipient Institutions, by Total Foundation Awards, 2001*

Institution	Number in data set	Share of total (percent)	Total grant dollars	Share of total grant dollars (percent)
Stanford University	290	1.54	504,237,105	8.15
University of California	533	2.83	154,740,096	2.50
Harvard University	379	2.01	141,443,687	2.29
New York University	227	1.21	108,957,951	1.76
Robert W. Woodruff Health Sciences Center	2	0.01	88,821,151	1.44
University of Pennsylvania	228	1.21	68,751,634	1.11
University of Michigan	232	1.23	52,827,966	0.85
Duke University	150	0.80	51,668,772	0.84
Johns Hopkins University	191	1.01	48,008,796	0.78
Columbia University	276	1.47	47,307,369	0.76
University of Southern California	108	0.57	45,031,343	0.73
Kansas University Endowment Association	18	0.10	44,545,517	0.72
University of Texas	252	1.34	42,113,615	0.68
Emory University	59	0.31	41,617,210	0.67
Yale University	162	0.86	39,478,918	0.64
Rockefeller University	50	0.27	37,740,607	0.61
University of North Carolina	147	0.78	35,584,944	0.58
Weill Medical College of Cornell University	39	0.21	34,192,600	0.55
Georgetown University	97	0.52	32,938,305	0.53
Princeton University	103	0.55	32,867,199	0.53
Massachusetts Institute of Technology	124	0.66	32,488,465	0.53
Northwestern University	121	0.64	32,184,494	0.52
University of Washington	157	0.83	31,552,141	0.51
Foundation of the University of Medicine and Dentistry of New Jersey	15	0.08	31,520,549	0.51
Total	3,960	21.04	1,780,620,434	28.78

Source: Foundation Center Statistical Database 2001.

However, the vast majority of the largest grants clearly favor the leading institutions in the field.

This trend toward elite favoritism can be seen in a second way. A look at the colleges and universities that received the most grants in a single sample year (2001)—grants of all sizes, not just the largest ones historically—indicates that this trend of support for the biggest and strongest institutions continues. Table 5-2 underscores the favor shown by foundations toward the largest and most prestigious research institutions. The FC Stats data indicate that almost twenty-five hundred organizations involved in higher education received a foundation grant in 2001, but as table 5-2 shows, twenty-five of them—1 percent—accounted for almost 30 percent of the money. The list contains some of the most prestigious private research institutions in the nation—Harvard, Princeton, Stanford, Yale, Columbia, Penn, Duke, Johns Hopkins, and New York University. It also has some of the largest public flagship institutions from states like Texas, North Carolina, Kansas, California, and Michigan.

Much of this money supported research efforts, and since so much of the major research efforts in the nation take place among these twenty-five institutions, it is hardly surprising that this group would receive such large total donations. While the institutions at the bottom of this annual list may change from year to year, over time the top of the list remains remarkably stable, with only modest shifts in positions but not institutions.

Type of Support

Table 5-3 tabulates the kinds of education support that foundations awarded in the sample year of 2001. The categories are listed in order of the frequency with which they appear in the higher education grant data, but we have added a column allowing the reader to see how much money went for each of these support types.[13] We also organized the rows according to our access and institution-building dichotomy.

As we surveyed the current role of foundation money in higher education, it became apparent that foundations tend to give five main kinds of support, and we have grouped the grant types into these five categories. A first type of grant can be used to enhance access by setting up programs targeted at groups that have traditionally been underserved by higher education—minorities, women, and the poor. Second, universities are often active in their communities, and foundation resources can support community building and community-directed educational activities on the part of universities and colleges. A third kind of funding aims at enhancing the quality of delivery of education, from better technology to improved classroom support. A fourth type is targeted toward research

13. The data we analyzed using National Taxonomy of Exempt Entities codes total 13,530 grants, while the data we used include almost 19,000 grants to higher education. The Foundation Center data had more than five thousand missing values for the variable indicating the type of support the grant offered. So the most popular grant category was to not indicate or assign a grant category. Much of the blank values for the variable recording type of support can be attributed to the donor's not providing some short text describing the grant, although in a handful of instances, when the grantor did offer a brief description of the grant, the Foundation Center declined to code that grant with a support-type value.

Table 5-3. *Foundation Grants to Education, by Foundation Center Category, 2001*

Category	Support type	Frequency of award	Share of total awards (percent)	Total grant dollars
Access and social change funding	Underserved populations			
	—Scholarship funds	1,337	9.88	127,335,415
	—Fellowships	750	5.54	110,682,564
	—Student aid	73	0.54	12,059,830
	Subtotal	2,160	15.96	250,077,809
	Community building			
	—Electronic media/online services	108	0.80	30,355,855
	—Film/video/radio	54	0.40	6,544,308
	—Internship funds	54	0.40	4,129,966
	—Exhibitions	31	0.23	2,203,150
	—Performance/productions	30	0.22	1,156,531
	Subtotal	277	2.05	44,389,810
Mixed purpose funding	Educational services			
	—Program development	3,910	28.90	881,506,965
	—Faculty/staff development	248	1.83	84,760,627
	—Curriculum development	242	1.79	78,148,453
	—Professorships	163	1.20	69,403,983
	—Seed money	150	1.11	54,505,347
	—Management development	97	0.72	20,089,974
	—Program evaluation	83	0.61	32,240,480
	—Income development	60	0.44	5,202,400
	—Technical assistance	38	0.28	20,114,913
	Subtotal	4,991	36.88	1,245,973,142
Core capacity and institution-building funding	Research activities			
	—Research	2,223	16.43	454,903,127
	—Conferences/seminars	443	3.27	40,777,210
	—Publication	143	1.06	16,986,913
	—Awards/prizes/competitions	104	0.77	66,758,536
	—Commissioning new works	2	0.01	22,200
	Subtotal	2,915	21.54	579,447,986
	Institutional support and capital			
	—General/operating support	1,640	12.12	368,301,321
	—Building/renovation	664	4.91	371,912,518
	—Endowments	364	2.69	670,858,917
	—Capital campaigns	183	1.35	112,789,748
	—Equipment	162	1.20	25,919,151

Category	Support type	Frequency of award	Share of total awards (percent)	Total grant dollars
	—Computer systems/equipment	67	0.50	21,734,202
	—Collections management/preservation	53	0.39	9,959,465
	—Annual campaigns	33	0.24	1,324,349
	—Collections acquisition	14	0.10	2,873,925
	—Land acquisition	6	0.04	20,384,971
	—Debt reduction	1	0.01	63,821,151
	Subtotal	3,187	23.55	1,669,879,718
	Total	13,530	100	3,789,768,465

Source: Foundation Center, *FC Stats, Foundations Awarding Grants, by Subject Area, 2001*.

activities, which connects directly to the desire of many foundations to promote the advancement of knowledge. Finally, foundations do provide direct institutional support, by means of grants either for operations or for capital to finance major construction projects.

Table 5-3 suggests that much of foundation giving is devoted to institution building and the support of research. Forty-five percent of the grants and more than half of the grant dollars can be categorized as support for institutional infrastructure or research. Well over a quarter of the funds were directed toward the improvement of educational services. Less than 18 percent of the grants and $300 million worth of grant funds in 2001, much less than 10 percent of the total amount given, were directed toward enhancement of access or community building.

Virtually a third of the grants (and a fifth of grant dollars) went toward program development. This category also received the most funding in the Foundation Center classification, amounting to almost $1 billion in 2001. In some cases, grants that are designated program development seem to be a miscoding, as the accompanying text description clearly describes research activity. But the grant might have been made not as a research grant but as a more general grant that was applied to research by the institution; that might explain the discrepancy. Nevertheless, most of the program development grants appear to have gone to support ongoing activities or programmatic goals at the institutions receiving the grants. Since this ongoing activity was not general activity but specialized in nature, it was designated program development. For instance, one such grant from the Ford Foundation to Harvard University for $75,000 was made to bring Iranian officials to Harvard for a training program. Another grant, of $20,000 from the Citigroup Foundation, went to the University of Southern Mississippi for their Center for the Study of Financial Services project.

General operating support was the third most popular kind of funding granted. Scholarships and fellowships rounded out the top five kinds of support to higher education in terms of frequency. In terms of total dollars awarded, institutional endowment—capital to build up the financial base from which a school might draw future income—was the second most popular category. It received almost $700 million in total grants awarded. Another popular type of support was the financing of building construction and building renovation. This received almost $400 million. Research received about the same amount of funding as building and renovation, but research grants were awarded much more frequently. Hence most grants and most grant dollars went toward ongoing activities—research, program development, general operating support, endowments, and capital campaigns.

Only a small fraction of the program development grants appear to have been aimed at groups that have traditionally been underserved by higher education. In the program development area, however, foundations appear to be acting in concert with higher education institutions to develop innovative ways to achieve social change or innovative approaches to higher education. For instance, one grant supported college preparatory programs for disadvantaged youth living in areas adjacent to the campus. Another grant provided foundational support for a minority Master's in Business Administration program. Yet another set up a law clinic for elderly citizens living in the nearby community. Other categories provide similar flexibility and philanthropic support for innovation, but by and large program development, research, and capital projects appear to be the areas toward which most higher education and foundation philanthropic activity is directed.

Beneficiary Populations

One limitation of the Foundation Center data set stems from the failure of institutions, the grantors, or the center itself to code consistently the populations served by the grants. Although the data set explored here lists almost nineteen thousand grants, slightly less than three thousand of those grants record a beneficiary population. Most grants do not express their philanthropic tendencies by identifying and homing in on vulnerable target populations. We can say little about why grantors or coders so rarely identify target populations other than it does not appear to be a straightforward matter or a conscious concern of givers. Hence only one in every six grants can be said to specifically target a defined population.

What we can say, though, is that when foundations did record a target population with a grant, most of those grants were aimed at assisting the most vulnerable groups in the general population. Racial and ethnic minorities account for nearly 630 grants out of almost 3,000 and for more than $100 million of a total of $700 million designated for specific populations. Most of this targeted funding went in the form of broadly directed grants to the overall minority population rather than singling out a specific group. Children and youth received the most money, primarily through university and college programs that focus on social services or education policy. The economically disadvantaged and women round out the remaining groups in the list of the most frequently identified beneficiaries of foundation largesse. Programs targeted toward senior citizens and frail elderly were a less frequent recipient of grants, but this category did receive the third largest amount of money, narrowly edging out funding for women.

Most of the minority awards came in the form of direct grants to colleges and universities, but the purposes of these grants varied a great deal. A third of this funding went to three purposes—health care and health research, children's policy and services, and the general category of universities. Well over a third of them were for program development. Another 25 percent were for scholarships and fellowships, and about 8 percent were for research on minority issues.

Grant Purposes and Fields of Activity

The FC Stats data include several variables that measure the primary purpose of the grant. The underlying code is derived from the National Taxonomy of Exempt Entities. However, there are twenty-six general categories and more than two hundred such codes for grant purposes. To render straightforward analysis, we sorted through the designated grant purposes and sought to collapse them where possible. For instance, education policy, early child development policy, and developmental and educational services to the K–12 population were collapsed into children's policy and services. All of the various kinds of health care and medical research, as well as certain kinds of health treatments, were collapsed into a single health care and health research category. Using this approach, we were able to contain the many separate codes of grant purpose into a more concise listing of thirty-seven categories.

The leading purposes of these grants appear to be broad support of universities, colleges, professional education, and health care and health research. Hard sciences and a smattering of social and education policy initiatives make up the largest share of the rest of the grants. Of the grants that are designated as being for the purpose of the FC Stats category *University*, about half of these come with no further designation that might give us insight into what such funds were for.

The kind of support that these grants offered is, however, recorded in about half of the 4,090 grants to universities. Of these 2,000 or so grants, about a quarter (487 grants) come in the form of general operating support. Another quarter (440 grants) consist of support for scholarship programs, and an additional 5.5 percent (107 grants) support fellowships. About 18 percent (337 grants) go toward program development. Interestingly, more than half the money in 2003 went in the form of direct endowment support (79 grants—only 4.4 percent of the total grants awarded), but it is certainly the case that this figure was inflated in 2003 by the $400 million dollar grant to Stanford's endowment by the Hewlett Foundation. Absent this grant, the three categories that received the largest total dollar contributions were general operating support ($133 million—25.5 percent), program development ($97 million—18 percent), and endowments ($89 million—17 percent). Building and renovations also received a not insignificant share of these grants ($68 million—13 percent). Although scholarships constituted a quarter of the grant numbers, they made up a much lower fraction of the grant dollars—6.4 percent of total amount awarded in 2003, absent the $400 million Hewlett grant to Stanford.

Based on our analysis of available data, our general conclusion is that much of the giving observed has sought to maintain the core capacity needs of these institutions. However, a portion of this funding can be seen as oriented toward change. In some areas of program development, foundations and institutions of higher education appeared to be carving out interesting niches within the sector, targeting special needs populations, looking out for the vulnerable, or trying to leverage a role in social or policy change. Further study on the nature of grants in the area of program development is clearly needed to establish their scope in the sector and the trends and issues at the forefront of funders' minds in delivering this kind of support.

Up to this point we can draw two conclusions. First, foundations appear to serve a largely institution-building purpose in higher education. When they venture into funding greater access by underserved groups and the opening up of the university to the community, they do so on a limited basis. Overall, the data show that giving to higher education is seen as funding in support of an ongoing, friendly partnership with the sector (based in many instances on long-term familiarity) rather than support that is oriented toward changing the sector to serve some broader social purpose.[14]

Inside Foundation Intentionality

With sector data garnered at such a macro level, it remains difficult to do much more than render broad judgments about the purposes and intentions behind foundation support of higher education. Inferring and understanding this

14. This is consistent with the verdict from a series of focus groups in which foundation program officers explained their thinking in awarding grants to higher education (Gumport 2003).

activity from such a height inevitably leads to some imprecision and generalization. To address our core question about foundation activity in higher education, we collected additional qualitative data that allow us to approach this question from another angle.

One of the best sources of data on what foundations are seeking to accomplish with their grant making is the foundations themselves. We read and analyzed the foundations' own grant descriptions to discern the intentions and
objectives behind the largest grants in higher education. We scrutinized the
language used to announce grant awards and review them in year-end foundation reports. We looked at the annual reports, news reports, and press releases
related to the fifty largest grants to higher education over the past four decades.
After eliminating gifts by individuals, we were left with thirty-four very large
foundation grants. The documents related to these grants often included quota-
tions from foundation leaders and university presidents in which the underlying purpose of each grant was explained. We read these carefully and weighed
them against the distinction between core capacity, on the one hand, and access
and social change, on the other—that is, between unconditional support and
change-oriented giving.

It is clear that foundations have played a significant role in the growth and
development of higher education by funding a staggering array of new academic
and research projects, the construction of new buildings and campuses, and programs designed to increase college access and affordability. When one considers the largest gifts to colleges and universities coming from foundations, two
facts immediately surface. First, many of the largest gifts come from foundations
whose donors or their immediate families are still alive and active in foundation
decisionmaking—often having a personal connection to the recipient institution. Second, the vast majority of the gifts are for basic institutional development, including new academic programs, expanded research, hiring new faculty, the construction of buildings, and other needs that are connected with the
development of a college or university.

The William and Flora Hewlett Foundation's gift of $400 million to Stan-
ford reflects both the donor's personal connection to an institution and a neutral
desire to contribute to institutional capacity. Although the gift was made under
the leadership of Hewlett's son, it was clearly identified by the foundation as
reflecting the founder's commitment and attachment to the university. "This gift
honors my father . . . and honors his lifetime of philanthropy and his lifelong
devotion to Stanford and his passionate belief in the value of a liberal arts education."[15] The gift was made in support of Stanford's School of Humanities and

15. "Hewlett Foundation Makes History with $400 Million Gift," *Stanford Report*, May 2,
2001 (http://news.stanford.edu/news/2001/may9/gift-59.html [April 2006]).

Sciences ($300 million) and the university campaign for undergraduate educa-
tion ($100 million). The central purpose of the gift was to build the financial
resources and capacity of areas that had been neglected over the years and that
required renewed support. Unlike some gifts that come with significant precon-
ditions and requirements, the Hewlett Foundation support was aimed at fulfill-
ing its founder's commitment to supporting liberal arts education at Stanford.

In 2001 the Gordon and Betty Moore Foundation delivered a gift of $300
million to the California Institute of Technology, where Moore, the founder of
Intel, received his doctorate. Gordon noted at the time of the gift that a key
consideration was giving back and strengthening an institution that helped him
launch his career: "The education I received there has served me well. We are
hoping this gift will position the institute well as it moves forward." In addition
to the gift from their foundation, the Moores also made a matching personal
contribution of $300 million.[16]

In recent decades, many of the largest gifts to higher education have had very
broad intentions. The Walton Family Charitable Support Foundation made a
$300 million contribution to the University of Arkansas, most of which was
directed at the Honors College and designed to meet financial needs in the areas
of undergraduate and graduate student support, endowed faculty chairs, and
library and technology support. The Lilly Endowment has made several large
gifts to Indiana University that fit squarely in the large category of institution
building and that have no social agenda whatsoever attached to them. In 2000
Lilly made a grant of $105 million, the largest ever to Indiana University, to
strengthen the school's work in genomics research.

A relatively small number of the largest gifts to higher education have had
a recognizable social or political change agenda attached to them. By a change
agenda, we mean here an intent to make a gift to higher education that affects
the broader social order, either by reducing inequality or by shaping politics.
There are many ways that foundations could, in principle at least, use higher
education philanthropy to advance a change agenda. One way would be to
invest heavily in programs that serve the most disadvantaged populations and
offer them a chance to access quality education. Another might be to promote
research that aims to shape the public policy agenda. Foundations could also
use their resources to support work within higher education that might reflect a
commitment to public problem solving on behalf of the disadvantaged.

Among the largest gifts to higher education, the Bill and Melinda Gates
Foundation grant of $1 billion stands out. Not only is it the largest gift, but it

---

16. "Caltech Receives $600 Million in Two Gifts: Largest Academic Donations in History,"
Caltech Media Relations press release, October 29, 2001 (pr.caltech.edu/media/Press_Releases/
PR12193.html).

is the one that is most progressive and focused on equalizing access. Although the Gates Foundation has supported institution building in higher education in the past, at least one of its largest philanthropic commitments has been change oriented: a $1 billion gift to help minority students gain a top quality education. The Millennium Scholars program is administered by the United Negro College Fund with the support and participation of the Hispanic Scholarship Fund and American Indian College Fund. The program was launched in 2000 and serves one thousand students a year through the year 2020. In describing the gift, Bill Gates made a clear reference to the equity objectives of the grant: "It is critical to America's future that we draw from the full range of talent and ability to develop the next generation of leaders. The Millennium Scholars program is intended to ensure that we build a stronger America through improved educational opportunities."[17]

It is not surprising that the language of improved educational opportunity was central to the description of the grant's intended impact. What is interesting, however, is the nature of the rationale provided for the effort. While it would have been possible to make reference to racial equity or social justice in describing this massive scholarship program, Gates chose to explain his decision to give educational opportunity to twenty thousand minority students by pointing to the country's need for leadership and talent. Thus in one of the most progressive and change oriented of the largest grants to higher education, there is a clear preference for language that is not unnecessarily provocative.

Another large gift aimed at enlarging educational opportunity was the Duke Endowment's gift of $75 million to Duke University to support student financial aid. In announcing the gift, the endowment noted that a critical element in Duke University's ability to be a leader in higher education was access: "An essential part of that dream is providing financial aid so that the student body can be the best available within a wide range of backgrounds and talents, without any limitation of financial constraints."[18] Sometimes the desire to provide access is combined with the desire to build institutional capacity. In the case of the F. W. Olin Foundation, access was secondary to creating a new engineering college in Massachusetts. The foundation made a grant of $200 million to create a new college and campus focused on excellence in undergraduate engineering education. While starting a college from scratch is in some ways the most institutional of all funding strategies, the Olin gift was tempered by an equity concern that

17. "Bill and Melinda Gates Announce New Millennium Scholars Program to Bridge the Gap in Access to Higher Education," Bill and Melinda Gates Foundation, September 16, 1999.

18. "The Duke Endowment Gives Record $75 million to Duke for Student Financial Aid," Duke University News and Communications, October 3, 2005 (www.dukenews. duke.edu/2005/10/tdefinaid.html).

ultimately led the foundation to design the new college so that it would be as close to tuition-free as possible for all students who gained admission.

The Gates Foundation has also attempted to support equity and change by making gifts to higher education conditional on performance of research and related health care services in developing nations. In 1999 the foundation made a grant of $50 million to Columbia University's School of Public Health for work in developing countries. The grant will allow Columbia to work with local governments in Africa, Asia, and Latin America to analyze local needs and then improve medical resources to reduce death owing to inadequate emergency medical measures such as surgery, drugs, and blood transfusions. By funding comprehensive emergency obstetrical services, the Gates Foundation goal was to reduce preventable maternal death and disability. Focused on nations such as Mozambique, Bangladesh, and Peru, the grant has a decidedly equalizing intention in its goal to close the gap between the quality of medical care in rich and poor nations.

Not all donors shy away from provocative or ideological language. Among the largest and most ideologically charged gifts on the other side of the spectrum was one from Thomas Monaghan, the founder of Domino's Pizza. Working through the Ave Maria Foundation, Monaghan's Catholic philanthropy has been centered on higher education. One of his most ambitious undertakings has been the founding of the Ave Maria School of Law, located on Monaghan's office park outside of Ann Arbor, where the 270-acre headquarters for Domino's and surrounding office buildings are built in the style of Frank Lloyd Wright's Prairie School. Seeking to enact his faith and his belief in the importance of education, Monaghan's law school serves students who are interested in the moral dimension of the law and who have an interest in the intersection of faith and law. His critics contend that the law school is simply a tool for training the next generation of conservative lawyers who will go about trying to dismantle liberal jurisprudence. What is instructive about this gift is the extent to which the giving foundation represents the values and commitments of the founding donor.

The vast majority of large-scale foundation giving to higher education bears no social or political change imprint at all. Gifts of more than $100 million are largely directed at building academic programs in areas of interest to the funder and to erecting new buildings that will support new or expand research or teaching activity. What is notable is that of the thirty-four largest grants to higher education over the past four decades, all but five went to less controversial capacity-building efforts related to research and teaching.

There are many possible reasons for this distribution of grants. Perhaps the most plausible is related simply to the sheer size of the contributions that are on the list. Large gifts require large agendas and often take the form of endowment gifts. When funding endowments, it is often hard to do much that is radical or change oriented, since funding universities in perpetuity is by its nature a conservative approach to grant making. Rather than direct funds toward immediate programmatic ends, endowment funding puts only a small fraction (usually less than 5 percent) of funds in play each year. Thus in the end the largest gifts to higher education are inclined, like smaller grants in the field, toward long-term institution building, not social change.

Emerging Issues in Access to Higher Education

The world of higher education is changing, and the field faces a number of important challenges in the years ahead. While there are significant and complex obstacles to overcome in the areas of research and technology, many of the concerns that have been cited by experts relate to the issues of access. In compiling research for this discussion, we consulted essays, websites, and policy briefs produced by higher education scholars, trade associations, and policy think tanks to identify the major trends and concerns that face higher education today. Across this work several topics recur that can be identified as emergent access challenges for universities and colleges. Given that our analysis of past foundation support to higher education suggests that foundations have tended to favor core capacity and institution building rather than a social change agenda, it is not clear how well prepared or eager foundations will be to take on the following pressing problems in the field.

The growing and changing student body. The increase among the general population of the proportion of students pursuing higher education has been a persistent issue since colleges and universities were flooded with World War II veterans taking advantage of the G.I. Bill. During the 1960s higher education witnessed another surge in enrollment as the baby boomers came of age and college provided a way for male students to avoid the draft. This expansion continues as a trend today, but the imperatives arise from economic pressures and the increasing returns to a college degree relative to a high school diploma. Broader in scope, this trend does not simply constitute a change in the overall proportion of high school graduates going on to college.[19] Much of the enrollment growth today is concentrated among the ranks of nontraditional students.[20] Often they are second learners, meaning they have returned to school or decided to enter college to learn a new set of skills after the skills they previously relied on for work were rendered redundant by economic change. Such students challenge the traditional organization and delivery of higher education and call for a different mix of student services and amenities.

19. Western Interstate Commissioner for Higher Education (2003).
20. Kim (2004).

The coming demographic boom. In addition to the increasing inclusion of adult students, the racial and ethnic mix of the student body is likely to change rapidly in the next two decades. The birthrate of whites is falling as the birthrates of Hispanics, African Americans, and other minority groups are rising.[21] This change, together with immigration patterns, sets the stage for a rapid increase in the number and proportion of college students drawn from populations that typically have been underrepresented on campuses.[22] This poses potential challenges for higher education, as the needs of such groups may be different from those of the current majority-white population. The services and amenities these groups demand may require changes to traditional models.

The role of technology in teaching and distance learning. Many of the nontraditional students and second learners who will access higher education will not be sleeping in dorms or living near campus. They may be hundreds of miles away, seated in front of a computer. Distance learning is likely to be a source of significant revenue for universities, and it offers the potential for such institutions to expand their reach and the kinds of populations they serve. Yet such delivery requires new models of pedagogy and a better understanding of how to use technology to impart learning.[23] Market incentives may be insufficient to fund innovation and development in this area, and external grant-funding models may be necessary.

Rising costs. Tuition has increased at such a pace that the very accessibility of higher education has been jeopardized. One reason for this is that operating costs per employee have risen inexorably since 1970 and have significantly outpaced the growth in inflation, in government revenues, and in personal family incomes.[24] The college cost crisis has engendered national commissions, legislative policy initiatives, and popular concern. To the extent that it continues unabated, it threatens achievement of social equity goals and access to higher education for large segments of the population.

Privatization of public universities. Concurrent with the rapid increase in operating costs and the seemingly insatiable demand for financial resources has been a steady erosion of public financial support and changes in the delivery of the public subsidy. States are confronting the question of the public's role in public higher education. As more and more private and corporate support has flowed into public universities, some institutions have petitioned their states for changes to their legal status and for adjustment to the state's system of governing state campuses and multicampus systems. Yet privatization challenges the

---

21. Klein (2004).
22. Western Interstate Commissioner for Higher Education (2003).
23. Levine and Sun (2002).
24. Dickeson (2004).

administrative capacities of public institutions and the ability of states to regulate the sector for the attainment of public objectives.[25]

K–16 seamlessness. The demands of a global economy will continue to require an ever-wider set of skills and enhanced preparation for work within a knowledge economy. These economic demands challenge the entire education sector, but in particular they call for a need to improve K–12 preparation, so that more students are ready to learn in college, and to recraft the learning experience as a seventeen-year process.[26] More and more students will need to be college ready just when our primary and secondary schools seem to be slipping further and further behind their international counterparts. Colleges and universities will struggle to produce globally competitive students if they must invest significant resources in remedial education.

Advancement in science and math for female and minority students. As America lags behind foreign economic rivals in its performance in science and math, leaders in the field are turning their attention to three issues: enhancing student performance, increasing the proportions of students who choose majors in math and science, and increasing participation in these fields among groups that have traditionally been underrepresented, particularly women and minorities.[27] Institutions must learn how to make the study of these subjects more attractive, how to enhance student performance, and how to promote the advancement of minority and female students through related degree programs.

Although colleges and universities are among the largest and financially strongest organizations in the nonprofit sector, this hardly means that the field is static or that major challenges are not on the horizon. Pressures and profound challenges do in fact loom large, particularly in the area of accessibility. It is far from clear that foundations are ready to confront the challenges that face higher education. In fact, if past grant making is evidence of future philanthropic behavior, it is far from clear that foundations will step forward to help higher education solve the access challenges that lie just ahead.

The Major Impact of Foundations in Higher Education

Foundations can and do sometimes play a pioneering, cutting-edge role as change agents within higher education. As chapter 4 demonstrates, the early history of foundation philanthropy is filled with grants to higher education that changed the landscape of the field and of society at large. But as the foundation

25. Gabriel Kaplan, "State Fiscal Crises and Cuts in Higher Education: The Implications for Access, Institutional Performance, and Strategic Reengineering, September 2006 (www.wiche.edu/policy/ford/kaplan_paper.pdf).

26. Hoffman and Vargas (2005); Cohen (2001).

27. Oakes (1990).

sector has grown larger and become populated with many more players, much of the sector no longer plays a role in promoting social change and greater opportunity. Instead, most giving serves the purposes of providing broad institutional support, just as the oldest and most established foundations have done for decades. Foundations as a whole appear content to meet the core capacity and capital needs of higher education rather than to push these institutions to change and ready themselves for the major access issues that confront the field.

The evidence marshaled to support this conclusion here has been threefold. First, social change and access are simply not prioritized as highly as the goals of supporting core capacity and institution building. Second, community and technical colleges receive only marginal support from foundations. This is significant because these smaller institutions, which do not often have impressive research agendas or physical plants, are still the critical access points to higher education for families with the least economic means. These are also prime vocational training grounds for workers in the new economy who are unlikely to wade deeply into knowledge production. Third, only a small number of the largest foundation grants to higher education had an explicit social change or access agenda.

Foundation support of higher education is strikingly different from foundation support in the area of K–12 public education. When foundations turn their attention to public schools, they take an aggressive, change-oriented approach, including restructuring school districts, supporting charter schools to compete with mainstream public schools, and generally attempting to bring change to the field through a strategy that pressures and pushes from the outside for change on the inside of the system.[28] In higher education, this kind of outsider approach is hard to find. In its place is a much less confrontational, insider model that supports these institutions' stated needs and goals. One large question that we can only pose is whether there is any evidence that this insider model in giving for higher education is, in fact, more effective in the long term than the alternative. We suspect there may be little such evidence.

One question that we have not addressed in this chapter is why foundations might be inclined to accept higher education as it is rather than press it to meet the challenges it faces in the area of accessibility. One possible reason that foundation support of higher education is tilted substantially toward institution building and away from aggressive change agendas may be related to the leadership and recruiting patterns of the largest foundations. Going way back in the history of foundations and stretching all the way to the present, big foundations have long sought their leaders from the ranks of college and university presidents.[29]

---

28. F. M. Hess (2005b); McKersie (1999).
29. Hall (1999).

Today, the Carnegie Corporation is led by the former president of Brown University. The Rockefeller Foundation is headed by the former president of the University of Pennsylvania. The MacArthur Foundation chose the president of the New School University. The Hewlett Foundation is directed by the former dean of the Stanford Law School. The Mellon Foundation selected the president of the University of Chicago as its new leader, replacing another former university president. The Daniels Fund was headed by the former president of the University of Northern Colorado, who went on to become president of the University of Colorado when he left the foundation. The list of foundation leadership coming from college and university administration could go on and on. The fact is simply that there has long been a close and symbiotic relationship between elite foundations and major research universities. This tight relationship cannot help but steer to some extent foundation support toward grants that build capacity and support the capital infrastructure rather than demand from the sector social change and increased access.

In the end, foundations are primarily engaged with the sector in a gentle and supportive role, although some foundations do engage in more aggressive agenda-based giving on the margins. However, in their overall approach, foundations do not see their primary task as encouraging change, access, or equity in higher education. Rather, foundations appear to celebrate their historic relationship with colleges and universities and view them as reliable and trusted partners.

6

Foundations and Health: Innovation, Marginalization, and Relevance since 1900

DANIEL M. FOX

The ideas, political skills, and cash of the donors, directors, and staff of American philanthropic foundations have affected the health status of millions of people during the past century. Foundations in health have innovated and temporized. They have sustained some organizations, promoted radical change in others, and helped to invent more than a few. They have embraced public advocacy and avoided it. In doing their work in health, foundations have collaborated as well as contended with leaders in government, universities, hospitals, and the medical profession.

A history of health services and policy from the point of view of foundations would, however, exaggerate their importance, even though health has been second only to education among foundations' expenditures. Most foundations have been passive donors to health care organizations. They mainly responded to proposals to meet the immediate or short-term needs of medical schools, research organizations, hospitals, and, in the first four decades of the twentieth century, patients. Moreover, as the health sector grew to become the largest in the American economy, foundation giving declined in relative importance to spending by government, employers, and individual consumers.

A few numbers illustrate foundations' involvement in health. In 1936 Eduard C. Lindeman published a study of spending by one hundred foundations and community trusts between 1921 and 1930.[1] Most of what these foundations

1. Lindeman (1936).

spent for health had modest contemporary impact or historical significance. Similarly, most of the almost four hundred contemporary foundations whose grants are recorded in the electronic database maintained by Grantmakers in Health help individuals and organizations but are tangential to major issues in health policy.[2]

This chapter assesses the influence of leading foundations on health policy and practice rather than the overall significance of foundation spending for health. I define leading foundations as those whose trustees, staff, and money had, at least for some years, effects that can be documented on significant issues in health affairs, nationally as well as internationally. Some of these foundations have been among the largest endowments, others middle sized; a few have been relatively small.

The history of leading foundations in health during the past century can be summarized (though thereby necessarily distorted) in three words: innovation, marginalization, and relevance. From the early twentieth century through the 1920s, leading foundations collaborated on innovation with central actors in health policy and practice. They planned and implemented new ways to organize education for the health professions, basic and clinical research, and the delivery of services in hospitals and ambulatory settings. From the early 1930s through the 1980s, the work of leading foundations, though respected by central actors in health policy and practice, was marginal to the major issues that preoccupied them. Since the early 1990s, the work of leading foundations has been consistently relevant to major issues in health policy and practice in the United States and of growing importance in the area of global health.

An Overview of Foundations and Health Affairs

Since the 1890s, foundations have participated in changes in health affairs that have had enormous significance for Americans' lives. The most important of these changes have been advances in biomedical science and technology and their translation into clinical and public health practice, the increasing prestige of the medical profession and, as a result, its domination of the allocation of funds to maintain and improve health, and vast expansion in access to health services accompanied by political conflict. Significant consequences of these changes include increasing life expectancy and the problem of managing serious chronic disease for growing numbers of people; optimism about the conquest of infection and the subsequent realization that it was exaggerated; the dominance of clinical models of prevention, diagnosis, and treatment in public policy rather

2. Grantmakers in Health, Resource Center for Health Philanthropy (www.gih.org [April 2007]). Access to the Resource Center requires registration.

than broader determinants of health; and disparities in health services and health status by race, income, and social class, despite economic growth and increased protection of civil rights.

The histories of foundations and of the health sector converged at the beginning of the twentieth century because of changes in fundamental assumptions about the organization of both philanthropy and activities to improve health. New York state was the first to enact a law permitting the creation of new charitable endowments that had as their purpose the general improvement of human welfare.[3] Unlike existing charitable corporations, general-purpose foundations could choose charitable objectives and strategies for achieving them in response to the interests of their donors, directors, and staff as well as to changing external circumstances.

During the same years, a growing number of leaders among academic physicians began to advocate establishing or reorganizing health services in hierarchies within geographic regions to apply rapidly accumulating knowledge in the basic and clinical sciences. The first regional hierarchies had been organized in Germany and the United Kingdom (and imported during the 1890s) by faculty members at the recently established Johns Hopkins Medical Institutions who had trained overseas.[4]

According to the theory of hierarchical regionalism, knowledge moves in one direction, patients in another. Scientific findings from the laboratories of medical schools and wards of teaching hospitals at the top of each hierarchy would be disseminated to settings that were less technically sophisticated in geographic regions that usually coincided with political boundaries. These settings included hospitals, clinics supported by government and philanthropy, and physicians' private practices. Patients would be referred, according to the complexity of their needs, up a hierarchical array of physicians, clinics, and hospitals.

Public health work would, in theory, be separate from but integrated with regional hierarchies. This work, which would be performed by public agencies and charitable organizations, would be based on science and supervised by physicians. But public health activities would be divided into clinical prevention and treatment of low-income patients, which would be carried out in regional hierarchies of hospitals, clinics, and private medical offices, and population-based disease control, notably surveillance, quarantine or isolation, mass inoculation, and health education, which would be the responsibility of government.

In the first three decades of the twentieth century, general-purpose foundations and private donors who followed their example granted millions of dollars to academic institutions to create regional health hierarchies. This philanthropy

3. See chapter 1, this volume; Fremont-Smith (2004).
4. Fox (1986).

stimulated additional funding to organize, maintain, and expand these hierarchies, mainly from appropriations by local and state government and fees from middle- and upper-class patients and their families. In the 1930s commercial and nonprofit insurance companies began to finance services offered within regional hierarchies. During the 1940s, the federal government became a significant source of funding for hierarchical regionalism through grants and contracts.

Foundations made grants to implement and strengthen regional hierarchies because most donors, trustees, and staff assumed that the central problem of health policy was how to increase the supply of services that delivered to patients the benefits of advancing science and technology. To subsidize the supply of science and the capacity of the facilities and practitioners that applied it, foundations and subsequently government and insurers subsidized biomedical research, the construction and equipping of hospitals, and education for the health professions.

During the first half of the twentieth century, most foundation leaders, like their colleagues in government, business, and the health professions, believed that effective demand for a burgeoning supply of services would be financed by growth in the general economy. The profits and wages that resulted from economic growth would finance rising demand through an efficient combination of risk pooling by the insurance industry and out-of-pocket payments by individuals and families. When markets failed to finance demand for persons with low incomes or catastrophic illness, government at all levels would provide a safety net of public programs supplemented by private charity.

In the 1960s leaders in government and business modified their assumptions about the supply of and demand for health services. Regional hierarchies had been fragmented and inefficient since their inception as a result of competing interests and contradictory policies. After the 1960s, however, hierarchies flattened; in a new metaphor, they became networks. Specialized physicians and the facilities in which they provided sophisticated care proliferated across urban and suburban communities, often competing successfully with teaching hospitals.

The enactment of Medicare and Medicaid in 1965 challenged the assumption that economic growth alone would eventually provide access to health care for the poor and most of the elderly. As a result of this legislation, the federal government and the states soon became the major sources of payment for health services. Moreover, health cost inflation after the 1960s annually exceeded general inflation for reasons that included the proliferation of new technologies, the willingness of public and private payers to reimburse any physician and hospital for any procedure for which they billed, and the inefficiency of a fragmented system of public and private coverage.

Research documenting the contribution of human behavior to the rising cost of health services also challenged assumptions about policy priorities.

Researchers linked increasing numbers of cases of disease to smoking, overeating, physical inactivity, and industrial toxins in the environment. Studies suggested a strong association between social and economic disparities and illness. This evidence led a few leaders of foundations and government to consider modifying the priorities of philanthropic and public spending to address the multiple determinants of population health.

However, leading foundations and their allies in government, business, and the health professions continued to accord considerably higher priority to containing the costs of health services and improving its quality and safety than to improving population health. In the absence of strong public support for addressing broader determinants of health, interest group politics guaranteed the primacy of personal health services in health policy.

In the 1990s and into the new century, moreover, a growing number of influential persons in government, business, and a few foundations lost confidence in the long-standing assumption that clinically autonomous physicians would effectively and efficiently allocate resources for patient care. Public policymakers and business executives, often allied with leading foundations, began to test a new assumption: that improving the health of populations required physicians, researchers, and third-party payers for care to become more accountable to collective purchasers in government and business. The collective purchasers aroused considerable antagonism among physicians and hospital managers as they implemented policy to reduce the authority of the supply side of the health sector.

Most foundations had already been marginalized in the health sector when, in the 1960s, supply-side dominance began to erode. In part this was a result of increased government and business spending that dwarfed foundation contributions. More important, however, leading foundations had stopped innovating and became risk averse because of criticism from organized medicine in the early 1930s. As a result of their declining ability to influence policy and practice, foundations had contributed only modestly to the rapid growth in the supply of research, facilities, and professionals and hardly at all to increasing access to care or improving the health of populations.

In the 1990s executives of leading foundations in health, encouraged by supportive boards and allies in government, business, and the health sector, became important actors in controversial health issues. Their programs frequently engaged ideas and interest groups that inhibited access to effective and efficient health services in the United States and in low-income countries. At home, these foundations and their grantees challenged elements of the insurance industry, the medical profession, the hospital and nursing home industries, and manufacturers of pharmaceutical drugs, medical devices, and tobacco products.

Assertiveness was even more conspicuous in the work of leading foundations in global health. Several foundations tried, for example, to change laws that regulated intellectual property in the interests of multinational pharmaceutical companies rather than of patients. Officials of several foundations negotiated, often with success, with political elites, especially in Africa. Moreover, these foundations were frequently more effective than multilateral aid agencies and nongovernmental organizations that contracted with donor agencies to provide health services in low-income countries.

By the beginning of the twenty-first century, leading foundations in health were again, as they had been during the first quarter of the twentieth century, participating in a substantial reorientation of assumptions about what policies are most likely to improve and maintain health. They had exchanged marginalization for relevance and, for some foundations, for influence on health policy and practice; on a few issues foundations were even once again sources of innovation. The renewal of foundations' relevance had two sources: the political experience and knowledge about health affairs of their senior executives and the trustees who hired them and new sources of endowment and other funds.

Innovation, 1900–1932

During the first three decades of the twentieth century, a small number of foundation trustees and executives collaborated with leaders of the medical profession and government to reorganize the supply side of the health sector. Foundations helped their allies in medicine to increase capacity to conduct biomedical research and apply its results to patients and populations, to reorganize medical schools and hospitals to take account of advancing scientific knowledge, and to devise for persons with low incomes what would later be called a safety net of services informed by science.

By the late 1920s foundations and their allies could look back on significant achievements in reorganizing supply. They now tried to innovate in making policy to assist consumers to pay for care of the highest quality. Only a few years later, they had dismaying evidence that organized medicine had defeated their efforts to reorganize and expand access to the services and institutions of the health sector.

Three organizations exemplify the contributions of foundations to the reorganization of the health sector from the late 1890s to the early 1930s: the philanthropies financed and led by John D. Rockefeller (Sr. and Jr.), Andrew Carnegie, and Elizabeth Milbank Anderson. A substantial literature, both contemporary and historical, describes how these philanthropies evolved. This account emphasizes how their philanthropic strategies promoted innovation in the health sector.

Leaders of the Rockefeller, Carnegie, and Milbank philanthropies believed that science, properly applied, could improve the health of the public. John D. Rockefeller Sr. established an institute for medical research in New York City in the mid-1890s (now Rockefeller University), and Rockefeller philanthropies applied laboratory discoveries at home and abroad in the first decade of the century to prevent yellow fever and hookworm.[5] Andrew Carnegie's philanthropies focused on reorganizing higher education to produce, teach, and disseminate scientific knowledge more effectively. In 1909 the Carnegie Foundation for the Advancement of Teaching commissioned Abraham Flexner, brother to the director of the Rockefeller Institute for Medical Research, to visit every medical school in the United States and Canada to assess how well their faculties studied, taught, and applied the sciences basic to medicine. The American Medical Association, which had begun a campaign of its own to eliminate inferior schools of medicine and poorly trained physicians, collaborated with the Carnegie project. In 1910 the Carnegie Foundation published Flexner's report detailing the shortcomings of medical education. The report, which attracted considerable attention, concluded that scientific medicine should be taught according to the theory of the new "progressive education."[6] Students and house staff should, Flexner insisted, be active learners rather than passive recipients of didactic instruction.

This recommendation became the basis of policy innovation a year later, when the General Education Board, a Rockefeller philanthropy, and its allies in academic medicine proposed to pay full-time salaries to senior faculty in clinical disciplines as an incentive for them to do scientific research, which would make them better practitioners and teachers. Most of the physicians who taught medical students, even at Hopkins and other reforming institutions, had no economic incentives to do research. Clinical teachers were usually prominent community practitioners whose incomes came from the fees patients paid directly to them. The proposal of full-time salaries threatened their incomes and, by extrapolation, their autonomy. Many of them predicted, accurately, that if deans and hospital managers collected fees from their patients and paid them an annual salary, they would lose cash, control over how they allocated time, and, their ultimate nightmare, absolute autonomy in making clinical decisions. The most famous, like William Osler, who left Hopkins for Oxford as a result of the controversy, would lose the contemporary equivalent of millions of dollars.[7]

During the second decade of the century and into the 1920s, the General Education Board enabled senior full-time clinicians and their allies in the basic sciences (anatomy, biochemistry, microbiology, and physiology) to control the resources allocated to medical education, teaching hospitals, and research. Senior clinicians and deans of leading medical institutions negotiated modifications in

5. Corner (1964); Fosdick (1989); Ettling (1981); Lagemann (1999); Fox (2006b, pp. 5–36); Sealander (1997).

6. Bonner (2002).

7. Fox (1980, pp. 475–96); Wheatley (1988).

the board's strict full-time model. These modifications, labeled *geographic full time,* permitted clinicians (or their departments) to retain a percentage of their fees in exchange for restricting their hospital and outpatient practice to institutions affiliated with medical schools.

The modification of strict full time to geographic full time helped to create formal and informal hierarchies made up of medical schools, affiliated hospitals, and specialty practices in urban regions across the country. Community physicians who wanted to enhance their prestige among peers and wealthier patients by being professors now taught and practiced in environments that were controlled by full-time faculty members who conducted, or at least respected, research.

In 1918 the General Education Board, after intense internal debate, for the first time awarded grants to public universities to subsidize the conversion of their medical schools to the full-time system. The board justified this change in policy on the pragmatic ground that supporting full-time faculty practice in public universities was the most effective way to create networks of health institutions headed by medical scientists whose clinical research and practice would ultimately improve the health of all Americans.

The Memorial Fund Association, established by Elizabeth Milbank Anderson and led by her and her cousin Albert G. Milbank from 1905 to 1920, also collaborated with government. Anderson and Milbank worked with officials of New York City and with the Association for Improving the Condition of the Poor, a major charity, to build and operate public baths, create new models of serving sick children, and design and construct subsidized housing in which persons with tuberculosis could live with their families while receiving decentralized health and social services. Similarly, they worked with New York state government to commission and implement studies of the most effective methods of ventilating schools to reduce the transmission of infections among children.[8] After Anderson's death in 1920 the Memorial Fund Association, renamed the Milbank Memorial Fund, hired John A. Kingsbury as its first chief executive. Kingsbury initiated a program to demonstrate the benefits of applying biomedical science to health care and public health.

In 1922 the Milbank Memorial Fund implemented demonstration projects in New York state that modeled the organization of science-based health services for underserved populations. In consultation with leaders of government and the medical profession in New York City, Syracuse, and rural Cattaraugus County, the fund organized three projects that helped create public health clinics, health education and preventative services, and the first rural public health department in the state. The fund financed rigorous evaluative studies of the three demonstrations and disseminated their results in articles, books, and press releases.

8. Fox (2006b, pp. 6–9).

By the mid-1920s the Rockefeller, Carnegie, and Milbank philanthropies, along with the more recently established Commonwealth and Rosenwald funds, were widely recognized innovators in health policy in the United States. However, the staff and trustees of the innovative foundations collectively misjudged their ability to influence the politics of policymaking for health in the United States. After consulting leaders in academic medicine and public health, they decided to leverage their success in creating hierarchies of health providers in geographic regions. The newly created hierarchies and the scientific advances that flowed from the academic institutions at their apex would, they assumed, help to solve the growing problem of access to health services.

Health services were becoming more expensive as a result of advancing science and new technologies for hospital and ambulatory care. Advocacy had failed to push through changes in state laws that would create insurance pools enabling consumers to manage growing health care costs. In response, seven foundations and their medical advisers appointed, funded, and guided a Committee on the Costs of Medical Care (CCMC) between 1927 and 1932. They wanted the committee, which comprised physicians and a few social scientists, to recommend policy that would make hierarchies of health services more efficient and expand access to care. These foundations were the Carnegie Foundation for the Advancement of Teaching, the Commonwealth Fund, the Josiah Macy Jr. Foundation, the Milbank Memorial Fund, the Rockefeller Foundation, the Rosenwald Fund, and the Russell Sage Foundation.[9]

The CCMC seemed to have support from the medical profession, the federal government, and even the public. Foundation leaders and most of the members of the committee had, however, severely underestimated physicians' hostility to its major recommendations: to strengthen regional provider hierarchies and to pool insurance premiums to spread the cost of care. Hierarchies threatened physicians' clinical autonomy, and insurance, or prepayment, threatened their financial autonomy. Most physicians in community practice believed that combining hierarchy and prepayment would destabilize their relationships with patients, hospitals, and colleagues by inserting "third parties" into examining rooms. The medical press amplified their fears.

Physicians' antagonism to the CCMC was profound. Most had been trained and licensed before the reforms of medical education stimulated by the Carnegie and Rockefeller philanthropies. They feared supervision by colleagues who knew more science than they did. Even graduates of reformed schools suspected that insurance carriers would create and reinforce hierarchy by restricting reimbursement for particular procedures to certain members of the multispecialty group practices recommended by the CCMC majority.

9. Engel (2002, chap. 2, pp. 11–53).

Officers of state and local medical societies, encouraged by their counterparts in the American Medical Association and the editor of its journal, orchestrated coverage in the medical and general press condemning the report of the CCMC majority. They also endorsed a report by a minority of committee members that defended physician autonomy and opposed prepayment. Most of the foundations that had sponsored the CCMC reacted to vilification in the medical and general press by ceasing to support discussion or even analysis of controversial issues of organizing and financing health services. For the remainder of the 1930s and several subsequent decades, foundations prioritized less controversial issues, especially laboratory research, capital funding for hospitals, medical education, and subsidizing health care for the unemployed.

After the CCMC disaster, the foundations in health that had engaged in what, in twenty-first century language, would be called institution building, social entrepreneurship, and policy development became risk averse. Although never as passive as the vast majority of foundations, they were considerably less ambitious than they had been between 1900 and 1932, whether their endowments were comparatively large (Rockefeller, Carnegie), mid-sized (Commonwealth, Rosenwald), or small (Macy, Milbank, Russell Sage).

Marginalization, 1933–1990

The rejection of the recommendations of the Committee on the Costs of Medical Care's majority report by organized medicine initiated a period during which foundations were marginal to the central issues of health affairs. The committee was not the only cause of their marginalization. Government and the private sector assumed roles previously played by the innovating foundations. From the late 1930s public spending to increase the supply of research, hospitals, and health professionals grew rapidly and uninterruptedly. During and after World War II, moreover, government and private employers asserted leadership in expanding access to health services.

The humiliation of the Milbank Memorial Fund between 1933 and 1935 exemplified the risks of attempting to innovate in health policy. The fund's chief executive, John A. Kingsbury, advocated national policy to increase access to health services by subsidizing prepayment. His efforts were met with scathing criticism from leaders of organized medicine. This very public controversy, including a boycott of Borden condensed milk urged by state medical societies (because the Milbank Fund held considerable stock in the Borden Company), taught the most prominent foundations that their money and prestige could not guarantee significant changes in policy. A CCMC study had calculated that, nationally, philanthropic funding for health services was never more than 5 percent of total spending in the 1920s. In that decade patients paid 79 percent of costs directly and government at all levels only 14 percent.[10] But grants by foundations that collaborated with powerful reformers in medicine and government leveraged innovation in the decades before government and employers had substantial purchasing power in health.

Spending for health by government and employers (the latter through commercial and nonprofit insurance companies) became increasingly important as foundations retreated from seeking policy change. As hospitals grew in number, size, and complexity, their leaders sought public subsidies, including public debt and predictable revenues for patient care from government and insurers. The changing politics of the health sector was, however, the major cause of the marginalization of the innovating foundations. Between the 1930s and the 1970s, an informal, mutually beneficial alliance between practicing physicians and their colleagues in academic medicine dominated the agenda for health policy across the country. The rejection of the report of the CCMC majority had been an early sign of the political strength of this alliance between town and gown that dominated the agenda for health policy and translated into practical political beliefs about science and technology shared by the medical profession and the public.

Since the late nineteenth century, popular culture and media had proclaimed and frequently exaggerated the beneficent advance of medical science. The application of business principles of organization and management to hospitals and clinics reinforced the belief that health services were efficiently extending life and reducing suffering.[11] Foundations and their allies had promoted and financed the creation of institutions that provided education, research, and patient care at the apex of what most experts in health affairs believed would eventually be coordinated regional hierarchies.

During these years, however, leaders of the American Medical Association, state medical societies, and the growing number of specialty societies began to devise a political response to hierarchical regionalism that served the interests of the profession more than the vision of foundation leaders. Most physicians resisted the organizational logic of hierarchical regionalism even though they accepted or at least respected its scientific basis. They insisted on governing clinical decisionmaking, licensure, professional discipline, and the setting of fees for their services, adamantly refusing to cede control of these activities to colleagues with better training and more knowledge. They preferred, that is, to work in a fragmented health care system in which the scientific basis of hierarchical regionalism was axiomatic but formal hierarchical arrangements were limited to

10. Fetter (2006, p. 54) citing the CCMC.
11. Sturdy and Cooter (1998, pp. 421–66) is the best account of the mutual reinforcement of the principles of scientific management and hierarchical regionalism.

medical schools and their affiliated teaching hospitals. Even attending physicians at affiliated hospitals expected medical schools to accept their clinical and business autonomy in exchange for voluntarily teaching.

For many years neither foundations, government, employers, nor insurance companies wanted to challenge the alliance of town and gown that fragmented hierarchical regionalism. The CCMC's majority report was the last coherent national effort to rationalize health service delivery and payment. For the next seven decades, most of the organizers of alliances to increase access to health services, contain costs, and rationalize delivery appeased organized medicine by endorsing clinical autonomy and professional self-regulation.

Leaders of academic medicine had no alternative to working in fragmented hierarchies. Under the town-gown compromise, academics controlled undergraduate medical education and research, usually with support for increased funding from organized medicine. Academics remained silent, in public and often within the profession, about the quality and accountability of medical care in the regions they served.

This compromise defined feasible health policy for almost half a century. From the 1930s through the 1960s, the American Medical Association, most state medical societies, and specialty societies endorsed public subsidies to finance biomedical research in academic centers and to construct, renovate, and equip hospitals. These organizations opposed or tried to modify most proposals for government subsidies of health care. They thwarted efforts by reformist physicians and a few labor leaders and business executives to create integrated delivery systems in which physicians would be paid by capitation or salary. Community physicians and the organizations that represented them supported increased enrollment in medical schools and the establishment of new schools in states and regions in which they did not fear competition from new graduates.[12]

For a generation this compromise satisfied the interests of most community and academic physicians. From the mid-1930s to the early 1960s, the federal government and the states awarded ever-larger subsidies to the supply side of the health sector (that is, for education and research and the clinical and laboratory facilities they required) while making only modest contributions to creating effective demand.

By the end of the 1930s federal subsidies to construct hospitals exceeded foundation spending for this purpose. The Hill-Burton Program, authorized by the Hospital Survey and Construction Act of 1946, provided unprecedented subsidies to construct hospitals and related facilities. Although Congress intended Hill-Burton to create more rational regional hierarchies of hospitals and clinics, in practice it reinforced fragmented regional hierarchies. In 1957 the

12. Fox (1993, pp. 56–83).

Ford Foundation, pressed by news media to increase spending as its endowment grew, appropriated $170 million to subsidize the capital budgets of hospitals and medical schools.[13] These grants reinforced existing policy under Hill-Burton as well as state appropriations for hospitals and higher education.

The federal government, moreover, replaced foundations as the major source of innovation and funding for biomedical research. The law that established the National Cancer Institute in 1937 authorized grants to investigators who were affiliated with hospitals, universities, and research centers. Revising the Public Health Act in 1943, Congress authorized the National Institutes of Health to award grants. Spending under this new extramural research program began in 1946 when the agency converted federal contracts to procure medical research for the war effort into investigator-initiated grants to medical schools. These grants carried generous overhead payments to the receiving institutions. In the next several years, Congress authorized new national institutes to address, among other issues, mental health, heart disease and stroke, arthritis, and kidney disease.[14] The Office of Naval Research established biomedical research centers at medical schools across the country and assigned administrative personnel to assist academic researchers.

By the late 1950s the federal government, pharmaceutical companies, and organizations that raised private money in behalf of curing particular diseases were the major sponsors of research at academic medical centers. Research grants from foundations, which were usually smaller than federal awards and paid lower overhead rates, became more important to their recipients than to their host institutions.

Since the 1940s, foundations have been more important as advocates for additional federal spending for research and as disseminators of its results than as funders.[15] The Albert and Mary Lasker Foundation, the most prominent foundation in research advocacy, lobbied effectively for increases in National Institutes of Health budgets and the creation of new institutes and has awarded annual prizes to investigators who were funded mainly by government and disease associations. The Howard Hughes Medical Institute, established in 1953, is the largest of a diminishing number of foundations that provide substantial financing for biomedical research.

Other foundations helped to disseminate research findings and facilitate discussion of their practical implications. The Milbank Memorial Fund, for example, disseminated findings on nutrition and mental health; the Carnegie Corporation of New York, the Rockefeller Foundation, the Milbank Fund, and others helped translate research on reproduction into programs of family planning;

13. Fleishman (2007, pp. 225–26).
14. Fox (1987, pp. 447–66).
15. Fleishman (2007, p. 75).

the William T. Grant Foundation sponsored and disseminated research in child development and the prevention of mental illness in children.

Foundations were similarly marginal to the making of policy that influenced the direction of academic medicine and regional hierarchies. After World War II, community and academic physicians collaborated to promote new and expanded medical schools in regions in which there were substantial shortages of physicians' services. State governments, eager to promote economic development, health, and upward mobility for voters and their children, acquired land for new or expanded schools and teaching hospitals, subsidized their construction with public debt, and appropriated funds to operate them.

Public funding for the growth of supply and public and private funding for effective demand for care crowded out foundations. A foundation in Maine, for example, had in 1932 established the Bingham Program to expand a regional hierarchy by linking teaching hospitals in Boston to hospitals and clinics in that state. After World War II this program narrowed its purpose in response to the expansion of academic medical centers in New Hampshire and Vermont and the creation of a teaching hospital and graduate medical education in Portland, Maine.[16] In the 1950s the Commonwealth Fund and local philanthropies helped to organize the Rochester Regional Hospital Council in upstate New York. This organization was a national model of hierarchical regionalism for several decades until its influence eroded as a result of changes in reimbursement policy and in the economy of the region.[17]

Most foundations preferred to support less controversial aspects of medical education and service integration. Between the 1940s and 1970s, for instance, the Commonwealth Fund, the Josiah Macy Jr. Foundation, and the Carnegie Corporation awarded numerous grants to study the experience of medical education and to introduce into the education of physicians such neglected subjects as public health, nutrition, and sex and the disciplines of the humanities and social sciences.[18] A substantial number of these grants had positive results, but they did not address sharply contested issues of policy for access, quality, and cost.

Foundations were mainly absent from national and state debates about access to health services between Kingsbury's departure from the Milbank Memorial Fund in 1935 and the reorganization of the Robert Wood Johnson Foundation into a national philanthropy in 1973. In the first three decades of the twentieth century the innovating foundations had financed or conducted studies that documented problems of access to care for persons with low incomes. The

16. Fox (1986, p. 165); "The Bingham Program: Investing in a Healthy Maine," Bingham Program News, Spring–Summer 2005 (www.binghamprogram.org/Pages/about).

17. Rosenfeld and Makover (1956).

18. Bloom (2002, pp. 181–213).

federal government assumed responsibility for investigating problems of access and related issues in 1934 and 1935, when staff of the U.S. Public Health Service conducted a comprehensive national health survey. Their central finding was that chronic disease management was replacing treatment for infections and injuries as the major policy challenge in financing, organizing, and increasing access to care.[19] Foundations were more interested in commissioning analyses of this fundamental shift in the burden of disease than in devising practical programs to address it.

During the middle decades of the century, other nonprofit organizations had a significant influence on policy to increase access, often spending from their surpluses as well as their public affairs and marketing budgets. Blue Cross and Blue Shield plans pioneered in creating employment-based health coverage and in some locations, the New York metropolitan area, for example, organized public-private insurance partnerships to increase access for people with low incomes. Integrated delivery systems, notably Kaiser Permanente, the Group Health Cooperative of Puget Sound, and the Health Insurance Plan of New York, demonstrated that they could provide care to diverse populations effectively and efficiently. The efforts of these nonprofits, in contrast to the work of foundations, helped to build support during the 1950s and 1960s for federal intervention to increase coverage for seniors and the poor. Moreover, leaders of these organizations helped to develop and implement landmark legislation, particularly the amendments to the Social Security Act that created Medicare and Medicaid in 1965 and an act of 1971 subsidizing new health maintenance organizations.

The marginalization of foundations in addressing issues of access and financing made the program of the Robert Wood Johnson Foundation unusual. After its reorganization and the injection of new assets, the foundation became the largest endowment in the health sector (and remained the largest until the establishment of the Bill and Melinda Gates Foundation two decades later). It accorded highest priority to increasing access to medical care for underserved populations. Early programs helped to spread 911 emergency response systems, to support new midlevel health professions in order to improve access to primary care (in collaboration with the Commonwealth Fund), and to subsidize health services in schools. In the 1980s the Robert Wood Johnson Foundation began to subsidize programs to expand health insurance coverage in states and localities. In the early 1990s the foundation risked censure from public officials and the media by promoting national discussion and more informed debate of the Clinton health plan.[20]

19. Fox (1993, pp. 34–36).
20. Chapter 7, this volume.

Relevance, 1990–Present

Foundations spent less, relative to their assets, to address the most controversial issues of health policy between the 1930s and the 1980s than they had before or have done subsequently. In the first quarter of the twentieth century the innovating foundations collaborated with academic institutions to reorganize and strengthen the supply side of the health sector. Their counterparts at the end of the century prioritized, using the best available evidence from research to address problems of access to health services and their quality and cost across the world. Significant events in the health sector in which many foundations participated included the Clinton administration's universal health care plan and its failure, the rejection of managed care by consumers unwilling to accept restrictions on their coverage and choice of providers, the growth of the uninsured population, the enactment of a federal-state Children's Health Insurance Program, the growing cost of pharmaceutical drugs, the expansion of Medicare to include prescription drug coverage in 2003, and the dissemination of evidence that many Americans are at risk of care that is unsafe.

Two less visible clusters of events increased opportunities for foundations to join government, large employers, and labor unions in changing the distribution of power and money in the health sector. One was the maturation of research methods that enabled collective purchasers for health care services to hold providers accountable for the effectiveness and efficiency of their services. The other cluster was changes in law and regulation that curtailed physicians' monopoly control of their services.

By the 1990s the methodology of what people in the field called "evidence-based health research" enabled researchers to evaluate and systematically compare the effectiveness of interventions to prevent, diagnose, and treat illness.[21] These methods could also measure the quality and safety of services provided by physicians, individually and in groups, and by hospitals. By the end of the 1990s collective purchasers and many citizens had access to persuasive evidence that many Americans received care that was unsafe or inappropriate and that contributed to rising costs.[22]

In the 1970s a few foundations began to support education and training in this new method of research, clinical epidemiology. The Rockefeller Foundation established "its largest health program ever," the International Clinical Epidemiology Network, which conducted training around the world.[23] Between

21. Daly (2005).
22. Fox (2005, pp. 114–22).
23. White (2007).

1978 and 1985, the Milbank Memorial Fund sponsored fellowships to recruit young academic physicians to careers in clinical epidemiology. The Nuffield Trust, a British foundation, supported important contributions to the methodology of health services research.[24] However, government, primarily in Canada, the United Kingdom, and the United States, financed most of the advances in research methodology that became relevant to health policy in the 1990s and paid for most training of researchers.

Changes in antitrust law and regulation that also began in the 1970s enabled collective purchasers in government and business to increase their authority over suppliers of services. Innovations in antitrust law, and the court decisions that affirmed them, effectively ended physicians' monopoly on the regulation of their work and encouraged competition in markets for health services. The new regulatory regime, like the new capacity to measure the quality and effectiveness of services, encouraged purchasers to challenge the formidable political influence and public support of organized medicine and its allies in the hospital, pharmaceutical, and medical device industries.[25]

The goals and methods of foundations in health also changed. A new generation of chief executives had considerable experience in making and implementing policy and conducting research. Most of their immediate predecessors had been leaders in academic medicine or had spent their careers working for foundations. The boards that chose these new chief executives were increasingly led by professionals in business and finance who demanded evidence that their foundations' work was relevant to policy.

The new chief executives and their staffs were eager to engage central issues of health policy and were familiar with the quantitative and qualitative methods of evaluation that members of their boards used in conducting business. They sponsored publications, conferences, and projects that addressed alternative policies for access, quality, and cost. Many of them sought opportunities to discuss policy with decisionmakers. Some of the chief executives had strong policy preferences, about which they spoke and wrote publicly. But they also knew how to avoid polarizing advocacy.

Foundations' programs were also changing because they had different financial sources from those of traditional endowments. Some were financed by individuals who maintained control over programs and projects by paying their costs directly rather than from an endowment (for example, the Open Society Institute, financed by George Soros). A variant on this model is the William Jefferson Clinton Foundation, which solicits funds from many wealthy donors. The controversial conversion of nonprofit health plans, insurers, and hospitals

24. Cochrane (1972).
25. Ameringer (2008).

to investor-owned corporations during the 1990s led to the creation of about a hundred new endowed foundations (ranging in size from the multibillion-dollar California Endowment to the nine-figure Kansas Health Foundation to smaller foundations focused on local communities).

New endowments are also being created by the courts as a result of the settlement of class action lawsuits (for example, the Physicians' Foundation, created by a settlement between organized medicine and managed care companies, and the American Legacy Foundation, a result of the settlement between the tobacco industry and most of the states). In distributing funds from the settlement of suits, state attorneys general frequently act as de facto foundation executives (for example, distributing grants from a settlement that resulted from a drug company's promoting off-label use of Neurontin, a painkiller). Another new funding model is the Kaiser Permanente Community Benefit program, for which the largest nonprofit integrated delivery system earmarks an annual philanthropic budget. Among foundations, the Kaiser Permanente program is exceeded in size only by the budgets of the Bill and Melinda Gates and the Robert Wood Johnson foundations.

Although there is evidence that foundations' relevance to health affairs has increased, it is difficult to identify changes in policy and practice that would not have occurred, or would have occurred more slowly, absent the efforts of a particular foundation. For the past ten years the Robert Wood Johnson Foundation has published annual anthologies that describe and evaluate its work.[26] Some foundations describe their achievements on the web: for example, the California Endowment, the Commonwealth Fund, the John A. Hartford Foundation, and the Kaiser Family Foundation. A recent monograph assesses the work of twelve foundations to inform policy for reducing the number of persons who lack health insurance.[27] I have described some of the work of the Milbank Memorial Fund in collaboration with decisionmakers in the public and private sectors.[28] Whatever judgments readers, decisionmakers, and historians subsequently make about the significance of this work, they are likely to agree about its relevance.

Although prominent foundations in health are addressing central issues of health policy, most of them are unlikely to be major forces in health affairs within the United States. Whether these foundations have endowments of billions or hundreds of millions or fewer dollars, their total annual spending is trivial in a sector that accounts for 17 percent of domestic product. Whatever influence foundations have on health policy in the future will be entirely a result of the ability of their boards and staffs to understand the politics of policy well

26. Isaacs and Knickman (2006).
27. Oliver and Gerson (2003).
28. Fox (2006a, pp. 1724–29); Fox (2010); Fox and Greenfield (2006, pp. 531–50).

enough to assist actors who have more power and money to innovate in the public interest.

The Promise of Foundation Influence on Global Health

American foundations may be more likely to influence policy and practice in global health in the next several years. Between 1995 and 2005, funding for international projects by American foundations increased by 80 percent; foundations allocated a third of this new money to improving global health. The Gates Foundation, the largest funder, spent $6.6 billion for global health programs, mainly to prevent and treat HIV/AIDS, malaria, and tuberculosis.[29]

Foundations can exert more influence on policy to improve global health than on domestic health policy. By 2006 the Gates Foundation's annual spending for global health exceeded the core budget of the World Health Organization, a United Nations agency.[30] The Gates Foundation's annual spending is expected to double as a result of contributions from Warren Buffett, the second-wealthiest American, after Gates. From his base in the Carter Center, former president Jimmy Carter has since the 1980s mobilized funds from foundations and individual donors and led effective campaigns in Africa against major diseases such as guinea worm infestation and river blindness. Similarly, former president Bill Clinton has used his political skills, access to powerful people, and ability to raise money to persuade multinational pharmaceutical companies to reduce the price of antiviral drugs for persons with AIDS/HIV in low-income countries.

American foundation spending in developing countries has a long history. Most projects earlier in the century applied the results of their activities in the United States. Examples include Rockefeller Foundation projects early in the century to devise a vaccine for yellow fever and to organize health professionals and services in regional hierarchies in Canada, China, and Scotland.[31] In the 1950s Carnegie, Milbank, and a Rockefeller family foundation created the Population Council to promote family planning abroad, modeled on projects in the United States.[32] A notable exception to the transfer of projects from the United States was the Rockefeller Foundation's sponsorship in the 1950s and 1960s of research on hybrid corn by Norman Borlaug. This program propelled a "green revolution" estimated to have saved a billion and a half lives.[33]

29. Chapter 11, this volume.
30. Levine (2006, pp. 1015–17).
31. Fedunkiw (2005); Farley (2004); Stewart (2006, pp. 513–39).
32. Critchlow (1999, pp. 13–49).
33. Fleishman (2007, p. 194).

Recent foundation expenditures to promote global health have different purposes from those of the past. Foundations are trying to succeed where public agencies and their private and nonprofit contractors have failed by improving on the methods of multilateral agencies such as the World Health Organization and the World Bank, donor countries' aid agencies, and host governments that lack adequate health infrastructure or have insufficient political commitment for reform. Moreover, foundations are systematically applying lessons from successful programs in global health in the recent past, notably the smallpox eradication campaign of the 1970s and more recent work to control tuberculosis in Peru and other countries.[34]

Foundations that work in global health share with domestic foundations a commitment to adapting contemporary methods of management and measures of accountability. As Warren Buffett told *The Economist* shortly after announcing his donation to the Gates Foundation, "Philanthropy is a 'tougher game' than business. . . . The most important problems are those which have already resisted both intellect and money. . . . In philanthropy measuring performance can be fiendishly tricky and take a lot longer."[35] In the months before Buffett's donation and interview, the Gates Foundation had begun to expand its focus from funding potential breakthrough technologies of prevention and therapy to include strengthening health systems and services in low-income countries.

American foundations' recent work in developing countries is also evidence of a new consensus among leaders of government, business, and the media that improving global health serves the self-interest of the United States and other industrial countries. This consensus is grounded in apprehension about the rapid spread of epidemic disease through international travel and economic exchange, awareness that healthier consumers and workers contribute to the growth of the global economy, and concern that poor health threatens international security because it helps destabilize weak regimes in low-income countries.[36] As a result of this consensus, since 2001 development assistance for health improvement has increased from each member nation of the Organization for Economic Cooperation and Development as well as from foundations.

Retrospect and Prospect

Although many foundations are no longer marginal to health policy, none of them are, as a few were a century ago, significant agents of innovation, except

34. Rosenberg and others (2010).
35. "The New Powers in Giving," *The Economist*, July 1, 2006, pp. 63–65; Okie (2006).
36. Horton (2006).

possibly in global health. The politics of health policy in the early twenty-first century, both domestically and globally, are more complicated than they were in the first quarter of the twentieth century. The stakes are higher: each year sees more science, more technology, more institutions, more professionals, and especially more money. The stakes are also higher because knowledge is available that could, if effectively and efficiently implemented, improve the health of more people than ever before.

This chapter has examined the history of foundations in the context of the history of the health sector, emphasizing the politics of policy for access to health care, its quality, and its cost. My principal finding is that foundations influenced the resolution of significant problems in health affairs when their goals were congruent with the goals of key decisionmakers in health affairs and when these decisionmakers judged foundation staff to be trustworthy and their cash to be helpful. Foundations have sometimes helped to make history, but they have rarely made it themselves. Foundations are likely to be as innovative, marginal, and relevant in the future as they have been during the past century.

7

The Robert Wood Johnson Foundation's Efforts to Improve Health and Health Care for All Americans

JAMES R. KNICKMAN AND STEPHEN L. ISAACS

In 1972 a small local foundation that had been doing limited grant making in the New Brunswick, New Jersey, area became the nation's second largest foundation, with an endowment of $1.2 billion from the estate of Robert Wood Johnson, a former president of Johnson and Johnson. The Robert Wood Johnson Foundation, with assets that have grown to roughly $9 billion, is now the nation's fourth largest foundation. Its mission—to improve the health and health care of all Americans—is easy to state. Carrying out the mission is difficult and complex, requiring the attention of a fifteen-person board of trustees and a staff of approximately 250 people headquartered in Princeton, New Jersey, and providing support, as of the end of 2005, to thirteen hundred grantees. The foundation's strategic priorities have evolved since 1972 and along with them the mechanisms that the foundation has adopted to realize its goals. In the 1990s these priorities and mechanisms came together in one area—tobacco control—in which the foundation is widely considered to have played a significant role.

Foundations working to bring about social change have a limited number of tools in their arsenals: grant making for programs, advocacy, core support, research, fellowships, conferences, and the like; communications and public affairs activities; bringing people and organizations together; and playing a leadership role on important issues. The Robert Wood Johnson Foundation has used all of these at one time or another. Its trademark has been large, multisite demonstration programs administered by outside program offices and expert advisory boards. The foundation, which has always taken evaluation seriously, developed a number of tools to assess the impact of its programs, to measure its programmatic bottom line, and to share its findings with the public.

The Evolution of Strategic Priorities at the Robert Wood Johnson Foundation

This section explores the foundation's strategic priorities and how they have evolved since 1972. We discuss the choices that the foundation has made and why it made them.

The 1970s through the Mid-1980s

In 1972 the new staff of the Robert Wood Johnson Foundation, under the leadership of David Rogers, found itself in the enviable position of having to distribute roughly $50 million a year. To do this, it adopted a program strategy based on three priorities, which, with some variations, lasted through the mid-1980s.

The first priority was increasing the access of underserved populations to medical care. Its early programs helped catalyze the nation's 911 emergency response system, develop the new professions of family nurse practitioner and physician's assistant, and provide health care services to underserved children in schools.

The second priority was improving the quality of medical care. Recognizing the importance of building a strong corps of experts—physicians and nonphysicians alike—who would have the skills to understand health policy and the desire to improve it, in 1973 the foundation funded two fellowship programs that continue to the present day. The Clinical Scholars Program enables young physicians to gain research and social sciences skills so that they will be able play leadership roles in health policy or in academic medicine, and the Health Policy Fellowship Program offers young health care professionals the opportunity to work in the Washington office of a senator or representative.

The third priority was improving public policy and the research that would guide it. This goal has endured to the present day. In fact, the Robert Wood Johnson Foundation was intimately involved with the growth of the field of health policy research, whose roots date back to research programs developed in the 1970s.

The Mid-1980s through 1990

By the mid-1980s, new presidents served both the nation and the Robert Wood Johnson Foundation, and the foundation's strategic priorities had changed. Instead of three priorities, the foundation, led by Leighton Cluff between 1986 and 1990, listed eleven. Improving access to care remained a priority, but the foundation's approach to it had shifted. After the 1980 election it became clear that state governments, rather than the federal government, were going to take the lead in developing innovative ways to increase access to medical care. While not neglecting change at the federal level, the foundation's attention turned increasingly toward the states and localities as it looked for model programs that could be widely replicated. As a result, the foundation funded state and local coalitions of business, labor, insurers, and hospitals to find innovative ways of keeping health care costs down and state-based programs to find innovative ways to encourage employers to provide lower-cost insurance coverage for their employees. It also supported medical groups that were the forerunners of today's health maintenance organizations and developed new programs to attract qualified members of minority groups to become physicians.

A new priority was destructive behavior, including substance abuse and violence. As the nation became alarmed about the dangers of substance abuse, the Robert Wood Johnson Foundation developed programs that supported community coalitions working to improve neighborhoods, curb crime, and reduce drug and alcohol abuse.

During this period, the foundation also addressed the problem of HIV/AIDS by replicating a prevention model that had been successfully used in San Francisco and, as part of its focus on medical ethics, funded a research study on the treatment of dying people in hospitals. The disappointing results of this study launched a major initiative in the 1990s to improve end-of-life care for hospitalized patients.

The 1990s

In the first half of the 1990s, with the arrival of a new president, Steven Schroeder, the Robert Wood Johnson Foundation homed in on three objectives. The first, increasing access to health care services, continued the foundation's work in an area that had been its primary concern since its very first days. The second, improving services for people with chronic illnesses, although new as a strategic priority, incorporated elements of past programs. The third, reducing the harm caused by substance abuse, including tobacco, was new and raised some trepidation among board and staff members when first introduced.

To increase access to care, the foundation adopted a variety of approaches:

—It funded programs to encourage physicians to become generalists, that is, doctors who would offer primary care to underserved patients.

—It strengthened its commitment to increase the opportunities of minorities to become health care professionals.

—It continued working to expand health insurance coverage. In the debate about health reform in the early years of Bill Clinton's presidency, many foundation grantees (and some staff members, including the foundation's president) provided advice to the health reform commission and to representatives and senators involved in the legislative process. With the demise of the proposal for health reform in 1994, the foundation adopted a more cautious stance that supported state initiatives to expand health insurance coverage.

—It supplemented federal programs to insure children. After passage of the State Children's Health Insurance Program in 1997, the foundation authorized a program called Covering Kids to publicize the availability of the insurance program and Medicaid and to make it easier for families of eligible children to enroll.

—To improve care of people with chronic illnesses, the foundation's grant making included five key strategies. First, in response to the foundation-funded study mentioned earlier confirming that dying people were not getting the care they wanted, the foundation adopted a wide-ranging strategy to improve the care of terminally ill people. Second, to encourage people to buy long-term care insurance, the foundation funded a new concept—partnerships of private insurers and Medicaid that would protect people against the potentially staggering cost of a nursing home or home health care. Third, to help homebound chronically ill people, the foundation greatly increased its support to Faith in Action, a program in which volunteers from interfaith coalitions served their homebound, usually elderly, neighbors. Fourth, it funded experimental programs that gave homebound individuals the opportunity to pay relatives, friends, and others of their choosing—rather than caretakers provided by agencies—for their home care. Fifth, it invested in programs that integrated and coordinated medical and supportive care of people with chronic conditions.

A growing endowment during the 1990s allowed the foundation to increase its funding for the health side of its mission as well as the health care side. Without having to take money away from programs to expand coverage or to improve chronic care, the foundation found itself in the enviable position of being able to address some of the behaviors that lead to poor health. This reflected a growing awareness that health is influenced more by behaviors, lifestyles, and social and environmental factors than by the delivery of medical care. Michael McGinnis, one of the nation's leading thinkers on health, was named as a senior vice president of the foundation, and in 1999 the foundation reorganized into health and health care groups, with McGinnis as head of the health group. Risa Lavizzo-Mourey, a future president, headed the health care group. The commitment of resources to encourage healthy behaviors and environments led the foundation to increase funding of community anti–substance abuse coalitions and programs to curb alcohol abuse among college and high school students and to initiate programs that tested different approaches to increasing people's physical activity.

The Twenty-First Century

Lavizzo-Mourey, who became president and chief executive officer of the Robert Wood Johnson Foundation in January 2003, emphasized the importance of impact, focus, and strategy. She organized the foundation's grant making into an "impact framework" consisting of four portfolios. Three of those concentrate on broad areas, reflecting elements of the foundation's core commitments. The "human capital portfolio" brings together a broad range of programs designed to improve the quality of the health and health care workforce and leadership. The "vulnerable populations portfolio" supports and tries to improve programs that deliver services to needy populations, such as the elderly, the poor, the mentally ill, and those living in underserved inner cities or rural areas. The "pioneer portfolio" represents the foundation's commitment to innovative ideas that may have a high payoff in the future. The "targeted portfolio" is the largest, representing more than 50 percent of the foundation's grant making. The targeted portfolio specifies eight objectives, each having a strategy, a multiyear budget to implement the strategy, and a team of foundation staff members to develop and monitor programs.[1] Four of the objectives—childhood obesity, public health systems, addiction prevention and treatment, and tobacco control—focus on improving health, and four—health insurance coverage, quality of care, racial and ethnic disparities, and hospital nursing—on improving health care.

Having learned that social change does not come quickly, the foundation takes a long-range perspective. It has set long-term goals for each of its portfolios and strategic objectives. Some—such as those having to do with expanding health insurance coverage, reducing childhood obesity, and improving hospital nursing—stretch out a decade.

The Mechanics of Grant Making, Execution, and Monitoring

The night that newspapers ran the story of the creation of the Robert Wood Johnson Foundation with a $1.2 billion endowment, burglars broke into the foundation's headquarters and tried to make off with the cash. There was no cash there, of course (the endowment consisted of shares of Johnson and Johnson stock), and the burglars left empty handed. Even though the money was not physically stored at the foundation headquarters, the board and staff felt great pressure to set up a system that would distribute 5 percent of the foundation's endowment quickly, efficiently, and fairly.

They hit upon a system whereby a significant percentage of the money would be allocated to large national demonstration programs conducted in a number of sites that would be carefully evaluated and whose results would be communicated to the field. The programs would be administered partly in-house but mainly by outside national program offices (frequently housed in universities)

---

1. In mid-2006, the foundation reduced the number from eight to four: insurance coverage, quality and inequality, public health, and childhood obesity.

counseled by advisory committees consisting of recognized experts. This struck a balance between the desire to have a lean headquarters staff and to be able to monitor the work of grantees and provide technical assistance to them. With some modifications and with significant variations from program to program, this system has characterized the foundation's program management for more than thirty years. Currently, 83 percent of allocations to programs goes to national programs.

The idea of large national demonstration programs probably came from the early trustees, nearly all of whom were members of the Johnson and Johnson board, who viewed demonstration programs as the social analogue to the pharmaceutical trials they were accustomed to. The concept appealed to the staff, too. They saw large demonstration programs as a way of testing ideas, or variations on a single idea, which, if successful, could be widely replicated and perhaps even picked up by the federal government. In fact, that is exactly what happened with the foundation's very first national program, the Emergency Medical Services Program. The newly hatched Robert Wood Johnson Foundation, aware of a groundswell of interest and impressed with small experimental projects in several communities, made grants averaging $350,000 to forty-four communities to try different approaches to responding to emergencies. The foundation worked hand in glove with the federal government, which picked up the program and expanded it throughout the nation.

This model of testing innovations that could, if successful, be funded on a large scale by the federal government worked in a number of early cases. In the 1970s, for example, the foundation worked to strengthen the nascent professions of family nurse practitioner and physician's assistant by funding pilot programs in a half-dozen communities, each of which used a different approach to deploying these new classes of health care practitioners. It did not take long for the government to appreciate the value of these new health professionals and to pick up funding for their training. During the AIDS epidemic in the 1980s, the Robert Wood Johnson Foundation tested variations of an apparently successful model, pioneered in San Francisco, of providing HIV prevention and treatment services. The program provided a model for the Ryan White Act, the primary federal AIDS legislation. Similarly, the Health Care for the Homeless Program (funded jointly with the Pew Charitable Trusts) was a multisite demonstration program that led to the McKinney Act, initially passed in 1987, which has been the federal government's major legislative response to homelessness. The Fighting Back program led the federal Center for Substance Abuse Prevention to fund more than six hundred communities that formed coalitions to fight substance abuse.

As noted earlier, in the 1980s it became increasingly rarer for the government to pick up successful demonstration programs, and the foundation began to refocus its efforts on states, communities, school districts, and health care providers. Many of the ideas tested in the 1980s and in later years also attempted to redirect existing money rather than look for new sources of financing. For example, a demonstration program called Cash and Counseling, whose objective was to give frail and disabled people more control over the long-term care services they receive, was designed to cost no more than traditional long-term care services.

In other cases, the foundation expanded the purpose of multisite demonstrations and invested sufficient resources to make a difference without the necessity of government funding. The Urban Health Initiative, for example, provided ten years of substantial funding to communities in Baltimore, Detroit, Oakland, Philadelphia, and Richmond in the hope that the initiative would have a measurable impact on children's health in these cities. In one sense, the idea behind the Urban Health Initiative was to demonstrate new approaches to improving children's health; in another sense, it was to help young people directly in these five cities. Other initiatives, too, focused on improving people's health directly rather than on the concept of demonstrating new approaches. The Faith in Action program, which was for a time the foundation's costliest initiative, is one example.

Although the foundation devotes a significant portion of its grant-making budget to multisite demonstration programs, that is not the only approach it takes. A small portion of its grant-making budget goes to fund ad hoc programs—smaller efforts such as, say, conferences or specific items of research, some of which are requested by foundation staff members, others of which arrive as unsolicited ideas. The foundation devotes roughly 16 percent of its grant funds to fellowships and other ways of strengthening human resources. Although it is difficult to prove statistically, the foundation believes in the long-term effectiveness of strengthening the health care workforce. As it has worked to develop priority fields such as nursing, health policy research, and epidemiology, the foundation has funded, as part of its field-building strategy, fellowship programs whose purpose is to develop a corps of leaders and experts.

Research, evaluation, and communications form an important and integral part of program development. Since its earliest days, the Robert Wood Johnson Foundation has evaluated the programs it funds and has shared its findings with the public. As a rule, national initiatives are evaluated by outside experts, who are given wide latitude and are asked to come to independent conclusions about impact. Moreover, the foundation has funded a massive amount of research in health and health care and is widely considered to have been a force behind the development of the field of health policy research. The foundation devotes 26 percent of its budget to research and evaluation.

The foundation has an active communications office that lets the public know what it is doing and what it has learned through various means, including publications, such as the annual *Robert Wood Johnson Foundation Anthology* and the *Robert Wood Johnson Foundation Health Policy Series;* a website; grants results reports published on the foundation's website; and, of course, an annual report. What makes the foundation's communications office unique is its involvement in programs from their earliest stages of development through their conclusion. In addition, the foundation sometimes builds initiatives around communications strategies. The Covering Kids and Families campaign, for example, supplements the federal government's Medicaid and State Children's Health Insurance programs by mounting public information campaigns to let families know that their children might be eligible and to help them surmount the bureaucratic hurdles. Cover the Uninsured Week is a massive communications campaign aimed at keeping the issue of the uninsured on the front burner. Communications grants account for 16 percent of the funds awarded by the foundation.

Based on its three decades of experience, the foundation has come to appreciate the importance of taking a multipronged approach to health and health care issues. Writing checks certainly remains central to its work, but the foundation is now more consciously using all the tools available to it—what Lavizzo-Mourey refers to as the "five C's": communicating openly and honestly with the field and the public; convening people who would not ordinarily be talking to one another (as it has done in bringing together what the foundation calls "the strange bedfellows"—health insurance experts with differing perspectives who are all seeking ways to cover the uninsured); coordinating various groups, including government and foundations, who have an interest in the same topic; connecting the dots so that individual grantees understand how their program fits into a larger strategy; and counting, or measuring impact and results.[2]

The Foundation's Contribution to Tobacco Control Initiatives

The Robert Wood Johnson Foundation entered the tobacco arena timidly. The harm caused by tobacco was hardly a secret, however, what with the great publicity given to it by a succession of reports by the surgeon general, negative publicity generated by antismoking advocacy groups, federal legislation requiring warning labels on cigarette packs, and extensive media coverage. When Steven Schroeder, interviewing for the job of foundation president and later as the foundation's head, suggested that the organization should be doing more to address the damage to health caused by smoking, the idea met with immediate resistance. After all, it was argued, tobacco was a legal substance—unlike, say, crack cocaine or heroin—and available to anybody with the money to buy a pack. Moreover, some staff and board members feared that by entering this field and pitting itself against the powerful tobacco industry, the foundation might be

2. Lavizzo-Mourey (2006).

mired in controversy and its other work overshadowed. Nonetheless, the damage to health that resulted from smoking—then as now the number-one cause of premature death in the United States—was compelling. What tipped the balance, however, was the undeniable fact that smoking was unhealthy for kids. The board was comfortable establishing a goal in 1991 that included reducing smoking as long as the focus was on reducing smoking by minors. When the staff was polled about who wanted to work on substance abuse issues, only four of thirty-one volunteered to do so.

The foundation's early grant making reflects its initial reticence. The first tobacco control grant, awarded in 1991, was a relatively small one to reduce teenage smoking in four communities. The next grant, awarded the following year, was given to Stanford University to coordinate a research program on tobacco policies. From these beginnings, the foundation became increasingly emboldened and, over the decade, developed a five-part strategy to reduce tobacco use. The components of the strategy were research to understand effective policy interventions; advocacy aimed at counteracting the tobacco industry's influence on children and bringing about policy change; development and dissemination of tobacco-cessation standards; demonstration programs; and communications activities.

Policy research. The Robert Wood Johnson Foundation, which does not fund basic or clinical research, built on its history of funding social sciences research to develop a new field of tobacco policy research. The foundation funded the Tobacco Policy Research and Evaluation Program, the Substance Abuse Policy Research Program, the Research Network on the Etiology of Tobacco Dependence, and the Bridging the Gap program. These research programs looked at tobacco addiction and how to overcome it from different angles. The research disclosed, for example, that raising the price of cigarettes would cut down the number of youthful smokers and that nicotine had many of the attributes of a drug. This kind of policy-oriented research provided the basis for legislation (for example, excise taxes on cigarettes and clean-air ordinances) and government regulation (such as the Food and Drug Administration's attempt to regulate cigarettes as a device that passed a drug—nicotine—to people). In addition, the foundation's funding attracted a corps of highly skilled researchers who focused their efforts on tobacco policy. The foundation also awarded a series of grants to establish and maintain the National Center on Addiction and Substance Abuse at Columbia University; under the leadership of former Health, Education, and Welfare secretary Joseph Califano, the center conducted research—some of it involving addiction to nicotine—that it used to promote policy change.

Advocacy and policy change. Although direct advocacy is not a strategy employed frequently by foundations, the Robert Wood Johnson Foundation developed two major national programs—SmokeLess States and the National

Center for Tobacco-Free Kids—whose purpose was advocacy and policy change. SmokeLess States, which the foundation first authorized in 1993, became one of its largest programs. With the American Medical Association serving as the national program office, SmokeLess States financed the work of state coalitions seeking to bring about policy changes, such as increasing the tax on cigarettes or banning smoking in restaurants. In mounting this program, the foundation had to be keenly aware of the laws regulating lobbying and to be vigilant in assuring that it and its grantees were always on the right side of the line. As the two foundation officials who oversaw the program concluded, advocacy can be an effective way to improve health, yet it is messy and time-consuming and requires astute legal assistance and strong leadership.[3]

In 1996 the foundation funded the establishment of the National Center for Tobacco-Free Kids as an advocacy organization, based in Washington, D.C., that would serve as a policy counterweight to the Tobacco Institute. By 1999 the National Center for Tobacco-Free Kids had launched the highly visible Campaign for Tobacco-Free Kids, developed alliances with more than a hundred health, education, civic, and religious organizations dedicated to reducing tobacco use among children, and sponsored what has become the annual Kick Butts Day. Perhaps most noticeably, the center became a key player in trying (unsuccessfully) to broker an agreement among public health advocates, state governments, and the tobacco industry in the negotiations over the Master Settlement Agreement.

Tobacco-cessation standards. Research in the tobacco policy field in the 1990s had shown the benefits of a combination of pharmaceuticals and counseling in helping smokers to quit. Building on this, and the work of the federal Agency for Health Care Policy and Research (now the Agency for Health Care Research and Quality), the foundation funded conferences and publications to promote the development of federal smoking-cessation standards. The government adopted these guidelines, known as the five As (ask, advise, assess, assist, arrange), and the foundation provided funds to give the five As wide publicity. To make the guidelines a regular part of medical practice, the foundation gave a grant to the National Committee for Quality Assurance to incorporate smoking cessation into its Health Plan Employer Data and Information Set, which many large companies use in selecting health plans for their employees. The standards were adopted in 1996.

Demonstration programs. To put the research on tobacco cessation into practice, the foundation funded a program called Addressing Tobacco in Managed Care. This program, launched in 1997, tested different approaches to introducing the five As into visits to physicians in managed care practice. Complementing the effort to incorporate smoking cessation into standard managed care

---

3. Gerlach and Larkin (2005).

practice is the foundation's Smoke-Free Families program, which looks at different approaches to reduce smoking among pregnant, low-income women.

Communications activities. Beyond these initiatives, the foundation used a number of tools to catalyze the field and help coordinate its activities: funding conferences, bringing people together, providing advice, promoting the activities of advocates, and engaging in a wide variety of communications and public information activities, including support of the PRISM awards, given by the Entertainment Industry Council to its members for outstanding contributions in accurately depicting substance abuse and addiction. The foundation's president was a visible spokesman on the subject of tobacco control. Recognizing the influence of athletes on young people, the foundation developed a partnership with Major League Baseball to reduce ballplayers' reliance on chewing tobacco.

Behavioral change comes slowly and only with great difficulty. The change in behavior that resulted in the steady drop in the number of Americans who smoke is a remarkable public health victory, and the Robert Wood Johnson Foundation is widely considered to have played an important role in it. While the foundation's approach developed in a piecemeal fashion, it has the elements of a grand strategy. Reviewing its work in tobacco control, James Bornemeier, a writer in the health care field, concludes that "seen in retrospect, [the Foundation's strategy] could rightfully be held up as a model—blending policy research, state-based advocacy and coalition building, and a national communications and strategic command center—for others seeking social change against formidable odds."[4]

Assessing Performance at the Robert Wood Johnson Foundation

Given the interest of the Robert Wood Johnson Foundation in identifying ideas that may serve as models to improve health and health care, it is not surprising that evaluation emerged as a central feature of its approach to grant making over the years. The foundation came of age in the 1970s, a time of ferment in the area of social science research when the field of public policy analysis was emerging. The purpose of public policy analysis is to subject social interventions in the public arena to careful testing analogous to scientific or clinical trials. In the 1970s, for example, the federal government financed a range of "social experiments" that tested new ideas in welfare reform, national health insurance models, and workforce training.

Throughout the 1970s and 1980s, the Robert Wood Johnson Foundation invested consistently in evaluations of most of its multisite demonstrations to develop evidence about the success and failure of each initiative. In the 1990s, however, interest in performance assessment evolved as the foundation's trustees explored a number of questions:

4. Bornemeier (2005).

—What impact is the foundation having?

—How does the foundation know whether it is making progress toward a specific grant-making objective?

—Are the programs supported by the foundation logical and appropriately selected?

—How does the foundation know whether it is effective as an organization?

—Is the foundation treating grantees and staff effectively and fairly?

—Are the activities the foundation funds actually helping people?

This interest in assessing the outcomes of foundation-funded programs led to an expansion of evaluative activities and the development of a family of evaluation efforts, including program evaluations that measure the impact of specific programs; performance indicators that track progress toward broad objectives; a "balanced scorecard" that reviews the impact and effectiveness of the organization; and publications and web-based series that examine the foundation's strategies and programs and what they have and have not accomplished.

Measuring the Impact of Specific Programs

When a foundation-funded national program tests a new idea or innovation, the foundation often funds a program evaluation in addition to the program itself. It awards a grant to an outside team of experts—often one situated in a university or an independent research team—to conduct a rigorous, objective evaluation. The expectation is that at the end of the initiative, the evaluation team can present evidence showing whether the program achieved an outcome of interest and explain why (or why not).

Program evaluations also look at implementation issues to learn why outcomes are achieved or not achieved and to document how the grantee goes about working on the initiative. Implementation analysis sometimes can help grantees midstream; but most important, they create a road map of dos and don'ts that can help in the replication of successful programs.

Program evaluations at the Robert Wood Johnson Foundation use social science and epidemiological research design concepts to assess whether an outcome of interest occurs through a program supported by the foundation. At the heart of program evaluation is comparison: whenever possible, the evaluation team compares outcomes in sites supported by the foundation with those in similar sites not supported by the foundation. In the ideal program evaluation, either random assignment or some other mechanism is used to ensure that the comparison sites are as similar as possible to the foundation-supported sites.

Over the years, the foundation has learned how difficult it is to mount believable and practical evaluations in the real world. The perfect evaluation design is generally elusive, and second-best strategies for selecting comparison groups and measuring outcomes are often necessary. Even with the best of intentions, national programs tend to evolve over time as priorities change, expected outcomes are revised, or grantees shift their focus. Interpersonal tensions can complicate the evaluation process, and the burden on grantees and program staff to meet the needs of evaluators is frequently more difficult than projected at the start. Often, the findings that emerge are tentative or inconclusive or are reported too late to influence decisions about next steps in grant making.

Evaluations do, however, result in learning, and having an external, independent team measuring outcomes keeps the learning process honest. It would be easy for a foundation's program staff and its grantees to become overly invested in a program and reluctant to admit that it has not achieved the outcome desired. Moreover, when an intervention is successful, the presence of an independent evaluation team offers credibility among audiences considering replication.

Tracking the Progress toward Broad Objectives

While program evaluations can assess success and failure of specific program investments, trustees, staff, and the public often want to know what impact the foundation's grant making is having in a specific area. For example, when the foundation sets an objective such as reducing tobacco use, people will want to know whether smoking rates have gone down and what contribution the foundation's programs have made to the decline.

As discussed earlier, the Robert Wood Johnson Foundation has developed an impact framework to guide each area of its grant making. In the case of health insurance coverage, for example, the objective is enactment of a national policy ensuring stable and affordable coverage for all by 2010; in the case of disparities, it is to reduce by 50 percent racial and ethnic disparities in cardiovascular disease, diabetes, and depression in ten to twelve health care plans.

The performance measurement system is designed to track progress toward these kinds of long-term objectives, as well as short- and medium-term objectives set by the relevant team of staff members and approved by senior management and the board of trustees. Senior management and the board use the performance measurement system to assess the progress of each of the grant-making portfolios. The performance measures serve as signposts that help the staff and the board assess whether positive change is likely or not likely to occur over the long term. If short- and medium-term targets are not met, it is an indication that the long-term objectives are unlikely to be met as well. The assessment of short- and medium-term objectives can lead to an alteration in the strategy (and the logic model guiding it) or perhaps a reconsideration of the feasibility of reaching the ultimate goal.

The performance measurement process is difficult. It is challenging to identify tangible targets that can be measured and may actually change in the short or intermediate run but do not seem trivial. Sometimes the targets are process measures (for example, fielding a set of grants or convening key players), and sometimes the targets are intermediate outcomes. In managing the process, there is constant concern that focusing on measurable outcomes could lead the foundation to address less important (though more easily measurable) problems or to adopt less risky program strategies. The board, however, recognizes the importance of intangible goals and keeps them in mind even as it reviews quantitative indicators of progress. Of course, even if the targets are met, it does not prove that the foundation-supported activities are the primary cause of the social change.

Assessing Organizational Effectiveness

In developing its balanced scorecard, the foundation adapted a concept developed by Harvard Business School professor Robert S. Kaplan and businessman David P. Norton to develop strategies and measure performance in the business world. Typically, in the business sector these dimensions include financial strategies, internal business, innovation and learning, and customers. The Robert Wood Johnson Foundation, whose bottom line is social change rather than profitability, translated these dimensions into program impact, program development, customer (that is, grantee) service, and financial and human capital. The scorecard, presented to the staff in the spring and to the board in July, elaborates on each dimension:

—The impact section considers whether the foundation is achieving the goals it set for itself in each portfolio and program area.

—The program development section considers whether the foundation is working in areas that its key constituencies (for example, grantees, government decisionmakers, the general public, and foundation staff) think are important.

—The customer service section considers how grantees view the foundation.

—The financial performance section reviews the state of the endowment, and the employee survey measures the staff's satisfaction with the foundation as a place to work.

Over the years, the foundation has developed measures that support each section of the scorecard. The staff commissions surveys of grantees, staff members, decisionmakers, and public opinion. It summarizes the results of performance indicators as a measure of impact. Finally, it reviews data from the foundation's internal grant management system to see how many applications are coming in, how many are being funded, and how the results are being disseminated.

The scorecard helps the Robert Wood Johnson Foundation in many ways. It creates a time for formal reflection on the organization's performance. It provides staff members and trustees with a forum for identifying areas for follow-up and discussing how this follow-up will occur. It engages the foundation's trustees in meaningful discussion of foundation accountability.

Providing Programmatic Accountability

In 1996 the foundation's director of evaluation and the director of communications initiated a series of products that would tell the stories of how grantees went about using the funds awarded to them, what they accomplished, when they failed, and what lessons emerged from programs and portfolios of investments.

The Grant Results reports document what happened under specific grants or national programs. The reports describe the problem addressed, objectives and strategies adopted by the foundation, results, communications efforts, and post-grant activities. Most reports include a bibliography. To date, nearly two thousand reports have been prepared and posted on the foundation's website. The Grant Results section of the website is the second most visited area of the site, after guidelines for applying for grants.

The second set of products to assess grantee activities is *The Robert Wood Johnson Anthology* (the formal name of the book is *To Improve Health and Health Care: The Robert Wood Johnson Foundation Anthology*). Published annually by Jossey-Bass, the book contains ten to twelve chapters written by noted journalists, program evaluators, or foundation staff members. Each chapter provides an examination of an area of grant making—sometimes a number of grants addressing a specific issue and sometimes an individual grant or program. Anthology authors sift through the written record, interview key players, visit sites, and make an informed judgment about what the program or programs accomplished and what lessons can be drawn. They are asked to write an interesting, jargon-free chapter—one that a person interested in the subject, but not expert in it, will understand and appreciate. The foundation distributes the book to approximately ten thousand health care experts, foundation staff members and trustees, and government officials and places the chapters on its website.

Taken as a whole, the anthology series, the Grant Results reports, and publications that emerge from foundation-funded evaluators (their reports are also available on the foundation's website) offer an extensive record of the foundation's successes and failures. Serving as a guide to policymakers, health care leaders, researchers, foundation staff members, and the general public, they represent one way in which the foundation tries to be accountable and transparent.

Conclusion

The Robert Wood Johnson Foundation has been steadfast in pursuit of its mission to improve the health and health care of all Americans and has used a variety of strategies to accomplish that goal. For the first twenty years or so of its life, the foundation concentrated on the health care side of its mission by working to expand access to ambulatory care, improve quality of care, strengthen health policy research, and improve the health care workforce. These all remain important priorities, and their echoes can be heard currently in the foundation's strategic objectives. Although it took some steps—through its community-based anti–substance abuse programs—to improve health in the 1980s, the foundation began seriously looking at the health side of its mission in the 1990s. It was able to do this, in part, because the endowment was higher and its traditional health care programs were not threatened. Thus in the 1990s the foundation was able to mount initiatives aimed at reversing people's unhealthy behaviors such as smoking, drug addiction, and lack of exercise. In the past ten years, with the commitment to both health and health care ingrained in the foundation, the organization's leadership developed an impact framework to give coherence to the foundation's programming and allow results to be more easily measured.

The evolution of the Robert Wood Johnson Foundation's strategic priorities reflects both the leadership within and the environment outside of the foundation. While the foundation is always guided by its mission, the paths that lead to attaining the mission—its strategic priorities—have been heavily influenced by its presidents. David Rogers, the president from 1972 through 1986, focused largely on out-of-hospital medical care; improving services, research, and human resources; and working with the academic medical community. Leighton Cluff (1986–90) broadened the focus to incorporate community-based anti–substance abuse programs, AIDS treatment, and mental health services. Steven Schroeder (1991–2002) took the foundation in the direction of reducing tobacco use, improving care of terminally ill patients, and improving generalist medicine; he reorganized the foundation into health and health care divisions. Risa Lavizzo-Mourey, who became president in 2003, developed an impact framework to guide the foundation's grant making; within that framework, the foundation has made substantial commitments to reducing obesity in children, strengthening the public health system, improving quality of care, and reducing racial and ethnic disparities.

As important as, and perhaps more important than, the foundation's leadership, the institution's grant making has been influenced by the nation's health and social environments. Working within a trillion-dollar-plus health economy, this almost has to be the case. Some of its most successful initiatives have resulted from the foundation's sensing an emerging field or social trend, homing in on it, and helping to shape its development. Tobacco is one example. End-of-life care is another. In the mid-1970s the case of Karen Ann Quinlan, a comatose young woman being "kept alive" by feeding tubes, gave national attention to an issue that had been percolating below the surface for a while. The growth of organizations such as the Society for the Right to Die and the Hemlock Society, along with the rise of the hospice movement, the publicity given to Jack

Kevorkian, the writings of more mainstream physicians such as Timothy Quill, and the Supreme Court's 1986 decision in the Nancy Cruzan case (another young woman in a persistent vegetative state who was being sustained artificially) gave increased prominence to the question of whether a person could refuse medical treatment even if it meant his or her own death.

When a foundation-funded research study called SUPPORT concluded, in 1994, that the wishes of terminally ill patients and their families were routinely ignored, the foundation's leadership decided to make a substantial investment into improving the treatment people received (or chose not to receive) toward the end of their lives. It made grants to establish a network of hospital-based palliative care centers, to rewrite medical and nursing textbooks, to publish series on care of the dying in medical and nursing journals, and to create a national coalition of activists—all of which led the *New York Times* to conclude that the work of the Robert Wood Johnson Foundation and the Soros Foundation "demonstrates the growing power of philanthropy almost to create an academic field."[5]

In other cases, too, such as emergency medical systems, tobacco control, and managed care, the foundation has been ahead of the curve and has helped shape the development of an emerging area. However, this is not always the case. Despite many years of commitment to increasing the number of physicians in generalist practice, there has been little progress. And notwithstanding a consistent record since 1972 of programs aimed at reducing the number of uninsured Americans, their number keeps rising. In cases such as these, even though the societal wind is not at its back, the foundation maintains its commitment—as a matter of principle and in the hope that society will catch up with it.

5. Judith Miller, "When Foundations Chime In, the Issue of Dying Comes to Life," *New York Times*, November 22, 1997.

8

Foundations and Social Welfare in the Twentieth Century

WOLFGANG BIELEFELD AND JANE CHU

Foundations have been involved with a diverse group of programs and services referred to by a variety of terms, including *social welfare services, welfare services, social services,* and *human services.* The term *social welfare* has been the most widely used over the twentieth century, although its specific definition has varied over that time period, and its use has recently waned in some contexts. Social welfare has been an important focus for American foundations since the initial establishment of this organizational form.

Definitions of *social welfare* vary. Relatively narrow definitions usually equate social welfare with services to the poor or needy. For example, Gerald Handel notes that social welfare is a term "used by a relatively small number of people: government officials, social planners, social workers, social scientists, and others who work to understand and solve problems of poverty and other social problems."[1] Broader definitions have also been offered, however, such as Phyllis Day's: "American social welfare is the social institution that provides society's sum total of all goods and services to enhance the social and economic well-being of society's members or to ensure their conformity to current societal norms, standards, and ideologies."[2]

The diversity of services at issue and the various definitions of what should or should not be included in a given categorical scheme pose substantial challenges

1. Handel (1982, pp. 4–5).
2. Day (1997, p. 35).

for policymakers, analysts, and those seeking to provide services. In general, however, it is acknowledged that both the public and the for-profit (market) sector are major contributors to the social welfare status of society. The nonprofit sector's activities on behalf of social welfare have generally been seen as carried out in relation and reaction to the other sectors.[3]

This is clearly displayed in the case of American foundations. Social conditions at the turn of the twentieth century and concerns for social welfare were central to the early establishment of the foundation as well as its subsequent development. The foundation as a legally and operationally distinct organizational form appeared at a particularly turbulent point in time in the history of the United States. The provision of social welfare in response to this turbulence was an important rationale given for the establishment of the foundation form in the early twentieth century. The conditions of the time demanded institutional solutions to social problems.[4]

The importance of founding conditions has long been recognized by organizational theorists. The events surrounding the creation of new organizations and forms have a lasting effect on their subsequent development.[5] According to Richard Scott, "New organizational forms are constrained by conditions present in the environment (material and institutional) at the time of their founding. Because they confront similar circumstances, organizational cohorts arising during a given period tend to exhibit similar structural features."[6]

At the turn of the twentieth century, problems resulting from urbanization and unregulated industrialization combined with great fortunes and corporate wealth led to the establishment of a new environmental niche, which foundations came to fill.[7] In addition, societal and business norms and values at the time established the institutional expectations for foundations' approach to social welfare. The result was the rapid establishment of a new set of organizations with distinct ideas about their role in the provision of social welfare services.

Moreover, once an organizational form is established it may persist because of a competitive advantage over alternatives or in response to "traditionalizing forces," including vested interests or institutionalization. The latter will infuse structures and routines with values and legitimacy, thereby making them resistant to change.[8] This pattern can be seen in foundations, as well. While foundation involvement with social welfare changed with changes in the American society, polity, and economy, their basic underlying orientation to social welfare

3. Gronbjerg and Salamon (2002).
4. Zucker and Kreft (1994, p. 295).
5. Stinchcombe (1965).
6. R. Scott (2003, p. 171).
7. Aldrich (1999).
8. R. Scott (2003, p. 172).

remained consistent. This orientation has led foundations to play particular roles in the provision of social welfare; while these roles have been carried out in a variety of ways, the roles themselves have been maintained.

A number of approaches to the provision of social welfare can be distinguished. An institutional (strong government) perspective holds that every person in society has the right to its services, through universal programs.[9] Alternatively, conflict perspectives (such as Marxism, socialism, and feminism) see recalcitrant social structures and the conflict between social groups as the source of social problems, with social welfare as one aspect of the struggle.[10] Finally, a residual perspective holds that people are responsible for themselves, and aid should be given only in emergency situations, when other social institutions fail, on a short-term basis, and as a stopgap measure until "normal" social institutions respond. An examination of foundation roles and impacts shows that, for the most part, foundations have operated with such a residual perspective on social welfare.

This orientation has led foundations to focus on particular roles in relation to social welfare. They have tended to rely on other institutions (the family, church or synagogue, social work, government, and so on) to directly address the needs of the disadvantaged. That being the case, their limited role in the provision of direct aid can be characterized as complementary. With this outlook, they have provided assistance to particular groups that they have identified as underserved by other institutions.

Their major outlook on social welfare can be characterized as philanthropic—a focus on what is perceived as larger or more general social issues. Foundations have primarily seen themselves as social innovators, developing or promoting new, experimental, or entrepreneurial approaches to the issues of concern to them. They have pursued this role through their own programs, through funding, and by establishing new partnerships or relationships for this purpose. As part of this, foundations have sought to respond to new social issues and problems as they arose over time. They have also at particular times played advocacy roles, promoting social or policy changes on behalf of the constituencies they have identified with.

These roles have been played out with a tremendous amount of diversity and with changes over time. The limited research that has been done has found that foundation funding for human services is highly fragmented. Kirsten Gronbjerg concludes from a study of funders in Chicago that funders "differ in how they focus their efforts, structure their grantmaking, modify priorities and grant structures, and select agencies to fund. . . . The portrait of philanthropic funders

9. Day (1997, pp. 36–41).
10. For example, Piven and Cloward (1993).

that emerges suggests we should not expect coherent and coordinated responses by philanthropic funders to major developments in the human services field."[11]

We also discovered this fragmentation and diversity. Our goal, consequently, was not to arrive at a single conclusion regarding foundations and social welfare but to provide a historical framework within which to locate the variety we found. Even in this task it will be necessary to limit the discussion. A detailed analysis of the historical evolution of foundation involvement in all the types of services considered under the umbrella of social welfare is beyond the scope of one chapter. To delineate the study and attain as much consistency as possible we focused on the particular types of services contained in the Human Service category of the most prominent classification system of nonprofits used today, the National Taxonomy of Exempt Entities. The categories covered by this rubric include children and youth services, family services, personal social services, emergency assistance, residential care, and services to support the independence of specific populations. Examples of particular services include adoption and foster care support, services to keep families together and support healthy family development (such as parenting education), homeless services, and homes and services for the aged or disabled.

As we examined the data on foundation giving to social welfare, two general patterns emerged. One is that the percentage of grants given to social welfare has remained quite consistent over the course of the twentieth century. We drew data from a wide variety of sources. The data did not allow us to tabulate total social welfare funding by all foundations in a given year (those data are not available). Within the data sets that are available, however, the percentage of grant dollars given to social welfare has averaged 15.8 percent. Two notable deviations are seen in the data. Over the 1960s, the percentage averaged 11.1 percent, and over the 1980s, 25.1 percent. These deviations reflect shifts in the priority foundations gave social welfare during these periods.

The second pattern is that the percentage given to social welfare varies systematically with foundation size, with smaller foundations giving proportionately more to social welfare. Information from the 1960 *Foundation Directory* indicates that the percentage going to social welfare was twice as high for foundations of intermediate size as for the largest foundations and almost three times as high for the smallest foundations. In addition, the percentage of grant dollars going to social welfare was decreasing for large foundations, while it was increasing for intermediate and small foundations. In the discussion that follows, we consider primarily the largest foundations. While these large foundations dominate the financial dimensions of foundation activity, their priorities cannot be seen as representing those of smaller foundations.

11. Gronbjerg (2004, p. 253).

The Social Welfare Basis of Foundation Formation

The period from the late 1870s to 1920 was a time of momentous changes that laid the groundwork for the modern era. These changes were inextricably bound up with social welfare. During this period, social conditions were turbulent, and the problems of uncontrolled urbanization and industrialization became apparent. Great extremes of need and wealth were found.[12] The rise in power of industrialists and the unregulated operations of large corporations brought a sharp response. Peter Hall notes that "by the 1880s, groups of urban workers, intellectuals, farmers, and small businessmen in the South and West began organizing a coherent political opposition. Focusing first on national fiscal policy including hostility to big business and its cultural components, it became widespread."[13]

Coming at a time when Bolshevism and socialism were spreading in Europe, anticapitalist radicals and strikes in the United States were viewed with alarm by the press and business community. In response, the latter developed an approach that Hall calls "the private-sector alternative to socialism."[14] Not willing to adopt the European solution to social welfare problems (government intervention in the economy), the private sector solution in the United States entailed the fundamental tenet that to deal with the inequality of conditions that capitalism can create, social justice should come through the actions of the private sector, assisted, but not directed, by government. This led to two closely related major philanthropy initiatives from the business community: that firms themselves, in addition to functioning efficiently, should support the public good, in part, at least, by giving to nonprofit organizations and establishing corporate foundations—what has come to be called welfare capitalism; and that the philanthropy of the wealthy should be used to address social problems, particularly to prevent them, through the use of charitable foundations. These developments augmented the preexisting provision of social welfare by earlier foundations and foundation-like institutions.

Early Foundations and Social Welfare

Reports on grant distribution of foundations established before 1920 were intermittent. Of the 149 foundations created before 1920 that were listed in the Russell Sage Foundation's 1946 directory of American foundations, more than half (52 percent) provided no information on either assets or grants. Following initial legal establishment, some foundations took time to develop their mission

12. Landon (1986, pp. 89–90).
13. Hall (1987, p. 9).
14. Hall (1987, p. 11).

statements and guidelines before making grants. Additionally, foundations did not generally produce annual reports until after the implementation of the Tax Reform Act of 1969. A few foundations tracked their grant distributions in retrospect, combining the amounts over twenty to forty years.[15]

Some general patterns of foundations' giving to the field of social welfare in the early decades of the twentieth century can nevertheless be identified. In a classification of 335 foundations in the Harrison and Andrews directory, 45 foundations established before 1920 identified themselves as interested in social welfare, child welfare, or family welfare.[16] In addition, 13 foundations established before 1920 with assets of $1 million or more focused the bulk of their giving on subjects such as health and education, giving proportionately smaller grants to social welfare causes. Those foundations that contributed a greater proportion to social welfare directed their dollars to general causes. For example, the New York Foundation applied its grant dollars to "altruistic, charitable and benevolent purposes." The Nathan Hofheimer Foundation promoted "the improvement of living conditions of unfortunate persons by research and publications as well as by the establishment of benevolent activities and agencies."[17]

Eduard Lindeman, in his 1936 study of one hundred foundations and community trusts, reports that between 1921 and 1930 the fields of education, health, and social welfare consistently received the largest contributions from foundations. Education ranked highest, averaging 43 percent of the total grants made to all fields. Health grants ranked a close second, with an average of 33 percent of the total grants made. The social welfare category ranked a more distant third, averaging 14 percent of contributions to all fields.[18]

The Development of Foundation Roles

In the social welfare field, before 1900 foundations tended to focus on direct giving for relief assistance. For example, the goal of the Magdalen Society of Philadelphia, formed early in the nineteenth century, was to help "wayward" females.[19] Several early twentieth-century foundations (especially those established by Carnegie, Rockefeller, Elizabeth Milbank Anderson, Margaret Olivia Sage, and Julius Rosenwald) insisted that they were introducing new approaches. Direct donations to the poor decreased. Efforts to leverage grants to better conditions for the future increased. In addition to mitigating public distrust of government, foundations moved to streamline and standardize grant-making

15. Harrison and Andrews (1946, pp. 103–85)
16. Harrison and Andrews (1946, p. 186).
17. Harrison and Andrews (1946, pp. 140, 158, 169).
18. Lindeman (1936, p. 21).
19. Harrison and Andrews (1946, p. 17).

processes in response to the barrage of requests. And as government increased its social welfare role, foundations decided not to duplicate government efforts.

Studies of early twentieth-century foundations reveal flexible and shifting grant-making policies, with foundations adapting to ongoing societal changes.[20] Foundations adopted very general mission statements, intentionally crafted with broad, sweeping statements rather than narrow guidelines. For example, the Commonwealth Fund was established in 1918 "to do something for the welfare of mankind." The Rockefeller Foundation was established in 1913 "to enrich and sustain the lives and livelihoods of poor and excluded people throughout the world."[21]

However, in spite of these broad mission statements, Harold Coffman notes, larger foundations that started out giving to general purposes soon moved toward specific projects. The newer foundations made grants to fewer projects but in larger dollar amounts. Rather than commit operating dollars to specific social welfare projects in perpetuity, many large grants now went for a specific purpose, with funds provided between stated beginning and ending dates.[22]

Many foundations saw the value of grants in helping launch new activities but discouraged an agency from becoming financially dependent on grants for financial sustainability. Robert de Forest, the vice president of the Russell Sage Foundation board of trustees, advocated for one-year grants with no commitment for renewal, encouraging grant recipients to become self-sustaining. At a public dinner in 1908, de Forest reiterated that "the Foundation's policy in assisting a new 'cause' was not to 'support' it but to win its own support. Otherwise it would be pretty well demonstrated that this particular machine was not worth starting."[23]

Even when foundations focused their grant guidelines on specific projects, they maintained the flexibility to build into their funding priorities the pressing social concerns of the day. The Carnegie Hero Fund Commission, created in 1904 to honor heroic, life-saving acts by individuals, also appropriated funds for disaster relief for those injured in tragic accidents.[24] The Milbank Memorial Fund's overall emphasis on health evolved from early projects with a bent

---

20. Coffman (1936); Harrison and Andrews (1946).

21. Coffman (1936, p. 36).

22. Coffman (1936).

23. Quoted in Glenn, Brandt, and Andrews (1947, p. 45). In practice, however, the Russell Sage Foundation committed most of its funds to quasi-permanent efforts—its own extensive policy research and consultation activities; the organizational infrastructure for the new profession of social work including its many specialties; the Regional Plan of New York; and others. See Hammack and Wheeler (1994).

24. Carnegie Hero Fund Commission (1907, p. 11).

toward welfare of the poor (1905 to 1921) to health advocacy demonstrations and emphasis on general public welfare in the 1920s.[25]

Finally, foundations began to expand their methods of grant making. While more than 75 percent of grants were made to outside agencies, foundation directory data show an alternative approach to disbursing grants through the creation and operation of programs within the foundation. By 1930–31 between 37 and 42 percent of foundations made grants to support the operations of their own internal programs directed toward their selected field of interest, in addition to funding outside agencies.[26] Foundation trustees believed there could be a greater impact if their internal staff operated the service programs. The J. C. Penney Foundation moved from solely giving donations to outside charities to development of its own vocational guidance project.[27] By 1931 the J. C. Penney Foundation had assigned an employee to run the guidance program as its vocational director.[28] Originating with its founding in 1907, the Russell Sage Foundation began to extend its method of making grants to external social service agencies to include operation of internal programs under a social service wing of the foundation. By 1909 the foundation had created three internal departments, with dedicated foundation staff, developed from external programs previously funded.[29]

Notable Trends

In many ways, foundations had a blank canvas in 1900 because they had relatively few well-known precedents and because several states gave them wide latitude. This combination of circumstances encouraged both entrepreneurship and experimentation. As long as they were giving for good public causes, foundations could be flexible and creative in how and to whom they made grants. And foundation dollars could have a substantial impact on specific and targeted projects.

As foundations increased in size and number, more also moved from being charitable to philanthropic—that is, seeking to create new institutions, transform old ones, and promote more effective practices and government policies rather than directly subsidizing the mission of immediate aid. The Russell Sage Foundation's philanthropic approach was demonstrated through its internal operating activities, with a focus on ameliorating the living conditions of the poor, professionalizing the social service sector, and increasing the awareness of underrepresented children. By tackling deteriorating living conditions, the foundation understood that other welfare issues would also improve. Tenement

25. Coffman (1936, p. 61); Andrews (1956, p. 159); Fox (2006b, p. 5).

26. Clark (1931, 1932).

27. Coffman (1936, p. 56).

28. Clark (1932, p. 38).

29. Glenn, Brandt, and Andrews (1947, p. 63).

houses were constructed and refurbished. Education was provided for landlords and tenants. By supporting the publication of a journal on social work, the Sage Foundation was able to inform the public of current social welfare conditions and unify the field of social work. Schools for training social workers in Boston, Chicago, St. Louis, and New York were supported by the foundation, strengthening the teaching staff and educational curriculum. Through the use of research materials and sector conferences, the foundation called attention to the plight of children who were neglected or delinquent. By studying 1,350 orphan homes across the nation, Sage was able to assess and shed light on inconsistent operational standards. Having become nationally recognized for its expertise in children's issues, the Russell Sage Foundation participated in the 1909 White House Conference on the Care of Dependent Children, laying the framework for future resolutions to improve child welfare.[30]

To the extent that their orientation was to the provision of aid, most foundations adhered to a residual orientation toward social welfare, supporting causes that were complementary to what government was doing in the same area without replicating or partnering with government. They looked for areas in social welfare where government did not go.

Foundations in the Great Depression

The Great Depression had profound implications for social welfare. Responses to the Depression were seen in both the public and private sectors. The public sector, especially, underwent significant and lasting change as the crisis ushered in the beginnings of the welfare state in America.

Private local nonprofits undertook to meet the needs of the jobless. Their efforts were, however, woefully inadequate, since most of them did not provide the basic services needed by the newly poor, their combined resources were insufficient to meet the huge needs, and their own funding from philanthropic sources decreased drastically.[31]

Through the early years of the Depression, the federal government was slow to respond, primarily owing to Hoover's opposition to the provision of widespread federal aid (preferring private aid). States, however, did respond in many cases. Nevertheless, as Walter Trattner notes, "as a result of federal inaction, by the fall of 1932, the nation faced a serious threat. Disorder spread and talk of revolution was heard. . . . Then came the federal election—a decisive popular rejection of many of Hoover's conservative shibboleths."[32] Franklin D. Roosevelt's ideal that

30. Glenn, Brandt, and Andrews (1947).
31. Trattner (1999, p. 273).
32. Trattner (1999, p. 280).

in a civilized society "public assistance was not a matter of charity but a matter of justice that rested upon the individual's right to a minimum standard of living" led to an unprecedented expansion of the federal government into social welfare and its provision of major aid and social welfare programs.[33]

Pattern of Foundation Funding for Social Welfare

According to David Hammack, "Philanthropists and their organizations, especially the new foundations and federated fund-raising agencies like the Community Chest, strongly resisted the expansion of federal authority."[34] Moreover, during the Depression foundations did not change the focus they had developed earlier. Hammack concludes that American's wealthiest donors maintained their "devotion to individual responsibility and self-help and to what they viewed as universal values." Their mission was to "promote science, scientific standards, and professional values as well as opportunity and personal responsibility" while seeking "to limit the power of federal regulations and of federal officials."[35]

As in the previous decade, foundation grants to social welfare issues in the 1930s ranked third behind those for health and education. At the same time, however, the Great Depression induced foundations to increase their grants to social welfare. Analyses by the Twentieth Century Fund and Raymond Rich Associates, however, reveal that during the height of the Depression years (1929–35) foundation grant dollars to health and education proportionately decreased while grants to social welfare increased.[36] The Twentieth Century Fund also notes an increase in the field of social sciences between 1930 and 1934, suggesting foundation interest in studying projects that addressed social problems. The same interest in the social sciences began to wane by 1937, after the height of the Depression.[37]

Early community foundations, with their focus on local community issues, were consistently responsive to social welfare concerns. Community foundations in the 1930s designated from 42 to 54 percent of their total grants to address social welfare issues.[38] Community foundations mirrored private foundations by shoring up the systems that surrounded the social welfare causes, and they provoked interest in research of social welfare issues. The Committee of the Permanent Charity Fund, later known as the Boston Foundation, worked to professionalize social agencies by strengthening their internal operational infrastructure and coordinating community agencies to reduce duplication of social

33. Trattner (1999, p. 281).
34. Hammack (2003, p. 269).
35. Hammack (2003, p. 280).
36. Clark (1931, 1932, 1935); Seybold (1939).
37. Clark (1931, 1932).
38. Clark (1935, 1931); Seybold (1939).

services.[39] In addition to directly supporting social welfare programs, the Cleveland Foundation published in 1939 a directory of social agencies to inform the community of the scope of work being done and encourage collaboration and the reduction of duplicative services.

Notable Trends

Coffman's 1936 study of American foundations supporting the child welfare field uncovered a diversity of approaches to giving. The first involved providing support to services that directly affected children, particularly in the areas of health, relief, recreation, and leadership training. Lesser giving focused on special needs, such as "crippled" children and child labor issues. Second, foundation grants encouraged collaborations among agencies working in the child welfare field. Partnership services allowed child welfare services to consolidate information. Third, foundations began to initiate their own experimental projects and leadership programs through grants channeled to organizations, such as the Boy Scouts of America, Camp Fire Girls, the Child Study Association of America, the Child Development Institute, and the New York School of Social Work.[40] Finally, an interest in understanding the issues surrounding child welfare drew foundations to seek advice from specialists in the child welfare field. Universities and other organizations researching the effects of child welfare were sought after for consultations. The Social Science Research Council, comprising seven professional societies, served in an advisory capacity to foundations.[41]

Overall, foundation appropriations for direct relief of welfare issues diminished as government agencies increased allocations for public social service programs. Given their limited resources in comparison with government funding, foundations were reluctant to see their role as the main provider of ongoing welfare services in society.[42]

In addition, their emphasis was shifting from curing social ailments to preventing their expansion. The Magdalen Society of Philadelphia, established in 1800, was formed to directly assist women who were trying to reform from a life of prostitution. By 1918 the society had shifted its focus from providing direct relief, reestablishing itself as the White-Williams Foundation and providing educational scholarships for children and youth in need.[43] The Children's Fund of Michigan, established by Senator James Couzens, extended its focus from direct support of child welfare in Michigan to creating change by leveraging social policy. When the governor of Michigan declined Senator Couzens's request to

39. Keele and Kiger (1984).
40. Coffman (1936, p. 44).
41. Coffman (1936, p. 62).
42. Harrison and Andrews (1946, p. 92).
43. Harrison and Andrews (1946, p. 17).

allocate state funds for the support of children's health welfare, the senator established a public-private partnership by offering to the mayor of Detroit a contribution of up to $1 million, giving one dollar for every ten dollars raised by the
mayor's Emergency Relief Committee. The committee ultimately raised $1 mil-
lion, of which $200,000 was given by the Children's Fund of Michigan.[44]

Over a twenty-five-year span (1930–55), foundations began to direct even
greater support toward research and education, no matter what the field of interest. Those foundations that operated programs began to decrease their internal
relief activities. Immediately after World War II, the Russell Sage Foundation
ended its grants to the organs of the social work profession and to the Regional
Plan of New York. It continued to support studies of philanthropy but now put
its chief emphasis on the development of social science.[45] A decade count by the
foundation directories (*American Foundations and Their Fields*) reveals a decrease
in the number of foundations with internal operating programs. By 1954, partially
owing to the exponential increase in the number of foundations, few were operating their own programs. Five such remained, though their programs were not
necessarily operating in the area of social welfare.[46] These included the Rockefeller
Foundation, the Ford Foundation, the Carnegie Foundation for the Advancement of Teaching, the Josiah Macy Jr. Foundation, and the Trexler Foundation.

Foundations, the War on Poverty, and the Great Society

The post–World War II era was characterized by economic prosperity for the
middle and upper classes. The gross national product rose from $100 billion
in 1940 to $286.5 billion in 1950 and $400 billion in 1960.[47] Real wages grew
2.5 to 3.0 percent a year, and union contracts greatly expanded the pension and
health insurance benefits of production workers.[48] Pent-up demand and deficit
spending fueled the economy. Joel Blau and Mimi Abramovitz conclude that

> by the 1950s and early 1960s, a comfortable feeling of normality had set-
> tled over many homes: work was regular, and there were baby boomers to
> raise. . . . Americans felt secure enough to extend some of the benefits they
> enjoyed to previously excluded racial minorities. This psychology explains,
> in part, the timing of the Great Society. For a brief moment in the mid-
> 1960s, the economy made people feel that giving to others took very little
> away from themselves.[49]

44. Richards and Norton (1957).
45. Rich (1955, p. 459); Hammack and Wheeler (1994).
46. Rich (1955, p. xxviii).
47. Day (1997, p. 310).
48. Blau and Abramowitz (2004, p. 259).
49. Blau and Abramowitz (2004, p. 260).

A number of factors brought about developments in social welfare in the 1960s. As the postwar period proceeded, cautious cold war liberalism was increasingly challenged by a more activist democratic left, which vigorously pushed for additional social programs.[50] Michael Harrington's *The Other America* appeared in 1962. The book was a stark reminder that poverty had not been eliminated and prompted debate both inside and outside government on the causes and responses to poverty.[51] President John F. Kennedy declared the abolition of poverty a major domestic goal and set the stage for the War on Poverty. Legislation and major spending increases followed in the mid-1960s. Significant new programs included food stamps, federal aid to education, Medicaid, and Medicare. Other initiatives included the Office of Economic Opportunity, Head Start, Model Cities, and the Job Corps.

In addition, three significant social movements galvanized public and private actions: the struggle for racial equality, the women's movement, and opposition to the Vietnam War. Besides the specific civil and equal rights legislation at issue in these movements, each also had implications for social welfare. African Americans and Latinos demanded more jobs, housing, and education. The women's movement pushed for more economic independence for women, which, at the same time, implied a greater need for an expanded social welfare safety net. Finally, one of the arguments of the antiwar movement was that the war was draining funding from needed social welfare programs at home.[52]

Government social welfare funding reflected these developments. Between 1965 and 1980, government spending on social welfare showed a pattern of steady and rapid growth. Social welfare spending by all levels of government grew by 637 percent in current and 259 percent in inflation-adjusted dollars, expanding from 11.5 percent to 18.5 percent of gross national product.[53] While most of this expansion was accounted for by Social Security and Medicare, funding was also significantly increased for programs to aid the poor. The expansion of government spending had important impacts on the nonprofit sector. Lester Salamon identifies a broad pattern of government–private sector relationships in the United States, which he terms "third-party government." This is characterized by the use of government-funded nongovernmental entities to carry out governmental purposes.[54] Given this pattern, Salamon notes, "when public aid expanded in the 1960s, it often did so in ways that promoted, rather than displaced, the nonprofit sector."[55] Nonprofit social service providers benefited through contracts with federal agencies to deliver social welfare services.

50. Blau and Abramowitz (2004, p. 262).
51. Harrington (1962).
52. Blau and Abramowitz (2004, p. 265).
53. Salamon (1999, pp. 59–61).
54. Anheier and Salamon (2007, p. 110).
55. Salamon (1999, p. 62).

Pattern of Foundation Funding for Social Welfare

The increase in government funding of social welfare programs, in conjunction with major portions of the War on Poverty and other social policy initiatives, had an influence on the amount of foundation giving to social welfare as reported during the 1960s. A second development, however, made the exact impact of such spending difficult to assess. That development was a major change in how foundation data were gathered and reported. The third edition of the *Foundation Directory*, published in 1967, marked an increase in the level of precision with which foundation grants were tracked by using financial data reported on foundation IRS 990-PF forms. Previously, data were gathered by using foundation annual reports and media clippings. Access to Internal Revenue Service data now allowed the consistent inclusion of many foundations that had been only sporadically included in previous directories.

Although changes in record-keeping in the 1960s disclosed patterns in foundation giving that had previously gone unrecorded, thereby increasing reported funding, overall foundation giving to welfare causes in the 1960s decreased as public funds through government social welfare programs increased. The Foundation Center's 1960 *Foundation Directory* notes that large foundations had reduced the percentage of grant dollars going to social welfare. The directory had this to say about social welfare funding: "From its traditional position among the major three fields of foundation interest, it has now dropped to a minor position. Undoubtedly, the expansion of social security and heavy government intervention in other areas traditionally supported by voluntary welfare services has accelerated this decline."[56] This was echoed in the 1964 edition: "Welfare, like health, has been declining in proportion of foundation grants. Evidence accumulates that the expansion of social security, the private insurances such as Blue Cross, Blue Shield, welfare funds, retirement plans, and increased governmental involvement in relief and similar fields formerly supported largely by voluntary contributions, have accelerated the decline in this area."[57]

Data from the *Foundation Directory* illustrate the priorities of foundations for social welfare funding in 1966. Foundation grants supporting the local Community Chest or United Fund accounted for 38 percent of all funding. Youth agencies received the second-highest amount of funding (17 percent), followed closely by community planning (13 percent), relief and social agencies (8 percent), and interracial relations (8 percent).[58]

56. Foundation Center (1960, p. xxxiii).
57. Foundation Center (1964b, p. 40).
58. Foundation Center (1967).

Top Funders

The Foundation Center compiled an index representing the giving priorities of foundations included in the third edition of the *Foundation Directory*.[59] We identified the top ten funders of social welfare, using information from IRS 990-PF forms and annual reports, and examined in detail the giving of the top five. The top ten funders are shown in table 8-1.

The top five foundations supporting social welfare causes concentrated their efforts on the protection and sustenance of children and youth, notably those from low-income homes, who lacked opportunities for education, physical or mental health care, or constructive family support. From its inception in 1948, the Vincent Astor Foundation reflected a carte blanche approach to giving. Grants were to be used for alleviating human misery. Beyond that, foundation trustees were given the freedom to select the most worthy causes relative to the issues of the day. Still, Astor's penchant for children in need motivated him to make $50,000 in annual grants to the Astor Home for Children in Rhinebeck, New York, which served as a psychiatric institution for preteen-age boys. He gave real estate valued at $1 million to the City of New York, in support of a park and playground for children in Harlem. Grants of $250,000 and $350,000 supported the youth center of the West Side YMCA and the Madison Square Boys Club.[60]

Both the Charles Hayden Foundation in New York and the Turrell Fund in New Jersey supported the underprivileged, neediest children. Hayden supported schools for children with behavior problems, homes for children with no families, and camps for low-income inner-city youth. From 1937 to 1977, the Charles Hayden Foundation distributed nearly $85 million toward the educational, recreational, and moral needs of youth. Skill development in word and information processing was given to five hundred children. A reading academy was established for functionally illiterate youth. From 1935 to 1964, Turrell made grants of $8.5 million for projects ranging from operational support of group homes for children with behavior problems to vocational training for the children of migrant workers. In 1969 the Duke Endowment developed intense treatment programs for children with emotional barriers and provided ongoing support for more than forty child care institutions in North and South Carolina, servicing 5,129 children and spending almost $9,000 on each child.[61]

Challenge grants from the Kresge Foundation were typically made for construction projects; yet such undertakings often supported disadvantaged and alienated people living in poverty. A $20,000 grant assisted in constructing a

---

59. Foundation Center (1967).
60. Vincent Astor Foundation (1961, 1968).
61. Charles Hayden Foundation (1974, 1977); Turrell Fund (1965); Duke Endowment (1965).

Table 8-1. *Top Ten Foundation Funders of Social Welfare, 1967*

Foundation	Social welfare grants (thousands of dollars)	Share of grants to social welfare (percent)
Vincent Astor Foundation	2,290.8	60
Charles Hayden Foundation	1,719.1	55
Turrell Fund	1,145.4	94
Duke Endowment	806.8	4
Kresge Foundation	607.2	12
Eugene and Agnes E. Meyer Foundation	466.1	57
Sears-Roebuck Foundation	409.5	6
Woods Charitable Fund, Inc.	295.5	20
Robert R. McCormick Charitable Trust	272.3	19
Rockefeller Brothers Fund	270.5	4

Sources: IRS 990-PF forms (1967, 1968); annual reports (1967, 1968).

camp facility for three hundred emotionally challenged children, and a $25,000 grant expanded a child guidance clinic. In 1968 a $500,000 grant supported programs for residents living in urban Detroit.[62]

Notable Trends

The increased government funding for welfare and basic social needs left foundations free to focus their efforts in directions they found compatible with their philanthropic goals. Foundation activities were in tune with the social climate of the time and included advocacy and services to underserved populations.

Some foundations adopted a more activist orientation during this period, and their funding became more consistent with a liberal political agenda. As Randall Holcombe notes, "In the decades following World War II foundations spearheaded a liberal agenda in the United States. . . . Foundations were attempting to steer the course of public education, they were trying to impose their vision of race relations on the nation, they were actively involved in political campaigns, and they were influencing the course of foreign nations through their grants."[63]

The Conservative Ascendance

During the 1970s, the prosperity of the earlier decade began to wane, largely owing to inflation brought on by insufficient tax revenues to support spending

62. Kresge Foundation (1969).
63. Holcombe (2000, pp. 117–18).

for the Vietnam War and new 1960s social programs. Other factors included high energy prices, rising unemployment, increasing federal budget deficits, increased foreign competition, and a sagging stock market. Beginning in 1979 the Federal Reserve Board clamped down on the money supply, interest rates rose, borrowing slowed, and the economy fell into deep recession.[64]

In time, inflation eased, and by 1983 the economy had rebounded. Economic conditions continued to improve through the 1990s. However, the economic upheaval of the late 1970s and early 1980s had major political and social consequences. It ushered in a period during which the market had a freer hand and both political parties, taking a step back from the social welfare gains of the 1960s, advocated a reduced social welfare role for the government. Mainstream economics became more conservative, promoting the belief that markets, to operate best, must be free to self-adjust. Basic principles guiding economic policy included privatization and deregulation, restraints on social welfare spending, and the commercialization of social costs.[65]

Embracing the conservative economic agenda, the Reagan administration began a series of retrenchments in federal social service spending. Lester Salamon documents these cuts. Between 1977 and 1982, the inflation-adjusted value of spending for social services dropped 31 percent at the federal level and 14 percent at the state level. In addition, whereas government social welfare spending increased 145 percent from 1965 to 1977, it increased only 21 percent from 1977 to 1989, and over the same period, government spending for social services decreased 28 percent. Given the continued growth of health and pension spending, Salamon concludes, "the retrenchment of the 1980s . . . shifted the center of gravity on the social welfare system more towards the middle class and away from the poor, and more towards health and away from human services."[66]

The downward trends were somewhat moderated in the early 1990s, in part owing to increases in some programs during the Clinton administration. Nevertheless, federal spending on social services and education in 1994 was still 30 percent below what it had been in 1977,[67] despite the increasingly healthy economy of the late 1980s and 1990s.

Pattern of Foundation Funding for Social Welfare

The top three categories of foundation giving identified in previous decades—health, education, and social welfare—also took precedence in the first half of the 1980s, although funding priorities were reordered. Foundation grants to social welfare categories increased in both dollars and number of grants in the

64. Conte and Karr (2001).
65. Blau and Abramowitz (2004, pp. 267–70).
66. Salamon (1999, pp. 64–65).
67. Salamon (1999, p. 67).

first half of the 1980s, reflecting foundations' acknowledgment of a financial gap in assisting the poor following the severe reduction of federal welfare dollars instigated by the Reagan administration.[68] The Foundation Center reports overall grant dollars to welfare as the top-ranked category of giving between 1982 and 1986, with a mean of 27.8 percent of total dollars granted, followed by 22.8 percent to health and 19 percent to education. The welfare category was also first ranked in the number of grants made.[69]

To assess social welfare funding in the 1980s, the *Source Book Profiles* generated by the Foundation Center categorizes and totals contributed dollars over a two-year publishing cycle for the grant priorities of the one thousand foundations largest in asset size for 1987, 1988, or 1989. Nearly three-quarters (71.5 percent) of the foundations examined had made grants to social welfare by 1989. Of the 715 foundations so identified, 12 devoted 50 percent or more to social welfare causes, suggesting that some foundations were willing to respond to increased social needs. Foundations with assets of $25 million to $1 billion apportioned the largest dollar amounts, representing 70 percent of all grants to social welfare causes. Five foundations with assets of $1 billion or more appropriated 6.5 percent of their total grant dollars.[70]

Top Funders

Table 8-2 lists the top ten foundations among those that funded social welfare projects in 1989. According to Foundation Center data, five of these (Ford Foundation, Lilly Endowment, Pew Charitable Trusts, Robert Wood Johnson Foundation, and Kresge Foundation) were also among the top ten largest foundations and the top ten largest grant makers overall. Two other foundations (McKnight and Surdna) designated more than 50 percent of their total grants to the social welfare category.[71]

During the decade of the 1980s, foundations independently decided how best to dedicate their grants on behalf of the public good, and at the same time assessed whether their grants would duplicate already-established government programs or fill in gaps in government funding. The McKnight Foundation focused its greatest proportion of funding on agencies in the Minneapolis–St. Paul region. Beginning with modest grant making of $1.9 million collectively during the first twenty years of its existence (1953–73), the foundation grew from nearly $8 million in assets to $338 million by 1981. Despite such rapid growth, the foundation continued to make human service programs its funding priority, through operating support, project support, and direct assistance. Some

68. Foundation Center (1975).
69. Foundation Center (1987).
70. Jones (1989).
71. Jones (1989, 1990).

Table 8-2. *Top Ten Foundation Funders of Social Welfare, 1989*

Foundation	Social welfare grants (millions of dollars)	Number of social welfare grants	Share of grants to social welfare (percent)	Total assets (millions of dollars)
McKnight Foundation	14.2	74	70	764.3
Ford Foundation	9.4	37	5	583.2
Surdna Foundation	8.5	15	58	312.5
Pew Charitable Trusts	7.2	40	5	3,321.9
Meadows Foundation	5.3	68	27	405.9
Lilly Endowment	5.3	17	7	3,357.9
Edna McConnell Clark Foundation	5.1	37	25	414.3
Skillman Foundation	4.8	41	37	298.8
Kresge Foundation	4.5	28	8	1,261.1
Robert Wood Johnson Foundation	4.1	18	4	2,608.3

Sources: Jones (1989, 1990).

grants were given to stimulate additional public and private support from others. Most, however, were selected in support of local causes in the area.[72]

The Ford Foundation's high-ranked position in amount of dollars given to social welfare was not representative of its main giving priorities (international issues and the arts). Yet the foundation remained attentive to emerging social issues in the 1980s, with a domestic agenda.[73] Research undertaken by the foundation on the social problems of the 1980s prompted Ford to nearly double its allocated funds to urban poverty. The foundation's watchful eye on the effect of government cutbacks to social programs identified unmet needs in the area of childcare for single mothers who were recipients of Aid to Families with Dependent Children.[74] Local community development organizations and programs addressing teen pregnancy and offering support to children in high-risk families were founded as a result of their assessment.[75]

This pattern of independently supporting specific charities and projects continued with the other top funders of social welfare. In addition to addressing problems of the disadvantaged, children, and the aged, the Surdna Foundation provided extant operational support for the Andrus Children's Home and a home for the elderly, both based in its home state of New York. Coupled with other such grants for the underrepresented, the foundation distributed between

72. Keele and Kiger (1984).
73. Ford Foundation (1988, p. 11).
74. Ford Foundation (1988, p. 12).
75. Keele and Kiger (1984, p. 133).

58 and 75 percent of its grants to social welfare concerns.[76] The philanthropic paternalism of the seven Pew Charitable Trusts was reflected in the design of specific trusts to represent their contribution preferences, from higher education to conservation to emphasis on the values of a free economy, extending from their Philadelphia home base to national and international reach. Even with the varied interests of the Pew trusts, human services remained a commitment, ranking fourth in its grants to program areas. In 1985 the Pew Charitable Trusts made $14.2 million in human service grants, representing 10 percent of grants made to all fields.[77] Rather than identifying a major field of interest, the Meadows Foundation in Dallas maintained its five categories—arts, social services, health, education, and civic and cultural affairs—and moved toward a parity distribution formula, giving equal amounts to each category in Texas.[78]

The pattern of the 1990s continued the trends seen in the 1980s, with health, education, and welfare listed as the top three foundation giving categories. However, social welfare funding, which was ranked as the top category in the early to middle 1980s, dropped to third place behind the other two categories. Within the social welfare category, the human services–multipurpose subcategory, representing programs and services for individuals, families, and special populations, received an average of $425 million annually between 1991 and 1995. At the same time, the number of grants given to human services–multipurpose issues increased steadily, from 6,348 grants in 1991 to 9,009 grants in 1995. The top 100 foundations in 1995 gave more than 2,300 grants totaling $239 million to human services–multipurpose issues. An additional 912 smaller foundations awarded approximately the same amount—$242 million—to human service–multipurpose programs through 6,647 grants.[79]

Research was conducted by the Foundation Center on the grant-making activities of the one thousand largest foundations in the United States and compiled into a directory, *The Foundation 1,000*.[80] Based predominantly on 1993 data, we extracted information on the grants each foundation gave to the human services–multipurpose category for analysis of the trends and patterns of social welfare giving. The top three social welfare funders were the Annie E. Casey Foundation ($20.5 million to social welfare), the Pew Charitable Trusts ($15.3 million), and the Skillman Foundation ($11.8 million).

The Annie E. Casey Foundation and the Skillman Foundation each designated 50 percent or more of their total grant dollars to social welfare. Moreover, through their grant making they played key roles in calling attention to

76. Surdna Foundation (1985–86, 1988).
77. Pew Memorial Trust (1985).
78. Keele and Kiger (1984, p. 295).
79. Jones (1995).
80. Jones (1995).

the plight of children in need. Over a span of fifty years from its beginning in 1948, the Annie E. Casey Foundation would shift its role from charity support to philanthropic grant making yet never lose its commitment to disadvantaged children.[81] The Skillman Foundation combined efforts in welfare reform and devolution with its ongoing involvement with children, youth, and families in the Detroit area.[82] Both foundations focused on issues of infrastructure and information. Child welfare initiatives created by Casey focused on the system surrounding children in need, from support for their families and the agencies that served them to innovative policy reform. As a result of their experience in supporting child service programs the foundations were able to publish information that would assist in the formation of policy reforms. Casey's Kids Count program not only addressed the needs of vulnerable children living in poverty but also furnished state and national indicators on children's well-being, thus setting the stage for assessing and monitoring measurable results.[83] The Skillman Foundation supported the publication of annual information data books concerning the welfare of children in Michigan. Building on the Casey Foundation's initiative, the Skillman Foundation funded the publication of the *Kids Count Data Book* about the needs of Michigan children.[84]

Notable Trends

Trends in grant making over the 1980s, tracked by the Foundation Center, indicate that increases in foundation grants to social welfare programs came as a response to the cuts in federal welfare programs by the Reagan administration. At the same time, foundations managed to support the widening human services funding gap by focusing on welfare causes that aligned with the scope of their individual interests. In addition, after decades of trying to distinguish themselves from government, some foundations made a greater attempt to create some public-private partnerships, which made available more services for people in need.[85]

In August 1996 sweeping welfare reform legislation was passed, ending the system in place since the Great Depression. Under this system, the federal government had provided fairly uniform benefits to the nation's poor without regard to the details of their personal circumstances and with no time limit. State contributions to welfare, however, varied widely, and until the 1970s county officials could discriminate based on race and other factors. The new federal welfare rules required most recipients to be employed within two years of receiving assistance, limited most assistance to a total of five years, and let states establish family caps

81. Keele and Kiger (1984, p. 25).
82. Skillman Foundation (1998, p. 20).
83. Annie E. Casey Foundation (1995, p. 34); Jones (1995, p. 415).
84. Skillman Foundation (1998, p. 20).
85. Renz and others (2001).

to deny additional benefits to mothers for children born while the mothers were already on public assistance.[86]

In addition, federal money allocated for public assistance would be sent to the states in block grants. The federal role would be limited to setting goals and establishing financial penalties and rewards. A number of concerns were voiced about the new system, including the possibility that people who deserved assistance would be denied it; that without standardization, some social groups might not be dealt with fairly, and some with legitimate reasons for not being able to work might nevertheless be cut off from assistance; and that all the variation in public assistance could lead to migrations of welfare recipients to places where benefits were more generous. The result could be a race to the bottom as local governments reduced benefits in an attempt to avoid attracting more poor people—or even drove them out entirely. Foundations shared these concerns. A group of fifteen foundations funded an early Urban Institute study of the effects of the legislation.[87]

The top foundations supporting social welfare in the 1990s embodied an entrepreneurial spirit. Each foundation reflected a pattern of particular preferences, based on the generally entrepreneurial inclinations of its founder. The first of the Pew Charitable Trusts was set up in 1948 by the children of Joseph N. Pew, the founder of Sun Oil Company, and was expanded by the Pew children to accommodate the range of commitments to varied social issues.[88] Harry Weinberg, an immigrant from Galicia as a young boy, amassed a real estate fortune and through the Harry and Jeanette Weinberg Foundation provided aid in Maryland, Hawaii, northeast Pennsylvania, New York, Israel, and the former Soviet Union.[89] The Joseph B. Whitehead Foundation was chartered by family members to honor Coca-Cola founder Joseph Brown Whitehead. The $1.2 billion foundation gave 17 percent of its $24 million in grants awarded in 1998 to education, health, public affairs, and environmental issues, along with $20 million to human services.[90] These foundations supported a mix of programs, allowing them to remain flexible in responding to the needs of the community.

Total giving by foundations was only about 12 percent of all private giving in 2004, and foundation grants to social welfare in that year were only about 13 percent of total foundation grants.[91] Foundations, however, made significant impacts through other strategies, especially by encouraging collaboration

86. Sawhill (2002).

87. Long and others (1988).

88. Pew Memorial Trust (1985).

89. Harry and Jeanette Weinberg Foundation, *Annual Report,* 2007, p. 3 (www.hjweinberg-foundation.org/publications/annual.php).

90. Keele and Kiger (1984).

91. American Association of Fundraising Counsel Trust for Philanthropy (2005); Foundation Center (2006).

and promoting effectiveness. By the 1990s foundations had several decades of experience in responding to shifting government agendas and differentiating themselves from government activity. Foundations responded to gaps caused by decreased federal funds by investing in partnerships with business corporations, nonprofit agencies, and government actors.

Foundations brought a number of advantages to these partnerships. They did not have to go through the same bureaucratic steps as government agencies. Their freedom to start and field-test small, focused programs enabled foundations to absorb risks by launching initiatives in housing and community development, housing for the elderly, and child care that government could take to scale, if they proved successful, or take into account in setting new policy.

For example, in 1998 the McKnight Foundation sponsored a conference at which three hundred participants, representing community partnerships with government and nonprofit agencies, considered approaches to welfare reform. That same year, the William Penn Foundation gave a $2.7 million grant to support a government-initiated network of neighborhood prevention services, along with numerous grants ranging from $50,000 to $100,000 to community agencies supporting Temporary Assistance for Needy Families recipients and the immigrant population. By leveraging an active collaboration of other public and private agencies, foundations supported a broader system of services for those in need.[92]

Conclusion

Looking over the course of the twentieth century, we can identify a number of patterns in foundation involvement in the provision of social welfare. Despite some occasional and transitory shifts, foundation support of social welfare issues generally ranked third in popularity behind education and health. Children and youth attracted significant giving in each decade.

So far as we can tell from the fragmentary available data, foundations with larger assets have generally contributed proportionately less than small and mid-sized foundations to social welfare causes. Nevertheless, the small proportions from large foundations dominated in dollar amounts the social welfare grants of the smaller foundations. There did seem to be a shift from the 1930s and 1940s to the decades beyond, however. During the 1930s and 1940s, foundations giving the most to social welfare causes were also among the foundations with the largest assets. As foundations increased in both number and assets in more recent decades, the earlier pattern reasserted itself.

Overall, foundations have displayed an orientation toward social welfare that emphasizes self-help and private social service organizations rather than

---

92. Internal Revenue Service Form 990s are available online at www.guidestar.org.

an expansion of government institutions or political mobilization. They have sought to differentiate themselves in their grant making from government funding and see their efforts as complementary to government, not as a substitute. Their approach to social welfare has been philanthropic and involved the roles of social innovator and, at times, advocate.

Foundations have responded to changing social conditions (the Depression, the Great Society, recent welfare reform) but have not changed their basic orientation or approach. They have adjusted funding priorities, and during economic downturns they have temporarily narrowed their scope.

This modest degree of change should not be surprising. Foundations retained their initial orientation to social welfare over the course of the century. Organizational change is usually externally driven, and for most organizations the most significant factor is the need for continued acquisition of scarce resources from the environment. Foundations, though, are not subject to the same resource constraints or market conditions as are producers of goods and services. Consequently, to the extent that they experience pressures for significant and lasting change, these are produced internally—through the shifting attitudes and goals of founders, trustees, or staff. Changes, therefore, are more likely to be incremental and slow.

As we move into the twenty-first century, a number of issues and trends have implications for the provision of social welfare by both public and private actors, including foundations. A partial listing of the current trends includes the following:

—great new wealth plus persistent poverty and widening income inequality
—new societal challenges, such as immigration, the environment, and globalization
—continued austerity in government programs and funding
—welfare limits
—pay-for-performance contracting
—a push for a market orientation in social service provision
—the movement of for-profits into service provision
—a push by funders for evaluation, accountability, and impact analysis
—coexistence of a variety of orientations toward philanthropy

Some observers feel that there have been significant and far-reaching changes both in the nature and the extent of societal needs and attitudes as well as in the numbers and orientation of the wealthy and those controlling foundations. Perhaps the conjunction of these two factors will produce responses in existing foundations as well as the birth of new foundations with different approaches to social welfare.[93]

93. Ellsworth and Lumarda (2003).

9

The Role of Foundations in Shaping Social Welfare Policy and Services: The Case of Welfare Reform

JENNIFER E. MOSLEY AND JOSEPH GALASKIEWICZ

Foundations play a key but often overlooked role in influencing and implementing social welfare policy. They shape knowledge and preferences for policy solutions by funding specific kinds of research, driving community development initiatives, and supporting selected forms of social services. Strategic involvement and monitoring of public policy debates and thoughtful responses to policy changes are crucial for them to meet their goals in a changing environment. This is especially important in areas of social welfare in which government is heavily involved. In this chapter we use the case of the 1996 welfare reform legislation to explore the charitable (that is, giving to those in need) and philanthropic (that is, giving to spur innovation and social change) orientations of foundations before, during, and after this major policy change. Comparing how foundations adopted these two roles also sheds light on how foundations leverage their comparative advantages as social entrepreneurs, institution builders, mediators, and risk absorbers in the field of social welfare.[1]

We would like to thank Helmut Anheier, David Hammack, and the Center for Civil Society at University of California, Los Angeles, for providing funding to collect these data; Loren Renz, Steven Lawrence, and Brenda Burk for assistance with the data and responding to our endless queries; Colleen Grogan, Zeke Hasenfeld, and Paul-Brian McInerney for providing helpful feedback on earlier drafts; and Eve Garrow and Marcus Lam for help with preparing the data for analysis.
1. Chapter 1, this volume.

The charitable and philanthropic roles of foundations in the United States are well illustrated in the case of welfare reform because this ideologically charged policy change explicitly juxtaposed the two approaches to serving society. The welfare debate involved overt public discussion of the role of cash assistance, including the question of whether it was a vital safety net, a handout to lazy parents, or a potential tool to foster self-sufficiency in troubled families. How foundations responded to this discussion and intervened in the process reveals how they saw their own role in shaping and supporting social welfare policy and services.

Welfare Reform

The 1996 welfare reform legislation, formally known as the Personal Responsibility and Work Opportunity Reconciliation Act of 1996, was the largest U.S. social policy shift in decades and was years in the making. Efforts to reform welfare (then known as Aid to Families with Dependent Children, or AFDC) with an emphasis on work participation began during the Nixon administration and accelerated during the 1980s, notably with the Family Support Act of 1988. During this time, research on poverty and its causes and consequences was also growing rapidly.[2]

The 1996 law abolished AFDC and replaced it with Temporary Assistance for Needy Families (TANF) block grants. This changed welfare from an entitlement program to a work program and devolved responsibility for welfare from the federal government to the states. The most significant changes in the welfare law were lifetime limits on welfare receipt and work requirements for all recipients, generally sixty months of total lifetime aid, and the full-time participation in work or educational activities in order to receive aid. States were allowed wide leeway in how they structured their programs and were also encouraged to be more restrictive by augmenting federal regulations through the implementation of sanctions, family caps, and the denial of benefits to adolescent parents.

The policy resulted in a large outcry from the left, as well as from many social science researchers and policy experts, who worried that it was overly punitive, would negatively affect the well-being of vulnerable children in particular, and did not recognize the struggles of many poor families who cycled on and off welfare or mixed welfare with work.[3] Another concern was that the time limits were not sensitive to the multiple barriers to work that many families on welfare faced, such as lack of work experience, education, and consistent child care, as well as transportation problems, violence in the home, illness, and substance abuse.[4]

2. Weaver (2000).
3. Duncan and Brooks-Gunn (2000); Hershey and Pavetti (1997).
4. Danziger and Seefeldt (2003).

Over time, welfare reform did prove to be successful at moving families off the welfare rolls, but it was not so successful in raising families out of poverty.[5]

The Role of Foundations in Welfare Reform

Given the significance of welfare policy in the lives of low-income children and families, it is important to understand the role foundations have played in both shaping and responding to this policy change. It is always difficult, however, to ascertain the roles actors play within an institutional context. One approach is to look at the motivation or purpose behind foundations' actions by using narratives and firsthand accounts to infer the rationales behind foundation grants or other actions. The other is to observe their behavior and then try to infer motivation or purpose. Neither approach is totally adequate, so in this research we pursue both strategies. In the first section we present quantitative data on foundations' funding patterns both before and after welfare reform, looking at differences in giving trends over time and among foundations. In the second section we present archival evidence gleaned from annual reports, looking at how foundations discussed and framed their work at the time.

In discussing the work of foundations, we pay special attention to the issues of philanthropic versus charitable orientation, ideology, and framing. First, knowing whether foundations played a charitable or philanthropic role during the welfare reform era helps us understand their approach to social change. By assuming a charitable role, foundations provide public benefit by helping the needy or disadvantaged, alleviating suffering, and providing services that government cannot or will not provide. Foundations that take a charitable orientation to giving often serve as risk absorbers and mediators. Examples of this behavior include giving to social service programs, highlighting the need to maintain safety net services, funding niche services, and supporting programs that ease the transition of former welfare recipients returning to work.

Foundations assume a philanthropic orientation when they experiment with new programs, develop new models of service, fund needed research, and push policymakers to implement policy change. This orientation takes advantage of the fact that foundations can take risks that government cannot because they are accountable only to their boards of directors and they have permanent, independent sources of revenue. This allows them unparalleled freedom to express individual and organizational preferences through their giving choices and considerable power in bringing attention to new ideas, service technologies, or organizations. Foundations that take a philanthropic orientation to giving often act

5. Corcoran and others (2000).

as social entrepreneurs or institution builders. Knowing whether foundations assumed a primarily charitable or philanthropic orientation and how they carried out those different roles is key to helping us understand the unique contributions foundations made in the policy reform process.

Second, it is also important to understand how these orientations and roles may differ depending on the ideology of the foundation. Scholars have argued that conservative foundations have played an important role in sparking social change over the past forty years or so through careful organization, coordinated giving, and funding of specific conservative institutions.[6] Strategic giving to a network of increasingly influential conservative think tanks like the Heritage Foundation and the American Enterprise Institute has been a key part of this effort. The reports and monographs these think tanks have produced, and their related media campaigns, have been extraordinarily successful in reframing how specific social problems are understood as well as what should be done about them.[7] This leads us to expect that conservative foundations would assume a mostly philanthropic role around the issue of welfare reform. In contrast, centrist and progressive foundations may have had a more mixed orientation, playing roles associated with both philanthropy and charity, by attempting to balance traditional notions of providing for those in need while working to ensure that new service models and policies were reflective of their ideological preferences. Discovering how different kinds of foundations approached their work will reveal important information about systematic variation in the field and how ideology may mediate the way foundations conceptualize both roles and impact.

Finally, the statements that foundations make about their giving in their annual reports play a dual role. They reflect organizational values and provide indications of how the foundation wants to be seen in the larger funding community. More important for the policy process, however, these statements are also attempts to influence policy decisions by framing the debate in ways foundations expect will resonate with their supporters and help sway policymakers. Foundations reinforce certain ways of conceptualizing the problem and possible solutions by providing different rationales for their giving. For example, framing the welfare debate as a problem of dependency emphasizes a very different set of solutions than framing it as a problem of barriers to employment. In the archival findings section of this chapter we investigate the values and norms foundations of different ideologies were trying to appeal to when invoking different frames in the rationale for their giving.[8]

6. Rich (2004); Covington (1997); Miller (2006); O'Connor (2007).
7. Rich (2004); Stefancic and Delgado (1996).
8. Benford and Snow (2000).

Evidence from Quantitative Data

Quantitative data on what activities foundations gave to, how much they gave, and how that changed over time help us see broadly what roles foundations played during the welfare reform era and how that differed by foundation ideology. Looking at overall patterns of giving also sheds light on the way the foundation sector as a whole conceptualized both responsibility and opportunity in the welfare reform era and thus how foundations affected society during this time. For this reason, before delving into how foundations framed their giving and the intention behind it, we look at the overall giving patterns of foundations by presenting aggregate amounts of funding given nationally for specific activities relevant to welfare reform from 1995 to 2001. We use data from the period before 1997 to see whether funding patterns changed before and after the legislation. We stop at 2001 because the events of 9/11 and the subsequent recession were important exogenous shocks to the foundation world that disrupted business as usual.

Data, Sample, and Methodology

These analyses were done using data procured from the Foundation Center, an infrastructure organization supported by foundations.[9] Each year the Foundation Center compiles information from one thousand of the largest private and community foundations in the United States. The annual data set includes information on each grant of more than $10,000 given by the selected foundations in that year. Although it does not provide a full representation of grant-making activities in the United States, it is the largest database of its kind and accounts for about half of the total dollars given by foundations in the United States each year. The information in the Foundation Center's data file is organized by grant and includes the National Taxonomy of Exempt Entities (NTEE) classification system codes describing the activities of the recipient organization and the grant's purpose, among other things.

Two samples are used in this analysis. First, we use the full national data set to investigate the activities of foundations broadly. Second, to explore the effect of ideology and to corroborate our findings with the archival annual report data, we chose a purposive sample of fourteen major foundations to investigate more closely. The fourteen foundations were not chosen at random and thus should not be considered representative of foundations as a whole. We had a particular interest in larger foundations with significant assets that have a history of engaging with public policy or are widely considered to be important and trendsetting. Our rationale for choosing these foundations was that they would be most

9. The data are proprietary and were provided by the Foundation Center to the Center for Civil Society at the University of California at Los Angeles for this study.

likely to act and have the capacity to make an impact. The financial and cultural capital of the selected foundations positioned them to be meaningful players in the debate.

We also specifically chose foundations that reflected a variety of centrist, progressive, and conservative viewpoints. Foundation ideology is an important variable to explore in this case because of the highly charged debate surrounding welfare and how best to reform it. Foundations were categorized as progressive, centrist, or conservative based on statements found in the foundations' annual reports and how they have been categorized in prior research.[10] For example, foundations espousing support for individual liberties and traditional values were classified as conservative, and foundations calling for greater public investment in reducing inequality or promoting social justice were classified as progressive. Foundations that were not clearly identified as belonging to one side or the other were classified as centrist, but it should be noted that ideology is not naturally categorical and the centrist group is highly heterogeneous. For example, the Ford Foundation is close to the progressive group and the Lilly Endowment is close to the conservative group, but both are coded as centrists. Of the fourteen foundations selected for inclusion in the study, the Annie E. Casey Foundation, the Joyce Foundation, the McKnight Foundation, the Open Society Institute, and the Charles Stewart Mott Foundation were identified as progressive; the Ford Foundation, the Lilly Endowment, the Andrew W. Mellon Foundation, the Pew Charitable Trusts, and the Russell Sage Foundation as centrist; and the Lynde and Harry Bradley Foundation, the Sarah Scaife Foundation, the Smith Richardson Foundation, and the John M. Olin Foundation as conservative.

We looked at giving patterns in five specific areas relevant to welfare reform. An analysis of giving in these five areas can tell us whether foundations were more concerned about workforce development, such as preparing former welfare recipients to take part in full-time paid work; maintaining the safety net through support of emergency assistance programs; work supports like day care for children; social services, such as family services to adolescent parents; or research on poverty and welfare policy. Since we were interested only in grants to these five areas, we used the NTEE codes to define each general funding area and to select the specific grants of interest from the larger grants data file.

Workforce development. New work requirements were the most dramatic change of welfare reform. All recipients of cash assistance were required to participate in work-related activities to maintain their eligibility. Ensuring that recipients complied with these requirements was vital to reform. This meant training former welfare recipients and finding jobs for them. The NTEE codes

10. Covington (1997); Rich (2004); O'Connor (2007).

selected were J20 (Employment procurement assistance and job training), J21 (Vocational counseling, guidance, and testing), J22 (Vocational employment training), and J23 (Retraining program).

Safety net. Many scholars and activists were concerned that with welfare no longer an entitlement program, the lack of a safety net would throw some families into abject poverty and thus create a greater need for emergency assistance and food programs. The NTEE codes selected were K30 (Food service/Free food distribution), K31 (Food banks and pantries), K33 (Commodity distribution services), K34 (Congregate meals), K35 (Eatery, agency/organization sponsored [for example, soup kitchens]), P24 (Salvation Army), and P60 (Emergency assistance [food, clothing, cash]).

Child day care. Despite increased federal subsidies, the new work requirements left many mothers with no place to leave their children during the day. Lack of access to quality, affordable day care is a major barrier to work, decreasing labor force participation and number of hours worked.[11] The NTEE code selected was P33 (Child day care).

Family services to adolescent parents and pregnancy prevention. A major goal of the legislation for conservative policymakers was reducing the number of children born outside of marriage, particularly the teenage pregnancy rate. The 1996 act allowed states to set special rules for adolescent parents to discourage adolescent pregnancies. Most frequently, they had to stay in school and live at home to receive benefits. The NTEE codes selected were P35 (Prevention of adolescent pregnancy) and P45 (Family services for adolescent parents).

Research on welfare reform policies and poverty. Major demonstration programs took off in a variety of states both before and after the 1996 act, reflecting increased interest in the conditions of the poor in America, including the role of welfare in their lives. Findings from these projects gave direction to lawmakers, advocates, and administrators during the policy formulation phase, and research on the implications of welfare reform continued after the law was passed. The NTEE codes selected were V39 (Poverty research/studies) and W21 (Welfare policy and reform).

Giving in each area implies a slightly different role for foundations. Funding for workforce development, child day care, and family services to adolescent parents and adolescent pregnancy prevention could reflect either a charitable or a philanthropic orientation, depending on the purpose of the grant. For example, it would be philanthropic if the grant supported an innovative new jobs program but would reflect a charitable orientation if it funded the opening of a new day care center in a low-income area. Safety net funding is clearly a charitable

---

11. Meyers, Heintze, and Wolf (2002).

Figure 9-1. *Giving to Welfare Reform Activities, by the 1,000 Largest Foundations, 1995–2001*

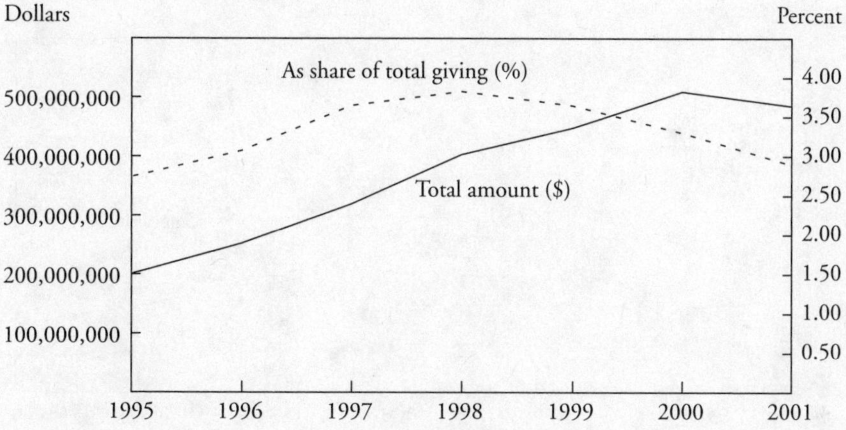

Dollars   Percent

As share of total giving (%)

Total amount ($)

Source: Data from Foundation Center Statistical Database 2001.

risk absorber response, while funding research clearly reflects a philanthropic orientation.

In the Foundation Center data set, grants can receive up to five NTEE codes. Because we wanted to tally the dollar amounts by general funding area, if the Foundation Center coded the grant using any of the codes listed for a general funding area we recoded it as going to that funding area, and the dollar amount was assigned to that activity.[12] All data are presented in 2001 constant dollars, and the inflator is the average consumer price index for urban consumers for a given year.

Trends in Giving Patterns

Figure 9-1 shows the giving patterns of the one thousand largest private and community foundations each year from 1995 to 2001. In terms of the total amount of dollars given, the chart shows that giving to the five areas began increasing immediately following passage of the welfare reform bill of 1996 and did not tail off until 2000. The line showing the amount as a percentage of total

12. Sometimes the grant was assigned codes from two different general areas; for example, a grant might be coded as research on poverty (V39) and as related to job training (J21). When this happened, we assigned the grant amount to both of the general categories, for example, work-force development and research on welfare reform policies and poverty. Thus the grant was double counted in the charts showing giving to the five areas. However, double counting is not present in figure 9-1, where the five areas are summed.

Figure 9-2. *Giving to Specific Welfare Reform Activities as a Share of Total Giving, by the 1,000 Largest Foundations, 1995–2001*

Percent

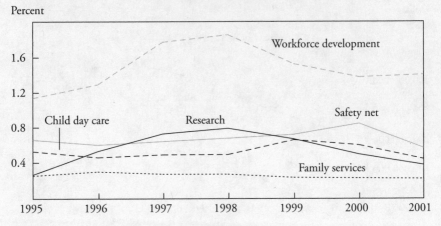

Source: Data from Foundation Center Statistical Database 2001.

grant making, however, is more revealing. This chart indicates that while the total dollars given may have been rising, foundations started turning away from welfare reform funding as early as 1998, decreasing the percentage of their giving in these areas in comparison with their giving to other areas.

Figure 9-2 shows the percentage of total giving that went to each of the five areas. Overall, foundations gave the highest percentage of their welfare reform dollars to workforce development programs, with a large increase in giving in the years 1997 and 1998. Giving to research followed a similar pattern, with a boost in giving from 1996 to 1998. Thus it seems that foundations played a primarily philanthropic role by supporting research for policymaking, tracking the outcomes of policy change, and smoothing the transition by supporting workforce development.

To explore how ideological differences among foundations might have affected the areas to which funding was primarily directed, figures 9-3, 9-4, and 9-5 show the average amounts given to each welfare-related giving area by type of foundation, using the purposive sample of fourteen major foundations.[13] The most obvious finding is the relatively small amount of money given to all five areas by the conservative foundations during this period. For example, the average annual amount given by the ten progressive and centrist foundations to welfare

13. We took the total amounts given by foundations of a particular type over a two-year period and divided that by double the number of foundations in each category. For 2001 we divided simply by the number of foundations for which we had data.

Figure 9-3. *Average Giving by Conservative Foundations to Welfare Reform Activities, 1995–2001*

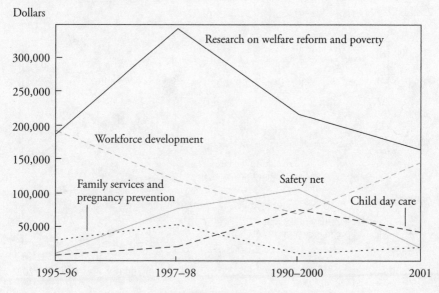

Dollars

Source: Data from Foundation Center Statistical Database 2001.

reform activities in 1997–98 was $9.8 million, while the average annual amount given by the three conservative foundations was $546,000. This disparity is evident throughout the study period. It is important to note that many of the centrist and progressive foundations we studied were among the twenty-five largest foundations in the country. While the conservative foundations we studied were chosen for their prominence, conservative foundations on the whole tend to be much smaller. The smaller asset size and giving of the conservative foundations is crucial to understanding the overall implications of these data. Finally, these foundations frequently gave grants for general operating support, which would not have been coded as welfare reform giving, although it is extremely likely that these funds would have been used for welfare-related research and publications by influential think tanks like the Heritage Foundation during this era.

Despite the smaller size of their grant making overall, a comparison of figures 9-3, 9-4, and 9-5 suggests conservative foundations spent a much larger percentage of their welfare-related funding on research than the other two types of foundations. Although the absolute dollar amounts were smaller in size, in 1995–96 they spent 53 percent of their welfare-related grants on research as against about 32 percent for progressive foundations and a little more than 24 percent for centrist foundations. This demonstrates their clear philanthropic orientation and

Figure 9-4. *Average Giving by Centrist Foundations to Welfare Reform Activities, 1995–2001*

Dollars

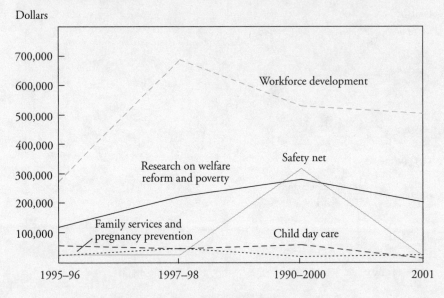

Source: Data from Foundation Center Statistical Database 2001.

may be a reason why they have garnered so much attention for their efficacy in impacting policymaking. Conservative foundations increased their support for research after the legislation passed (63 percent of the amount given to welfare reform activities in 1997–98), as did progressive foundations (52 percent of the amount to welfare reform in 1997–98). In contrast, the pattern of giving among centrist foundations did not change in response to welfare reform legislation (23 percent in 1997–98). The absolute dollar amounts for research dropped in 2001 for all foundations, following an earlier decline in research funding by the conservative foundations.

Workforce development activities also received considerable foundation attention, but child day care, family services and pregnancy prevention, and safety net programs did not. The figures show that both progressive and centrist foundations significantly increased their funding for workforce development in response to the policy change, but their giving to other areas showed little or no change over the period, with the exception of an increase in safety net funding by centrist foundations well after the policy passed.[14] The conservative

14. The increase in funding in 1999–2000 resulted from a single grant by the Lilly Endowment of $25 million to Goodwill Industries for an emergency assistance heating program.

Figure 9-5. *Average Giving by Progressive Foundations to Welfare Reform Activities, 1995–2001*

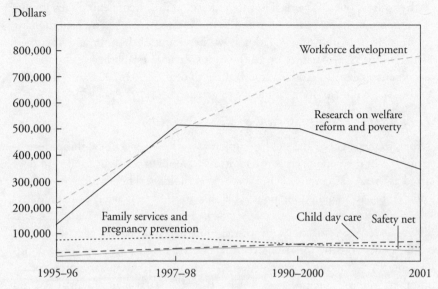

Source: Data from Foundation Center Statistical Database 2001.

foundations also gave to workforce development programs before passage of the legislation, but they exhibited a sharp drop in this spending as soon as it passed and spent little on child care, family services and pregnancy prevention, and safety net programs. These patterns are similar to our findings in figure 9-2 for the national sample of foundations.

The data support the finding that conservative foundations played an explicitly philanthropic role, which facilitated their moving away from the issue more quickly than the other foundations once the new law was passed. The findings also imply that progressive foundations played a more philanthropic role than centrist foundations, which spent comparatively smaller amounts on research. Interestingly, none of the groups assumed a clear charitable role, as none showed significant increases in safety net and social service funding during the 1990s.

Evidence from Archival Data

While aggregate numbers like those presented above are informative, they do not provide a complete account of the role foundations played in the welfare reform era. We found that a philanthropic orientation was more evident than a charitable one, particularly for conservative and progressive foundations. Their public statements reveal much about how intentional they were about this orientation, as well as what roles, such as mediator or institution builder, they played as they carried out this work. Thus to understand the intent behind their giving, it is important to probe deeper into the philanthropic and charitable rationales given by foundations, investigating how they frame their work and how their stated priorities change over time. To do this we used established techniques for document analysis to produce data from each of the 1993–2001 annual reports of the fourteen major foundations we targeted.[15]

Foundations as Shapers of Welfare Policy, 1993–1996

Efforts to shape policy and public opinion are reflective of a philanthropic orientation, so in the period preceding reform we would expect foundations to have acted as social entrepreneurs and institution builders. These actions are key to their ability to shape public policy, because prohibitions against direct lobbying for foundations mean that many may be reluctant to engage with legislators directly. Despite restrictions on formal lobbying, foundations play important public policy roles by convening critical stakeholders, building coalitions, funding and disseminating important research, and building capacity for advocacy in other nonprofit organizations.[16] This is exactly what many foundations did in the years immediately preceding welfare reform. In particular, they expressed philanthropic social entrepreneurship and institution building by funding demonstration programs, think tanks, and public intellectuals.

Indeed, as was expected, a charitable orientation was less evident among the selected foundations during this time. Across ideology, there were few statements in the foundations' annual reports that the poor needed to be supported from a purely charitable viewpoint or that foundations needed to step in as risk absorbers. That does not mean they were not participating in charitable giving, however. Many of the centrist and progressive foundations, particularly Mott, Ford, Casey, and McKnight, gave to nonprofit human service providers for their work with low-income populations. However, they did not frame their giving in charitable language and instead talked about their work in terms of promoting reform, initiating change, and developing knowledge. In contrast, there is little evidence that the conservative foundations favored a charitable orientation at all. The conservative foundations gave few purely social service grants and did not explicitly discuss grants of this type.

Foundations clearly saw a strong role for themselves as social entrepreneurs in this period. By funding research, foundations took the opportunity to create "facts" that could then be mobilized in support of their ideas. In the annual

15. Prior (2003).
16. Arons (2007).

reports we analyzed, several major demonstration projects stood out as widely supported before 1996, with outcomes that were most likely useful to policy-makers on both the left and the right. Particularly well funded demonstration programs include the New Hope project, which provided support for the work-ing poor, and Parents Fair Share, which helped noncustodial fathers get jobs and better parent their children.[17] Evaluations of these demonstration projects, often by Manpower Demonstration Research Corporation, were also widely sup-ported. Interestingly, these demonstration projects were funded by many of the centrist and progressive foundations but less so by the conservative foundations, with the single exception of the Smith Richardson Foundation, whose mission is specifically devoted to research. Demonstration programs are often intended to pave the way for future government-funded projects, so the absence of support by conservative foundations may at least partially reflect the limited government ideal espoused by many in the conservative movement, and that is noted in the Bradley Foundation's mission statement.

The strategic funding of think tanks was another way foundations on both the right and the left acted as social entrepreneurs and institution builders in the case of welfare reform. It has been argued that think tanks, which often function as a type of interest group, can be particularly effective in popularizing particular policy proposals because of their capacity to produce knowledge and expertise while also marketing and framing ideas.[18] Furthermore, during this time the number of think tanks in Washington was growing, as was their influence on national-level policymaking.[19] It makes sense, then, that foundations saw think tanks as an ideal vehicle for pursuit of their philanthropic goals.

Several influential think tanks in Washington, D.C., played particularly important roles in shaping welfare reform, and foundations facilitated their pol-icy activities by providing consistent funding.[20] In his comprehensive history of the welfare reform era, Kent Weaver notes that the Heritage Foundation, the American Enterprise Institute, and the Cato Institute were particularly impor-tant to political conservatives.[21] Data from the annual reports shows that the Olin, Bradley, and Scaife foundations funded all of these groups at some point between 1993 and 1996, often with general operating support. The American Enterprise Institute was also funded by the Smith Richardson Foundation. On the left and in the middle, the Brookings Institution, the Urban Institute, the Center on Budget and Policy Priorities, and the Center for Law and Social Pol-icy all played important roles in the policy process, and annual report data show

17. Duncan, Huston, and Weisner (2007); Johnson, Levine, and Doolittle (1999).
18. Stone (1996); Rich (2004).
19. Ricci (1993).
20. Rich (2004).
21. Weaver (2000).

that these organizations were widely supported by the progressive and some centrist foundations, albeit usually not with general operating support. We found that key funders of these organizations included the Annie E. Casey Foundation, the Charles Stewart Mott Foundation, and the Ford Foundation, among others.

Conservative foundations also built the intellectual infrastructure for policy change by funding key individuals active in the debate. Some examples of the support that conservative foundations gave influential scholars working on welfare policy issues were the Olin Foundation's funding of Charles Murray and his widely influential book, *Losing Ground,* and the Bradley Foundation's annual (from 1992 to 1997) grants to Lawrence Mead, the author of *Beyond Entitlement.*

Indeed, scholars have argued that conservative foundations and the think tanks and scholars they supported were extraordinarily effective in both shaping welfare reform policy and setting the stage for its eventual acceptance.[22] This was partly because of the strategic nature of their highly coordinated giving. In his 2006 book on the Olin Foundation, *A Gift of Freedom,* John Miller writes that conservative foundations, including Olin, Bradley, Smith Richardson, and Sarah Scaife, came to make up a "full-fledged movement." Sally Covington also argues that these four constitute the "core group" of a larger movement.[23] Covington notes that several features of their giving patterns stand out: these foundations have had a clear political agenda, they have been committed to building strong institutions outside themselves, they have invested heavily in national policy debates rather than local concerns, and they have strongly supported scholars and policy leaders who work to advance conservative ideas. Data from the annual reports of these foundations confirm that in the case of welfare reform all of these patterns held true. Although their overall giving was far less in dollar amounts than most centrist and progressive foundations, they often gave in concert and seemed to put a premium on strategic, philanthropic grant making rather than on charitable giving. They gave to fewer organizations but were more likely to give general operating and long-term support for specific individuals.

Other than these general trends in giving, however, the annual reports of the conservative foundations give little away in terms of how they framed the debate. In general, the conservative foundations, unlike the centrist and progressive foundations, stayed away from making ideologically charged comments or even stating specific goals for their grant making in their annual reports. Rather, they seemed to leave that activity to the institutions and individuals they supported. While the other foundations' annual reports increasingly came to resemble glossy magazines, with stirring photographs and personal stories, the conservative

22. Stefancic and Delgado (1996).
23. Miller (2006, p. 7); Covington (1997, p. 4).

foundations' annual reports were thin and plain, with little commentary or narrative. This was particularly true for the Olin and Scaife foundations.

The progressive Annie E. Casey Foundation is a prime example of the opposite approach in reporting and is also an interesting case with regard to how a philanthropic orientation and focus on social entrepreneurship was framed by progressive foundations during this time. The Casey Foundation used its lengthy annual report to make strong statements about what the foundation stood for, what it was trying to accomplish, and what success would look like. For example, in 1993 the foundation argued that "experimentation, risk-taking, and innovation are necessary to realign existing systems and policies" and noted it was laying the groundwork for a new funding initiative to focus on the "economic viability of families." In 1994 this program was launched for "the development of policies and programs that provide poor families an adequate level of income without discouraging work, savings, or the formation of strong families." The foundation explicitly discussed the need for welfare reform and chronicled in depth its significant giving in this area. By 1995 it reported that 58 percent of its funding was going to addressing "major problems and systems failures" (up 20 percent from the year before). This focus on barriers to work, disadvantage, and economic viability, while explicitly addressing the need for innovation, made clear both how the foundation would prefer the debate be structured and framed and its commitment to social entrepreneurship.

Located in Flint, Michigan, the Charles Stewart Mott Foundation has had a long-term commitment to funding in the area of poverty, and its 1993–96 reports contain explicit frames revealing its preferences and values about poverty policy. In 1994, for example, the foundation launched a five-year initiative to address poverty concerns, framed in terms of "reconnecting," "strengthening families," and "expanding economic opportunity." In 1995 it stated that the welfare reform debate had "tended to scapegoat the poor for their poverty" and that the nation had taken out "our national frustrations on the most vulnerable members of society." These statements clearly reflect the progressive viewpoint that the structural barriers faced by the poor are often severe and that eliminating these barriers should be the starting point for any national policy. As is clear from the organizations and projects the foundation gave to during this time, its concern with both ameliorating and reducing structural barriers was reflected in its orientation to giving, which contained a mix of charitable and philanthropic roles.

One innovative strategy that progressive and centrist foundations like Casey and Mott used to shape public opinion and policy during this time was the funding of documentaries and public television specials. In the annual reports, grants for films featuring the lives of the poor and the work of social service agencies in low-income communities were generally reported as initiatives tied to welfare reform funding, not as grant-making programs earmarked for media projects. It seems reasonable to assume that foundations made these grants because this type of work promoted specific frames through which they wanted the welfare reform debate to be viewed.

A shift in framing by the Russell Sage Foundation is a powerful example of how foundations attempted to shape the debate around policy solutions to poverty during this time. Russell Sage played a prominent role in funding poverty research beginning in 1987, and in contrast to most of the other centrist foundations overwhelmingly funded university-based research rather than think tanks. The foundation also frequently funded specific individuals, a trend found more often among conservative foundations. In 1993 Russell Sage spent almost $2.5 million on its poverty research program and was supporting many of the leading poverty researchers in the country, including Katherine Newman, Sheldon Danziger, and Gary Sandefur. However, in its 1994–95 annual report, just when the welfare reform debate was starting to take off, the foundation announced that the program was "successfully concluded." Although this funding shift may have ultimately served to distance it from the debate, it also reflected Russell Sage's desire to change the focus of that debate. The foundation wrote that "although the national debate about poverty has focused almost exclusively on welfare use and single parenthood, [Russell Sage Foundation]–sponsored studies . . . have repeatedly shown that the main culprit is not a change in family structure. Instead the principal cause has been the virtual collapse of wages among workers with limited educational background." The foundation then announced that the poverty program was being replaced by a program on the "future of work." Rather than disengagement, this move signaled a desire to reframe the debate and push it in a new direction.

The Public Response of Foundations to Welfare Reform, 1997–2001

When welfare reform was signed into law, foundations were not particularly outspoken in either their support or criticism. The lack of detail in the conservative foundations' annual reports makes it difficult to judge their response, but given that the law contained time limits and work requirements that were widely supported by conservatives in general, one can assume a fairly positive evaluation. It appears that most centrist and progressive foundations were supportive to the extent that they felt existing welfare policy was not working, but they were concerned about the punitive nature of the policy and possible negative outcomes for children.

For the centrist and progressive foundations, this concern was evident in the way they talked about welfare in their annual reports and also in more public messages. Annie E. Casey wrote in 1996 that "as a result" of the law, the foundation "deepened its support for promising reform directions that both increase employment and safeguard the interests and condition of dependent children." The Open Society Institute, previously silent in its annual reports regarding the domestic welfare agenda, spoke up in 1996, writing that in response to the recent legislation, it gave a $2 million grant to "build coalitions to safeguard the needs of poor children." Lynn Williams, president of the Eisenhower Foundation, weighed in on the debate in a letter to the editor of the *New York Times* on November 20, 1995, explicitly responding to a previous op-ed by Charles Murray. She did not challenge the need for reform, but she was highly critical of the proposed plan as not going far enough in providing appropriate supports for parents.

After passage of the legislation, the annual reports reveal a slight move toward a charitable orientation among the progressive and centrist foundations. Some, drawing on their capabilities as risk absorbers, announced funding initiatives to support families transitioning off welfare or stepped up funding for child care and work development programs. Others used their advantage of being outside the political system to act as mediators, bringing multiple groups together to fashion a more coordinated and streamlined response. These findings highlight that in the postreform period, the increase in funding for workforce development seen in the quantitative data was indeed reflective of both charitable and philanthropic concerns of the centrist and progressive foundations. In contrast, it appears that the conservative foundations began slowly moving away from welfare-related funding altogether.

The Charles Stewart Mott Foundation stated in its 1996 annual report that it was paying close attention to how welfare reform had changed the "landscape" for low-income Americans. It actively framed the issue in saying that its effort "was focused on helping to reshape thinking about welfare recipients, not as burdens and dependents, but as people with untapped assets and human potential." Its grant making represented a mixed charitable and philanthropic orientation, with continued funding for research endeavors but also funding for a host of programs whose mission was to help transition former welfare recipients into full-time workers. For example, the foundation's 1997 report describes its support for microenterprise opportunities for former welfare recipients, a funding area that reflects the role of social entrepreneur as well as risk absorber. In 1998 Mott continued to put welfare reform issues at the center of its grant making, stating that its "ultimate goal" was to "focus greater attention on these [employment] barriers, in order to help shape welfare policies and service delivery programs so they better address recipients' limitations and capacities for full-time work." In 1999 the foundation restructured grant-making initiatives again, announcing a new six-year plan focusing on the three areas it felt best represented "pathways out of poverty." This progressive foundation did not move away from welfare reform at all but rather adjusted its grant making to account for the policy change and continued to try to influence the way poverty was framed and addressed as a social problem in the United States.

The McKnight Foundation is also emblematic of foundations that met the challenge of welfare reform head on, taking both a social entrepreneurship and a mediator approach and assuming a combined charitable and philanthropic orientation. Immediately after welfare reform passed, in early 1997, the McKnight Foundation made a major commitment to give $20 million over two years to help facilitate welfare reform in Minnesota, where the foundation is based. This demonstrated a clear mediator approach and resulted in the funding of twenty-two state-level partnerships, formed among employers, social services agencies, and government entities. The foundation also sponsored several major conferences, hosted regional meetings, maintained an e-mail list, and put out a periodic newsletter, all to facilitate and report on the work of McKnight-funded partnerships. This huge influx in funding has been credited with helping spur a $53 million state grant modeled after the McKnight program and contributed to Minnesota's being considered a leader in transitioning families off welfare.[24]

The Chicago-based Joyce Foundation was also a leader in helping to shape welfare reform policy and outcomes in the Upper Midwest. The Joyce Foundation has a specific commitment to a philanthropic orientation, focusing on public policy rather than grants for service provision. The foundation acted as a social entrepreneur by funding think tanks that produced policy research and supporting evaluations to monitor the impact of welfare reform on families. Its giving in this area actually grew after the bill passed, and Joyce reported overall spending of $8 million on welfare-related research between 1996 and 2002. The foundation also acted as a mediator, helping to create a network of state welfare officials across the Midwest and ensuring that every grant made for research and evaluation also funded a communications strategy to disseminate results.[25] Finally, Joyce strategically distributed a report on the overall findings of Joyce-sponsored research to policymakers, right before the welfare reform legislation was to be reauthorized in 2002, and funded advocacy groups to provide an additional layer of outside monitoring and reporting on the issue.

A final example of creative action in the period following welfare reform enactment was the Lilly Endowment, which demonstrated how social entrepreneurship can play out even in foundations without an explicit commitment to social policy work. The Lilly Endowment played an important philanthropic role during this period through its large commitment to funding faith-based organizations and facilitating the growth of faith-based initiatives. Although

24. Clyde (2002).
25. O'Connell (2007).

"charitable choice" provisions, which allow explicitly faith-based organizations to compete for federal contracts, are now common in federal social policy legislation, the 1996 welfare reform was the first legislation to explicitly allow them. The Lilly Endowment jumped on these initiatives immediately and has consistently funded programs to help support faith-based organizations. Other than the faith-based funding, Lilly largely stayed away from welfare reform funding both before and after the legislation passed. It did, however, give some grants that indirectly supported welfare reform goals, for example, funds for workforce development programs embedded in larger projects, such as funding for a new convention center.

That many foundations remained silent during the debate over welfare reform or else continued to focus on other funding initiatives speaks to the diversity of interests of foundations and their desire to stick to stated funding priorities. The Mellon Foundation is a stand-out example of this, never mentioning issues related to welfare in its annual reports at any time between 1993 and 2001 and spending the vast majority of its public affairs grant making on issues related to Eastern Europe and immigration. That many foundations did not change course during this period of dramatic policy change is an important cautionary tale for those who call for private charity to step in and fill the gap created by government cutbacks or policy shifts.[26]

For many foundations, interest in framing the welfare reform debate faded quickly, even those who continued to fund research and evaluation programs. For most foundations in this study, discussion about issues relating to the poor and sparking system change was much more explicit in annual reports before 1996. This move away from explicit framing of welfare-related issues supports the idea that foundations were strategically discussing this funding in advance of the legislation. Once the policy passed, there was little need to spotlight these issues in the same way, and many foundations began to focus their annual reports around other issues, even if they were still funding in the area.

The conservative foundations seemed to back off the issue more quickly than the progressive and centrist foundations, although this is truer for Olin and Scaife than for Smith Richardson and Bradley. This may be related to the more specifically philanthropic orientation the conservative foundations took. If the conservative foundations considered the passage of the legislation the ultimate goal of their grant making, then it makes sense that they then moved on to other issues. In contrast, the centrist and progressive foundations, with their more mixed orientation to grant making, continued to fund programs and projects that were intended to maximize whatever positive benefits the new policy might have.

26. Tanner (1996); Olasky (1992).

Conclusion

This research addresses the issue of what U.S. foundations did in anticipation of and in response to the historic Personal Responsibility and Work Opportunity Act of 1996. Overall, we found that foundations took a primarily philanthropic approach and that foundation ideology did have some impact on funding patterns and in how they framed their work. In both analyses we found strong evidence that foundations were not passive bystanders during the welfare reform era. Giving to welfare reform–related activities increased in response to the legislation, and foundations clearly acted as social entrepreneurs throughout this time. They promoted particular policy trends, such as workforce development programs, supported key demonstration programs, funded influential think tanks and opinion makers, and directed funding overall toward projects and institutions that helped shape both welfare reform policy and the outcomes of that policy.

The quantitative data suggest that foundations assumed primarily philanthropic roles by funding major research and demonstration projects and helping support workforce development programs, rather than taking on the charitable role of providing support services to needy households or otherwise acting as risk absorbers. Only workforce development and research-related grants actually increased in response to the policy shift. This strategy makes sense, given that the overall amount of money foundations had to spend on welfare reform–related activities was minuscule compared with government welfare and safety net spending. In the case of welfare reform, foundations may have realized that they could make a greater contribution by affecting policy instead of individuals and families. Additionally, while the type of welfare-related projects foundations chose to support was noteworthy, the speed with which many foundations turned away from these issues is also an important finding. Overall, our research suggests a strong caution for those who call for decreasing public investment in social services so as not to crowd out increased private involvement.[27] Clearly, around this policy shift at least, foundations did not see a charitable orientation as their primary role.

Our analyses also make clear that foundation ideology had a strong impact on the giving patterns, orientation, and preferred roles of foundations. Conservative and progressive foundations were more likely than the centrist foundations to take on a philanthropic orientation by funding research. Additionally, the foundations with the least involvement in the debate, such as Lilly and Mellon, were centrist foundations. Perhaps because of the ideologically charged

27. Kingma (1989).

nature of the welfare reform debate, the foundations with more extreme political views were more invested in the outcome than foundations with a less-defined political identity.

Some foundations see having a charitable impact as an important part of their public identity. Many centrist and progressive foundations highlighted both their efforts to support new innovations and their funding of charitable social service activities. It is interesting, then, that quantitative data reveal that overall spending on areas such as social services, safety net, and child day care did not change during this time. Clearly, although many progressive and centrist foundations wanted to be seen as at least partially charitable, more attention was paid to philanthropy and social entrepreneurship.

Overall, the way centrist and progressive foundations discussed their welfare reform giving in their annual reports only partially corresponded with their giving patterns. There was less framing of the welfare debate overall in the years after the legislation passed, and the quantitative data show that many foundations moved away from funding in this area after two or three years. The tendency of progressive and centrist foundations to make statements in their annual reports emphasizing their philanthropic roles and work as social entrepreneurs also corresponded with their giving, but the increased discussion of the need to safeguard the interests of children after passage of reform was not. Although there was a large increase in workforce development funding, we saw no evidence of a corresponding increase in funding for safety net provision, day care, or family services.

The conservative foundations' strong philanthropic orientation was demonstrated by greater spending as a greater percentage of their welfare reform dollars on research than either progressive or centrist foundations, both before and after passage of the legislation. They gave much less, relatively speaking, to workforce development than the other two types of foundations and only minimally to the other areas. This group of foundations clearly saw their contribution as based in philanthropy, not charity. Because conservative foundations tended to have smaller assets than the centrist and progressive foundations, they had to think carefully and strategically about where to put their money to make the most impact. In this case, they gave less overall but focused heavily on research. This strategic, philanthropic orientation allowed them to make a much larger impact on the policy debate than they might have if they had followed a more diversified funding strategy. This may have also contributed to the fact that the conservative foundations were much quicker than the other foundations to back away from funding in this area after the law passed.

There is no doubt that as well as making their policy preferences explicit through their funding choices, foundations of all ideologies contributed greatly to framing the public debate and shaping policymakers' opinions on welfare reform. Many centrist and progressive foundations chose to frame their welfare-related giving in explicit ways in their annual reports, emphasizing the structural barriers that low-income families faced. The conservative foundations, on the other hand, chose not to say much about their philosophy or ideology in their public documents. They let their viewpoint be known by the institutions they supported and in the use of some conservative master frames when talking about their overall mission, such as emphasizing personal responsibility and traditional values. It is unclear exactly why the conservative foundations were so reticent about the rationale behind their giving. This could be an isomorphic effect, with foundations mimicking the plain style of the foundations they considered their peers. Alternatively, they may have felt that their more limited and strategic giving was clear in its intent and needed no further explanation.

In sum, in the context of welfare reform, foundations played a set of heterogeneous roles that focused more on philanthropy than on charity, differing slightly by ideology. We may see these patterns in other areas where government funding far outweighs private spending, such as education and health care for the elderly. This is a pragmatic approach, given that foundations can never serve as an adequate substitute for government spending on social services. Their overall response to welfare reform supports the argument that foundations are primarily concerned about strategic impact and innovation. Their effort to support innovation by funding research or complementary programs was an example of this, as was their role as promoters of policy change, shaping arguments and providing data to guide policy choices. As a result, however, foundations' focus on philanthropic goals may have left some of the neediest populations in the United States without a charitable safety net during the welfare reform era.

10

The State and International Philanthropy: The Contribution of American Foundations, 1919–1991

STEVEN HEYDEMANN WITH REBECCA KINSEY

The historian Eric Hobsbawm has called the period from the end of World War I to the end of the cold war the "short twentieth century."[1] At the start of the period covered here, few professionally staffed, multipurpose foundations of any kind existed. Beginning with the interwar period, however, private foundations proliferated and became increasingly engaged with issues that extended beyond America's borders. By the 1990s the number of U.S. foundations working internationally, or addressing international issues through domestic grant making, had expanded significantly. Today, more than 60 percent of the one thousand largest grant-making foundations in the United States are involved in international activities of one kind or another. As the scale of international activities expanded, so did their scope. U.S. foundations are now active in every part of the world and address a vast array of issues, from peace and security, economic development, and public health to education, the environment, migration, humanitarian assistance, refugee relief, and political advocacy—among many others. These activities are carried out by organizations ranging from large, professionally staffed foundations with multibillion-dollar endowments and offices spread across the world to foundations sponsored by multinational firms to local

---

1. Hobsbawm (1994). This periodization also makes sense from a foundation perspective. The Rockefeller Foundation was created in 1913, marking the extension of scientific philanthropy into international affairs. The end of the cold war marked an even more formative turning point in the history of U.S. international foundations.

religious organizations and small, community-based groups frequently staffed by volunteers. To do justice to the dense and diverse landscape of international philanthropy in the United States would far exceed what it is possible to cover in a single chapter. As a result, we limit our focus to the largest, professionally staffed, multipurpose grant-making and operating private foundations.

The scope of this chapter is further limited by the inadequacy of data on international foundations and their work, especially for the interwar and immediate postwar periods. Foundations' record-keeping and reporting practices vary considerably, leaving an uneven historical account of their activities. And national-level data collection efforts did not begin in earnest until the 1970s. Thus although a small but important secondary literature and some key archival holdings are available, it is not possible to provide comprehensive data on the scale and scope of international philanthropy in the United States for the period before 1980. One effect of these gaps is that the story of international foundations and their contribution is biased in favor of the largest and best-funded among them, pushing into the background the work of smaller and less well endowed foundations.

Despite these limitations, tracking the emergence and growth of international foundation activities sheds significant light on broader questions about foundations and their contribution to society in the United States. What foundations choose to work on and how they do their work provide insight not only into the roles and functions of foundations in society but also, and crucially, into the relationship between private foundations, society, and the state. In the priorities they establish, in the movement of issues onto and off foundation agendas, and in their own conceptions about how most effectively to achieve their aims, international foundations offer an exceptionally useful platform from which to view shifts and movements in America's role in the international system; to assess how the government has responded to, and worked to manage, the presence of nonstate actors in the international arena; and to explore how the role of the third sector—nonprofit organizations—in international affairs has changed over time. Moreover, given the centrality of the state in the management of foreign relations, in the regulation of international flows, and in global governance, the state-foundation relationship takes on particular prominence.

At the same time, the contribution of international foundations extends beyond the direct (and often elusive) impact of their grant making and programs to include their role in creating space within the international arena for nonstate and nonmarket actors to shape the trajectory of international affairs, however modestly, and to influence how Americans think about the world. In this sense, foundations matter not only for what they do but for what they are: civil society actors that constitute one element of an international third sector. Whether foundations are national institutions that undertake international work or transnational actors headquartered in the United States is an important distinction, with significant implications for how we understand the relationship between state, society, and foundations. We explore both aspects of international foundations—their relations with the state and their role as nonstate actors—in the following sections.

Defining Key Terms

Our first obligation, however, is to define some of the terms used in this chapter. In particular, we need to specify what we mean by *international* and clarify how we define the roles and contributions of international foundations.

When is a U.S.-based foundation international? Despite our commonsense understanding of the term, the question is not entirely straightforward. How we answer it is important in establishing the size and composition of the sector that falls within the scope of this chapter and in addressing questions about its roles and contributions.

The conventional definition of an *international foundation* would include private organizations that are legally registered in the United States as nonprofit charitable foundations and that make grants or otherwise use their funds for the direct support of activities taking place in other countries. The central element of this definition is that funds cross borders, and the vast majority of what we think of as international foundations fall within this definition. It encompasses the Ford Foundation, the John D. and Catherine T. MacArthur Foundation, the Rockefeller Foundation, the Open Society Institute, the Bill and Melinda Gates Foundation, the Carnegie Corporation of New York, the Charles Stewart Mott Foundation, and many others that have long-established roles in cross-border grant making.

Yet the definition could also include foundations whose international grant making is indirect: their funds might not cross borders, but their grantees do. This category could include a community foundation that funds international exchange programs for local students or an operating foundation, such as the Kettering Foundation or the Stanley Foundation, that hosts international meetings involving participants from around the world.

Funders that address international issues within a domestic American context—supporting public outreach, publications, educational activities, or other work within the borders of the United States—would also fit our definition. This category would include the Ford Foundation, the Carnegie Corporation, and the Rockefeller Foundation, which helped to build the infrastructure of area studies in the United States, worked to promote international exchange programs, supported U.S. engagement with international institutions, and sought to strengthen U.S. expertise on foreign affairs by creating think tanks and policy research organizations. Recently, foundations advancing conservative ideas have played a prominent role in this regard through grant making that is almost entirely domestic but supports activities with an international focus, including advocacy research in areas such as U.S. foreign policy, international security, market-based economic development, and the limits of global governance.

In many respects, these foundations adopted the earlier strategy of their counterparts, creating a network of conservative think tanks, policy research institutes, and affiliated scholars. This group includes the John M. Olin Foundation and the Sarah Scaife Foundation—both of which make grants only to U.S. organizations.[2] It could also include the Lynde and Harry Bradley Foundation.[3] While the activities of these foundations might fall outside a strict definition of *international*, their impact on the international arena through their influence on elite opinion and foreign policy debates in the United States suggests that they cannot easily be excluded from our sample. Defining them as out of scope, moreover, could have serious implications for our findings, skewing our conception of foundations' international impact by neglecting an influential set of actors.

These three sets of organizations (funders whose grants cross borders; funders whose grantees cross borders; and funders whose domestic activities address international issues) vary significantly, yet they fall relatively easily within the scope of this chapter. However, for other kinds of international organizations, such as those engaged in corporate philanthropy or international aid and charitable organizations like the Red Cross, the fit is less clear. To keep the category within manageable limits, we adopt four criteria in defining international foundations. Thus for the purposes of this chapter we define an *international foundation* as a private, independent organization whose assets are held in the form of an endowment, whose principal activity is to disburse funds either in the form of grants or in support of foundation-initiated activities, and whose grants or activities have a significant international dimension.

This group includes both private independent grant-making foundations, such as the Ford Foundation and the William and Flora Hewlett Foundation, and also private operating foundations like the Twentieth Century Fund (now the Century Foundation) and the Stanley Foundation. However, our definition rules out organizations such as the National Endowment for Democracy, which maintains an active international grant program but is funded on an annual basis by the U.S. Congress. It also excludes organizations such as the Washington-based office of the Friedrich Ebert Stiftung, a leading German political party foundation, as well as the Catholic Church and the Red Cross. Corporate foundations are similarly excluded from our consideration here: as the agents

2. Based on a review of their annual reports and tax returns for the 2000–04 period.

3. Although Bradley makes a negligible number of grants outside the United States (largely in Rome for issues relating to the Catholic Church), its grant making is largely limited to U.S.-based grantees.

of private businesses, they lack the independence and typically the endowment needed to qualify under our criteria. Also out of scope are foundations that depend on voluntary contributions to support their international activities. While these criteria skew our sample in ways that privilege the small number of large, professionally staffed, multipurpose foundations, it does capture most grant-making and program expenditures by American foundations that do international work.

Roles and Contributions of International Foundations

In much of the developing world, social indicators are significantly better today than they were a century ago. Literacy is up. Life expectancy has increased. Educational attainment has improved. Fewer people are living below the poverty line. Polio has been all but eradicated. A network of institutions exists to strengthen global governance, including, prominently, the United Nations. Nuclear stockpiles have been reduced. Global environmental protections have been strengthened. Almost one hundred and fifty countries have ratified a treaty banning the production and use of land mines, an outcome that resulted in part from the advocacy efforts of an emerging global civil society: transnational activists who collaborated across borders to change international law.[4] Innovations in agricultural technology, microcredit and other unconventional financial systems, and the spread of communications and information technologies have improved the well-being of the world's least well off peoples.

Foundations claim a prominent role in the achievement of all these outcomes. Do they deserve such credit? Judging from what foundations themselves tell us, there can be little doubt. Their annual reports overflow with references to foundation impact, strategic grant making, and the crucial roles foundations play as innovators, risk takers, advocates in behalf of worthy international causes, and facilitators of global social change. Even foundation critics, from both left and right, are inclined to depict them as powerful actors whose work has decisive consequences.[5] Whether foundations are derided as plutocratic bastions of the power elite or castigated for their failures in international fields such as refugee relief, economic development, and democracy promotion, the underlying assumption is that they possess significant influence and power.[6]

4. See Keck and Sikkink (1998), Anheier and others (2005), and other editions of *Global Civil Society*.

5. For critical accounts that stress the unrecognized power of foundations and direct particular attention to international grant makers, see Dowie (2001) and Roelofs (2003). Additional critical views (both lacking balance) are from the left, Berman (1983), and from the right, Fonte (2004).

6. Harrell-Bond (1986) focuses only in part on foundations, saving much of its criticism for state-led relief efforts. See also Escobar (1995) and Quigley (1997).

Such assumptions, however, are open to question. In the international arena, as in every other domain of foundation activity, outcomes rarely have singular causes. Moreover, foundations typically lack the resources or the leverage unilaterally to bring about significant change. As one thoughtful observer of philanthropy has noted, "Foundations cannot operate at a scale that is transformative except perhaps in the rare instance when a foundation-funded technological breakthrough, such as the green revolution, is taken to a massive scale when adopted by the market. Such exceptions aside, the major strategic interventions made by foundations—policy analysis, policy advocacy, social movements, social empowerment, public education—are swamped by larger social, cultural, and economic forces."[7]

Despite their self-described role as innovators, foundations are, as a rule, risk averse. More often than not, they swim downstream rather than fight the current, and they tend to swim in packs. International foundations have long been concerned in general with issues of peace and security, public health, and economic development. In specific areas of work, however, such as the global ban on land mines, HIV/AIDS, global economic governance, international migration, or microcredit, foundations typically enter the scene only after other actors create the conditions needed to spark their interest—and these conditions often include the emergence of organizations able to serve effectively as the recipients of foundation support. [8] This is not to say that foundation work in these or other controversial areas carries no risks at all. The political and social context in which foundations operate has, along with many other domains of life, become increasingly politicized and polarized over the past two decades; liberal and progressive foundations in particular confront a less congenial political landscape today than in the period from the 1970s to the 1990s. Moreover, international grant making is subject to substantial federal oversight and scrutiny. Foundations risk significant sanctions, for example, if they are found to violate post-9/11 homeland security guidelines of the U.S. Treasury Department.[9] What this does suggest, however, is that foundations often act less as true innovators than as supporters of trends that are already percolating widely in different locations in American society and, increasingly, in the international system at large.

Foundations also hedge their bets, making relatively small commitments in a range of issue areas rather than concentrating their resources. They tend to have

7. Prewitt (1999a, p. 25).

8. Foundation agendas are heavily influenced by organizational cultures and constraints. Certain kinds of problems look more tractable than others to organizations with a limited repertoire of strategies. Even quite pressing international concerns, therefore, may not receive attention if they require responses that foundations feel they are institutionally ill equipped to make.

9. See "Philanthropy and Homeland Security," transcript of a panel discussion sponsored by the Center for Democracy and Civil Society, Georgetown University, March 11, 2004, Washington, D.C.

short attention spans. They shift priorities and grant dollars from issue to issue or region to region in relatively short funding cycles, further mitigating the long-term impact of their presence in a particular field—though with some important exceptions, such as support for the struggle against apartheid, the Ford Foundation's decades-long commitment to area studies in American higher education, the long-term effort of conservative foundations to influence American foreign policy, and the Gates Foundation's attention to HIV/AIDS.[10]

Rethinking Foundation Roles

If international foundations deserve less credit and less blame and wield less power than is sometimes attributed to them, a balanced assessment would nonetheless acknowledge a number of important contributions that international foundations have made and positive roles that they have played. Foundations serve an important legitimation role. Through their grant making and other activities, foundations lend their reputations to particular issues, institutions, and individuals. In their willingness to commit resources and to identify particular problems or people as deserving of foundation—and, by implication, public—attention, they confer their own institutional legitimacy on the causes, ideas, and grantees with which they affiliate. The inverse of this is the gate-keeping role that foundations perform in the ways they allocate and withhold their resources. Foundations typically, and not unreasonably, justify this process as strategic philanthropy: it permits them to concentrate limited resources and maximize the potential impact of their work. Inevitably, however, this gate-keeping function—delimiting the boundaries of foundation interests or the pool of eligible applicants—excludes and even marginalizes issues and organizations that find themselves screened out by foundation filters. It is also designed, often quite explicitly, to discipline potential grant seekers, creating incentives to define activities in terms that reflect the priorities of funders.

International foundations also serve as amplifiers. They publicize the activities of grantees; mobilize public and official interest in their issue agendas; help to validate international issues as deserving of attention, both within elite policy networks and among the media; promote their own international engagement with particular activities, values, and organizations; and, through the legitimacy that foundation support confers, provide international grantees with valuable symbolic, public relations, and financial resources.

10. Early in the current decade, for instance, both the MacArthur and the Rockefeller foundations publicly proclaimed their interest in issues of global economic governance. Within only three or four years, both had shifted their attention away from this area and toward a focus on the next critical issue area: global migration. Major programmatic shifts have also occurred recently at the Atlantic Philanthropies, the Carnegie Corporation, and other large international foundations.

Related to this, they have a role as importers and exporters of ideas and practices. By virtue of their location within national and global networks of expertise, advocacy, public policy, and communications, international foundations facilitate the transnational movement of ideas, technologies, values, and policy options and serve as models of problem solving, social change, advocacy, institution building, and program development. They serve, in effect, as conveyor belts of ideas, helping to move them from their origins in one location—geographic, institutional, disciplinary, social—outward to broader publics.

Few foundation roles have been as important, however, as their contribution as institution builders. Indeed, building institutional infrastructure and creating organizational and human capacity across a wide range of fields may well have been the most significant contribution of international foundations during the twentieth century. These efforts include some of the most prominent and influential organizations in the world that address international issues, including think tanks and public policy institutes such as the Council on Foreign Relations, the Foreign Policy Association, the Brookings Institution, the American Enterprise Institute, the Royal Institute of International Affairs (London), and the Carnegie Endowment for International Peace. Foundations have played a pivotal role in creating the infrastructure that supports area studies centers at universities across the United States, as well as university-based research and policy centers in the fields of peace and security, development, foreign affairs, and conflict resolution. International foundations took the lead in establishing a vast array of international medical, social science, cultural, artistic, technological, and agricultural institutes.

Closely associated with this has been the work of foundations as coalition builders. Exploiting their location as key nodes in select organizational and social networks, international foundations foster ties among organizations and individuals, helping to create epistemic communities, spread ideas about "best practice" in particular fields, facilitate collaboration among groups with similar aims, and bolster local grant recipients through their participation in broader organizational networks. Finally, foundations have also contributed to society through their symbolic and representative role. As nonprofit organizations, international foundations occupy a visible and influential position as representatives of an international third sector. Through their grant making, and in carrying out the roles outlined above, foundations express the possibility for nonstate, nonmarket actors to intervene in and to help shape the trajectory of international affairs.

As a result of their contributions through these seven roles, international foundations themselves have become visible and influential elements of the infrastructure of global civil society. They have become more effective not only in exporting American norms and models around the world but also in bringing non-U.S. possibilities and experiences to the attention of Americans. They both represent and promote the diffusion of international authority away from state actors—even while occasionally seeking partnerships with states. Indeed, in certain issue areas foundations have exercised more influence than, and outspent, national governments.[11]

The State and the Contingent Autonomy of International Foundations

Private foundations typically are described as highly autonomous institutions—economically independent, responsible neither to voters nor to stockholders, and able to chart their own course with relative impunity. Yet the history of international foundations during the twentieth century challenges this conventional view. Despite their significance as nonstate actors, the international experiences of foundations reveal as much about the limits of foundation autonomy and the constraints under which they operate as about the scope and breadth of foundation power. In the international arena, whether in efforts to shape foreign policy, bring about change in local settings, or educate Americans about global affairs, the autonomy of foundations is far more contingent than is often assumed.

State-foundation relations can vary widely over time and across issue areas. They can involve cooperation and collaboration between state agencies and international foundations, as exemplified by the post–World War II reconstruction efforts of the Rockefeller and Carnegie foundations in Europe and by the Ford Foundation's engagement with development efforts in South Asia from the 1950s to the 1970s.[12] They can involve co-optation, as in the use by American intelligence agencies of private foundations to influence international affairs and engage in low-level espionage.[13] Relations are also on occasion confrontational, as in foundation efforts during the 1970s and 1980s to end the nuclear arms race and contain the destructive power of both the United States and the Soviet Union.[14]

Nonetheless, the state is always present, and it bears heavily both on what foundations are able to do internationally and how they conduct themselves. International foundation activities are not only scrutinized and regulated by

11. For more than a decade before 2001, the philanthropic networks created by financier George Soros, including the Open Society Institute, outspent the U.S. government in the area of democracy promotion. Soros's commitments have been estimated at some $500 million a year at their peak. See Melia (2006, pp. 122–30).

12. Sutton (1987, pp. 41–91); G. Hess (2005, pp. 51–71).

13. Diamond (1992).

14. Writing on the early Reagan period, the former executive director of the Winston Foundation for World Peace noted, "Clearly, the polite discussion of the Council on Foreign Relations or the Brookings Institution was unlikely to stop this careening juggernaut of the renewed Cold War. Something more public, and far more confrontational, was required." Tirman (2000, p. 3).

the U.S. government, they are also actively, sometimes aggressively, policed by elected officials and bureaucrats seeking to reestablish the authority of the state over foundations, to tighten the accountability of foundations to government, to impose controls over their activities, and to sanction foundations that appear—whether accurately or not—to have transgressed the limits of their autonomy.[15] At times, international foundations have intentionally pushed the boundaries of their autonomy and challenged the state on important matters of international concern (the Vietnam War and issues of nuclear nonproliferation stand out in this regard). At other times, however, they engage the state more cautiously. Aware of their vulnerability, international foundations exhibit self-censorship—refusing to enter fields of work that are seen as especially likely to draw unwelcome attention from the state and voluntarily imposing constraints on grantees in an effort to appear responsive to the concerns of politicians and state agencies. This behavior on the part of international foundations was evident during the McCarthy era and is again visible in the responses of some international foundations to new, post-9/11 restrictions on their grant-making autonomy.[16]

Seen in this light, what moves to the fore in the history of international foundations during the short twentieth century is not the gradual, linear expansion of foundation roles internationally or the steady accretion of foundation assertiveness and confidence as autonomous nonstate actors in the international arena. What emerges, instead, is the story of a complex and often unsettled association between the U.S. state and foundations, in which the latter struggled to create domains of autonomy and influence while reacting to the evolving configuration of state institutions, roles, and authorities as the United States acquired an increasingly prominent international presence. Over time, and increasingly in the period after World War II, as the foreign policy and international development apparatus of the U.S. government itself expanded, states came to impinge even more profoundly on the international work of U.S. foundations. With the establishment of the U.S. Agency for International Development during the Kennedy administration, for example, the management of U.S.-Indian relations with respect to development assistance—an arena in which the Ford and Rockefeller foundations had occupied roles comparable to government agencies—tended to be assimilated into the growing development aid bureaucracy of the U.S. government.[17] This shifting balance of authority and influence away from foundations was reinforced by developments outside the United States: decolonization, the growing authority of "new states" in areas previously under

15. See Nielsen (1972, especially pp. 5–20).

16. This behavior stands in contrast to the willingness of multipurpose foundations to challenge the United States with respect to domestic policy, even as they adopt more submissive relations on international policy.

17. G. Hess (2005, pp. 51–71).

European control, and the increasing prominence of state-led international institutions, many of which foundations had played a role in creating.

In the twentieth century, therefore, state-foundation relations were marked by the growing presence and authority of state agencies in fields in which foundations had earlier established their visibility and influence, including international disaster and humanitarian relief, postwar reconstruction, higher education, advanced scientific research, international exchange, and development assistance. This shift was marked, in part, by the declining reliance of agencies like the U.S. Department of State on foundation partnerships to accomplish diplomatic purposes that the state had previously lacked the capacity to pursue independently.

Certainly, foundations like Rockefeller, Carnegie, and Ford, among others, did not disengage from international activities as the government's presence grew. But the balance of funding, influence, and visibility shifted decisively toward the state, leaving private foundations in a less prominent position internationally by the 1960s and 1970s. Moreover, this trend was accompanied by heightened levels of state regulation of foundations—in part the result of changes brought about in the wake of the Filer Commission and the 1969 Tax Reform Act—but also as a partisan political response to the role foundations played in the 1960s in support of civil rights and against the war in Vietnam.

As the state expanded its international engagements and capacity, foundation roles underwent change, as well. Within the United States, private foundations emerged during the interwar and postwar periods as key supporting actors in the construction of American internationalism and the promotion of global governance—building domestic support for an assertive American role internationally—even as their presence and grant making overseas began to be overshadowed by U.S. diplomatic aid and military activities related to the cold war. They became especially active in the field of cultural diplomacy, working to mitigate cold war tensions by promoting international exchange and dialogue in a wide range of fields—activities that were most often framed as contributions to the broader anticommunist aims of U.S. foreign policy.

Above all, however, large foundations transformed the landscape of American higher education and public policy research, creating the institutional infrastructure domestically that was seen as an essential support for America's role as a global superpower. Beginning in the early interwar period, and increasing in scale after World War II, large international foundations underwrote the development of international expertise in areas such as public health and natural and agricultural sciences but also, and centrally, in language and area studies within American universities. These and other foundations funded cultural, academic, and diplomatic exchange programs, created international think tanks (both in the United States and overseas), and fostered U.S. engagement with international institutions. They advanced ideas about the possibilities for international cooperation and global governance that helped pave the way for the creation of, among other institutions, the United Nations.

Their successes, in turn, fueled growing antagonism toward foundations among anti-internationalist conservatives in the United States and, later, helped spark the rise of conservative foundations and the "counterintellectuals" they funded to challenge internationalism as the basis of U.S. foreign policy and to promote a more limited conception of America's role in the world—perspectives that found increasing purchase with the ascendance of the conservative wing of the Republican Party in American political life in the 1970s and 1980s.[18]

Thus the twentieth century was marked by the ongoing struggle of foundations to identify international domains in which they might continue to exercise influence as state roles and authorities evolved. Their strategies sometimes converged with official preferences (in economic and social development, international public health, and support for international research infrastructure) but often diverged from or collided with U.S. policies (in areas such as peace and security, arms control, and challenging military interventions in Asia and Latin America). This mix gave rise to a complicated matrix of interactions between foundations and the state, simultaneously collaborative and conflictual, throughout the postwar period.

Foundation strategies also included movement during the cold war period and beyond toward nonstate spheres of activity. This took the form, in particular, of a growing role in the development and thickening of transnational civil society and advocacy infrastructure, often with the stated aim of containing the authority of states, rendering states accountable to civil societies, and raising the visibility of nonstate priorities within international institutions. If, in the interwar period, the elites who ran international foundations had often seen them as private means for the pursuit of national purposes, from the 1960s onward their successors began, slowly, gradually, and unevenly, to develop a keener sense of themselves as transnational and nonstate actors.

Throughout these years, we find variation in the intensity of state intervention in and regulation of foundation activities. Yet distinct patterns are evident when we review the development of international foundations in the twentieth century during three periods: the interwar period; the period from post–World War II to the 1960s; and the period from the 1960s to the end of the cold war, around 1989.

18. For a conservative perspective on the rise of one prominent conservative foundation, see Miller (2006). See also, from a critical perspective, the publications of the National Committee for Responsive Philanthropy, including Krehely, House, and Kernan (2004).

The Emergence of International Foundations
in the Interwar Period

Long before the creation of the first international foundations, American philanthropy had a well-established presence outside the United States.[19] Charitable campaigns, humanitarian relief, reconstruction, missionary activity, education, public health, and social service provision were all well-established spheres of international philanthropy by the turn of the twentieth century. Yet the emergence of what are known as private, professional, multipurpose, international foundations in the first decades of the twentieth century marked the intersection of three trends that were transforming American philanthropy and society at the time, including both elite and popular conceptions of America's role in the world.

The first of these was the move toward scientific philanthropy in the United States around the turn of the century and the appearance, with the founding of the Russell Sage Foundation in 1907, of formal, permanent, bureaucratic organizations, professionally staffed and permanently endowed, with a mandate to identify and address the "root causes" of social ills.[20] The second was the growing influence of liberal internationalist sensibilities among American elites in the late nineteenth and early twentieth centuries, precursors to the rise of Wilsonian internationalism as the (short-lived) framework for the organization of American foreign policy following World War I. The third was the increasing visibility of new ideas about social reform and novel conceptions about possibilities for the amelioration of problems like illiteracy, disease, intolerance, hunger, and the exploitation of labor, both in the United States and overseas.

The confluence of these trends had an indelible impact on the formation of international foundations, shaping their identities in enduring ways. World War I, in particular, and the rapid collapse of the international system into conflict in 1914 gave urgency and direction to international foundations in their initial decades. It drove their agendas toward a concern with issues that, in one form or another, have remained central to their work ever since: avoiding the renewal of international conflict, taming the power of states, constructing a vision among elites, experts, and the public of a common destiny and shared humanity, and identifying and overcoming the root causes of conflict, with an emphasis on

19. The history of American philanthropy, including international philanthropy, has been told elsewhere and is beyond the scope of this chapter. See, among other works, Curti (1988); McCarthy (2003); Bremner (1960); Friedman and McGarvie (2003).

20. Hammack and Wheeler (1994). This moment in the shift from charitable giving to scientific philanthropy is also illustrated by some of the Rockefeller Foundation's earliest activities in support of humanitarian relief efforts in Europe during World War I—activities toward which it contributed some $22 million between 1914 and 1918 (almost $300 million in 2006 dollars).

understanding the relationships that link economic development, the arts, education, and health to global cooperation and security.

We can trace to this period the idea that the application of expert knowledge could achieve the systematic betterment of humankind, not only in the United States but universally, melding neatly with the conviction that U.S. experiences provided the appropriate model for the social and economic development of non-Western societies.[21] Properly applied, reason and rationality would ameliorate the impulses that drove nations and peoples into conflict. In 1911, for example, Nicholas Murray Butler, a board member of the recently established Carnegie Endowment for International Peace, provided "the first authoritative and detailed statement of the work to be undertaken and the method pursued" by the endowment: "The establishment of the Carnegie Endowment for International Peace," he noted, "marks an epoch, in that it furnishes the organization and the means for a sustained and systematic effort to reach and convince the public opinion of the world by scientific argument and exposition. Talk about the evils of war there has been in plenty; we are now ready and anxious for something more constructive."[22] Echoing this sentiment several decades later, the Rockefeller Foundation declared that

> to speak of research in the field of international relations in such an anxious and disillusioned hour as this may seem almost like a jest. Everywhere reason is on the defensive and we live in danger that mass hysteria will completely overwhelm it at a time when it is most needed as a safeguard. . . . Friendly relations between nations must be based on an intelligent understanding of the contribution which each is in a position to make to the other.[23]

These comments underscore the liberal sensibility of the era: the post–World War I urgency that drove concerns about achieving international understanding and managing armed conflict; the positive contribution science, including social science, would assuredly make to world peace; the commitment to institutions as mechanisms of global governance; and the certainty, in the aftermath of World War I, of the need to create frameworks that might strengthen international coordination and render the world more secure—in particular, the notion that nonstate actors, linked through networks of expertise, dialogue, research, and mutual exchange, could advance the aims of economic, social, and human

21. For example, the early work of the Phelps Stokes Fund to strengthen education in Africa. See Berman (1971, pp. 132–45); Holmes (1938, pp. 475–85); Yellin (2002, pp. 319–52); and Davis (1976, pp. 87–99). The experience of the Phelps Stokes Fund in African education is one of many instances in which U.S. experiences were explicitly exported as models to be emulated.

22. "Carnegie Endowment for International Peace" (1911, p. 757).

23. Rockefeller Foundation (1938), cited in Curti (1988, pp. 305–06).

development and of global security. In the view of their founders, the affairs of nations and problems of social and economic development had become sufficiently complex to require the formation of elite specialists. These experts, in turn, required institutional arenas within which they could deploy their skills, interact with others of similar outlook, training, and sensibility, and communicate their ideas to government and the public.[24] All of these became lasting elements of international foundation activity.

The interwar period was formative in other ways, as well. As early as the second decade of the twentieth century, for example, international philanthropy already reflected a bifurcated structure, with a tiny number of large foundations occupying dominant positions and pursuing broad agendas while a larger number of small foundations engaged in niche activities. Yet enduring patterns are also evident in other, more important, respects. The earliest international foundations fashioned a template that has influenced the trajectory of international philanthropy for much of the past century—in the self-characterizations of foundation founders and the rhetoric they used to justify themselves; the design of their programs; their thematic priorities; their organizational arrangements; and their ambivalent relationship to the state. In this, the development of international foundations in the United States has been strikingly path dependent. Early choices about the rhetoric, form, and content of international philanthropy established adaptive but resilient organizational frameworks that have constrained successor generations, ensuring that for the most part, foundations today do indeed bear the clear imprint not only of their founders' intentions but of the institutional arrangements they designed.

Four elements of this template stand out: the organizational form that international foundations established to conduct their activities; an explicit focus on public policy, elite opinion, and public education as domains in which to exert influence and on the potential of knowledge to achieve social and political change; the grant-making strategies international foundations pursued to advance their aims, notably creating institutions, promoting the formation of expert knowledge, disseminating knowledge to state elites and the public, and sponsoring international networks of policy and knowledge elites; and a hybrid pattern of state-foundation relations combining an uneasy mix of partnership, autonomy, conflict, and constraint.

During these years, international foundations consolidated an institutional model that became widespread and remains largely intact. The founders of international foundations defined their creations in terms of broad, benign

24. Karl (1997, pp. 207–20). International foundations and their role in the production of policy elites were part of a broader process of elite formation in which private foundations exercised considerable influence.

public purposes while fashioning an institutional form—the multipurpose grant-making or operating foundation, governed by prominent members of the political, academic, and business elite, organized around a mix of thematic and regional programs, and staffed by experts in specific areas of work—that provided both for continuity of institutional structure and also for extraordinary flexibility in the specific issues that would make up the foundation's priorities. Moreover, from the outset, and despite their embrace of science and expertise, international foundations exhibited a shared commitment to doing over talking—the imperative of applying research to problems in the public arena. As Butler stressed, the value of science lay in its potential to "convince the public opinion," not simply as means for generating new knowledge.

In addition, the earliest international foundations adopted grant-making strategies that established important and lasting precedents, as institution builders and coalition builders, in particular. During the interwar years international foundations played a crucial role in creating the organizational infrastructure and global policy networks that supported the management of international affairs.[25] They gave substance to the notion that global governance constituted a profession that demanded its own specially trained cadres of experts. Indeed, it is hard to overestimate the extent to which a handful of major foundations in the United States created international affairs as a field of study and a domain of professional expertise, including its organization into component parts such as international law, conflict resolution, area studies, security studies (and, later, peace studies), international public policy, diplomacy, and others.[26]

The emergence and early expansion of international foundation activities also benefited significantly from a fortunate confluence during the interwar period of foundation priorities, on one hand, and the dominant strands of U.S. foreign policy at the time, on the other. The alignment between the two was not, of course, the product of serendipity: it was in part a product of the shared worldview and social backgrounds that linked leading philanthropists and state elites and led both to view as eminently appropriate the idea that private institutions could supplement and enhance state capacity in addressing international concerns. The alignment was not complete and certainly did not preclude tensions between foundations and state agencies. Nonetheless, these conflicts took place

25. Indeed, they also played a role in creating the physical infrastructure to support international peace. Carnegie was responsible for the construction of several "palaces of peace," including the International Court of Justice at The Hague, "hoping that these forums for friendship and discussion would lessen the strife that led to war." Lagemann (1989, pp. 20–21).

26. In other areas, notably international scholarly and cultural exchange, smaller foundations contributed much to their institutional development, for example, the World Peace Foundation in Boston, the Institute of Current World Affairs in Chicago, and the Watumull Foundation in Hawaii.

in the context of a state-foundation relationship that reflected a high degree of symmetry between the two. Woodrow Wilson's commitment to global governance, to the importance of permanent international institutions for the resolution of conflict, and to the value of mutual understanding as a pillar of international security extended significant legitimacy to private foundations that, broadly speaking, defined their international goals and activities in similar terms. As a result, questions of foundation autonomy and state authority were less pressing in these years than they were to become in the post–World War II period, when cold war tensions infused the practices and politics of international philanthropy.

The contributions of international foundations during this period were substantial and enduring, not least because of the close ties between political and philanthropic elites. They included not only new institutions and the rise of foreign policy as a field of knowledge production and technical expertise but also, and perhaps even more important, the enactment and consolidation of norms that legitimated nonstate participation in the management of international relations. International foundations played a critical role in the promotion of new ways of thinking about international affairs, of the possibilities for global governance, and of the role of the United States in pursuit of this aim, a role that proved nothing less than transformative. They helped to embed within U.S. foreign policy a liberal internationalist sensibility that has persisted ever since—a defining element of what Tony Smith calls "America's mission."[27]

The Cold War and America's International Foundations

The investment of U.S. foundations in international understanding, the establishment of international institutions, and the formation of a global, cosmopolitan elite charged with guiding national governments toward more peaceful relations proved ineffective in the face of the world's descent into World War II. Yet the war itself, and in particular the use of nuclear weapons against Japan, cemented even more firmly among leaders of international foundations the urgency of strengthening and expanding the institutions, principles of governance, expert networks, and forms of knowledge that might sustain peace and security in the international system—and, not coincidentally, reinforce U.S. power and prestige around the world.[28] The collapse of global governance in 1938 thus reinforced postwar commitments to more encompassing and more

27. Smith (1994).

28. Parmar (2002, pp. 13–30). Like Berman's study, Parmar's work contains much of value but adopts far too simplistic a notion of the relationship between foundation activities and the state. Intentionality and agency in linking foundation activities to state purposes requires more careful and more critical use of foundation documents than they receive from either Parmar or Berman.

authoritative frameworks for securing world order—firmly anchored in American military and economic power.

In the early postwar period, the close relationship between government and foundations served these purposes well. Leading international foundations drew for their leadership and senior staff on men who had gained managerial experience in government agencies during the war. This generation of foundation executives, including Paul Hoffman at the Ford Foundation and Dean Rusk at the Rockefeller Foundation, carried into their positions commitments honed during wartime and postwar government service to American leadership in the international system and to international philanthropy as a means to advance the policy priorities of the state. Government, in turn, benefited from foundation support in fashioning the institutional infrastructure of postwar global governance, including the Bretton Woods system and the United Nations. The intellectual justifications for and institutional architecture of a liberal internationalist order found ample support not only through the grant making of large international foundations but also from the networks of policy institutes, research centers, and university-based programs that were created with foundation support during the interwar period and expanded enormously in the decades after the war.[29] As in the prewar period, this role in shaping the postwar order can be seen as a major contribution of international foundations during the period from 1945 to 1965.

Continuity from prewar to postwar contexts, however, should not be exaggerated. The expansion of state-governed international institutions alongside America's emergence as a global superpower transformed state-foundation relations in profound ways. This shift was evident in the creation in 1948 of the World Health Organization, in 1950 of the National Science Foundation, and in 1951 of the National Institutes of Health. All three organizations were chartered to take on roles in research, field building, and infrastructural development in which the Rockefeller and Carnegie foundations had earlier been prominent players. In 1951, only three years after the creation of the World Health Organization, Rockefeller shut down its own prestigious International Health Division.[30]

29. Latham (1997).

30. After World War II, Dwight Macdonald writes, the government increased its research budget from $90 million to $2.1 billion. "Some $150,000,000 of the total goes to universities for government-sponsored projects; trivial though this sum is in comparison to what the government is spending directly, it is more than all the foundations combined contribute to university research. The Department of Commerce now undertakes the national-debt surveys that were initiated by Edward A. Filene's Twentieth Century Fund as well as much of the statistical work on national income that was originally done by the Rockefeller-financed National Bureau of Economic Research; the General Education Board's farm and home programs have long since become part of the Department of Agriculture's extension services; and the Point Four program dispatches American experts and techniques to backward countries on a scale that no foundation can begin to match." Macdonald (1989, p. 48).

The shift was also evident in official efforts to centralize, professionalize, and more tightly control the conduct of international affairs, a trend that was marked by the growing assertiveness of both government agencies and political actors in the policing and oversight of international foundations. If this originated, initially, in the concerns of the isolationist-populist wing of the Republican Party, it was later picked up, in a different form, by their populist counterparts on the left.

Yet beyond the more spectacular examples of official encroachment on foundations of the McCarthy period and the Reece Commission, a more pervasive and more powerful process was set in motion after the war of adaptation to and accommodation with state-defined national security agendas that came to be reflected throughout the international activities of foundations in these years. Driven by the growing centrality of the cold war as an organizing principle of U.S. foreign policy, the engagement of international foundations during the prewar period in economic development, peace and security, democratization, public health, education, and science were all reframed in the postwar era as expressions of the global struggle against communism.

Thus even as the number of international foundations grew during the postwar period at a rapid pace—with some four thousand new foundations created between 1945 and 1960—it was also during this period that the contingent nature of foundation autonomy became most starkly visible. To an unprecedented degree, the cold war brought about the subordination of international foundation activities to the foreign policy priorities of the state. The emergent prewar role of international foundations as autonomous nonstate actors eroded as national security and anticommunism came to dominate America's international engagements. It was only with the Vietnam War, the civil rights movement, and the emergence of grassroots opposition to nuclear proliferation that international foundations reasserted their nonstate identities and their autonomy from a policy agenda defined by state interests.

On the ground, cold war considerations had a deeply uneven impact on foundation programs and grants. Major programs were often designed and implemented without visible regard for the politics of anticommunism: the Rockefeller Foundation's role in eliminating malaria and in supporting the green revolution were not simply exercises in cold war diplomacy. Yet the rhetoric that international foundations adopted to legitimate their international work after World War II reflects how powerfully the cold war influenced international foundations and how they themselves defined their contributions to society. Strengthening education in the developing world, for example, an early priority of international foundations, was now viewed as pivotal not only to counter ignorance and prejudice but also to equip societies to resist Soviet propaganda. Economic development was now characterized not as an end in itself, a self-evident good, but as the means for overcoming inequalities that might foster the spread of communism. In the words of the Ford Foundation's trustees, "Men submit to dictators when hunger and frustration undermine their faith in themselves and in the existing order."[31] As early as 1949, virtually every area of the Ford Foundation's international work—in development, public health, education, culture and the arts—was framed in terms of the global struggle against communism and the prevention of war.

Priorities that had long featured among the principal concerns of international foundations were thus redefined in the context of the cold war as contributions to the pursuit of security, freedom, and the global struggle against communist aggression.[32] Nor was the embrace of anticommunism as a rationale for foundation work unique to Ford.[33] Contrary to the charges often leveled against them by isolationist conservatives during the McCarthy era, the Ford Foundation under Hoffman, the Rockefeller Foundation under Rusk, and the Carnegie Corporation under Charles Dollard viewed their foundations as instruments that could and should be used to advance the national interest at a time of conflict between communism and democracy.[34] In some limited areas, moreover, the relationship between government and international foundations went beyond a generalized sense of shared purpose to include the abuse of international foundations by intelligence agencies for covert programs, notably in higher education, area studies, scientific research, and cultural and artistic exchange.[35]

The commitment of international foundations to the cold war policies of the American government was not sufficient, however, to insulate them from the domestic politics of anticommunism during the McCarthy era. International foundations came under sharp and sustained attack from the House Un-American Activities Committee. They were investigated by the short-lived Cox Committee, launched in 1952, and by its successor, the Reece Committee,

---

31. Ford Foundation (1950).

32. Bolling and Smith (1982).

33. In adopting this language, international foundations reflected a view that was also widely championed in government at the time. In 1952 no less a figure than associate justice of the Supreme Court William O. Douglas gave a speech proposing that the United States use Point Four assistance to promote peasant revolutions "in underdeveloped areas to end economic serfdom." Otherwise, U.S. foreign aid was "'only underwriting the status quo' and perpetuating the conditions on which communism grew." Felix Belair, "Peasants' Revolts Urged by Douglas," *New York Times*, April 8, 1952, p. 1.

34. In Rockefeller's 1953 annual report, the foundation defended its investment in research by pointing out that "at a period when free institutions came under challenge from totalitarian ideology of both the left and the right, it was felt that penetrating studies of our own free economic and political institutions would help them to withstand assault." Fisher (1980, p. 256).

35. Diamond (1992); see also Sutton (1977, pp. 94–120), which argues that "the relative magnitude of CIA funding should not be exaggerated" and suggests that the Ford, Rockefeller, and Carnegie foundations, in particular, were not recipients of CIA funds.

created in 1953 to demonstrate to the American public the purported complicity of tax-exempt foundations in the spread of Soviet propaganda and their efforts to disseminate suspiciously cosmopolitan, internationalist, empiricist, relativist, and collectivist ideologies both within the United States and internationally.[36]

This chapter in the history of American foundations has been adequately recounted elsewhere. It continues to animate debate, often more heated than informed, about the role of foundations in American politics. Far more relevant, from our perspective, is what these episodes reveal about the cold war's effects in destabilizing prewar conceptions of the legitimacy and autonomy of international foundations and their contributions to American society. Then as now, the rise of national security as a pervasive attribute of domestic life fueled political concerns about the autonomy of international foundations and the potential abuse of that autonomy by foundation executives for purposes viewed as seditious or corrosive of core American values. Targeting their tax-exempt status and association with wealth, privilege, and power but also their identity as cornerstones of liberal cosmopolitanism, populist and isolationist politicians from both parties viewed international foundations' "globalistic" outlook and support for international institutions as ample evidence of their subversive intent.[37]

Combined with the expansion of state agencies and increasingly state-centric modes of global governance, the cold war and the rise of anticommunism as a defining feature of U.S. foreign policy marked a critical juncture in the life of international foundations. In much of the literature, international foundations during this period are cast as straightforward agents of state power, as mechanisms through which U.S. policies were implemented abroad and legitimated at home and, not coincidentally, as nodes in elite networks that linked government, the private sector, and philanthropy. Certainly, international foundations continued to be governed and staffed by elites, overwhelmingly white and male, who represented broadly similar social, educational, and professional backgrounds and who circulated easily in the upper reaches of government and the private sector.

---

36. For more on the Cox and Reece committees and their relationship, see Kiger (2000).

37. In the report of the Reece Commission, sections on the internationalism of foundations and their "globalistic" outlook are immediately followed by sections on "communism and subversion." U.S. House (1954). Despite their significant impact on the everyday work of foundations, these efforts had little effect on public opinion. In fact, surveys taken at the time showed an increase in public support for foundations in the wake of McCarthyite attacks of the Cox and Reece commissions. Macdonald (1989, p. 34–35). According to Macdonald, the three-month-long Reece Committee hearings "were devoted largely to the animadversions of obscure crackpots and the scarcely more lucid testimony of the Reece Committee's staff" (p. 31). It should be noted that among the committee staff was René A. Wormser, author of a subsequent screed (Wormser 1958) that remains influential within isolationist-populist factions of the American right.

Yet the impact of the postwar period on international foundations should not be read in simplistic or one-dimensional terms. Foundations confronted a more complex, more heavily regulated, and more deeply ambiguous relationship to the state that now included stricter oversight and new demands for accountability. They contended, as well, with a much denser institutional environment—where state agencies now overshadowed foundations in many spheres and imposed on them a process of organizational adaptation and adjustment as well as a rescaling of activities and of substantive priorities.[38] International foundations also faced a drastically altered international context, marked not only by the rise of the United States as a global superpower but also by the rapid spread of decolonization and the diffusion of anti-Western nationalisms that transformed the local contexts in which international foundations operated.

Despite these shifts, however, and despite the charged political climate at home, the 1950s and 1960s brought a significant expansion in international grant making and in support for deeper international engagement among Americans (see figure 10-1). Building on initiatives launched during the war, international foundations undertook programs that would come to represent some of their most influential and lasting contributions as institution builders, coalition builders, amplifiers of ideas, and exporters of ideas from the United States to other parts of the world—not least to postwar Germany, Japan, and across postwar Europe, where foundations were active participants in reconstruction programs.[39]

As early as 1950, the Ford Foundation had established programs in overseas development, international training and research, and international affairs. Between 1950 and 1975, Ford alone made international grants totaling $1.5 billion, with some $1 billion for purposes relating to international development. Ford's activities had a particular focus on India, specifically, "the installation and improvement of public management to serve development" and "the building of economic planning competences."[40] Programs on a similar scale (relative to its endowment) were undertaken by the Rockefeller Foundation, which supported institution building in newly independent states and higher education

---

38. One element of this environment was the appearance of foundations created explicitly to advance conservative ideas, and several were established in the interwar period. The Earhart Foundation (founded in 1929) counted among its earliest grantees the conservative pro-market economist Friedrich Hayek. The Smith Richardson Foundation (1935) and the Scaife Foundations (1941) were joined in the same period by the Bradley Foundation (1943) and the Olin Foundation (1953). By the early 1950s, therefore, the pillars of conservative philanthropy were already in place. It would be another two decades before they achieved the visibility and impact of their more established counterparts.

39. Yamamoto and others (2006); Gemelli (1998).

40. Sutton (1977, p. 99). See also McCarthy (1984).

Figure 10-1. *Total Grant Dollars Directed to International Affairs, 1930–88*

Millions of dollars

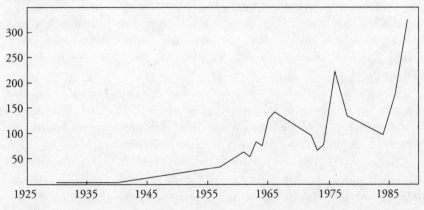

Source: Data for 1930–40 were drawn from Rich (1931–55). Data for 1957–88 are from *The Foundation Directory* (Foundation Center 1960, 1946, 1967, 1975, 1985, 1987, 1989). The 1976 and 1978 percentages were two-year aggregates, from 1975–76 and 1977–78. The 1930–40 percentages and grant dollar totals were drawn from very limited samples of foundations reporting activities by field area. The sample disproportionately reports on relatively large foundations, so that percentages are likely to be upwardly biased, and dollar totals may be slight underestimates. The directories used here adapted their minimum asset requirements for foundations reported on as the total number of foundations and their average assets grew.

and human capital development in Africa, Latin America, and South Asia. The core of Rockefeller's postwar international activities, however, was the field of agricultural development, with a particular focus on research to improve crop yields—what would later come to be called the green revolution. The success of these initiatives provided the impetus for the foundation's long-term engagement with institution building in the field of agricultural research, investments that transformed the global landscape of agricultural science.[41]

Perhaps the signal domestic contribution of international foundations in the first two decades after the war, however, was the expansion of international studies in the United States, including the formation and consolidation of area studies as a distinct field of study in American higher education. As early as 1945, the Rockefeller Foundation provided a grant to Columbia University to establish a Russian studies center within the newly created School of International

41. See Fosdick (1989). Rockefeller was joined by Ford in many of these institution-building activities in the field of agricultural research. The two were joint founders, for instance, of the International Rice Research Institute in the Philippines in 1957. This remains a central area of interest for Rockefeller, which has announced an initiative to extend the benefits of the green revolution to Africa. Rockefeller Foundation (2006).

Affairs—the first of several grants from Rockefeller to Columbia to support research on world regions. The Carnegie Corporation joined in these efforts, awarding a grant to Harvard in 1947, also in support of Russian studies. Both foundations also provided support to the Social Science Research Council in New York, which created a Committee on Latin American Studies in 1947 and soon expanded this interdisciplinary, regional framework to include Slavic and Eastern European Studies (in 1948), Southern Asia (in 1949), and the Middle East (in 1951).

These early efforts were relatively modest in scale (Harvard's Russian Research Center was established with a grant of $740,000) until, in 1952, the Ford Foundation established the Foreign Area Fellowship Program, which supported the professional development of scholars working on the Middle East, Africa, the Soviet Union and Eastern Europe, and Asia. Fellowship funding was followed almost immediately by support for international academic exchange programs and by grants in support of university programs in international and area studies. In contrast to some other areas of foundation interest, however, the emergence of large federal initiatives to strengthen international education (notably, the National Defense Education Act of 1958 and the 1961 Fulbright Hays international fellowship program) did little to displace or overshadow the presence of international foundations in international and area studies. Collectively, foundation initiatives in the development of these fields, with Ford in the lead, transformed American higher education and continue to exert significant (if declining) influence over the production of international knowledge in the United States. They also came to define professional pathways within higher education, institutionalizing a set of discrete, self-governing, and typically self-referential area-centric silos (African Studies, Middle East Studies, and Asian Studies, for example) as the basis for undergraduate and graduate education and for faculty hiring and promotion.

Although foundations were occasionally in direct competition with federal programs, higher education was sufficiently decentralized to leave space for both governmental and foundation programs to operate, even as federal funding rapidly outpaced the scale of foundation investment. Here too, however, foundation grant making was heavily influenced by U.S. foreign policy priorities of the postwar era: funding for international education was anchored in the twin imperatives of the cold war and the rise of the United States as a global superpower.[42] International and area studies were explicitly envisioned as frameworks for the production of expertise needed to support America's role as leader of the

---

42. Oren (2003). The regional frameworks that Ford and other foundations helped to consolidate within American universities meshed neatly with the parallel organization of agencies such as the U.S. Department of State, the Central Intelligence Agency, and the World Bank.

free world—a nation with interests and engagements that had become global in reach yet demanded intimate knowledge of the histories, cultures, languages, politics, societies, and economies of virtually every country in the world.[43] Nonetheless, the impact and influence of these foundation initiatives soon transcended the contexts that gave rise to them. They outgrew their origins in the cold war to provide a significant impetus for the development of the social sciences and humanities in the United States, Europe, and the developing world.

International Foundations from the 1970s to the End of the Cold War

The period from the 1970s to the end of the cold war was no less transformative for international foundations than for American society in general. New international foundations made their presence felt during these years, including the MacArthur Foundation (in 1971) and some of the first West Coast foundations created by the earliest of the high-tech entrepreneurs, notably the David and Lucile Packard Foundation (in 1964) and the William and Flora Hewlett Foundation (in 1968).[44] Conservative foundations also achieved new visibility during the latter part of this period, benefiting significantly from Ronald Reagan's election as president in 1980.

In addition, relations between international foundations and the state shifted yet again during these years in a direction that has proved both durable and formative, initiating a transition in the form and content of international philanthropy that became even more prominent with the end of the cold war. While continuing to act as institution builders, legitimators, coalition builders, gatekeepers, and amplifiers and exporters of ideas, international foundations placed increasing stress on their role as nonstate and transnational institutions and on their contribution to the development of civil societies as agents of change on both the domestic and the international levels.

As part of this process, and with some important exceptions, international foundations adopted more explicitly oppositional—though far from radical—positions with respect to U.S. foreign policy. They displayed a new willingness to challenge state priorities, to support the development of critical alternatives to U.S. foreign policy—especially with respect to arms control, nuclear nonproliferation, and U.S. defense policy in Southeast Asia—and to present themselves and their grantees as agents of public accountability in the face of unresponsive state institutions. Foundation leaders continued to be drawn overwhelmingly

43. See Mitchell (1991, pp. 77–96).

44. These dates reflect IRS "ruling years," as indicated by GuideStar. In some cases, foundations remained largely inactive for years after their formal recognition as 501(c)(3) organizations.

from elite networks of business leaders and senior government officials, yet the organizations they managed now expressed a new awareness of, and concern to overcome, what they identified as a history of elitism and U.S. centrism in their staffing, governance, and grant making.[45] Internationally, they worked to enlarge their networks of grantees to include more non-U.S. recipients, advocacy organizations, and grassroots civil society groups than they had in the past, to broaden the perspectives represented on foundation boards, and to develop funding priorities based on concerns originating outside the United States and outside small, and often inward-looking, elite networks.

In his presidential review of 1966, for example, McGeorge Bundy set out a major shift in Ford Foundation priorities away from support for higher education and toward funding for crucial domestic issues such as integration and civil rights. Bundy noted the foundation's ongoing interest in advancing world peace, but in contrast to some of his predecessors, he stressed that Ford did not "have a department for peace," or "confuse [itself] with the Government of the United States, and still less with the United Nations." Having invested hundreds of millions of dollars in international and area studies, Ford was now taking "its men and money to the next table," though it would continue to invest in some areas of international studies on a smaller and more selective scale.[46]

If in earlier periods international foundations made crucial contributions in building institutional capacity in areas such as foreign affairs, university-based research, agricultural science, and the arts, both in the United States and internationally, from the mid-1960s onward their attention slowly shifted toward support for institution building in the third sector. Over the next two decades, international foundations complemented established patterns of grant making with new efforts designed to promote, give direction to, and coordinate activities among a select set of advocacy, grassroots, and social-change organizations. To be sure, these new priorities emerged only gradually, and not all foundations embraced them with equal enthusiasm. Ford and Rockefeller moved more quickly and more visibly in this direction than did Carnegie.[47]

In some instances, changes of direction meant setting aside established international commitments—at least rhetorically—leading to what is characterized

45. This shift was evident in the appointment in 1979 of Franklin Thomas, Ford's first black president and the first black leader of a major private foundation in the United States. His background is also illustrative of the changes then under way among international foundations. He moved to Ford following ten years as head of the Bedford Stuyvesant Restoration Corporation.

46. Ford Foundation (1966). This marked a shift from the days of Paul Hoffman, whose "delegations" to India sometimes resembled those of a head of state. G. Hess (2005, pp. 51–71).

47. Nielsen suggests that the changes at Rockefeller under George Harrar, president from 1961 to 1971, might have been less meaningful than the foundation indicated and also notes the slow pace at which the Carnegie Corporation moved "beyond elitism." Nielsen (1972, pp. 46, 66).

today as a period of drift and loss of impact.[48] In general, however, shifts in grant making did not displace the long-standing engagement of international foundations with global problems such as economic development, poverty reduction, population, public health, and world peace or with funding for international research, science, and education. Rather, these new trends signaled an important shift in foundation thinking about how best to advance a relatively stable set of long-term aims and in the language international foundations adopted to define their interests and priorities. For instance, by 1979, when Ford issued a report on its international programs, the language it used bore the clear imprint of the civil rights and antiwar movements in noting the foundation's intent to "give greater attention to . . . activities that help to promote peace, freedom, and justice throughout the world."[49]

At Ford and elsewhere, earlier commitments to ideas and expert knowledge as agents of change in the international system—a perspective that granted privilege to universities, think tanks, and research institutes—were slowly giving way to an appreciation for the role of grassroots organizations, policy institutes, advocacy groups, and activist networks. This changed intention was captured in the Mott Foundation's annual report for 1967–68: "A review of the past year can be summed up in one word: Action! Action against war, against poverty. Action involving money, race, jobs, education, crime, urbanization. Never before has the status quo received such attack."[50]

In part, this transformation among international foundations reflected their awareness of and responsiveness to an emergent public disillusionment with the place of expertise and specialist knowledge in the management of international affairs. Even as the appeal of science and technology remained strong in the United States, the country experienced growing popular mobilization against U.S. foreign and defense policy, including the central role played by the "best and the brightest" such as Secretary of Defense Robert McNamara.[51] This societal trend eroded the authority and legitimacy of the expert networks and elite institutions—both public and private—that had long dominated the day-to-day work of global governance.

Yet this new focus on the third sector can also be understood as a by-product of two additional factors. The first of these was the massive investment by

48. "By the early 1970s most of the Rockefeller Foundation's greatest achievements were in the past and a long period of drift had begun. Ms. Rodin inherited a foundation that was no longer the best nor the biggest—in its early years it gave more foreign aid than the American government. There was a danger of 'becoming marginal in our impact,' says Ms. Rodin. 'Impact needed to be reasserted as a fundamental criterion for everything we do.'" *The Economist,* December 13, 2006.

49. Ford Foundation (1979).

50. Cited in Nielsen (1972, p. 300).

51. Halberstam (1972).

foundations throughout the course of the twentieth century in the creation of international nongovernmental institutions that could now provide third sector frameworks for international grant making in virtually every world region. The presence of these institutional networks, with which international foundations had long and well-established ties, created readily available platforms for program development as foundations redirected their resources into new areas.

The second was simply state expansion—the growth of state regulation and the increasing prominence of state agencies, resources, and funding in the international arena. In a context in which international foundations in particular had conceded considerable ground to states, were concerned to preserve (or restore) a sense of their autonomy, and no longer possessed their earlier influence in shaping the international arena, they found themselves pushed to adapt by identifying new domains in which their more limited resources and staffing would permit them to make meaningful contributions.[52] International foundations, moreover, now viewed the state less in terms of partnerships and more as a force to be managed with care and with the interests of the foundation foremost in determining how that relationship would be defined. Bundy's final presidential review makes a useful bookend to his sense a decade earlier concerning Ford's limits relative to the state and international institutions. What was needed in managing relations with the state, Bundy stressed, was for foundations "to keep their nerve" if they were to "manage [their] relation to the federal government with independence and integrity." Where foundation activities intersected with state interests, as was often the case, foundations should be prepared to assert their role as independent, nonpartisan providers of expertise, not to act as adjuncts of Congress or the executive branch.[53]

This view framed a new sense among international foundations concerning the issues and approaches that shaped their grant making. Beginning in the late 1960s, the contributions of international foundations were evident in their support of policy research and public engagement in areas such as conflict resolution, arms control and disarmament, population, agricultural development, and public health. International foundations directed support toward new areas of interest as well, including the struggle against apartheid and the effort to address its consequences, women's issues, and refugees and international migration. All three represented the entry of international foundations into areas that have become visible and important aspects of their grant making for the past thirty years. Other notable initiatives of this period include the Mott Foundation's support for the development of community foundations

52. Described as a move "from criticism to new NGO empowerment." Shiao (2005, p. 186).
53. Ford Foundation (1978).

in South Africa; support from international foundations for the newly created Union of Concerned Scientists (founded in 1969 by faculty and students at MIT); the MacArthur Foundation's founding grant in 1982 to create the World Resources Institute in response to environmental concerns; and MacArthur's efforts, beginning in 1984, to improve research and public policy on international peace and security.

As this highly selective list suggests, international foundations remained active as institution builders, legitimators, gatekeepers, and coalition builders during the 1970s and 1980s. Yet the pace and scope of their work as midwives to new international institutions had diminished considerably in comparison with previous decades. It would not pick up steam until the post–cold war era.[54] By the 1970s, international foundations were able to make use of well-established networks of grantees around the world, including think tanks, universities, and research centers that they had been largely responsible for creating—and to do so using well-established strategies of grant making. The presence of these institutions is itself an important indicator of how much international foundations had transformed the landscape of policymaking, research, and international affairs since their founding in the first decades of the century. It underscores the difference in the environment in which a foundation like MacArthur emerged in the early 1980s, one densely packed with viable institutions able to advance foundation agendas, relative to the conditions that existed when the first international foundations began their work in the early decades of the century.

If this thriving ecology of international grant making with its own norms, values, and practices contributed to an underlying sense of continuity and stability in the work of international foundations (and reinforced a sense of international foundations as risk averse), it also sometimes masked the extent to which the content of international grant making had changed during the tumultuous years of the late 1960s and early 1970s. At the same time, this pattern speaks to the underlying flexibility of both foundations and the general-purpose think tanks and research centers they supported. As the founders of what would become major international foundations envisioned, they had created highly adaptive frameworks for the organization and management of philanthropy, understood as a domain of expert knowledge that could be picked up and moved from issue to issue as needs and problems shifted.

Among conservative foundations with an interest in international affairs, however, institution building remained a core priority from the 1960s onward.

---

54. In contrast, the pace of institution building on the domestic front remained higher during the 1970s, as leading foundations worked to build institutional capacity in areas such as civil rights, poverty reduction, and urban policy.

In an effort to counter what they characterized as the dominance of liberal perspectives in foreign and domestic policy and in university-level teaching and research on world affairs, conservative foundations helped to create a number of research centers and think tanks, including the Center for Strategic and International Studies (created in 1962), the Heritage Foundation (1973), the Cato Institute (1977), the Manhattan Institute (1985), and the Olin Institute for Strategic Studies at Harvard University (1989), among others. Along with the American Enterprise Institute (1943), these organizations were instrumental in producing the knowledge, intellectual rationales, and policy recommendations that underpinned the foreign policies of the Reagan administration and led to the consolidation of neoconservatism in American foreign policy. Following America's withdrawal from Vietnam in 1975 and the Carter administration's embrace of human rights and democracy promotion as cornerstones of its foreign policy, the work of these think tanks helped to ensure that conservative perspectives were well represented in post–Vietnam War debates about the role of the United States in the world.

Despite the ferment that surrounded efforts to shape U.S. foreign and defense policy during the late 1970s and early 1980s, it is hard to avoid the impression that for international foundations, the period from the 1970s to the end of the cold war was not their finest hour. In comparison with earlier periods—when foundations had been instrumental in establishing the institutional frameworks of global governance, created the fields of policy research and area studies, sponsored the green revolution, and built transnational networks of research institutions in fields such as population, economic development, and public health—the scope of foundation innovation and the impact of international grant making in the 1970s and 1980s appears relatively modest (see figure 10-2). More vitality and influence are visible on the domestic scene during these years than in the international activities of major private foundations.

It was not until the 1990s and the end of the cold war—with democratic transitions unfolding across Eastern Europe, the former Soviet Union, Africa, and Latin America; the rise of democracy promotion as a leading international concern; a renewed interest in civil society as an agent of democratic transformation; an emerging consensus about the need to reconceptualize global governance in an era of globalization; the growing urgency associated with the spread of HIV/AIDS; and new interest in transitional migration among a host of other post–cold war concerns—that the established international foundations recovered their earlier vitality in international grant making. However, the initiatives of international foundations during the 1970s and 1980s to redefine their relationship to the state, reaffirm their standing as autonomous institutions, adopt the language of social justice, and shift their attention to the challenges of

Figure 10-2. *Grants Directed to International Affairs as Share of Total Foundation Giving, 1961–88*

Percent

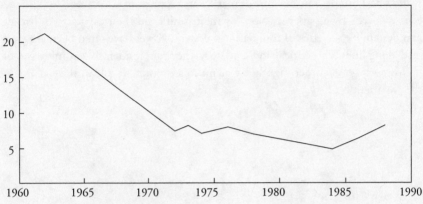

Source: See note to figure 10-1.

sustaining and coordinating social change at the local level left America's major international foundations well positioned for the challenge of supporting and participating in an international third sector once the cold war ended.

Conclusion

The historical contribution of international foundations to society can be measured by the institutions and ideas they helped to create during the short twentieth century. Large swaths of the institutional landscape that we now take for granted in addressing international concerns in the sciences, in higher education, and in public policy are the product of international foundation support. So are many of the ideas that continue to shape public and official debate about the prospects for advancing the aims of international security, economic development, public health, and civic engagement. These represent the enduring legacy of the early foundation leaders, who believed in the possibilities of global order and the importance of international institutions.

Their contribution, moreover, was as much a result of the broader liberal and cosmopolitan worldview they helped to construct through their grant making as it was the product of any particular grant or program. They expressed and helped to popularize a distinctly modern conception of social problems as tractable, as having root causes that experts could identity and, through the application of their particular expertise, overcome. Foundations reflected a vision of global security anchored in mutual understanding, knowledge, and shared interests. An end to disease, poverty, and war, the triple scourge of modern civilization, was not only imaginable but feasible and thus demanded the urgent attention of the world's best minds. The benefits of market and state were understood and valued but tempered by an appreciation for their limits and their capacity to disrupt and destabilize societies. If foundation roles and power have often been exaggerated along lines both critical and laudatory, they can, in their role as midwives of the postwar global order, rightly lay claim to a prominent role in the making of the twentieth century.

11

For the World's Sake: U.S. Foundations and International Grant Making, 1990–2002

LEHN M. BENJAMIN AND KEVIN F. F. QUIGLEY

The last decade of the twentieth century and the first few years of this new century have been marked by significant global changes. The move to more open societies marked symbolically by the fall of the Berlin Wall and animated by widespread democratization movements presented foundations with new grant-making prospects. These openings, coupled with governance models that shifted greater responsibility for development to the private sector, spurred foundations to support a variety of institution-building efforts, including supporting civil society in countries around the world. Rapid technological advances made international giving easier; at the same time, this more open and connected world drew foundation attention to new global problems, including environmental degradation and health pandemics.

Yet geopolitical changes resulting from the events of September 11, 2001, have presented new challenges for international grant makers. The global war on terror shifted national priorities and changed perceptions about the role of the United States in the world.[1] These events spurred foundations to give greater attention to issues in the Middle East, including efforts to foster peace

We would like to thank Carissa Lenfert for her work in formatting the citations and bibliography and to Steven Lawrence, at the Foundation Center, who graciously gave his time and assistance in preparing the data for this analysis. Errors and omissions remain the sole responsibility of the authors.

1. The Pew Charitable Trusts' Pew Research Center for the People and the Press has been tracking changing attitudes toward America, Americans, and American institutions.

and understand Islam.[2] But logistically, foundations faced more stringent documentation requirements to ensure their grants were not supporting what could be considered terrorist activities.[3]

Civil society and democracy assistance was a substantive focus of many large private foundations engaged in international grant making between 1990 and the present. The analysis that follows draws on data presented in a series of publications on international grant making published by the Foundation Center; a specialized data set of grants for democratization obtained from the Foundation Center; information provided by the foundations themselves; one author's experiences directing international grant making for one of the largest U.S. foundations; and independent research on foundation support for democratization in Eastern Europe.[4]

Internationally U.S. foundations take on philanthropic roles, seeking to promote innovation or social and policy change. Only in relatively rare circumstances, such as international disaster relief, are foundations' resources designed to serve charitable purposes to meet basic human needs. In their efforts to build global civil society and support democratization efforts, foundations have often acted as first responders, conveners, and social entrepreneurs. They have also been institution builders, especially building national policy–oriented nongovernmental organizations (NGOs) and education-related institutions.

---

2. This shift in focus has been challenging. Some foundations have not been able to find appropriate partners or develop effective programs. Others have been criticized for funding groups that may have links to terrorist organizations.

3. "Foundations Check Grant Recipients against Terrorist Watch Lists," *Philanthropy News Digest,* September 9, 2004 (www.foundationcenter.org/pnd/news/story.jhtml?=78800006 [November 22, 2009]).

4. Renz (1997); Renz, Samson-Atienza, and Lawrence (2000); Renz, Lawrence, and Smith (2004). The Foundation Center (www.fdncenter.org) has the most comprehensive set of grants data, although it is incomplete. The data are based on a sample of grants of $10,000 or more from 821 foundations in 1990, 1,020 foundations in 1994, 1,009 foundations in 1998, and 1,005 foundations in 2002. All dollar amounts are reported in current figures and are not corrected for inflation, unless noted. In the specialized data set we requested from the Foundation Center, we pulled out grants that were coded Q99, which functions as an "other" category, that did not also have the code R, I, W, T, or Q70/71. This resulted in fifty fewer grants and 5,844,687 fewer dollars in 1990; thirty-five fewer grants and 2,060,370 fewer dollars in 1996; and thirteen fewer grants and 232,564,449 fewer dollars in 2001. We used the primary code to analyze grants going to different functional areas. When a grant was coded international or public affairs, we used the secondary code. To identify the top grant recipients, we aggregated those grants that went to grantees with the same name and the same place but we did not aggregate those grantees with the same name but in a different location (unless it was clear that the two organizations were not separately incorporated) or those grantees with the same name in the same place but indicating separate incorporation. Finally, we aggregated consumer protection grants with civil rights, dispute resolution grants with intergroup relations grants, and general public affairs grants under civil society grants.

On the other hand, most U.S. foundations involved in supporting democratization efforts are less successful as risk absorbers or mediators, although there are examples where they have done both. The challenges confronting foundations active internationally mirror those acting domestically, although these challenges can be especially daunting in a charged foreign political environment. These challenges include insufficient resources to meet the foundation's goals, lack of professional skills necessary to accomplish ambitious tasks in a foreign context, a narrow programmatic focus, and paternalism.

As a consequence of these disadvantages, these specific interventions on the part of U.S. foundations involved in international grant making do not necessarily have a major societal impact. These foundations do, however, make a positive contribution, primarily through their role as influential advocates for social and policy change and in building key institutions that can help ensure democratic consolidation.

Recent Trends in International Grant Making

With technological advances and the end of the cold war, the world has witnessed dramatic changes since the 1990s.[5] The nations and the people of the world have become increasingly connected economically, culturally, and politically. This connectivity is evident in the rise of foreign direct investment, increased international travel and migration, greater media exposure, the ratification of international treaties by more countries, and even the way citizens organize to express their views. One need only look at the coordinated worldwide protests on February 15, 2003, against the invasion of Iraq, or the development of the World Social Forum to understand some of globalization's effects.

Yet global integration has also raised concerns. We see even greater disparity between rich and poor. We face greater risks from health and environmental problems that are not contained within national borders. At the same time, the twin trends of globalization and localization have raised questions about state sovereignty, new governance models, and whether we have adequate mechanisms to ensure democracy when key decisions that affect citizens are made by supranational actors such as the World Trade Organization.

Reflective of these developments, the kinds of programs U.S. foundations support and how they engage in international work has changed. Not only has the number of foundations and the amount of funding for international work increased (despite concerns about terrorism) but also foundations have shifted

---

5. This section draws primarily on the International Grantmaking series from the Foundation Center. See Renz (1997); Renz, Samson-Atienza, and Lawrence (2000); Renz, Lawrence, and Smith (2004).

their programmatic focus from cold war concerns to global issues such as health and governance and have realigned their grant-making strategies to reflect an increasingly interdependent world.

Growth in Proportion of Giving to International Causes

Between 1990 and 2002 the dollar value of international giving increased 200 percent, from $765 million to $2.3 billion, while the increase in overall giving during this same period was only 154.8 percent.[6] The Bill and Melinda Gates Foundation contributed significantly to this trend, its giving rising from $5.5 million in 1998 to $525.8 million in 2002. Yet even if Gates is excluded, the increase in international giving was still greater than the increase in overall giving. Despite these trends, international grant making remains a modest proportion of overall grant making, representing approximately 14 percent of the $240 billion total grants given in 2002.[7]

Putting the giving of U.S. private foundations in the context of overall U.S. international assistance sheds more light on these contributions. According to the 2006 report of the Index of Global Philanthropy, the United States provided $71 billion in private support from foundations, universities, volunteer groups, and religious and relief organizations in 2004.[8] This amount is roughly two and a half times the official U.S. government–sponsored international support of $30 billion, which includes military-related assistance. So-called official development assistance was approximately $19 billion in 2004.[9] Private foundations provided $3.8 billion in 2005, just 5 percent of all private giving.[10]

Increase in the Number of International Grant Makers

To present a general picture, between 1994 and 2002 the number of foundations allocating at least 50 percent of their grant dollars to international issues increased by 29 percent (from 31 to 40), and the number allocating at least 10 percent of their overall giving to international issues increased by 26 percent between 1994 and 2002 (from 153 to 193).[11] More specifically, table 11-1 shows the giving of the top twenty-five international grant makers in 2002. Reflecting a snapshot of the history of twentieth-century American philanthropy, the table

---

6. Renz (1997); Renz, Lawrence, and Smith (2004).

7. Renz, Lawrence, and Smith (2004, p. 20–21).

8. The Index of Global Philanthropy is an imprecise measure, and it is extremely difficult to determine the amounts provided directly by U.S. private foundations. It does provide rough orders of magnitude and relative size. For more information, see www.hudsoninstitute.org.

9. Organization for Economic Cooperation and Development, "Aid Statistics" (www.oecd.org/dac/stats [April 11, 2005]).

10. See Renz, Lawrence, and Marino (2006).

11. Renz (1997); Renz, Lawrence, and Smith (2004).

Table 11-1. *Top Twenty-Five International Grantmakers, 2002*
Units as indicated

Foundation	Established	Total value (dollars)	Number of grants
Bill and Melinda Gates Foundation	1994	525,754,545	90
Ford Foundation	1936	324,734,119	1,701
Rockefeller Foundation	1913	82,362,412	464
John D. and Catherine T. MacArthur Foundation	1970	61,577,024	230
Freeman Foundation	1978	60,795,048	201
William and Flora Hewlett Foundation	1966	57,427,877	193
W. K. Kellogg Foundation	1930	56,559,766	205
Starr Foundation	1955	52,617,840	118
David and Lucile Packard Foundation	1964	52,609,195	174
Lincy Foundation	1989	41,556,927	7
Turner Foundation	1990	39,244,018	115
Andrew W. Mellon Foundation	1940	38,278,750	139
Carnegie Corporation of New York	1911	37,818,500	123
Charles Stewart Mott Foundation	1926	33,762,429	254
Harry and Jeanette Weinberg Foundation	1959	22,341,763	38
Pew Charitable Trusts	1948	18,328,000	12
The AVI CHAI Foundation	1984	17,996,815	7
Righteous Persons Foundation	1994	17,660,387	191
Lilly Endowment	1937	15,937,150	8
Open Society Institute	1993	15,893,500	99
Arthur S. DeMoss Foundation	1955	15,441,174	328
Citigroup Foundation	1994	15,397,300	258,313
Gordon and Betty Moore Foundation	2000	14,351,100	3,211
Packard Humanities Institute	1987	12,940,550	6,224
Buffett Foundation	1964	12,478,832	11

Source: Data from Renz, Lawrence, and Smith (2004), p. 35.

includes institutions with recognizable names and long histories of international giving (Carnegie, Ford, Kellogg, Mellon, and Rockefeller) as well as a number of newly established foundations. Many of the new large foundations have been created by giants in the tech industry. The Gates Foundation, established in 1998 by Microsoft's founder Bill Gates and his wife, Melinda, with almost $30 billion in assets, has focused its grant-making efforts on international health. The Lincy Foundation, established in 1989 by the media mogul Kirk Kerkorian, supports Armenian charities, while the Gordon and Betty Moore Foundation, established in 2000 by Gordon Moore, the founder of Intel, supports environmental conservation. The 1990s also saw the emergence of the Open Society

Network of Foundations (also known as the Soros Foundation), created by the financier George Soros, which has devoted almost all of its resources internationally, with a particular focus on promoting democracy.[12]

Programmatic Shifts to Post–Cold War Priorities

Before 1990, international grant making reflected the concerns of the cold war era: promoting international understanding, development, and peace and security (see chapter 10 in this volume). With the fall of the Berlin Wall in 1989 and the emergence of democratization movements around the globe, foundations responded by decreasing funding for international affairs (for example, international exchanges, area studies) and peace and security and increasing support for democratization, especially the development of civil society in formerly communist countries. Coupled with the opening up of previously closed societies, globalization drew foundation attention to worldwide health issues (especially HIV/AIDS) and pressing environmental problems. Not reflected in these data are the consequences of post-9/11 concerns and interests.

These shifting priorities are illustrated in table 11-2, which shows the total grant dollars that went to major areas of international giving between 1990 and 2002. Health (led by the efforts of the Gates Foundation), public affairs, and religion saw the greatest increase in support, while international affairs, social sciences, and science technology saw fairly small increases in comparison.[13]

New Strategies in International Grant Making

Foundations use a variety of tools or strategies to facilitate their international grant-making activities. Historically, foundations relied heavily on U.S. nonprofits to meet their international goals, in part because political conditions or legal restrictions often precluded direct foundation giving in a country. They often operated in isolation from other foundation efforts, pursuing their own geographic, programmatic, and institutional interests. During the 1990s, however, foundation strategies started to change.

Greater cooperation to address global problems. Reflecting a world characterized by increasing interconnections across national boundaries and problems that have global implications, U.S. foundations have increasingly worked in concert with other foundations, governments, and local actors to address problems of global significance.[14] Perhaps the most prominent recent example is the major role played by foundations in establishing the Global Fund to Fight AIDS,

12. It is difficult to determine the size and scale of the Foundation Network because Soros-related organizations can be funders or recipients, and funds can be from the United States or off shore.

13. "Public affairs" includes grants for public affairs and the development of civil society.

14. Renz, Lawrence, and Smith (2004, p. 12).

Table 11-2. *International Grant Spending, by Purpose, Selected Years, 1990–2002*

Dollars, except as indicated

Purpose	1990	1994	1998	2002	Percent change, 1990 to 2002
International affairs	115,201,325	103,187,396	138,279,771	190,045,991	65
International development	73,945,553	124,258,970	186,473,921	276,151,221	273
Health	67,278,720	108,463,661	158,013,649	693,797,861	931
Social sciences	56,701,683	68,929,888	105,764,673	167,940,071	196
Education	49,416,338	83,928,151	116,614,582	167,088,349	238
Environment	43,259,230	55,492,099	89,133,678	183,351,385	324
Arts and culture	30,535,108	43,288,596	91,786,561	141,568,902	364
Science and technology	23,848,230	15,622,914	16,426,664	35,196,532	48
Human rights, civil liberties	21,017,912	36,633,277	82,689,446	122,238,737	482
Public affairs, society benefit	17,726,810	25,360,408	51,755,263	149,735,124	745
Religion	8,777,864	13,739,685	2,887,589	64,448,374	634
Other	512,699	524,477	604,800	239,539	

Source: Data from Renz (1992; 2000; 2004, p. 56). The data are based on a sample of grants of $10,000 or more from 821 foundations in 1990, 1,020 foundations in 1994, 1,009 foundations in 1998, and 1,005 foundations in 2002. All dollar amounts are reported in current figures and therefore not corrected for inflation.

Tuberculosis, and Malaria. This cooperative effort pioneered an innovative approach to financing international health as it sought "to dramatically increase resources to fight three of the world's most devastating diseases, and to direct those resources to areas of greatest need."[15]

Another important example is Transparency International, an international NGO that addresses problems of transparency and corruption in governments across the globe and is supported by foundations such as the Ford Foundation, the Tinker Foundation, the United Nations Foundation, and the Rowntree Trusts, along with a host of other agencies and organizations (for example, the United States Agency for International Development [USAID], the Swedish International Development Cooperation Agency, the Canadian International Development Agency, and the Australian Agency for International Development).[16]

15. Global Fund, "Who We Are" (www.theglobalfund.org/en/whoweare/?lang=en [November 22, 2009]).

16. Anheier and Daly (2005, p. 169). Partially as a consequence of this foundation-supported work the issue of corruption has received much greater attention in the international arena.

Focused giving. Longtime supporters of international issues, like the Ford and Rockefeller foundations, historically set up field offices to support grant making in a particular region. Field offices enabled foundations to hire staff who understood the local context and could more effectively address particular problems, but at considerable administrative cost. Foundations created in the 1990s introduced more strategic grant-making styles and innovative grant-making tools by targeting fewer issues, concentrating their resources in ways that increased the probability of impact and leverage, and generally doing so without a large administrative infrastructure. For example, in 2002 the Gates Foundation made 90 international grants totaling $526 million, for an average grant of $5.8 million. This approach stands in contrast to the Ford Foundation, the number-two international grant maker, which provided $325 million through 1,701 grants, for an average grant of $191,000 (see table 11-1). The Gates Foundation, in its primary focus on health, is also in contrast to the more traditional international grant makers like Ford, which addressed a wide variety of international issues from health to education to security to agriculture. Given the large size of Gates's grants and the fact that it has only one overseas office (in contrast to Ford, which has field offices in twelve countries), Gates can operate with a much lower overhead.[17]

Increased direct giving overseas. While most internationally focused grants still support U.S.-based nonprofits, the number of grants going directly to overseas recipients increased from 1,537 in 1990 to 4,484 in 2002 (that is, 192 percent).[18] Several conditions have supported the growth in direct overseas giving, including the increase in the number of nonprofits in countries around the globe, the development of local technical assistance groups or intermediaries that make direct giving easier for foundations, improved communications and technology, and the growing concern that foundation resources be devoted to programmatic rather than administrative activities.

Despite its increase, the practice of direct overseas giving is not uniform among foundations. Perhaps not surprisingly, foundations with longer histories of international giving do more direct grant making overseas. In 2002, for example, Ford and Rockefeller made 70 and 58 percent of their international grants directly overseas, respectively. Yet newer foundations are also giving directly overseas. For example, 29 percent of Gates's funding went directly to overseas organizations.[19] Other foundations that are extremely active in international grant making are actually precluded by their establishing documents (trust indentures)

17. The Gates Foundation's overhead is changing substantially as a result of Warren Buffett's recent gift. Within the next few years, its staff will grow from six hundred to more than a thousand, and it is building new headquarters in Seattle, Washington.

18. The trends actually show a slight decrease in 2002, from a high in 1998.

19. Renz, Lawrence, and Smith (2004, p. 44–51).

or policies from direct giving overseas. Examples include the Carnegie Corporation of New York, the Andrew W. Mellon Foundation, and the Pew Charitable Trusts. Foundations with these restrictions must necessarily find intermediaries.

Growing use of intermediaries to support direct giving. To facilitate their international grant-making efforts, foundations often use intermediary organizations—nonprofit organizations that secure funding for the purpose of regranting those funds to other organizations.[20] An intermediary can ease a foundation's burden of documenting that the organizations it supports overseas meet 501(c)(3) criteria and newer Department of Homeland Security requirements and can couple grants with technical assistance to build the organizations they serve.

U.S. foundations have actively supported the growth of intermediaries like community foundations.[21] Before 1990, community foundations were concentrated in the United States, the United Kingdom, Australia, and Canada. With the active support of foundations, a number of community foundations have now been established in Eastern Europe and Africa. One of the most interesting examples is the Environmental Partnership for Central Europe, a collaboration of a group of foundations (including the Charles Stewart Mott Foundation, the German Marshall Fund of the United States, the Pew Trusts, and the Rockefeller Brothers Fund) that were familiar with the community foundation experience and wanted to create a "regional community foundation" with a specific substantive focus because of the declining public interest in and support of environmental issues in the immediate aftermath of the political transitions in the region.[22]

Support for Democratization and Global Civil Society

In the last decade of the twentieth century, there was probably no more salient issue drawing the attention of U.S. private foundations than democratization and support for the burgeoning of civil society around the globe. This area did not capture the largest portion of grant dollars, nor did it see the greatest increase in giving during this period; but it probably received the most public attention, in part because of the emphasis on civil society by three successive U.S. presidents, beginning with President George H. W. Bush in 1989. Broadly speaking, U.S. private foundations' efforts targeted three overlapping areas: supporting open and competitive democratic processes, strengthening formal and informal institutions that make democracy more robust, and encouraging civic values and practices that undergird democracy, like tolerance and respect for minorities.

20. Renz, Lawrence, and Smith (2004, p. 48).
21. Sacks (2005).
22. For more information on the Environmental Partnership for Central Europe, see Quigley (1997, p. 74–78).

In our examination of foundation grant making to support democratization and civil society, we draw on the Foundation Center's grants database for the years 1990, 1996, and 2001, specifically those grants targeted to human rights and public affairs.[23] We use the terms *civil society* and *democratization* more broadly than does the Foundation Center, which uses *civil society* and *democracy* to refer to a narrow subset of grants related to civic participation.[24] Our use is consistent with other analyses of democracy assistance.[25]

Programmatic Areas

Overall support for democracy and civil society increased from $26.48 million in 1990 to $232.56 million in 2001, a more than sevenfold increase (see table 11-3).[26] Foundation support for democratization was small, relative to overall U.S. government support for these transitions, but nonetheless important, because the funding was targeted more intensely to building the capacity of democratic institutions, both public and private. U.S. support for these transitions focused more on economic restructuring. For example, during the 1990s the U.S. government, under the authority of the Support for Eastern European Democracy program, provided Eastern Europe with approximately $6.7 billion in three major areas: strengthening democratic institutions, economic restructuring, and improving the quality of life.[27] Economic restructuring received 70 percent of the funding. Projects to improve the quality of life (housing, environment, emergency services, and the like) received 21 percent, and support for strengthening democratic institutions received 9 percent.

U.S. private foundation programs focused more intensely on building independent institutions, especially developing civil society and an independent media. For example, the financier George Soros was providing more than $250 million annually in support of open societies and democracy through his country foundations, almost five times as much as USAID. These amounts did not include the approximately $40 million annually Soros was contributing to support higher education and libraries in Eastern Europe—critical elements in a

23. The data set includes grants for human rights and civil liberties (coded Q70, 71, R, and I) and public affairs and society benefit (coded T, W, and a portion of Q99). The human rights and civil liberties category includes civil rights, legal services, migration and refugee issues, and human rights. Public affairs and societal benefit includes public affairs and government, philanthropy and volunteerism, and civil society and democracy.

24. The Foundation Center includes National Taxonomy of Exempt Entities (NTEE) code W24 (civic participation) and a subset of Q99 (international other) grants in their civil society and democracy category.

25. Burnell (2000).

26. Programmatic areas not discussed here, but included in the data set, include refugees and migration, reproductive health and rights, financial services, military, and transportation.

27. Finkel and others (2005).

Table 11-3. *Foundation Support for Democratization, Civil Society, and Human Rights, Selected Years, 1990–2001*

Units as indicated

Item	1990	1996	2001
Total grants given (dollars)	26,477,081	90,812,091	232,564,449
Range of grant size (dollars)	10,000–1,493,600	10,000–2,892,617	10,000–7,658,175
Average grant size (dollars)	78,800	113,942	141,980
Number of grants given	336	797	1,638
Number of grants made outside United States	68	392	866
Number of grants made in United States	268	405	772
Number of foundations giving	106	134	218
Number of grantees receiving	208	523	1,019

Source: This data set was requested as a special query run by the Foundation Center. The search set is based on the Foundation Center's grants sample (circa 1990 and 1996), which includes all of the grants of $10,000 or more awarded to organizations by a sample of 832 larger foundations for 1990 and 1,010 foundations for 1996. For community foundations, only discretionary and donor-advised grants are included. Grants to individuals are not included. All dollar amounts are reported in current figures and therefore not corrected for inflation.

democratic society as they help to ensure that citizens have access to information.[28] But private foundations were limited by political and tax constraints from supporting direct party building and elections. Support for direct political change came from publicly funded foundations affiliated with the National Endowment for Democracy.[29]

As indicated in table 11-4, foundation support for citizen participation, election regulation, and voter participation—that is, issues of civil society and democracy—increased from $3.57 million in 1990 to $33.36 million in 2001, an 836 percent increase, while support for philanthropy and volunteerism grew from $5.17 million to $33.95 million, an increase of 557 percent. In addition, foundations poured money into building effective and viable nonprofit sectors in countries around the globe by supporting the development of local philanthropies and promoting volunteerism. These grants created and supported organizations like CIVICUS, a global civil society organization in South Africa, and the Information Network for the Third Sector, in Brazil.

The promotion and protection of human rights, civil liberties, civil rights, and legal services are all critical to democratization efforts, and all received

28. Quigley (1997).

29. See USAID, "Democracy and Governance" (www.usaid.gov/our_work/democracy_and_governance/ [November 24, 2009]) for an analysis of the U.S. government's democracy-related work.

Table 11-4. *Foundation Support for Democratization, Civil Society, and Human Rights, by Programmatic Area, Selected Years, 1990–2001*
Dollars

Area	1990	1996	2001
Democracy and civil society	3,565,228	6,065,964	33,363,233
Philanthropy and volunteerism	5,165,400	25,269,100	33,946,086
Civil liberties	993,435	1,613,750	3,217,916
Civil rights	1,069,323	5,678,367	20,743,012
Human rights	9,472,500	27,785,650	70,523,499
Legal services	2,091,093	2,258,982	8,304,712
Government and public administration	693,528	4,924,220	9,988,080
Leadership development	326,847	859,727	5,241,383
Telecommunications and media	. . .	1,459,249	3,015,435
Public policy	935,300	3,543,715	10,801,404
Public finance	105,000	521,540	1,847,250
Other public affairs[a]	410,500	1,171,000	5,961,356
Other[b]	1,398,927	8,986,827	23,175,418

Source: Data from the Foundation Center. See note to table 11-3.

a. Includes grants to support public affairs with a secondary focus on information services, public education, military affairs, international exchange, international affairs, ethics, management.

b. Includes programmatic areas less related to democratization and civil society: child abuse, transportation, financial services, military, reproductive rights/right to die, international migration. Our analysis by programmatic area does not include these grants.

increasing attention from U.S. grant makers over the 1990s. For example, the Ford Foundation, among others, supported the work of the American Bar Association's Central and Eastern European Legal Institute and the International Center for Not-for-Profit Law, which worked to ensure freedom of assembly; the Soros Foundation, among others, provided support for independent media.

Of all the programmatic areas related to democratization and the development of civil society, support for civil rights saw the greatest percentage increase of 1,840 percent, going from $1.07 million in 1990 to $20.74 million in 2001. Support for human rights also increased substantially, going from $9.47 million in 1990 to $70.52 million in 2001, a more than sevenfold increase. Foundation support for legal services increased 297 percent, from $2.09 million in 1990 to $8.30 million in 2001, and support for civil liberties saw a similar increase of 224 percent, from a little less than a million to $3.22 million.

Foundations also supported efforts to build the capacity of the public sector. The Ford Foundation provided a grant to the University of Witwatersrand in South Africa to examine the postapartheid governance capacity in the country and its impact on socioeconomic transformation. In fact, foundation support in these areas increased more dramatically than foundation support for civil society–related efforts described above, although civil society efforts received a greater share of the total grant dollars overall. Foundation support for government and public administration, for example, increased 1,340 percent, from approximately $700,000 in 1990 to almost $10 million in 2001.

Reflecting the dynamism and the complexity of building civil society and democracy, there was considerable evolution among the programs developed by U.S. private foundations. Many private foundations active in Eastern Europe, for example, started out supporting efforts to build democratic institutions and processes. Projects included leadership training and capacity-building support to parliaments and other governmental organizations as well as support for organizations, like the Freedom Forum, that help ensure an independent media. The Mellon Foundation did some extremely interesting work in strengthening citizen access to information—a critical prerequisite of democracy—by designing an innovative library consortia.[30]

Over time, U.S. foundations increasingly focused on developing civil society as a means of strengthening democracy. This included support for the civil society sector itself, including legal infrastructure and sector-serving institutions. While some may argue that support for political parties is more germane to developing political debate and deepening democracy, U.S. foundations eschewed direct support for political parties because it is contrary to U.S. law and potentially to the laws of the recipient country.

Work on civil society relates to an important role that foundations have played in other contexts, namely, their role in redistributing resources. In this Eastern European democracy-assisting case, foundation support helped develop the resiliency of civil society. As a direct consequence, civil society was in a much stronger position to hold the public sector accountable to the interests of its people. Foundations, especially Soros and Ford, made a special effort to support the participation in public life of individuals, including women and the Roma minority, who had previously played little substantive political role. Similarly in South Africa, a number of European governments and U.S. foundations like Ford, Kellogg, and Carnegie supported the Women's National Coalition—a broad-based coalition of women's organizations intended to ensure that the new legal and institutional frameworks were attentive to gender equality.[31] In this respect, U.S. foundations played an important role in promoting redistribution of power among groups as well as sectors within democratizing societies.

30. See Quigley (1997); Quandt (2002).
31. Gershater (2001).

Foundations Supporting Democratization

In the 1990s many foundations responded to the call to promote democracy in Eastern Europe, southern Africa, and elsewhere. These foundations included many of the twenty-five largest international grant-making foundations and some smaller foundations with a long history of international grant making, such as the Rockefeller Brothers Fund, which in many ways provided a leading example for grassroots and community-based grant making essential to civil society and democratic development.

This support was not consistent or uniform across foundations. The Ford Foundation's growth in grant dollars dedicated to these efforts is striking, as the total dollar contribution grew from $6.47 million in 1990 to $108.12 million in 2001, more than a sixteenfold increase. MacArthur and Mott total grant dollars directed to these efforts also increased substantially over this period. Pew's contribution declined over this ten-year period, going from $2.7 million to no grant dollars dedicated to this work in 2001, owing to its decision to cease international grant making in 1995.[32]

Regions and Countries Receiving Democratization Support

Globally, these democracy assistance programs occurred in three different contexts: supporting democratic breakthroughs in former authoritarian states, consolidating democratic progress once those breakthroughs had occurred, and, much later in the decade, encouraging democracy in fragile states. Most foundation programs occurred in the second context, as part of efforts to consolidate democracy. Poland is an example of the first context; there, foundation support started in late spring and early summer of 1989, immediately after the Round Table Talks but before elections. A small number of foundations are encouraging democracy in authoritarian or fragile states like Burma, Cuba, and China.

Foundations also provided democracy assistance in countries before and after their transitions from authoritarian rule. For example, foundation giving for the democratic transition in South Africa reflected the changing context of the country and supported both breakthrough and consolidation. Before the transition to democracy in 1994, private foundations largely supported organizations based on a commitment to fight apartheid.[33] With the first democratic elections and the African National Congress's transition from a movement organization to the dominant political party, early analysis suggests that foundations continued to support civil

32. Renz (2004).
33. Shubane (1999).

society organizations, while support from official state aid sources, like USAID, were redirected to the new legitimate government.[34]

The countries receiving the bulk of support for democratization and civil society issues include South Africa, Israel, Poland, and Brazil as well as Hungary, Russia, and Mexico. Both Canada and England received a significant amount of grant makers' dollars. This support went to universities and international organizations as well as charity and philanthropic initiatives. For example, the Charities Aid Foundation in England received $1 million in 1990 for an endowment to support the development of community foundations.[35]

As noted in the previous section, historically most international grants went to support U.S. nonprofits engaged in international work. In the 1990s, as the number of nonprofits grew dramatically around the globe, foundations increasingly gave directly to overseas nonprofits. Yet this change was even more dramatic in the area of democratization and civil society. While the number of grants going to overseas recipients increased 192 percent between 1990 and 2002, the number of grants for democratization and civil society increased by 1,172 percent between 1990 and 2001, an elevenfold increase. By 2001 the number of grants going directly overseas to support this work actually exceeded giving to U.S.-based nonprofits.

Over these same years, the dollar volume of direct giving by U.S.-based foundations increased from almost $7 million to more than $128 million, a 1,760 percent increase. Yet the change in the number of grants going overseas, from 68 grants worth $6.90 million in 1990 to 865 grants worth $128.27 million in 2001, is more revealing because the transaction costs for each of these grants are higher. In other words, it would be easier for a foundation to give a large grant to an intermediary overseas than to give smaller grants to several overseas recipients.

Roles and Contributions of International Grant Making

Recognizing that U.S. foundations' support for democratization and civil society could never be more than modest, given the scope and size of the changes they sought to support, what contribution did they make to these monumental changes? Our analysis shows that U.S. foundations almost exclusively sought to promote social and policy change, that is, to play a philanthropic rather than a charitable role. This makes sense, since democratization movements sought

---

34. See Stacey and Aksartova (2001). Initial data suggest that U.S. foundation support for civil society has actually increased since the transition and there are many examples of foundations' continued support in this area.

35. Sacks (2005).

to make fundamental societal changes. At times, foundation funding complemented public resources—as when foundations directed their resources to building democratic institutions while U.S. government funding focused on economic restructuring. Although it is difficult to draw general conclusions, based on an analysis of the data presented above and more in-depth casework in Eastern Europe, we suggest that in this philanthropic role foundations acted as first responders, conveners, institution builders, and social entrepreneurs.

First Responders

One thing that foundations did was respond early and quickly. After the political opening in Eastern Europe, they were often first responders, providing resources for new leadership and creating programs that were designed to lead to some momentum for change. Unlike U.S. government agencies, these foundations did not need congressional authorization to act and, because they required a lot less cumbersome and time-consuming feasibility work before beginning programs. While a few foundations (for example, the Soros Foundation and Rockefeller Brothers Fund) had modest programs in the region when the epochal changes took place in 1989, within a matter of months they were joined by the Mellon, Ford, and Mott foundations and the Pew Charitable Trusts, among others.

This nimble response was important in laying the groundwork for other public and private funding sources to move in and support these efforts. For example, foundations identified issues like support for the legal and information infrastructure of civil society as well as advocacy organizations that were later a focal point for public funding. Similarly, USAID's signature Democracy Network Project, the DemNet, drew heavily on the experiences of private foundations. In DemNet, USAID selected a U.S.-based NGO partner for each Eastern European country that essentially acted as a regranting entity, providing small grants and technical assistance to embryonic civil society organizations.[36]

Conveners

Foundations also played three critical convening functions: attracting other donors, identifying institutional or individual partners, and advancing specific project objectives. First, U.S. foundations did a considerable amount of missionary work, in which they took proactive roles in encouraging investment. Foundations like Carnegie in December 1989 and Ford in January 1990 convened important meetings of private and corporate philanthropists to encourage them to broaden and deepen their engagement in transitioning societies. U.S.

---

36. For example, the Academy for Educational Development administered the program in Poland, the Charter Seventy-Seven Foundation in the Czech Republic, the Institute for Sustainable Communities in Bulgaria, and so on. For more about DemNet see Quigley (1997).

governmental representatives, as well as officials from the World Bank and the United Nations, also participated. These meetings helped reduce the time and resources some public agencies required in their feasibility efforts and leveraged the foundations' investments by attracting significant additional resources.

Second, other U.S. foundations, like the Rockefeller Brothers Fund and the Mott Foundation, convened or supported meetings of local NGOs in various countries, which provided U.S. foundations and international donor agencies with opportunities to identify the most salient issues in a particular country context and to locate appropriate institutional and individual partners. Finally, U.S. foundations were adept at convening institutions around project-specific goals. The Mellon Foundation, for example, brought together numerous higher educational institutions in then Czechoslovakia, Hungary, and Poland around an effort to develop consortiums dedicated to the automation of card catalogues, enhanced interconnectivity among these disparate collections, and improved access to libraries throughout the region.

Institution Builders

U.S. foundations frequently provided seed capital for new institutions. These initial investments were often followed by large public investments either from USAID or the World Bank. As a consequence, foundations played an important role in identifying individuals, institutions, and issues that warranted further investment. Some of the best examples are educational institutions, for example, support from the Soros Foundations Network for the Central European University in Budapest and the Mellon and other foundations' support for the Center for Economic Research and Graduate Education in Prague.

U.S. private foundations also supported a set of independent policy research institutions that broadened and deepened the public debate about important policy issues. Throughout the region, these think tanks helped make the policymaking process more open.[37] Initially, many of these think tanks focused on economic issues. These include the Gdansk Institute in Poland, the Institute for Economics in Hungary, the Center for Economic Development in Slovakia, and the Market Institute in Lithuania. Later, think tanks began to focus more on political issues and included organizations like the Civic Institute in the Czech Republic. None of these think tanks would have been established without the financial support, technical assistance, and collaborations encouraged by U.S. private foundations, especially Ford, Mellon, Soros, and Pew.

Along with public donors like USAID, U.S. foundations also established a network of resource centers on civil society, the independent nonprofits—the so-called third sector. These centers were advocates for the sector, providing

37. For further discussion of the role played by think tanks in Eastern Europe, see Quigley (1996b).

training for sector leaders as well as invaluable information regarding donor and other kinds of support for sector members. The Slovak Academic Information Agency, founded by Pavol Demes, is a well-known example of this type of organization that received critical support from U.S. foundations.

Besides building institutions, U.S. private foundations also helped identify new sets of leaders who were not tainted by affiliation with the prior communist regimes and whose skills, experiences, and attitudes were encouraged by U.S. private foundations and instrumental in the integration of this region into Europe. These individuals, many of them early economic reformers, like Lezek Balcerowicz in Poland, Vaclav Klaus in Czechoslovakia, Martin Tardos in Hungary, and Pavol Demes in Slovakia, all received private foundation support before and after their tenures in government. This support included technical assistance, travel tours to examine particular issues, and direct support to the fledgling institutions that these leaders established.

The importance of supporting these leaders, both for the country as well as for the foundations' own work, cannot be overstated. For example, Juraj Mesik is a community activist from Banska Bystrica in central Slovakia. He encouraged foundations to focus more resources outside of capital cities and on new issues, such as the environment, as well as to test the community foundation model in the region. Through his efforts, a variety of foundations supported the Environmental Partnership in Central Europe, of which Mesik was the first executive director. After establishing the organization, Mesik became one of the key staff in the World Bank's community foundation initiative. None of this would have happened without the impetus and support from U.S. private foundations.

Social Entrepreneurs

U.S. private foundations' grant making in Eastern Europe was quite innovative, relying on a variety of different strategic and structural approaches. Many foundations, like Ford and Mott, primarily provided support through local organizations. Other foundations, like Pew and Carnegie, exclusively provided support through U.S.-based organizations. The Soros Foundations gave directly to local organizations, making an explicit point of beginning work in a particular country by first creating a local board, hiring local staff, and placing foundation offices in cities outside the capital city as well as in the capital. This was an innovative model for philanthropy—although one not widely replicated by other foundations, who either administered their programs from the United States or created a small number of field offices in the region (the Ford Foundation in Moscow and later Sofia; the Mott Foundation in Prague, later in Johannesburg; and others).

As social entrepreneurs, these private foundations were ambitious, results oriented, risk absorbing, and highly collaborative. In fact, foundations often took risks that the public and business sectors were unwilling to take in establishing new institutions. Without them, many independent institutions would never have been created, thereby limiting the pluralism essential to democratic development. For example, many projects, such as the establishment of the first independent educational institutions, were the results of collegial efforts from Pew, Ford, Mellon, and Soros, among others. These institutions included the American University in Blagoevgrad, the Central European University, which initially had multiple campuses in the region, and the Center for Economic Research and Graduate Education in Prague. At the same time, foundations advocated for institutional support and policy change around controversial issues for which there was little or no popular support. These included support for minority rights, especially for groups like the Roma, which was generously provided by the Mott, Ford, and Soros foundations. It also included support for addressing the region's horrific environmental degradation, especially from foundations like the German Marshall Fund and the Rockefeller Brothers Fund.

Limitations of International Grant Making

Although the response of private foundations was significant, it was not as large as expected or needed. Eastern Europeans, who were hoping that the epochal nature of the political and economic changes in the region would elicit a response similar to the Marshall Plan, were gravely disappointed. While private foundations provided more resources than some European bilateral assistance programs, the funding was simply insufficient for the problems at hand. Despite their many contributions, U.S. private foundations did not accomplish as much as they might have in their efforts to promote civil society and democracy in Eastern Europe, owing in large part to insufficient resources (including time) relative to the challenges associated with their ambitious goals, amateurism, and, to a lesser extent, paternalism.

Insufficiency

Foundations' advantage to act as first responders had a downside: they often did not stick around to ensure the long-term sustainability of the institutions they helped build. They moved on, either to other programmatic areas within the country or to other budding democracies. For example, the focal point for private foundations' democracy assistance programs that began in Central Europe in 1990 quickly shifted north to the Baltics and south to the Balkans as political openings occurred. And far too many of these democracy assistance programs were of very short duration.

By 1995 a number of private foundations like Pew and Mellon, which were extremely active in the immediate aftermath of the transition, announced plans to phase out of Central Europe, mirroring USAID's decision to "graduate" some

Eastern European countries. These foundations were motivated by a strong sense that their relatively scarce resources could be used better in other contexts. Mellon devoted more resources to support postapartheid South Africa. The Pew Trusts, on the other hand, focused more of its attention on the United States, devoting greater resources to environmental concerns like global warming and the protection of endangered ecosystems.

This relatively quick departure from some Eastern European countries left the foundations' partners in the region in awkward circumstances, often without the necessary resources. It also left the democracy assistance projects far from complete. For foundation critics, this reinforced the impression that foundation efforts are compromised by insufficiency: their attention spans and resources are far too limited for major efforts like the promotion of civil society and democracy, especially given their lofty ambitions.

Amateurism

Based on the expressed popular wishes and the public comments of the newly elected leaders, most private foundations thought that in Eastern Europe the movement to democracy should be relatively swift and easy. It turned out to be neither. As a consequence of this assumption, many democracy assistance programs were not designed to address the longer and more intractable challenges of transitioning from centrally planned and authoritarian states to more open societies. While there was widespread understanding about the need to develop democratic institutions and processes, there was less understanding about the requirement to encourage democratic values like tolerance and commitment to the rule of law and even less expertise to accomplish these much more challenging goals.

This problematic assumption about the ease of the transition process was not unique to U.S. private foundations. Other donors, such as the European Union, the World Bank, and the U.S. government, shared this assumption. Yet the double transition—economic and political—in post-communist countries was unprecedented. So it is understandable that U.S. private foundations, along with bilateral and multilateral institutions, lacked the essential experience that might have enabled them to design more effective assistance strategies and programs.

Moreover, because of the relatively closed nature of Eastern Europe, many private foundations did not have the deep regional competence in terms of relationships and understanding that would have enabled them to take a more sophisticated approach. Foundations assumed a level of homogeneity across the region that was simply inaccurate. Individual countries in Eastern Europe had vastly different experiences with democracy. Poland, Czechoslovakia, and Hungary had a brief experience between the two world wars, while other countries, such as Ukraine, Yugoslavia, Bulgaria, and Romania, had no prior experience. At the same time, individual countries had very different experiences with mass movements, often the precursors of civil society.

In Poland, for example, more than 25 percent of the population was involved in the trade union that became known as Solidarity.[38] The Catholic Church also played a strong role as an alternative source of power and influence. In Czechoslovakia, the state controlled virtually all aspects of social, cultural, and economic life. Robust institutions operating outside of the state simply did not exist. Romania had no prior experience with civil society or power centers distinct from the Nicolae Ceauşescu regime. Despite these differences, many foundations provided a common program across countries. This monochromatic view of countries was especially pronounced in the early 1990s. However, as private foundations gained experience, they generally did a better job in adapting their programs to local circumstances.

Paternalism

Another related shortcoming of the private foundations seeking to promote democracy in Eastern Europe was their implicit application of the U.S. model of democracy. Most private foundations advocated for federal presidential systems with strong checks and balances, including a robust civil society. While this democratic model works relatively well in the U.S. context, it is not easily exportable. There was an implicit sense that U.S. foundations were involved in helping make Eastern Europe "more like us," in large part because many Eastern Europeans were espousing their interest in developing a market democracy comparable to that of the United States. This instinct was understandable in that many of the foundations involved in this effort did not have deep experiences of non-U.S. democratic systems or the political culture of Eastern Europe.

Impact

Given the relatively short time horizons (especially if democracy takes sixty years or more to build, as Ralf Dahrendorf and others suggest), the modest resources of time and money (hundreds of millions instead of billions), and the lack of clear measurable outcomes, it is difficult to assess precisely the impact of U.S. private foundations' international grant making in democracy assistance.[39] This problem is not unique to private foundations. A report by the Center for Global

---

38. Solidarity, led by Lech Walesa, a worker from Gdansk, was the mass workers' movement in Poland that brought about change in the country's political circumstances.

39. Dahrendorf (1990).

Development in May 2006 stated that despite hundreds of billions invested by governments, foundations, and NGOs, the net impact of development support is still not known.[40]

Our assessment of the effectiveness of U.S. private foundation work to assist democracy in Eastern Europe is based on in-depth casework conducted during the mid-1990s.[41] This work involved intensive collaboration with leaders of civil society in Central Europe, and since it has been translated into Czech, Hungarian, Polish, and Slovak, it was broadly disseminated through the region.[42] Our observations about the impact of foundations' international grant making are tempered by the very different programming interests pursued by foundations, the fact that results are more difficult to trace in an international context, and the breadth of a focus like democratization. We cannot draw definitive conclusions about the impact of foundation international grant making. A robust assessment of impact would also involve much closer scrutiny of the foundations' putative goals, the resources provided, and the programmatic results.

With these caveats, however, some broad observations are in order. We can begin to understand the contributions of U.S. foundations to democratization efforts in Eastern Europe by reflecting on the benefits of this work at the individual, institutional, and societal level. In terms of their impact on individuals, there is evidence that Eastern Europeans who had the opportunity to participate in various training programs in situ—or, especially, international programs—benefited enormously from foundation-supported efforts. Examples include those individuals who participated in foundation-supported fellowships targeted at Eastern Europeans and conducted at institutions of higher education in the United States, including the Hoover Institution at Stanford University, the Kennedy School at Harvard University, the School of Foreign Service at Georgetown University, and many other locations.

As the earlier discussion suggested, there is also ample evidence that foundations had an impact in enriching the institutional landscape and, therefore, in deepening democratic development. This impact was particularly notable on independent educational and research institutions, as well as on the general development of civil society. It would be difficult to argue the counterfactual, that is, that civil society in Eastern Europe would be as developed as it is if U.S. private foundations had not been involved in supporting its development.

It is most difficult to gauge foundation impact on major democratic ideas. At times and in certain contexts, U.S. foundations had an impact in playing a

40. Savedoff, Levine, and Birdsall (2006).
41. The results of this work are discussed more fully in Quigley (1997).
42. Quigley (1996a).

supporting role for the idea of civil society—although the major role was played by the leaders who wrought these transitions, such as Vaclav Havel in Czechoslovakia, Adam Michnik in Poland, and Arpard Goncz in Hungary. The impact on other democratic ideas like competition and participation is very difficult to determine without extensive research. Our supposition is that much of this impact from external factors was derived from Eastern Europeans' greater exposure to Western ideas through travel and access to the international media, as well as support from the more official efforts of the European Union and the U.S. government.

Undoubtedly, lowering the rhetoric about private foundations' ability to affect global issues would be helpful. A bit more humility about what we expect to accomplish would probably have a positive effect on these programs. If foundation leaders and staff understand the complexity, time, and resources required to advance democracy, combat major health challenges, and enhance understanding of other cultures, they might provide greater resources and present a different attitude that would engender greater cooperation and results.

Still, U.S. private foundations' international grant-making efforts in assisting civil society and democracy could have been strengthened by better matching the needed resources with the problem and staying the course long enough so that tangible and sustainable results were left behind. Moreover, this sustainability would have been furthered by opportunities for local participation in every phase of the program: from conception and design to execution, communication, and evaluation. Of course, this would require that foundations work directly overseas and rely less on intermediaries, although that may conflict with regulatory and accountability pressures or even the foundation's own organizing documents or concerns about controlling administrative expenses.

Despite this ambiguity about the overall impact of foundation efforts to support democratization and the development of a global civil society, one of the most important things that U.S. private foundations did was simply be there, if not during, then immediately after the moment of democratic breakthrough. This provided an important point of reconnection for these countries and Europe and North America. There are many reports of the empowerment of leaders of civil society in Eastern Europe.[43] At the same time, foundations were able to carry their experience in Eastern Europe into other contexts; for instance, the Mott and Mellon foundations took their work to South Africa, and the Rockefeller Brothers Fund shifted from Central and Eastern to southeastern Europe. Perhaps one of the best indicators of their success will be the

43. See Quigley (1997) for further amplification.

long-term sustainability of the projects, programs, and institutions they have supported.[44] In this respect, final conclusions have yet to be drawn.

Conclusion

Dramatic changes on the world stage in the past fifteen years have spurred significant shifts in international grant making by U.S. foundations. This chapter just begins to scratch the surface of these trends and their implications. Philanthropic support for international issues has increased tremendously. More foundations are supporting these issues, including smaller and newer foundations. Foundations are granting more dollars to international concerns, and this support is increasingly given directly to overseas recipients in many more countries. Foundations are also more strategic in how they approach their international grant making, focusing more intensely on a few key programmatic areas, cooperating with other private funders and public agencies to address global problems, and building and using intermediaries to support international grant making.

Foundations' international grant making to support democratization and the development of a global civil society does offer evidence of positive results, although certainly not as great as rhetoric suggests. Foundations that responded to the call to promote democracy were generally nimbler than government donors, took more risks, were less politicized, and were willing to look beyond the government for partners. They made important contributions in building the first set of independent institutions in Eastern Europe. In fact, considerable evidence suggests that civil society in these countries was more pluralistic and vigorous in 2002 than it was in 1990, and this would have been unlikely without the help of U.S. private foundations. Foundations also developed approaches that were mirrored by public funders, who took them to a much larger scale. Finally, foundations' efforts to advocate for social and policy change drew attention to certain issues, such as minority rights and the environment, that were receiving only the most modest attention.

Yet foundations' contributions would have had greater impact if some of the underlying assumptions about the transition process had not been so limited and foundations' resources were more in line with their lofty ambitions for democracy in the region. At this point, few private foundations—notable exceptions being Soros and the German Marshall Fund—are still deeply engaged in strengthening democratic values and processes in Eastern Europe. Time will

44. Kevin F. F. Quigley, *Conversations on Democracy Assistance,* Woodrow Wilson Center, Washington, D.C., 2006. This monograph was translated into Czech, Hungarian, Polish, and Slovak, and the point on sustainability was strongly endorsed during a series of press conferences around the region to release the monograph.

tell more clearly, but it does seem that some of the most innovative democracy-assisting work was done by private foundations.

Foundations involved in international grant making have great ambitions. Despite these ambitions and the growing resources and numbers of foundations involved in overseas grant making, U.S. private foundations alone are unlikely to have a determinative impact in solving the world's problems. If strategic and focused, with long-term commitments, working in concert with other public and private institutions, and eschewing some of the limiting consequences of amateurism and paternalism, U.S. private foundations can and will play an important supporting role in addressing some of our most pressing global challenges.

12

Foundations as Cultural Actors

JAMES ALLEN SMITH

America's largest foundations arrived late on the cultural scene.[1] When the major philanthropic enterprises of Rockefeller, Carnegie, Sage, Harkness, and Rosenwald got under way in the years around 1900, their principal focus was on medicine, public health, education, and social science. Long before these endeavors, however, many wealthy Americans had already been hard at work establishing museums, libraries, symphonies, and opera companies. Foundations were not their preferred vehicle for supporting cultural interests. Only in the 1920s, with foundations well established, did some foundation leaders begin to ponder their own absence from the cultural sector. The head of the Rockefeller Foundation's Division of Studies, Edwin R. Embree, asked plaintively, "Of what good is it to keep people alive and healthy if their lives are not to be touched increasingly with something of beauty?"[2]

Why the neglect? What inhibited the major foundations in their support of arts and culture in the early decades of the twentieth century? The most obvious answer is that large general-purpose foundations represented an institutional

---

1. *Culture* and *cultural* are problematic words. They invite a separate essay, if not another book. For the sake of convenience, this chapter relies on the "arts, culture, humanities" definition from the National Taxonomy of Exempt Entities of the National Center for Charitable Statistics. But it should be remembered from the outset that usages change. Much of this chapter covers ground that precedes these classifications. In the first half of the twentieth century, when foundation staff members spoke of the humanities, they subsumed the arts under that rubric.

2. Quoted in Fosdick (1989, p. 238).

and intellectual break with past charitable practices. The founders famously described their work as scientific philanthropy, seeing their role as a search for the root causes of social problems. They were explicit in rejecting older notions of charity that had brought about only temporary amelioration of human suffering and had made little headway in analyzing or solving systemic social ills. As they focused on building research institutions and bolstering various professional domains, they often described their philanthropy as wholesale rather than retail giving. Arts patronage was clearly old hat. The realms of arts and culture thus remained marginal to the interests of the turn-of-the-century foundations.

But other realities also inhibited the large foundations in supporting the nation's cultural life. By the early 1900s, some of the nation's most prominent cultural institutions were already flourishing. They were the product of post–Civil War economic growth and the expanding cultural horizons of Americans. Wealthy and even not-so-wealthy citizens had begun to travel abroad for pleasure and study. In their European wanderings they had discovered all sorts of urban amenities. They had seen magnificent museums and art collections while visiting London and Florence, heard symphony orchestras in Berlin and Leipzig, strolled through parks and zoos in Paris and Antwerp. Some began to collect books, manuscripts, and works of art as they traveled; some stayed abroad to study music at European conservatories.

Long before general-purpose foundations entered the scene, new patterns of cultural philanthropy had taken shape. Urban elites undertook projects for civic betterment—museums, libraries, botanical gardens, parks, and war memorials—enlisting their peers, engineering broad-based public fund-raising campaigns, and often turning to municipal governments for help. Although the precise forms varied from place to place, public-private partnerships were common, with city governments donating a building site or agreeing to pay specific operating costs. According to one estimate, municipal governments provided as much as 40 percent of aggregate museum construction costs between 1870 and 1910.[3] Individual donors, large and small, gave the rest. Major cultural institutions emerged: Boston's Museum of Fine Arts (in 1870) and Symphony Hall (1900), the New England Conservatory of Music (1867), New York's Metropolitan Museum (1870) and Metropolitan Opera (1880), Chicago's Art Institute (1879), and Detroit's Institute of Arts (1882), among others.

A number of smaller and still vital cultural institutions also took nascent shape in the late nineteenth century. Zealous private collectors brought enduring institutions into being, including New York's Morgan Library (built from 1902 to 1906) and Frick Collection (created in 1919 and opened in 1931) and Boston's Isabella Stewart Gardner Museum (opened in 1903) among them.

3. Fox (1963, p. 51).

Music lovers also had roles to play. Henry Higginson, the founder of the Boston Symphony Orchestra and the guiding force behind the city's Symphony Hall, was effectively the owner and manager of the orchestra, hiring musicians, paying them, and covering debts when necessary. In the 1910s Elizabeth Sprague Coolidge was patron of a string quartet and organized summer music festivals in the Berkshires before turning to larger-scale patronage.

Cultural giving was robust, but it was not akin to the scientific philanthropy or wholesale giving described by a John D. Rockefeller Sr. Cultural projects were conceived in different contexts and relied on different resources. Sometimes they were civic endeavors, involving city governments and a broad community of donors; sometimes they were private obsessions that yielded legacies that would benefit the public. While cultural institutions depended on generous gifts of money, artwork, and volunteer labor, they were not exclusively or even primarily supported by charitable largesse. The U.S. cultural economy has always been more complex.

Culture has been viewed in the United States not as a public good but rather as a hybrid, providing a mix of private and public benefits. Some economists think of culture as a merit good rather than a public good because some individuals will pay to attend plays, concerts, and museums and enjoy the exclusive benefits. Indeed, American culture—whether P. T. Barnum's thriving museums or Jenny Lind's wildly popular tours—has long had a market orientation. In the late nineteenth century, orchestras, opera companies, and touring theatrical groups were all organized on a commercial basis. Distinctions between highbrow and lowbrow vanished in the pursuit of paying audiences.[4] Organizers and promoters—orchestra conductors, famous singers, and leading actors among them—assumed the financial risks, hoping to profit while expecting little or no philanthropic subsidy.

Even those we now think of as the era's most magnanimous philanthropists brought a strong commercial sensibility to their cultural giving. Andrew Carnegie had generously acquired the land and provided the construction funds for New York's Music Hall, as it was modestly named at first. It was intended as a rental hall for visiting lecturers, touring musical groups, and New York's rival orchestras, the Symphony and Philharmonic. Events there were expected to pay their way. Carnegie dutifully served on elite cultural boards, including both New York orchestras and the Metropolitan Opera and Real Estate Company. However, like many of his contemporaries he felt that the performing arts were a business venture, insisting bluntly that "the greatest patronage of music should come from a paying public rather than from private endowment."[5] Cultural patronage, commercial entrepreneurship, and civic pride were intimately intertwined.

4. Levine (1988).
5. Quoted in Dizikes (1993, p. 285).

As the great foundations took shape around the turn of the century, cultural philanthropy was already following its own distinctive trajectory. Looking back at an earlier generation's contributions, a 1935 report for the Carnegie Corporation described the state of patronage well in discussing Carnegie Hall:

> [It] was no philanthropy; it was a business venture, far-seeing perhaps, yet designed to pay its own way. At that time of his life Carnegie felt, as so many other magnates have felt, that one essential proof of a public need was public support; that a city should not be ahead of its citizens; that if they really wished an extension of their cultural lives they must signify their wish by their patronage.[6]

Whether seated in the orchestra or the highest balcony, the paying public, no less than the wealthy donor, could be described as patrons.

Herein lies an important clue to the complexity of America's cultural philanthropy and the attitudes that have shaped it. The paying public has been the paramount source of cultural revenue. Philanthropy has been important, but it has often been a mere adjunct to the larger cultural economy. Much of the nation's cultural life—film, Broadway theater, music recording, and book publishing—is still organized on a for-profit basis. But even the aspects of cultural life that are organized on a nonprofit basis must look to the market, competing for audiences and seeking diverse ways to augment earnings. Current watchwords in the nonprofit arts and cultural sector—"earned income" and "sustainability"—echo this ingrained market sensibility, as do the many complex interactions between nonprofit organizations and commercial entities.

In the aggregate today (although acknowledging wide variations across arts disciplines and among individual organizations), some 50 percent of revenues for the nonprofit cultural sector is earned from ticket sales, admissions fees, gift shops, and other ventures.[7] Private donations yield roughly 40 percent of the sector's revenue, but foundations account for only one-third of total philanthropic dollars, a mere 13 percent of the overall revenue stream. At times, the public sector has been a direct funding partner, beginning with municipal support for museums and libraries in the nineteenth century. But governments have been fitful and generally reluctant cultural patrons. Today, only about 10 percent of the aggregate revenue for the cultural sector comes directly from government sources, and the contribution varies greatly across arts disciplines.[8] Typically, government's role has been indirect, predominately through the tax code and its various incentives for charitable giving.

6. Clark (1935, pp. 234–35).
7. Seaman (2002, p. 18).
8. Renz, Lawrence, and Marino (2003, p. 1).

The cultural role of foundations is played out within the larger context of individual and corporate giving and within the still broader cultural economy. Much of what foundations do—providing money for capital projects, commissioning new works and sponsoring exhibitions, awarding prizes or travel grants, supporting arts education, acquiring art for museums, and contributing to general operations—is indistinguishable from what individual donors are constantly doing.[9] Moreover, existing cultural grants have a range of purposes: charitable aims (enabling disadvantaged children to attend concerts or creating after-school arts programs in public schools); goals that complement or substitute for public sector programs (paying for arts teachers in schools, funding individual artists or controversial exhibitions); conservation objectives (historic preservation and art authentication); and innovative purposes (commissioning new works or expanding the reach of music and art through digital archives). But the classification of diverse foundation grants—even if a large sample is aggregated and categorized—does not tell us about the distinctive role and impact of foundations. To begin to understand that role, two enduring realities must be acknowledged.

First, foundations are patrons in a market-oriented cultural sector. Over the decades the boundaries have shifted and blurred between commercial and nonprofit culture. Whether commercial or nonprofit, cultural organizations have always earned much of their livelihood in the marketplace. The impact of the large foundations has been most consequential when foundations have attempted to expand, reshape, or redefine the cultural economy. They have done so by drawing new resources into the cultural economy, by encouraging the nonprofit organizational form, by strengthening professionalism in the cultural sector, and by laboring to improve the capacity of individual organizations to survive within a very competitive marketplace.

Second, the role of government has been episodic and, in our federal system, highly variable across states and localities. To speak of foundations playing consistent roles of complementarity or substitution is meaningless when government has been inconsistent in its direct cultural support and when policymakers have not generally viewed culture as a public good. In most other fields, foundations have played an important—in fact, an innovative—role in shaping public policy. But cultural policymaking has always faced an uphill battle in the United States, and foundation support of cultural research and policy innovation has been erratic. Basic questions about the public purposes of the arts remain unresolved: they are not posed in the commercial cultural marketplace, and they have been considered only fitfully in the public arena.

9. Weber (1993). This and subsequent arts funding studies by the Foundation Center and Grantmakers in the Arts itemize the largest grants.

Setting the Stage

In the early twentieth century, the general-purpose grant-making foundation offered no clear institutional or legal advantage to the nation's major cultural donors, many of whom were diligent students of art or music. The professionalization and bureaucratization of cultural patronage thus developed at a different pace and along different lines from those of foundation activity in other fields. Cultural donors responded to their own philanthropic muses, many of them establishing single-purpose operating entities. Collectors created museums to house their treasures or augmented the collections of existing museums. Music lovers founded some of the nation's famous conservatories, sometimes with endowments to rival those of the larger foundations. In 1924 the Curtis Institute of Music received a gift of $12.5 million from Mary Louise Bok, the daughter of the founder of Curtis Publishing. George Eastman donated some $20 million between 1918 and 1932 for the Eastman School of Music. Augustus Juilliard's fortune ultimately found its way to the conservatory that bears his name.

Juilliard's bequest was reported on the front page of the *New York Times* as the largest single sum ever devoted exclusively to music, later determined to be some $13.5 million. His 1919 will specified that he wanted to support the Metropolitan Opera, finance concerts, and "aid worthy students of music in securing a complete and adequate musical education, whether at appropriate institutions now in existence or hereafter created."[10] Another donor, Elizabeth Sprague Coolidge, pursued her own pioneering path. Born into a prosperous Chicago family in 1864, Lizzie Coolidge was a talented pianist and serious student of composition. In the 1910s, after her parents and husband died, she inherited approximately $4 million. Aware of musicians' often wretched economic status, her first gifts, totaling some $200,000, went to the Chicago Symphony Orchestra, where she established a pension fund for the players.[11]

Over the years Coolidge learned much about being a patron-impresario. As her biographer notes, "Hers was never a remote patronage, a kind of antiseptic dispensing of humanitarian assistance from a safe clinical distance." But she did begin to think about the need to institutionalize or, as she put it, to "impersonalize" her philanthropy so that the activities would "not be dependent upon the life, the good will, or the bank account of any individual."[12] As is the case with other cultural donors, the desire to preserve creative works and to make them accessible to the public determined her philanthropic choices. She would go on

10. Quoted in Garraty and Carnes (1999, pp. 314–15).
11. Barr (1998).
12. Barr (1997, p. 7).

to build an auditorium at the Library of Congress and create an endowment for concerts, although it took an act of Congress to allow the library to receive and hold her funds in trust and to secure a venue in Washington for the performance of chamber works.

Coolidge's patronage reminds us of the continuing role played by both serious amateurs and successful professional musicians and artists. While the assets of their foundations do not approach those of the largest foundations, they are an important part of the philanthropic ecosystem. They provide the resources for both artistic innovation and the preservation of traditions.

Examples of foundations operating in this manner abound. After Edgar Leventritt's death in 1939, his wife and daughter sustained his musical passions; the Edgar M. Leventritt Foundation has supported music festivals and a prestigious competition for pianists and violinists. Serge Koussevitzky, the music director of the Boston Symphony Orchestra from 1924 to 1949, used his personal resources to commission new works for the orchestra and subsequently established a foundation that has assisted many composers, among them Béla Bartók, Paul Hindemith, Benjamin Britten, and Aaron Copland. When the Boston Symphony Orchestra concerts at Tanglewood were threatened with cancellation during World War II, Koussevitzky's foundation subsidized them.

In the visual arts, artist-endowed foundations now include the Pollock-Krasner Foundation, the Jerome Foundation, and the Andy Warhol Foundation for the Visual Arts. Among these, the Warhol Foundation is far and away the largest, with more than $200 million in assets. Since its creation in 1987 it has funded projects to defend artistic freedom of expression and supported exhibitions of challenging and experimental works. When the National Endowment for the Arts curtailed much of its funding for individual artists, the Warhol Foundation stepped forward with a $10 million financial commitment to get the Creative Capital Foundation and its programs for funding individual artists off the ground. Today, with booming art markets and various royalty streams enriching some of the most successful artists, there are signs that artist-endowed foundations will proliferate.

Whether created by devoted amateurs or endowed by famous artists or musicians, these foundations have been an important source of artistic support in the United States, serving as a bridge between individual patronage and the interventions in the cultural economy of better-endowed and more fully staffed foundations. Any account of the cultural role of American foundations must acknowledge the presence of these small yet vital patron- and artist-endowed foundations. While their financial resources are not vast, their intellectual and social capital are enormous. Their existence hints at a philanthropic division of labor.

These smaller foundations can specialize. They can be venturesome in nurturing creativity. Indeed, they have identified new talent, sustained first-class training, fostered artists' careers at every stage, and commissioned new creative works. In contrast, the efforts of the large foundations in supporting individual artists—the innovative role at its most basic—have been erratic and limited. The Rockefeller Foundation had a significant postwar program of individual support for artists, and the Ford Foundation has recently taken the lead in a newly announced project, United States Artists, which completed its first round of grants in late 2006. According to Foundation Center data, however, less than 5 percent of large foundation grants (based on 1,172 of the nation's largest foundations) goes for the commissioning of new works, prizes, residencies, competitions, and other sorts of professional development for artists.[13] This situation leads one to pose the persistent question: What distinctive roles have the large foundations played?

Enter the Leading Players

In 1922 Frederick Keppel, the president of the Carnegie Corporation of New York, asked how his foundation could "further the understanding of that deeper structure of knowledge and feeling which involves philosophy, art, and the comprehension of human relations."[14] He was not alone in worrying that cultural funding was lagging behind other fields. For his study *Wealth and Culture,* Eduard C. Lindeman had collected data throughout the 1920s on approximately two hundred foundations. Cultural giving was so inconsequential—or so intimately connected to higher education—that it did not merit its own category.[15] Another survey of giving, conducted in 1931 by the Twentieth Century Fund, was able to catalogue $52 million in foundation grants, estimating that less than $1 million was going to the "humanities," a term that included the arts.[16]

These are the best early benchmarks that exist for cultural giving by foundations. In all likelihood, cultural support was less than 2 percent of total foundation giving during the 1920s and the early 1930s. The data are clearly crude and should be accepted cautiously. Nevertheless, they are a gauge against which to measure the roughly 13–15 percent share of foundation giving currently going to the cultural sector.[17] The story of the expansion of cultural giving as a share of foundation giving is central to appreciating the role and impact of the large foundations over the long run: these foundations have expanded the ranks of cultural donors.

13. Renz, Lawrence, and Marino (2003).
14. Keppel (1936, p. 81).
15. Lindeman (1936, pp. 13–14).
16. Clark (1931).
17. Weber (1993, p. 33).

When Keppel first turned Carnegie's attention toward culture, he followed patterns set in other fields. Grants went to leading universities, where the foundation aimed to improve college teaching and raise professional standards. Keppel was especially interested in improving graduate training for art historians and museum curators. After work in the visual arts got under way, the foundation began to explore a program in music. Its forays followed a similarly academic path. Carnegie dispatched Randall Thompson to visit some thirty colleges, asking deans, professors, and students, "What should a college attempt to do in music?"[18] The foundation posed even broader questions in a second survey: "What aspects of music in America to-day seem the most important? How can music best be furthered?"[19]

Among the general-purpose foundations at work in the early 1930s, Carnegie was far and away the largest single donor to art and music, providing an estimated 80 percent or more of all foundation funding for those fields. The dollars flowed mostly toward universities. As Evans Clark observed at the time, "The Corporation drifted into [music] through its wish to encourage music as it was encouraging other subjects."[20] Carnegie's strategy in this as in other fields was to encourage professional training and development. Indeed, a strategy when pursued single-mindedly and across diverse fields begins to constitute a role—in this case, building human capital.

As the economic crisis of the 1930s deepened, foundation leaders were compelled to confront elemental questions about their aims and role. With individual human suffering so glaring, they asked whether foundations should shoulder some of the burden and revert to providing charitable assistance during a national emergency. Alternatively, with the lingering economic crisis, should they maintain their commitment to philanthropy, which they understood primarily as long-term support for basic research, social and economic investigation, and knowledge building? In either case, with the responsibilities of the federal government expanding, how should they now define their relationship to government?

By and large, Carnegie stuck to its program. Keppel explained that a foundation's task was always to balance "desperate present necessity" against the long term. Foundation trustees, he said, should never forget that they must "determine what *in the long run* represents the wisest use of the funds at their disposal."[21] In contrast, the president of the Rockefeller Foundation, Raymond Fosdick, seemed

18. Thompson (1935, p. xii).
19. Clark (1935, p. vi).
20. Clark (1935, p. 240).
21. Keppel (1936, p. 85).

more troubled by the nation's near-term economic woes. He questioned the foundation's commitment to research, wondering whether the foundation had uncritically supported "aristocratic traditions" of culture to the neglect of contemporary concerns. Rockefeller's cultural funding had focused on classical archaeology, with contributions to the American Academy in Rome, the American School of Classical Studies in Athens, and the University of Chicago's Oriental Institute. One trustee was prompted to ask bluntly whether the foundation had persisted too long in pursuing "the snobbishness of the classical tradition."[22]

David Stevens, who moved in 1932 from the General Education Board to the Rockefeller Foundation's humanities program, was also critical, arguing that the foundation was simply "buttressing scholasticism and antiquarianism in our universities."[23] He wanted to broaden the audiences for culture: "The humanities should contribute to a spiritual renaissance by stimulating creative expression in art, literature, and music; by setting and maintaining high standards of critical appreciation; and by bringing the intellectual and spiritual satisfactions of life within the reach of greater numbers."[24] The foundation funded the study of American literature, experimental programs in radio and film, and communications studies. Stevens seemed proudest of the foundation's role in theater, helping university departments at Yale, Iowa, and North Carolina, reviving a group called the National Theatre Conference, and turning to the Authors League of America to aid playwrights and directors and to build bridges between nonprofit and commercial theaters.[25]

Rockefeller was not alone in creating cultural programs with national scope and purpose during the Great Depression. Samuel Kress's "Gift to the Nation," Andrew Mellon's even more magnanimous donations to the National Gallery in Washington, and Elizabeth Coolidge's work with the Library of Congress exemplify the national aims of some donors. The Samuel H. Kress Foundation, still active today in supporting art scholarship and conservation, was established in 1929 against the backdrop of the economic crisis. Like other collector-driven philanthropies, its programs were structured around the donor's acquisitions. Convinced that too few Americans had enjoyed opportunities to travel and view European masterpieces, and believing that great art possessed moral force, Kress embarked on a series of projects in the 1930s that spanned the continent. He selected fifty Italian artworks from his extensive collection and created a traveling exhibition that was seen in two dozen cities.

22. Fosdick (1989, p. 241).
23. Fosdick (1989, p. 239).
24. Fosdick (1989, p. 240).
25. Yahnke (1978, p. 30).

His foundation gradually dispersed his holdings to the National Gallery of Art, regional museums, and universities.[26] But how does one categorize the role of his foundation? Kress's aims were, in a broad sense, charitable in the audiences he hoped to reach. But the goals were also philanthropic in the moral and aesthetic transformation he hoped to bring about. His gifts to museums supplemented certain government ambitions. In the end, the work of his foundation could be seen as innovative in its effects on regional museums and universities, even while remaining deeply conservative in its conception of art.

More important than affixing broad labels to philanthropic activities is understanding how foundations have interacted with the larger cultural economy and how they have come to terms with government's episodic cultural interventions. The New Deal cultural programs offer a first glimpse at the complicated interdependence of private philanthropy and government programs. For roughly a decade the various New Deal programs, most notably the Works Progress Administration's Federal Project Number One, were of such a scale and national reach that they temporarily altered the cultural landscape. Foundations were clearly operating in a different environment. But would their role be best described in terms of complementarity or substitution?

Federal One created projects to assist artists, musicians, writers, actors, and scholars who, like other workers, faced tenuous employment prospects. Less a signal of an incipient federal cultural policy than a work relief experiment, the programs nevertheless aspired to something more. They sought to inculcate an appreciation for the arts in the American public. By 1938, thirty-four symphonies funded by the Music Project had drawn fourteen million people to concerts. The Arts Project established arts education centers that drew eight million people to classes. The Theater Project also drew millions to its productions.

The scale of the federal programs could never be matched by foundations, but the objectives were often similar, shaped by common concerns. Foundation efforts often intersected with federal initiatives. But collaboration was typically a matter of opportunism, an occasional intertwining of public and private aims, rather than of clearly conceived roles. A foundation might loan a staff member, augment a project budget, or speed the purchase of a piece of equipment. In several instances, the Rockefeller Foundation helped the government to coordinate hastily conceived or understaffed activities, such as the frenetic efforts of the Writers Project to collect folk tales, then inventory and archive them. Indeed, the greatest resource that Rockefeller and a handful of other foundations brought to bear on the federal cultural activities of the Depression era was an intellectual

26. Kress Foundation, "History of the Kress Collection" (www.kressfoundation.org/collection/default.aspx?id=70 [November 25, 2009]).

one—the expertise of staff and the capacity to mobilize the extensive professional networks that Rockefeller and other foundations had built during the 1920s.

Although World War II brought an abrupt end to this episode of federal cultural support, Federal One's legacy would linger. But it was a legacy that government would have to share with the leading foundations: the definition of American culture had been broadened, and the seeds had been planted for a wider geographic reach, better understanding of regional cultures, and larger audiences for theater, music, and the visual arts. And there would be deeply etched memories—some favorable, some skeptical—of the federal government as cultural patron. Whether working together or on parallel paths during the Depression, the federal government and private foundations were setting the stage for the cultural boom of the 1950s and 1960s.

A West Side Story

The nation's postwar cultural boom resonated most loudly and philanthropically in the project that brought New York's Lincoln Center for the Performing Arts into being. The project, which transformed New York City's cultural economy, was soon replicated in performing arts initiatives in other cities. It showed how major foundations, when fully committed to an enterprise, could stimulate and reshape philanthropy and thus dramatically alter the cultural marketplace. In its grand scale, the Lincoln Center project broke fiscal barriers for the arts and began to align cultural giving with schemes for urban renewal and economic development. By 1966 more than $125 million had been raised, which, in its day, was the largest cultural project ever undertaken in the United States. Looking back, one participant recalled the uncertainty: "There was no formula available to determine the center's fund-raising potential, for there was no defined group of prospective donors, whose contributing potential could be gauged."[27]

The project's masterminds—with the Rockefeller and Ford foundations playing leading roles—cultivated new categories of donors. They drew in corporate donors, who supplied nearly 6 percent of the funding. Foundations also discovered innovative ways to bring government funding to the table, with city, state, and federal commitments providing about 20 percent of the total. The project propelled the two lead foundations to levels of giving that far exceeded their past cultural commitments: Ford contributions totaled $25 million, and Rockefeller giving reached $15 million. The appeals to other foundations—some one hundred and sixty of them giving more than $62 million—greatly expanded the universe of foundation donors to cultural causes.

27. Young (1980, p. 61).

The dual streams of financial resources commanded by the public and private sectors interacted in complex ways. Without the initial prospect of public funding through Mayor Robert Wagner's Committee on Slum Clearance, there might never have been a way to initiate the project and push it forward. Substantial as the private sums ultimately proved to be, they were clearly inadequate to sustain or complete a project on the scale of Lincoln Center. Neither sector could execute so vast a project alone. By the early 1960s various government agencies had provided approximately $40 million for Lincoln Center. Federal money helped acquire the land and relocate the people living there; state money built the New York State Theater by drawing on funds appropriated for the World's Fair; and city money was used to acquire important parcels of land, build the new performing arts library, pay for the State Theater, construct a parking garage, and pay for various neighborhood amenities.

Foundation money also had diverse uses. It funded some of the initial conceptual work and over the years kept the project alive and on a disciplined fiscal track whenever doubts surfaced about skyrocketing costs. Ford and Rockefeller insisted several times that there be complete reviews of costs and potential overruns. Foundation staff members also worked hard to articulate and insist upon a core mission for the arts complex: encouraging artistic innovation, fostering international cultural exchanges, and expanding the audience for the arts. Finally, in putting the finishing aesthetic touches on Lincoln Center, smaller foundation grants added such embellishments as the plaza's central fountain, Richard Lippold's sculpture of Orpheus and Apollo in Philharmonic Hall, and the Chagalls at the Metropolitan Opera House.

Despite the financial scale of this New York project, private philanthropic contributions for the arts nationwide budged only slightly in real terms from 1955 to 1964. In some quarters, this provoked legitimate doubts about the extent of the nation's cultural "boom." Historical data are imprecise and difficult to compare, but the data collecting that started at the Foundation Center in 1956 provides a reasonably sound point of departure for understanding foundation giving. By the late 1950s, foundation support for the humanities, a rubric that included music and the visual arts, was estimated to be about 4 percent of all foundation giving. The percentage had grown, perhaps doubling, since the rudimentary surveys of foundation giving in the 1920s. But the Foundation Center's annual report for 1961 concluded woefully, "The humanities, in spite of new expressions of interest and the substantial programs initiated by several foundations, remains a minor field."[28] If culture were indeed to boom nationally, much more would have to be done to trigger the explosion.

28. Foundation Center (1962, p. 15).

Ford's Soliloquy

The Ford Foundation, founded in Michigan in 1936, took its place on the national stage only in the early 1950s, becoming the nation's first billion-dollar foundation. It got under way with programs described by one observer as "scientific rather than cultural, utilitarian rather than aesthetic."[29] But significant arts and cultural initiatives gradually emerged. In late 1956, even before the first Lincoln Center grants were made, the foundation's trustees approved a five-year exploratory program in the arts and humanities, allocating $2 million a year for a series of studies, surveys, and conferences that, in the end, reached out to approximately one hundred seventy-five organizations and five hundred individuals. Ford wanted to know what the visual and performing arts most needed. In the absence of a ministry of culture, Ford filled a gap, first with systematic research and later with unrivaled financial resources and a vision of strengthening cultural organizations across the nation. Over the course of two decades beginning in the late 1950s, always firmly guided by W. McNeil Lowry, the director and then vice president of the foundation's humanities and arts program, Ford would expend more than $400 million for the arts, often requiring matching grants that would greatly leverage the impact of Ford dollars.

The foundation acted briefly as a traditional patron, commissioning new symphonies and operas. But seeing the need for a more substantial and targeted infusion of money into the arts, the foundation launched a larger initiative in 1962, budgeted at $8 million to $10 million a year. The impact on specific disciplines was enormous. Ford's $7.7 million ballet development program was the largest investment ever made in that field. It aimed to raise standards of dance training by sending teachers from New York's School of American Ballet into the heartland, where they taught, recruited talented young dancers, and seeded new training programs. Money also went to eight dance companies, including Washington's National Ballet, the New York City Ballet, and companies in Boston, San Francisco, and Houston. A Ford program for symphony orchestras, funded with a grant of $85 million, sought similar long-term effects, elevating professional standards, extending seasons, and raising salary levels. Ford's commitment to regional theater companies also strengthened a number of amateur and semiprofessional groups that had been founded years earlier but still struggled financially.

Throughout, Lowry and his colleagues were gaining insights into the economics of individual cultural organizations while beginning to understand some of the structural needs of the arts community as a whole. One of the most

29. Macdonald (1989, p. xiv).

exemplary and enduring efforts to emerge from this era of grant making was the Theater Communications Group, created in 1961 with the aim of aiding the regional theater movement. Service organizations for other arts disciplines soon followed, helping to professionalize managerial practices, improve communications and marketing, and foster best practices.

By 1972 the many changes spurred by Ford led it to undertake a systematic review of its program. Instead of providing operating funds, which were cut back, Ford began to concentrate on helping nonprofit organizations eliminate their accumulated deficits and establish cash reserves that would see them through periods of constrained cash flow. This so-called stabilization strategy was an innovative way of relieving cultural organizations from the annual scramble to cover operating deficits. The strategy assumed that operating needs could best be met by expanding the base of local donors, working with the growing numbers of public arts agencies, helping organizations acquire long-range planning and management tools, and encouraging them to look toward five-year time horizons. By 1981 some forty-three organizations had gone through Ford's stabilization process, all showing improvements on their balance sheets. With $9 million from a consortium of foundations, Ford spun the program off to an independent National Arts Stabilization Fund in 1983. Ford's approach, which acknowledged the market environment in which cultural organizations must operate, exemplifies an enduring strategic use of foundation resources: helping nonprofit organizations to sustain themselves in the cultural marketplace.

Seeking financial stability for cultural organizations—expanding the resources within the cultural economy and broadening the base of support—was the unifying thread in Ford programs. Lowry and his colleagues knew that Ford would have to draw additional private money into the cultural sector, not merely foundation resources but corporate and individual dollars. Total private giving to the arts began a steady climb in the 1960s, doubling within two decades. In 1964, according to *Giving USA,* the arts received 3.2 percent of philanthropic dollars, a share that rose to 4.5 percent in 1974 and 6.5 percent in 1984.[30] The infusion of Ford money into the arts was clearly a major factor in moving cultural giving to a 15 percent share of large foundation grant dollars. Since attaining that level more than forty years ago, the share of foundation giving for arts and culture has fluctuated in a relatively narrow band, approximately 13 to15 percent. By the late 1990s, some 90 percent of large U.S. foundations were making grants to the arts, a hugely expanded and more diverse framework of philanthropic support.[31] Ford supplied the initial push, though by the late 1960s and early 1970s it was increasingly difficult to disentangle Ford's impact from that

30. Cobb (1996, p. 11).
31. Renz, Lawrence, and Marino (2003, p. 6).

of the National Endowments for the Arts and Humanities, whose budgets grew steadily throughout the 1970s.

This expansion of cultural support, from both private and public sources, would have another notable effect: nonprofit organizations, increasingly professional in their work, would become the dominant mechanism for organizing cultural activity in the United States. A predominantly nonprofit cultural economy, relying on multiple streams of philanthropic support as well as significant earned income, took shape in these decades. It is within this cultural system that foundations have operated for two generations. But it is a system now undergoing significant change. Indeed, it is a system under considerable stress. The pressures are not only financial—they are *always* financial—but they also arise from inexorable demographic changes, rapid technological advances, heightened competition with commercial enterprises, and a changing legal and public policy landscape. Whether foundations will be compelled to reassess their historic roles and to define new goals in a changed cultural economy is the unanswered question.

Exeunt Omnes

Few foundations have devoted serious attention to the workings of the cultural economy. Theoretical and applied cultural research projects have rarely been funded, and when they have been supported, foundation commitments to research have been erratic. Engagement with public policy processes, which has been so enduring and consequential a role for foundations in other fields, has never been consistent in the cultural realm. In this arena it is a role largely neglected; indeed, in the United States cultural policymaking has been downright suspect. A $50 million cultural policy research program announced by the Pew Charitable Trusts in 1999 inspired a *New York Times* headline, "Heavyweight Foundation Throws Itself behind Idea of a Cultural Policy." Pew's critics leapt to the conclusion that "cultural policy" could mean nothing less than the creation of a large federal agency, a "bureaucratic behemoth" with a "gruesomely bureaucratic approach" and "more centralized regulation of the arts and their institutions," according to the overheated allegations of one skeptic. Ever since the New Deal, nightmarish visions of Soviet cultural commissars have served to restrict government's role and to inhibit debates about cultural policy.[32]

After funding several useful studies by the Rand Corporation, Pew withdrew abruptly and unceremoniously from the cultural policy field. An earlier effort in the 1990s to create an independent Washington-based cultural policy think tank, the Center for Arts and Culture, received support from nearly a dozen

---

32. Judith H. Dobrzynski, "Heavyweight Foundation Throws Itself behind Idea of a Cultural Policy," *New York Times,* August 2, 1999.

small and midsize foundations. But after a decade of work, it too faltered when foundations lost interest in building a stable cultural research infrastructure. A few foundations—most notably the Wallace Foundation—have made serious commitments to evaluating cultural programs.[33] But cultural research, with all its potential for policy innovation, has been a fitful pursuit.

Nevertheless, one early research endeavor did have considerable impact. It still resonates intellectually and continues to shape our conception of how the U.S. cultural economy works (and why it needs growing sums of contributed income). The study was undertaken by William J. Baumol and William G. Bowen, with financial support from the Twentieth Century Fund (an operating foundation established in 1919, now called the Century Foundation). Nearly six hundred pages long, *Performing Arts: The Economic Dilemma* was published in 1966.[34] It proceeded in tandem with a project of the Rockefeller Brothers Fund that yielded a 1965 report on dance, music, and theater, *Performing Arts: Problems and Prospects*.[35] Together, these two studies helped shape private sector arts-funding strategies as well as the government initiatives that got under way after the 1965 legislation creating the National Endowments for the Arts and Humanities.

Baumol and Bowen explored why costs in the performing arts almost always exceed earned income and why the "income gap," as they termed it, would continue to widen. The performing arts, they explained, are unable to capture productivity increases as readily as other economic sectors do: "Whereas the amount of labor necessary to produce a typical manufactured product has constantly declined since the beginning of the industrial revolution, it requires about as many minutes for Richard II to tell his 'sad stories of the death of kings' as it did on the stage of the Globe Theatre."[36] They predicted that by 1975 there would be an income gap in the performing arts of between $48 million and $61 million, a gap that would continue to grow rapidly.[37]

If the challenge in the arts was conceived as filling a widening income gap, then both public and private sectors needed to step forward with more money. By 1970 direct public support for the arts had risen to $85 million. It continued to grow at impressive rates, reaching some $282 million in 1975. This amounted

33. Among the larger foundations with significant arts programs, the Wallace Foundation has had a strong commitment in recent years to understanding and measuring impact. Its work in encouraging greater arts participation has yielded several reports, including K. McCarthy (2004).

34. Baumol and Bowen (1966).

35. Rockefeller Brothers Fund (1965).

36. Baumol and Bowen (1966, p. 164).

37. Baumol and Bowen (1966, pp. 387, 389).

to a thirteenfold increase in public support for the arts in only a decade.[38] Much as the Ford Foundation had been doing, the National Endowment for the Arts was expanding and altering the flows of money into the cultural sector.

But even as its budget was expanding, the National Endowment for the Arts had to make clear what it would not do with its money: no general operating support, no capital grants, no deficit covering, and all project support would have to be matched by other donors. By the mid-1970s, viewed in the aggregate, performing arts organizations saw their income from government sources grow from 5 to 13 percent; earned income from the box office dropped from 44 to 35 percent; nonperformance earned income fell from 9 to 5 percent; and private contributions grew from 33 to 37 percent. Analyzing these figures for the Twentieth Century Fund in the late 1970s, Dick Netzer concluded that increased government support, contrary to some predictions, had not substituted for private contributions. It seemed instead to have created less reliance on certain earned income sources while drawing in more gifts from individuals, corporations, and local foundations.[39] Although the percentages of income that performing arts organizations received from the large national foundations had declined over the decade from 1965 to 1975, this was almost entirely a consequence of changes in grant making at the Ford Foundation as some of its largest initiatives wound down. But whose resources served as the lever? Where was the fulcrum situated?

The fulcrum clearly moves over time. From McNeil Lowry's perspective in the early 1980s, it seemed that national cultural leadership had passed from foundations to government: "The requisite size that allows for long-range planning is no longer located at foundations, but at the [National Endowment for the Arts] which since 1976 has become the single largest source of annual funding of the arts."[40] But national leadership would prove to be a fleeting opportunity for the federal government. Declining and stagnant budgets for the National Endowments for the Arts and Humanities (owing to the shifting of federal dollars to state agencies and the abandonment of most grants to individual artists) as well as contentious debates surrounding the proper federal cultural role, the so-called culture wars, flared in the 1980s and 1990s. Although there now seems to be a

---

38. The National Endowments for the Arts and Humanities were not the only federal agencies involved in supporting the nation's cultural life. Federal cultural expenditures were situated in more than a dozen cultural agencies, including the Smithsonian Institution, the Library of Congress, and the Kennedy Center, and there were cultural programs in several cabinet-level departments, including Interior, State, Transportation, and Education.

39. Netzer (1978, p. 102).

40. Cobb (1996, p. 18).

truce in the culture wars, the issues surrounding government funding have never been fully resolved for Americans.

What can be concluded with long historical perspective is that funding for cultural activities has secured a place among foundation priorities that it did not have one hundred or even fifty years ago. Although such funding fluctuates as a share of overall foundation giving, it now does so in a relatively narrow band, hovering around 13 percent. The dollar figures tell a dramatic story of recent growth: estimated arts grant making by foundations was about $660 million in 1983, slightly more than $1 billion in 1989, $1.6 billion in 1995, and nearly $4.2 billion in 2001.[41] Cultural projects have drawn in thousands of new foundation donors while also spurring individual and corporate donors to greater giving. Of the roughly one thousand large foundations that make up the universe regularly studied by the Foundation Center, some 90 percent are now making some grants for arts, culture, humanities, and media. Viewed more broadly, the cultural share of overall American charitable giving has been around 6 percent in recent years, a figure somewhat lower than in the early 1980s but nearly twice what it was in 1960.

The sheer numbers of foundations and the variety of their cultural programs make it difficult to generalize about their roles. It is possible to find foundations whose arts education projects complement or substitute for government activity; to discover conservation and restoration projects preserving traditional cultural practices and artifacts; and to uncover foundations engaging in cultural policy research and advocacy. A picture of diverse foundation interventions in the cultural sector emerges. But is the role of foundations in our cultural life best judged by looking at single foundations, whether large or small, national or regional? Is their role instead about the aggregate impact of foundation dollars in the larger cultural sector?

With respect to both a single foundation's activities and the totality of the foundation sector's impact, it is difficult to isolate the effects that foundation resources have had when they so often work in conjunction with government grants, individual donations, and corporate contributions. Aims and purposes are often similar. Rarely do foundations seem to have any comparative advantage over individual cultural donors, who can act with speed and flexibility and on a scale of giving that often surpasses foundation activities in this field.

Perhaps it is the simple fact of diverse funding streams that is noteworthy. It is one of the most distinctive and enviable traits of the U.S. cultural economy: cultural institutions are not reliant on only a few sources of philanthropic income, nor dependent exclusively on earned income, nor fatally vulnerable to

41. Renz, Lawrence, and Marino (2003, p. 4).

cuts in government support. Foundations have functioned over the long term to expand and sustain the diversity of resources available to the cultural sector. To enable organizations to take advantage of these diverse funding streams, foundations have propelled cultural institutions to adopt nonprofit status, enlarging the ranks of nonprofit cultural groups from a few thousand in the 1960s to some fifty thousand today. The American cultural terrain has always been shared by both commercial and nonprofit entities, boundaries shift and blur, the topography changes. New digital technologies, commercial opportunities, changing tastes, new forms of audience engagement, and globalization are among the host of forces altering the terrain once again. It would be presumptuous for this historical chapter to predict how foundation roles might or should change with so much in flux.

But it is useful to conclude with a perception about why foundation interventions in the cultural realm have seemed different from work in scientific research, public health, education, and welfare. Why was it so difficult, early on, for culture to gain traction inside the large foundations? From the beginning, foundation funding for culture faced a conceptual obstacle—an obstacle grounded in commercial realities. American cultural institutions have never been able to turn their backs on the marketplace. In the United States, culture has been treated less as a public good than as a "merit good." Merit goods are those that can be supplied to some extent by the market simply because some individuals, presumably with good taste and discernment, are willing to pay for them. They are willing to buy tickets to the opera and ballet and to pay admissions fees to museums or to purchase DVDs and see films. Unlike public goods, merit goods provide the ticket buyers and performance attendees with something they desire, something that offers them exclusive private pleasures. But while providing obvious private benefits, merit goods are also deemed to generate social benefits that will spill over to the advantage of a wider community.

Merit goods prompt many questions, most of them arising from this inextricable mix of public and private benefits. This melding of benefits remains at the nettlesome core of our perennial debates about culture—and our continuing uncertainties about foundation and government roles in supporting it. Americans have not yet decided emphatically that culture is a pure public good. Thus they have limited government's cultural role, preferring a more substantial role for the private sector. But markets fail, and it has never been entirely clear what market failure means in the cultural sector. By what criteria should the adequacy or inadequacy of the supply of a merit good be judged? What is the nature of the wider public benefits that cultural investments can provide? Is public benefit grounded in social and economic utility, or can it be conceived in essentially aesthetic terms? How are culture's public benefits to be valued? And how should access to merit goods for those who cannot pay be expanded and allocated? Neither the market nor democratic decisionmaking processes provide ready solutions to such fundamental and perennially unanswered cultural questions as who should pay, for what, and how much. In the end, it is the role of foundations to keep these questions alive, to refine and clarify them, to offer persuasive evidence about both private and public benefit, and to supply answers, however tentative, about the role of culture in our lives.

13

Roles of Foundations and Their Impact in the Arts

STEFAN TOEPLER

In 1957 the Ford Foundation, soon to be followed by other private founda-tions, launched an arts program aimed at leveraging new forms of support for the arts, establishing the arts as a legitimate recipient of public funds and a rele-vant policy issue.[1] In a way, Ford's program was a reaction to the rapid growth of the arts sector. Many new organizations were emerging, established institutions were expanding their services, and there was a growing recognition that the arts could not be sustained by private sector income alone owing to the economic characteristics of the services they provided.[2] The effects of Ford's efforts consti-tute an example of significant policy innovation: not only did the program vali-date the arts as a legitimate field for government involvement and jump-start its postwar expansion, it also encouraged the movement away from its roots in the marketplace and toward the nonprofit sector. While the nonprofit form in the arts had already developed in the late nineteenth century, it became the norm when it was made a precondition for receiving grant funding.[3]

Four decades after the Ford Foundation took the first steps toward a new national program that would dramatically alter the cultural ecosystem, and three decades after the federal government's reentry into the field with the creation

---

1. DiMaggio (1986, pp. 113–39).

2. Cummings (1991); Baumol and Bowen (1966).

3. For example, commercial dance companies converted to nonprofit status to become eligible for Ford Foundation grants. Chujoy (1969, pp. 316–28).

of the National Foundation on the Arts and Humanities, the tacit policy consensus that had propelled the post–World War II growth of the arts came to an end. Following several years of heated debate about the appropriateness of government support for "blasphemous," "indecent," or "obscene" art, Congress reduced the National Endowment for the Arts (NEA) appropriations by 40 percent, from $162.0 million in fiscal year 1995 to $99.5 million in fiscal year 1996, leading to a similar cut in agency staff and a fundamental restructuring of endowment programs. The loss of some $60 million in federal subsidies for the arts from one year to the next was relatively small in a nonprofit arts and cultural economy that had reached $7.7 billion in current operating expenditures in 1992 and that would continue to grow to $12 billion in 1997.[4] More significant was that the NEA had been the core of an implicit policy paradigm that kept most policy actors focused on the funding and support needs of the nonprofit cultural infrastructure.

However, in the post-NEA era, a new policy paradigm has yet to emerge.[5] The past decade has seen a welcome broadening of the cultural policy discourse beyond the past's narrow obsession with funding. Overall, arts policy issues have become considerably more diffuse. They now range from intellectual property protection and cultural heritage preservation to media concentration and regulation, the role of creativity in workforce and economic development, cultural diplomacy, and addressing cultural diversity in an increasingly interconnected world, to name but a few. In addition, questions are emerging about whether the carefully nurtured nonprofit arts infrastructure is beginning to show signs of crumbling and may, at least in part, have become overextended. In this cacophony of issues, it has become more difficult to assess the contributions of foundations.

The Changing Arts Economy of the Post–World War II Era

Before the mid-1960s, public support for the arts was largely limited to indirect subsidies through tax exemption for arts organizations and comparatively generous deductions for benefactors in a system of private policymaking. Among the reasons for the traditionally low involvement of government are the lack of a feudal-aristocratic heritage of cultural institutions, puritanical beliefs that regarded the arts as an unnecessary luxury, and a strong republican tradition of limited government. Until well into the middle of the twentieth century, the relationship between government and the arts remained both extremely limited and politically disputed. This deeply ingrained reluctance was exemplified in the

4. Independent Sector and Urban Institute (2002, pp. 96–97, table 4.2).
5. Cherbo and Wyszomirski (2000).

torturous reception of James Smithson's bequest to the United States in 1835. In the words of Milton Cummings, "President Jackson ignored it; and several senators . . . declared that it was unconstitutional."[6] In the end, it would be another ten years before the Smithsonian Institution was founded.

With no public tradition or predisposition toward patronage, arts and culture were largely left to the marketplace until the latter half of the nineteenth century, when the beginnings of the nonprofit institutional form evolved. High-culture institutions, such as museums and symphony orchestras, remained tightly controlled and financially dependent on the local urban elites that had founded them.[7] Wealthy patrons, accordingly, controlled key resources, including individual gifts and occasionally municipal appropriations. Local elite control was a source of resistance to broader private and governmental involvement in the arts.[8] It was not until the 1960s that foundations became systematically involved in funding the arts. In 1965 the federal government established the National Endowment for the Arts, spurring the development of new state- and local-level public funding agencies. With the entrance of corporations as sponsors, the 1970s saw the rise of new public and private funding mechanisms that began to diminish the domineering role of local elite patrons and municipalities.

This remarkable shift in the economics of high-culture institutions is exemplified in the changing revenue structure of the Metropolitan Museum of Art over this period. The Metropolitan relied almost exclusively on endowment income and city subsidies for its operating budget well into the 1960s. Individual gifts went largely into the endowment funds, and external grants barely existed. The early 1970s, however, represented a tipping point: while the museum expanded its operations, rising inflation eroded the purchasing power of endowment income, and economic recession undercut the city's support.[9] The relative decline of these two financial pillars led the museum to pursue a broader range of public funding sources, including gifts and grants, membership, and earned income. Within the space of two decades, the share of gifts and grants from foundations, corporations, and public funders began to equal the endowment income and became the single largest source of net operating revenues in the early 1990s.

While revenue structure varies considerably among various artistic disciplines, the Metropolitan Museum of Art is nevertheless indicative of a fundamental change in the way the arts are financed: whereas early arts institutions relied on either elite philanthropy or market-based revenues for core funding, the more recent past has seen a substantial diversification that has turned the financing of the arts into a highly fractured patchwork. The National and Local Profiles of Cultural Support

6. Cummings (1991, p. 39).
7. DiMaggio (1986).
8. Cummings (1991).
9. Toepler (2006, pp. 95–109).

Project details disciplinary and regional variations in funding sources for arts organizations. The project's findings suggest that the source of more than 53 percent of all revenues is earned income, followed by endowment and investment (12%) and individual and miscellaneous private support (12%), then by government (9%), foundation funding (9%), and finally, corporate support (5%).

The post–World War II period also saw a significant expansion of public demand for the arts. Attendance at art museums increased from 11 million in 1952 to 50 million by 1979 and to 225 million by 1993.[10] Spurred by available funding and growing demand, the nonprofit arts sector grew significantly. Joni Cherbo and Margaret Wyszomirski summarize this growth:

Dance troupes have grown from 28 in 1958 to over 400.

Opera companies with budgets of over $100,000 have grown from 29 in 1964 to 209 by 1989.

Chamber music groups, most formed in the last twenty years, now number around 1,120.

Half of America's eighty-two hundred museums have come into existence since the 1970s.

The nonprofit regional theater movement, begun in the 1960s, now consists of more than nine hundred theater groups.

At least thirty-seven mixed-arts complexes have sprung up nationally in various urban centers in the last twenty years.[11]

This growth spurt over the past fifty years has led to greater numbers of arts organizations with a broader geographical spread and greater variety in the number and size of available funding sources in a system that is both diverse and decentralized. Against this background, where do foundations fit in? Are they acting in leading roles, or are they merely among the supernumeraries in the production of art and culture in the United States? During the period from the 1970s to the early 1990s, the National Endowment for the Arts dominated center stage, and the role of foundations was largely reduced to the question of how much money they provided amid individual and corporate supporters. With the NEA's fortunes reversed over the past ten years, however, a reexamination of foundation contributions appears timely.

Potential Impacts and Roles

As James Allen Smith notes in the preceding chapter, foundation impacts can be sought at many different levels: a fellowship may affect the career of a particular artist; a general operating grant may put an arts institution on secure financial

10. Heilbrun and Gray (2001, p. 191).
11. Cherbo and Wyszomirski (2000, pp. 5–6).

footing; support for service organizations may elevate a whole artistic discipline; investments in arts education may create future audiences; large-scale policy interventions may restructure the support system for the arts. Any assessment of foundation impact thus depends on the unit of analysis. Specific examples of foundation impacts are easily found but do not lend themselves to generalization. Nevertheless, it may be useful to distinguish between three types (or levels) of impact:

Economic impact. Foundation support can be crucial for the economic viability and financial sustainability of individual arts organizations. Whereas large-scale individual patrons and corporate donors are frequently motivated to support projects that provide recognition, such as bricks-and-mortar naming opportunities, foundation support can help underwrite less visible activities, from paying secretaries to conserving artwork.

Artistic impact. Foundation grants can play a role in affecting aesthetic or artistic development and excellence through supporting new work that challenges the boundaries of art forms, disciplines, and canons. Grants might back emerging schools, genres, or techniques, support avant-garde artists, commission new plays, or underwrite contemporary music composition and performance.

Policy impact. Finally, foundation interventions can aim at changing the nature of the cultural ecosystem through emphasizing and legitimating specific aspects of the creative economy, such as the nonprofit infrastructure; advocating for specific topics and issues in legislation (for example, arts education); influencing participation patterns; or addressing broad moral or regulatory concerns, such as free expression or intellectual property rights.

Several different impacts can occur simultaneously. A grant to a choreographer, for example, may support the development of new work (artistic impact) while financially stabilizing her dance company (economic impact). In the early twentieth century, the Carnegie Corporation of New York focused on raising interest in the arts, particularly in colleges and universities.[12] Arguably as a result of this policy-level intervention, universities became major providers of artistic programming, kept certain art forms alive (for example, modern dance), and provided a measure of economic security to artists in residence programs or employed as teachers.[13]

Applicability of Roles and Their Relationship to Impacts

Foundation roles such as innovation, complementarity, and institution building also apply in the context of the arts. Not all are equally salient, however, and some take a different meaning in this field. As Smith observes in the preceding

12. Chapter 12, this volume; DiMaggio (1986).
13. Rockefeller Brothers Fund (1965).

chapter, the latter is the case with complementarity and substitution. Both roles presuppose government dominance in a field of foundation activity. Given the limits of government funding for the arts, particularly at the federal level, this presupposition does not hold. By contrast, with creativity and imagination the bedrock of the arts, the innovation function most genuinely applies to fostering artistic creativity. Although the United States has strenuously resisted developing an explicit arts policy, there are nevertheless a range of public and private policies in place. The pursuit of policy change is also a role in which foundations engage.

Generally, the arts are not a prime area for income redistribution either directly or indirectly (through subsidization of essential welfare services for the poor). However, support of nonelite art can be considered redistributive since it directs resources toward traditionally neglected areas. Although not a function that has received much attention in the foundation debate, asset protection is also a role that has some bearing in the arts. For the most part this role plays out in conjunction with public institutions, such as museums, libraries, and universities.[14] The association of private foundations with public institutions allows the latter to maintain assets outside the political control of legislatures and the regulations of public fiscal policy while providing a tax advantage to donors who might be otherwise reluctant to give to a government agency.

What is the relationship between roles and impacts in the arts? Certain impacts can be associated with certain roles, providing some degree of guidance about what types of impacts can be expected depending on which roles dominate. For purposes of this chapter, economic impact is equated with asset protection, complementarity, and substitution, since all three relate to institutional financing; artistic impact with the innovation role, although there is also policy innovation; and policy impact with the roles of social change, innovation, and redistribution. In other fields, redistribution may be economic, but in the arts it is oriented toward social change in the sense of providing creative or participatory opportunities outside the mainstream.

In the following discussions of economic and artistic impact and the associated foundation roles, I primarily relied on the analysis of data contained in a series of arts funding reports prepared by the Foundation Center in conjunction with the foundation affinity group Grantmakers in the Arts. The first of these reports covers much of the 1980s, and subsequent reports update trends at various points in the 1990s and early 2000s. The availability of these reports offers a unique opportunity to chart arts funding over a twenty-year period between

14. For example, the "Virginia Museum of Fine Arts Foundation . . . manages private assets, including equities, fixed income securities, and certain real property on behalf of the Virginia Museum of Fine Arts . . . , an agency of the Commonwealth of Virginia. In addition, the foundation has the responsibility of administering ongoing fund-raising activities that benefit projects identified by the museum's board of trustees" (www.guidestar.org).

1983 and 2004. In each of these reports, the Foundation Center used a sample of grants of $10,000 or more derived from the Foundation Grants Index and extrapolated the results for the arts funder universe.

Economic Impact

Foundations often contribute to the economic viability and sustainability of arts organizations, assuming various roles with respect to financial intermediation, complementarity, and substitution.

Financial Intermediation

First and foremost, foundations are important financial intermediaries in a field that relies more heavily on private philanthropy than most others; this gives them an important asset-protecting role.[15] In 2003 the one thousand largest foundations contributed about $1.8 billion to arts and culture, or 13 percent of total foundation giving that year.[16] The lion's share of foundation support is directed toward the performing arts and the museum field, which account for a combined 60 percent of all grant dollars. Of the remainder, multidisciplinary activities and media and communications receive substantial shares, whereas support for history, the humanities, and the visual arts (other than museums) is rather limited (see table 13-1).

In dollar terms, art museums receive the largest share of foundation giving, with almost a quarter billion dollars a year, followed by multidisciplinary arts (including institutions like the Kennedy Center) and music (including symphony orchestras and opera companies). Theater, dance, and media and communications also draw substantial foundation support. On the other end, support for the humanities and all of the visual arts (other than museums) hovers around the $100 million mark each, dance receives about half that, and support for various museum types (other than art museums) is even lower.

Funding shares and aggregate grant dollar amounts are nevertheless not necessarily the most useful indicators of the relative importance that foundations accord to the various fields of artistic activity. In those few fields where foundation spending can reasonably be measured against total revenues, a slightly different picture emerges. Although foundations spend approximately ten times more on museums than on dance companies, the share of foundation support of total field revenues is proportionally considerably higher for the latter (nearly 13 percent) than for the former (less than 9 percent). Foundation giving to music is almost twice as high as that for theater, though the difference in terms of total

15. Salamon (2002a, pp. 3–61).
16. Grantmakers in the Arts (2005).

Table 13-1. *Foundation Giving to the Arts, by Discipline, 2003*
Thousands of dollars

Discipline	Share of arts giving by (percent)[a]		Arts giving by		Total foundation revenues by		Foundation giving as share of total revenues by (percent)	
	Category	Discipline	Category	Discipline	Category	Discipline	Category	Discipline
Performing arts	32		572,800		4,639,534		12.3	
Music		38		217,664		2,365,490		9.2
Theater		22		126,016		1,821,898		6.9
Dance		9		51,552		405,573		12.7
Other		30		171,840		...		...
Museums	27		483,300		5,540,305		...	8.7
Art		51		246,483	...	...	...	...
Science and technology		9		43,497	...	...	...	...
Specialized, such as maritime, sports		9		43,497	...	...	...	...
Natural history and other science		9		43,497	...	...	...	...
History		8		38,664	...	...	...	...
Multipurpose		6		28,998	...	...	...	...
Children's		5		24,165	...	...	...	...
Ethnic and folk art		3		14,499	...	...	...	...
Multidisciplinary arts	13		232,700	...	...	...	...	...
Media and communications	9		161,100	...	...	...	...	...
Historical activities	6		107,400	...	...	...	...	...
Humanities	6		107,400	...	...	...	...	...
Visual arts	5		89,500	...	...	...	...	...
Other	2		35,800	...	...	...	...	...

Sources: Dollar figures for foundation support were calculated from the Foundation Center's giving estimate for 2003 of $1.79 billion by applying the respective percentages for the categories given. Grantmakers in the Arts (2005). Total revenues are taken from the U.S. Census Bureau (2002), table 1. Included are the North American Industry Classification System codes for establishments exempt from federal income tax: Performing Arts: 7111 Performing Arts Companies; Music: 7111101 Opera Companies, 7111301 Symphony Orchestras and Chamber Music Groups, 7111309 Other Music Groups and Artists; Theater: 7111102 Theater Companies; Dance: 71112 Dance Companies; Museums: 71211 Museums.

a. Owing to rounding errors, percentages may not total 100 percent.

revenue shares is only 2 percent. Yet in some fields, such as the humanities or visual artists, the perception remains that support levels are less than adequate.[17]

With a roughly 10 percent stake in the financing of the nonprofit arts economy, the financial intermediation role of foundations is therefore highly consequential for the sector's economic sustainability and viability. This was demonstrated during the 2001 economic recession, which threatened private giving, foundation grants, and corporate support; it curtailed state-level arts support and, to a lesser degree, local government funding—both typically important sources of general operating revenues. In addition, the stock market slump reduced the size of endowments; and the impact of the events of September 11, 2001, on travel and tourism contributed to fewer visitors and lesser earned income, forcing even major institutions to make cutbacks. Although the arts survived the brief crisis, there is a long-term financial squeeze at work in parts of the performing arts and the visual arts.[18] In the museum case, for example, Adrian Ellis recently predicted a bust following a long-running boom, as museums tend to be both overextended and undercapitalized.[19]

Complementarity

While in their financial intermediation functions foundations do generate a significant economic impact, the same cannot be said as far as the complementarity and substitution functions are concerned. In fact, given the nature of the American arts policy system, federal intervention in the form of the National Endowment for the Arts was by design intended to complement existing private support rather than the other way around.

The NEA's original enabling legislation in 1965 set out a number of broad goals, including fostering artistic excellence, increasing accessibility to the arts, and creating a decentralized public support system. Although the economic problems endemic to high-culture institutions provided the main rationale for the agency's establishment, the preamble of the National Foundation on the Arts and Humanities Act explicitly reiterates the preeminence of private and local initiative.[20]

17. Renz (2004); Jackson (2003).

18. McCarthy (1998)

19. Adrian Ellis, "American Museums in Financial Crisis," *Forbes* (www.forbes.com/2003/05/05/cx_0506hot_print.html [October 2006]).

20. Wyszomirski and Mulcahy (1995, p. 122). More specifically, "The encouragement and support of national progress and scholarship in the humanities and the arts, while primarily a matter for private and local initiative, are also appropriate matters of concern to the Federal Government. [20 U.S.C. §951 (2)] It is necessary and appropriate for the Federal Government to complement, assist, and add to programs for the advancement of the humanities and the arts by local, State, regional, and private agencies and their organizations [20 U.S.C. §951 (5)]."

The importance of local and private initiative is reflected in the forms of support that the National Endowment for the Arts has traditionally provided. The NEA—in contrast to state and local arts agencies—does not provide statutory funding or operating support for arts institutions. Projects are only partially underwritten, through matching or challenge grants. The most important aspect of the NEA's funding was not the actual dollars but what was referred to as its "imprimatur": public grants were perceived as a recognition of quality and facilitated the grantee organization's fund-raising from private sources.

Fostering new private support was only one goal of the NEA; the other major goal related to increasing access to the arts, especially geographically, by stimulating new public support at the state and local levels. The largest single share of the endowment's budget has therefore been designated as block grants to state arts agencies, substantially decentralizing the public support system and generating additional public arts spending at the state and local levels that has far outdistanced the annual NEA appropriations over the past forty years.

Although government spending on the arts has increased significantly since the 1960s, government involvement remains comparatively low in terms of spending levels. Federal, state, and local outlays account for no more than 10 percent of total revenues of the arts sector. Over the past decade, moreover, public funding has remained more or less static. The 2006 estimate of $1.1 billion is essentially the same as it was in 1995.[21] The complementarity role thus makes little sense in this field (see chapter 12 in this volume), a fact borne out by direct comparison between foundation and public spending levels. Foundations consistently outspend the public sector at local, state, and federal levels combined, and the gap has grown exponentially since the mid-1990s.

Substitution

As concerns about public spending for the arts emerge, the question of whether private philanthropy will be able to fill the gap gains in salience.[22] However, such concerns rarely translate into an expectation that foundations should fill a substitution role. In arts and culture in particular, the more common expectation is for organizations to seek ways to increase earned income.[23] The museum community is one of the trendsetters in this respect, where commercialization strategies range from expansion and modernization of museum shops and restaurants to off-site retailing and direct merchandising, although the actual financial

21. Cobb (1996).

22. For instance, an influential study commissioned by the President's Committee on the Arts and the Humanities demonstrates that the anticipated drainage of public spending on the arts was unlikely to be replaced by comparable increases in donative income from individuals, corporations, and foundations. Cobb (1996).

23. Stevens (1996, pp. 101–14).

impact of increased commercialization remains somewhat doubtful.[24] Moreover, the creeping marketization of the arts is also driven by the shift of corporate support from philanthropic giving to cause-related marketing and sponsorships requiring a direct quid pro quo.

Some foundations do pursue the substitution role, and the past decade has seen a number of prominent substitution projects. Among the largest was the Annenberg Foundation's Challenge to the Nation. In response to a precipitous decline of arts education in public schools, Walter Annenberg, the former ambassador to Great Britain, announced an unprecedented $500 million challenge at the end of 1993. Operating between 1995 and 2002, the program aimed at improving school-based arts education, particularly in disadvantaged urban and rural districts. Other foundations also took up arts education funding, with levels peaking at almost $250 million in 2002.[25]

Another prominent example of substitution was the Andy Warhol Foundation–initiated response to the elimination of most of the NEA individual fellowship programs in the mid-1990s, which resulted in the formation of the Creative Capital Foundation in 1999. The latest artists' support initiative— United States Artists (USA), launched with seed money by the Ford, Rockefeller, Rasmuson, and Prudential foundations—is another example. Despite these few exceptions, current data suggest that the foundation field at large has not significantly increased its support for individual artists, despite policymakers' expectations that foundations and private donors would fill the gaps left by the NEA.[26] Rather, their actions are consistent with funders' perceptions that it is not an appropriate role for foundations to replace lost government support.[27]

Measures of Impact

Beyond this, the economic impact of foundation support for individual institutions is not easily measured. However, the willingness of foundations to provide unrestricted general operating support is a measure of concern for the financial viability of arts institutions, as are technical assistance grants or stabilization programs.

By these measures, the economic impact of foundation funding is substantial, as shown in table 13-2. In 2004 foundations devoted one-fifth of arts dollars to general operating support, about the same share as twenty years earlier. While general operating support declined in relative terms during the 1980s, to just 13 percent in 1989, it reached twice the 1989 share of total arts dollars,

24. Toepler and Kirchberg (2002); Toepler and Dewees (2005, pp. 131–46).
25. Renz and Atienza (2005).
26. Galligan and Cherbo (2004, pp. 23–42).
27. Renz and Atlas (1999).

Table 13-2. *Foundation Support for the Arts in General Operating, Capital, and Technical Assistance, 1983–2004*

Thousands of dollars

Item	1983	1986	1989	1992	1996	2001	2003	2004
General operating support[a]								
Grant dollars	49,281	52,469	66,179	119,327	158,979	360,334	461,995	401,170
Share of total arts support (percent)	20.8	16.3	13.2	16.4	17.9	18.2	27.2	20.3
Number of grants	1,294	1,372	1,271	1,867	2,727	3,976	4,869	4,972
Average grant size (dollars)	38	38	52	64	58	91	95	81
Technical assistance[b]								
Grant dollars	25,075	17,998	23,532	...	46,872	59,035	78,089	79,128
Share of total arts support (percent)	10.5	5.6	4.7	...	5.2	4.0	4.4	3.9
Number of grants	364	467	499	...	367	718	770	918
Average grant size (dollars)	69	39	47	...	128	82	101	86
Capital support								
Grant dollars	90,285	141,949	161,720	223,169	286,564	711,606	484,002	671,669
Share of total arts support (percent)	38.0	44.1	32.2	30.7	32.2	36.0	27.0	33.9
Number of grants	831	1,178	1,162	1,192	1,505	2,121	1,836	1,910
Average grant size (dollars)	109	121	139	187	190	336	264	352

Sources: Compiled from Weber and Renz (1993); Renz (1995); Renz and Lawrence (1998, 2003, 2006); Renz and Atlas (1999); Grantmakers in the Arts (2005).

a. General operating support and annual campaigns.

b. Income and management development.

or 27 percent, by 2003. However, the 2003 high point appears to have been a short-term reaction to the 2001–02 financial crisis that led to large reductions in state arts budgets, declining individual giving, and investment losses of arts organizations.

The share of funding for technical assistance support dropped by nearly half between 1983 and 1986 and has since been relatively stable, although there was a slight relative decline over the period. During the 1980s, technical assistance was predominantly in the form of fund-raising support. As such, the high 1983 level reflects a reaction to the Reagan administration's proposed cuts in arts funding and foundation attempts to help prepare grantees to generate more private resources. By the beginning of the new century, however, management assistance had become predominant, signaling a greater interest in strengthening organizational capacity. Technical assistance spending for organizations consti- tuted more than twice the total direct support for artists (table 13-3), suggesting

Table 13-3. *Foundation Support for Individual Artists, 1983–2004*
Thousands of dollars

Item	1983	1986	1989	1992	1996	2001	2003	2004
Fellowships and residencies								
Grant dollars	8,634	13,218	18,539	20,411	34,703	22,203	...	25,315
Total arts support (percent)	3.6	4.1	3.7	2.8	3.9	1.1	...	1.3
Number of grants	106	143	153	161	196	212	212	230
Average grant size	81	92	121	127	177	105	...	110
Awards, prizes, and competitions								
Grant dollars	600	1,674	4,026	...	3,727	4,570	5,897	14,482
Total arts support (percent)	0.3	0.5	0.8	...	0.3	0.2	0.3	0.7
Number of grants	33	37	39	...	81	98	108	92
Average grant size	18	45	103	...	46	47	55	157
Professorships								
Grant dollars	1,364	2,588	3,660	4,509	3,895	5,041	9,882	20,638
Total arts support (percent)	0.6	0.8	0.7	60.0	0.4	0.3	0.6	1.0
Number of grants	12	14	16	17	14	24	16	15
Average grant size	114	185	229	265	278	210	618	1,376
New work commissions								
Grant dollars	1,886	3,843	9,556	...	5,618	11,762	11,040	12,328
Total arts support (percent)	0.8	1.2	1.9	...	0.6	0.6	0.6	0.6
Number of grants	54	91	93	...	81	175	173	130
Average grant size	35	42	103	...	69	67	64	95
Total arts support as share of all foundation funding	5.3	6.6	7.1	...	5.2	2.2	...	3.6

Sources: Compiled from Weber and Renz (1993); Renz (1995); Renz and Lawrence (1998, 2003, 2006); Renz and Atlas (1999); Grantmakers in the Arts (2005).

that foundation priorities lie more with the maintenance of the organizational infrastructure than with furthering the arts.

Moreover, capital support typically outranks general operating support by large measures, accounting for one-third of foundation support. In 2001 capital support ($711.6 million) was more than thirty-two times the foundation spending ($22.2 million) on artistic fellowships (tables 13-2 and 13-3). Again, this provides a strong indication that bricks-and-mortar infrastructure concerns, rather than artistic creation, constitute the focal point of foundation support.

This economic impact orientation also holds true in comparison with government support (table 13-4). For instance, foundation-provided general operating support alone was considerably more in 2004–05 than total state arts spending;

Table 13-4. *Foundation and State Arts Agency Grant Spending,*
2004–2005[a]

Thousands of dollars

Purpose	Foundations		State arts agencies	
	Grant dollars	Share of grant dollars (percent)	Grant dollars	Share of grant dollars (percent)
Acquisition	213,141	10.8	596	0.2
Building and construction	242,638	12.3	10,501	3.8
General operating support	401,170	20.3	102,896	37.3
Capital campaigns, endowment, stabilization	189,222	9.6	149	0.1
Technical assistance and management	84,661	4.3	17,712	6.4
Performance and exhibition	96,227	4.9	39,921	14.5
All other	230,882	38	103,772	37.7
Total	1,979,541	100	275,547	100

Sources: Renz and Lawrence (2006); National Assembly of State Arts Agencies (2006), Final Descriptive Report data as submitted annually to the National Assembly of State Arts Agencies and the National Endowment for the Arts.

a. Foundation data are 2004; state arts agency data are fiscal year 2005. The two data sources are coded differently, and the comparison should be regarded with caution. State arts agency data reflect only grant making by state arts agencies, not their total appropriations.

and foundations outspend state arts agencies on general operating support by a factor of four. Moreover, while the relative shares of technical assistance funding were similar, state support for capital items such as acquisitions, building, and construction barely registers, whereas almost a quarter of foundation support is vested in these areas. It bears noting that state legislatures often provide line-item funding for capital projects at specific arts institutions, which are not included in these data. Nevertheless, line items amounted to $31 million, or about 10 percent of state arts agencies appropriations, in 2005 and do not fundamentally alter the overall picture.[28]

Artistic Impact and Innovation

As corporations and many traditional patrons tend to favor the popular rather than the provocative,[29] and governments steer away from the new and the

28. National Association of State Arts Agencies (2006).
29. Alexander (1996).

controversial—as made evident by the fate of the NEA during and after the culture wars—one avenue for significant foundation impact is the support of art that is new, controversial, and outside the established canon. Foundations have degrees of freedom that neither governments nor corporations enjoy because of their permanent, independent sources of revenue and assets.

Tracing artistic impact is beyond the scope of this chapter. Assuming that artistic creativity and innovation are lodged in individual artists (rather than organizations), the degree to which foundations provide individual support, fellowships, prizes, and competitions for artists can serve as an imperfect stand-in for the pursuit of (though not actual) artistic impact. Similarly, with many artists finding stable employment within universities, foundation-sponsored professorships also indicate artistic support. Finally, artistic impact can be measured by the level of support dedicated to the commissioning of new work.

Foundation Support Benefiting Individual Artists

Table 13-3 traces foundation funding for these measures from 1983 to 2004. Before evaluating these data, however, another caveat is in order. The data used here cover the largest foundations, and little, if any, of the support geared toward individual artists is actually directly awarded to them. Rather, support is largely funneled to and through intermediaries, such as artist support organizations or universities. Other foundations, particularly smaller ones, are more likely to support individuals directly through grants and awards. The activities of these grant makers are better reflected in other data sources, such as the Foundation Center's *Foundation Grants to Individuals*.[30] Using this publication, Ann Galligan and Joni Cherbo identify as much as $57 million in direct grants to artists in 1999, considerably more than reflected in our data.[31]

According to our data, however, foundation funding for fellowship and residency programs increased from less than $9 million in the early 1980s to a peak of close to $35 million in 1996. This peak represented a sharp increase from the 1992 level of $20 million, though the increase did not prove sustainable. By 2001 support was down to essentially pre-1996 levels. What is more, although funding of fellowship programs in the early years of this century was about twice what it was in the first half of the 1980s in absolute terms, proportionally, fellowships lost considerable ground.

The situation with other types of support targeting artists was not much better. Foundation monies for awards, prizes, and competitions grew tenfold in dollar terms from a mere $600,000 in 1983 to nearly $6 million in 2003, and the number of grants for such purposes more than doubled over the time period. Yet

30. Edelson (2003).
31. Galligan and Cherbo (2004).

the share of total support in 2003, 0.3 percent, was the same as it had been in 1983. From 2003 to 2004, the available foundation resources more than doubled in the space of a year, to $14.5 million, but did not raise the relative share beyond 0.7 percent. For the most part, funding for professorships matched or slightly exceeded award, prize, and competition funding over the period and saw a similar spike—more than doubling from less than $10 million to more than $20 million between 2003 and 2004.

Finally, commissions attracted foundation interest during the 1980s, growing from less than 1 percent of arts funding to almost 2 percent. In 1996 commissions dropped sharply in dollar terms, from almost $9.6 million in 1989 to $5.6 million, as well as proportionally. This may reflect a short-term redirection of foundation resources from commissions to fellowships at the time, but support for new work never recovered the relative shares of total arts support it had seen in the middle to late 1980s. Proportionally, foundation support for individual artists lost considerable ground over the twenty-year period. While roughly 7 percent of foundation arts funds were geared toward support of individual artists in the later 1980s, the share had dropped to little more than 2 percent in 2001.

The sudden uptake in 2004—primarily benefiting the awards and professorship categories, and to a much smaller extent fellowships—may signal a reawakening of foundation interest in supporting artists. In fact, there have been a number of recent initiatives intended to boost artist support. The loss of NEA fellowship programs led the Ford Foundation to explore ways to improve the economic and working conditions of individual artists. A coalition of more than thirty funders cosponsored a major research study that explored avenues by which to ascribe value to the work of artists and analyzed market demand, support systems, and training needs, as well as networks and available data sources on individual artists.[32] As a follow-up, in 2003 a number of foundations launched a ten-year initiative, Leveraging Investments in Creativity, that aimed at

—"expanding financial supports for artists' work;

—improving artists' access to essential material supports such as live/work space, insurance, equipment and professional development; and

—bolstering knowledge, networks and public policies that enhance artists' work and their contributions to communities."[33]

Rather than to establish an institution that would seek to improve the status and working conditions of artists, the purpose of the initiative is to create and connect relevant networks at the national and local levels that will foster artistic creativity in a sustainable way. A very different approach is embodied in United

32. DiMaggio (1986, 113–39).

33. Leveraging Investments in Creativity (LINC) (www.lincnet.net/about/mission [November 24, 2009]).

States Artists. Launched in 2005 with $20 million in foundation seed money, the organization aims at building a permanent endowment from private contributions. Hoping to make a long-range contribution toward improving innovation and creativity ("100 years and beyond"), United States Artists pursues a strategy of awarding unrestricted fellowship grants—fifty awards of $50,000 each year—to the best living artists across a range of diverse disciplines.[34] In a way, this strategy emulates the functions of the NEA's former fellowship programs by validating and lending prestige to leading artists.

Despite such efforts, artists as creative innovators have largely been sidelined. Support benefiting artists most directly was relatively small in the 1980s and has since declined significantly in relative terms. While the overall arts-funding pie increased dramatically in the 1990s, the share of artist support declined dramatically. This may be a response to the political backlash against the small number of controversial artists that received NEA funding, setting a cautionary tone for foundations as well. If current initiatives prove sustainable, this may change. Even so, artistic impact does not appear to be high on the philanthropic agenda.

Program Development, Seed Money, and Concentration of Arts Funders

Tying the question of artistic impact to these measures is not without peril. First, and as noted above, direct support for individual artists is not represented in these data. What direct support exists is generally funded by very small foundations. Moreover, artistic creation takes place in organizations, and much project support can be aimed at innovative productions or avant-garde exhibitions, providing venues for and access to new art; alternatively, foundations may provide general operating support to organizations that are perceived as innovative. Unfortunately, current foundation data do not allow a fuller assessment. Nevertheless, the provision of program development support and seed money can be interpreted as a stand-in for foundation interest in developing new artistic initiatives at the organizational level.

A quite different way of approaching the question of the foundation field's capacity to support artistic innovation is to measure the degree of concentration in the funding field. Considering the time and staff resource constraints that even large funders face, high degrees of concentration—that is, a few large funders—can negatively affect the ability of the foundation field to spot artistic innovation.

Table 13-5 shows the trends in program development and seed money support from 1983 to 2004. Program development support grew eightfold between 1983 and 1996 in dollar terms and more than doubled as a share of total

34. United States Artists, "We Are United States Artists" (www.unitedstatesartists.org/Public/Home/index.cfm [June 2006]).

Table 13-5. *Foundation Support for Program Development and Seed Money, 1983–2004*

Thousands of dollars

Item	1983	1986	1989	1992	1996	2001	2003	2004
Program development								
Grant dollars (thousands)	24,163	29,218	86,074	142,962	198,004	314,083	300,695	302,497
Share of total arts support (percent)	10.2	9.1	17.1	19.7	22.2	15.9	16.8	15.3
Number of grants	642	897	1,508	1,880	2,323	3,803	3,654	3,799
Average grant size (thousands)	38	33	57	76	85	83	82	80
Seed money								
Grant dollars (thousands)	2,699	5,145	3,230	10,619	3,633	13,738	8,937	22,432
Total arts support (percent)	1.1	1.6	0.6	15.0	0.4	0.7	0.5	1.1
Number of grants	35	58	56	78	34	51	69	59
Average grant size (thousands)	77	89	58	136	107	269	130	380

Source: Compiled from Weber and Renz (1993); Renz (1995); Renz and Lawrence (1998, 2003, 2006); Renz and Atlas (1999); Grantmakers in the Arts (2005).

foundation giving to the arts. Over the same period, the number of these grants quadrupled, indicating a growing interest on the part a number of foundations in supporting new programs. After 1996 program development support grew by half again, to a high of $314 million in 2001, and then dropped back to the $300 million mark. However, despite the considerable increase in dollar terms, the share of program development of total support fell to 15 percent in 2004 compared with 22 percent in 1996. To the extent that foundations pursue the innovation role, it is most strongly apparent in program development support.

Compared with their relatively heavy investment in program support, foundations have seemed less interested in providing seed money. In dollar terms, seed money grew more than eightfold from $2.7 million in 1983 to $22.4 million in 2004. The 2004 funding level represents a significant increase and brought seed monies' share of total support back up to the 1983 level of 1 percent. Judging from the number of grants each year, providing seed money appears to be the domain of a fairly small number of foundations. As seed money is primarily aimed at new organizations and initiatives, this may indicate a certain risk aversion in the foundation field, as the liability of "newness" brings greater risks of failure. Both in terms of total funding shares and the apparent recent uptake in 2004, seed money seems closer to the individual artists funding categories than program development. Assuming that the 2004 data are not a fluke, this may indicate a growing willingness among some foundations to refocus on artistic innovation, even if it involves greater risk than funding established organizations.

Finally, the degree of concentration among funders has somewhat decreased since the early to middle 1980s, when the twenty-five largest arts funders accounted for slightly more than half of all arts giving. The largest-funder share declined to around 40 percent from the late 1980s to the middle of the 1990s. After reaching a low of just one-third in 2001, the share of the twenty-five largest funders has since risen again to just below 40 percent. This indicates "that the base of large funders has grown and means that support for the arts is less concentrated among a small number of foundations than in most earlier years."[35]

Despite these encouraging signs, there is no firm indication in the aggregate that innovation and artistic impact is an area of pronounced foundation impact. The main exception is the resources devoted to program development. However, program development grants are not necessarily geared toward achieving artistic impacts as defined here and are a relatively safe way of providing support because they typically benefit established institutions. Arts foundations thus emerge, on balance, as more risk averse than entrepreneurial.

Policy Impact

Exploring policy impacts in the arts is a more complicated undertaking than in other fields. Ideological positions against centralizing interventions by the federal government and policy of any kind, as well as the belief in markets as suitable mechanisms to foster creativity, remain significant and historically rooted barriers to explicit policy development.[36] This aversion to an explicit and formal policy framework is manifested most clearly in the authorizing legislation for the National Endowments for the Arts and Humanities:

> The purpose of the Foundation shall be to develop and promote a broadly conceived national policy of support for the humanities and the arts in the United States. . . .
>
> In the administration of this Act no department, agency, officer, or employee of the United States shall exercise any direction, supervision, or control over the policy determination, personnel, or curriculum, or the administration or operation of any school or other non-Federal agency, institution, organization, or association. [20 U.S.C. §953 (b–c)]

Despite these statutory limitations, the NEA played a major role in delineating an implicit policy through the "support for the arts" or "public leveraging

---

35. Grantmakers in the Arts (2005, p. 9).
36. Marquis (1995); Cowen (1998).

arts" paradigms that kept all funding sources squarely focused on the financial needs of nonprofit arts organizations and their expansion.[37] Grants from the NEA in discrete artistic disciplines and fellowships for individual artists signaled to other donors where artistic excellence was to be found and provided private donors with guidance about allocating resources. With the NEA's restructuring in the mid-1990s, all disciplinary grant-making programs and most fellowships were eliminated;[38] the NEA lost its ability to define the parameters of the policy field; and private donors lost their ability to delineate their own roles within the framework set by the NEA.

This has been especially true for foundations. With the NEA as a central guidepost until the late 1980s, private foundations had unambiguous choices in defining their own roles: whether to follow and complement the NEA's programmatic and grant decisions by providing matching or challenge grants; to substitute for government contributions with grants supporting artists or organizations overlooked by the NEA; or to innovate by designing programs to address artistic and cultural endeavors outside the framework of the agency. The presence of the NEA facilitated the work of foundations in one core respect. With its national scope and breadth of resources, the agency was able to gather, summarize, and evaluate information on a scale that private foundations rarely can;[39] and whatever a foundation's individual focus in relation to the NEA, this information was a valuable resource for the philanthropic field.

Although they might arguably be among the beneficiaries of a more coherent national policy, foundations have made few efforts to develop a new cultural policy framework at the national level that could alleviate the gap left by the NEA. Among the exceptions was the announcement of a five-year, $50 million cultural policy initiative by the Pew Charitable Trusts in 1999.[40] External reaction to this effort was uniformly negative, as the former Metropolitan Museum of Art director Thomas Hoving and others declared any attempts at developing a policy framework to be a waste of resources better spent on supporting artists directly. This, in turn, signaled a near complete lack of policy readiness in the arts field that foundations have not been able to overcome.

Rather than seek national policy changes, some foundations have resorted to supporting private policymaking, on the one hand, and market-augmenting initiatives, on the other.[41] Foundations have supported various efforts by trade associations to increase the community access, diversity, and engagement of

37. Cherbo and Wyszomirski (2000).

38. Kimbis (1997).

39. DiMaggio (1986, pp. 113–39).

40. Judith H. Dobrzynski, "Heavyweight Foundation Throws Itself behind Idea of a Cultural Policy," *New York Times,* August 2, 1999.

41. Wyszomirski and Cherbo (2003).

cultural institutions. Foundations have also sponsored studies exploring audience development, arts participation, and education issues, seeking strategies for cultural organizations to augment market-based revenues by increasing access to nontraditional audiences or by developing future audiences.

The advantage of both approaches is that they allow foundations to pursue certain policy goals, such as diversity and access, without encountering resistance to systemic policy interventions. Their drawback lies in the inherent limitations of private policies in enforcing broad policy goals. Accordingly, most private efforts to move cultural institutions toward greater cultural diversity have more or less failed, and large-scale policy impacts are not readily discernible.

Conclusion

In the post-NEA era, foundations are finding themselves in an ever-expanding free philanthropic market, characterized by a growing diversity of issues and a blurring, if not outright lack, of boundaries.[42] Foundation arts funding is becoming less concentrated as new foundations enter the market. However, the market is not (yet) sending clear signals, and information about where resources are best deployed to maximize impacts is diffuse and hard to come by. In principle, this free-for-all market of cultural philanthropy may bode well for future innovation, as some current foundation investments will pay off and others will wither away. So far, it remains uncertain who the new gatekeepers will be to determine funding priorities and where the areas of greatest potential impacts lie. The information problem in the emerging marketplace may also play against future innovation, given the organizational limitations of foundations. As Paul DiMaggio has phrased it, "The cost of information—of getting it and of evaluating it—is as substantial a constraint on foundation innovativeness as any other."[43]

While the field of arts and culture has grown and potential policy issues have become more complex, information is arguably scarcer than it was two decades ago. As a result, and with requisite exceptions for a few national foundations, there are no strong indications that the foundation field at large pursues innovation—as defined here in terms of artistic or policy impacts—at a significant scale. Rather, the data suggest a fairly high degree of continuity of foundation funding priorities over the past twenty years, despite the major public policy upheavals of the 1990s. On one hand, this may mean that most foundations are impervious to larger policy changes. With about half a century of past investments in the nonprofit cultural infrastructure to protect, foundations may be too vested to consider changing course. On the other, it may mean that foundations

---

42. Cherbo and Wyszomirski (2000).
43. DiMaggio (1986, pp. 113–39).

have not yet fully adapted to post-NEA realities and will continue past work and priorities until a new framework emerges to guide future efforts.

In either case, this analysis suggests that foundations are heavily focused on their economic impact, and their intentions are clearly traceable in this respect. Foundation funding appears to be more traditional (charitable) than forward looking (philanthropic) in the arts. This is, however, not problematic in and of itself. While it might be desirable to see larger funders providing more artistic and policy leadership, the economic needs of the arts field are substantial, and addressing them remains a valid and important task. The core challenge in this regard is to find ways to nurture the cultural infrastructure without encouraging overextension. Arguably, the postwar growth rate is not sustainable, but there are no internal safeguards inherent in the nonprofit form that would discourage growth. Finding ways to use foundation resources to set limits to, rather than providing further incentives for, growth may thus prove to be the area where the need for innovation will meet the need for economic impact in the future.

14

The Role of Foundations in American Religion

ROBERT WUTHNOW AND D. MICHAEL LINDSAY

Although American religion has been studied extensively, little attention has been paid to its financial underpinnings until recently, and even less has been devoted to understanding its relationships with foundations.[1] Given the larger neglect of religion in sociological treatments of nonprofit organizations, it has been easy for scholars to assume that foundations and other centers of philanthropy were relevant to studies of higher education, the arts, health, welfare, and social advocacy but not to religion. This assumption is reinforced by summary statistics suggesting that religion is a relatively small part of total foundation giving and that foundation grants represent a small share of total revenue for religion. According to figures compiled by the Foundation Center, 3,498 foundation grants were given for religious purposes in 2003, amounting to $340 million—seemingly a sizable amount. However, these grants represented a mere 2.9 percent of all foundation grants and in dollar value constituted only 2.4 percent of total foundation giving. In the same year, giving to religion from all sources totaled $84.3 billion, meaning that the share from foundations amounted to only 5.1 percent.[2]

Although they provide a small proportion of overall funding for religion, foundations play an important role in American religion. This chapter examines that role by considering which foundations are currently the most active in the

---

1. Chaves and Miller (1999); Ronsvalle and Ronsvalle (1996).
2. U.S. Census Bureau (2005, pp. 365, 364).

religious sphere, who the major recipients of these foundations are, the kinds of activities these foundations are supporting, and what major challenges currently face foundation leaders interested in religion. In considering these questions, we argue that foundations' role in American religion extends well beyond the 3 to 5 percent of their giving that might be assumed from summary statistics. Foundation-based philanthropy in religion is both highly concentrated and strategically deployed, reaching into many realms, and thus goes uncaptured by statistical classifications alone into such areas as education, welfare, and international affairs. Religion-oriented foundations face serious challenges, however, as a result of secular, legal, and governmental considerations and responses to such developments as globalization, increasing religious and cultural pluralism, and continuing demands for accountability and effectiveness.

The Major Foundations

The twenty-five foundations that gave the most money to religion between 1999 and 2003 are listed in table 14-1.[3] The most notable feature about the foundations listed is the enormous variation among them. They differ dramatically from one another in the overall size of their assets, in the extent to which their grant making focuses on religion, and in the number and amount of grants to religion. The largest two foundations, Ford and Lilly, had total assets of $9.3 and $10.8 billion respectively in 2003. Five foundations had assets of more than $1 billion. At the other extreme, eleven had assets of less than $100 million. These differences indicate that religion is a higher priority for some (especially the smaller ones) than for others, as is illustrated by the percentage of total grant dollars each foundation spends on religion. Here, the range is as low as 1 percent for the Ford Foundation to 99 percent for the Eagle's Wing Foundation.

In terms of the number of grants to religion, the Koch Foundation, for instance, gave nearly three thousand grants between 1999 and 2003, whereas the Florik Charitable Trust gave only eight. The mean number of grants to religion

3. Such designations as these are subject to several sources of possible error. We discovered, for instance, that the Foundation Center omitted information from several foundations that were included in the Foundation Search database. In these instances, we incorporated the missing data we could find from Foundation Search and from IRS Form 990s. We also observed a number of discrepancies between Foundation Center and Foundation Search figures. We had no way of independently reconciling these discrepancies and thus opted for Foundation Center figures for consistency and because they are more widely publicized and used. We did not question whether grants were properly classified into National Taxonomy of Exempt Entities categories, although we discuss some of these ambiguities below. We based our decision to rank foundations using five-year totals from 1999 to 2003 on the considerable variation among annual reports. We focused on the top twenty-five foundations after examining the next twenty-five and seeing a significant increase in missing information.

Table 14-1. *Total Grants for Religion, by Top Twenty-Five Foundations, 1999–2003*

Foundation name	Assets (dollars) 2003	Total religion grants	
		Number	Dollar value
Lilly Endowment	10,849,406,670	1,473	677,304,580
Arthur S. DeMoss Foundation	329,859,393	349	94,706,661
Pew Charitable Trusts	4,100,000,000	57	70,420,000
Koch Foundation	110,826,905	2,988	48,336,101
Richard and Helen DeVos Foundation	35,154,452	150	45,747,899
Duke Endowment	2,052,396,108	1,035	44,461,044
Dan Murphy Foundation	199,498,742	108	43,411,549
Florik Charitable Trust	4,088,839	8	40,892,819
Karfunkel Family Foundation	13,649,158	52	40,848,499
Grace Foundation	26,208,446	120	39,732,393
Community Foundation of Greater Memphis	184,276,432	730	39,494,779
Open Doors International	8,506,215	45	38,324,917
Maclellan Foundation	170,132,456	96	35,369,261
Harry and Jeanette Weinberg Foundation	1,790,172,593	203	35,062,733
Eagle's Wing Foundation	8,182,098	18	33,604,263
Ford Foundation	9,300,140,000	177	32,857,259
Garmar Foundation	2,690,659	67	31,044,857
Orville D. and Ruth A. Merillat Foundation	60,680,954	291	25,613,122
Foundation for the Carolinas	312,258,194	547	24,767,682
John Templeton Foundation	337,359,840	114	23,368,851
Communities Foundation of Texas	392,612,287	397	23,229,414
Mary Stuart Rogers Foundation	28,782,645	102	20,103,820
Edgar and Elsa Prince Foundation	30,952,880	160	19,907,829
Rushing Wind	218,843	37	17,918,014
Stewardship Foundation	115,204,238	545	15,914,172

Source: Data from Foundation Center; adjusted for missing data with information from Foundation Search America and IRS Form 990s; religion grants as percentage of all grants is based on dollar value (Foundation Search America; Rushing Wind estimated from IRS Form 990).

for these twenty-five foundations was 375, or an average of 75 a year. The dollar value of all grants to religion between 1999 and 2003 also varies dramatically, ranging from a high of $677 million from the Lilly Endowment to just under $16 million from the Stewardship Foundation. Half of the $1.2 billion given to religion by these twenty-five foundations came from only the top five. Because the total value and number of grants vary so greatly, the average size of grants also varies considerably. Given that these twenty-five foundations are the largest of the hundreds of organizations that give grants to religion, it is striking that so much variation exists among them.

A second trend that emerges from the figures in table 14-1 is the volatility of grant making to religion. By volatility we mean fluctuations from year to year, as illustrated even within the five years under consideration. For instance, only 7 of these 25 foundations were among the top-ranked 25 in each of the years between 1999 and 2003. When we examined the top 50 foundations for each of these years, we found that 114 foundations had been among the top twenty-five at least once. Two other indications of volatility are shown in table 14-2. Total dollar value of grants for religion in the highest year and lowest year between 1999 and 2003 is shown for each of the top 25 foundations. In fifteen of the twenty-five comparisons, the amount granted in the lowest year was less than 50 percent of the amount given in the highest year.

Another measure of volatility is the average percentage by which the amount given each year differed from the amount given in the preceding year.[4] In fourteen of the twenty-one instances for which data were available, the average annual percent change was 25 percent or more (and in an equal number of cases the number of grants given also changed by this much). One implication of this volatility is that strategic religious philanthropy employed by these foundations does not entail long-term financial commitment. For example, Eagle's Wing Foundation awarded eighteen grants to various groups between 1999 and 2003, totaling more than $33 million, but by 2004 the foundation had been dissolved. The Florik Charitable Trust, which was dissolved in 2005, followed a similar trajectory.

There is no reason to think that volatility in grant making is any greater in religion than in other arenas. These fluctuations might be attributable to larger uncertainties in financial markets, especially those associated with the attacks of September 11, 2001. This possibility appears unlikely, however, since there was no discernible pattern in the years in which religion grant making was highest or lowest (six foundations' giving was highest in 1999, three in 2000, four in 2001, seven in 2002, and five in 2003; five gave the least in 1999, four in 2000, four in 2001, two in 2002, and ten in 2003). Nor was the apparent volatility attributable to sheer growth. Not a single foundation increased its giving for religion every year between 1999 and 2003. The volatility of grant-making patterns is underscored by the fact that 51 of the 100 annual comparisons in both dollar value and number of grants represented decreases over the previous year, while 49 represented increases. Whatever the sources of this volatility (it is not

4. For 1999 and 2000, 2000 and 2001, 2001 and 2002, and 2002 and 2003, we calculated the absolute difference (plus or minus) between the amount granted in paired years, divided that figure by the amount given in the first year to obtain a percentage value, summed those four values, and divided by four to obtain the average annual percent change.

Table 14-2. *Volatility in Foundation Grants for Religion, 1999–2003*

Foundation	Highest year (dollars)[a]	Lowest year (dollars)[b]	Average annual percent change
Lilly Endowment	233,457,403	81,819,011	53
Arthur S. DeMoss Foundation	24,746,095	13,040,791	32
Pew Charitable Trusts	19,483,000	10,405,000	25
Koch Foundation	16,879,447	6,252,998	28
Richard and Helen DeVos Foundation	13,825,100	6,254,312	20
Duke Endowment	13,123,165	5,287,400	42
Dan Murphy Foundation	9,982,244	6,530,105	12
Florik Charitable Trust	15,418,221	3,521,756	. . .
Karfunkel Family Foundation	17,621,249	2,195,000	. . .
Grace Foundation	13,409,556	775,145	225
Community Foundation of Greater Memphis	12,741,227	5,199,929	54
Open Doors International	8,576,700	5,743,886	11
Maclellan Foundation	16,290,029	222,500	1,439
Harry and Jeanette Weinberg Foundation	9,718,467	5,157,000	32
Eagle's Wing Foundation	9,127,131	7,700,000	29
Ford Foundation	7,929,000	5,597,500	17
Garmar Foundation	11,793,547	4,832,352	. . .
Orville D. and Ruth A. Merillat Foundation	10,435,622	2,215,227	71
Foundation for the Carolinas	6,136,909	4,212,868	15
John Templeton Foundation	6,844,727	1,998,767	67
Communities Foundation of Texas	6,232,689	3,362,717	20
Mary Stuart Rogers Foundation	6,734,983	292,000	47
Edgar and Elsa Prince Foundation	6,460,000	2,125,500	90
Rushing Wind	7,428,579	2,918,383	. . .
Stewardship Foundation	3,661,630	2,804,500	14

Source: Data from Foundation Center; adjusted for missing data with information from Foundation Search America and IRS Form 990s (some percentage values are missing because no grants for religion were recorded in at least one of the studied years).

a. Foundation was ranked among the top twenty-five foundations in dollar value of funding.

b. Foundation was ranked among the lowest twenty-five foundations in dollar value of funding.

significantly correlated either with overall assets or total dollar value of grants), it is clearly a reality of the grant-making world.[5]

Combined giving by the twenty-five large foundations listed in tables 14-1 and 14-2 accounts for approximately two-thirds of all foundation grants to

5. Correlations of −.015 and −.004, respectively.

religion, according to Foundation Center statistics. That proportion is sufficient to sponsor major agenda-setting programs in American religion. The remaining third of foundation grants is also supplied by some major contributors. For instance, fifteen foundations each gave at least $5 million to religion between 1999 and 2003, and another five each donated more than $2 million. Smaller foundations—beyond these top twenty-five—also play an important role in American religion. Many of these are local foundations, established by families or single congregations, and often are too small or informal to have been captured in Foundation Center statistics. Many do not have professional staffs or formal boards. As religious organizations, many claim exemption from reporting to the Internal Revenue Service and function as nonprofit organizations that rely on donations rather than serving as primary sources of funds to other organizations. Although most of these foundations promote Christian or Jewish activities, a growing number reflect the increasing diversity of American religion. For example, Muslim foundations include the Ah Lul Bayt Foundation of Houston, the Arizona-based Al-Mahdi Benevolent Foundation, the Alhuda Foundation of Indianapolis, and the Al-Makarim Islamic Foundation of Erie, Pennsylvania.

According to data from the National Center for Family Philanthropy, family foundations are more likely than independent foundations to give to religious nonprofits. Building campaigns at local houses of worship, fund-raising drives, and religious festivals in the community have all been supported with funds from small, local foundations that, owing to constraints in organizational capacity, prefer to support local initiatives and benefit from community ties. Just as most of the activity within the realm of religion takes place locally, so too is the largest number of foundations that give to religion found among smaller foundations, ones that do not have large, professional staffs or bureaucratic structures. However, these foundations also do not use standardized reporting procedures, which is why they are often overlooked in examinations of foundation philanthropy.

The variation and volatility evident among foundations engaged in grant making for religion point to the importance of understanding the distinctive characteristics of these organizations. Donor intent is a significant factor for many foundations. The reason they are among the top donors to religion is that religion mattered to foundation founders. For example, the Lilly Endowment has been supporting religious causes since its founding in 1937. The three founders of the Lilly Endowment were active Episcopalians in their home state of Indiana and believed that church involvement was an important dimension of active citizenship. Over the years, Lilly has prioritized leadership development and support for religious institutions within its religious division. Like other private foundations, the Lilly Endowment tends to direct most of its funding toward one major religious tradition, not religious causes in general. Indeed, a survey of foundation philanthropy across the religious landscape reveals the prevalence of a "silo effect": that is, recipients of religious grants from a single foundation tend to resemble one another, as well as the granting foundation, in terms of religious tradition. This silo effect creates a context in which religion serves as a unifying element among disparate organizational actors. Nonprofit organizations and funding agencies that would not normally interact with one another, either because of geography or organizational size and scope, partner together. Shared religious tradition and commitment serves as an important bonding agent. In an era of significant institutional differentiation, this kind of unifying principle is noteworthy; indeed, this silo effect is one of the distinctive elements of religious philanthropy.[6]

The Recipients

The twenty-five organizations that received the most money for religion from foundations between 1999 and 2003 are listed in table 14-3. As with the donor list, there is huge variation among these organizations. The United Jewish Appeal Federation, at the top, received nearly $185 million, more than the combined amounts awarded to the bottom ten organizations on the list. It is also evident that these organizations are quite diverse religiously—some span specific religious traditions; others are unaffiliated with any tradition.

The right-hand column of table 14-3 shows the foundation that gave the most money during this period to each of the top twenty-five recipient organizations. In nearly every case, private foundations served as the source of at least 85 percent of the recipient organization's grants and in some cases provided all of its grants. This fact is noteworthy because it contrasts rather sharply with the picture of volatility that emerged from considering foundations' overall giving to religion. It appears that each recipient organization has one major foundation to which it can look as a somewhat stable source of support. Of course, funding may fluctuate from year to year owing to different needs or grant durations. We must also qualify this observation by emphasizing that we do not have information about long-term funding patterns. What is clear is that these recipient organizations are not having to piece together major funding from dozens of different foundations every year.

Although there is some overlap between the donor organizations listed in table 14-3 and the top foundations listed in table 14-1, it is notable that this overlap is not greater than it is. Only ten of the top twenty-five foundations considered earlier appear on this list. Not surprisingly, the Lilly Endowment, with its

---

6. On institutional differentiation, see Friedland and Alford (1991, p. 232).

Table 14-3. *Top Twenty-Five Recipients of Grants for Religion, 1999–2003*

Recipient Name	Total grants (dollars)	Top donor
United Jewish Appeal Federation	184,788,159	Jewish Communal Fund
American Jewish Joint Distribution Committee	66,512,678	Harry and Jeanette Weinberg Foundation
National Christian Charitable Foundation	58,106,896	Maclellan Foundation
Campus Crusade for Christ	56,590,703	Corman Foundation
Associated Jewish Community Federation	50,379,136	Blaustein Thalheimer Foundation
Power for Living	49,342,051	Arthur S. DeMoss Foundation
Archdiocese of Chicago	44,613,166	Florik Charitable Trust
Minneapolis Jewish Federation	34,902,654	Minneapolis Foundation
Educational Broadcasting Corporation (for Religion and Ethics Newsweekly)	33,665,170	Lilly Endowment
Jewish Federation of Greater Atlanta	31,135,462	Marcus Foundation
Roman Catholic Archbishop of Los Angeles	27,442,781	Dan Murphy Foundation
Fund for Theological Education	24,969,328	Lilly Endowment
Chesed Foundation of America	22,505,249	Karfunkel Family Foundation
Center for Theology and the Natural Sciences	21,676,289	John Templeton Foundation
Louisville Presbyterian Theological Seminary	21,214,378	Lilly Endowment
Chabad of California	19,982,671	Revokip Foundation
Duke University (Divinity School)	18,405,992	Lilly Endowment
Union Theological Seminary	18,156,347	Lilly Endowment
Watch Tower Bible and Tract Society	16,696,685	K. H. Foundation
Third Sector New England	15,087,640	Robert Wood Johnson Foundation
Emory University (Candler School of Theology)	14,517,225	Lilly Endowment
Prison Fellowship Ministries	13,519,322	Arthur S. DeMoss Foundation
Living Stones Charitable Trust	13,434,000	Living Stones Foundation
Wabash College (for Wabash Center of Teaching and Learning in Theology and Religion)	13,349,521	Lilly Endowment
Samaritan's Purse	12,764,939	Arthur S. DeMoss Foundation

Source: Foundation Search America.

sizable grant making for religion, appears as the top donor for three of the recipient organizations named in table 14-3. The Arthur S. DeMoss Foundation is the major source for two of these recipients, and the Richard and Helen DeVos, Dan Murphy, Karfunkel Family, Maclellan Family, Harry and Jeanette Weinberg, Garmar, and John Templeton foundations and the Florik Charitable Trust also serve as principal donors.[7] One implication is that most of the top recipient organizations are receiving significant grants from foundations that direct their giving to only one (or a few) beneficiaries. Another is that some of the largest overall givers to religion distribute their grants to several different recipients (and thus do not appear here). These observations in themselves do not reveal much about grant-making patterns but once again underscore the diversity that exists among the top foundations and recipients in the religion arena.

That the top two recipient organizations are Jewish—and that seven of the top fifteen are Jewish—is undoubtedly a matter of some interest. On one hand, it underscores the importance of Jewish foundations and Jewish federations at the national and municipal level. On the other, the presence of these organizations among the top recipients of foundation support is an artifact of the federated structure of these organizations as opposed to the more dispersed pattern among Protestant and Catholic organizations. For instance, if all recipient organizations with "Catholic" or "archdiocese" in their titles were combined, the total foundation funding they received for religion between 1999 and 2003 would be $464 million. During the same period, Presbyterian organizations received $275 million; Baptist organizations, $219 million; Methodist organizations, $200 million; "Christian" organizations, $199 million; Episcopal organizations, $149 million; and Lutheran organizations, $114 million. These figures show the considerable amount of foundation funding that goes to Catholic and Protestant organizations. The total for all these Christian organizations is $1.6 billion—virtually identical to the foundation support received by Jewish organizations.

Unlike the Christian community, American Jews unite in significant measure in support of the United Jewish Appeal Federation's annual campaign. This campaign funds a variety of Jewish causes—from welfare assistance for destitute Jews in Argentina to travel funds for American Jewish youth to visit Israel for the first time. Whereas American Christianity tends to rely on smaller entities with their own appeals to foundations for funding—often competing with one another—this is not nearly as much the case for American Jewry. Indeed, the top five Jewish recipients of religion grants are all part of the United Jewish Appeal Federation in one way or another. United Jewish Communities (recently renamed the Jewish Federations of North America) serves as an umbrella organization for 157 local Jewish federations in North America. Each local federation, in turn, functions as an alliance of various Jewish social service agencies, educational organizations, and similar groups. Collectively, these federations are significant voices within the Jewish community. As such, they make important decisions about

7. The Jewish Communal Fund would qualify as a top religion foundation; its absence from table 14-1 reflects the criteria used by the Foundation Center for determining whether or not an organization should be regarded as a foundation.

which projects should receive funding, which organizations should expand or downsize, and how resources should be allocated in a given year. In the American Christian community, this decisionmaking process is more diffuse through numerous funding streams and myriad organizational structures. In sum, a streamlined funding process distinguishes Jewish philanthropy. Significant support for these various Jewish clearinghouses comes from important Jewish foundations including the Harry and Jeanette Weinberg and the Alvin and Fanny Blaustein Thalheimer foundations and the Jewish Communal Fund.

The remaining recipients of major religious grants fall into three broad categories. The first involve specific projects such as DeMoss's support for the book *Power for Living* and Templeton's underwriting of the Center for Theology and the Natural Sciences. Not all of these recipients are explicitly religious entities. Third Sector New England, for example, serves an array of nonprofit organizations through educational programs, consulting services, and fiscal oversight. Among its clients are several religious groups, including an interfaith partnership against domestic violence.

Second among the remaining grants are those directed to large religious institutions. Roman Catholic archdioceses such as those in Chicago and Los Angeles have benefited from private foundation grants in recent years. In fact, the Dan Murphy Foundation regularly awards significant grant dollars to large entities like Roman Catholic archdioceses and Catholic universities. Also among this class of grants are those awarded to faith-oriented special purpose organizations (also called parachurch organizations). Campus Crusade for Christ, Prison Fellowship Ministries, and Samaritan's Purse have all received large foundation grants. Indeed, within the world of evangelical foundation philanthropy, there appears to be a preference for funding large, existing organizations. Foundation executives report a desire to choose "safe" funding options, which involve institutions that they believe will deliver measurable outcomes for their investment. As one executive confided, "Very few of these [evangelical] foundations are willing to take a risk. . . . Some of the big ones like DeMoss and Ahmanson might try something new, but most of us are too nervous that smaller [projects and] groups won't deliver what they promise."[8]

The third category of religious grants includes those awarded to build and maintain institutions. Lilly's support of Union Theological Seminary, which has faced a series of financial crises in recent years, is representative of this trend. The seminary, located next to Columbia University on the Upper West Side of

---

8. Interview with an evangelical foundation executive conducted in 2006 in conjunction with a research project carried out by D. Michael Lindsay. The interviewee refers to the philanthropic work of the Arthur S. DeMoss Foundation and Fieldstead and Company, a private philanthropy of Roberta and Howard Ahmanson.

Manhattan, once served as the institutional home for several theological luminaries in American Protestantism, including Reinhold Niebuhr and Paul Tillich.
Over the years, though, declining enrollments and waning financial support from
mainline denominations contributed to significant fiscal hardships for the seminary. Lilly's grants, which include an award of $8 million in 2000, have sought to
slow the seminary's decline and to keep the venerable institution solvent.

Two organizations that did not make the top twenty-five list also merit comment. One is Teen Challenge, the substance abuse recovery program that provides addicts with faith-based life-transforming religious training. Between 1999
and 2003, Teen Challenge received 435 foundation grants totaling $10.4 mil-
lion. Had these grants all been given to a single organization, Teen Challenge
would have been among the ten or so recipient organizations just below the
top twenty-five. However, Teen Challenge is separately incorporated in different
locations—Arizona, Iowa, the cities of Sacramento, Midland, Milwaukee, and
so on. Hence even though it was the recipient of considerable funding, Teen
Challenge's relationships with foundations could easily be missed.

A similar example is Catholic Charities. In total, Catholic Charities received
$118 million in foundation grants, an amount larger than the awards to most of
the top twenty-five recipients. Like Teen Challenge, though, Catholic Charities
is not a single organization. The Southern Nevada chapter received $11.3 mil-
lion, nearly all from the Donald W. Reynolds Foundation in Las Vegas. Catholic Charities of Baltimore received $6.5 million, including significant donations
from the Weinberg Foundation—one of the few examples of giving across religious lines. Catholic Charities of San Francisco received $5.3 million in a single
grant from the Y. and H. Soda Foundation. Other chapters receiving sizable
foundation grants included those in Minneapolis, San Jose, Oakland, New York,
and Boston.

Nonreligious "Religious" Giving

Thus far we have focused on foundations, recipients, and grants that qualify as
religious groups according to National Taxonomy of Exempt Entities catego-
rization. Other activities, however, also have strong connections with religion,
even though they fall into different tax-exempt categories. A study of foundation funding for social service activities illustrates one way in which the religious
interests of foundations overlap with and influence other aspects of their programs.[9] Using Foundation Center data, our study identified fifty large foundations that provided funding both for social services and for religious organizations. Analysis of the grant making of these faith-friendly foundations shows

9. J. Scott (2003).

Table 14-4. *Giving by Largest Foundations, by Field, 2001*

Percent

Field	Lilly Endowment	Arthur S. DeMoss Foundation	Pew Charitable Trusts	Koch Foundation	Richard and Helen DeVos Foundation
Education	58.0	6.0	44.0	22.0	39.0
Health	...	...	2.0	3.0	1.0
Social and human services	14.0	3.0	5.0	4.0	21.0
International giving	0.1	9.0	1.0	37.0	0.1
Environment	0.8	...	21	...	0.1
Arts and culture	9.0	0.2	8.0	0.4	7.0
Religion	6.0	63.0	2.0	32	23.0
Community development	12.0	18	14.0	1.0	9.0
Sports and recreation	0.2	1.0	...	...	...
Miscellaneous philanthropy	1.0	0.4	2.0	1.0	...

Source: Data from Foundation Center. Owing to rounding, some column totals do not equal 100 percent.

that few of them had formal restrictions against giving money to faith-based social service organizations and that several provided substantial funding to such organizations. The best example of such funding would be grants to the Salvation Army, which totaled $306 million between 1999 and 2003, including sizable grants from such faith-friendly foundations as the Lilly Endowment, the Marcus Foundation, and the Robert Wood Johnson Foundation.

Table 14-4 illustrates the distribution of grant categories among the largest foundations awarding grants to religious causes in 2001. There is a wide variation around the percentage of grant dollars being allocated to the religious category among these five foundations—from 63 percent at the Arthur S. DeMoss Foundation to 2 percent at the Pew Charitable Trusts. As discussed earlier, however, grants are often misclassified by the Foundation Center. As previously noted, the Maclellan Foundation is probably the best example.[10] Among the "big five" foundations, a large number of grants under the education category could be considered grants to religion. These include grants to religiously affiliated colleges and universities, such as those given by Lilly and Pew, as well as dollars devoted to parochial schools and educational initiatives for young people, such as those funded by the Charles G. Koch Charitable Foundation and the DeVos Foundation.

10. Indeed, an interview with the Maclellan Foundation's executive director confirmed that "100 percent of Maclellan's grants should be counted as grants to religion." Telephone interview conducted by D. Michael Lindsay with Tom McCallie in 2006.

In addition, what counts as international giving can sometimes be considered religious grants. Consider the financial support for religious workers and programs abroad that are funded by certain foundations. One example is the DeMoss Foundation, which gave five grants between 1999 and 2003, totaling $23.8 million, to an organization called the Confederation of Independent States Ministries. These grants were classified as "international giving," but the Confederation of Independent States Ministries is a missionary organization devoted to spreading an evangelical-style Christian gospel in former Soviet Union countries. These illustrations show the prevalence of substantial funding for projects classified differently but with apparent religious aims. The chances for misclassification for grant categories are likely to be greater within the realm of religion, because many staff members at places like the Foundation Center are not as knowledgeable about religious institutions and faith-based programs—as is the case for the philanthropic world in general. What these staff members classify as support for a hospital or a school may, in fact, be a religious grant. Knowing both the donor and the specifics of the grant are essential to understanding the extent to which religion is the principal criterion for a particular grant.

By the same token, recipient organizations may not be identified as religious ministries but may function in ways that emphasize religious goals and principles. This contributes to additional blurring of the boundaries within religious philanthropy. One of the most important "nonreligious" religious organizations in the United States is Focus on the Family, headquartered in Colorado Springs. Between 1999 and 2003, Focus on the Family received 645 foundation grants totaling $25.9 million. These were all classified as "social and human services" grants. God's Gift, located in Temecula, California, gave seven grants worth $4.2 million. The Richard and Helen DeVos Foundation in Grand Rapids, Michigan, gave nine grants totaling $2.6 million. The Edgar and Elsa Prince Foundation in Holland, Michigan, gave four grants also totaling $2.6 million. Other foundation donors included the Orville D. and Ruth A. Merillat Foundation, Huizenga Family Foundation, Corman Foundation, and Stewardship Foundation. Focus on the Family's "primary reason for existence," according to its website, is "to spread the Gospel of Jesus Christ through a practical outreach to homes." This goal is underscored by the ministry's stated belief that "the ultimate purpose in living is to know and glorify God and to attain eternal life through Jesus Christ our Lord, beginning within our own families and then reaching out to a suffering humanity that does not know of His love and sacrifice."[11]

A contrasting example is the Family Research Council, which received two hundred foundation grants between 1999 and 2003 totaling $7.8 million, none

11. "About Us," Focus on the Family (www.focusonthefamily.com/about_us.aspx [November 27, 2009]).

of which were classified as religious. Many of the foundations contributing to
Focus on the Family also funded the Family Research Council, including the
Prince, Bolthouse, Johan DeVries, and Merillat foundations. Unlike Focus on
the Family, the Family Research Council does not explicitly emphasize promoting religion in its mission statement. Nevertheless, Family Research Council
leaders have been in the forefront of efforts by conservative religious organizations to promote marriage, instill traditional values, and reform policies toward
abortion. Among its core principles, the Family Research Council also emphasizes its conviction that "God exists and is sovereign over all creation [and that]
human life is, therefore, sacred and the right to life is the most fundamental of
political rights."[12]

The upshot of these considerations is that foundation giving that at least indirectly serves religious purposes is considerably larger than the amounts derived
from National Taxonomy of Exempt Entities classifications. Of course, grants
can serve more than a single purpose, as can recipient organizations. The more
important point, however, is that religion does not conform easily to academics' attempts to pigeonhole it. Churches, synagogues, mosques, and theological
seminaries may be readily classified as religious organizations. Other organizations that span the increasingly porous boundaries between institutional sectors
are not so easily categorized. An organization with a religious word in the title
may be engaged entirely in social service activities, while a service organization
may promote faith as part of its implicit mission. The same may be true of educational programs and international relief organizations. The proliferation of
organizational variety in response to financial and legal concerns is but one of
the ways in which foundation practices are being challenged.

Foundations' Contributions

In the parlance of foundation discourse, the contribution of foundation grant
making to religion is best described as countercyclical. Specifically, the goal of
much foundation funding for religion has been to maintain, revitalize, or renew
religious traditions thought to be endangered by secularism (or by other religions). In other words, foundations help support the preservation of particular
traditions within a context of rising religious pluralism. Foundations' countercyclical religious contributions fall into several distinct categories, but *institution builder* is the term that would most readily apply, followed by *social entrepreneur*. Institution building includes such activities as supporting seminaries
and divinity schools, training clergy, sponsoring religiously oriented hospitals

12. "Over Twenty Years Defending Family, Faith, and Freedom," Family Research Council
(www.frc.org/get.cfm?i=WX07C17 [November 27, 2009]).

and health clinics, providing for the preservation of historic religious buildings, helping low-income congregations, and financing new congregations and missions activities. Entrepreneurial activities range from supporting special social programs that might not elicit contributions from members (such as gay rights, environmental, or antiwar advocacy) to launching special-purpose organizations aimed at capturing new religious markets (such as campus ministries, religious broadcasting, and motion pictures). Because of the legal demands of separation of church and state, foundations' religious activities can seldom be described as pioneering programs for government. However, there are notable examples in the past, such as the settlement house movement at the end of the nineteenth century, the temperance movement, and the civil rights movement.

Foundations' contributions to religion are sometimes viewed as particularistic, paternalistic, and amateurish by scholars used to studying more professionalized aspects of philanthropy and the nonprofit sector. However, particularism also generates competition among religious groups, which sometimes invigorates their planning and activity to stretch into other philanthropic realms. Such activities include education and leadership training, research and information gathering, promoting the public role and services of religious organizations, general support for religious institutions, and a miscellaneous category of special projects. Through its sizable grants, the Lilly Endowment has provided countless hours of leadership development and continuing education for religious leaders—all centered around maintaining a vital leadership cohort for American congregations. For Lilly, talented and well-educated leaders are the key to strengthening the country's religious life. Templeton and Pew also fund major research initiatives for the academic study of religion, believing that breakthroughs in research can yield results in the spiritual realm. These grants have advanced knowledge in multiple domains, including the sciences, humanities, social science, and the arts, not to mention ethics and religious studies. Thousands of foundation grants have enabled religious institutions to provide social services to members of particular religious communities as well as the general public. Many other foundation grants address societal concerns through general support of religious institutions. In general, religious philanthropy cannot be pigeonholed into a category of strictly religious purposes.

The Lilly Endowment illustrates the considerable role that foundations can play as institution builders that serve to ensure a future cadre of religious leaders and constituents and to preserve a base of support for the foundation itself. Although not sectarian, the Lilly Endowment has a long-standing affiliation with various mainline congregations, including the more moderate and liberal branches of Presbyterians, Episcopalians, Lutherans, Methodists, and Baptists. Across the Lilly Endowment, most grants are awarded to institutions within Indiana, and grants from the religion division are no exception. Religious tradition trumps geography in some of Lilly's decisionmaking process, once again illustrating how religious grant making can be stratified according to maybe more, but at least different, factors than occur in other philanthropic sectors.

Chief among Lilly's institution-building priorities are initiatives designed to cultivate and sustain future generations of church leadership. Over the last decade, the endowment has allocated nearly $500 million to various programs across the country, with the goal of recruiting, training, and sustaining high-caliber ministry professionals. Beginning with high school students interested in exploring a religious vocation, Lilly has launched a series of initiatives to support future and current pastors through college, seminary, and into the early and middle parts of their careers. These include grants to eighty-eight church-related colleges and universities and fifty-four theological schools, along with hundreds of local congregations. In addition to these disparate institutional bases, Lilly has established organizations like the Louisville Institute and the Indianapolis Center for Congregations, which exist almost entirely to support Lilly priorities. Through the process, the endowment has sought to cultivate a sense of community among participants, funding a number of initiatives for relationship building and creating a coalition of institutions that support religious organizations and their leaders. In total, this sustained initiative represents the largest financial commitment made by a single foundation in the United States toward a particular religious goal.

In similar measure, although technically not classified as a foundation, the Jewish Communal Fund represents one of the nation's largest ongoing philanthropic initiatives. The American Jewish Joint Distribution Committee allocates monies to hospitals, nursing homes, social service agencies, and a host of religious institutions that build and strengthen the Jewish community. Jewish Community Centers, which serve as hubs of Jewish life in cities across America, have particularly benefited from the institution-building impulse of the United Jewish Appeal Federation Campaign. The unified approach of this annual appeal, which has drawn extensive support from wealthy foundations such as Weinberg and Karfunkel, is without parallel among other faith traditions in this country.

Entrepreneurial initiatives aimed at spreading religious values through new media and into different social niches are best exemplified through the Arthur S. DeMoss Foundation, which has devoted more than $100 million toward raising the nation's religious conscience through media campaigns. Perhaps most notable among these is its advertising campaign featuring celebrity endorsements for a book called *Power for Living*. DeMoss contracted with a Christian pastor to write the book in 1983; it includes profiles of prominent Christians, including popular Dallas Cowboy Roger Staubach. DeMoss has published subsequent editions, and between 1999 and 2003 the foundation allocated $49.3

million for publication and marketing of *Power for Living*. DeMoss also funded a national television campaign—entitled "Life. What a beautiful choice"—aimed at curbing the number of abortions in the United States. Such media campaigns are informed by the foundation's bylaws to "promulgate the Christian Gospel throughout the world by any and all proper means."

The Pew Charitable Trusts provides one of the clearest examples of attempts by a foundation with interests in religion to influence public policy. The foundation has remained nonpartisan and has seldom sponsored projects aimed at specific policies (an exception was campaign finance reform), but it has sought to bring religious values into the public arena through educational programs and public opinion research. Whereas Lilly has focused on issues surrounding leadership and religious institutions and DeMoss on evangelism and public relations, Pew has devoted significant funds to the academic study of religion, with special emphasis on research conducted by scholars at leading institutions and of relevance to the wider public.[13] Founded by the evangelical oil magnate J. Howard Pew in 1948, the foundation has been particularly supportive of studies undertaken by evangelical academics as well as evangelical-leaning institutions of higher education. In 1988 Pew's religion division commissioned a paper on the status of evangelical scholarship and developed a ten-year plan for raising the intellectual stature of the evangelical movement. In the end, Pew spent more than $14 million toward revitalizing the movement's intellectual life, including conferences, research for scholarly publications, graduate student mentoring, and campus lectures.[14] It also funded Centers of Excellence for the academic study of religion at several major universities including Yale, Emory, and New York University, thereby legitimating such studies, even in thoroughly secular settings. Under the leadership of Joel Carpenter—who later became provost at Calvin College—Pew established programs and networks for evangelical academics, introducing younger scholars to senior scholars.

Like Lilly, Pew believed that long-term achievement of their goal required relationship building and strategically placed social networks. Pew sought dramatic improvement for evangelical intellectual activity and widespread recognition of its legitimacy. An internal study suggests that the foundation accomplished that goal, concluding that publications in secular (that is, nonreligious) outlets grew from 33 percent to 80 percent among Pew program participants between 1990 and 2001. Moreover, the study notes an increasing number of

13. The Lilly Endowment has also been a significant benefactor of academic studies on religion. However, this support has arisen from Lilly's more fundamental commitment to religious institutions and religious leadership.

14. Alan Wolfe, "The Opening of the Evangelical Mind," *Atlantic Monthly*, October 2000.

observers referring to "a visible evangelical presence" in the academy and a general "opening of the evangelical mind" as a result of Pew's philanthropy.[15] In recent years, Pew has moved increasingly into sponsoring high-profile public opinion surveys, forums in the nation's capital about religion and politics, and websites concerned with publicizing information about policies affecting faith and public welfare. Pew's commitment to evangelical causes even after the death of the foundation's benefactor also reveals the important role that board members can play in sustaining the original donor's intent.

In considering the contributions of foundations, it is again important to remember that activities not labeled as religious often involve an application of religious values to broader social needs. For instance, only 1 percent of Ford Foundation grants were spent on religion between 1999 and 2003; most of that supported two religious traditions: African American spirituality and Islam, both of which it regarded as historically marginalized and holding moral resources that could benefit the wider society. Closer inspection of grants made by Ford, though, reveals that religion enters a wider spectrum of its awards. For example, a grant made to the Archbishopric of Guatemala in 2002 is classified as international, not religious, giving, even though it is given to an explicitly religious entity.

National Taxonomy of Exempt Entities grant categories are noticeably imprecise on many major foundations that support religious causes. Consider the Maclellan Foundation—a highly religious foundation, complete with its own statement of faith.[16] A review of the Maclellan grant categories might suggest that religion is not very important to the foundation; between 1999 and 2003 only 8 percent of all Maclellan grants were allocated to "religious" causes. But a closer review of the foundation's funding priorities reveals that all Maclellan grantees outside its hometown of Chattanooga, Tennessee, must be evangelical Christian ministries. Instead of seeing their total number of religious grants between 1999 and 2003 as approximately $35 million, as National Taxonomy of Exempt Entities grant categories would suggest, it is more accurate to regard their religious grants as more than double that amount. The entire $76 million Maclellan awarded during those five years should be counted as religious grants, serving some type of religious purpose. This one example reveals the dubious nature of grant categories, for many programs and initiatives that are religious or spiritual in nature are not counted as religious grants. By the same token, many grants deemed religious may, in fact, be more accurately described as educational initiatives or social service programs.

15. For Pew performance, see Kroll and Cornejo (2003). For "visible evangelical presence," see James Turner, "Something to Be Reckoned With: The Evangelical Mind Reawakens," *Commonweal,* January 15, 1999; for the "opening of the evangelical mind," see Wolfe (2000).

16. "Statement of Faith," Maclellan Foundation (www.maclellan.net/about/statementoffaith. asp [November 24, 2009]).

Conclusion

Funding for religion amounts to less than 3 percent of total foundation grant making, and receipts from foundations constitute only about 5 percent of all giving to religion. Thus it is important not to exaggerate the role of foundations in American religion. It is nevertheless the case that a few foundations with an interest in religion have strategically deployed enormous resources to promote programs that would most likely have been impossible through other means. The Lilly Endowment is the most substantial of these contributors. Other foundations that have invested heavily in religion include the DeMoss and DeVos foundations and the Pew Charitable Trusts. The major recipients of religion-oriented foundation funding are quite varied, ranging from local congregations to large enterprises such as Campus Crusade for Christ and Chabad of California.

The objectives of foundation funding for religion can be summarized largely as efforts to reinforce and revitalize religious organizations and practices that appear to be threatened by secular social trends or by other religions. In pursuing these objectives, foundations have contributed significantly to institution building and to entrepreneurial activity within religion, serving a preservation function that has helped maintain religious traditions and customs in the midst of increasing religious pluralism. Beyond these specifically religious objectives, foundations also direct funding toward activities that reflect religious values, such as community service and international relief and development. Current changes in the relationship between religion and U.S. society do not appear to raise fundamental questions about the role of foundations but do challenge foundation leaders to consider new opportunities and challenges. These developments include possible secularization, changing church-state relationships, increasing pluralism, and globalization.

The philanthropic dollars of private foundations have had several different impacts on the world of religion.[17] Among these, two are particularly prominent—the institutional and the expressive. Institutional impact corresponds to foundation roles of innovation, complementarity, and preservation. In terms of institutional impact, private foundations have funded new organizational forms (such as parachurch groups) and built innovative programs that are part of a larger agenda (such as scholarship programs for young people). Through this, these foundations have fulfilled the innovation role of strategic philanthropy. Their grants complement the income that comes from other funding streams,

17. Although assessing the impact of foundations' philanthropy can be particularly challenging within the realm of religion, where sectarian differences and competing objectives exist, the financial support they provide has shaped both the religious sector and the reception of religious expression within wider society. These twin focuses frame our assessment of foundation impact.

often spurring new initiatives and meeting institutional needs when funds from other sources are insufficient. Through this, private foundations fulfill a role of complementarity—often associated with traditional charity. The Lilly Endowment's significant support of Union Theological Seminary as other funding streams have dried up in recent years is an example of this kind of institutional impact. And as often is the case, this complementary funding seeks to secure the preservation of religious institutions, especially ones within the donor's own tradition.

At the same time, private foundations have also directed grant dollars to support the symbolic-expressive component of religious life. The expressive impact of foundations corresponds to roles of innovation, complementarity, preservation, and social and policy change. The DeMoss Foundation, for example, has directed significant funds to supporting religious expression in the public square, as in its *Power for Living* campaign using celebrity endorsements in support of personal spiritual transformation. Because foundations like DeMoss have such significant and independent asset bases, they have noticeable degrees of freedom to innovate new forms of religious expression. DeMoss was the first to pay for commercials on cable television in which professional athletes and celebrities spoke of their evangelical faith. As in the institutional arena, private foundations fulfilled the strategic philanthropic role of innovation through their support of symbolic-expressive initiatives in mainstream media.

Private foundations also amplified other funding streams, carrying out a role of complementarity. The United Jewish Appeal Federation receives significant support from Jewish foundations, but this merely complements the larger share of funds that come from individual donors. Within this federated system, monies are directed toward maintaining Jewish traditions and customs, reflecting the preservation function of many religious grants. In nearly every case, the religious orientation of the foundation's principal determines the religious branch that receives these preservation dollars, leading to the rise of philanthropic silos across the religious landscape, by which grant recipients resemble one another and the granting foundation in terms of faith tradition. These grants become public symbols for a particular faith as mainstream media make the public aware of these religious expressions. Finally, some foundation initiatives in the symbolic-expressive arena of American religion have worked to produce social and policy change, yet owing to tensions surrounding the separation of church and state, foundation religious activities rarely make major forays into public policy. Regardless, President George W. Bush's faith-based initiatives have provided an opportunity for foundation dollars to be used for programs that advocate certain social and governmental policies.

The theoretical implications suggested by considering the role of foundations in American religion are largely conceptual and underscore the ambiguities involved in determining what counts as a foundation and what does not. Whereas the Lilly Endowment fits the pattern of having been founded by a single family and concerned with making annual gifts from the income derived from its endowment, organizations such as the Baptist Foundation of Arizona or the Foundation for New Era Philanthropy deviate from this pattern. They illustrate the difficulty of drawing a clear line between foundations and donor-advised funds, mutual aid societies, and socially oriented investment opportunities. Because religious causes are often supported by small contributions from large numbers of donors, these alternative patterns may be especially common in the religious realm. At the same time, an important theoretical implication for the study of religion is that elite sources of funding, whether from foundations or individual philanthropists, matter more than is generally acknowledged in studies concerned with the membership, attendance, and giving habits of ordinary religious participants.

For public officials and other policymakers, the role of foundations in American religion is probably an insignificant consideration compared with foundations' place in furthering education, the arts, or social advocacy. Nevertheless, policymakers are increasingly aware of the great extent to which the American public cares about religion and can be mobilized by religious appeals and programs. The Pew Charitable Trusts' initiative to collect and disseminate information about faith-based initiatives illustrates the extent to which a government-funded program may succeed, falter, or simply be ignored, depending on the kind of information made available through foundation funding. Similar activities include the Pew Forum on Religion and Politics and Pew-funded national surveys about religion's relationship to social issues. Whereas Pew officials appear quite comfortable with the public role implied in these programs, other foundations have preferred to distance themselves from potentially controversial policy debates.

Foundation practice is largely oblivious to the centrality of religion in American culture, with the exception of the few foundations that focus a considerable share of their attention on religion. That foundations have been established to promote science, public health, or museums is a reflection of their founders' interests and cannot be criticized insofar as these aims contribute to the broader good of the nation and world. What can legitimately be questioned is whether these interests can be pursued without consideration of their relation to religion. For instance, it is obvious that foundation-funded science raises ethical considerations about which religious people feel deeply, that reproductive and other health-related technologies promoted by foundations evoke both support and opposition from religious communities, and that foundation priorities can either undercut or reinforce the role of religion in higher education. The time when foundation officials could imagine themselves promoting a brave new world in which religion could be relegated to the past clearly has ended. If the role of conservative Protestants in American politics has not made this abundantly clear in recent decades, the rising prominence of Muslims, Hindus, and other groups certainly will do so in the future.

Foundations that do focus on religion must continue to invest their resources strategically. One way to think about strategic investment is to consider those aspects of religion that are unlikely to be funded in other ways. The most costly of these—namely, clergy salaries, construction, building maintenance, and congregational programs—generally do not qualify, except in low-income communities or instances in which start-up funds are needed. Although a few more millions of dollars for salaries and construction are always welcome, these costs are routinely covered by the donations of members themselves. Cutbacks and expansion reflect demographics and other dynamics of the religious marketplace. With an overall tab in the tens of billions of dollars, a few million from foundations would make little difference. A second arena in which foundation funding is unlikely to be of strategic value is the entrepreneurial ministry, especially those earning vast sums from a large constituent base. Prominent megachurch pastor Rick Warren's Purpose Driven Ministries is an example. Having earned tens of millions of dollars from book royalties, including his *Purpose Driven Life,* Warren elected to donate up to 90 percent of his royalties to initiatives related to his organization. These include serving those infected and affected by AIDS, training for church leaders in developing countries, and a global initiative to fight poverty, disease, and illiteracy. With large sums of money already in hand, these entrepreneurial ministries are not likely to need foundation support.

That foundations generally have not invested heavily in church construction, ordinary congregational programs, megachurches, television ministries, or even the kind of faith-based service programs that qualify for government subsidies suggests that program officers have been strategic in their thinking. Foundation funding has instead emphasized three areas in which other support is relatively unavailable. One, illustrated most clearly by the Lilly Endowment, is research. United States government restrictions on collecting information about religion through the Census Bureau, plus government hesitancy about including religion in broader research programs, has meant that nearly all religion research has depended on foundation grants. Some of this support has been of considerable practical value to religious organizations themselves—for instance, in determining clergy needs or anticipating social trends. In addition, research about religion has documented the recent history of religion for future generations, thus serving an archival function much like that of museums and galleries.

A second area, also illustrated by the Lilly Endowment, is leadership training. Leadership has proved to be an important area of strategic investment, both because of its potential for shaping the future of religious organizations and because of the relative paucity of such funding from other sources. A third strategic area is what might be termed start-up costs for innovative religious programs, such as interfaith dialogue centers, urban ministries, and new educational organizations. These are sometimes high-risk ventures that need foundation funding at the start, after which they either fail or continue to prosper through other sources of support. In this way, foundations act as risk absorbers within the religious realm.

Foundations provide a small proportion of the total funding to religious causes, but they are disproportionately influential within American religion. They have incubated new organizational forms and funded novel programs that extend far beyond local congregations. Foundation-based philanthropy has also furthered the symbolic-expressive component of American religion, innovating new kinds of religious discourse as well as alternative distribution channels for religious expression. Even as cultural shifts such as secularization, religious pluralism, and growing demands for accountability have challenged foundations in the religious sector, foundations have drawn upon their strengths as institution builders and capacity developers and become strategists for social change, the effects of which are felt not only within the religious sector but also in wider society.

15

Foundations, Social Movements, and the Contradictions of Liberal Philanthropy

ALICE O'CONNOR

Few issues in the history of organized philanthropy have been as fraught with conflict, controversy, and apparent contradiction as the role of foundations in movements for equal rights, social justice, and political democracy in the twentieth-century United States. Foundations, after all, have been subject to frequent criticism as inherently elite and undemocratic institutions, politically unaccountable, and reliant for their very existence on an economic system that produces huge concentrations of individual and corporate wealth. Run by highly educated professionals and governed by well-networked members of what sociologist C. Wright Mills has memorably called the "power elite," the most prominent hold tremendous, mostly unacknowledged power over the considerably less well heeled constituents of the rights and social justice movements they occasionally subsidize.[1] Such disparities only confirm and reinforce the establishment image that major foundations, ironically by supporting social movements, seem so eager to shed. Meantime, the support that foundations provide for social justice movements has drawn considerable criticism from the political right for being subversive of so-called traditional values or for overstepping the boundaries of a more properly charitable purpose.

Foundation support for social movements also points up uncomfortable contradictions from the philanthropic past. Early philanthropic programs aimed at

---

1. For analyses that put foundations squarely within the networks of the power elite, see Mills (1956) and Domhoff (2006).

"Negro" education and "uplift," for example, were undertaken in the name of "advancing the race." Nevertheless, they upheld and helped to institutionalize the principles of Jim Crow and inferior "industrial" education throughout the South, leaving critics to wonder whether the objective was indeed to make sure the "uplift" only went so far.[2] Northern white philanthropic support for scholarship and higher education similarly, if more subtly, upheld prevailing racial hierarchies and relegated black scholars and institutions to the second tier—much to the frustration of the intended beneficiaries.[3] Early feminist philanthropy was also deeply segregated by race and divided by class, operating less often to empower working-class women than to underscore their dependence on upper-class donors whose interests and ideology differed from their own.[4]

A review of organized philanthropy's role in social movements must also reckon with the fact that in the historic twentieth-century struggles for minority and women's rights, foundations were notoriously behind the curve. With a few notable exceptions, the major campaigns of the interwar and post–World War II black freedom struggle—for equal access to jobs and wages, integrated housing and schools, and elimination of racially motivated restrictions in Social Security, fair labor standards, collective bargaining, and other pillars of the New Deal welfare state—were initiated and orchestrated without substantial funding from the organized, white, and at that point overwhelmingly male-dominated philanthropic sector.[5]

Far more significant than even the crucial support from progressive white philanthropies such as the Garland Fund (to establish the NAACP's first legal defense fund in the 1920s) were the thousands of small donations raised on the local "chicken and greens circuit" and through black churches and targeted publicity campaigns.[6] The larger and most prominent foundations—even, indeed especially, those that presented themselves as being in the vanguard of social reform—were exceedingly cautious when it came to challenging the racial status quo until well into the 1960s. Here, as in the struggle for women's rights, foundations came in with major and explicit support only after these movements had gained a degree of public acceptance and political legitimacy, and, crucially, had built up the activist networks and coalitions to translate years of organizing

2. Gaines (1996); Kluger (1976, p. 392); Woodson (1931).

3. See, for example, comments by W. E. B. DuBois quoted in Jackson (1990, p. 25) and by E. Franklin Frazier (1957, pp. 96–97).

4. Gordon (1991); Kirkby (1992).

5. Among the major works on the black freedom struggle that emphasize the centrality of economic as well as social and political rights are Hamilton and Hamilton (1997); MacLean (2006); Jackson (2007); Goluboff (2007). On foundation reluctance to join the struggle to make racial inequity a major issue in social welfare reform, see Mittelstadt (2005, pp. 69–106).

6. Boyle (2004, pp. 203–06); Kluger (1976, pp. 221–26).

and advocacy into concrete legislative gains.[7] When the leading foundations did come in with more substantial support for the civil rights movement in the 1960s, that support remained heavily concentrated in what to more progressive and grassroots movement leaders appeared to be the important but comparatively safe vehicles such as voter education, policy analysis and advocacy, leadership training, and public interest law.[8]

Nevertheless, the notion that foundations can play, have played, and should play a leading role in making the United States a more just and democratic society—and specifically, in advocating the interests of minorities, women, poor people, and otherwise disadvantaged or underrepresented groups—has become a central tenet among the leadership of mainstream organized philanthropy since the 1960s. Then, pressed by a widening range of social movements, alarmed by the explosion of protest and racial violence, and subject to investigation from congressional critics left and right, foundation leaders began to invoke their support for freedom and equality movements as a warrant for official, public sanction of private philanthropic wealth. Funding streams that had hitherto been the province of a handful of smaller, often family-run foundations were swelled by the entry of the philanthropic giants, led by the Ford, Rockefeller, and Carnegie foundations, as well as a number of less prominent funds.

While never more than a tiny percentage of overall foundation giving (slightly more than 1 percent in 1990 and today), given the simultaneous growth in the sector itself, the major expansion that started in the 1960s brought considerably greater funds: according to the most systematic studies, from less than $100,000 in the mid-1950s, on the eve of the Montgomery, Alabama, bus boycott, to $88 million in 1990 and $346 million in 2001 (in current dollars).[9] Equally important, funding for civil rights and social justice became a recognized, increasingly institutionalized and professionalized part of the philanthropic repertoire. The image of foundations as a force for social justice, equal rights, and even social change has since been embraced as a point of pride and self-definition by a sector that has come to think of and characterize itself as a significant "third force" in American life. For this, the big, generally liberal foundations have earned the undying enmity of the conservative right, whose leading grassroots outpost, the National Conservative Union, continues to monitor the activities of the foundations it labeled the "financiers of revolution" in 1969.[10]

7. On the timing of major foundation support for the civil rights and women's movements, see Jenkins and Halci (1999, pp. 247–55); Goss (2007, pp. 1182–86).

8. Haines (1984); Jenkins (1998); Marquez (2003).

9. Jenkins and Halci (1999, pp. 230–39); chapter 16, this volume.

10. O'Connor (2006, pp. 244–45). The conservative Capital Research Center, established in 1984 to target nonprofit organizations "that promote the growth of government," maintains a monthly newsletter entitled "Foundation Watch" (www.capitalresearch.org/pubs/index.html?t=5 [November 24, 2009]).

In this chapter I seek to make sense of (which is not to say resolve) the tensions and apparent contradictions in the historical relationship between foundations and social movements while also providing a framework for understanding foundations' varied roles in promoting movement goals. Aimed more at developing a conceptual and historical framework than at measuring the impact of foundation support (an issue taken up in the next chapter by Debra Minkoff and Jon Agnone), my analysis traces shifts in the overall pattern of foundation funding—and in the relationship between social movements and organized philanthropy—at three critical junctures in social movement politics. Clearly, the second of the junctures I consider, the 1960s, was a major turning point in drawing more, and more overt, foundation support for movement goals. And yet, by taking a longer historical perspective, I aim to consider such major shifts in foundation support for social movements in the broader context of a political culture that has veered dramatically—and not always in progressive directions— in its receptivity to the demands of civil rights, feminist, and labor movement organizations as well as to affirmative government measures to promote social and economic equity.

Philanthropic support for civil rights and social justice movements can be viewed as part of a larger historical project that was deeply conflicted, if not contradictory at its core: the project of continually reinventing twentieth-century liberalism as at once a program of broad-based political, economic, and—especially after midcentury—social and cultural reform and also as the embodiment of a more limited ideological, institutional, political, and cultural consensus that, especially as the cold war against communism reached its height, was defined around a shared commitment to capitalism, political democracy, cultural pluralism, and a mildly redistributive welfare state. It was a project that both motivated and delimited foundations in their engagement with civil rights and social justice movements while putting leading foundations at odds with the more radical, confrontational, and direct action aspects of movement politics.

In their role as arbiters of liberalism, the largest and most prominent foundations positioned themselves both as agents of accommodation—between corporate capitalism and the liberal welfare state, social movements and the political establishment—and as agents of change.[11] Operating as much out of ideological and institutional as of a discernible class interest, the country's largest and most prominent foundations established themselves as important influences in the post–World War II "rights revolution" and, more significantly, in shaping the pluralistic, rights- and identity-based social and political liberalism within which movements for equal rights and social justice would find mainstream access, legitimacy, and avenues for reform. In turn, the civil and social rights liberalism

11. On foundations as accommodating the relationship between capitalism and the welfare state, see O'Connor (2006); on foundations as change agents, see O'Connor (1999).

embraced by the major foundations in the 1960s sought to respond to and accommodate the demands of social movements while also containing them: within an ideological frame anchored in commitments to nominally color- and gender-blind cultural and political pluralism and within a politics that emphasized gradualism over militancy, litigation and legislation over protest, and individual and group access to the benefits of the existing political and economic system over structural reform.

The result was a relationship in which foundations, late and reluctant as they were to provide direct, movement-building support, instead exercised their influence on the course of social movements indirectly and through interventions that reflected the essential conflicts and contradictions of their simultaneously accommodative and confining task. It was a relationship, moreover, in which the philanthropic encounter with the postwar African American civil rights movement proved foundational (so to speak), both in capturing the tensions and in generating a template for philanthropic activism that would later be applied to other groups and in other areas (environment, gender, and sexuality, for example) of movement activism. The resulting template was historically more rights-than social justice–oriented; positioned liberal foundations more prominently as legitimators, institution builders, and professionalizers than as either an intellectual vanguard or a movement-building force; and engaged foundations in indirect efforts to influence values, public discourse, and political culture more than in such overtly movement-building activities as community organizing or political mobilizing.

It is all the more ironic, then, that the funding strategies that emerged from this indirect and often ambivalent relationship between liberal foundations and social justice movements should provide a template for two very different forms of movement philanthropy that have emerged over the past three decades as self-conscious alternatives to the more mainstream foundations and their approach to social change. In one, the aim was to transcend the comparatively cautious, apolitical veneer of the major liberal foundations to provide support for the direct action and organizing activities the establishment foundations were reluctant to pursue. Such more explicitly left or progressive movement funders as the Haymarket People's Fund tended also to be more deliberatively democratic and grassroots in their own organization, in contrast to the more top-down hierarchies of their liberal counterparts.[12] In the other, explicitly conservative movement philanthropy, the aim was, paradoxically, even more radical and self-consciously revolutionary than for its progressive counterparts: no less than to dethrone liberalism—and specifically the very civil rights, feminist, environmentalist, and other expressions of movement liberalism the most prominent foundations had come

12. Ostrander (1995, 1999).

to stand for since the 1960s—as the reigning orthodoxy of the day. Although developed very much and very consciously in opposition to what its chief strategists saw as rights-and-advocacy philanthropy, the conservative foundation movement achieved its most significant successes using funding strategies borrowed from the liberal left to pursue a rights-based agenda of its own.

Foundation Roles in Social Movements

To understand the complex role foundations have historically played in social movements, it is helpful to distinguish between foundation support for the goals and institutions of social movements, on the one hand, and explicitly movement philanthropy, on the other. In the former, a comparatively small number of foundations came to embrace movement goals as part of a broader commitment to what might loosely be called social betterment—and indeed as an indicator of the changing meaning of that overly generalized term. In the latter, an even smaller number of foundations have dedicated themselves to an explicit and more overtly politicized movement-building agenda. Although they are usually associated with the liberal left in discussions of social movement philanthropy, in this chapter I argue for a more expanded conceptualization of these movement funders to include foundations that have aligned themselves with the political and ideological right.

This distinction between movement philanthropy and philanthropy that supports movement goals points to the degree to which social movement funding has taken foundations out of, or at least pushed at the limits of, their traditional roles. Those roles, conceptualized throughout this volume as involving charity (complementarity and substitution) on the one hand and philanthropy (innovation and policy change) on the other, are not always so easily distinguishable in the foundation engagement with social movements. Thus in the context of the Jim Crow South, even grant making that remained safely within the confines of racially segregated charity could be discerned as a potentially subversive act—if for no other reason than that it funneled resources to deliberately disenfranchised, resource-starved African American communities. Nevertheless, the distinction between more traditional charity and philanthropy is apt, in that it parallels an important and ever-lingering tension in the way foundations have approached social movements in a relationship that over the course of the post–World War II decades has expanded the role of foundations from self-appointed agents of traditional uplift to self-described agents of social change. Within this general framework of shifting yet frequently overlapping roles, foundations aimed to bring the movements they funded into the political and cultural mainstream even as they tried to reshape mainstream values and institutions through support for a more expansive vision of civil and social rights and of the role of government in protecting and enforcing them.

It is also important to recognize the degree to which engaging with civil rights and social justice movements drew foundations into unfamiliar territory—where, at least momentarily, those holding the purse strings could not always rely on what they understood to be their unique advantages and certainly could not readily predict the political forces their interventions might unleash. To be sure, in promoting the values of civil rights and social justice, foundations relied extensively on such familiar strategies as social research, institution building, and public education and more generally on building resources within the realm of civil society. But meaningful social change, especially in light of stubborn and organized resistance, would require more and would confront foundations with the question of just how direct a political role and just how much political risk they were willing and able to absorb. Only occasionally did foundations venture to position themselves as agents of change and risk absorbers by providing direct support for a variety of community and political empowerment strategies in the 1960s. By the 1980s, in an atmosphere of political reaction and federal retreat from active civil rights enforcement, foundations, like the social movements they funded, found themselves once again in a defensive mode, leaving less room for experimentation and insisting on a more traditional philanthropic role, this time of backstopping increasingly diminished public resources with private support.

Finally, it is important to recognize that foundations have historically sought to engage with social movements at least in part through their own readiness— or reluctance—to themselves be influenced and to some degree reformed by the values and principles of the movements they support. With increasing assertiveness since the 1980s, foundations positioned themselves as moral standard bearers of sorts—within the nonprofit sector if not in society writ large—embracing the cultural values of racial and ethnic diversity, gender equity, social tolerance, and inclusiveness in their own institutional practices and in the institutional practices they required of grantees (for example, minority representation on boards and staff).[13]

According to comprehensive surveys conducted in the early and late 1990s, the results of such efforts were reflected in substantially higher representations of women and racial minorities in professional foundation positions than in other fields. Here again, though, foundations have come up against, and publicly struggled with, the limits of political capacity and will. Those same surveys revealed far more limited diversity gains on boards of directors and among chief executive officers, particularly for racial minorities, while qualitative surveys raised serious questions about whether advances in numbers have translated into more genuinely representative decisionmaking and lines of authority.[14] Sectorwide diversity

13. Frumkin (1999, pp. 82–83).
14. Kasper, Ramos, and Walker (2004).

measures also encountered unexpected, and at least somewhat organized, opposition from a number of conservative foundations, which cited affirmative action standards endorsed by the Council on Foundations, along with its so-called liberal bias, in breaking from the organization in the early 1980s.[15] Nor, as critics on the left have pointed out, did visible moves among foundations to embrace the values of social justice movements necessarily extend to equalizing the relationship between grantor and grantee.

Yet much as we might explain the various roles, capacities, and limitations of foundations in terms of their internal features or structural position within the polity, they need also be understood as having been shaped and driven by the changing dynamics of the major civil rights and social justice movements in their own struggles to gain legitimacy, voice, political power, and organizational stability—and to use foundation funds toward those ends. By the same token, foundation involvement with social movements was also shaped, limited, and at times facilitated by the changing political environment, particularly by widely varying degrees of receptivity to movement goals on the part of key government actors and agencies. It is in this light, and focusing principally on the postwar African American civil rights movement, that I view the changing roles and contributions of foundations as inextricably tied to the conflicting pulls within liberalism at critical junctures in movement history.

From Uplift to Rights

Judging from the sector as a whole and the volume of funders and dollars, the 1960s proved pivotal in the emergence of a social change orientation in organized philanthropy. Important changes had begun earlier, however, starting with the foundation role in an initial, post–World War II shift in the public framing of the "race question" to emphasize civil rights and political democracy alongside, if not in place of, more traditional racial uplift. What made the moment ripe was a combination of factors, most profoundly the searing contradiction posed by a segregationist United States, with a segregated army, assuming a position of leadership in the worldwide fight against Nazism—a fight for the very principles of freedom and democracy denied to racial minorities at home. African American civil rights activists had made the most of the contradiction, launching the Double V (victory abroad, victory at home) campaign. Largely ignored in the New Deal reform agenda, movement leaders allied with labor to demand equal treatment in wartime jobs, if not in housing, achieving at least temporary gains with the creation of the Fair Employment Practice Committee in 1940. Calls for racial equality were also bolstered by the massive demographic

15. Miller (2006, pp. 128–33).

and economic transformations wrought by wartime migrations that brought millions of African Americans to industrial jobs in the major manufacturing centers in the urban North, Midwest, and West. Those transformations were also stirring all-too-familiar racial fears, leading to violent outbreaks in Detroit, New York, and Los Angeles, among other major cities, and bringing the "race problem" to the fore nationwide.

Within this alternately hopeful and volatile context, the Garland Fund, governed since its creation in 1922 by a multiracial board of left-liberal activists, remained virtually unique in its willingness to fund civil rights activism directly. Others, however, including the Julius Rosenwald Fund and, more famously, the Carnegie Corporation of New York, found a more comfortable and indirect venue in efforts to bring research and social scientific understanding to the visibly changing "Negro problem"—albeit not necessarily with the intention of supporting the movement for civil rights, jobs, and freedom. Intentionally or not, such efforts did involve foundations in laying out the contours of a more socially egalitarian, rights-oriented racial liberalism than could be accommodated within the confines of an earlier racial uplift ideology. Especially important in this regard was the support foundations offered to a way of framing the problem of racial (although, notably, not class) inequality as itself a contradiction—of the American dream, of the promise of postwar affluence, and most resoundingly, of the American creed of freedom and democracy. By taking it upon themselves— or turning to outside "experts" rather than to movement activists—to formulate America's contradictory problems, dilemmas, and paradoxes as crises of conscience, foundations lent urgency and sanction to movement grievances but also kept those grievances in check. They also, not coincidentally, framed the issues in ways that were amenable to philanthropic as well as liberal policy intervention and that ultimately proved influential in public policy debates.

For this among other reasons, no philanthropic act of framing was more influential in the future course of rights-based liberalism than Gunnar Myrdal's Carnegie Corporation–funded *An American Dilemma* (1944). Although few subsequent projects matched it in ambition and scope, that massive social scientific reformulation of the "Negro problem" effectively created the rhetorical and strategic template for innumerable subsequent appeals to conscience and action. Equally important, by framing the "Negro problem" as a series of overlapping pathologies—irrational white racial attitudes and the economic and cultural isolation they fomented—Myrdal's tome offered a kind of political and cultural reassurance that would also reverberate in later expressions of rights-based liberalism: that the source of the dilemma lay in the hearts and minds, individual attitudes and actions, of white Americans; that racial inequality could be rooted out by awakening white Americans to the necessity of applying, rather than fundamentally revising, the basic tenets of the American creed; and that eliminating discriminatory barriers to opportunity could be accomplished without recourse to radical change in existing political institutions or economy. In this emphasis, with its implicit critique of very powerful, more militant voices within the movement, *An American Dilemma* proved a harbinger for later foundation interventions that sought to strengthen the hand of movement moderates and integrationists against the emergence of black power activists.[16]

From Protest to Politics

For more than a decade following its original publication, however, the limited and indirect engagement with civil rights activism brought by *An American Dilemma* did not sit well with the Carnegie Corporation, which did virtually nothing to follow up on the study's implications and continued to treat it as a rigorous, politically neutral statement of social scientific fact.[17] While such distancing did not stave off a steady barrage of right-wing attack, it does suggest the extraordinary caution with which even the best endowed foundations, those presumably best suited to be bold and independent, approached the issue of race through the 1950s. Such was the case as well with the largest and newest of the philanthropic giants, the Ford Foundation, which for most of the decade kept its race-related funding off-site and under the auspices of separately created intermediaries.[18] Extreme caution, if not downright resistance, was certainly the tone set by federal officials: having sparked a segregationist split within the Democratic Party in the 1948 presidential race, President Harry S. Truman's civil rights platform (which called for an end to discrimination in employment, housing, voting rights, and other vital areas of social and political life) remained dormant; in the aftermath of the 1954 *Brown* v. *Board of Education* decision, the Eisenhower administration proved reluctant to take a stance against organized resistance in the South.

It was not until a second critical juncture in movement politics in the 1960s, from "protest to politics" to borrow Bayard Rustin's famous phrase, that the unspoken taboo was officially broken, and large as well as smaller foundations visibly stepped in with support for civil rights litigation, policy analysis, advocacy, and reform.[19] Once again, such intervention came at a moment filled with hope, based on the mass mobilizations and legislative achievements the movement had been able to sustain. While there was much to be done and substantial

16. Myrdal, Sterner, and Rose (1944); Jackson (1990); Lagemann (1989); O'Connor (2001, chap. 3; 2002).

17. Lagemann (1989, p. 146).

18. Raynor (1999, pp. 201–06); O'Connor (1999).

19. Bayard Rustin, "From Protest to Politics: The Future of the Civil Rights Movement," *Harper's*, February 1965.

political differences remained, President Lyndon B. Johnson's Great Society put federal government more in sync with movement liberals than at any time since post–Civil War Reconstruction. But it was also a moment filled with tension and trepidation—both within the movement and within the liberal establishment that had lent its support—based on divisions and growing radicalization among activists as well as the ever-looming threat of racial violence and political backlash. In this context, foundations positioned themselves to facilitate the movement's shift in focus from grassroots organizing and mass protest to legislative politics and policy in a number of ways.

One was by supporting movement-generated policies, strategies, and programs that sought to use existing institutions of law, civil society, the market, and, especially, the federal legislature and courts as vehicles for social change. Foundation support for civil rights and advocacy organizations, in turn, helped to underwrite increasingly expansive visions of political and social (if not economic) rights while laying the groundwork for extending rights-based strategies to welfare, feminist, environmental, and other arenas of movement activism. In all of these interventions, foundation grants helped to underwrite and strengthen what, in the radicalized atmosphere of the middle to late 1960s, were emerging as the more moderate voices within social movements.[20] Meantime, in a host of community-based programs aimed at addressing the root causes of racially concentrated poverty and disadvantage, Ford and other foundations sought to deflect growing militancy, in part by funding nominally apolitical, consensus-based avenues to empowerment that emphasized social services, job training, economic development, and variations on what has more recently come to be referred to as building social capital as a means of opening access to mainstream opportunities.[21]

A second major channel for philanthropic support of social movements was creating, and opening access to, a more pluralistic political and public sphere. Here again, building on activist networks that emerged through the earlier course of movement work, foundations invested extensively in voter education as a legislatively sanctioned approach to expanding the minority and women's vote.[22] Foundations also provided extensive funding to create a more established, formalized minority and women's political and policy sector—one that, in the

20. Haines (1984); Jenkins and Eckert (1986); Lagemann (1989, pp. 248–52); Jenkins and Halci (1999, pp. 239–41); MacLean (2006, pp. 270–71, 292–93). On efforts to build on the law and legislative gains for various movement purposes, see Davis (1993) and Handler (1978).

21. O'Connor (1996); Countryman (2006, pp. 120–30); Ferguson (2007).

22. In the wake of tightened restrictions on political activity imposed by the Tax Reform Act of 1969, foundations steered clear of voter registration or related activities that could be construed to influence the outcome of elections in favor of more broad-gauged educational programs.

eyes of critics, lost touch with the needs and priorities of its working-class and locally based constituents.

As such criticism suggests, foundation funding streams fed into tensions within movement politics that became more exaggerated with growth and institutionalization. They also favored more moderate, professional development and leadership-building strategies over grassroots organizing and training.[23] Premised on a pluralistic interest-group model of political representation and influence, philanthropic support favored political moderation in other ways as well, emphasizing change from within existing institutions and through conventional rather than more confrontational modes of political participation and representation. It is somewhat ironic, then, that in other, more academically focused expressions of philanthropic support for introducing movement values and ideas into the public sphere, foundations—deliberately or not—helped to underwrite the development and institutionalization of the feminist, ethnic studies, and critical legal scholarship that challenged the premises of pluralism.[24]

Third and more generally, through these and other initiatives foundations provided support for a host of institutions within civil society—and, indirectly, within the liberal state—variously established to fight for, extend, implement, and ultimately to defend movement gains and goals. While most readily apparent in the vast expansion of such professional social movement organizations as legal defense funds, public interest law firms, policy research and advocacy institutes, the institutionalization and professionalization of movement activity can also be seen in the post-1960s reconfiguration of foundation program areas to include programs to promote equal rights and opportunities for minorities, women, and the disadvantaged as well as such causes as environmental justice. Through such program areas, moreover, foundations became sources of social and cultural as well as financial capital for the networks of professional individuals and public and private agencies that would pursue movement work within establishment venues.

In each of these ways, foundations played a role in creating the space—ideological, discursive, institutional, political—for legitimating but also for what the sociologist Craig Jenkins refers to as "channeling" and containing the more radical implications of movement activism.[25] Foundation programs, for example, tended to segment the struggle for civil and social rights from that for economic rights, equality, and justice while focusing more heavily on institution building and professionalization than on organizing or other grassroots, rank-and-file

23. Marquez (2003, p. 332).
24. See, for example, Proietto (1999).
25. Jenkins (1998).

movement-building strategies. Indeed, foundations generally proved wary of confronting the class dimensions of movement work and either sidestepped or ignored the intersecting disparities of status and power embedded in their own relationships with movement petitioners and grantees.

At the same time, with stepped-up support for a widening range of rights and advocacy organizations beginning in the 1960s, foundations also created the space for rechanneling considerable amounts of philanthropic wealth into social movements, in the process reconceptualizing organized philanthropy's role in liberal democratic society as an agent not merely of social amelioration but of social change. In this rechanneling, to be sure, foundations hardly spoke with one voice, differing not only on appropriate methods for promoting equal rights and social justice but also on whether philanthropy should involve itself in the struggle at all.

Such differences were among the motives for the emergence of networks of self-consciously alternative, progressive, or social movement funders and funding networks beginning in the 1960s and 1970s—generally distinguished from their more mainstream counterparts by their willingness to fund direct action and political organizing, by their emphasis on "change, not charity," and by their attentiveness to democratizing the relationship between patron and grantee organizations.[26] Among the earliest and most prominent of these alternative funders were the Haymarket People's Fund, the Tides Foundation, the Funding Exchange, and a number of community-based funders associated with the National Network of Grantmakers. Notably, many of these funds eschewed the traditional single-donor model in favor of more cooperative and collaborative funding networks and community-based funds with multiple donors. They were also more willing to acknowledge, and consciously to question if not entirely to transcend, disparities in power and perspective embedded in the traditional philanthropic relationship. At their most alternative, such funds have brought grantees more fully into the priority-setting and grant-making process.

Still, for all their differences, progressive and more mainstream foundations operate in sync in basic respects; indeed, in what could be seen as an act of co-optation—or of pluralistic tolerance—the philanthropic establishment expresses respect and appreciation for the alternative funding movement, ceding to it, as if in tacit agreement, the riskier movement grant-making that mainstream foundations are unwilling to take on.[27] In this regard, it is not surprising that such major multiracial and ground-up movements as those for living wages and immigrant rights have looked more to alternative than to mainstream philanthropic

---

26. Jenkins and Halci (1999, pp. 234–39); Ostrander (1995). "Change, not charity" is a catch-phrase used by the Funding Exchange. See www.fex.org.

27. See, for example, Goldberg (2002).

funding networks for support. The emergence of progressive movement philanthropy underscores the deeply, historically contested nature of the relationship between organized philanthropy and civil rights and social justice movements. On the one hand, movement philanthropy seeks to use foundations (like the law, traditionally conservative institutions) to push rights and justice agendas toward aspects of the status quo otherwise unchallenged by the philanthropic mainstream. On the other, it uses the principles and values of civil rights and social justice movements to push foundations into confronting and changing the practices within the philanthropic sector that perpetuate inequality.

From Politics to Consolidation

Operating as moderating influences though they might be, foundation grants for social movement organizations were increasingly sought-after resources by the late 1960s and 1970s, both for the financial stability and for the legitimacy they seemed to promise. And they were beginning to show considerable institutional effects beyond the fate of particular organizations or movements, playing a part in establishing an expanding, diverse, and at times internally conflicted organizational sector committed to representing the interests of historically disenfranchised groups and incorporating the values of equal rights and diversity into the broader political culture.[28] At the same time, and at least in part thanks to the kind of institutional learning foundation grants promoted, growing numbers of organized constituencies were competing for the still relatively small proportion of philanthropic dollars available for the kinds of advocacy, analytic, litigation, and public outreach projects foundations were wont to fund.

Much was at stake, then, both for foundations and for social movement organizations, when the very existence of a civil rights and social justice "establishment" became fodder in the polarizing political and culture wars that accompanied the conservative counterrevolution in the closing decades of the twentieth century and threatened to bring the momentum of rights and social justice liberalism to a halt.[29] Facing new and renewed battles over rights once considered to have been won, foundations and grantees alike turned more to protecting and consolidating past gains than to funding innovative change agendas (as discussed in the following chapter, by Debra Minkoff and Jon Agnone).

Equally significant in this period of social movement funding was the wholly unanticipated emergence of a new expression of movement philanthropy that openly contributed to a well-mobilized, ideologically and politically conservative

28. Minkoff (1997).

29. For more on the conservative counterrevolution and its impact on philanthropy, see O'Connor (2007).

campaign against liberalism in all but its presumably classical free-market forms. This still-ongoing campaign, ironically, uses the approaches and models culti- vated by the civil rights–feminist–environmentalist establishment as a template for a much different kind of rights-based, social movement philanthropy that has proved far more radically alternative than any challenge from the left. More- over, professedly conservative-movement philanthropy gained considerable trac- tion beginning in the 1980s with the election of President Ronald Reagan by organizing its work around two complementary goals. One was to "defund" the left by advocating a massive withdrawal of government support for legal services, public interest advocacy, civil rights enforcement, and the welfare state more generally.[30] The other, more ambitious, was to mount an aggressive counterof- fensive against the "rights revolution" by building an alternative infrastructure of conservative thought, jurisprudence, "private"-interest law, legal defense funds, policy advocacy, and public policy think tanks. Indeed, operating with fewer resources and over a shorter time period than the major liberal foundations, conservative-movement philanthropy mounted a virtual counterrevolution in rights-based advocacy, this one based on the defense of "traditional" cultural values, strictly color-blind social policy, and above all, individual and property rights. This marked, in effect, a return to an older rights-based liberalism in which there is no contradiction between inequality and political democracy.

The origins of this counterrevolution are deeply rooted in the history of the post–World War II, anti–New Deal, and hard-line anticommunist right. Much like their early civil rights counterparts, the foundations anchoring initial phil- anthropic support for the movement were few and far between, visible chiefly to movement activists and often focused on targeted goals such as preserving free-market economics within the academy or distributing anticommunist man- ifestos to legions of "suburban [cold] warriors."[31] But the key period of mobili- zation that channeled right-wing opposition into a conservative philanthropic movement started in the 1970s. That was when elite groups of conservative activists set out to mobilize the grass tops, as it were, in an unapologetically top-down effort to redirect philanthropic wealth to more "pro-American"—and procapitalist—causes. Although not necessarily—again, like their progressive counterparts—speaking with one voice, they were united in their opposition to the so-called liberal establishment and found common cause for protest against philanthropic "social engineers."

McGeorge Bundy, the Ford Foundation's president (from 1966 to 1979) and a national security adviser in the Kennedy and Johnson administrations, proved

---

30. On defunding the left, see Himmelstein and Zald (1984); Esther Kaplan, "Follow the Money," *The Nation,* November 1, 2004.

31. Van Horn and Mirowski (2009); McGirr (2001).

an especially potent target in this regard: having already come under fire for backing the foundation's move into unprecedented (albeit, by some lights, limited) degrees of activism in civil rights, environmentalism, and public interest law, Bundy was still presiding when Henry Ford II resigned from the board in 1977, citing the staff's disengagement from the foundation's capitalist roots. Few episodes, it seems, could do more to confirm what conservatives had long been charging than to have Bundy's foundation, the ultimate symbol of the Ivy League liberal establishment, unmasked as a bastion of collectivism. In the annals of conservative philanthropy, moreover, Henry Ford's resignation is considered one of the central events in galvanizing a more energized opposition.[32] Yet Bundy's activism became something of a backhanded inspiration in other ways as well, as an emblem of how foundations could institutionalize and move forward a political agenda outside the standard venues of political accountability.[33]

Indeed, in calling for and organizing an alternative philanthropic force, conservative movement activists sounded contradictory themes. One was that liberal philanthropy had overstepped its bounds, both in straying from traditional charity and, especially, in violating donor intent with funding for progressive causes.[34] The other, more directly significant for purposes of this chapter, was that conservatives had to be more aggressive about using their own philanthropic resources to promote limited government, free enterprise, hard-line anticommunism, "traditional" family values, and individualism as prevailing political norms. For this, of course, conservative foundations proved eminently willing and able to break out of their charitable roles, embracing the tools of social change philanthropy to build a decidedly alternative organizational sector and to cultivate the political class to carry out its goals. In the process, they surely complicated the meaning of "social movement philanthropy," if not redefining it, not in the least by using the nominally apolitical tools of liberal philanthropy to turn the political tides against liberalism in several ways.

Among the most important of these was to reframe the core issues that animated the major twentieth-century civil rights and social justice movements, ironically by appropriating the rights-based language and logic of liberal movement culture and turning it on liberalism itself. Nowhere was this more evident than with reference to what scholars and writers from across the political spectrum took to calling a "new American dilemma" in the 1980s and early 1990s, in debates about a presumably new form of racial inequality, the "urban underclass."[35] Elsewhere, much has been written about the origins and ideological

32. On Bundy's tenure at the Ford Foundation, see Bird (1998, pp. 376–95). On Ford's resignation inspiring conservative philanthropic organizing, see Miller (2006, pp. 188–90).

33. James Piereson, "You Get What You Pay For," *Wall Street Journal,* July 21, 2004.

34. Lienesch (1993, pp. 124–38); Bork and Nielsen (1993).

35. Glenn Loury, "The New American Dilemma," *New Republic,* December 31, 1984, pp. 14–18.

complexities of this debate.[36] What is most relevant here is the work of such foundation-backed conservative writers as Charles Murray and Dinesh D'Souza to use the debate as a venue for challenging what they deemed to be liberal conventional wisdom: first, by declaring all but the tiniest and most recalcitrant vestiges of white racism to be a thing of the past; second, and related, by holding postwar and especially Great Society liberalism responsible for having coddled a whole complex of behavioral and cultural "pathologies" that were said to be the true source of enduring inequality.

Indeed, in the inversions that continue to reverberate in contemporary political discourse, liberalism was demonized as the source of a "new racism" that held nonwhites to lower standards and singled them out for preferential treatment. Affirmative action, by the same token, was a violation of the true intentions of color-blind civil rights.[37] Such contentions, in turn, became the basis of conservative "civil rights initiatives" across the country aimed at dismantling affirmative action and related antidiscriminatory government interventions, as well as at challenging the underlying legal, legislative, and policy edifice that liberal foundations relied on as the vehicle for achieving movement goals.

A similar appropriation of the values of liberal rights and social justice movements can be seen in conservative efforts to insist on, and in some instances to legislate, ideological as opposed to race, gender, and cultural diversity in such presumably orthodox liberal holdouts as public universities. Far more effective in this regard, however, has been the longer-term work of conservative foundations toward building a dense and proliferating array of explicitly conservative movement organizations within civil society. In recent years many of these organizations, including the religious, culturally conservative Focus on the Family and the antigovernment National Taxpayers Union, have drawn attention for their ties to the conservative political establishment. Similarly, organizations such as the Federalist Society, the National Right to Work Legal Defense Foundation, and a number of regional conservative public interest law firms—established and sustained with the help of conservative foundation grants—have been credited with laying the groundwork for the "counterrevolution" in law and jurisprudence favoring individual, corporate, and property rights.[38]

But more striking within the historical framework of philanthropy and social movements is the degree to which these organizations have come to constitute an alternative, oppositional, foundation-sponsored organizational sphere for the wide-ranging conservative movement establishment that has come to dominate much of political life. Thus in addition to the proliferation of the kinds of

36. Katz (1993); O'Connor (2001).

37. Charles Murray, "Affirmative Racism: How Preferential Treatment Works against Blacks," *New Republic,* December 31, 1984, pp. 18–23; D'Souza (1996); O'Connor (2004).

38. Miller (2006, pp. 88–102).

advocacy, legal defense, and public outreach organizations through which liberal foundations have funneled their movement work, conservative foundations have made a huge investment in public policy think tanks—the Heritage Foundation, the Cato Institute, the American Enterprise Institute, and the Hudson Institute are perhaps the best known—that have played an integral part as the self-appointed intelligentsia of the counterrevolution. While hardly the first and hardly alone in using such organizations to advance a policy agenda, conservative foundations were far more explicit than their postwar counterparts in acknowledging and focusing on the ideological and political nature of such work—and in positioning philanthropy not as a politically or ideologically neutral agent but as itself a movement-building and movement-mobilizing force.

The extraordinary success of this conservative philanthropic counteroffensive points back to a lingering contradiction in the relationship between liberal foundations and the movements for civil rights and social justice they fund. For in positioning themselves as politically and ideologically neutral protectors of the public interest, all but the more explicitly progressive foundations have proved reluctant to challenge the rightward shift in public discourse, social philosophy, and political culture that has done so much to undermine the legitimacy of civil rights and social justice movements and of the rights-based liberalism that, however partially and inadequately, sought to bring their values into the political mainstream. At the very least, this raises difficult questions that liberal foundations have been reluctant to address: can they be fully supportive of movements for civil rights and social justice without engaging more directly in these deeply political and ideological debates? Is the emphasis on consolidation, discussed in chapter 16 of this volume, a sign of a deeper aversion to political risk? Although the historical record would provide support for this conclusion, it also offers a further insight: that such caution was not organizationally or institutionally inbred but instead stemmed from political and ideological proscriptions that themselves were subject to change.

Conclusions

Other conclusions can be drawn from this historical overview that speak to the broader nature of foundations' relationship to social movements and support for their goals. First, organized philanthropy's roles and contributions have not occurred in a historical vacuum. What foundations have been able or willing to contribute (or not) to civil rights and social justice movements has shifted considerably over time, as much in response to changes in the political climate and movement dynamics as in response to shifts within foundations themselves. Nor have foundations been above or immune to the internal politics of the movements they fund. Each of these factors has variously limited and created opportunities for grant programs—as have the structural shifts in political economy that affect the shape of inequality over time.

Second, the contributions or influence foundations have had on social movements have not always been a reflection of intent. While unintended consequences (good and bad) abound in virtually all areas of foundation grant making, in the case of social movements in particular they have generated an ongoing, historically rooted tension in the way foundations have carved out their role as change agents, the consequences of which are discussed in chapter 16. Third, although measurements of foundations' efficacy in funding social movements are subject to dispute, for civil rights and social justice movement activists, in particular, the credibility and legitimacy of foundations as social movement funders has been affected by their willingness to incorporate the values of diversity, equity, and inclusiveness into their own institutional practices.

Finally, although the historical mobilization of conservative foundations points to philanthropy's potential as an oppositional force, the leverage that foundations have been able to exercise as movement funders at particular historical moments has been tremendously affected by the political priorities of elected governmental officials and their willingness to ally themselves with movement goals. The most effective movement funders have taken this into account: not, to be sure, by pulling back in the face of an adverse political establishment but by anticipating future moments of expanded political possibility with resources for activists to develop more innovative change agendas.

16

Consolidating Social Change: The Consequences of Foundation Funding for Developing Social Movement Infrastructures

DEBRA MINKOFF AND JON AGNONE

T he crux of the dilemma regarding social movement philanthropy is that despite expressed good intentions, foundation funding for social movements is thought to be inherently conservative, channeling movement groups in more moderate directions with the consequence that social dissent is diffused.[1] One version of this narrative posits that such heavy-handedness on the part of foundation funders is a more or less explicit strategy as they seek to ensure social stability and thus their elite standing in society. A different account, which leads to roughly the same result, is that the moderating influence of foundation support reflects the tendency of all organizations (and nonprofits in particular) to adopt conventional structures and practices to meet the expectations of major organizational stakeholders in their fields so as to ensure organizational survival. Either way, the results are substantially the same: the privileging and reproduction of more acceptable modes of doing political work at the expense of the development of more progressive or innovative social change organizations.

This chapter explores recent foundation involvement in the fields of women's and civil rights, two sectors of activity linked historically to highly mobilized and socially significant political movements. Given that the broad grassroots involvement that previously animated these movements has subsided, the consolidation of collective gains in the context of persistent racial and gender inequalities is heavily reliant on the activities of formal organizations. Although foundation

1. Jenkins (1998).

funding represents only one source of support for groups committed to social and political change, it may be particularly crucial when social movements are in "abeyance"[2] or when they become more accepted as institutional actors and individual sources of enthusiasm and support diminish.

As a more general point, foundations represent a potentially critical source of both stability and innovation in the organizational field, although one that may not best promote the interests of foundations and social change organizations alike. Given the demonstrated role that organizations play as carriers of social movement goals, collective identities, and protest potential, understanding the contribution that foundations make to these organizational projects is central to understanding the potential for both shoring up and furthering the gains of these historically important collective mobilizations.[3]

Foundation Roles and Contributions in the Social Movement Arena

When considering foundation involvement in the social movement arena, one finds that the distinction between *charity* and *philanthropy* animating the chapters in this volume becomes analytically and empirically blurred. As Alice O'Connor demonstrates in chapter 15, the investment of organized philanthropy in the social movements of the 1960s represented a departure in the field's self-definition as well as a new set of opportunities and risks for support-seeking organizations. Arguably, it was at this historical juncture that philanthropy— one of whose roles, as defined by David Hammack and Helmut Anheier in the introduction to this volume, is the encouragement of innovation and social and policy change—began to supplant charity, summarized as complementarity and substitution, as the orienting framework of both established and newly created foundations interested in promoting social change.[4]

In some cases, this shift from charity to philanthropy represented a significant departure from past practices and promoted a restructuring of the "social relations of philanthropy" in those fields that historically had been the focus of charitable support.[5] So, for example, foundation programs for such "charitable" purposes as social welfare services to poor blacks, English language courses for immigrants, or employment counseling for unmarried women was presumably replaced by "philanthropic" support for the civil rights and feminist movements in the form of voter education projects, cultural empowerment, and class-action litigation, mapping onto the development of new forms of organization and

2. Taylor (1989).

3. Minkoff (1997).

4. Chapter 15 in this volume describes this shift as a field-level redefinition of the role of foundations as agents of accommodation to agents of social change.

5. Ostrander (1995); Chambré (2006).

action by these constituencies.[6] In other cases, the shift to philanthropy as innovation and policy change in the 1960s created the opportunity for new constituencies and funding areas to become established almost entirely along the philanthropic model. Funding initiatives in the areas of the environment, consumer protection, civil liberties, or patients' rights, for example, have little or no earlier charitable equivalent.

For substantial components of the American social movement arena, then, it may make little sense to evaluate the relative balance between charitable and philanthropic roles. For other subfields, including those that are the focus of this chapter, it is important to consider the tensions between these two dominant objectives (on the part of both foundation actors and nonprofits seeking their support). Although O'Connor makes a cogent argument for the historical shift in the orienting social change mission of foundations, newer models of organization and action tend to coexist with, and do not completely replace, older ones;[7] this is as true of foundation funding priorities as of the kinds of nonprofits receiving support. Foundation support for social change in the areas of women's and civil rights during this period illustrates the effectiveness of foundation funding priorities in promoting the development of a more innovative, change-oriented organizational infrastructure, thereby clarifying one dimension of the relative balance between philanthropy and charity in this sector.

Comparative Advantages and Disadvantages of Foundations

Proponents of a strong role for foundations in society posit a set of comparative advantages that uniquely position foundations to act as social entrepreneurs, institution builders, risk absorbers, and mediators. In principle, their permanent and independent revenues give them greater room for maneuvering and enable them to play potentially significant philanthropic and charitable roles. Such comparative advantages would seem to be especially crucial in leveraging foundation resources for the purposes of innovation and social and policy change. Sponsorship of social movement projects would seem to represent a clear route of influence. However, as the debates discussed in the next section suggest, the comparative advantages of elite foundations are blunted by the distinctive dilemmas inherent in sponsoring collective initiatives that, in different ways and to different degrees, challenge the status quo. The result is that those groups that may most require the infusion of external support cannot count on it, largely because of institutional and organizational constraints on foundation action.

The approach taken here precludes claims about the disadvantages of foundations and the way funding dynamics play out at the level of relations between

6. Minkoff (1995).
7. Clemens (1993); Minkoff (1995).

foundation and grant recipient. Even if it were possible to identify organization-specific models of successfully implemented philanthropic programs or evidence of foundation actors using their power to co-opt or moderate more activist political projects, it is too soon to generalize from particular cases or to assume that they represent dominant tendencies in the field.

Foundation Impact

We employ a relatively narrow conceptualization of foundation impact that emphasizes how funding patterns contribute to organizational maintenance and the development of an infrastructure for mobilization. Rather than analyzing the direct influence of foundation support on a limited number of cases, we seek a more comprehensive, "bird's-eye" profile of the kinds of organizations—or, more accurately, organizational characteristics—that are favored by large foundations. We do not think it is meaningful to posit intentionality between foundation action and outcomes. Our view is that there is an outer bound on the ability of foundations to promote fully innovative philanthropic support in the social movement arena, with the result being a more conventionally structured set of priorities, practices, and organizational forms.

Current Debates

In tandem with the involvement of elite foundations in a variety of social movement causes since the early 1960s, analysts and activists have questioned both the intentions and the consequences of foundation sponsorship. Although grudgingly acknowledging the importance of resource mobilization from "conscience constituents," the key concern of scholarship has been whether foundation support operates as a form of social control that defuses or contains significant challenges to the status quo.[8] Early research on the civil rights movement, for example, documents a reactive pattern of support whereby foundation funding not only followed the upsurge of civil rights activism in the mid-1960s but was primarily directed at more established and moderate reform groups, such as the NAACP and the Southern Christian Leadership Conference.[9] These funding patterns were characterized as evidence of a "radical flank effect": as social movements radicalize, foundations step in to contain them by bolstering more politically moderate organizations.[10] Rather than initiators or philanthropic innovators, then, foundations were understood to be primarily interested in containing dissent, motivated to get involved only when their interests were threatened.

8. McCarthy and Zald (1977).
9. McAdam (1982).
10. Haines (1984).

Subsequent research by Craig Jenkins and his collaborators, on a broad range of movements active since the 1960s, took a middle ground and introduced the concept of "channeling," whereby foundation support tends to push social movements into relatively narrow (and, by extension, less threatening) directions but not necessarily because of a set of explicit social control intentions on the part of funders.[11] Examining aggregate trends in what they refer to as social movement philanthropy (funding by foundations that have an explicit commitment to progressive social change), Jenkins and Abigail Halci document a significant expansion of foundation support beginning in the late 1960s and continuing over the following decades.[12] Their findings suggest that social movement philanthropy has become effectively institutionalized since the 1960s, providing valuable resources to new and ongoing social movement initiatives but at the same time favoring more professionalized and politically moderate organizations in ways that diminish—but do not entirely undermine—the impact of progressive social movements.

As exemplified by Daniel Faber and Deborah McCarthy's edited volume, *Foundations for Social Change: Critical Perspectives on Philanthropy and Popular Movements,* scholars continue to be skeptical of the willingness and ability of both mainstream and alternative foundations to facilitate social change.[13] However, this newer body of research moves beyond an either-or dichotomy and attempts to situate the power of both grant makers and grant recipients in the "social relations of philanthropy," which create a space for collaboration and strategic action that promotes the goals of both sets of actors.[14] From this perspective, the promise of social change philanthropy remains unfulfilled but not necessarily unthinkable.[15]

Nonetheless, the constraints on what can be considered the philanthropic (that is, innovative and change-oriented) potential of foundation support for social movements and social change remain substantial. These constraints are not specific to the field of social movement philanthropy but reflect more general organizational processes that limit the innovative role of foundations operating throughout the nonprofit sector. As powerful as they may be, foundations are subject to pressures for institutional conformity that inform their programmatic priorities as well as their evaluation of potential grant recipients.[16] Innovative action on the part of foundations, therefore, is constrained by legitimacy

---

11. Jenkins and Eckert (1986); Jenkins (1998); Jenkins and Halci (1999).

12. Jenkins and Halci (1999, pp. 230–40).

13. Faber and McCarthy (2005a).

14. Ostrander, Silver, and McCarthy (2005); see also Chambré (2006); D. McCarthy (2004); Silver (1998).

15. Faber and McCarthy (2005b).

16. See, for example, Powell and DiMaggio (1991).

concerns similar to those that all organizations face, especially those that operate in nonmarket arenas. Legitimacy concerns are especially pronounced with
respect to supporting organizations associated with social movements, which
"almost always entail a possibility of political controversy."[17] In this sense, foundations tend to be naturally risk averse when it comes to innovative action in the
social movement arena. Such caution implies an outer bound on the comparative advantage they may have in other sectors, where they can function as risk
absorbers as they seek to play a role as institution builders.[18]

Whereas a great deal of scholarly attention has focused on the role of institutionally powerful actors (such as foundations) in the development of nonprofit
organizations, only limited attention has been paid to the other side of the equa-
tion.[19] Sada Aksartova has observed that one way foundations can avoid the risks
of sponsoring more controversial issues is to target grants to organizations that
adopt more conventional organizational structures, that is, those that are more
professionalized and work through institutionalized channels (a channeling
effect that, as noted, is evident across the nonprofit sector but arguably exaggerated within the social movement arena).[20] The consequences of this tendency to
favor specific organizational forms over others cannot be overstated: less conventionally structured groups or those with more controversial goals are excluded or
marginalized, whereas conventional forms are reproduced through processes of
organizational formation, adaptation, and survival.[21] Such processes of selection
and reproduction are likely to translate into the consolidation of an organizational base that is characterized by a built-in reluctance to pursue policy innovation and comprehensive social change and is, by extension, potentially less capable of serving as an infrastructure for more institutionally confrontational forms
of political action. Put differently, foundation reluctance to innovate promotes
the reproduction of organizations that may also be risk averse when it comes to
political or organizational innovation.

Foundation Contributions to Civil Rights, Social Action, and Advocacy

Civil rights, social action, and advocacy make up a central component of the
social movement sector in the United States—defined as "private nonprofit organizations whose primary purpose is to protect and promote the broad civil rights

17. Aksartova (2003, p. 30).
18. See Bartley (2007) for a more positive view of the potential for foundations to play an innovative role in social movement projects.
19. Minkoff and Powell (2007).
20. Aksartova (2003).
21. Minkoff (1995, 1999); Faber and McCarthy (2005b).

and civil liberties of individuals, to work for the realization of specific social or political goals, or to encourage the participation of people in the public policy debate."[22] In broad terms, these groups can be understood as making an explicit commitment to social change, coming closest to what analysts understand to be social movement organizations.

The civil rights, social action, and advocacy category includes groups that "work to improve relations between racial, ethnic, and cultural groups; advocacy and citizen action groups that work to change public policy and opinion in a variety of areas; and organizations that promote voter education and registration."[23] Grants in this category go to organizations that advocate in behalf of the rights of women, immigrants, ethnic and racial minorities, the elderly, gay men, and lesbians and to those that promote a reproductive rights agenda as well as the alternative right-to-life position and a range of civil liberties issues. It excludes, however, legal service groups, environmental organizations, animal rights groups, and groups that use advocacy to achieve institution-specific changes, such as education reform or housing advocacy.[24]

Using data on grants compiled by the Foundation Center, we are able to more closely examine the distribution of funding across the civil rights and social action sector in 2001 (see appendix C).[25] In aggregate terms, the domestic civil rights and social action sector received 3,458 grants in 2001, totaling more than $346 million—only a fraction of the foundation funds invested annually into civil society in recent years. The average grant was for slightly more than $100,000, although the median grant of $35,000 provides a better indicator of the relatively modest levels of funding going to grant recipients in this sector. Also of note, though not shown, is that slightly less than 20 percent of grant

22. McCarthy and Zald (1977); National Taxonomy of Exempt Entities, "(R) Civil Rights/ Social Action, Advocacy (R)" (http://fdncenter.org/ntee/ [December 2005]).

23. Foundation Center, "National Taxonomy of Exempt Entities: (R) Civil Rights/Social Action, Advocacy (R)" (http://fdncenter.org/ntee/ [December 2005]).

24. Employing this National Taxonomy of Exempt Entities R classification is problematic for developing a comprehensive overview of foundation involvement in the social movement sector, especially given the increasing visibility of such movements as environmentalism and animal rights, as well as mobilizations within institutions and organizations that characterize many contemporary social change initiatives (see Clemens and Minkoff 2004). Nonetheless, our operationalization is consistent with that employed by Helmut Anheier and Jennifer Mosley in their empirical overview, presented during the winter 2006 meeting of this volume's authors at the Aspen Institute.

25. These data are compiled from the Foundation Center 2001 Grants Database, which includes grants of $10,000 or more awarded by a set of just more than a thousand of the largest U.S. foundations. This sample constitutes approximately one-half of all grant dollars awarded by the country's foundations each year and thus represents funding at the most elite levels. We include all grants whose primary, secondary, or tertiary purpose was coded as within the R classification by Foundation Center staff; our baseline number of grants and grant amounts are therefore higher than those presented by Anheier and Mosley.

Figure 16-1. *Foundation Funding for Civil Rights and Social Action,*
by Category, 2001

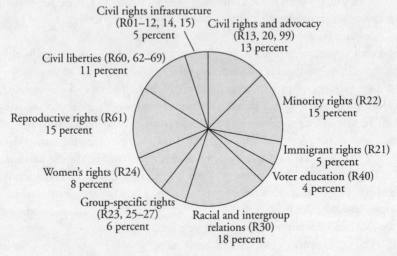

Source: Data from Foundation Center 2001 Grants Database.

recipients were located in Washington, D.C., and only 17 percent received
grants for general operating support. Putting this in a larger context, in this same
year there were 3,438 registered nonprofits operating in this sector, representing
only 0.3 percent of all registered nonprofits.[26]

Figure 16-1 illustrates funding patterns with respect to key issue areas
(National Taxonomy of Exempt Entities codes corresponding to these issue areas
and grant information are detailed in appendix C). Civil rights and advocacy
groups and civil liberties groups received modest amounts of support, while
women's rights, specific group rights, civil rights infrastructure, immigrant rights,
and voter education each received 8 percent or less of foundation support. The
remaining support was targeted to such areas as reproductive rights, minority
rights, and racial and intergroup relations. In fact, this last subfield received the
largest share of funding distributed over the largest number of grants. In terms
of the distinction between philanthropy and charity, it is unclear how to inter-
pret this funding priority. Perhaps it represents a commitment to social change,
as opposed to political change, which is a component characteristic of philanthropy as defined here. However, the concomitant focus on increased harmony

26. Urban Institute, National Center for Charitable Statistics (http://nccsdataweb.urban.org/
NCCS/Public/index.php [December 2005]).

and understanding is one that, especially in the field of race and ethnicity, has been historically linked to cultural enrichment and charitable purposes rather than advocacy and social reform—arguably the hallmark traits of such initiatives as the civil rights movement.[27]

Focusing on grants that support women's and minority rights, overall funding for minority rights was almost double that for women (approximately $53 million compared with $28 million), the average grant in support of minority rights being close to $120,000 (based on 447 grants) compared with $81,000 for women's rights (343 grants). Women's rights supporters were, however, slightly more likely to receive general operating support (16 and 12 percent, respectively; see appendix C). In general terms, then, it appears that organizations working for minority civil rights are more advantaged with respect to levels of funding and number of grants but organizations working on women's issues are favored with respect to receiving general operating support grants. Given the premium that nonprofits place on hard-to-get unrestricted grants, this signals somewhat greater support for infrastructural development in the women's rights sector.[28]

Who Is Funding Social Change?

Table 16-1 lists a selection of foundations that funded minority civil rights in 2001. The top ten funders allocated 22.5 percent of grants and 64.3 percent of total funding within this issue area. Among these top foundations, the one with the most issue-specific mission is the Charles Stewart Mott Foundation's race and ethnic relations program, which aims to, among other things, "enhance the organizational capacity and impact of leading nonprofits in the antiracism and race relations field."[29] Other funders have more diffuse missions related indirectly to minority civil rights. The Rockefeller Foundation, for example, targets its funding toward poverty-related issues, such as "improving opportunities for poor people," while the domestic branch of the Open Society Foundation "focuses on civil liberties in the United States."[30] The California Endowment's "multicultural approach to health" is clearer in its focus on racial and ethnic

27. Minkoff (1995).

28. On the importance of unrestricted grants for progressive social change groups see, for example, Dreier (2002) and Michael Shuman, "Why Do Progressive Foundations Give Too Little to Too Many?" *The Nation,* January 12, 1998, pp. 11–16.

29. Charles Stewart Mott Foundation, "Race and Ethnic Relations U.S. Program" (http://mott.org/programs/cs_us.asp [August 2006]).

30. Rockefeller Foundation, "About Us" (www.rockfound.org/about_us/about_us.shtml [August 2006]); Open Society Foundation (www.soros.org/initiatives/washington [August 2006]).

Table 16-1. *Foundation Funding of Minority Rights, 2001*

Foundation	Assets (dollars)[a]	Number of grants	Value of grants (dollars)
Top ten funders			
Ford Foundation	11.4 billion	34	12,793,000
California Endowment	3.7 billion	5	9,388,456
Lannan Foundation	241 million	9	2,390,000
Rockefeller Foundation	3.4 billion	13	2,290,254
General Motors Foundation	255 million	7	1,925,000
Charles Stewart Mott Foundation	2.4 billion	3	1,473,550
John D. and Catherine T. MacArthur Foundation	5.5 billion	7	1,121,000
Open Society Foundation	329 million	14	1,064,595
DaimlerChrysler Corporation Fund	37 million	7	975,000
Kresge Foundation	2.7 billion	2	825,000
Median funders			
ExxonMobil Foundation	110 million	1	60,000
Avon Foundation	52 million	2	55,000
J. P. Morgan Chase Foundation	122 million	3	55,000
Compton Foundation	79 million	2	55,000
George Gund Foundation	475 million	2	51,500
Baseline funders			
Cooper Industries Foundation	8 million	1	10,000
David Geffen Foundation	612,335	1	10,000
Koret Foundation	247 million	1	10,000
3M Foundation	39 million	1	10,000
Steelcase Foundation	113 million	1	10,000

Source: Data from Foundation Center 2001 Grants Database.

a. Assets data from most recent year available through foundation annual reports or Foundation Center database.

minorities, in contrast to the more general goal of the Kresge Foundation to "strengthen nonprofit organizations that advance the well-being of humanity."[31]

Median and baseline supporters of minority civil rights have substantially lower assets than do the top ten foundations, although there are clearly a few, such as the George Gund Foundation and the Koret Foundation, that control comparably high assets. The mission statements of these foundations indicate that their grant making is less directly targeted toward minority rights.

31. California Endowment (www.calendow.org [August 2006]); Kresge Foundation (www.kresge.org/content/displaycontent.aspx?CID=15 [August 2006]).

Table 16-2. *Foundation Funding of Women's Rights, 2001*

Foundation	Assets (dollars)[a]	Number of grants	Value of grants (dollars)
Top ten funders			
Ford Foundation	11.4 billion	55	10,132,865
Atlantic Foundation of New York	3.1 billion	2	1,968,300
Rockefeller Foundation	3.4 billion	17	1,920,592
Open Society Foundation	329 million	13	1,260,000
William and Flora Hewlett Foundation	7.3 billion	4	720,000
Charles H. Revson Foundation	200 million	1	690,000
John D. and Catherine T. MacArthur Foundation	5.5 billion	2	663,000
Public Welfare Foundation	473 million	11	598,000
Moriah Fund	163 million	19	595,000
Charles Stewart Mott Foundation	2.4 billion	6	555,000
Median funders			
Carnegie Corporation of New York	2.2 billion	2	50,000
CIGNA Foundation	475,000	1	50,000
Jacobs Family Foundation	38 million	1	50,000
Seattle Foundation	470 million	1	50,000
Walton Family Foundation	733 million	1	50,000
Baseline funders			
Buffett Foundation	318 million	1	10,000
Avon Foundation	945,777	1	10,000
Alan B. Slifka Foundation	7.7 million	1	10,000
Stoddard Charitable Trust	75 million	1	10,000
Alphawood Foundation	137 million	1	10,000

Source: Data from Foundation Center 2001 Grants Database.

a. Assets data from most recent year available through foundation annual reports or Foundation Center database.

For example, the Gund Foundation—the largest of this selection of median and baseline foundations, with $475 million in assets—focuses on "advancing human welfare" through its human services and economic development and community revitalization programs.[32]

Data on foundations sponsoring initiatives that promote women's rights are shown in table 16-2. The top ten funders—five of which (Ford, Rockefeller, MacArthur, Open Society, and Mott) are also top sponsors of programs in minority rights—distributed 37.9 percent of the grants and 68.4 percent of

32. George Gund Foundation (www.gundfdn.org/what.asp [August 2006]).

the total funding within this issue area. Four of the top ten funders have mission statements or programs explicitly focused on women's rights. Among these foundations, the Open Society's Washington, D.C., initiative specifically targets women's rights, while the Revson Foundation identifies "the changing role of women" as a funding priority, and the Moriah Fund seeks to "promote women's rights and reproductive health."[33] The Ford Foundation, the fourth of these foundations, is discussed in greater detail below.

The foundations listed as median and baseline financial supporters of women's rights also tend to have fewer assets compared with the top ten foundations active in this area, with the notable exception of the Carnegie Corporation of New York, with $2.2 billion in assets. Like the median and baseline foundations to minority civil rights giving, many of the foundations that support women's rights appear to have diffuse funding priorities. Only the CIGNA Foundation aims to fund issues directly related to women's rights through a women's and children's health program.[34]

Figure 16-2 presents data on overall funding for women's and minority rights and also separately identifies the amount of aggregate funding by the top ten foundations and the Ford Foundation individually. A clear picture emerges: grant recipients competing for elite funding for women's and minority rights activities are overwhelmingly reliant upon a small number of foundations for a large percentage of their financial support, with disproportionately high levels of support coming from the Ford Foundation. Organizations sponsoring programs in the area of minority rights secured thirty-four grants and nearly $13 million from Ford in 2001, while women's rights supporters received fifty-five grants and just over $10 million. The Ford Foundation, in contrast to other elite foundations identified here, more explicitly invokes social movements in its mission. As the foundation states in discussing its human rights program, funding for "women's rights and racial justice . . . builds on the historic victories of these movements in the United States." Furthermore, one of the foundation's aims, noted under its asset building and community development program, is to "support vibrant social movements, institutions and partnerships that analyze contemporary social and economic opportunities and devise responses to them."[35]

Based on this brief examination of the missions of Ford and other large foundations that actively support women's and minority programs, it may seem that

33. The Open Society (www.soros.org/initiatives/washington [August 2006]); A. Balla, "3rd President for Revson Foundation," *New York Sun,* October 16, 2007; Moriah Fund (www.moriah-fund.org/ [August 2006]).

34. CIGNA (www.cigna.com/general/about/community/contributions.html [August 2006]).

35. Ford Foundation, "Human Rights Program" (www.fordfound.org/program/humanr.cfm [August 2006]); Ford Foundation, "Asset Building and Community Development Program" (www.fordfound.org/program/asset_main.cfm [August 2006]).

Figure 16-2. *Foundation Funding for Women's and Minority Rights, 2001*

Dollars

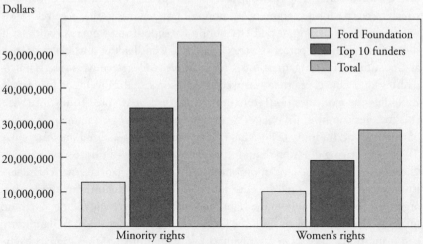

Source: Data from Foundation Center 2001 Grants Database.

there is a set of elite sponsors that explicitly seek to consolidate the gains of these historically important social movements. It also suggests a commitment to take on a philanthropic, as opposed to charitable, role in the women's and civil rights sector. Such a conclusion, however, is premature without a more systematic examination of the organizational outcomes of foundation support.

Who Is Getting Funded?

For a more in-depth look at the impact of foundation funding practices on organizational developments, we created a database of grant recipients in the areas of women's and minority rights, starting with the Foundation Center grants data. We then conducted supplementary research to learn more about the organizational profiles of grant recipients working on projects in these two areas. In moving from foundation grant to grant recipient as the unit of analysis, we created a single record for each grantee that included a measure of combined support if the grantee received more than one grant as well as measures indicating the number of grants received and whether any of these grants were made for general operating support. Additional information on these organizations, such as founding date, focus of activities, financial information, and so forth, was collected from such sources as GuideStar, Associations Unlimited, and organizational websites.[36]

36. GuideStar (www.guidestar.org [September–December 2005]); Associations Unlimited (www.gale.com [September–December 2005]).

For the purposes of data collection, we excluded grantees that operated outside of the United States. The resulting sample included 395 organizations (some of which received multiple grants): 214 nonprofit organizations that received funding for minority civil rights and 181 nonprofits supporting women's rights.[37] Of these, forty-eight (12 percent) were classified as what Jenkins and Halci refer to as "institutionalized organizations," for example, colleges, universities, municipalities, and churches, that themselves sponsor social movement projects.[38] Excluding these organizations from our sample (except as noted below), we were able to collect some additional data on 296 of 347 grant recipients in the areas of women's and minority civil rights that are not institutionalized organizations.

The underlying question that motivates the remainder of this section is which kinds of organizations—or, more specifically, which organizational characteristics—seem to be favored by elite foundations when it comes to supporting organized efforts to promote the rights and interests of women and racial-ethnic minorities. Is it the case, as both the literature on social movement philanthropy and institutional approaches to organizations would predict, that more conventional (older, more professionalized, less political, and so on) organizations benefit more from foundation funding? To the extent that this is the case, an argument can be made that particularism and insufficiency characterize the efforts of elite foundations to contribute positively to social change. Alternatively, evidence of a tendency to support nonprofits that fit a less institutionally acceptable profile—with respect to either their operating procedures or their approaches to social change—could indicate some ability on the part of these same foundations to capitalize on their comparative advantages in channeling resources into less conventional, or more innovative, organizational forms.

Table 16-3 presents descriptive information on the sample of grantee organizations derived from the Foundation Center Grants Database. Although there are a fair number of missing data on key characteristics of interest, the data in the table provide a valuable first step toward a detailed profile of grantee organizations in these two areas.[39] Looking first at formal organizational characteristics, one finds supporters of minority rights are older, on average, than nonprofits involved in women's rights (thirty-one years as against twenty years). Approximately 40 percent of organizations in both categories employ at least one paid staff member. Although similar on this dimension, there is a striking difference with respect to

37. Eleven of these recipients received funding for both women's rights and minority civil rights projects. We treat them as separate organizations in the analyses presented below.

38. Jenkins and Halci (1999, p. 245).

39. To address the problem of missing data on a number of dichotomous measures, each variable was coded as zero unless there was clear evidence that the group had the characteristic of interest. This is a relatively conservative approach that most likely underestimates the prevalence of organizational characteristics across the sample.

Table 16-3. *Grant Recipients in Minority Civil Rights and Women's Rights, 2001*

Item	Civil rights Mean (percent)	Median	N	Women Mean (percent)	Median	N	Total Mean (percent)	Median	N
Formal characteristics									
Age of recipient group (years)	30.9	26	79	19.7	16	80	25.3	21	159
Number of staff	10.8	1	92	22.4	12	56	15.2	3	148
Any staff	42	...	159	40	...	137	41	...	296
Membership	39	...	159	26	...	137	33	...	296
Volunteers	30	...	159	36	...	137	32	...	296
Financial characteristics									
Revenue (in millions of dollars)	8.6	1.3	128	7.7	0.7	112	8.2	0.9	240
Governmental support									
Any support	32	...	159	24	...	137	28	...	296
Value (millions of dollars)	0.9	0	125	2.1	0	81	1.4	0	206
Assets									
Net (millions of dollars)	10.2	7	128	6.2	0.4	114	8.3	0.5	242
Total (millions of dollars)	15.1	1.2	119	7.6	0.5	111	11.5	0.9	230
Locus of activity									
National	18	...	159	52	...	137	34	...	296
Local	50	...	159	51	...	137	51	...	296
Washington, D.C., based	13	...	159	23	...	137	18	...	296
Tactics									
Protest	34	...	159	14	...	137	25	...	296
Advocacy	61	...	159	53	...	137	57	...	296
Service	30	...	159	60	...	137	44	...	296
Community origin	48	...	159	30	...	137	40	...	296

Source: Data from Foundation Center 2001 Grants Database.

how staff intensive these organizations are: the average staff size of grantee organizations in the minority rights sector is eleven, compared with twenty-two for those operating in the women's rights sector. Also, a higher proportion of minority civil rights supporters indicate that they are membership organizations (39 percent compared with 26 percent), although slightly more grantees in the women's rights arena indicate some reliance on volunteers (36 percent as against 30 percent).

Minority rights grantees are slightly advantaged financially, reporting average revenues of $8.6 million compared with $7.7 million (the median revenues reported by minority rights grantees being twice as high as for women's rights grantees).[40] A somewhat higher percentage of organizations in the minority rights sector report receiving some governmental support (32 percent, as against 24 percent for women's rights), although the average amount of governmental funding for women's rights grantees is more than twice that of civil rights supporters. In terms of financial stability, measured with respect to both total assets and net assets, grantees in the area of minority rights are clearly in better shape: the average net assets reported by these organizations are in excess of $10 million and the average total assets are close to $15 million (compared with $6.2 million and $7.6 million for women's rights grantees). Median net and total assets paint a more circumspect picture, although it is clear that nonprofits that support minority rights are more financially secure than those operating in the area of women's rights.

Grant recipients in the area of women's rights are more likely to indicate that they operate at the national level—52 percent, compared with 18 percent of minority rights grantees. This may correspond with differences in recipient: 13 percent of recipients of funding for minority rights are located in Washington, D.C., compared with 23 percent of women's rights grantees. Differences with respect to activities are also marked: 34 percent of civil rights grantees indicate some involvement in protest, in contrast to only 14 percent of women's rights grantees; 61 percent of civil rights grantees do some form of advocacy compared with 53 percent of women's rights grantees; and almost twice as many recipients working in the area of women's rights indicate involvement in service provision. More minority rights grantees, in contrast, indicate a commitment to grassroots community organizing compared with women's rights supporters (48 and 30 percent, respectively).

On the face of it, there seem to be clear differences in the organizational profiles of grant recipients pursuing social change projects in the areas of women's and minority rights. However, the key question is, which organizational features make a concrete difference with respect to mobilizing foundation support? No less important, how does this differ for supporters of minority civil rights and women's rights? The logic of our approach is to isolate those recipient characteristics that represent the extent of professionalization or institutional standing, as well as those that reflect a more or less explicit commitment to political and social change, and then to examine whether these features of organizational structure and strategy provide, on average, significant advantages (or disadvantages) with respect to mobilizing foundation support.

40. Based on reported IRS revenue. In most cases, these data correspond to the 2001 tax year to match the Foundation Center database or, if not available, the most proximate year following.

First we examine differences in mean levels of foundation support in terms of key features of organizational structure and activities. Looking at the implications of professionalization, it is fairly clear that organizations that employ some paid staff are at an advantage: mean support for staff-run minority rights grantees is $219,000 compared with $145,000 for organizations run by volunteers and $213,000 for staff-run women's rights grantee organizations compared with $113,000 for those that rely on volunteers. The difference between minority rights and women's rights supporters, however, is relatively negligible. In contrast, the pattern of support for groups that rely on volunteers indicates a significant divergence across fields. Volunteer-based organizations within the minority rights field appear to be less attractive to foundations, while the opposite pattern holds for supporters of women's rights projects. Mean support for volunteer-based organizations in this sector is approximately $185,000, compared with $135,000 for those that provide no indication that they rely on volunteer labor. This result contrasts with organizations in the minority rights arena, where the mean grant for organizations that indicate a reliance on volunteer labor is about $116,000 compared with $200,000 for those that do not. Possibly related, minority rights grantees coded as membership organizations receive lower levels of average funding—$150,000 as against $192,000 for those with no members.

We also expected there to be differences in terms of where these organizations focus their efforts, namely, at the national or local level. Looking at those nonprofits that indicate they target some of their work at the national level (compared with either local or international involvement) reveals only a slight difference between minority rights supporters but a significant difference among organizations supporting women's rights. Those organizations with some national focus receive, on average, a "bonus" of more than $100,000 over those with no national-level involvement. In addition, the mean funding for national groups focusing on women is slightly higher than that for nationally oriented organizations that support minority rights ($205,000 as against $188,000). There are also some notable differences in the other direction. Within the minority rights field, grants for organizations with some local focus are higher than for those operating nationally or internationally. Moreover, organizations involved in local efforts to improve minority rights are clearly getting more than those focusing on women: here the bonus comes close to $100,000 ($200,000 and $104,000, respectively).

Next we explore differences along the dimension of what grantee organizations do, with the primary distinction between activities that signal a direct engagement in political and social change and those that reflect a more traditional nonprofit orientation of service provision or community-based work. The extent to which foundations tend to favor the former set of activities can be taken as some evidence of their commitment to a philanthropic agenda; alternatively, more extensive support for service and community groups signals continued investment in charitable forms of activity. Among organizations coded as engaging in some advocacy-related activities, it seems clear that more funding goes to groups that support women's rights—compared both with those that do not engage in any advocacy ($216,000 and $84,000, respectively) and with minority rights supporters who do ($160,000). In contrast, minority rights advocates get, on average, almost $40,000 less than those that apparently stay away from advocacy as an explicit strategy. Regarding the few protest groups in the sample, the limited evidence suggests that within the minority rights sector there is no substantial difference between organizations willing to engage in protest and those that are not (mean support of $173,000 and $177,000, respectively). However, there is a substantial penalty for protest organizations within the women's rights sector, with such groups receiving an average of $75,000 in foundation support compared with $166,000 for those that keep a distance from protest activities.

Two other related strategies characterize nonprofits oriented toward women's and minority rights: service provision and community organizing. As a first point of note, it appears that average levels of funding for organizations involved in advocacy are higher (between $200,000 and $215,000) than for either service provision or community organizing (between $125,000 and $150,000). There is, however, not much difference between the two sectors with respect to average levels of foundation funding for service or community-organizing projects, although in both cases minority rights supporters that do not identify themselves with these more grassroots types of activities seem to experience a substantial benefit. The evidence also suggests that all groups that are engaged in community organizing get comparatively low levels of support. Although provisional, the observed differences in funding patterns with respect to key strategies suggest that elite foundations appear to invest somewhat more intensively in organizations that align with their objectives of policy innovation and social change. At the same time, service provision and community-based action continue to represent foundation-sponsored initiatives among nonprofits involved in the fields of women's and minority rights.

A final set of characteristics isolate three dimensions of what can be considered the institutional standing of grantee organizations: whether they locate their base of operations in Washington, D.C., whether they receive any financial support from the government, and whether the organizations themselves are institutionalized actors that sponsor social movement projects in contrast to independent nonprofits that can be considered more closely aligned with the civil rights and women's movements. Washington-based supporters of women's rights have a clear advantage over those located outside the Beltway, receiving foundation support of $214,757, on average, as against $134,742, and over groups working in the area of minority civil rights and with main offices in Washington, which receive support of $170,715, on average. Based on a simple measure of whether or not the organization reports any government support in its annual revenue, the average level of foundation support for civil rights supporters that receive government funding is somewhat higher, at $158,966, than for women's rights supporters that rely on government support, at $148,385. In both cases, foundations seem to direct their money to those organizations that do not receive additional support from the government, with a more pronounced advantage for grantees involved in minority civil rights projects—providing some evidence of complementarity and substitution as an incentive for foundation involvement in this area in particular.

Finally, to examine differences between institutional actors and independent nonprofits, we reintroduce the forty-eight "institutionalized" organizations that were excluded from new data collection. Institutional actors receive slightly more funding within the minority rights area, $228,248, on average, whereas in the women's rights field, foundation support averages only $80,761. Noninstitutionalized organizations supporting women's rights receive average support of $165,000 compared with the $204,000 going to minority rights.

These data, although limited, provide a first step toward a better understanding of the targeting of foundation funding to organizations active in consolidating the gains of the civil rights and women's movements. One of the key findings is that professionalization does seem to pay: organizations experience a bonus for having formal staff (especially for supporters of women's rights) and, in the case of minority rights grantees, a penalty for relying on volunteers. In addition, institutional actors that work in behalf of minority rights get more for their activities than those focused on women's rights. More money is directed to groups that are not getting government support, a finding that is more pronounced among minority rights supporters. And whereas a national focus benefits organizations supporting women's rights, a local focus is more rewarding, in terms of foundation support, for minority rights supporters. Activities also matter: advocates for women's rights benefit, whereas advocates for minority civil rights do not; protesters for women's rights are relatively penalized; and service and community organizing do not seem particularly attractive to the elite foundations—a finding that points in the direction of foundation investment in philanthropy along with some continued, but less substantial, support of more traditional forms of charitable activity in these sectors.

Conclusions

In this chapter, new data have been brought to bear on a question that has occupied social movement researchers, nonprofit scholars, and activists since the involvement of major foundations in organized efforts for social change starting in the 1960s. This concern with the consequences of external support for the viability of social movements and their organizational carriers has been articulated most starkly in the contrast between co-optation and channeling, the presumption being that foundation support has some, most likely negative, influence on the ability of activist organizations to maintain fidelity to their mission. This is a general dilemma for nonprofit organizations, but one that is arguably more acute for social change organizations that depend on external resources and, at root, seek to alter existing power arrangements.[41]

At least two decades after the height of the black civil rights and contemporary feminist movements, nonprofits that carry on the missions of these historic mobilizations continue to garner a substantial share of foundation support targeted to civil rights and social action, broadly defined. That said, notable differences exist across sectors in terms of the profiles of grant recipients and the benefits (or penalties) that correspond with adopting certain organizational attributes.

In the broadest strokes, it appears that grantees in the area of women's rights fit closely to the image of Washington-based "professional advocates" and that those organizations that locate themselves and their efforts nationally, employ a paid staff, and limit their involvement in more disruptive forms of social protest reap substantial financial benefits.[42] Staff-run and nonmembership organizations also receive a bonus for adopting a professionalized model, but Washington-based and nationally focused advocates for minority civil rights do not seem to be especially attractive to foundation supporters. In fact, here the advantage seems to go to those groups operating locally and to those organizations that seem to lack direct support from the federal government. In this regard, elite foundations can be seen as taking a supportive role with respect to private initiatives that might not otherwise be viable, although this conclusion is tentative at best.

Taking a supportive role, however, is distinct from active sponsorship of, or engagement in, innovative practices and social and policy change. Here it appears that elite foundations favor more familiar programmatic goals and organizational forms over pushing the boundaries of social change philanthropy, although foundations active in the areas of women's and minority civil rights do seem willing to sponsor advocacy over traditional forms of service provision. Taken as a whole, such selectivity in funding priorities reflects a form of particularism and insufficiency. These tendencies (or what have been referred to as disadvantages throughout this volume) reflect the more general pressures toward conformity that face nonmarket organizations—pressures that elite foundations interested in promoting social change are hard pressed to resist under the best of circumstances, and especially when faced with the choice of supporting

41. Minkoff and Powell (2007).
42. Skocpol (2003b).

less familiar organizational forms over those that adopt conventional operating structures (political and administrative).

Although some of the foundations profiled here appear to "talk the talk" of a more extensive commitment to social movements overall, most of them embed their social change priorities in more diffusely defined missions. Rather than using their unique resources to serve as risk absorbers, the most elite foundations active in the civil rights and social action sector appear to be relatively risk averse. Even taking into account that an explicit commitment to more comprehensive social change may be too risky—politically and institutionally—for even the most powerful foundations, recent work on conservative foundations suggests that these legitimacy concerns are not insurmountable.[43] In fact, one clear message from Alice O'Connor's chapter 15 is that foundations can and do capitalize on their distinct advantages to serve as a "movement-building and movement-mobilizing force." However, in contrast to the relatively risk-averse patterns of elite foundations active in the fields of women's and minority civil rights (both historically and currently), conservative foundations appear capable of taking a more proactive, institution-building role in sponsoring social movement activism. This case suggests that, when foundations do make an explicit commitment to social movement philanthropy, adherence to this mission can help overcome—or at least buffer—the disincentives to innovation identified in this chapter. In fact, the historical trajectory of liberal foundations itself demonstrates the potentially powerful link between mission and effectiveness, since their very commitment to political neutrality seems to have operated as a formidable barrier to more innovative forms of philanthropy.

The minority and women's rights "grants economy" is dominated by a relatively small set of large and resourceful foundations that provide the bulk of financial support for consolidating the gains of the earlier civil rights and feminist movements.[44] Although such reliance on a delimited set of foundation sponsors clearly creates vulnerabilities and dependencies on the part of grant-seeking organizations, the existence of such a concentration of asset-rich supporters could, in principle, facilitate the development of a more coordinated network of philanthropic initiatives in the social movement sector. In this sense, foundations active in this field of private, nonprofit action have the potential to serve as more effective mediators and institution builders with respect to consolidating a stable field of organizations committed to more progressive forms of political or social advocacy and activism. Whether they are willing to translate this potential into a set of stable funding priorities, however, is still an open—and critical—question.

43. Chapter 15, this volume; Krehely, House, and Kernan (2004).
44. Chambré (1996).

PART **III**

Conclusion

17

Foundations and Public Policy

STEVEN RATHGEB SMITH

The broad restructuring of the American state, together with the evolution of public policy toward foundations and the nonprofit sector in general, are changing the capacity of foundations to support policy reform, innovation, and social change. Foundations operate in an increasingly complex environment that reflects the diversification of the American government's policy tools. For operating nonprofit organizations, such policy tools include contracting with nonprofit and for-profit organizations, tax deductions and credits, loans, and bonds. For foundations, such tools have long included the tax deductibility of donations, which promotes the creation of foundations, and the greatly reduced tax on foundation assets. In exceptional circumstances, as in the case of German chemical patents seized by the United States during World War I, the government itself has used a foundation to distribute important assets. More recently, some foundations have partnered with public entities to support low-income housing or economic development, through local community organizations, or conservation goals, through land trusts. And as government-funded and private purchases of services have diversified the sources of nonprofit income, foundations have been forced to reevaluate their grantees and pay more attention to public policy.

The author would like to thank Beth Lovelady, Benjamina Menashe, and Skip Swenson for assistance in the preparation of this manuscript. In addition, the author is indebted to Helmut Anheier, Putnam Barber, Mary Ann Colwell, Mary Kay Gugerty, David Hammack, David Harrison, Stephen Page, and Cory Sbarbaro for input on earlier versions of this paper. The Nancy Bell Evans Center on Nonprofits and Philanthropy, Evans School of Public Affairs at the University of Washington, provided important funding support.

The greater complexity of the organizational and funding environment reflects significant shifts in citizen and donor attitudes. For example, the United Way has instituted a policy of donor choice, which offers donors much greater control over the destination of their donation than was previously the case. Donor-advised funds, often located within community foundations, are designed to give donors greater control over their donations. The venture philanthropy movement is predicated in part on the idea that donors should have much more direct engagement with their grantee organizations than is typical with traditional foundations.[1] More broadly, the movement for greater donor choice and involvement reflects the widespread concern among policymakers, foundation and nonprofit leaders, and scholars of public and nonprofit management about the need to be more responsive to citizens.

The increasingly diverse and complicated organizational and policy environment, as well as the steep recent drop in the value of foundation assets, challenges foundations to craft new strategies to respond to urgent public problems. In many cases it has become more difficult for foundations to identify a distinctive niche or role in their funding of specific agencies. Foundations have responded to this changed policy environment in several ways. They have increased emphasis on evaluation. They have made deliberate efforts to influence public policy. They have collaborated with government to support new program initiatives. Foundations have also undertaken to build nonprofit capacity.

Foundations and the Changing Role of Government

The federal and state governments provide the context for American foundations.[2] In chapter 10 of this volume, Steven Heydemann and Rebecca T. Kinsey emphasize the complex and ever-shifting relationship between the federal government and foundations in the field of international relations, one that is equally critical for domestic affairs. Major events such as the McCarthy hearings, the Vietnam War, and the cold war profoundly influenced foundations, as several writers have noted. However, the state's growing regulatory and funding role also has significant consequences. Many judicial decisions and legislative actions have legitimated and encouraged a more extensive regulatory and funding role for government. Incrementally, these actions have alternately expanded and restricted the scope for foundations.

The 1960s brought more rapid change. Major new health legislation creating Medicare and Medicaid provided funding for nonprofit hospitals and related programs. Many other social and health programs were also established,

---

1. Letts, Ryan, and Grossman (1999).
2. Fremont-Smith (1965, 2004).

including Head Start, community action agencies, and community mental health centers. In addition, many existing nonprofit agencies that had formerly relied on private gifts now had access to government contracts and government-provided fees. During the 1960s and early 1970s, Congress also increased federal regulatory authority through landmark legislation in the fields of civil rights, consumer protection, clean water, and clean air, far extending the regulatory reach of the federal government.

In short, the American public-private mix shifted, with more regulation of private organizations and more direct public funding—particularly from the federal government—of nonprofit organizations. New federal funding spurred the creation of many entirely new nonprofit organizations, such as community mental health centers and neighborhood health clinics. The rise of government funding allowed service organizations in such fields as humanitarian assistance, antipoverty relief, and child welfare to expand—just as the rapid growth of federal investment in scientific and medical research also underwrote the rapid proliferation of nonprofit and state university research facilities. At the same time, federal funding and consumer spending for health care and college education allowed hospitals and universities to grow rapidly. All this reduced the role of private philanthropy, but many of the new and expanded organizations would soon seek foundation funding as they evolved and sought to diversify their programming and revenue base.[3]

The greater willingness of Congress to pass new federal regulations during the 1960s is also reflected in the landmark Tax Reform Act of 1969. This act imposed on foundations stricter reporting requirements, restrictions on political activity, and minimum payout requirements.[4] These requirements remain the basic framework of the federal regulatory regime for foundations. Foundations are required to file an annual information return, Form 990-PF, with the federal Internal Revenue Service (IRS), whose principal concerns are, not surprisingly, tax related. Foundations are required to pay unrelated business income tax on revenue of more than $1,000 from business activities that are not related to their tax-exempt mission. Private foundations are required to pay out annually at least 5 percent of a moving average of their assets in distributions that qualify as charitable. A private foundation must also pay an annual excise tax equal to 2 percent of its net investment income.[5] Foundations are prohibited from "self-dealing," that is, engaging in major business relationships with their donors, donors' families, or staffs. Federal law also prohibits foundations from

3. See chapters 3 and 10, this volume.
4. Frumkin (1998); Troyer and Varley (2002); Gravelle (2003); Fremont-Smith (2004); Brilliant (2000).
5. Boris and Steuerle (2004).

attempting to influence legislation or the outcome of an election. Overall, private foundations face substantially higher levels of accountability and regulation than do ordinary nonprofit organizations, supporting organizations, or donor-advised funds within community foundations. Supporting organizations and community foundations are defined as public charities rather than as foundations, and like all such entities in the United States they are required to file IRS Form 990, to avoid self-dealing, and to disclose much information about their finances.[6]

Since passage of the Tax Reform Act of 1969, Congress has largely remained silent on matters pertaining to foundations. In the past five years, some individual members of Congress, notably Senator Charles Grassley (R-Ia.), have been active in investigating foundations and introducing proposals to increase government regulation of foundations and other nonprofits. Grassley's efforts, and those of others, produced a substantial discussion of the regulation of foundations during 2004–06 and encouraged a significant IRS revision of Form 990 in 2009.

Federal regulation arguably affects the incentives of philanthropic donors. John Simon argues that the 1969 federal regulation encouraged the diversion of charitable dollars away from foundations to other uses, including public charities such as hospitals or universities, other philanthropic instruments, and even foundation staff (because the heightened accountability demands of government forced foundations to spend more on lawyers and accountants).[7] The incentives embedded in the 1969 federal regulatory regime thus acted, in combination with other factors, to broaden the diversity of philanthropic instruments and diminish the centrality of foundations to philanthropic giving. The 1969 Tax Reform Act also created an incentive for foundations to organize themselves, to provide a collective representation of their views to those who implement the new regulatory regime, and to improve their ability to anticipate new policy or regulatory threats. Both the expansion of direct funding and the associated regulatory activity have encouraged foundations, like other institutions and individuals, to mobilize politically.[8]

The growth of the federal government and its regulation of foundations reduced, in part, the relevance of state regulation to foundation activities. (For instance, for several decades, Texas and other states gave advantageous tax treatment to foundations that confined their grants to their home state and imposed certain other regulations.) Nonetheless, states remain important to foundations. Private foundations must incorporate as tax-exempt entities at the state level.

6. Bjorklund (2003); Simon (2000).

7. Simon (2000).

8. Salisbury (1984); Skocpol (2003a).

States regulate some aspects of investment and spending decisions for all charities, including foundations. State attorneys general have general responsibility for the oversight of foundations and other charities. However, state oversight has usually entailed little detailed scrutiny of foundations.

Some of the larger states with a more extensive history of regulatory action have increased their monitoring of foundations. The state of California brought suit against the James Irvine Foundation and has thoroughly investigated the operations of the J. Paul Getty Trust in Los Angeles.[9] Texas, Illinois, Indiana, Massachusetts, and New York have brought recent enforcement actions against foundations for violating laws against self-aggrandizement.[10] In New York State, the attorney general's office under Eliot Spitzer floated proposals to substantially change the regulation and operations of foundations, including setting minimum asset levels for family foundations.[11] Yet most states, including the largest, continue to devote only modest staff to regulating charitable and other exempt entities, limiting their focus to fund-raising.[12]

State and local courts do get involved in foundation regulation if a change is proposed or necessary in the governance or disposition of foundation assets. Among the most notable recent examples are health conversion foundations created by the shift of nonprofit assets as a condition of the sale of a nonprofit hospital or nonprofit insurance provider to a for-profit entity. Health conversion foundations are created under the order of state courts as a condition for the sale of nonprofit hospitals, and insurance companies constitute some of the largest new foundations of recent years.[13]

Since the 1960s foundations have continued to respond to the restructuring of the American state. When the Nixon administration undertook to reduce federal funding for legal assistance and for community action programs, some of the affected organizations looked to foundations for aid. When Reagan administration legislation reduced funding for many federal programs and devolved some

9. Todd Wallack, "Attorney General Clears Irvine Foundation: Former CEO's Compensation Deemed Proper," *San Francisco Chronicle,* December 11, 2003, p. B1.

10. Katz (2006).

11. Grant Williams, "Making Philanthropy Accountable," *Chronicle of Philanthropy,* June 26, 2003.

12. Wells (1990); Attorney General of California, *Laws and Regulations,* 2007 (http://ag.ca.gov/ charities/statutes.php [March 2008]).

13. Indeed, three of the largest foundations in California—the California Endowment, the California Healthcare Foundation, and the California Wellness Foundation—are conversion foundations. "Conversion Foundations" (1997); Ferris and Melnick (2004). A related case concerns the Barnes Foundation, actually an operating nonprofit, whose board persuaded a Pennsylvania court to approve moving its entire art collection to a new building in downtown Philadelphia, despite the donor's original stipulation that the collection be housed in his home. Debra E. Blum, "Court Ruling Appears to End Dispute over Donor's Guidance," *Chronicle of Philanthropy,* May 12, 2005.

administrative responsibility for these programs to state and local government in the 1980s, those affected again turned to foundations. The Reagan administration's efforts to curtail federal regulation and to encourage privatization of government services also led to calls for foundation response. Over time, though, federal funding for health care, job training, and, until recently, low-income housing steadily increased. Lacking the resources to replace lost federal revenue and eager to help make the best possible use of new funding, several foundations have responded with greater direct engagement in public policy related to such matters as homelessness, AIDS, early childhood education, low-income housing, and community development. Often, foundation engagement with such matters comes in partnership with state or local governments. Nationally, the Milbank Memorial Fund has helped several state legislatures work on health policy, while the Robert Wood Johnson Foundation has supported many health-related research and demonstration projects.[14]

In the 1980s and 1990s, many government agencies embraced the Reinventing Government initiative, which emphasized greater attention to performance, accountability, and market-oriented policy instruments to address public policy problems (such as contracting for services and the use of vouchers), as well as more attention to community and citizen engagement in the delivery and evaluation of public services.[15] Governments at all levels responded with new evaluation requirements, performance-based contracting, and new demands for accountability and effectiveness. Some of the most notable foundation responses came from the Edna McConnell Clark, Annie E. Casey, and Robert Wood Johnson foundations, each of which invested millions of dollars in rigorous social science evaluations of their grant programs.[16] Joel Fleishman, a former leader of Atlantic Philanthropies, recently received widespread attention for his call for much greater foundation investment in evaluation.[17]

This restructuring of the American state and the new relationship between government and the nonprofit sector has had important effects on the role of foundations in contemporary American life. Two key developments are the diversification of public policy and the growth of more complex and varied philanthropic and charitable organizations.

Foundations and the Diversification of Public Policy

The use of tax deductions to encourage charitable giving in the United States has a long history, and other direct and indirect government support of nonprofit

14. Chapters 6 and 7, this volume.
15. Osborne and Gaebler (1993); Behn (2001).
16. Chapter 7, this volume; Connell and others (1995).
17. Fleishman (2007); see also Brest, Harvey, and Low (2009).

organizations, including various direct subsidies such as gifts of land, dates to the colonial era.[18] Since the 1960s the intentional use of policy to encourage giving and other desired behaviors has increased in scope and scale. Motivated by market-oriented approaches and demands for consumer choice, American governments at all levels have increasingly relied on such policy tools as tax credits, tax deductions, bonds, loans, vouchers (as for child care and housing), and quasi-vouchers such as Medicaid payments.[19]

Of particular relevance to this volume, this diversification of policy tools has promoted an increased engagement of foundations in public policy concerns. The 1986 Low Income Housing Tax Credit allows private investors to reduce their tax liability by purchasing tax credits; their payments are pooled with public and private funds to support low-income housing projects. The tax credit structure provides substantial funds to match foundation grants, such as those the Ford Foundation directs through the Local Initiatives Support Corporation and Enterprise Community Partners.[20] Many local community development corporations and other nonprofit housing entities have also received foundation funding.[21]

Several land conservation and preservation initiatives also pool foundation grants and private (and tax-deductible) individual and corporate philanthropy. The nonprofit Trust for Public Land, a national organization with many local chapters, has successfully protected hundreds of thousands of acres of land. Under its sometimes complicated land deals, an individual or corporate donor sells land to the trust (often at below-market price), which then sells or gives the land to a public or nonprofit organization. Often, a foundation provides the crucial funds.[22] The David and Lucile Packard Foundation, for example, has spent more than $175 million since 1998 for the Conserving California Landscape Initiative, joining Trust for Public Land chapters and local land trusts in preserving more than 342,000 acres.[23]

This mixing of direct and indirect public support with foundation support is apparent in the cultural arena as well. Government in the United States has never provided substantial direct funding for the arts. The federal government's role increased with the 1965 creation of the National Endowment for the Arts, but foundations continue to outspend government by a wide margin in their support of the arts.[24] The growth of cultural institutions has been made possible

18. Simon (1987); Hammack (2002).

19. Salamon (2002c).

20. Sviridoff (2004). Enterprise Community Partners was formally called the Enterprise Foundation, although it has always been a private 501(c)(3) charity.

21. Keyes and others (1996).

22. Richard King Mellon Foundation (2008).

23. Delfin and Tang (2006); David and Lucile Packard Foundation (2000).

24. See chapters 12 and 13, this volume.

through often elaborate and complex public-private partnerships involving private foundations, individual donors, and state and municipal government. These projects typically rely upon a mix of tax incentives, bond financing, direct government aid, foundation grants, and private donations.[25]

The diversification of policy tools evident in the public sector is mirrored in foundations themselves. Many foundations use a diverse mix of policy tools, including predevelopment loans, planning grants, and loans as well as grants for acquisition and construction of facilities. Furthermore, several foundations have revived a tradition of program-related investments (PRIs) from the late nineteenth and early twentieth centuries. In the Tax Reform Act of 1969, Congress imposed heavy taxes on investments by foundations that were considered so speculative or risky as to jeopardize the foundation's tax-exempt purpose. However, the law allowed higher-risk investments if they met three key conditions: they had a charitable purpose; they did not have as their primary goal the production of income or property appreciation; and they were not connected in any way to lobbying or electioneering.[26]

The Packard Foundation, for example, used the Conserving California Landscape Initiative as an opportunity to increase its commitment to program-related investments, using loans and other financing vehicles to purchase or facilitate the purchase of land or, in some cases, conservation easements. Packard also used a PRI in the form of a guaranty-collateral deposit with a local bank to secure a construction line of credit for the Community School of Music and Arts in the San Francisco Bay area. The Ford Foundation has used PRIs in its asset and community development programs to fund land trusts, revolving loans, microfinance programs, loan guarantees, and sometimes equity investments in for-profit companies with a social mission. Reflecting the diversification of policy tools as well, the Ford Foundation used a PRI to support the purchase by local communities of new public radio station licenses; the loan was then repaid by the station, using money raised through capital campaigns, the sale of tax-exempt bonds, and commercial capital. More recently, several foundations have used a PRI as a rapid-response strategy to address the serious problems resulting from the current financial crisis. For instance, the John D. and Catherine T. MacArthur Foundation responded to the homeowner foreclosure crisis with $34 million in program-related loans, including $15 million to Chicago's Shore-Bank, which specializes in loans and assistance to disadvantaged individuals and communities.[27]

25. Smith (2006).

26. Grantcraft, *Program-Related Investing: Skills and Strategies for New Funders,* 2006 (www.grantcraft.org/index.cfm?fuseaction=Page.viewPage&pageID=821 [November 28, 2009]); David and Lucile Packard Foundation (2006); Internal Revenue Service (2006); Schmalbeck (2004).

27. Lawrence (2009).

Many other foundations have used PRIs, although the total amount of grant funds devoted to such investments is still a relatively small part of total foundation giving. Nonetheless, PRIs are part of the more general effort by foundations to obtain greater leverage for their funds in a more complex era of denser organizational relationships and a much more extensive regulatory and funding role for government. Program-related investments—and, more broadly, foundation funding of public-private partnerships, social enterprises, and collaborations—can be crucial to the viability of important initiatives, even if the actual dollar amount of the foundation investment is relatively modest.

The diversification of foundation tools and the policy response to their use are also evident in the growth of new charitable instruments and opportunities. Donor-advised funds grew rapidly in recent years, contributing greatly to the growth of community foundations and commercial gift funds. Rapid growth and some well-publicized abuses drew the scrutiny of Congress, resulting in new regulations governing donor-advised funds in the Pension Protection Act of 2006.[28]

New and More Complex Organizational Options

Several developments illustrate the broader trend toward more complex organizational forms within the foundation world. Donor-advised funds, for example, exemplify the increasing use of choices that offer wealthy donors more flexibility in their gifts and give them greater control over the use of these funds even after they have received the benefit of tax deduction. Community foundations have become complicated institutions, with hundreds or even thousands of donors and generally with limited discretionary grant-giving resources. Supporting organizations, a complicated type of 501(c)(3) charity that qualifies as a public charity, also allow donors to avoid the stricter regulations that apply to private foundations.[29] Because supporting organizations report to the IRS through the charities they support, it is difficult even for the IRS to track their growth or monitor their activities.[30]

28. Bjorklund (2003); Council on Foundations, *Council Summary of the Charitable Provisions in HR 4,* 2006 (www.cof.org/Action/content.cfm?ItemNumber=5275&navItemNumber=5276 [March 2008]).

29. Bjorklund (2003); Korman (1994).

30. In one highly publicized case in Utah, a lawyer created eight supporting organizations, which in turn made large loans to the directors. Harvy Lipman and Grant Williams, "One Utah Lawyer Helped Create 8 Groups That Lent Money to Donors or Officers," *Chronicle of Philanthropy,* February 5, 2004. In other much-criticized cases, foundations have made grants to supporting organizations that are controlled by the foundation directors or public charities that they control. Foundations have then counted these grants toward their 5 percent minimum payout requirements. But this is arguably counter to the intent of Congress in the Tax Reform Act of 1969, which tried to encourage higher payouts and more community benefit broadly defined.

Congress has increased the regulation of supporting organizations.[31] But the substantial growth of supporting organizations and of advised funds underscores the increased complexity and hybridization of foundations (and nonprofit organizations more generally). Thus many nonprofit and public entities have created affiliated "foundations"—in reality, 501(c)(3) public charities that mostly raise annual funds but in some cases have also accepted supporting organizations and endowed funds.[32]

Health conversion foundations provide another example of the trend toward greater organizational diversity. Health conversion foundations present many difficult, complex issues for state regulators, especially in terms of the relationship between the boards of directors of nonprofit hospitals and health plans and the acquiring for-profit entity. Indeed, some transactions are structured as complicated mixed combinations of for-profits and nonprofits. State regulators do not typically have extensive capacity for monitoring health conversion foundations, whose focus is on fund-raising.[33]

Corporate foundations also exemplify this trend toward greater organizational complexity. The employees of the foundation are often employees of the corporation; the corporation provides direct cash support or in-kind assistance (or both), such as office space and utilities, and the boards of corporate foundations are typically controlled by the corporation. Predictably, the grant-making policies of corporate foundations are closely tied to the priorities of the corporation. Generally, corporate foundations have no endowment but depend upon annual allocations from the corporation.

Even as they have grown more complex, foundations have also contributed to the increasing diversity of nonprofits (although the rise of government funding has been perhaps an even more important factor). Many foundations prefer to fund program innovation and start-ups, promoting the creation of more local nonprofit organizations. As Robert Wuthnow and D. Michael Lindsay note in chapter 14, foundations have funded many new so-called parachurch groups. As several other contributors to this volume have documented, the Carnegie Corporation of New York, the Commonwealth Fund, and the Rockefeller, Ford, MacArthur, and Charles Stewart Mott foundations, among many others, helped

31. Council on Foundations, *Council Summary;* Independent Sector (2006).

32. Tribal governments are considered sovereign nations and as such are often ineligible to receive various types of public and private grants. Consequently, some tribal governments have created affiliated foundations to receive grants and donations, especially for capital purposes. For instance, the Port Gamble (Washington) S'Klallam Tribe created the S'Klallam Foundation as a public charity to raise money for a new career and education center and a new library, among other projects.

33. DeLucia (2001).

create extensive networks of nongovernmental organizations throughout the world.[34] And as noted, foundations have also supported collaborations, joint ventures, and partnerships in a variety of policy areas.

Finally, the increase in the number and scope of intermediary associations and groups representing foundation interests is worthy of emphasis as part of the changing organizational universe of foundations. Most visible is the Council on Foundations, created out of an older association of community foundations in response to the developments that led to the Tax Reform Act of 1969. As the major advocate for foundations, the council represents the foundation viewpoint on proposed regulation, provides technical assistance to members, and helps convene members around matters of common concern.

The Council on Foundations has also been a major force for self-regulation by foundations. For instance, it issued a Statement of Ethical Principles that seeks to encourage greater accountability on the part of foundations. The council recently developed national standards and ethical principles for community, corporate, and independent foundations and also for international grant making and initiated training programs focusing on best practices for foundation managers. Some of its affinity groups, such as the community foundation group, have also tried to promote ethical practice among their members.[35] Other intermediary organizations range from the Association of Small Foundations to Independent Sector, which seeks to represent organized philanthropy and nonprofit organizations as a whole, especially pertaining to public policy issues related to philanthropy, before Congress and the IRS.[36]

Overall, the growth of foundations and their complexity has attracted increased policymaker interest. Legislation provides foundations with the subsidy of tax advantages, so legislators ask what foundations are doing to justify those advantages. As conservative legislators in Congress have sought to reduce the role of government, especially in the social policy arena, they have called upon philanthropy, including foundations, to replace government in addressing social problems. The highly partisan atmosphere of contemporary American politics creates an atmosphere in which foundations and their ties to politicians are scrutinized and debated. The general push for higher levels of accountability in government, with its attendant focus on performance measures and outcome evaluation, has encouraged some policymakers to call for tighter regulation of private foundations and nonprofit organizations more generally.

34. Chapters 1–4, 6, 8, and 10–12, this volume.

35. For more detail on the Council on Foundations standards and ethical principles, see www. cof.org/templates/41.cfm?ItemNumber=16761&navItemNumber=14854 (November 26, 2009).

36. Independent Sector (2008).

Policy and Management Challenges

The growth in the number and nominal assets of foundations, the increase in the complexity of the foundation universe, and the changing political and economic environment for foundations create nettlesome policy dilemmas for foundation executives, policymakers, donors, and recipient organizations of foundations. Policymakers are tempted to demand more and more from foundations, even as their total wealth has declined sharply in relation to the sums that flow through the fields they address. This decline was marked as early as the 1960s, even before passage of the Tax Reform Act of 1969; the present financial crisis has further reduced these resources.

Transparency

The Tax Reform Act of 1969 was designed to greatly increase the accountability of private foundations to government and the taxpayers. But the regulations embodied in the legislation encourage donors and foundation executives to seek more flexible options, including greater use of supporting organizations, public charity status, and donor-advised funds. Furthermore, many foundations have complex relationships with their grantees and with intermediary organizations serving these grantees. To date, the government regulatory structure for foundations is not well positioned to monitor this increased complexity. First, the staff capacity and resources of the IRS and state regulatory agencies have not kept pace with the growth in foundations, although efforts have been made in recent years to add more staff to improve monitoring and enforcement.

Second, and related, the existing reporting system for foundations needs to be revisited. At the federal level, the principal form of oversight of the IRS is the annual filing of its Form 990-PF. The IRS reviews the information in a foundation's annual filing, but the data requested in the form are ill suited to ongoing monitoring and regulation of foundations; the standard Form 990, relevant to the rapidly growing donor-advised funds and supporting organizations, is even less useful for this purpose. Because donor-advised funds of community foundations and supporting organizations of public charities have not been subject to detailed reporting, the IRS (like the relevant state authorities) has found it difficult to evaluate compliance with rules governing the relationship of the donor to the fund's investments, loans, and grants.[37] Most states also need a more detailed reporting system to better inform their regulatory decisions.

Third, transparency is a more pronounced challenge for citizens owing to the increased diversity of the foundation and philanthropic world. Many private, nonoperating foundations, especially larger foundations such as the Ford, Bill

---

37. U.S. Government Accountability Office (2006, p. 3).

and Melinda Gates, and Rockefeller foundations, have detailed reporting procedures that go well beyond the requirements of federal law. These foundations publish annual reports and provide extensive information for citizens and potential recipient organizations on their grant-giving activities. But many smaller foundations, especially family foundations as well as donor-advised funds and supporting organizations, often do not provide easily accessible information on their grant-giving policies and awards. Smaller nonprofit organizations without substantial staffs may find it especially challenging to identify appropriate grant-giving opportunities. In short, citizens are not well positioned to exercise accountability vis-à-vis these foundations.

Politics, Public Policy, and Foundations

The issue of transparency is directly related to the concern in Congress and at the state level with the grant-giving policies of foundations. Part of this concern stems from belief that foundations are very rich and that they are not making appropriate use of their wealth. As several of the chapters in this volume note, however, foundation resources have been shrinking, especially in relation to the American economy as a whole and in relation to the sums involved in addressing issues in the fields of religion, health, education, the arts, international affairs, and social welfare. The financial crisis of the early twenty-first century has led to steep declines in these assets, though the total holdings of American foundations do remain quite large. The foundation world is complex and diverse; it does not speak with a unified voice, it supports a wide range of initiatives (many of which celebrate minority interests), and it can be difficult to understand. Moreover, as noted above, political interests critical of some foundation work would like to see foundation assets diverted to the support of other programs.

From a number of motives, some members of Congress in recent years have discussed or even formally submitted proposals to increase the regulation of foundations. Some favor an increase in the current 5 percent yearly payout rate for private foundations. A hotly debated proposal in 2003 and 2004 would have changed the current rules under which foundations can count a substantial part of their administrative costs against that 5 percent requirement.[38] In related arguments, those who believe that tax-advantaged charity should largely be directed to the relief of poverty point out, for example, that where school districts rely on private giving, wealthy school districts have a definite advantage.

38. William A. Schambra, "The New Politics of Philanthropy," *Chronicle of Philanthropy,* November 13, 2003; Pablo Eisenberg, "Don't Cry for Thee, Foundations," *Chronicle of Philanthropy,* May 29, 2003. In 2003 the former New York attorney general Eliot Spitzer similarly proposed a minimum asset size for foundations in an effort to encourage, at least in part, more grant giving. Williams, "Making Philanthropy Accountable."

The Greenlining Institute, based in San Francisco, has sharply criticized foundations for their lack of giving to communities of color.[39] Critics of the foundation preference for capital expenses, program innovation, specific projects, and start-up also raise questions of equity and redistribution, rejecting foundation arguments that their limited resources make it impossible for them to underwrite most operating costs of nonprofit agencies.[40]

As noted, foundations are strictly prohibited from engaging in electioneering or directly seeking to influence legislation. By contrast, public charities can devote up to 20 percent or more of their budgets to advocacy designed to influence legislation.[41] The Tax Reform Act of 1969 reinforced the view in most private foundations that it was important to avoid direct engagement in politics or advocacy activity. Yet in 2005, *Roll Call,* the newspaper reporting on Congress, noted that more than four dozen foundations were connected to members of Congress. Some of these foundations were created long before the person was elected to Congress. However, some were created with unspent campaign funds, and others had close connections to political contributors. Critics argue that some foundations are supporting politicians or political candidates in a way that violates at least the spirit of current federal and state law.[42]

New regulations pertaining to international grant making by foundations in the wake of 9/11 have also raised concerns about the relationship between foundations and government. In 2002 the U.S. Treasury Department issued voluntary guidelines to ensure that no funds were going to groups that supported terrorism.[43] Many foundations raised concerns about the original guidelines, which were eventually revised to incorporate feedback from the philanthropic community. Nonetheless, the guidelines have arguably had a substantial effect on foundation grant-giving behavior, especially giving to controversial nongovernmental organizations abroad.

Maintaining Relevance and Impact

The foundation community drew from the Tax Reform Act of 1969 the lesson that it needed to be more attentive to the policymaking process. Through the Council on Foundations and by other means, foundations have successfully met most subsequent legislative challenges. Nevertheless, the act has contributed

39. Reich (2005). Fulton and Blau (2006) have echoed this critique by noting that universities received 26.8 percent of the giving of the largest foundations, while only 9.7 percent went to human services. For the Greenlining Institute critique, see Pittz and Sen (2004).

40. Krehely and House (2005).

41. Reid (1999); Berry and Arons (2003).

42. Cohen and Krehely (2005); Leslie Lenkowsky, "How Washington's Political Scandals Could Harm Nonprofit Groups," *Chronicle of Philanthropy,* June 23, 2005.

43. U.S. Department of the Treasury (2006).

over time to a smaller and smaller role for foundations within the overall philanthropic world. Wealthy individuals and companies can now select from a wide array of charitable vehicles, including donor-advised funds, supporting organizations, charitable remainder trusts, and public charities.[44]

To be sure, foundations will continue to wield considerable policy influence, and some have the resources to address important issues. With its extraordinary assets, the Gates Foundation will continue to have the capability to make substantial contributions to the solution of important social and health problems around the world. More typically, though, most foundations are relatively small, with modest assets and few or no staff.[45] Most grants are modest in size. Philanthropy Northwest, the association for organized philanthropy in the six-state Pacific Northwest region, found that the median grant for all foundations was approximately $3,000.[46] With such small grants, it is difficult for foundations to have substantial policy or organizational impact. This is especially so when grants are scattered to many, many organizations and when so many of the newer grant seekers are small community agencies that lack adequate capital, infrastructure, and even grant-writing capacity.

Government policy compounds the problem of impact. The increased regulatory role of government and the growth of government funding in education, health care, social welfare, and other classic foundation fields necessarily reduce the influence of foundations and other forces.[47] Yet to the extent that resistance to taxes and other factors have shifted government's funding role to tax credits, bonds, vouchers, and competitive contracts, government has less capability to shoulder the funding responsibility for new programs. In many fields, the logic of foundation funding thus requires reconsideration.

Some foundations have seen their role as supporting innovation and program reform, with the expectation that government might then choose to support worthy programs once their effectiveness has been demonstrated. Scarcer, more targeted government funding forces a different approach. A number of foundations now place more emphasis on impact, logic models and other tools of evaluation, and capacity building as a way of promoting greater effectiveness. Some foundation approaches have become similar to those of the governments that dominate their chosen fields.

---

44. Indeed, the announcement that Google has created a for-profit company (Google.org) as its philanthropic arm underscores just how dramatically the field of philanthropy is changing and the challenges faced by private foundations in maintaining their relevance. Katie Hafner, "Philanthropy Google's Way: Not the Usual," *New York Times,* September 14, 2006; Fulton and Blau (2006).

45. In 2002 there were 64,843 private foundations, yet only 3,360 had paid staff. Fulton and Blau (2006).

46. Philanthropy Northwest (2008).

47. Chapter 3, this volume, addresses the role of government in funding and regulating education.

Foundations are also increasing their use of mission-based and program-related investing.[48] A foundation interested in helping low-income communities, for example, might invest a small part of its endowment in institutions or funding vehicles such as loans that benefit these same low-income communities. Such investments reflect foundation efforts to distinguish themselves by their ability to act quickly in support of a nonprofit's capital or start-up project.

Indeed, as foundations wrestle with an increasingly turbulent and difficult revenue environment, it is useful to consider their past policy roles as a guide to future directions and strategy. Collectively, the chapters in this volume provide an excellent overview of the varied ways in which foundations have tried to use resources that have always been limited in relation to their aims to influence public policy and promote social and policy change.

Given the prohibition on the direct engagement of foundations in the support of lobbying and political activity, it is perhaps not surprising that foundations have typically tried to influence policy indirectly. As noted, for example, in the chapters on international grant making, foundations played three crucial convening roles: bringing donors together, identifying institutional and individual partners, and advancing project goals.[49] Over the entire course of the twentieth century, foundations played similar roles in the fields of elementary and secondary education, higher education, and health care. In the field of social policy, foundations have often supported collaborative partnerships in the interests of attracting other resources.[50] In general, the growing interest in greater impact and leverage on the part of grantees and governments, as well as of foundation leaders, encourages foundations to collaborate.[51]

Foundations also support policy change through institutional support. This role is vividly evident in many newly democratizing countries in Eastern Europe during the 1990s, where foundations have supported the establishment of non-governmental organizations dedicated to promoting good government, democracy, and transparency.[52] As noted earlier in this chapter, foundations have also played a key role in supporting the development of new infrastructure of low-income housing and community development agencies as well as many other new community organizations in social and health services. They have aided national organizations supporting women's rights and civil rights.[53] More generally, foundations have encouraged the growth of nonprofits through their interest in organizational start-ups and innovation.

48. F. B. Heron Foundation (2007).
49. Chapters 10 and 11, this volume.
50. Chapters 7 and 8, this volume.
51. Fleishman (2007).
52. Chapter 8, this volume.
53. Chapters 15 and 16, this volume.

Concluding Thoughts

Foundations can influence public policy in many ways.[54] Indeed, one of the enduring concerns in American public policy is whether foundations are somehow supporting causes or influencing public policy in ways that are not transparent and consistent with their tax-exempt status. To a large extent, foundations have found their legitimacy and public support, despite these concerns, through their funding of nonprofit organizations and through a gradual increase in transparency.[55] Today's more complicated and diverse policy and organizational environment, together with increasingly constrained resources, push foundations to be more strategic and to seek to demonstrate value and impact.

Indeed, foundations are likely to face continuing pressure—both from government and from the competitive marketplaces of donors and recipient organizations—to undertake new strategies and policies to enhance impact. To be sure, many foundations will continue to fill particular market niches that may be quite unrelated to public policy and to view their role as strictly private.

Foundations appear to be at an important moment in their historical relation to public policy. Major new federal legislation pertaining to foundations appears unlikely in the near future, especially given the financial crisis. Yet pressure will continue for more self-regulation of foundations and more transparency, accountability, and impact. In the crowded marketplace of individual and organized philanthropy, foundations will need to distinguish themselves and maintain the trust and support of the community and policymakers. The diversification of public policy and the public and nonprofit organizational universe provides more opportunities for foundations to become engaged in addressing important public problems. This new landscape of organizations requires support if it is to be sustained. Foundations are focusing more attention on the institutional infrastructure and the capacity of recently created nonprofit organizations vital to the aspirations of struggling communities. Balancing support for sustainability, capacity building, and impact with the diverse roles that foundations continue to play in many fields will be one of the major challenges for foundations in an increasingly complex and uncertain political and economic environment.

54. Ferris and Mintrom (2002); Smith (2002); Bernholz (2002); Colwell (1993); Ylvisaker (1987); Fleishman (2007).

55. Hammack (2006).

18

Looking Forward: American Foundations between Continuity and Change

DAVID C. HAMMACK AND HELMUT K. ANHEIER

Over their long history, American foundations have created a considerable list of positive contributions to society, as the contributors to this book have shown. Foundations have also had a long time in which to record controversy, false starts, inconsistency, disappointment, futility, and sometimes failure. The American public has both celebrated and criticized foundations. It has celebrated them chiefly for their philanthropic contributions, their support of innovations, their sometimes critical support for new institutions, practices, policies, and creative individuals, and for new ideas generally. Foundations have also made vital (though too often ignored) efforts to control, invest, and preserve the traditional values of particular groups and communities, to preserve honored purposes, traditions, and identities, and to support and encourage those who devote themselves to valued purposes. They have supported individual achievement, helping tradespeople get a start in life and enabling talent to excel and break new scientific, artistic, and intellectual ground.

Americans have criticized foundations for all these things and also for their alleged conservatism, liberalism, elitism, radicalism, devotion to religious tradition, hostility to religion—in short, for commitments to causes whose significance can be measured, in part, by the controversies they provoke. Americans have also criticized foundations for ineffectiveness and even foolishness. Foundations have undertaken many ambitious and difficult projects. Success has almost always required the cooperation of other actors and outside forces in ways that, in hindsight, some foundations did not adequately appreciate. Most fundamentally, foundations can and in many cases do contribute to the vitality of American civil society.

Over the years, foundations have grown so numerous, and so diverse in size and in purpose, that it has become impossible to describe their contributions, positive or not, in a single set of phrases or statements, let alone in any set of numbers. At the same time, it is possible to offer some general observations about the larger grant-making foundations, which have been the focus of this book.

The first, and perhaps the most important, is that grant-making foundations have never held overwhelming amounts of money in relation to the fields they address. Throughout the history of U.S. foundations, there has been a persistent and significant mismatch between aspiration and available resources—a discrepancy that continues and is even widening today. Some foundation leaders have perhaps sought to increase their influence by cultivating the notion that foundations are very rich institutions. Some observers like to think that foundation wealth is so great that it demands seriously critical attention. In the second and third decades of the twentieth century a very few foundations were indeed sufficiently wealthy, in relation to other institutions in some fields of action, to launch major initiatives, even against strong opposition. The institutional constellation of the 1920s and 1930s was an exception in American history; yet the foundation experience of that relatively short and unsettled period continues to cast a shadow on current perceptions and practices. By contrast, the experience of more recent decades shows that foundation resources—despite significant growth and despite the vast resources added to the field by the Bill and Melinda Gates and other foundations—are quite limited, relative to their ambitions, and are likely to remain so for the foreseeable future.

Given this persistent mismatch between objectives and means, it is no surprise that foundations have rarely made contributions, positive or negative, on their own; rather, they work, typically and necessarily, in some form of partnership or another.[1] This is an important observation, for since the middle of the

1. In chapter 8, Wolfgang Bielefeld and Jane Chu note that for forty years the Russell Sage Foundation worked closely with many groups in the social welfare field. In separate work, Judith Sealander (1997) explores the failures of several sustained foundation campaigns to improve America's morals during the 1920s and 1930s. As James Allen Smith observes in chapter 12, foundations worked with other donors to create America's networks of orchestras and museums. The Guggenheim Foundation, like the later MacArthur Foundation, continues to make grants to individuals, but both rely on expert advisers and expect winners to work through the nation's institutions for the arts, sciences, humanities, and social change. In chapter 10, Steven Heydemann and Rebecca Kinsey note foundation support for international initiatives that were necessarily led by the federal government, including the new United Nations and America's engagement with the "new nations" in the postcolonial period of the cold war. Small clusters of foundations have done much in recent years, as chapters 15 and 16 emphasize, to create such new fields as women's studies and African

twentieth century, foundations have worked with institutions whose resources have grown far larger. In 2004–05, for example, Americans spent a total of $536 billion on elementary and secondary education, some $350 billion on colleges and universities, and $1,894 billion on health care.[2] By comparison, total foundation giving came to just $36.4 billion in 2005—or less than 1 percent of the total spent on these and other fields of foundation interest, such as social services, arts and culture, or the environment.[3] Ten percent of total foundation giving consisted of the value of drugs provided to needy patients through patient assistance foundations of pharmaceutical corporations.[4] Much more was strictly limited in purpose. So how can relatively small amounts of resources make a difference, and in what way?

Could the difference foundations make simply be in the form of voluntary redistribution from those who have more money to those who have less? The evidence and the studies presented in this book indicate that foundations do indeed redistribute some money but in a rather limited way. Rather than as significant agents of redistribution, it is more useful to think of foundations as devices for holding, investing, and dispensing charitable and religious funds over time.

In addition to money, the contributions of foundations also include intangible resources. Foundations create new institutional realities, make practices routine, and help shape diverse public spheres. To the extent that they become accepted, foundation initiatives contribute to the institutional blueprints by which the United States addresses social problems, makes policy, and reviews its progress. Foundation-created institutional realities also include the competitive grant-seeking and grant-making process itself and the notion that nonpartisan nonspecialists are capable of evaluating the worthiness of ideas and initiatives.

American studies in American colleges—and in the process, to shape those fields in ways that have sometimes been more compatible with academic culture and American society in general than with the most transformative demands of the civil rights movement. In particular communities, clusters of foundations typically provide valuable long-sustained support for local universities and colleges, hospitals and clinics, museums, theaters, orchestras, and dance companies; but given the limits of their resources, foundations must accept the greater influence of consumers and governments on such institutions.

2. U.S. Department of Education, "No Child Left Behind: 10 Facts about K–12 Education Funding," June 2005 (www.ed.gov/about/overview/fed/10facts/index.html [November 28, 2009]); Organization for Economic Cooperation and Development, "Country Statistical Profiles: United States" (http://stats.oecd.org/wbos/viewhtml.aspx?queryname=485&querytype=view&lang=en).

3. Amy Blackwood, Kennard T. Wing, and Thomas H. Pollak, "The Nonprofit Sector in Brief" (http://nccsdataweb.urban.org/kbfiles/797/Almanac2008publicCharities.pdf), p. 6.

4. Foundation Center estimate of $3.2 billion for 2005 (foundationcenter.org/gainknowledge/research/pdf/fgge07.pdf [January 22, 2010]).

Through their actions, foundations can help give credibility, value, and attention to particular ideas, perspectives, disciplines, individuals, even professions. Intangible as well as monetary resources enable foundations to bring people and institutions together, to encourage dialogue, to mediate, to seek consensus. Foundations can also act to withhold recognition, to exclude people and institutions, to withdraw support, and to ignore needs and opportunities if they so choose. By playing the roles of broker and gatekeeper foundations help shape the development of American society.

The contributions to this book show that foundations have indeed provided sustained and sometimes creative and effective support for the educational, health-related, research, social service, religious, and related activities that have always been legally defined as charitable in the United States. As noted in the introduction, the very availability of the foundation form, reinforced by the example of much foundation work, has increased the total amount of wealth given to charitable and philanthropic causes in the United States.[5] Much evidence in this book demonstrates that foundations, together with the endowment funds of nonprofit organizations, have made it possible to set aside funds for long-term efforts, despite the sometimes dramatic ups and downs of the American economy.

In this way foundations have helped build self-sustaining institutions and corresponding professional communities, ranging from schools, hospitals, clinics, research institutes, social service agencies, and arts organizations to religious groups. Through these institutions and professions, some foundations have relieved immediate need, sometimes over long periods of time and to relatively large numbers of people; some have played philanthropic roles though the support of innovation and policy change. Frequently, foundations have helped shape the control of charitable funds for the benefit and the protection of others.

As is clear from the work discussed in this book, the common notion that foundations do their work chiefly by making discrete grants is inadequate. Foundations necessarily work in concert with other institutions. And foundations have made the most impressive philanthropic contributions when they

5. Expanding philanthropy has been a classic foundation purpose. John D. Rockefeller's Cleveland associate Frank Goff started the Cleveland Foundation so that less wealthy people could participate in foundation philanthropy; the Cleveland and other community foundations gave sustained early support to the Community Chest (later United Way) workplace giving movement; more recently, the Lilly, the Charles Stewart Mott, and other foundations have given substantial support to efforts to create new community foundations; and in the 1980s and 1990s Lilly, Mott, Atlantic Philanthropies, and several other major foundations underwrote much of the cost of developing an infrastructure for the fields of philanthropic and nonprofit studies and professional education.

committed substantial funds, expertise, and recognition to sustained work for larger, and clearly articulated, purposes.

Examples reach back to the beginnings of the Republic and are found throughout U.S. foundation history. Some of the earliest funds, launched after the American Revolution ended British control of church establishments, underwrote salaries and pensions for the clergy and teachers of America's newly formed Protestant denominations. In the last decades of the nineteenth century, the Peabody Education Fund promoted public education in the southern states by working with local school advocates and government officials, as Pamela Barnhouse Walters and Emily A. Bowman show in their chapter. At the beginning of the twentieth century, Andrew Carnegie used a foundation-like office to build America's national system of locally supported public libraries, while the Carnegie Foundation for the Advancement of Teaching worked with scores of private colleges to set up the Teachers Insurance and Annuity Association, the chief retirement program for professors, and to launch the College Board to coordinate key aspects of the college admissions process. As Daniel Fox notes, the Rockefeller Foundation took up Carnegie's plan of creating the modern, university research–based medical center, enlisting local foundations in a dozen or more states to create the larger system, while the Commonwealth Fund worked closely with medical researchers. The Rockefeller, Julius Rosenwald, and Guggenheim foundations and related funds did much to establish America's research universities and related associations of professional researchers, a history ably reviewed in this volume by Steven Wheatley. A specialized group of foundations, as Steven Heydemann and Rebecca Kinsey note, did much to underwrite the development of area studies and international affairs at American universities.

Foundations also exercise a controlling role by shielding special interests or groups and generally by increasing the odds that a valued activity or cherished value will persist despite the vicissitudes of the economy and government and the frailties of human beings. Foundation control complicates the direction not only of social movements but also of nonprofit organizations and government agencies. This is the necessary and inevitable result of the fact that foundations make their own decisions, retain the ability to reconsider a given grant program, and can shift funds, sometimes on very short notice, from one activity, organization, field, or locale to another. Foundations have the legal right to ignore the concerns or plans of a supported nonprofit's board and employees, of government agency leaders, and of members of a beneficiary community.[6] Peter Frumkin and Gabriel Kaplan note that a number of foundations do not believe a university has done anything significant unless it turns away from its traditional commitment to research and teaching and emphasizes efforts to advance social change. We would

6. For this view, see Douglas and Wildavsky (1978); for an analytic account, see Wheatley (1988).

add that most foundations derive their legitimacy not from a commitment to science but from their more general reputations for probity, commitment to the values of their communities, and wealth. Thus foundations almost by definition celebrate the virtues of the public-spirited generalist and the well-meaning amateur rather than the trained scientist, professional, or policy expert.

These are broad conclusions about the general character of foundation contributions. Of course, foundations have highly diverse records. We and our associates have not found evidence that foundations in any field have been especially notable for facilitating tax evasion or financial skullduggery—though foundation donors and staffs are certainly not exempt from human weakness. Nor do we know of evidence that foundations are notable for political offenses: business and professional firms and government agencies, many of which command more resources than almost any foundation, also find themselves used for illegitimate and abusive purposes.[7]

According to other critics, foundations are or have been too far to the political left or right or have failed to honor their founders' purposes.[8] Such critiques are fundamentally political. They entail many assumptions, often generalize far beyond available data, and encourage speculation about motives. As civic actors, foundations are subject to public evaluation, criticism, and exhortation. Our collaborators in this book have noted occasions when observers have given foundations credit for results—the development of segregated and unequal public schools in the South, the creation of the modern research university and medical center, the creation of the Educational Testing Service, or the expansion of university extension—for which many other actors share responsibility. Our collaborators and others have also identified occasions when foundation contributions fell short of what would have been required to overcome those who opposed particular reforms, as, for example, in the improvement of public morals during the 1920s and 1930s and of the morality of university faculties in the 1950s, the promotion of something like universal health care in the 1930s, the improvement of public education in one important way or another in every decade since the 1920s, the creation of an effective system of foster care in any decade, or the significant reduction of federal funding for the arts in the 1990s.

The U.S. Constitution's protections of speech, belief, and property rights make foundations possible; by definition, to have large foundations is to have centers of effective action outside of elected governments. The legal and political

7. Lehman Brothers Holdings, for example, in its Form 10-K for November 30, 2007, reported more than $691 billion in assets and liabilities—considerably more than the assets of all U.S. foundations together. U.S. Securities and Exchange Commission Edgar website (www.sec.gov/edgar.shtml [November 28, 2009]). See McDonald (2009, pp. 298–99). The total value of U.S. residential mortgages, to take another number, is about $10 trillion.

8. Olasky (1992); Colwell (1993); Covington (1997); Wooster (1994).

ideas and arrangements of American society, including the arrangements that support foundations, reinforce what the historian Norman Silber describes as "a corporate form of freedom" and the political scientists Robert Dahl, Kenneth Prewitt, and others describe variously as "polyarchy" and "pluralism."[9] It is therefore not surprising that for more than a hundred years, American courts, regulators, and legislators have steadily agreed that nonsectarian, general-purpose foundations have a right to independent existence and indeed to substantial tax exemption privileges, so long as they do not advance the personal wealth of donors and their families and so long as they devote their resources to a wide range of charitable purposes and in general contribute constructively to American pluralism.

The dominant American political traditions have never required that foundations (or other charities) seek specifically to relieve immediate need, reduce poverty, or, in economic terms, play a role in the general redistribution of wealth. American law and regulation have always insisted that donors, and the foundations they create, have the right to advance a range of beliefs or virtues, whatever pressing needs society might have. In general, American traditions encourage donor commitments across a spectrum of fields and concerns that range from the religious and cultural to health and social welfare and the study of public policy. While some voices urge that the relief of poverty or the redress of discrimination ought to be the chief foundation purpose, others press the case for innovative medical research, effective and innovative social policy, and fundamental religious or cultural values.

The acceptable range of views has changed over time, reflecting the fortunes and misfortunes of American history; nonetheless, it suggests a general trajectory. The acceptable range of views was significantly limited under slavery, during the Jim Crow era of racial segregation, and to some extent in times of war, but it has always been relatively wide and has generally expanded over the decades. Challenges to foundation autonomy, such as those raised during the cold war, have generally failed to impose severe or continuing restrictions. This is partly, no doubt, because foundation leaders have anticipated criticism (as Pamela Walters and Emily Bowman and Dan Fox note), thereby earning later censure for bending to the pressures of a political moment. American foundations, like other charities, justify their existence and their privileges not so much by such specific achievements as reducing poverty or relieving taxpayers of the expense of public facilities and services as by enriching America's varieties of religious, scientific, cultural, and policy initiatives and action.

9. Silber (2001); Dahl (1971); Prewitt (2001). One of the present authors has developed a closely related analysis in Hammack (1978).

As we argue in the introduction to this volume, American foundations have made their contributions in four quite distinct eras. Foundations appear to us to be in the early phase of the fourth era, characterized by acceptance of variety and a focus on measurable results. Foundations today differ more widely from one another than ever in size, operations, and purposes. The contexts in which foundations seek to make their mark appear to have stabilized in many ways. Consumers and federal and state taxpayers continue to pay for the great bulk of education, health care, social services, recreation and the arts, and income support for the young, the elderly, and the disabled. Many interests support the continued use of vouchers and voucherlike arrangements (food stamps, rent supplements, Medicare and Medicaid payments for medical services, grants to college students, and so on). Schools, hospitals, teachers, nurses, doctors, and others essential to the provision of services in these fields are strongly institutionalized. Religious communities continue to show great strength and resilience in American society. The movement toward government funding of faith-based activities and its use of voucherlike funding arrangements reinforces government's defining role in these fields. Strong advocates urge various reforms of elementary and secondary education, collegiate education, health care, foster care, and care for the elderly. If they succeed, likely reforms will probably not change the relevance of American foundations.

Responding to their reduced relative wealth and to the maturation of their fields of interest, many foundation leaders have accepted new realities. They understand the complexity of their fields. They emphasize the need to focus, to pursue objectives that fit their resources, to find niches in which they can achieve measurable and sustainable results. Many foundations promote social innovations that markets, including markets funded with government vouchers, will support. Others develop wide-ranging engagements with government policy and civil society. Still others seek above all to preserve cultural, artistic, environmental, social, and religious values. In short, a new foundation era may well be emerging, an era characterized by acceptance of foundation variety, an understanding of the severe limits on foundation resources and capabilities, a strong commitment to distinctive values, a search for leverage, and a focus on measurable and sustainable results.

An extensive and widely discussed literature urging "venture" or "strategic" action from foundations is one reason for our sense that we are entering a new era. Christine Letts, William Ryan, and Allen Grossman have won considerable attention for their call for "venture philanthropy," their argument that what they broadly label as "traditional philanthropy" has performed in lackluster fashion and that foundations would benefit from the infusion of venture capital techniques. These include adopting performance measures, avoiding "scatterization" by placing large bets on chosen organizations, working closely with them to produce results, and exiting at the appropriate time.[10] At the center of this model is the concept of treating funding as an investment rather than a discrete charitable gift, with corresponding expectations of return on investment, operating efficiencies, and management oversight that this shift requires.

As we have seen, many of the most successful foundation interventions over the past 150 years have, in fact, shared many of these characteristics. That can certainly be said about such recent initiatives as those seeking to improve health care in the United States (including the Robert Wood Johnson Foundation's efforts, described in this volume by James R. Knickman and Stephen L. Isaacs, as well as the Kaiser Family and Gates foundations, the Milbank Memorial Fund, and several others). It can as well be said of those seeking in sometimes competing ways to improve the effectiveness of elementary and secondary education (including efforts discussed in this volume by Elisabeth Clemens and Linda C. Lee, whose varied funders include the Annenberg, Lynde and Harry Bradley, Ford, Thomas B. Fordham, Gates, and Walton Family foundations and the Carnegie Foundation for the Advancement of Teaching, among others) and of the John M. Olin and other foundations that have supported the broad-based effort to create a network of conservative think tanks and policy advocates (discussed in this volume by Alice O'Connor).[11]

Such an approach clearly appeals to confident, aggressive venture capitalists who—much like the entrepreneurial industrialists and university builders of the early twentieth-century foundations—view philanthropy as investment intended to produce specific social changes. Consistent with this view, they demand business plans, explicit "logic models" showing how and why projected actions are expected to produce desired results, and specific measures to demonstrate whether their funds produce the intended return on investment.[12]

Bruce Sievers and other critics have raised questions about notions of venture and strategic philanthropy.[13] Sievers also points out that nonprofit and

10. Letts, Ryan, and Grossman (1997).

11. See also the thoughtful insider's account by Miller (2006).

12. The International Network on Strategic Philanthropy, a virtual think tank project that operated from 2001 to 2005, developed the perspective that venture philanthropy involves an emphasis on social justice; "model solutions, new ways of thinking, and new understanding [that] include both blueprints and a focus on practical implementation"; "a ["proactive"] concern for the effectiveness" and on "capacity building and organizational learning"; a "public policy orientation driven by the potential of taking project results to scale"; and "investment in the production of public goods, preferably aiming at innovations or increased effectiveness" (www.bertelsmann-stiftung.de/cps/rde/xchg/SID-766DBA9C-E076E429/bst_engl/hs.xsl/prj_7504_7512.htm [November 28, 2009]).

13. Sievers (2001); see also Karoff (2004). Bruce Sievers observes that venture capitalists expect that many of the enterprises in which they invest will fail and have not yet demonstrated that their approach makes business success more likely. A careful staff report for the Federal Reserve Bank of

government entities, unlike many business firms, provide services widely seen as indispensable (above all, health care, schooling, and care for the young and the disabled) and adds that nonprofit entities seek multiple goals rather than a single bottom line that can be measured as clearly as we try to measure profit.[14] Some of these goals can be measured but not, perhaps, the gains in insight won by a foundation-supported visitor to a foreign land or the quality and ultimate value of the music composed at a foundation-supported artistic retreat.[15] Finally, while it is appropriate for the owner to call the shots in a business, nonprofit organizations do not have owners in the same sense and by definition should not be entirely beholden to donors, because they exist to serve particular communities or the public at large.

It does strike us that demands for immediate and demonstrable results, and for other forms of direct control, may sometimes reflect donors' recognition of the fact that the fields in which they hope to realize their ambitions are large and complicated. Most donors understand that they cannot expect to impose their will on a nonprofit organization or government agency in the way a dominant investor can with a firm. Foundations support organizations that must take account of their largest sources of funds and are highly regulated by professional standards as well as by governments. As noted at the outset of this conclusion, the financial capacities of consumers and governments dwarf the resources of foundations.

Indeed, because government resources are so great and because alternative sources of funding are so unlikely to appear, many calls for taking new social initiatives to scale seem more likely to express dissatisfaction with current government policy, or with current taxes, than to succeed in reducing their importance. Many other institutional, professional, economic, religious, and community interests dominate the fields of health, education, economic development, and social and family relations. They often overwhelm foundation influence.

Discussions of foundations too often ignore such contextual factors. What Nassim Nicholas Taleb has been trying to persuade us about markets applies to philanthropy as well: we are easily "fooled by randomness" into believing

---

New York observes that "the 1990s . . . witnessed the proliferation of many chancy high-growth technology and Internet issuers" and a significantly increased rate of failure among new firms in those fields. This report also notes that sponsorship by a firm of venture capitalists was associated with an increased risk of failure. Peristiani (2003).

14. We would add that in many cases the public rightly asks that nonprofit organizations, whether religious, educational, cultural, scientific, or medical, not only make use of the "newest and best" but also stand for enduring values.

15. Sievers (2001) quotes an Annie E. Casey Foundation official's warning against "a system in which we now cannot admit that evidence is scant and shaky and have to continue pumping up expectations about not only our successes but about our ability to measure success."

false claims about cause and effect. That is, highly publicized juxtapositions, often involving striking and plausible but in reality unique and poorly understood cases, seem to demonstrate that certain actions will always bring specific consequences. Taleb reminds us of the large role played in the investment markets by inertia, chance, and poorly understood relationships.[16] We would add that in charitable fields as well, outcomes are often shaped by factors that most participants are not equipped to understand. Thirty years ago James Coleman demonstrated, for example, that family origins shaped student achievement to a much greater degree than anything done by schools; later experience showed that schools could be made even less effective if reforms disrupted their internal workings and their relationships with their communities.[17] Campaigns to improve public health, literacy, the standard of living, civility or other virtues, or world peace (as our colleagues Steven Heydemann and Rebecca T. Kinsey note) are at least as complicated as the affairs of commerce and industry. Foundations serve many purposes, and it is difficult to specify direct measurements for their effectiveness in advancing the arts and other "merit goods," the term used by James Allen Smith in his chapter on arts and culture, or religion, well discussed in the chapter by Robert Wuthnow and D. Michael Lindsay.

Several trends identified in this volume further suggest the arrival of a new era. A number of foundations have revived older ways to leverage their assets. Program-related investments and mission-based loans, often used in the nineteenth and early twentieth century but neglected for many years (in part because government regulation strongly discouraged the mixing of commercial and nonprofit activity) reappeared with strong Ford Foundation support in the mid-1970s.[18] Rejecting the notion that foundations should start pilot projects as models for government—sometimes out of general opposition to government, sometimes out of fear that government funding would prove inadequate—a number of foundation leaders have sought to help their grantees look instead for alternate funding sources: sweat equity, earned income, hitherto untapped sources of private contributions, or wealthy but previously disengaged major donors. Where alternative sources are difficult or impossible to find (as in efforts to help disadvantaged and scorned populations or to uphold and advance cherished values strongly held by a particular cultural or religious community), some foundations have been choosing to commit themselves to longer-term funding relationships.[19] Cleveland's Mandel Foundation, for example, has made

16. Taleb (2004).
17. Schneider and Coleman (1993); Bacchetti and Ehrlich (2006).
18. Ford Foundation (1974).
19. Anheier and Leat (2006).

continuing (but annually reviewed) "evergreen" grants to a small number of key organizations.[20]

As a number of our colleagues have shown in their chapters for this volume, many foundations have seen the provision of comprehensive, reliable data sets designed to be useful to policy analysts and policymakers as one thing they are better placed than governments, universities, or other entities to provide. By supporting the creation of reliable data, a relatively small foundation investment can make a big contribution. In their chapter Elisabeth Clemens and Linda Lee note examples of this tendency in their analysis of foundation funding for the reform of elementary and secondary education. Jennifer Mosley and Joseph Galaskiewicz also discuss this phenomenon in their chapter on the response of several foundations to the End of Welfare as We Know It campaigns of the 1980s and 1990s. The Annie E. Casey Foundation's Kids Count program constitutes another important example. Yet another is the sustained support for the study of the contemporary sources of persistent poverty funded by several foundations, including the Rockefeller, Smith Richardson, William T. Grant, John D. and Catherine T. MacArthur, and Annie E. Casey foundations and the Foundation for Child Development.[21] In their chapter, Wuthnow and Lindsay note the role of the Lilly Endowment and others in supporting the collection of data about religious behavior. Stefan Toepler describes similar foundation efforts in the arts.[22]

Other efforts seek more directly to evaluate the impact of foundation initiatives. In their chapter for this volume, James Knickman and Stephen Isaacs exemplify the search for reliable information and serious analysis of impact characteristic of their own work on the R. W. Johnson Foundation's health care initiatives.[23] The Wallace Foundation encourages people to examine its evaluations of its own programs and places extensive evaluation reports on its website. Foundations concerned with elementary and secondary education have made a small industry of evaluations of the impact of initiatives in that field, though our colleagues Elisabeth Clemens and Linda Lee argue that this is a difficult task, one that is still a long way from completion.[24]

Still others continue the long-standing foundation tradition of working with government. Such work takes many forms. As Lehn M. Benjamin and Kevin

20. Edelsberg (2009).

21. See, for example, Brooks-Gunn, Duncan, and Aber (1997).

22. In writing this volume, all contributors made extensive use of data collected and made available by the Foundation Center, the National Center for Charitable Statistics, and GuideStar. Foundations made this work possible, as well.

23. See Isaacs and Knickman (2006).

24. See, for example, the debates in F. M. Hess (2005a, 2005b) and Bacchetti and Ehrlich (2006).

F. Quigley show, in international affairs foundations continue to try to meet daunting challenges by working with government, supporting research and education, and working to build effective institutions abroad. One of the most striking is the Milbank Memorial Fund, whose efforts have helped state legislatures find the information they need to shape effective health care policy.[25] It is also clear from the essays in this volume, and from even a casual reading of current debates, that significant government action will be needed if we are to meet major challenges in health, education, housing, and most other fields of foundation interest.

Finally, in working to complete this volume, we have become more and more aware of the differing purposes of much writing about foundations and of the diversity of the audiences. This is inevitable because foundations have many stakeholders. We think it is essential to keep in mind these differing purposes—as well as the widely differing sizes and purposes of foundations themselves—as we try to evaluate the field as a whole. As the economist Richard Steinberg has observed, the "list of arguably legitimate stakeholders" is "staggeringly long": donors, of course, board members, and staff, but also members of whole classes of beneficiaries, both individuals and institutions, both potential grantees and those destined to benefit from grantee work—local, state, and national governments and the general public.[26]

All foundation stakeholders share an interest in the large body of literature concerned above all with the broad topic of government and foundations. What are the current laws and policies relevant to foundations? What does government demand from foundations? What does the law encourage or permit them to do? What policies should governments adopt? How can governments use foundations for government purposes? We have said something about this topic, but current policy questions have largely been left to the chapter by our colleague Steven Rathgeb Smith and the other specialists he cites.

A second body of writing is concerned chiefly with foundations. It asks what foundations actually do and what they have done in the past. It also contains many arguments about what foundations, their donors, their boards, their staffs, ought to do. Interestingly, much of this writing consists of exhortations to foundation leaders—to board members and executive directors—to "do the right thing," as the writer understands the right thing to be. Our effort in this volume to learn something about what foundations actually do, about their real contributions to American society, persuades us that foundations vary widely in capacity and, especially, in purpose. They vary so widely that it is very difficult to determine what the right thing might be in any general sense.

25. Fox (2005, 2006a, 2006b).
26. Steinberg (2008).

One important camp among those who exhort foundation leaders to do the right thing offers what we might call a vision critique, urging foundations to adopt bold agendas that address what the writers see as the really important issues. Waldemar Nielsen, Mark Dowie, Joel Fleishman, and others argue that foundations too often adopt weak, poorly defined agendas, that they fail to seek bold ends, and that they all too rarely take strong action designed to make a big difference.[27] These writers scold foundations either for inertia, conformity, and lack of imagination or for capriciousness, inconstancy, inconsistency, and pushiness.

Still other critics have objected that foundations have often been feckless, unreliable, overambitious, even arrogant or vain, sometimes stupidly modest, and frequently ineffective. In a variation of this critique, Peter Frumkin points to the frequent gap between intentions and outcomes, between the lofty ambitions reflected in foundation rhetoric and the modest results of their efforts.[28]

A third group presses foundation leaders to manage more effectively, emphasizing process and achievement. Michael Porter and Mark Kramer express less concern about vision, legitimacy, and transparency than about outcomes and impact.[29] For them, foundations have a responsibility to achieve a social impact disproportionate to their spending, not least because some of the money they give away belongs to the taxpayer. They argue that too few foundations work strategically to achieve this disproportionate impact and that it can be costly to society to hold charitable funds rather than spend them on immediate needs. We would note, however, that foundations (like charitable endowments) exist not only to meet immediate needs but more often to provide stable, continuing support to longer-term projects or to undergird continuing values, whether traditional, universal, or particular.

There is something to be said for each of these and other critical perspectives on American foundations. Certainly foundations, like other institutions created by human beings, can be deeply flawed. Like other human institutions, foundations call for constant attention and for continuous, engaged, serious evaluation. But at their best, foundations are creative, independent agents encouraging social innovation or solidly defending honored traditions and values. The signature characteristic of foundations—their autonomy—reflects their freedom from the constraints of both the market and the state. Autonomy allows foundations to support strongly held values and also to seek the new. Their lack of accountability to government, and their liberation from the obligation to earn profits for their shareholders, is central. It is the very source of their freedom to seek the

27. Nielsen (1972; 1985); Porter and Kramer (1999); Dowie (2001); Fleishman (2007).
28. Frumkin (2006).
29. Porter and Kramer (1999); Letts, Ryan, and Grossman (1999); Frumkin (2006).

common good in whatever way they choose, so long as they respect the law and the dictates of public opinion.[30]

At the same time, and based on the findings of these chapters, neither the vision critique nor the management critique of foundations fully captures the current development of American foundations. A historical perspective is useful here. As the various chapters in this volume have made clear, the evolution of the American economy and especially of American governments has had enormous impact on the role of foundations, but this relationship has never been a one-way street. Foundations have not been passive bystanders or agents of government. Foundations have supported religious, cultural, ethical, scientific, and artistic purposes that American governments have not addressed at all. And foundations have themselves pushed new ideas and new approaches. By no means have foundations simply mirrored government's use of a diverse mix of policy tools.

Whereas government has relied on tax credits, tax deductions, bonds, loans, and vouchers to address public problems, foundations have used their own array of tools, adding more recently such devices as predevelopment loans, planning grants, loans for acquisition and construction, program-related investments, permanent use, and many forms of collaboration across sectors. This diversification of private policy tools is also revealed in the growth of new philanthropic forms, including the rapid recent increase in community foundations, donor-advised funds, supporting organizations, donor giving circles, corporate social responsibility, and public-private partnerships.

As has been seen in this volume, when in the twenty-first century foundations act merely in response to immediate need, they simply complement government or substitute for government—and they do so with limited resources. It stands to reason that when foundations relate themselves closely to government, they will be held to the same accountability and performance standards as government agencies and as the nonprofit organizations and business firms that contract to serve as agents of government. The more creative foundations become, the more they commit to "philanthropic passion," the closer philanthropy comes to realizing its unique role as the protector of distinctive values and the innovative social engine of modern society.[31]

30. While we agree that foundation leaders must take care not to offend public opinion so as to invite excessive regulation, we would note that American regulators have always taken the view, in effect, that foundations are protected by the First Amendment. Regulation has sought to ensure that foundations truly serve the public by supporting the broad array of religious and charitable purposes long recognized by American law and American political culture. Beyond insisting that foundations avoid actions deemed to violate public policy, regulation has not tried to tell foundations what to do or how to do it.

31. See Anheier and Leat (2006); Tayart de Borms (2005) (emphasizing the convening power of foundations as their appropriate role in diverse, fragmented societies); Fleishman (2007).

Appendix A: Data Sources

Center for Effective Philanthropy

The Center for Effective Philanthropy provided access to data collected in February 2003 on grantee perceptions of foundations for their report *Listening to Grantees: What Nonprofits Value in Their Foundation Funders* (2004). This survey included questions addressing foundation impact in specific fields as well as impact on individual organizations. The data set provided included anonymized data collected for the 2003 grantee survey and information on total assets, total giving, foundation type, and the location (state) of foundations whose grantees were surveyed.

Foundation Center

The Foundation Center provided the Roles and Contributions of Foundations to Society project with complete grant records (in electronic format) for all 124,844 grants included in the Foundation Center's circa 2001 grants sample database. The grants were for $10,000 or more and were awarded to organizations by a sample of 1,007 of the largest private and community foundations. For community foundations, only discretionary and donor-advised grants were included. Grants to individuals were not included in the file. Each record had fields for foundation name, foundation state, recipient name, recipient city, recipient state or country (for non-U.S. recipients), recipient unit (for example, the medical school of a university), country of benefit (for grants to U.S. recipients for programs abroad), type of recipient, recipient population group, grant amount, grant duration, year authorized, text description, grant purpose, grant population group, type of support, matching support, and challenge support—alphabetically by foundation name and within foundation name by amount.

FoundationSearch

Information on foundation grants by subject category for 2004 was provided by FoundationSearch America, which developed an online database of grants by private U.S. and Canadian foundations. FoundationSearch classifies grants by subject category on the basis of its understanding of the activities of the recipient organization, not necessarily the grant itself. The database excludes grants of less than $10,000; grants made directly to individuals; expenditures for foundation-administered projects; community foundation grants from restricted or donor-designated funds; and grants awarded by a private or community foundation to another U.S. foundation. The database is designed to be useful to grant seekers; at the time we used it, it was continually evolving.

Appendix B: Cleaning the Foundations Data Set for Chapter 3

To clean the data set for chapter 3, we began with the Foundation Center's data set of 124,844 grants for 2000–01. From this set, we focused only on grants whose primary purpose codes fell in the education category (that is, National Taxonomy of Exempt Entities codes beginning with B). Of the 25,591 grants in education, we then cut out grants to non-U.S. recipients (grants to recipients in Guam and Puerto Rico remained in the data set) and grants whose primary purpose codes were not related to K–12 education (that is, related to college, graduate, professional, or adult education). Several primary purpose codes included both K–12 and higher education grants: Alliances and advocacy, Education management/ technical aid, Education association, Education administration/regulation, Education research, Education public policy, Education single organization support, Education fund raising, Education equal rights, Education information services, Education public education, Education volunteer services, Education government agencies, Early childhood education, Child development education, Education bilingual programs, Education ESL programs, Libraries/library science, Libraries (school), Scholarships/financial aid, Student services & organizations, Education alumni groups, Education services, Drop-out prevention, Reading, Education testing, and Education community/cooperative. For these categories, we included only those grants with a secondary grant purpose code of Elementary/secondary education, Elementary school/education, Secondary school/education, or Elementary/secondary school reform. The resulting data set contained ninety-three hundred grants, accounting for a total of $1,299,787,644.

Appendix C: Descriptive Information

The Civil Rights and Social Action Sector, 2001

Issue focus (NTEE code)	Total funding (dollars)[a]		Mean funding (dollars)	Median funding (dollars)	Number of grants[a]		Share operating grants (percent)
Civil rights infrastructure							
Civil rights, alliance (R01)	4,052,254	(1.17)	66,430	50,000	61	(1.76)	13.9
Civil rights, management/technical aid (R02)	3,637,967	(1.05)	93,281	41,643	39	(1.13)	19.6
Civil rights, association (R03)	40,000	(0.01)	13,333	10,000	3	(0.09)	75.0
Civil rights, research (R05)	575,000	(0.17)	57,500	47,500	10	(0.29)	20.9
Civil rights, public policy (R06)	1,823,608	(0.53)	95,979	50,000	19	(0.55)	49.1
Civil rights, single organization support (R11)	684,130	(0.20)	42,758	25,000	16	(0.46)	56.7
Civil rights, fund raising (R12)	765,000	(0.22)	85,000	25,000	9	(0.26)	32.7
Civil rights, information services (R14)	585,000	(0.17)	65,000	50,000	9	(0.26)	14.5
Civil rights, public education (R15)	4,603,562	(1.33)	97,948	40,000	47	(1.36)	24.1
Civil rights advocacy							
Civil rights, equal rights (R13)	2,715,950	(0.78)	123,452	45,000	22	(0.64)	7.4
Civil rights, advocacy (R20)	40,580,218	(11.71)	87,646	30,000	463	(13.39)	18.5
Civil rights (R99)	260,000	(0.08)	65,000	22,500	4	(0.12)	5.8
Minority rights							
Civil rights, minorities (R22)	53,264,014	(15.37)	119,159	35,000	447	(12.93)	12.4
Immigrant rights							
Civil rights, immigrants (R21)	16,562,558	(4.78)	67,055	40,000	247	(7.14)	14.5
Voter education							
Voter education/rights (R40)	14,478,303	(4.18)	108,859	25,000	133	(3.85)	7.4

Racial and intergroup relations						
Race/intergroup relations (R30)	64,082,309	(18.50)	104,369	33,233	614 (17.76)	6.5
Group-specific rights						
Civil rights, disabled (R23)	6,693,790	(1.93)	66,938	30,000	100 (2.89)	15.8
Civil rights, aging (R25)	4,143,440	(1.20)	96,359	50,000	43 (1.24)	5.1
Civil rights, gays/lesbians (R26)	7,201,750	(2.08)	50,362	25,000	143 (4.14)	28.0
Patients' rights (R27)	3,301,588	(0.95)	143,547	45,000	23 (0.67)	0.3
Women's rights						
Civil rights, women (R24)	27,921,015	(8.06)	81,402	35,000	343 (9.92)	16.4
Reproductive rights						
Reproductive rights (R61)	51,006,498	(14.72)	180,874	50,000	282 (8.16)	21.2
Civil liberties						
Civil liberties, advocacy (R60)	7,367,749	(2.13)	73,677	30,000	100 (2.89)	29.0
Civil liberties, right to life (R62)	1,024,804	(0.30)	31,055	20,000	33 (0.95)	38.2
Civil liberties, first amendment (R63)	15,590,219	(4.50)	192,472	30,000	81 (2.34)	42.5
Civil liberties, freedom of information (R64)	2,004,805	(0.58)	74,252	35,000	27 (0.78)	10.0
Civil liberties, freedom of religion (R65)	2,305,985	(0.67)	46,120	29,418	50 (1.45)	59.6
Civil liberties, right to privacy (R66)	1,589,859	(0.46)	144,533	40,000	11 (0.32)	n.a.
Civil liberties, right to die (R67)	3,507,624	(1.01)	146,151	75,000	24 (0.69)	9.3
Civil liberties, due process (R68)	1,327,300	(0.38)	165,913	72,500	8 (0.23)	n.a.
Civil liberties, death penalty issues (R69)	2,777,665	(0.80)	59,099	50,000	47 (1.36)	28.7
Total	346,473,964	(100.00)	100,195	35,000	3,458 (100.00)	17.4

Source: Data compiled from the Foundation Center 2001 Grants Database.

a. Percent to sector in parentheses.

References

Aksartova, Sada. 2003. "In Search of Legitimacy: Peace Grant Making of U.S. Philanthropic Foundations, 1988–1996." *Nonprofit and Voluntary Sector Quarterly* 32: 25–46.

Aldrich, Howard. 1999. *Organizations Evolving.* Sage Publications.

Alexander, Victoria D. 1996. *Museums and Money: The Impact of Funding on Exhibitions, Scholarship, and Management.* Indiana University Press.

Altbach, Philip G. 2005. "Patterns in Higher Education Development." In Altbach, Berdahl, and Gumport 2005.

Altbach, P. G., R. O. Berdahl, and P. J. Gumport, eds. 2005. *American Higher Education in the Twenty-First Century.* Johns Hopkins University Press.

American Association of Fundraising Counsel Trust for Philanthropy. 2005. *Giving USA 2005: The Annual Report on Philanthropy for the Year 2004.*

American Bankers Association. 1931. *Community Trusts in the United States and Canada: A Survey of Existing Trusts, with Suggestions for Organizing and Developing New Foundations.*

American Council of Learned Societies. 1964. "Report on the Commission on the Humanities." Council of Graduate Schools and United Chapters of Phi Beta Kappa.

Ameringer, Carl F. 2008. *The Health Care Revolution: From Medical Monopoly to Market Competition.* University of California Press.

Anderson, Eric, and Alfred A. Moss. 1999. *Dangerous Donations: Northern Philanthropy and Southern Black Education, 1902–1930.* University of Missouri Press.

Anderson, James D. 1988. *The Education of Blacks in the South, 1860–1935.* University of North Carolina Press.

Andrews, Frank Emerson. 1956. *Philanthropic Foundations.* Russell Sage Foundation.

———. 1961. "Growth and Present Status of American Foundations." *Proceedings of the American Philosophical Association* 105 (April): 157–61.

———. 1973. *Foundation Watcher*. Franklin and Marshall College Press.

Andrews, Kenneth T., and Bob Edwards. 2004. "Advocacy Organizations in the U.S. Political Process." *Annual Review of Sociology* 30: 479–506.

Anheier, Helmut K. 2005. *Nonprofit Organizations: Approaches, Management, Policy*. Routledge.

———. 2006. "Roles of Foundations in Europe: A Comparison." In Prewitt and others 2006.

Anheier, Helmut K., and Siobhan Daly. 2005. "Philanthropic Foundations: A New Global Force?" In Anheier and others 2005.

Anheier, Helmut K., and Diana Leat. 2006. *Creative Philanthropy*. Routledge.

Anheier, Helmut K., and Lester M. Salamon. 2007. "The Nonprofit Sector in Comparative Perspective." In Powell and Steinberg 2007.

Anheier, Helmut K., and others, eds. 2005. *Global Civil Society 2004/5*. Sage Publications.

Annie E. Casey Foundation. 1995. *Annual Report*.

Arons, David. 2007. "Public Policy and Civic Engagement: Foundations in Action." In *Power in Policy*, edited by David Arons. Fieldstone Alliance.

Ascoli, Peter Max. 2006. *Julius Rosenwald: The Man Who Built Sears, Roebuck and Advanced the Cause of Black Education in the American South*. Indiana University Press.

Astin, Alexander W., and others. 2000. *Leadership Reconsidered: Engaging Higher Education in Social Change*. W. K. Kellogg Foundation (www.wkkf.org/pubs/CCT/leadership/Pub3368.pdf [November 25, 2009]).

Ayers, Edward L. 1992. *The Promise of the New South: Life after Reconstruction*. Oxford University Press.

Ayres, Leonard Porter. 1909. *Laggards in Our Schools: A Study of Retardation and Elimination in City School Systems*. Russell Sage Foundation.

———. 1911. *Seven Great Foundations*. Russell Sage Foundation.

———. 1912. *The Measurement of Educational Processes and Products*. Russell Sage Foundation, Division of Education.

Bacchetti, Ray, and Thomas Ehrlich, eds. 2006. *Reconnecting Education and Foundations: Turning Good Intentions into Educational Capital*. Jossey-Bass.

Barley, Stephen R., Gordon W. Meyer, and Debra C. Gash. 1988. "Cultures of Culture: Academics, Practitioners, and the Pragmatics of Normative Control." *Administrative Science Quarterly* 33, no. 1: 24–60.

Barr, Cyrilla. 1997. "The Coolidge Legacy: A Speech Presented at the Library of Congress Festival." *Library of Congress Festival* (http://publicaffairs.cua.edu/speeches/barr97.htm [December 1, 2009]).

———. 1998. *Elizabeth Sprague Coolidge: American Patron of Music*. Schirmer Books.

Bartley, Tim. 2007. "How Foundations Shape Social Movements: The Construction of an Organizational Field and the Rise of Forest Certification." *Social Problems* 54, no. 3: 229–55.

Baumol, William J., and William G. Bowen. 1966. *Performing Arts, the Economic Dilemma: A Study of Problems Common to Theater, Opera, Music, and Dance*. Twentieth Century Fund.

Behn, Robert D. 2001. *Rethinking Democratic Accountability*. Brookings.

Bender, Thomas H. 1997. "Politics, Intellect, and the American University." *Daedalus* 126, no. 1: 1–38.

Benford, Robert D., and David A. Snow. 2000. "Framing Processes and Social Movements: An Overview and Assessment." *Annual Review of Sociology* 26:611–39.

Bergholz, David. 1992. "The Public Education Fund." *Teachers College Record* 93, no. 3: 516–22.

Berman, Edward H. 1971. "American Influence on African Education: The Role of the Phelps-Stokes Fund's Education Commissions." *Comparative Education Review* 15, no. 2: 132–45.

————. 1983. *The Ideology of Philanthropy: The Influence of the Carnegie, Ford, and Rockefeller Foundations on American Foreign Policy*. State University of New York Press.

Bernholz, Lucy. 2002. "Critical Junctures: Philanthropic Associations as Policy Actors." Research Paper 13, prepared for the Center on Philanthropy and Public Policy, December (www.blueprintrd.com/text/junctures.pdf [November 30, 2009]).

Berry, Jeffrey M., and David F. Arons. 2003. *A Voice for Nonprofits*. Brookings.

Biebel, Charles D. 1976. "Private Foundations and Public Policy: The Case of Secondary Education during the Great Depression." *History of Education Quarterly* 16, no. 1: 3–33.

Bird, Kai. 1998. *The Color of Truth: McGeorge Bundy and William Bundy, Brothers in Arms*. Simon and Schuster.

Bjorklund, Victoria. 2003. *Choosing among the Private Foundation, Supporting Organization, and Donor-Advised Fund*. Simpson Thacher.

Black, Marian Watkins. 1961. "Private Aid to Public Schools: The Peabody Fund in Florida, 1867–1880." *History of Education Quarterly* 1 (September): 38–42.

Blackwood, Amy, Kennard T. Wing, and Thomas H. Pollak. 2008. "The Nonprofit Sector in Brief, Facts and Figures from the Nonprofit Almanac, 2008: Public Charities, Giving, and Volunteering." Urban Institute.

Blau, Joel, and Mimi Abramovitz. 2004. *The Dynamics of Social Welfare Policy*. Oxford University Press.

Bloom, Samuel William. 2002. *The Word as Scalpel: A History of Medical Sociology*. Oxford University Press.

Bolling, Landrum Rymer, and Craig Smith. 1982. *Private Foreign Aid: U.S. Philanthropy for Relief and Development*. Westview.

Bond, Horace Mann. 1934. *The Education of the Negro in the American Social Order*. Prentice-Hall.

Bonner, Thomas Neville. 2002. *Iconoclast: Abraham Flexner and a Life in Learning*. Johns Hopkins University Press.

Boris, Elizabeth, and C. Eugene Steuerle. 2004. *Philanthropic Foundations: Payout and Related Public Policy Issues*. Washington: Urban Institute (www.urban.org/url.cfm?ID=311032).

————, eds. 1999. *Nonprofits and Government*. Urban Institute Press.

Bork, Robert H., and Waldemar A. Nielsen. 1993. "Donor Intent: Interpreting the Founder's Vision." Indianapolis, Ind.: Philanthropy Roundtable.

Bornemeier, James. 2005. "Taking on Tobacco." In *To Improve Health and Health Care: The Robert Wood Johnson Foundation Anthology.* Vol. 8, edited by Stephen L. Isaacs and James R. Knickman, pp. 1–28. Jossey-Bass.

Bowen, William G., and others. 2005. *Equity and Excellence in American Higher Education.* University of Virginia Press.

Boyle, Kevin. 2004. *Arc of Justice: A Saga of Race, Civil Rights, and Murder in the Jazz Age.* Henry Holt.

Bradford, Gigi, and Glen Wallach. 2003. "Promoting Research and Building a Cultural Policy Community: The Experience of the Center for Arts and Culture in Washington DC." In *The Arts in a New Millennium,* edited by V. B. Morris and D. B. Pankratz. Praeger.

Bremner, Robert Hamlett. 1960. *American Philanthropy.* University of Chicago Press.

Brest, Paul, and Hal Harvey. 2008. *Money Well Spent: A Strategic Plan for Smart Philanthropy.* Bloomberg.

Brest, Paul, Hal Harvey, and Kelvin Low. 2009. "Calculated Impact." *Stanford Social Innovation Review* (Winter): 50–56.

Brilliant, Eleanor. 2000. *Private Charity and Public Inquiry: A History of the Filer and Peterson Commissions.* Indiana University Press.

Brody, Evelyn. 2002. "Twilight of Organizational Form of Charity: Musings on Norman L. Silber, A Corporate Form of Freedom; The Emergence of the Modern Non-Profit Sector." *Hofstra Law Review* 30:1261.

Brooks-Gunn, Jeanne, Greg J. Duncan, and J. Lawrence Aber, eds. 1997. *Neighborhood Poverty: Context and Consequences for Children.* Russell Sage Foundation.

Bullock, Henry Allen. 1967. *A History of Negro Education in the South, from 1619 to the Present.* Harvard University Press.

Burke, Colin B. 2001. "Nonprofit History's New Numbers (and the Need for More)." *Nonprofit and Voluntary Sector Quarterly* 30:174–203.

Burnell, Peter J., ed. 2000. *Democracy Assistance: International Co-operation for Democratization.* Frank Cass.

Carnegie Corporation of New York. 1977. *Research Universities and the National Interest: A Report from Fifteen University Presidents.* Ford Foundation.

"The Carnegie Endowment for International Peace." 1911. *American Journal of International Law* 5, no. 3: 757–60.

Carnegie Foundation for the Advancement of Teaching. 1906. *1st Annual Report.* New York.

Carnegie Hero Fund Commission. 1907. *Annual Report.* Pittsburgh.

Center for Effective Philanthropy. 2004. *Listening to Grantees: What Nonprofits Value in Their Foundation Funders* (www.effectivephilanthropy.org/images/pdfs/ListeningTo-Grantees_reprint.pdf).

Chambré, Susan Maizel. 2006. *Fighting for Our Lives: New York's AIDS Community and the Politics of Disease.* Rutgers University Press.

Chapman, Paul D. 1981. "Schools Are Sorters: Testing and Tracking in California, 1910–1925." *Journal of Social History* 14, no. 4: 701–17.

Charles Hayden Foundation. 1974. *Annual Report for the Year Ended September 30, 1974.*

————. 1977. *Annual Report for the Year Ended September 30, 1977.*

Chaves, Mark, and Sharon L. Miller. 1999. *Financing American Religion.* AltaMira Press.

Cheit, Earl Frank. 1971. *The New Depression in Higher Education: A Study of Financial Conditions at 41 Colleges and Universities.* McGraw-Hill.

Cheit, Earl Frank, and Theodore E. Lobman. 1979. *Foundations and Higher Education: Grant Making from Golden Years through Steady State.* Ford Foundation and the Carnegie Council on Policy Studies in Higher Education.

Cherbo, Joni, and Margaret Wyszomirski. 2000. "Mapping the Public Life of the Arts in America." In *The Public Life of the Arts in America*, edited by Joni Cherbo and Margaret Wyszomirski. Rutgers University Press.

Chujoy, Anatole. 1967. "Philanthropic Foundations and the Dance." In Weaver and Beadle 1967.

Clark, Burton R. 1983. *The Higher Education System: Academic Organization in Cross-National Perspective.* University of California Press.

Clark, Evans and Geneva Seybold, eds. 1931–55. *American Foundations and Their Fields.* 1st–7th eds. Twentieth Century Fund.

Clemens, Elisabeth S. 1993. "Women's Groups and the Transformation of U.S. Politics, 1892–1920." *American Journal of Sociology* 98:755–98.

Clemens, Elisabeth S., and Debra Minkoff. 2004. "Beyond the Iron Law: Rethinking the Place of Organizations in Social Movement Research." In *The Blackwell Companion to Social Movements*, edited by David A. Snow, Sarah A. Soule, and Hanspeter Kriesi. Blackwell.

Cleveland Foundation. 1939. *The Cleveland Foundation: The First 25 Years, 1914–1939.*

Clotfelter, Charles T. 1996. *Buying the Best: Cost Escalation in Elite Higher Education.* Princeton University Press.

————. 2006. "Patron or Bully? The Role of Foundations in Higher Education." In Bacchetti and Ehrlich 2006, pp. 211–48.

Clotfelter, Charles T., and Thomas Ehrlich. 1999. *Philanthropy and the Nonprofit Sector in a Changing America.* Indiana University Press.

Clyde, Allan R. 2002. "Making Welfare to Work Work." *Foundation News and Commentary* 43, no. 3: 19–20.

Cobb, Nina K. 1996. "Looking Ahead: Private Sector Giving to the Arts and Humanities." *President's Committee for the Arts and Humanities.*

Cochrane, A. L. 1972. *Effectiveness and Efficiency: Random Reflections on Health Services.* Nuffield Provincial Hospitals Trust.

Coffman, Harold. 1936. *American Foundations.* General Board of the Young Men's Christian Association.

Cohen, Michael. 2001. "Transforming the American High School: New Directions for State and Local Policy." Report prepared for Jobs for the Future. Aspen Institute.

Cohen, Rick, and Jeff Krehely. 2005. "Reforming the United States Philanthropic Sector." Statement to the U.S. House of Representatives Ways and Means Committee, April 20.

Colvin, Richard Lee. 2005. "A New Generation of Philanthropists and Their Great Ambitions." In F. M. Hess 2005b.

Colwell, Mary Anna Culleton. 1993. *Private Foundations and Public Policy: The Political Role of Philanthropy*. Garland.

Commission on Foundations and Private Philanthropy. 1970. "Private Giving and Public Needs: Report and Recommendations." University of Chicago Press.

Commission on the Future of Higher Education. 2006. "A Test of Leadership: Charting the Future of U.S. Higher Education." Government Printing Office.

Commission on the Humanities. 1980. "The Humanities in American Life." University of California Press.

Connell, James P., and others, eds. 1995. *New Approaches to Evaluating Community Initiatives: Concepts, Methods, and Contexts*. Aspen Institute.

Conte, Christopher, and Albert Karr. 2001. *An Outline of the U.S. Economy*. U.S. Department of State International Information Programs.

"Conversion Foundations: A Listing." 1997. *Health Affairs* 16, no. 3: 238–42.

Coon, Horace. 1938. *Money to Burn: What the Great American Philanthropic Foundations Do with Their Money*. Longmans, Green.

Corcoran, Mary, and others. 2000. "How Welfare Reform Is Affecting Women's Work." *Annual Review of Sociology* 26:241–69.

Corner, George Washington. 1964. *A History of the Rockefeller Institute, 1901–1953*. Rockefeller Institute Press.

Countryman, Matthew. 2006. *Up South: Civil Rights and Black Power in Philadelphia*. University of Pennsylvania Press.

Covington, Sally. 1997. *Moving a Public Policy Agenda: The Strategic Philanthropy of Conservative Foundations*. National Committee for Responsive Philanthropy.

Cowen, Tyler. 1998. *In Praise of Commercial Culture*. Harvard University Press.

Cremin, Lawrence A. 1951. *The American Common School: An Historic Conception*. Columbia University, Teachers College, Bureau of Publications.

Critchlow, Donald T. 1999. *Intended Consequences: Birth Control, Abortion, and the Federal Government in Modern America*. Oxford University Press.

Cummings, Milton C. 1991. "Government and the Arts: An Overview." In *Public Money and the Muse,* edited by Stephen Benedict. W. W. Norton.

Cuninggim, Merrimon. 1972. *Private Money and Public Service: The Role of Foundations in American Society.* McGraw-Hill.

Curry, J. L. M. 1969. *A Brief Sketch of George Peabody and a History of the Peabody Education Fund through Thirty Years*. Negro Universities Press. [1898].

Curti, Merle Eugene. 1988. *American Philanthropy Abroad*. Transaction Books.

Dabney, Charles William. 1936. *Universal Education in the South*. University of North Carolina Press.

Dahl, Robert. 1971. *Polyarchy: Participation and Opposition*. Yale University Press.

Dahrendorf, Ralf. 2005. *Reflections on the Revolution in Europe*. Transaction Publishers.

Daly, Jeanne. 2005. *Evidence-Based Medicine and the Search for a Science of Clinical Care*. University of California Press.

Danziger, Sandra K., and Kristin S. Seefeldt. 2003. "Barriers to Employment and the 'Hard to Serve': Implications for Services, Sanctions, and Time Limits." *Social Policy and Society* 2: 151–60.

David and Lucile Packard Foundation. 2000. *Conserving California Landscapes: Midterm Report*.

————. 2006. *Using All Our Resources: The Packard Foundation's Program Related Investment History and Portfolio*.

Davis, Martha F. 1993. *Brutal Need: Lawyers and the Welfare Rights Movement, 1960–1973*. Yale University Press.

Davis, R. Hunt. 1976. "Charles T. Loram and an American Model for African Education in South Africa." *African Studies Review* 19, no. 2: 87–99.

Day, Phyllis. 1997. *A New History of Social Welfare*. Allyn and Bacon.

Delfin, Francisco, Jr., and Shui-Yan Tang. 2006. "Strategic Philanthropy, Land Conservation Governance, and the Packard Foundation's Conserving California Landscape Initiative." *Nonprofit and Voluntary Sector Quarterly* 35, no. 3: 405–29.

DeLucia, Michael. 2001. "Creating New Health Care Foundations." *Nonprofit and Voluntary Sector Quarterly* 30, no. 1: 130–36.

Diamond, Sigmund. 1992. *Compromised Campus: The Collaboration of Universities with the Intelligence Community, 1945–1955*. Oxford University Press.

Dickeson, Robert. 2004. *Collision Course: Rising Costs Threaten America's Future and Require Shared Solutions*. Lumina Foundation.

Dickinson, Frank G. 1970. *The Changing Position of Philanthropy in the American Economy*. National Bureau of Economic Research; distributed by Columbia University Press.

DiMaggio, Paul. 1986. "Support for the Arts from Independent Foundations." In *Nonprofit Enterprise in the Arts*, edited by Paul DiMaggio. Oxford University Press.

Dizikes, John. 1993. *Opera in America: A Cultural History*. Yale University Press.

Domanico, Raymond, and others, eds. 2000. *Can Philanthropy Fix Our Schools? Appraising Walter Annenberg's $500 Million Gift to Public Education*. Thomas B. Fordham Foundation.

Domhoff, G. William. 2006. *Who Rules America? Power, Politics, and Social Change*. McGraw-Hill.

Douglas, James. 1987. "Political Theories of Nonprofit Organization." In Powell 1987.

Douglas, James, and Aaron Wildavsky. 1978. "The Knowledgeable Foundations." In *The Future of Foundations*, edited by L. R. Bolling and others. Change Magazine Press.

Dowie, Mark. 2001. *American Foundations: An Investigative History*. MIT Press.

Drier, Peter. 2002. "Social Justice Philanthropy: Can We Get More Bang for the Buck?" *Social Policy* 33:27–33.

D'Souza, Dinesh. 1996. *The End of Racism: Principles for a Multiracial Society*. Free Press Paperbacks.

Duderstadt, James J. 2004. "Delicate Balance: Market Forces versus the Public Interest." In *Buying In or Selling Out?* edited by D. G. Stein. Rutgers University Press.

Duke Endowment. 1965. *Annual Report*.

Duncan, Greg J., and Jeanne Brooks-Gunn. 2000. "Family Poverty, Welfare Reform, and Child Development." *Child Development* 71, no. 1: 188–96.

Duncan, Greg J., Aletha C. Huston, and Thomas S. Weisner. 2007. *Higher Ground: New Hope for the Working Poor and Their Children*. Russell Sage Foundation.

Edelsberg, Charles. 2009. "An Insider's View of Public and Private Philanthropy." *Journal of Jewish Communal Service* 84, nos. 1–2.

Edelson, Phyllis. 2003. *Foundation Grants to Individuals.* 13th ed. Foundation Center.

Ellsworth, F., and J. Lumarda Jr., eds. 2003. *From Grantmaker to Leader: Emerging Strategies for Twenty-First Century Foundations.* Wiley.

Embree, Edwin R., and Julia Waxman. 1949. *Investment in People: The Story of the Julius Rosenwald Fund.* Harper and Brothers.

Engel, Jonathan. 2002. *Doctors and Reformers: Discussion and Debate over Health Policy, 1925–1950.* University of South Carolina Press.

Escobar, Arturo. 1995. *Encountering Development: The Making and Unmaking of the Third World.* Princeton University Press.

Ettling, John. 1981. *The Germ of Laziness: Rockefeller Philanthropy and Public Health in the New South.* Harvard University Press.

Everatt, D., and others. 2005. "Patterns of Giving in South Africa." *Voluntas* 16, no. 3: 275–91.

Faber, Daniel, and Deborah McCarthy. 2005a. *Foundations for Social Change: Critical Perspectives on Philanthropy and Popular Movements.* Rowman and Littlefield.

———. 2005b. "Foundations for Social Change: Critical Perspectives on Philanthropy and Popular Movements." Introduction to Faber and McCarthy 2005a.

Farley, John. 2004. *To Cast Out Disease: A History of the International Health Division of the Rockefeller Foundation, 1913–1951.* Oxford University Press.

F. B. Heron Foundation. 2007. *Expanding Philanthropy: Mission Based Investing at the F. B. Heron Foundation.*

Fedunkiw, Marianne. 2005. *Rockefeller Foundation Funding and Medical Education in Toronto, Montreal, and Halifax.* McGill-Queen's University Press.

Ferguson, Karen. 2007. "Organizing the Ghetto: The Ford Foundation, CORE, and White Power in the Black Power Era." *Journal of Urban History* 34, no. 1: 67–100.

Ferris, James M., and Glenn A. Melnick. 2004. "Improving the Health of Californians: Effective Public-Private Strategies for Challenging Times." *Health Affairs* 23, no. 1: 257–61.

Ferris, James M., and Michael Mintrom. 2002. "Foundations and Public Policymaking: A Conceptual Framework." Research Paper 10, prepared for the Center on Philanthropy and Public Policy. University of Southern California.

Fetter, Bruce. 2006. "Origins and Elaboration of the National Health Accounts, 1926–2006." *Health Care Financing Review* 28 (Fall): 53–67.

Finkel, Steven E., and others. 2005. *Effects of U.S. Foreign Assistance on Democracy Building: Results of a Cross-National Quantitative Study,* version 31. Report prepared for the U.S. Agency for International Development. Vanderbilt University, November 25.

Finkelstein, Martin, and Jack H. Schuster. 2001. "Assessing the Silent Revolution: How Changing Demographics Are Reshaping the Academic Profession." *AAHE Bulletin* 54, no. 2: 3–7.

Finkelstein, Martin. 2003. "The Morphing of the Academic Profession." *Liberal Education* 89, no. 4: 6–15 (www.aacu.org/liberaleducation/le-fa03/le-sfa03feature.cfm).

Finn, Chester E., Jr., and Marci Kanstoroom. 2000. "Lessons from the Annenberg Challenge." In Domanico and others 2000.

Fisher, Donald. 1980. "American Philanthropy and the Social Sciences: The Reproduction of a Conservative Ideology." In *Philanthropy and Cultural Imperialism*, edited by R. F. Arnove. Indiana University Press.

———. 1992. *Fundamental Development of the Social Sciences: Rockefeller Philanthropy and the United States Social Science Research Council*. University of Michigan Press.

Fisher, John E. 1986. *The John F. Slater Fund: A Nineteenth Century Affirmative Action for Negro Education*. University Press of America.

Fleishman, Joel L. 2001. "Public Policy and Philanthropic Purpose: Foundation Ownership and Control of Corporations in Germany and the United States." In Schluter and others 2001.

———. 2007. *The Foundation, A Great American Secret: How Private Wealth Is Changing the World*. Public Affairs.

Foner, Eric, and Joshua Brown. 2005. *Forever Free: The Story of Emancipation and Reconstruction*. Knopf.

Fonte, John. 2004. "Philanthropy and the American Regime: Is It Time for Another Congressional Investigation of Tax-Exempt Foundations?" Working Paper. Hudson Institute, Bradley Center for Philanthropy and Civic Renewal, November.

Ford Foundation. 1949. *Report of the Study for the Ford Foundation on Policy and Program*.

———. 1950. *Report of the Trustees of the Ford Foundation*.

———. 1966. *Annual Report*.

———. 1967. *Annual Report*.

———. 1974. "Program-Related Investments: A Different Approach to Philanthropy" (www.community-wealth.org/_pdfs/articles-publications/pris/report-ford74.pdf [December 1, 2009]).

———. 1978. *Annual Report*.

———. 1979. *Ford Foundation International Programs*.

———. 1988. *Annual Report*.

Fosdick, Raymond Blaine. 1989. *The Story of the Rockefeller Foundation*. Transaction Publishers. [Orig. published Harper and Brothers, 1952].

Foundation Center. 1960. "The Foundation Directory." 1st ed. Russell Sage Foundation.

———. 1962. *1961 Annual Report*.

———. 1964a. *1963 Annual Report*.

———. 1964b. *The Foundation Directory*. 2nd ed. Russell Sage Foundation.

———. 1967. "The Foundation Directory." 3rd ed. Russell Sage Foundation.

———. 1975. "The Foundation Directory." 5th ed.

———. 1981. "The Foundation Directory." 8th ed.

———. 1985. "The Foundation Directory." 10th ed.

———. 1986. "The Foundation Directory." 10th ed.

———. 1987. "The Foundation Directory." 11th ed.

———. 1989. "The Foundation Directory." 12th ed.

———. 2006. *FC Stats: The Foundation Center's Statistical Information Service* (http://fdncenter.org/fc_stats/index.html [September 4, 2006]).

———. 2007. "Foundation Giving and Growth Estimates: 2007."

Fox, Daniel M. 1963. *Engines of Culture: Philanthropy and Art Museums*. State Historical Society of Wisconsin.

———. 1980. "Abraham Flexner's Unpublished Report: Foundations and Medical Education, 1909–1928." *Bulletin of the History of Medicine* 54, no. 4: 475–96.

———. 1986. *Health Policies, Health Politics: The British and American Experience, 1911–1965.* Princeton University Press.

———. 1987. "The Politics of the NIH Extramural Program, 1937–1950." *Journal of the History of Medicine and Allied Sciences* 42, no. 4: 447–66.

———. 1993. *Power and Illness: The Failure and Future of American Health Policy.* University of California Press.

———. 2005. "Evidence of Evidence-Based Policy: The Politics of Systematic Reviews in Coverage Decisions." *Health Affairs* 24, no. 1: 114–22.

———. 2006a. "Foundation Impact on Health Policy." *Health Affairs* 25 (November–December): 1724–29.

———. 2006b. "The Significance of the Milbank Memorial Fund for Policy: An Assessment at Its Centennial." *Milbank Quarterly* 84, no. 1: 5–36.

———. 2010. *The Convergence of Science and Governance: Research, Health Policy and American States.* University of California Press.

Fox, Daniel M., and Lee Greenfield. 2006. "Helping Public Officials Use Research Evaluating Healthcare." *Journal of Law and Public Policy* 14, no. 2: 531–50.

Fraser, James W. 1992. "Preparing Teachers for Democratic Schools: The Holmes and Carnegie Reports Five Years Later; A Critical Reflection." *Teachers College Record* 94, no. 1: 7–40.

Frazier, Edward Franklin. 1957. *Black Bourgeoisie.* Free Press.

Fremont-Smith, Marion R. 1965. *Foundations and Government: State and Federal Law and Supervision.* Russell Sage Foundation.

———. 2004. *Governing Nonprofit Organizations: Federal and State Law and Regulation.* Belknap Press of Harvard University Press.

Friedland, Roger, and Robert R. Alford. 1991. "Bringing Society Back In: Symbols, Practices, and Institutional Contradictions." In Powell and DiMaggio 1991.

Friedman, Lawrence Jacob, and Mark D. McGarvie. 2003. *Charity, Philanthropy, and Civility in American History.* Cambridge University Press.

Frumkin, Peter. 1998. "The Long Recoil from Regulation: Private Philanthropic Foundations and the Tax Reform Act of 1969." *American Review of Public Administration* 28, no. 3: 266–86.

———. 1999. "Private Foundations as Public Institutions: Regulation, Professionalization, and the Redefinition of Organized Philanthropy." In Lagemann 1999.

———. 2006. *Strategic Giving: The Art and Science of Philanthropy.* University of Chicago Press.

Fulton, Katherine, and Andrew Blau. 2006. *Looking Out for the Future: An Orientation for Twenty-First Century Philanthropists.* Monitor Institute.

Gaines, Kevin Kelly. 1996. *Uplifting the Race: Black Leadership, Politics, and Culture in the Twentieth Century.* University of North Carolina Press.

Galligan, Ann, and Joni Cherbo. 2004. "Financial Support for Individual Artists." *Journal of Arts Management, Law, and Society* 34, no. 1: 23–42.

Garraty, John A., and Mark C. Carnes. 1999. *American National Biography.* Vol. 12. Oxford University Press.

Geiger, Roger L. 1990. "Organized Research Units: Their Role in the Development of University Research." *Journal of Higher Education* 61, no. 1: 1–19.

———. 2004a. *Knowledge and Money: Research Universities and the Paradox of the Marketplace.* Stanford University Press.

———. 2004b. *Research and Relevant Knowledge: American Research Universities since World War II.* Transaction Publishers.

Gemelli, Giuliana, ed. 1998. *The Ford Foundation and Europe, 1950s–70s: Cross-Fertilization of Learning in Social Science and Management.* Interuniversity Press.

General Education Board. 1915. *The General Education Board: An Account of Its Activities, 1902–1914.*

———. 1916. *Annual Report, 1914–1915.*

———. 1964. *Review and Final Report, 1902–1964.*

Gerlach, Karen K., and Michelle A. Larkin. 2005. "The SmokeLess States Program." In *To Improve Health and Health Care: The Robert Wood Johnson Foundation Anthology.* Vol. 8, edited by S. L. Isaacs and J. R. Knickman. Jossey-Bass.

Gershater, Darryl. 2001. "Sisterhood of a Sort: The Women's National Coalition and the Role of Gender Identity in South African Civil Society." Research Report 82, June. Center for Policy Studies.

Getz, Lynne Marie. 1992. "Extending the Helping Hand to Hispanics: The Role of the General Education Board in New Mexico in the 1930s." *Teachers College Record* 93, no. 3: 500–15.

Glenn, John M., Lilian Brandt, and Emerson Andrews. 1947. *Russell Sage Foundation 1907–1946.* Vol. 1. Russell Sage Foundation.

Glennan, Thomas Keith, and others. 2004. *Expanding the Reach of Education Reforms: Perspectives from Leaders in the Scale-up of Educational Interventions.* Rand.

Goldberg, Alison D. 2002. "Social Change Philanthropy and How It's Done." *Foundation News and Commentary* 43, no. 3.

Goluboff, Risa Lauren. 2007. *The Lost Promise of Civil Rights.* Harvard University Press.

Gordon, Linda. 1991. "Black and White Visions of Welfare: Women's Welfare Activism, 1890–1945." *Journal of American History* 78, no. 2: 559–90.

Goss, Kristin A. 2007. "The Foundations of Feminism: Philanthropy, Identity, and Gender Politics." *Social Science Quarterly* 88, no. 5: 1174–91.

Goulden, Joseph C. 1971. *The Money Givers.* Random House.

Graham, Hugh Davis, and Nancy Diamond. 1997. *The Rise of American Research Universities: Elites and Challengers in the Postwar Era.* Johns Hopkins University Press.

Grantmakers in the Arts. 2005. "Vital Signs: Snapshots of Arts Funding." Report.

Gravelle, Jane G. 2003. *Minimum Distribution Requirements for Foundations: Proposal to Disallow Administrative Costs.* Report RS21603. Congressional Research Service.

Greene, Jay P. 2005. "Buckets into the Sea: Why Philanthropy Isn't Changing Schools, and How It Could." In F. M. Hess 2005b.

Gronbjerg, Kirsten A. 1993. *Understanding Nonprofit Funding: Managing Revenues in Social Services and Community Development Organizations.* Jossey-Bass.

———. 2004. "Human Services and Philanthropy." In *Philanthropy in America,* edited by Dwight Burlingame. ABC-CLIO.

Gronbjerg, Kirsten, and Lester Salamon. 2002. "Devolution, Marketization, and the Changing Shape of Government-Nonprofit Relations." In Salamon 2002b.

Gumport, Patricia J. 2003. "Higher Education Research Priorities: Perspectives from Selected Foundations." Stanford Institute on Higher Education Research.

Haines, Herbert. 1984. "Black Radicalization and the Funding of Civil Rights." *Social Problems* 32, no. 1: 31–43.

Halberstam, David. 1972. *The Best and the Brightest*. Random House.

Hall, Peter Dobkin. 1987. "A Historical Overview of the Private Nonprofit Sector." In Powell 1987.

———. 1999. "Resolving the Dilemmas of Democratic Governance." In Lagemann 1999.

Hamilton, Dona C., and Charles V. Hamilton. 1997. *The Dual Agenda: Race and Social Welfare Policies of Civil Rights Organizations*. Columbia University Press.

Hammack, David C. 1978. "Problems in the Historical Study of Power in the Cities and Towns of the United States, 1800–1960." *American Historical Review* 83, no. 2: 323–49.

———. 1999. "Foundations in the American Polity." In Lagemann 1999.

———. 2001. "Growth, Transformation, and Quiet Revolution in the Nonprofit Sector over Two Centuries." *Nonprofit and Voluntary Sector Quarterly* 30, no. 2: 157–73.

———. 2002. "Nonprofit Organizations in American History: Research Opportunities and Sources." *American Behavioral Scientist* 45:1638–74.

———. 2003. "Failure and Resilience: Pushing the Limits in Depression and Wartime." In Friedman and McGarvie 2003.

———. 2006. "American Debates on the Legitimacy of Foundations." In Prewitt and others 2006.

Hammack, David C., and Helmut K. Anheier. Forthcoming. *The Roles and Contributions of Philanthropic Foundations*. Brookings.

Hammack, David C., and Stanton Wheeler, eds. 1994. *Social Science in the Making: Essays on the Russell Sage Foundation, 1907–1972*. Russell Sage Foundation.

Hammack, David C., and Steven Heydemann, eds. 2009. *Globalization, Philanthropy, and Civil Society: Projecting Institutional Logics Abroad*. University of Indiana Press.

Hanchett, Thomas W. 1988. "The Rosenwald Schools and Black Education in North Carolina." *North Carolina Historical Review* 65 (October): 387–444.

Handel, Gerald. 1982. *Social Welfare in Western Society*. Random House.

Handler, Joel. 1978. *Social Movements and the Legal System*. Academic Press.

Harlan, Louis R. 1958. *Separate and Unequal: Public School Campaigns and Racism in the Southern Seaboard States, 1901–1915*. Atheneum.

Harrell-Bond, Barbara E. 1986. *Imposing Aid: Emergency Assistance to Refugees*. Oxford University Press.

Harrington, Michael. 1962. *The Other America*. Macmillan.

Harrison, Shelby M. 1916. "Community Action through Surveys." Russell Sage Foundation.

———. 1931. "The Social Survey: The Idea Defined and Its Development Traced." Russell Sage Foundation.

———. 1949. "Foundations and Public Service." Russell Sage Foundation.

Harrison, Shelby M., and F. E. Andrews. 1946. *American Foundations for Social Welfare.* Russell Sage Foundation.

Harvey, A. McGehee, and Susan L. Abrams. 1986. *"For the Welfare of Mankind": The Commonwealth Fund and American Medicine.* Johns Hopkins University Press.

Havighurst, Robert J. 1980. "Foundations and Public Education in the Twentieth Century." In *Private Philanthropy and Public Elementary and Secondary Education,* edited by Gerald Benjamin. Proceedings of the Rockefeller Archives Center Conference, June 8, 1979. Rockefeller Archive Center.

Heald, Henry T. 1963. *In Common Cause: Relations between Higher Education and Foundations.* New York: Ford Foundation.

Heifitz, Ronald A., John V. Kania, and Mark R. Kramer. 2004. "Leading Boldly: Foundations Can Move Past Traditional Approaches to Create Social Change through Imaginative—and Even Controversial—Leadership." *Stanford Social Innovation Review* (Winter): 21–31.

Heilbrun, James, and Charles M. Gray. 2001. *The Economics of Art and Culture.* Cambridge University Press.

Hershey, Alan M., and LaDonna A. Pavetti. 1997. "Turning Job Finders into Job Keepers." *Future of Children* 7, no. 1: 74–86.

Hess, Frederick M. 2005a. "Inside the Gift Horse's Mouth: Philanthropy and School Reform." *Phi Delta Kappan* 87, no. 2: 131–37.

———, ed. 2005b. *With the Best of Intentions: How Philanthropy Is Reshaping K–12 Education.* Harvard Education Press.

Hess, Gary R. 2005. "The Role of American Philanthropic Foundations in India's Road to Globalization during the Cold War Era." In *Globalization, Philanthropy, and Civil Society: Toward a New Political Culture in the Twenty-First Century,* edited by Soma Hewa and Darwin H. Stapleton. Springer.

Heydemann, Steven, ed. 2002. "Preface." *American Behavioral Scientist* 45, no. 10: 1472–73.

Himmelstein, Jerome, and Mayer N. Zald. 1984. "American Conservatism and Government Funding in the Arts and Sciences." *Sociological Inquiry* 54:171–87.

Hobsbawm, E. J. 1994. *The Age of Extremes: A History of the World, 1914–1991.* Pantheon Books.

Hoffman, Nancy, and Joel Vargas. 2005. "Integrating Grades 9 through 14: State Policies to Support and Sustain Early College High Schools." Report prepared for Jobs for the Future.

Holcombe, Randall. 2000. *Writing Off Ideas: Taxation, Foundations, and Philanthropy in America.* Transaction Publishers.

Hollis, Ernest Victor. 1938. *Philanthropic Foundations and Higher Education.* Columbia University Press.

Holmes, D. O. W. 1938. "Twenty-Five Years of Thomas Jesse Jones and the Phelps-Stokes Fund." *Journal of Negro Education* 7, no. 4: 475–85.

Horton, Richard. 2006. "WHO: Strengthening the Road to Renewal." *Lancet* 367 (June 3): 1793–95.

Independent Sector. 2006. *Analysis of Charitable Reforms and Incentives in the Pension Protection Act of 2006.*

——. 2008. *Principles of Good Governance and Ethical Practice.*

Independent Sector and Urban Institute. 2002. *The New Nonprofit Almanac and Desk Reference.* Jossey-Bass.

Internal Revenue Service. 2006. *Program Related Investments* (www.irs.gov/charities/ foundations/article/0,,id=137793,00.html [December 3, 2009]).

Isaacs, Stephen L., and James R. Knickman, eds. 2006. *To Improve Health and Health Care: The Robert Wood Johnson Foundation Anthology.* Vol. 10. Jossey-Bass.

Jackson, Maria Rosario. 2003. "Arts and Culture in Communities: Systems of Support." Policy brief. Urban Institute.

Jackson, Thomas F. 2007. *From Civil Rights to Human Rights: Martin Luther King Jr. and the Struggle for Economic Justice.* University of Pennsylvania Press.

Jackson, Walter A. 1990. *Gunnar Myrdal and America's Conscience: Social Engineering and Racial Liberalism, 1938–1987.* University of North Carolina Press.

Jenkins, J. Craig. 1998. "Channeling Social Protest: Foundation Patronage of Contemporary Social Movements." In Powell and Clemens 1998.

Jenkins, J. Craig, and Craig M. Eckert. 1986. "Channeling Black Insurgency: Elite Patronage and Professional Social Movement Organizations in the Development of the Black Movement." *American Sociological Review* 51, no. 6: 812–29.

Jenkins, J. Craig, and Abigail Halci. 1999. "Grassrooting the System? The Development and Impact of Social Movement Philanthropy." In Lagemann 1999.

Jenkins, Lynn, and Donald R. McAdams. 2005. "Philanthropy and Urban School District Reform: Lessons from Charlotte, Houston, and San Diego." In F. M. Hess 2005b.

Johnson, Earl S., Ann Levine, and Fred C. Doolittle. 1999. *Fathers' Fair Share: Helping Poor Men Manage Child Support and Fatherhood.* Russell Sage Foundation.

Jones, F., ed. 1989. *The Foundation Center Source Book Profiles, 1989 Cumulation.* Foundation Center.

——, ed. 1990. *The Foundation Center Source Book Profiles.* Foundation Center.

——, ed. 1995. *The Foundation 1,000.* Foundation Center.

Jones, Howard Mumford. 1959. *One Great Society: Humane Learning in the United States.* Harcourt.

Julius Rosenwald Fund Papers. Fisk University Archives.

Kaestle, Carl F. 1983. *Pillars of the Republic: Common Schools and American Society, 1780–1860.* Hill and Wang.

Karl, Barry D. 1997. "Philanthropy and the Maintenance of Democratic Elites." *Minerva* 35, no. 3: 207–20.

Karl, Barry D., and Stanley N. Katz. 1981. "The American Philanthropic Foundation and the Public Sphere, 1890–1930." *Minerva* 19, no. 2: 236–70.

——. 1987. "Philanthropy, Patronage, and Politics." *Daedalus* 116, no. 1: v–xx.

Karoff, H. Peter, ed. 2004. *Just Money: A Critique of Contemporary American Philanthropy.* Philanthropic Initiative.

Kasper, Gabriel, Henry A. J. Ramos, and Constance J. Walker. 2004. "Making the Case for Diversity in Philanthropy." *Foundation News and Commentary* 45, no. 6.

Katz, Jamie. 2006. "State Regulation of Foundations." In *State of Philanthropy 2006*. National Committee for Responsive Philanthropy.

Katz, Michael B. 1993. *The "Underclass" Debate: Views from History*. Princeton University Press.

———. 2002. *The Price of Citizenship: Redefining the New American Welfare State*. Macmillan.

Keck, Margaret E., and Kathryn Sikkink. 1998. *Activists beyond Borders: Advocacy Networks in International Politics*. Cornell University Press.

Keele, H. M., and J. C. Kiger, eds. 1984. *Foundations*. Greenwood Press.

Keppel, Frederick P. 1936. *Philanthropy and Learning, with Other Papers*. Columbia University Press.

Kerr, Clark. 2001. *The Uses of the University*. Harvard University Press.

Keyes, Langley C., and others. 1996. "Networks and Nonprofits: Opportunities and Challenges in an Era of Federal Devolution." *Housing Policy Debate* 7, no. 2: 201–29.

Kiger, Joseph Charles. 1956. "The Large Foundations in Southern Education." *Journal of Higher Education* 27, no. 3: 125–73.

———. 2000. *Philanthropic Foundations in the Twentieth Century*. Greenwood.

Kihato, Caroline, and Thabo Rapoo. 1999. "An Independent Voice? A Survey of Civil Society Organisations in South Africa, Their Funding, and Their Influence over the Policy Process." Report. Centre for Policy Studies, Johannesburg, South Africa.

Kim, Kwang. 2004. *National Household Education Surveys of 2001: Participation in Adult Education and Lifelong Learning, 2000–2001*. U.S. Department of Education, Institute of Education Sciences, National Center for Education Statistics.

Kimbis, T. P. 1997. "Surviving the Storm: How the National Endowment for the Arts Restructured Itself to Serve a New Constituency." *Journal of Arts Management, Law, and Society* 27, no. 2: 139–58.

Kingma, Bruce R. 1989. "An Accurate Measurement of the Crowd-out Effect, Income Effect, and Price Effect for Charitable Contributions." *Journal of Political Economy* 97, no. 5: 1197–1207.

Kirkby, Diane. 1992. "Class, Gender, and the Perils of Philanthropy: The Story of Life and Labor Reform in the Women's Trade Union League." *Journal of Women's History* 4, no. 2: 36–51.

Klein, Steven. 2004. *Language Minorities and Their Educational and Labor Market Indicators: Recent Trends*. U.S. Department of Education, Institute of Education Sciences, National Center for Education Statistics.

Kliebard, Herbert M. 1995. *The Struggle for the American Curriculum, 1893–1958*. Routledge.

Kluger, Richard. 1976. *Simple Justice: The History of Brown v. Board of Education and Black America's Struggle for Equality*. Knopf.

Knight, Edgar Wallace. 1922. *Public Education in the South*. Ginn.

Knox, Ellis O. 1947. "The Origin and Development of the Negro Separate School." *Journal of Negro Education* 16 (Summer): 269–79.

Kohler, Robert E. 1991. *Partners in Science: Foundations and Natural Science, 1900–1945*. University of Chicago Press.

Korman, Rochelle. 1994. "Supporting Organizations to Community Foundations: A Little-Used Alternative to Private Foundations." *Exempt Organization Tax Review* 10: 1327–39.

Kousser, J. Morgan. 1974. *The Shaping of Southern Politics: Suffrage Restriction and the Establishment of the One-Party South, 1880–1910.* Yale University Press.

———. 1980. "Progressivism—For Middle-Class Whites Only: North Carolina Education, 1880–1910." *Journal of Southern History* 46 (May): 169–94.

Kramer, Ralph M. 1987. "Voluntary Agencies and the Personal Social Services." In Powell 1987, pp. 240-57.

Krehely, Jeff, and Meaghan House. 2005. *Not All Grants Are Created Equal: Why Nonprofits Need General Operating Support from Foundations.* Washington, D.C.: National Committee for Responsive Philanthropy.

Kresge Foundation. 1969. *Annual Report.*

Kroll, Janet L., and Rebecca A. Cornejo. 2003. "Onward Christian Soldiers." *Trust Magazine* (Spring).

Lagemann, Ellen Condliffe. 1983. *Private Power for the Public Good: A History of the Carnegie Foundation for the Advancement of Teaching.* Wesleyan University Press.

———. 1989. *The Politics of Knowledge: The Carnegie Corporation, Philanthropy, and Public Policy.* Wesleyan University Press.

———. 2006. "What Might Andrew Carnegie Want to Tell Bill Gates?" In Bacchetti and Ehrlich 2006.

———, ed. 1999. *Philanthropic Foundations: New Scholarship, New Possibilities.* Indiana University Press.

Landon, John W. 1986. *The Development of Social Welfare.* Human Sciences Press.

Latham, Robert. 1997. *The Liberal Moment: Modernity, Security, and the Making of Postwar International Order.* Columbia University Press.

Lavizzo-Mourey, Risa. 2006. Foreword to *To Improve Health and Health Care: The Robert Wood Johnson Foundation Anthology.* Vol. 9, edited by Stephen L. Isaacs and James R. Knickman. Jossey-Bass.

Lawrence, Steven. 2009. *A First Look at the Foundation and Corporate Response to the Economic Crisis.* Foundation Center.

Lawrence, Steven, and Leslie Marino. 2003. "Update on Funding for Higher and Graduate Educational Institutions." Report. Foundation Center (www.foundationcenter.org/gainknowledge/research/pdf/hiedupdt.pdf [December 2009]).

Leavell, Ullin W. 1933. "Trends of Philanthropy in Negro Education: A Survey." *Journal of Negro Education* 2 (January): 38–52.

Lee, Gordon C. 1963. "The Morrill Act and Education." *British Journal of Educational Studies* 12, no. 1: 19–40.

Leif, Beth. 1992. "A New York City Case Study: The Private Sector and the Reform of Public Education." *Teachers College Record* 93, no. 3: 523–35.

Leloudis, James L. 1996. *Schooling the New South: Pedagogy, Self, and Society in North Carolina, 1880–1920.* University of North Carolina Press.

Letts, Chris, William Ryan, and Allen Grossman. 1997. "Virtuous Capital: What Foundations Can Learn from Venture Capitalists." *Harvard Business Review* (March–April).

———. 1999. *High Performance Nonprofit Organizations: Managing Upstream for Greater Impact.* Wiley.

Levine, Arthur, and Jeffrey C. Sun. 2002. "Barriers to Distance Education." Report. American Council on Education and EDUCause (www.acenet.edu/bookstore/pdf/distributed-learning/distributed-learning-06.pdf *[December 2009]*).

Levine, Lawrence W. 1988. *Highbrow/Lowbrow: The Emergence of Cultural Hierarchy in America.* Harvard University Press.

Levine, Ruth. 2006. "Open Letter to the Incoming Director General of the World Health Organization: Time to Refocus." *British Medical Journal* 333 (November 11): 1015–17.

Lienesch, Michael. 1993. *Redeeming America: Piety and Politics in the New Christian Right.* University of North Carolina Press.

Lin, Ann Chih. 2000. *Reform in the Making: The Implementation of Social Policy in Prison.* Princeton University Press.

Lindeman, Eduard. 1936. *Wealth and Culture: A Study of One Hundred Foundations and Community Trusts and Their Operations during the Decade 1921–1930.* Harcourt Brace.

Link, William A. 1986. *A Hard Country and a Lonely Place: Schooling, Society, and Reform in Rural Virginia, 1870–1920.* University of North Carolina Press.

———. 1992. *The Paradox of Southern Progressivism, 1880–1930.* University of North Carolina Press.

Long, Sharon, and others. 1988. *Child Care Assistance under Welfare Reform.* Urban Institute Press.

Lucas, Christopher J. 1994. *American Higher Education: A History.* St. Martin's Press.

Macdonald, Dwight. 1956. *The Ford Foundation: The Men and the Millions.* Reynal.

MacLean, Nancy. 2006. *Freedom Is Not Enough: The Opening of the American Work Place.* Harvard University Press.

Magat, Richard. 1979. *The Ford Foundation at Work: Philanthropic Choices, Methods, and Styles.* Plenum Press.

Margo, Robert A. 1992. "Foundations." In *Who Benefits from the Nonprofit Sector?* edited by Charles T. Clotfelter. University of Chicago Press.

Marquez, Benjamin. 2003. "Mexican-American Political Organizations and Philanthropy: Bankrolling a Social Movement." *Social Service Review* 77, no. 3: 329–46.

Marquis, Alice Goldfarb. 1995. *Art Lessons: Learning from the Rise and Fall of Public Arts Funding.* Basic Books.

Mayhew, Lewis B. 1973. *The Carnegie Commission on Higher Education.* Jossey-Bass.

McAdam, Doug. 1982. *Political Process and the Development of Black Insurgency, 1930–1970.* University of Chicago Press.

McCarthy, Deborah. 2004. "Environmental Justice Grantmaking: Elites and Activists Collaborate to Transform Philanthropy." *Sociological Inquiry* 74: 250–70.

McCarthy, John, and Mayer N. Zald. 1977. "Resource Mobilization and Social Movements." *American Journal of Sociology* 82:1212–41.

McCarthy, Kathleen D. 1984. *Philanthropy and Culture: The International Foundation Perspective.* University of Pennsylvania Press.

———. 2003. *American Creed: Philanthropy and the Rise of Civil Society, 1700–1865.* University of Chicago Press.

McCarthy, Kevin F. 1998. *The Performing Arts in a New Era.* Rand.

———. 2004. *Gifts of the Muse: Reframing the Debate about the Benefits of the Arts.* Rand.

McCaughey, Robert A. 1984. *International Studies and Academic Enterprise: A Chapter in the Enclosure of American Learning.* Columbia University Press.

———. 2003. *Stand, Columbia: A History of Columbia University in the City of New York, 1754–2004.* Columbia University Press.

McDonald, Lawrence G. 2009. *A Colossal Failure of Common Sense: The Inside Story of the Collapse of Lehman Brothers.* Random House.

McGirr, Lisa. 2001. *Suburban Warriors: The Origins of the New American Right, Politics, and Society in Twentieth-Century America.* Princeton University Press.

McKersie, William. 1999. "Local Philanthropy Matters: Pressing Issues for Research and Practice." In Lagemann 1999.

McPherson, Michael S. 2005. "Response." In "Liberal Arts Colleges in American Higher Education: Challeges and Opportunities." Occasional Paper 59. American Council of Learned Societies.

Mead, Edward, Jr. 1972. "A Foundation Goes to School." Ford Foundation.

Mead, Lawrence. 1992. *The New Politics of Poverty.* Basic Books.

Melia, Thomas O. 2006. "The Democracy Bureaucracy." *National Interest* 1, no. 4: 122–30.

Menand, Louis. 2001. "The Marketplace of Ideas." Occasional Paper 49. American Council of Learned Societies.

Meyers, Marcia K., Theresa Heintze, and Douglas A. Wolf. 2002. "Child Care Subsidies and the Employment of Welfare Recipients." *Demography* 39, no. 1: 165–79.

Miller, John J. 2006. *A Gift of Freedom: How the John M. Olin Foundation Changed America.* Encounter Books.

Mills, C. Wright. 1956. *The Power Elite.* Oxford University Press.

Minkoff, Debra C. 1995. *Organizing for Equality: The Evolution of Women's and Racial-Ethnic Organizations in America, 1955–1985.* Rutgers University Press.

———. 1997. "Producing Social Capital: National Social Movements and Civil Society." *American Behavioral Scientist* 40, no. 5: 606–19.

———. 1999. "Bending with the Wind: Organizational Change in American Women's and Minority Organizations." *American Behavioral Scientist* 104, no. 6: 1666–1703.

Minkoff, Debra C., and Walter Powell. 2007. "Nonprofit Mission: Constancy, Responsiveness, or Deflection?" In Powell and Steinberg 2007.

Mitchell, Timothy. 1991. "The Limits of the State: Beyond Statist Approaches and Their Critics." *American Political Science Review* 85, no. 1: 77–96.

Mittelstadt, Jennifer. 2005. *From Welfare to Workfare: The Unintended Consequences of Liberal Reform, 1945–1965.* University of North Carolina Press.

Myrdal, Gunnar, Richard M. E. Sterner, and Arnold M. Rose. 1944. *An American Dilemma: The Negro Problem and Modern Democracy.* Harper and Brothers.

Najam, Adil. 2000. "The Four C's of Third Sector–Government Relations: Cooperation, Confrontation, Complementarity, and Co-optation." *Nonprofit Management and Leadership* 10, no. 4: 375–96.

National Assembly of State Arts Agencies. 2006. "Legislative Appropriations Annual Survey: Fiscal Year 2006."

National Evaluation of High School Transformation. 2004. "Executive Summary: Evaluation of the Bill and Melinda Gates Foundation's High School Grants, 2001–2004." American Institutes for Research and SRI International.

Netzer, Dick. 1978. *The Subsidized Muse: Public Support for the Arts in the United States.* Cambridge University Press.

Newbold, N. C. 1928. "Common Schools for Negroes in the South." *Annals of the American Academy of Political and Social Science* 140 (November): 209–23.

Nielsen, Waldemar A. 1972. *The Big Foundations.* Columbia University Press.

———. 1985. *The Golden Donors: A New Anatomy of the Great Foundations.* Truman Talley Books.

Oakes, Jeannie. 1990. "Opportunities, Achievement, and Choice: Women and Minority Students in Science and Mathematics." *Review of Research in Education* 16:153–222.

O'Connell, Mary. 2007. "Foundation Involvement in Welfare Reform." In *Power in Policy*, edited by David Arons, pp. 74–79. Fieldstone Alliance.

O'Connor, Alice. 1996. "Community Action, Urban Reform, and the Fight against Poverty: The Ford Foundation's Gray Areas Program." *Journal of Policy History* 22, no. 5: 586–625.

———.1999. "The Ford Foundation and Philanthropic Activism in the 1960s." In Lagemann 1999.

———. 2001. *Poverty Knowledge: Social Science, Social Policy, and the Poor in Twentieth-Century U.S. History.* Princeton University Press.

———. 2002. "Foundations, Research, and the Construction of 'Race Neutrality.'" *Souls* 4, no. 1: 54–62.

———. 2004. "Malign Neglect." *DuBois Review* 1, no. 2: 367–75.

———. 2006. "The Politics of Rich and Rich: Postwar Investigations of Foundations and the Philanthropic Right." In *American Capitalism*, edited by N. Lichtenstein. University of Pennsylvania Press.

———. 2007. *Social Science for What? Philanthropy and the Social Question in a World Turned Rightside Up.* Russell Sage Foundation.

Okie, Susan. 2006. "Global Health: The Gates-Buffett Effect." *New England Journal of Medicine* 355, no. 11: 1084–88.

Olasky, Marvin. 1992. *The Tragedy of American Compassion.* Regnery.

Oleson, A., and J. Voss, eds. 1979. *The Organization of Knowledge in Modern America, 1860–1920.* Johns Hopkins University Press.

Oliver, Thomas, and Jason Gerson. 2003. "The Role of Foundations in Shaping Health Policy: Lessons from Efforts to Expand and Preserve Health Insurance Coverage." Research Paper 15, prepared for the Center on Philanthropy and Public Policy. University of Southern California.

Oren, Ido. 2003. *Our Enemies and US: America's Rivalries and the Making of Political Science.* Cornell University Press.

Osborne, David, and Ted Gaebler. 1993. *Reinventing Government.* Plume.

Ostrander, Susan A. 1995. *Money for Change: Social Movement Philanthropy at Haymarket People's Fund.* Temple University Press.

———. 1999. "When Grantees Become Grantors: Accountability, Democracy, and Social Movement Philanthropy." In Lagemann 1999.

Ostrander, Susan A., Ira Silver, and Deborah McCarthy. 2005. "Mobilizing Money Strategically: Opportunities for Grantees to Be Active Agents in Social Movement Philanthropy." In Faber and McCarthy 2005a.

Parker, Franklin. 1972. "George Peabody, 1795–1869: His Influence on Educational Philanthropy." *Peabody Journal of Education* 49 (January): 138–45.

Parmar, Inderjeet. 2002. "American Foundations and the Development of International Knowledge Networks." *Global Networks* 2, no. 1: 13–30.

Peristiani, Stavros. 2003. "Evaluating the Riskiness of Initial Public Offerings: 1980–2000." *Staff Reports* 167, Federal Reserve Bank of New York.

Pew Memorial Trust. 1985. *Annual Report.*

Philanthropy Northwest. 2008. *Trends in Northwest Giving.*

Pierson, Paul. 2000. "The Limits of Design: Explaining Institutional Origins and Change." *Governance* 13, no. 4: 475–99.

Pittz, Will, and Rinku Sen. 2004. "Short Changed: Foundation Giving and Communities of Color." Report. Applied Research Center.

Piven, Francis Fox, and Richard Cloward. 1993. *Regulating the Poor: The Functions of Public Welfare.* Vintage Books.

Porter, Michael E., and Mark R. Kramer. 1999. "Philanthropy's New Agenda: Creating Value." *Harvard Business Review* (November–December): 121–30.

Powell, Walter W., ed. 1987. *The Nonprofit Sector: A Research Handbook.* Yale University Press.

Powell, Walter W., and Elisabeth S. Clemens, eds. 1998. *Private Action and the Public Good.* Yale University Press.

Powell, Walter W., and Paul DiMaggio. 1991. *The New Institutionalism in Organizational Analysis.* University of Chicago Press.

Powell, Walter W., and Richard Steinberg. 2006. *The Nonprofit Sector: A Research Handbook,* 2nd ed. Yale University Press.

President's Commission on Higher Education. 1947. *Higher Education for American Democracy: A Report of the President's Commission on Higher Education.* Government Printing Office.

Pressman, Jeffrey L., and Aaron B. Wildavsky. 1984. *Implementation: How Great Expectations in Washington Are Dashed in Oakland.* University of California Press.

Prewitt, Kenneth. 1999a. "Foundations as Mirrors of Public Culture." *American Behavioral Scientist* 42, no. 6: 977–86.

———. 1999b. "The Importance of Foundations in an Open Society." In *The Future of Foundations in an Open Society,* edited by Bertelsmann Foundation. Bertelsmann Foundation Publishers.

———. 2001. "The Foundation Mission: Purpose, Practice, Public Pressures." In Schluter and others 2001.

Prewitt, Kenneth and others, eds. 2006. *The Legitimacy of Philanthropic Foundations: United States and European Perspectives.* Russell Sage Foundation.

Prior, Lindsay. 2003. *Using Documents in Social Research.* Sage Publications.

Proietto, Rosa. 1999. "The Ford Foundation and Women's Studies." In Lagemann 1999.

Quandt, Richard E. 2002. *The Changing Landscape in Eastern Europe: A Personal Perspective on Philanthropy and Technology Transfer.* Oxford University Press.

Quigley, Kevin F. F. 1996a. *Conversations on Democracy Assistance.* Woodrow Wilson International Center for Scholars, East European Studies.

———. 1996b. "Think Tanks in Newly Democratic Eastern Europe." In Telgarsky and Ueno 1996, pp. 82–93.

———. 1997. *For Democracy's Sake: Foundations and Democracy Assistance in Central Europe; Woodrow Wilson Center Special Studies.* Woodrow Wilson Center Press.

Raynor, Greg. 1999. "The Ford Foundation's War on Poverty." In Lagemann 1999.

Reich, Rob. 2005. "A Failure of Philanthropy: American Charity Shortchanges the Poor, and Public Policy Is Partly to Blame." *Stanford Social Innovation Review* (Winter): 24–33.

Reid, Betsy. 1999. "Nonprofit Advocacy and Political Participation." In Boris and Steuerle 1999.

Renz, Loren, ed. 1992. *Foundation Giving: Yearbook of Facts and Figures on Private, Corporate, and Community Foundations.* Foundation Center.

———. 1997. *International Grantmaking: A Report on U.S. Foundation Trends.* Foundation Center.

———. 2000. *International Grantmaking II: An Update on U.S. Foundation Trends.* Foundation Center.

———. 2004. *International Grantmaking III: An Update on U.S. Foundation Trends.* Foundation Center.

Renz, Loren, and Josefina Atienza. 2005. *Foundation Funding for Arts Education.* Foundation Center.

Renz, Loren, and Carolyn Atlas. 1999. *Arts Funding 2000: Funder Perspectives on Current and Future Trends.* Foundation Center.

Renz, Loren, and Steven Lawrence. 2006. "Foundation Grants to Arts and Culture, 2004." *Grantmakers in the Arts Reader* 17, no. 2: 38-44.

Renz, Loren, Steven Lawrence, and Leslie Marino. 2003. *Arts Funding IV: An Update on Foundation Trends.* Foundation Center.

———. 2006. "Foundation Grants to Arts and Culture, 2004." *Grantmakers in the Arts Reader* 17, no. 2: 38–44.

Renz, Loren, Steven Lawrence, and James A. Smith. 2004. *Foundation Funding for the Humanities.* Foundation Center.

Renz, Loren, Josefina Samson-Atienza, and Steven Lawrence. 2000. *International Grantmaking II: An Update on U.S. Foundation Trends.* Foundation Center.

Renz, Loren, and others. 2001. *Foundations Today, 2001 Edition.* Foundation Center.

Resnick, Daniel P. 1981. "Educational Policy and the Applied Historian: Testing, Competency, and Standards." *Journal of Social History* 14 (Summer): 539–59.

Rhodes, Frank Harold Trevor. 2001. *The Creation of the Future: The Role of the American University.* Cornell University Press.

Ricci, David M. 1993. *The Transformation of American Politics: The New Washington and the Rise of Think Tanks.* Yale University Press.

Rich, Andrew. 2004. *Think Tanks, Public Policy, and the Politics of Expertise.* Cambridge University Press.

Rich, Wilmer Shields, ed. 1931–55. *American Foundations and Their Fields.* 1st–7th eds. American Foundations Information Service.

Richard King Mellon Foundation. 2008. *Richard King Mellon Foundation: History, Program Interests, and Geographic Focus* (www.foundationcenter.org/grantmaker/rk mellon/history.html [December 1, 2009]).

Richards, W. C., and W. J. Norton. 1957. *Biography of a Foundation: The Story of the Children's Fund of Michigan.* Children's Fund of Michigan.

Rockefeller Brothers Fund. 1965. *The Performing Arts: Problems and Prospects; Rockefeller Panel Report on the Future of Theatre, Dance, and Music in America.* McGraw-Hill.

Rockefeller Foundation. 1938. *Annual Report.*

———. 2006. *Africa's Turn: A New Green Revolution for the 21st Century.*

Roelofs, Joan. 2003. *Foundations and Public Policy: The Mask of Pluralism.* State University of New York Press.

Ronsvalle, John, and Sylvia Ronsvalle. 1996. *Behind the Stained Glass Windows: Money Dynamics in the Church.* Baker Books.

Rose, Kenneth W., and Darwin T. Stapleton. 1992. "Toward a 'Universal Heritage': Education and the Development of Rockefeller Philanthropy, 1884–1915." *Teachers College Record* 93, no. 3: 536–55.

Rosenberg, Charles E. 1997. *No Other Gods: On Science and American Social Thought.* Johns Hopkins University Press.

Rosenberg, Mark, and others. 2010. *Real Collaboration: What It Takes for Global Health to Succeed.* University of California Press and the Milbank Memorial Fund.

Rosenfeld, Leonard S., and Henry B. Makover. 1956. *The Rochester Regional Hospital Council.* Harvard University Press.

Rosenzweig, Robert M., and Barbara Turlington. 1982. *The Research Universities and Their Patrons.* University of California Press.

Rowan, Brian, Carol Barnes, and Eric Camburn. 2004. "Benefiting from Comprehensive School Reform: A Review of Research on CSR Implementation." In *Putting the Pieces Together*, edited by C. Cross. National Clearinghouse on Comprehensive School Reform.

Russo, Alexander. 2000. "From Frontline Leader to Rearguard Action: The Chicago Annenberg Challenge." In Domanico 2000.

Sabourin, Sophie. 1992. "Another Foundation Goes to School: The Panasonic Foundation's School Restructuring Program." *Teachers College Record* 93, no. 3: 463–71.

Sacks, Eleanor W. 2005. *International Connections: Resources That Support the Growth and Development of Community Foundations Globally.* Worldwide Initiatives for Grantmaker Support.

Salamon, Lester M. 1987. "Partners in Public Service: The Scope and Theory of Government-Nonprofit Relations." In Powell 1987.

———. 1995. *Partners in Public Service: Government-Nonprofit Relations in the Modern Welfare State.* Johns Hopkins University Press.

———. 1999. *America's Nonprofit Sector: A Primer.* 2nd ed. Foundation Center.

———. 2002a. "The Resilient Sector: The State of Nonprofit America." In Salamon 2002b.

———, ed. 2002b. *The State of Nonprofit America.* Brookings.

———, ed. 2002c. *The Tools of Government.* Oxford University Press.

Salamon, Lester M., and Alan J. Abramson. 1982. *The Federal Budget and the Nonprofit Sector*. Urban Institute Press.

Salisbury, Robert. 1984. "Interest Representation: The Dominance of Institutions." *American Political Science Review* 78 (March): 64–76.

Sarason, Seymour Bernard. 1990. *The Predictable Failure of Educational Reform: Can We Change Course before It's Too Late?* Jossey-Bass.

Savedoff, William D., Ruth Levine, and Nancy Birdsall. 2006. "Report of the Evaluation Gap Working Group." In *When Will We Ever Learn?* edited by W. D. Savedoff and others. Center for Global Development.

Sawhill, Isabel. 2002. *Welfare Reform and Beyond: The Future of the Safety Net*. Brookings.

Schlossman, Steven L. 1981. "Philanthropy and the Gospel of Child Development." *History of Education Quarterly* 21, no. 3: 275–99.

Schluter, Andreas, Peter Walkenhorst, and Volker Then. 2001. *Foundations in Europe: International Reference Book on Society, Management, and Law*. Brookings.

Schmalbeck, Richard. 2004. "Reconsidering Private Foundation Investment Limitations." *Tax Law Review* 58:59–110.

Schneider, Barbara, and James S. Coleman. 1993. *Parents, Their Children, and Schools*. Westview Press.

Scott, Jason D. 2003. *Private Sector Contributions to Faith-Based Social Service: The Policies and Giving Patterns of Private Foundations*. Research report prepared for the Roundtable on Religion and Social Welfare Policy. State University of New York, Rockefeller Institute of Government, June 22.

Scott, W. Richard. 2003. *Organizations: Rational, Natural, and Open Systems*. Prentice Hall.

Sealander, Judith. 1997. *Private Wealth and Public Life: Foundation Philanthropy and the Reshaping of American Social Policy from the Progressive Era to the New Deal*. Johns Hopkins University Press.

Seaman, Bruce A. 2002. "National Investment in the Arts." Issue paper. Center for Arts and Culture (www.culturalpolicy.org/pdf/investment.pdf [December 2009]).

Selznick, Philip. 1949. *TVA and the Grass Roots: A Study in the Sociology of Formal Organization*. University of California Press.

Seybold, G., ed. 1939. *American Foundations and Their Fields*. Vol. 4. Raymond Rich Associates.

Shiao, Jiannbin Lee. 2005. *Identifying Talent, Institutionalizing Diversity: Race and Philanthropy in Post–Civil Rights America*. Duke University Press.

Shils, Edward. 1973. "The American Private University." *Minerva* 11, no. 1: 6–27.

———. 1979. "The Order of Learning in the United States: The Ascendancy of the University." In Oleson and Voss 1979.

Shubane, Khela. 1999. "Local Content: The Politics of European and American Donor Intervention in South Africa under Apartheid." Social policy series 12, no. 3. Center for Policy Studies.

Sievers, Bruce. 2001. "If Pigs Had Wings: The Appeals and Limits of Venture Philanthropy." Address to the Waldemar A. Nielsen Issues in Philanthropy conference, Georgetown University.

Silber, Norman J., 2001. *A Corporate Form of Freedom: The Emergence of the Nonprofit Sector*. Westview.

Silver, Ira. 1998. "Buying an Activist Identity: Reproducing Class through Social Movement Philanthropy." *Sociological Perspectives* 41, no. 2: 303–21.

Simon, John G. 1987. "The Tax Treatment of Nonprofit Organizations: A Review of Federal and State Policies." In Powell 1987.

————. 2000. "Private Foundations as a Federally Regulated Industry: Time for a Fresh Look." *Exempt Organization Tax Review* 27, no. 1: 66.

Skillman Foundation. 1998. "Update 1998: The Status of Welfare Reform/Devolution in Michigan." Summary of a forum held March 6.

Skocpol, Theda. 1992. *Protecting Soldiers and Mothers: The Political Origins of Social Policy in the United States*. Belknap Press of Harvard University Press.

————. 2003a. "Advocates without Members: The Recent Transformation of American Civic Life." In *Civic Engagement in American Democracy*, edited by Theda Skocpol and Morris P. Fiorina. Brookings.

————. 2003b. *Diminished Democracy: From Membership to Management in American Civic Life*. University of Oklahoma Press.

Smith, James Allen. 1991. *The Idea Brokers: Think Tanks and the Rise of the New Policy Elite*. Free Press.

————. 2002. "Foundations and Public Policymaking: A Historical Perspective." Research Paper 11, prepared for the Center on Philanthropy and Public Policy. University of Southern California.

Smith, Steven Rathgeb. 2006. "Government Financing of Nonprofit Activity." In *Nonprofits and Government*, 2nd ed., edited by Elizabeth T. Boris and C. Eugene Steuerle, pp. 219–56. Washington: Urban Institute.

Smith, Steven Rathgeb, and Michael Lipsky. 1993. *Nonprofits for Hire: The Welfare State in the Age of Contracting*. Harvard University Press.

Smith, Tony. 1994. *America's Mission: The United States and the Worldwide Struggle for Democracy in the Twentieth Century*. Princeton University Press.

Snyder, Thomas D., ed. 1993. *120 Years of American Education: A Statistical Portrait*. U.S. Department of Education, Office of Educational Research and Improvement, National Center for Education Statistics.

Spring, Joel H. 1990. *The American School, 1642–1990: Varieties of Historical Interpretation of the Foundations and Development of American Education*. Longman.

Stacey, Simon, and Sada Aksartova. 2001. "The Foundations of Democracy: U.S. Foundation Support for Civil Society in South Africa, 1988–1996," *Voluntas* 12, no. 4 (December): 373–97.

Stefancic, Jean, and Richard Delgado. 1996. *No Mercy: How Conservative Think Tanks and Foundations Changed America's Social Agenda*. Temple University Press.

Steinberg, Richard. 2008. "Principal-Agent Theory and Nonprofit Accountability." Working Paper 2008-03. Indiana University–Purdue University at Indianapolis, Department of Economics.

Stevens, Louise. 1996. "The Earnings Shift: The New Bottom Line; Paradigm for the Arts Industry in a Market-Driven Era." *Journal of Arts Management, Law, and Society* 26, no. 2: 101–14.

Stewart, John W. 2006. "Child Guidance in Interwar Scotland: International Influences and Domestic Concerns." *Bulletin of the History of Medicine* 80, no. 3: 513–39.

Stinchcombe, A. L. 1965. "Social Structure and Organizations." In *Handbook of Organizations*, edited by J. G. March. Rand-McNally.

Stone, Diane. 1996. *Capturing the Political Imagination: Think Tanks and the Policy Process*. Routledge.

Strong, David, and others. 2000. "Leveraging the State: Private Money and the Development of Public Education for Blacks." *American Sociological Review* 65 (October): 658–81.

Sturdy, Steve, and Roger Cooter. 1998. "Science, Scientific Management, and the Transformation of Medicine in Britain, 1870–1950." *History of Science* 36:421–66.

Surdna Foundation. 1985–86. *Report for the Fiscal Year, July 1, 1985 to June 30, 1986.*

———. 1988. *Report for the Fiscal Year, July 1, 1987 to June 30, 1988.*

Sutton, Francis X. 1977. "The Foundations and Governments of Developing Countries." *Studies in Comparative International Development* 12, no. 2: 94–120.

———. 1987. "The Ford Foundation: The Early Years." *Daedalus* 116, no. 1: 41–91.

———. 1999. "The Ford Foundation and Columbia." Paper prepared for the University Seminar on Columbia University. Columbia University, November 16 (beatl.barnard.columbia.edu/cuhistory/fordfoundation.htm).

Sviridoff, Mitchell, ed. 2004. *Inventing Community Renewal: The Trials and Errors That Shaped the Modern Community Development Corporation*. New School University.

Taleb, Nassim Nicholas. 2004. *Fooled by Randomness: The Hidden Role of Chance in Life and in the Markets*. Thomson.

Tanner, Michael. 1996. *The End of Welfare: Fighting Poverty in the Civil Society.* Cato Institute.

Tayart de Borms, Luc. 2005. *Foundations: Creating Impact in a Globalised World*. Wiley.

Taylor, Verta. 1989. "Social Movement Continuity: The Women's Movement in Abeyance." *American Sociological Review* 54, no. 5: 761–75.

Telgarsky, Jeffrey, and Makiko Ueno. 1996. *Think Tanks in a Democratic Society: An Alternative Voice*. Urban Institute.

Thelin, John R. 2004. *A History of American Higher Education*. Johns Hopkins University Press.

Thompson, Randall. 1935. *College Music: An Investigation for the Association of American Colleges*. Macmillan.

Tirman, John. 2000. *Making the Money Sing: Private Wealth and Public Power in the Search for Peace*. Rowman and Littlefield.

Toepler, Stefan. 2006. "Caveat Venditor? Museum Merchandising, Nonprofit Commercialization, and the Case of the Metropolitan Museum in New York." *Voluntas* 17, no. 2: 95–109.

Toepler, Stefan, and Sarah Dewees. 2005. "Are There Limits to Financing Culture through the Market? Evidence from the U.S. Museum Field." *International Journal of Public Administration* 28, nos. 1–2: 131–46.

Toepler, Stefan, and Volker Kirchberg. 2002. "Museums, Merchandising, and Nonprofit Commercialization." Working Paper. National Center for Nonprofit Enterprise.

Trattner, Walter. 1999. *From Poor Law to Welfare State: A History of Social Welfare in America*. Free Press.

Troyer, Thomas. 2000. "The 1969 Private Foundation Law: Historical Perspective on Its Origins and Underpinnings." *Exempt Organization Tax Review* 27, no. 1: 52–53.

Troyer, Thomas A., and Douglas Varley. 2002. "Private Foundations and Policymaking: Latitude under Federal Law." Research Paper 12, prepared for the Center on Philanthropy and Public Policy. University of Southern California.

Turrell Fund. 1965. *Report of the First Thirty Years, 1935–1964.*

Tyack, David B. 1974. *The One Best System: A History of American Urban Education.* Harvard University Press.

Tyack, David B., and Larry Cuban. 1995. *Tinkering toward Utopia: A Century of Public School Reform.* Harvard University Press.

Una Roberts Lawrence Papers. Archives of the Southern Baptist Convention, Nashville, Tenn.

U.S. Bureau of the Census. 2002. *2002 Economic Census: Arts, Entertainment, and Recreation:* Subject Series (www.census.gov/econ/census02/guide/EC02_71.htm [December 2009]).

———. 2005. *Statistical Abstract of the United States, 2004–2005.* Government Printing Office.

U.S. Department of Education. 2006. *A Test of Leadership: Charting the Future of U.S. Higher Education.* Government Printing Office.

U.S. Department of the Treasury. 2006. *U.S. Department of Treasury Anti-Terrorist Financing Guidelines: Voluntary Practices for U.S.-Based Charities* (www.ustreas.gov/press/releases/reports/0929%20final revised.pdf [December 2009]).

U.S. Government Accountability Office. 2006. *Tax-Exempt Organizations: Collecting More Data on Donor-Advised Funds and Supporting Organizations Could Help Address Compliance Challenges* (www.gao.gov/cgi-bin/getrpt?GAO-06-799 [December 2009]).

U.S. House of Representatives. 1948. Special Subcommittee of the Committee on Un-American Activities. "Testimony of Alger Hiss and Whittaker Chambers before the House Committee on Un-American Activities." August 17.

———. 1954. Special Committee to Investigate Tax-Exempt Foundations. *Tax-Exempt Foundations: Report of the Special Committee to Investigate Tax-Exempt Foundations and Comparable Organizations.* Government Printing Office.

Van Horn, Rob, and Philip Mirowski. 2009. "The Rise of the Chicago School of Economics and the Birth of Neoliberalism." In *The Road from Mont Pèlerin: The Making of the Neoliberal Thought Collective,* edited by Philip Mirowski and Dieter Plehwe, pp. 139–80. Harvard University Press.

Vaughn, William Preston. 1974. *Schools for All: The Blacks and Public Education in the South, 1865–1877.* University Press of Kentucky.

Veyne, Paul, Oswyn Murray, and Brian Pearce. 1990. *Bread and Circuses: Historical Sociology and Political Pluralism.* Penguin.

Veysey, Laurence R. 1965. *The Emergence of the American University.* University of Chicago Press.

———. 1979. "The Plural Organized Worlds of the Humanities." In Oleson and Voss 1979.

Vincent Astor Foundation. 1961. *The Vincent Astor Foundation, 1949–1961.*

———. 1968. *The Vincent Astor Foundation, 1964–1968.*

Walton, Andrea. 2005. *Women and Philanthropy in Education*. Indiana University Press.

Weaver, R. Kent. 2000. *Ending Welfare as We Know It*. Brookings.

Weaver, Warren, and George M. Beadle, eds. 1967. *U.S. Philanthropic Foundations: Their History, Structure, Management, and Record*. Harper and Row.

Weber, Nathan. 1993. *Arts Funding: A Report on Foundation and Corporate Grantmaking Trends*. Foundation Center.

Wells, Catherine Pierce. 1990. "State Regulation of Charitable Solicitation." Paper prepared for the Charitable Solicitation: Is There a Problem? conference. New York University, October 12–13.

West, Earle H. 1966. "The Peabody Education Fund and Negro Education, 1867–1880." *History of Education Quarterly* 6 (Summer): 3–21.

Western Interstate Commission on Higher Education. 2003. "Knocking at the College Door: Projections of High School Graduates by State, Income, and Race/Ethnicity." Report.

Wheatley, Steven C. 1978. "Foundation Giving in Chicago, 1976: A Study of the Giving Patterns of 131 Large Illinois Foundations." Donors Forum of Chicago.

———. 1988. *The Politics of Philanthropy: Abraham Flexner and Medical Education*. University of Wisconsin Press.

White, Kerr L. 2007. "Health Services Research and Epidemiology." In *The Development of Modern Epidemiology*, edited by W. W. Holland, J. Olsen, and C. du V. Florey. Oxford University Press.

William and Flora Hewlett Foundation. 1999. *Annual Report*.

———. 2001. *Annual Report*.

Woodson, Carter. 1931. "The Miseducation of the Negro." *Crisis* 38 (August): 266–67.

Wooster, Martin Morse. 1994. *The Great Philanthropists and the Problem of "Donor Intent."* Capital Research Center.

Wormser, René Albert. 1958. *Foundations: Their Power and Influence*. Devin-Adair.

Wyszomirski, Margaret, and Joni Cherbo. 2003. "Understanding the Associational Infrastructure of the Arts and Culture." In *The Arts in a New Millennium*, edited by V. B. Morris and D. B. Pankratz. Praeger.

Wyszomirski, Margaret, and Kevin Mulcahy. 1995. "The Organization of Public Support for the Arts." In *America's Commitment to Culture*, edited by K. V. Mulcahy and M. J. Wyszmomirski. Westview.

Yahnke, Robert E. 1978. *A Time of Humanities: An Oral History*. Wisconsin House Book Publishers.

Yamamoto, Tadashi, and others, eds. 2006. *Philanthropy and Reconciliation: Rebuilding Postwar U.S.–Japan Relations*. Japan Center for International Exchange.

Yellin, Eric S. 2002. "The (White) Search for (Black) Order: The Phelps-Stokes Fund's First Twenty Years, 1911–1931." *Historian* 65, no. 2: 319–52.

Ylvisaker, Paul N. 1987. "Foundations and Nonprofit Organizations." In Powell 1987.

Young, Edgar B. 1980. *Lincoln Center: The Building of an Institution*. New York University Press.

Zemsky, Robert, Gregory R. Wegner, and William F. Massy. 2005. *Remaking the American University: Market-Smart and Mission-Centered*. Rutgers University Press.

Zook, George Frederick. 1945. *The Role of the Federal Government in Education.* Harvard University Press.

Zucker, Lynne, and Ita Kreft. 1994. "The Evolution of Socially Contingent Rational Action: Effects of Labor Strikes on Change in Union Founding in the 1880s." In *Evolutionary Dynamics of Organizations,* edited by J. A. C. Baum and J. V. Singh. Oxford University Press.

Zusman, Ami. 2005. "Challenges Facing Higher Education in the Twenty-First Century." In Altbach, Berdahl, and Gumport 2005.

Contributors

JON AGNONE
University of Washington

HELMUT K. ANHEIER
University of California–Los Angeles
and Heidelberg University

LEHN M. BENJAMIN
George Mason University

WOLFGANG BIELEFELD
Indiana University and Purdue
University–Indianapolis

EMILY A. BOWMAN
Indiana University–Bloomington

JANE CHU
Indiana University and Kauffman
Center for the Performing Arts

ELISABETH S. CLEMENS
University of Chicago

DANIEL M. FOX
President Emeritus, Milbank
Memorial Fund

PETER FRUMKIN
University of Texas–Austin

JOSEPH GALASKIEWICZ
University of Arizona

DAVID C. HAMMACK
Case Western Reserve University

STEVEN HEYDEMANN
United States Institute of Peace
and Georgetown University

STEPHEN L. ISAACS
Health Policy Associates

GABRIEL KAPLAN
University of Colorado–Denver

REBECCA KINSEY
U.S. Agency for International
  Development

JAMES R. KNICKMAN
New York State Health Foundation

LINDA C. LEE
University of Chicago

D. MICHAEL LINDSAY
Rice University

DEBRA MINKOFF
Barnard College, Columbia University

JENNIFER E. MOSLEY
University of Chicago

ALICE O'CONNOR
University of California–Santa
  Barbara

KEVIN F. F. QUIGLEY
National Peace Corps Association

JAMES ALLEN SMITH
Rockefeller Archive Center

STEVEN RATHGEB SMITH
University of Washington

STEFAN TOEPLER
George Mason University

PAMELA BARNHOUSE WALTERS
Indiana University–Bloomington

STEVEN C. WHEATLEY
American Council of Learned
  Societies

ROBERT WUTHNOW
Princeton University

Index

439